Synergy and Redundancy Measures: Theory and Applications to Characterize Complex Systems and Shape Neural Network Representations

Synergy and Redundancy Measures: Theory and Applications to Characterize Complex Systems and Shape Neural Network Representations

Guest Editor

Daniel Chicharro

MDPI

Basel • Beijing • Wuhan • Barcelona • Belgrade • Novi Sad • Cluj • Manchester

Guest Editor
Daniel Chicharro
Department of Computer
Science
School of Science &
Technology
City St George's,
University of London
London
UK

Editorial Office
MDPI AG
Grosspeteranlage 5
4052 Basel, Switzerland

This is a reprint of the Special Issue, published open access by the journal *Entropy* (ISSN 1099-4300), freely accessible at: https://www.mdpi.com/journal/entropy/special_issues/synergy_redundancy.

For citation purposes, cite each article independently as indicated on the article page online and as indicated below:

Lastname, A.A.; Lastname, B.B. Article Title. *Journal Name* **Year**, *Volume Number*, Page Range.

ISBN 978-3-7258-3613-0 (Hbk)
ISBN 978-3-7258-3614-7 (PDF)
https://doi.org/10.3390/books978-3-7258-3614-7

Contents

entropy

Article

Decomposing and Tracing Mutual Information by Quantifying Reachable Decision Regions

Tobias Mages * and Christian Rohner

Department of Information Technology, Uppsala University, 752 36 Uppsala, Sweden; christian.rohner@it.uu.se
* Correspondence: tobias.mages@it.uu.se

Abstract: The idea of a partial information decomposition (PID) gained significant attention for attributing the components of mutual information from multiple variables about a target to being unique, redundant/shared or synergetic. Since the original measure for this analysis was criticized, several alternatives have been proposed but have failed to satisfy the desired axioms, an inclusion–exclusion principle or have resulted in negative partial information components. For constructing a measure, we interpret the achievable type I/II error pairs for predicting each state of a target variable (reachable decision regions) as notions of pointwise uncertainty. For this representation of uncertainty, we construct a distributive lattice with mutual information as consistent valuation and obtain an algebra for the constructed measure. The resulting definition satisfies the original axioms, an inclusion–exclusion principle and provides a non-negative decomposition for an arbitrary number of variables. We demonstrate practical applications of this approach by tracing the flow of information through Markov chains. This can be used to model and analyze the flow of information in communication networks or data processing systems.

Keywords: partial information decomposition; redundancy; synergy; information flow analysis

Citation: Mages, T.; Rohner, C. Decomposing and Tracing Mutual Information by Quantifying Reachable Decision Regions. *Entropy* **2023**, *25*, 1014. https://doi.org/10.3390/e25071014

Academic Editor: Daniel Chicharro

Received: 29 May 2023
Revised: 27 June 2023
Accepted: 29 June 2023
Published: 30 June 2023

1. Introduction

A Partial Information Decomposition (PID) aims to attribute the provided information about a discrete target variable T from a set of predictor or viewable variables $\mathbf{V} = \{V_1, \ldots, V_n\}$ to each individual variable V_i. The partial contributions to the information about T may be provided by all variables (redundant or shared), by a specific variable (unique) or only be available through a combination of variables (synergetic/complementing) [1]. This decomposition is particularly applicable when studying complex systems. For example, it can be used to study logical circuits, neural networks [2] or the propagation of information over multiple paths through a network. The concept of synergy has been applied to develop data privacy techniques [3,4], and we think that the concept of redundancy may be suitable to study a notion of robustness in data processing systems.

Unfortunately and to the best of our knowledge, there does not exist a non-negative decomposition of mutual information for an arbitrary number of variables that satisfies the commutativity, monotonicity and self-redundancy axioms except the original measure of Williams and Beer [5]. However, this measure has been criticized for not distinguishing "the *same* information and the *same amount* of information" [6–9].

Here, we propose an alternative non-negative partial information decomposition that satisfies Williams and Beer's axioms [5] for an arbitrary number of variables. It provides an intuitive operational interpretation and results in an algebra like probability theory. To demonstrate that the approach distinguishes the same information from the same amount of information, we highlight its application in tracing the flow of information through a Markov chain, as visualized in Figure 1.

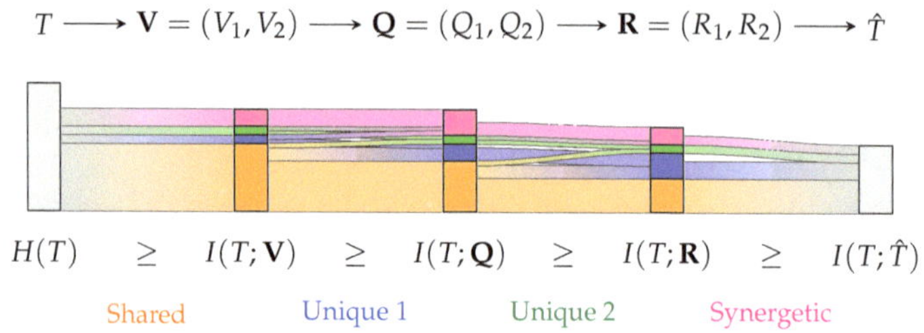

Figure 1. Visualization of a partial information decomposition with information flow analysis of a Markov chain as Sankey diagram. A partial information decomposition enables attributing the provided information about T to being shared (**orange**), unique (**blue/green**) or synergetic/complementing (**pink**). While this already offers practical insights for studying complex systems, the ability to trace the flow of partial information may create a valuable tool to model and analyze many applications.

This work is structured in three parts: Section 2 provides an overview of the related work and background information. Section 3 presents a representation of pointwise uncertainty, constructs a distributive lattice and demonstrates that mutual information is the expected value of its consistent valuation. Section 4 discusses applications of the resulting measure to PIDs and the tracing of information through Markov chains. We provide an overview of the used notation at the end of the paper.

2. Related Work

We briefly summarize partial orders and the four main publications which led to our proposed decomposition approach. This includes the PID by Williams and Beer [5], the quantification of unique information by Bertschinger et al. [10] and Griffith and Koch [11], the Blackwell order based on Bertschinger and Rauh [12], the evaluation of binary decision problems using Receiver Operating Characteristics and consistent lattice valuations by Knuth [13].

2.1. Partial Orders and Lattices

This section provides a brief overview of the relevant definitions on partial orders and lattices for the context of this work based on [9,13]. A binary ordering relation $\preccurlyeq$ on a set $\mathbf{L}$ is called a *preorder* if it is reflexive and transitive. If the ordering relation additionally satisfies an antisymmetry, then $(\mathbf{L}, \preccurlyeq)$ is called a *partially ordered set* (*poset*). For $\alpha, \beta, \gamma \in \mathbf{L}$:

$$\alpha \preccurlyeq \alpha \quad \text{(reflexivity)}$$
$$\text{if } \alpha \preccurlyeq \beta \text{ and } \beta \preccurlyeq \gamma \text{ then } \alpha \preccurlyeq \gamma \quad \text{(transitivity)}$$
$$\text{if } \alpha \preccurlyeq \beta \text{ and } \beta \preccurlyeq \alpha \text{ then } \alpha = \beta \quad \text{(antisymmetry)}$$

Two elements satisfy $\alpha \preccurlyeq \beta$, $\beta \preccurlyeq \alpha$ or may be incomparable, meaning $\alpha \not\preccurlyeq \beta$ and $\beta \not\preccurlyeq \alpha$. A partially ordered set has a *bottom element* $\bot \in \mathbf{L}$ if $\bot \preccurlyeq \alpha$ for all $\alpha \in \mathbf{L}$ and a *top element* $\top \in \mathbf{L}$ if $\alpha \preccurlyeq \top$ for all $\alpha \in \mathbf{L}$. For each element α, it can be defined a down-set ($\downarrow\alpha$) and up-set ($\uparrow\alpha$) as well as a strict down-set ($\dot{\downarrow}\alpha$) and strict up-set ($\dot{\uparrow}\alpha$) as shown below:

$$\downarrow\alpha = \{\beta \in \mathbf{L} \mid \beta \preccurlyeq \alpha\} \quad \text{(down-set)}$$
$$\dot{\downarrow}\alpha = \{\beta \in \mathbf{L} \mid \beta \preccurlyeq \alpha \text{ and } \alpha \not\preccurlyeq \beta\} \quad \text{(strict down-set)}$$
$$\uparrow\alpha = \{\beta \in \mathbf{L} \mid \alpha \preccurlyeq \beta\} \quad \text{(up-set)}$$
$$\dot{\uparrow}\alpha = \{\beta \in \mathbf{L} \mid \alpha \preccurlyeq \beta \text{ and } \beta \not\preccurlyeq \alpha\} \quad \text{(strict up-set)}$$

A *lattice* is a partially ordered set $(\mathbf{L}, \preccurlyeq)$ for which every pair of elements $\{\alpha, b\} \subseteq \mathbf{L}$ has a unique least upper bound $\alpha \curlyvee \beta = \sup\{\alpha, \beta\}$, referred to as *joint*, and a unique greatest lower bound $\alpha \curlywedge \beta = \inf\{\alpha, \beta\}$, referred to as *meet*. This creates an algebra $(\mathbf{L}, \curlywedge, \curlyvee)$ with the binary operators $\curlywedge$ and $\curlyvee$ that satisfies indempotency, commutativity, associativity and absorption. The consistency relates the ordering relation and algebra with each other. A *distributive lattice* additionally satisfies distributivity.

$$
\begin{array}{ccr}
\alpha \curlyvee \alpha = \alpha & \alpha \curlywedge \alpha = \alpha & \text{(indempotency)} \\
\alpha \curlyvee \beta = \beta \curlyvee \alpha & \alpha \curlywedge \beta = \beta \curlywedge \alpha & \text{(commutativity)} \\
\alpha \curlyvee (\beta \curlyvee \gamma) = (\alpha \curlyvee \beta) \curlyvee \gamma & \alpha \curlywedge (\beta \curlywedge \gamma) = (\alpha \curlywedge \beta) \curlywedge \gamma & \text{(associativity)} \\
\alpha \curlyvee (\alpha \curlywedge \beta) = \alpha & \alpha \curlywedge (\alpha \curlyvee \beta) = \alpha & \text{(absorption)} \\
\alpha \preccurlyeq \beta \Rightarrow \alpha \curlyvee \beta = \beta & \alpha \preccurlyeq \beta \Rightarrow \alpha \curlywedge \beta = \alpha & \text{(consistency)} \\
\hline
\alpha \curlyvee (\beta \curlywedge \gamma) = (\alpha \curlyvee \beta) \curlywedge (\alpha \curlyvee \gamma) & \alpha \curlywedge (\beta \curlyvee \gamma) = (\alpha \curlywedge \beta) \curlyvee (\alpha \curlywedge \gamma) & \text{(distributivity)}
\end{array}
$$

2.2. Partial Information Decomposition

This section summarizes Williams and Beer's general approach to partial information decompositions [5]. A more detailed discussion of the literature and required background can be found in [9] (p. 6–20).

Williams and Beer [5] define *sources* $\mathbf{S}_i \in \mathcal{P}_1(\mathbf{V})$ as all combinations of viewable variables ($\mathcal{P}_1(\mathbf{V})$ referring to the power set of $\mathbf{V}$ without the empty set) and use Equation (1a) to construct all distinct interactions between them $\alpha \in \mathcal{A}(\mathbf{V})$, which are referred to as *partial information atoms*. Equation (1b) provides a partial order of atoms to construct a *redundancy lattice* $(\mathcal{A}(\mathbf{V}), \preccurlyeq)$. As a convention, we indicate the visible variables contained in a source by its index, such as $\mathbf{S}_{12} = \{V_1, V_2\}$. The example of the redundancy lattice for two and three visible variables is shown in Figure 2.

$$\mathcal{A}(\mathbf{V}) = \{\alpha \in \mathcal{P}_1(\mathcal{P}_1(\mathbf{V})) \mid \forall \mathbf{S}_i, \mathbf{S}_j \in \alpha, \mathbf{S}_i \not\subset \mathbf{S}_j\}, \tag{1a}$$

$$\forall \alpha, \beta \in \mathcal{A}(\mathbf{V}), (\alpha \preccurlyeq \beta \Leftrightarrow \forall \mathbf{S}_j \in \beta, \exists \mathbf{S}_i \in \alpha \mid \mathbf{S}_i \subseteq \mathbf{S}_j). \tag{1b}$$

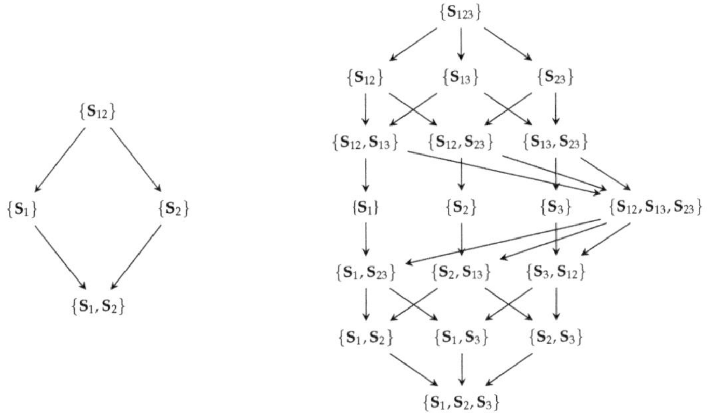

(a) (b)

Figure 2. The redundancy lattices for two (**a**) and three (**b**) visible variables. The redundancy lattice specifies the expected inclusion relation between atoms. The following function $I_\cap$ shall measure the shared information for a sets of variables such that the element $\{\mathbf{S}_1, \mathbf{S}_2\}$ represents the shared information between $\mathbf{S}_1$ and $\mathbf{S}_2$ about the target variable T.

A measure of *redundant information* $I_\cap$ shall be defined for this lattice as "[...] cumulative information function which in effect integrates the contribution from each node as one moves up through the nodes of the lattice" [9] (p. 15). Williams and Beer [5] then use the Möbius inverse (Equation (2)) to identify the *partial information* $I_\delta(\alpha; T)$ as the contribution of atom $\alpha \in \mathcal{A}(\mathbf{V})$ and therefore the desired unique/redundant/synergetic component.

A PID is said to be *non-negative* if the resulting partial contributions are guaranteed to be non-negative.

$$I_\delta(\alpha;T) = I_\cap(\alpha;T) - \sum_{\beta \in \downarrow \alpha} I_\delta(\beta;T). \tag{2}$$

Williams and Beer [5] highlight three axioms that a measure of redundancy should satisfy.

Axiom 1 (Commutativity). *Invariant to the order of sources (σ permuting the order of indices):*

$$I_\cap(\mathbf{S}_1,\dots,\mathbf{S}_i;T) = I_\cap(\mathbf{S}_{\sigma(1)},\dots,\mathbf{S}_{\sigma(i)};T)$$

Axiom 2 (Monotonicity). *Additional sources can only decrease redundant information:*

$$I_\cap(\mathbf{S}_1,\dots,\mathbf{S}_{i-1};T) \geq I_\cap(\mathbf{S}_1,\dots,\mathbf{S}_i;T)$$

Axiom 3 (Self-redundancy). *For a single source, redundancy equals mutual information:*

$$I_\cap(\mathbf{S}_i;T) = I(\mathbf{S}_i;T)$$

Finally, Williams and Beer [5] proposed I_{min} (Equation (3)) as a measure of redundancy and demonstrated that it satisfies the required axioms.

$$I(\mathbf{S}_i;T=t) = \sum_{s \in \mathcal{S}_i} p(s \mid t)\left[\log\frac{1}{p(t)} - \log\frac{1}{p(t \mid s)}\right] \tag{3a}$$

$$I_{\text{min}}(\mathbf{S}_1,\dots,\mathbf{S}_k;T) = \sum_{t \in \mathcal{T}} p(t) \min_{i \in 1..k} I(\mathbf{S}_i;T=t). \tag{3b}$$

However, the measure has been criticized for not distinguishing "the *same* information and the *same amount* of information" [6–9] due to its use of a pointwise minimum (for each $t \in \mathcal{T}$) over the sources.

2.3. Quantifying Unique Information

A non-negative decomposition for the case of two viewable variables $\mathbf{V} = \{V_1, V_2\}$ was proposed by Bertschinger et al. [10] (defining unique information) as well as an equivalent decomposition by Griffith and Koch [11] (defining union information) as shown in Equation (4) (modified notation). The function $\vartheta(V_1,V_2;T)$ acts as an information measure of the union for V_1 and V_2 (the minimal information that any two variables with the same marginal distributions can achieve), which is then used to compute the partial contributions using an inclusion–exclusion principle. Bertschinger et al. [10] motivated the decomposition from the operational interpretation that if a variable provides unique information, there must be a way to utilize this information in a decision problem for some reward function. Additionally, they argue that unique information should only depend on the marginal distributions $P_{(T,V_1)}$ and $P_{(T,V_2)}$.

$$\begin{aligned}
&\vartheta(V_1,V_2;T) = \min\ I(F;G_1,G_2) \ \text{ s.t. } P_{(F,G_1)} = P_{(T,V_1)} \text{ and } P_{(F;G_2)} = P_{(T,V_2)} \\
&S(V_1,V_2;T) = I(V_1;T) + I(V_2;T) - \vartheta(V_1,V_2;T) && \text{(Shared)} \\
&U(V_1;T) \quad = \vartheta(V_1,V_2;T) - I(V_1;T) && \text{(Unique)} \\
&C(V_1,V_2;T) = I(T;V_1,V_2) - \vartheta(V_1,V_2;T) && \text{(Complementing)}
\end{aligned} \tag{4}$$

We highlight this decomposition since our approach can be interpreted as its pointwise extension (see Section 4.1).

2.4. Blackwell Order

A channel κ can be represented as a (row) stochastic matrix wherein each element is non-negative and all rows sum to one (see Figure 3). In this work, we consider the sources to be the indirect observation of the target variable through a channel $T \xrightarrow{\kappa_i} \mathbf{S}_i$ while taking the joint distribution of the visible variables within $\mathbf{S}_i$. As a result, κ_i is obtained from the conditional probability distribution $\kappa_i = T \to \mathbf{S}_i = P_{(\mathbf{S}_i|T)}$. As for sources, we list the contained visible variables as an index such that $i = 12$ corresponds to $\kappa_{12} = P_{(\mathbf{S}_{12}|T)} = P_{(V_1,V_2|T)}$.

The Blackwell order $\kappa_1 \sqsubseteq \kappa_2$ is a preorder of channels, as shown in Equation (5) [14]. It highlights that a channel equivalent to κ_1 can be obtained by garbling the output of κ_2 (a chaining of channels as seen in Equation (5)). Therefore, there exists a decision strategy based on κ_2 for any reward function that performs at least as well as all strategies based on κ_1 [12].

$$\kappa_1 \sqsubseteq \kappa_2 \iff \kappa_1 = \kappa_2 \cdot \lambda \qquad \text{for some channel } \lambda \tag{5}$$

Bertschinger and Rauh [12] showed that the Blackwell order does not define a lattice in general since it does not provide a unique meet and joint element beyond binary inputs. However, binary input channels provide a special case for which the Blackwell order is equivalent to the *zonotope order* and defines a lattice. We use the notation κ^t to indicate that a channel has a binary input ($|\mathcal{T}| = 2$) or corresponds to the one-vs-rest encoding for one state t if $|\mathcal{T}| > 2$. In this case, the row stochastic matrix representing a channel contains a set of vectors $\vec{v}_s$ as shown in Equation (6). A zonotope Z_{κ^t} (Equation (6b)) corresponds to "the image of the unit cube [...] under the linear map corresponding to [κ^t]" [12] (p. 2), and the resulting zonotope order $\kappa_1^t \sqsubseteq \kappa_2^t \Leftrightarrow Z_{\kappa_1^t} \subseteq Z_{\kappa_2^t}$ is a preorder that is identical to the Blackwell order in the special case of binary input channels [12] as visualized in Figure 3. In the resulting lattice, the joint of two channels can be obtained as the convex hull $Z_{\kappa_1^t \sqcup \kappa_2^t}$ of the zonotopes $Z_{\kappa_1^t}$ and $Z_{\kappa_2^t}$, and the meet element $Z_{\kappa_1^t \sqcap \kappa_2^t}$ corresponds to their intersection.

$$\kappa_i^t = \begin{bmatrix} p(\mathbf{S}_i = s_1 \mid T = t) & p(\mathbf{S}_i = s_2 \mid T = t) & \dots & p(\mathbf{S}_i = s_n \mid T = t) \\ p(\mathbf{S}_i = s_1 \mid T \neq t) & p(\mathbf{S}_i = s_2 \mid T \neq t) & \dots & p(\mathbf{S}_i = s_n \mid T \neq t) \end{bmatrix} \tag{6a}$$

$$Z_{\kappa_i^t} = \left\{ \sum_{s \in \mathcal{S}_i} x_s \cdot \vec{v}_s \mid 0 \leq x_s \leq 1 \right\} \qquad \text{where} \quad \vec{v}_s = \begin{pmatrix} p(\mathbf{S}_i = s \mid T = t) \\ p(\mathbf{S}_i = s \mid T \neq t) \end{pmatrix} \tag{6b}$$

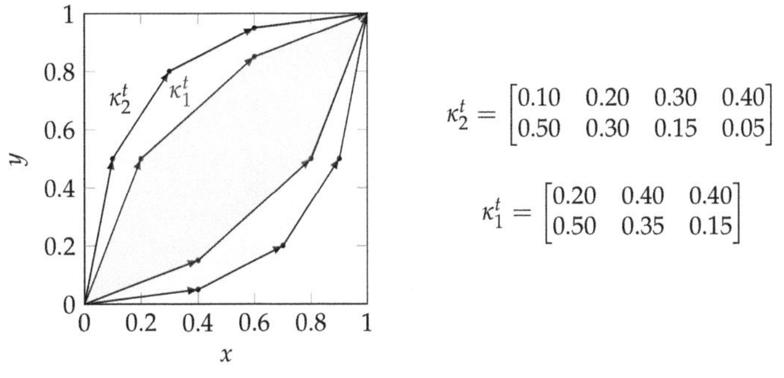

Figure 3. Visualization of the zonotope order for binary input channels. The channel κ_1^t is Blackwell inferior to κ_2^t ($\kappa_1^t \sqsubseteq \kappa_2^t$) since the corresponding zonotope $Z_{\kappa_1^t}$ (**green**) is a subset of $Z_{\kappa_2^t}$ (**purple**). As a result, the meet and joint elements of this example are: $\kappa_1^t \sqcap \kappa_2^t = \kappa_1^t$ and $\kappa_1^t \sqcup \kappa_2^t = \kappa_2^t$.

2.5. Receiver Operating Characteristic Curves

While any classification system can be represented as channel, this section focuses on binary decision problems or the one-vs-rest encoding of others ($T^t = t \Leftrightarrow T = t$). The binary label $t \in \mathcal{T}^t$ is used to obtain a sample $s \in \mathcal{S}_i$, which is processed by a classification system C to its output $o \in \mathcal{O}$ with $o = C(s)$, and applying a decision strategy d shall result in an approximation of the label $\hat{t} \in \mathcal{T}^t$ with $\hat{t} = d(o)$. This forms the Markov chain: $T^t \to \mathbf{S}_i \to O \to \hat{T}^t$. A common method of analyzing binary decision/classification systems is the Receiver Operating Characteristic (ROC). A ROC plot typically represents a classifier C with a continuous, discrete or categorical output range (by assigning distinct arbitrary values to each category) for a binary decision problem by a curve in a True-Positive Rate (TPR)/False-Positive Rate (FPR) diagram for varying decision thresholds τ_x with the decision rule for a sample s being $C(s) \leq \tau_x \Leftrightarrow$ False [15]. The resulting points are typically connected using a step function, as shown in red in Figure 4a. As a result of using a single decision threshold, the points of the ROC curve monotonically increase from $(0,0)$ to $(1,1)$; however, they are in general neither concave nor convex [16].

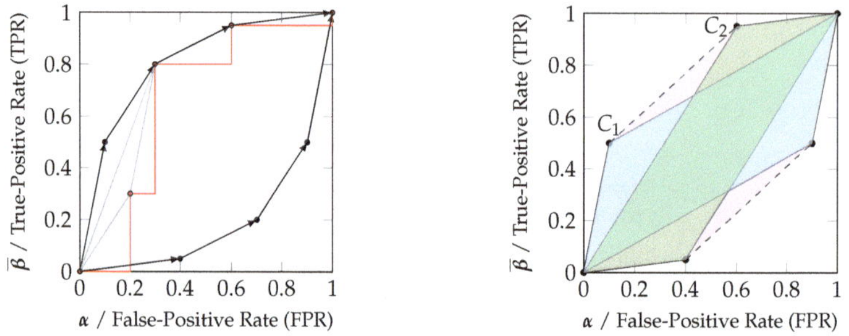

(**a**) (**b**)

Figure 4. Relating zonotopes and their convex hull to achievable decision regions. (**a**) A ROC curve (red) can be used to estimate the parameters of a channel, and the randomized combination of thresholds (Equation (7)) corresponds to an interpolation in the visualization (gray). The reachable decision region when utilizing all thresholds can be constructed using a likelihood ratio test, which corresponds to reordering the vectors by decreasing slope (in this case, swapping the first two steps) and taking the convex hull of reachable points. This reachable decision region is the zonotope of the channel. (**b**) The convex hull of any set of zonotopes is reachable by their randomized combination. Given two classifiers C_1 (blue) and C_2 (green), there always exists a randomized combination that can reach any position in their convex hull (purple).

We want to highlight the distinction between a ROC curve and the achievable performance pairs (TPR, FPR) based on the classifier. Any performance pair within the convex hull of the obtained points for constructing the ROC curve can be achieved since the decision strategy of Equation (7) results in an interpolation of the points corresponding to $\tau_1 \leq \tau_2$ with the parameter $0 \leq h \leq 1$ in the TPR/FPR diagram. Therefore, while a ROC curve *is not* convex in general, the achievable performance region *is* convex in general.

$$\begin{aligned} C(s) \leq \tau_1 &\Rightarrow \text{False}, \\ \tau_1 < C(s) \leq \tau_2 &\Rightarrow \text{Bernoulli}(h), \\ \tau_2 < C(s) &\Rightarrow \text{True}. \end{aligned} \tag{7}$$

When utilizing the set of all available thresholds on the classification output, we can identify the reachable decision regions within the TPR/FPR diagram using the likelihood ratio test, which is well known to be optimal for binary decision problems: Neyman–Pearson theory [17] states that the likelihood ratio test (Equation (8)) provides the minimal type II error (minimal $\boldsymbol{\beta}$, maximal TPR$=\overline{\boldsymbol{\beta}} = 1 - \boldsymbol{\beta}$) for a bounded type I error (FPR, $\boldsymbol{\alpha}$).

$$\begin{aligned} \frac{P(\mathbf{S}_i = s | T = t)}{P(\mathbf{S}_i = s | T \neq t)} &< \tau \Rightarrow \text{False}, \\ \frac{P(\mathbf{S}_i = s | T = t)}{P(\mathbf{S}_i = s | T \neq t)} &= \tau \Rightarrow \text{Bernoulli}(h), \\ \frac{P(\mathbf{S}_i = s | T = t)}{P(\mathbf{S}_i = s | T \neq t)} &> \tau \Rightarrow \text{True}. \end{aligned} \tag{8}$$

Notice that the decision criterion is determined by the slope of each vector in the row stochastic matrix that represents the binary input channel (Equation (6a)). This effective reordering of vectors based on their slope when varying the parameters τ and h results in the upper half of the zonotope discussed in Section 2.4 and as visualized in Figure 4a. The lower half of the zonotope is obtained from negating the outcome of the likelihood ratio test. Therefore, the zonotope representation of a channel corresponds to the achievable performance region in a TPR/FPR diagram of a classifier at binary decision problems. When reconsidering Figure 3, the channels $\kappa_1^t = T^t \to O_1$ and $\kappa_2^t = T^t \to O_2$ may correspond to two classifiers C_1 and C_2 whose channel parameters have been estimated from a ROC curve, and the achievable performance regions correspond to the zonotopes in a TPR/FPR diagram. Since the likelihood ratio test is optimal for binary decision problems, there cannot exist a decision strategy that would achieve a performance outside the zonotope. At the same time, the likelihood ratio test can be randomized to reach any desired position within the zonotope.

Finally, notice that the convex hull of any two classification systems is reachable by their randomized combination. We can view each classifier as an observation from a channel κ_1^t/κ_2^t about T^t and know that there always exists a garbling λ of the joint channel κ_{12}^t to obtain their convex hull $\kappa_1^t \sqcup \kappa_2^t = \kappa_{12}^t\lambda$. Using a likelihood ratio test on $\kappa_1^t \sqcup \kappa_2^t$, any position within the convex hull is reachable as a randomized combination of both classifiers. This has been visualized in Figure 4b. Due to this reason, we will say in Section 3.1 that the convex hull should be fully attributed to the marginal channels κ_1^t and κ_2^t.

2.6. Lattice Valuations

This section summarizes the properties of consistent lattice valuations based on Knuth [13]. The *quantification* of a lattice $(\mathbf{L}, \preccurlyeq)$ or $(\mathbf{L}, \curlywedge, \curlyvee)$ with $\alpha \curlywedge \beta = \alpha \Leftrightarrow \alpha \preccurlyeq \beta$ for elements of the set $\alpha, \beta \in \mathbf{L}$ is a function $q : \mathbf{L} \to \mathbb{R}$, which assigns reals to each element. A quantification is called a *valuation* if any two elements maintain an ordering relation: $\alpha \preccurlyeq \beta$ implies that $q(\alpha) \leq q(\beta)$. A quantification q is *consistent* if it satisfies a sum rule (inclusion–exclusion principle): $q(\alpha \curlyvee \beta) = q(\alpha) + q(\beta) - q(a \curlywedge \beta)$. If the bottom element of the lattice $(\perp)$ is evaluated to zero $q(\perp) = 0$, then the valuation of the Cartesian product of two lattices $q((\alpha;\beta)) = q(\alpha) \cdot q(\beta)$ remains consistent with the individual lattices. Finally, a *bi-quantification* can be defined as $b(\alpha,\beta) = q(\alpha \curlywedge \beta)/q(\beta)$. Similar to Knuth [13], we will use the notation $q([\alpha;\beta]) \equiv b(\alpha,\beta)$ which can be thought of as quantifying a degree of inclusion for α within β. The distributive lattice then creates an algebra like probability theory for the consistent valuation, as summarized in Equation (9) [13].

$$
\begin{aligned}
q(\alpha \curlyvee \beta) &= q(\alpha) + q(\beta) - q(\alpha \curlywedge \beta) && \text{(Sum rule)}\\
q([\alpha \curlyvee \beta;\gamma]) &= q([\alpha;\gamma]) + q([\beta;\gamma]) - q([\alpha \curlywedge \beta;\gamma]) && \text{(Sum rule)}\\
q((\alpha;\beta)) &= q(\alpha) \cdot q(\beta) && \text{(Direct product rule)}\\
q(([\alpha;\beta];[\tau;v])) &= q([\alpha;\tau]) \cdot q([\beta;v]) && \text{(Direct product rule)}\\
q([\beta \curlywedge \gamma;\alpha]) &= q([\gamma;\alpha \curlywedge \beta]) \cdot q([\beta;\alpha]) && \text{(Product rule)}\\
q([\gamma;\alpha \curlywedge \beta]) &= \frac{q([\beta;\alpha \curlywedge \gamma]) \cdot q([\gamma;\alpha])}{q([\beta;\alpha])} && \text{(Bayes' Theorem)}
\end{aligned} \tag{9}
$$

3. Quantifying Reachable Decision Regions

We start by studying the decomposition of binary decision problems from an interpretational perspective (Section 3.1). This provides the basis for constructing a distributive lattice in Section 3.2 and demonstrating the structure of a consistent valuation function. Section 3.3 highlights that mutual information is such a consistent valuation and extends the concept from binary decision problems to target variables with an arbitrary finite number of states. The resulting definition of shared information for the PID will be discussed as an application in Section 4.1 together with the tracing of information flows in Section 4.2.

We define an equivalence relation $(\sim)$ for binary input channels κ^t, which allows for the removal of zero vectors, the permutation of columns ($\mathbf{P}$ representing a permutation matrix) and the splitting/merging of columns with identical likelihood ratios (vectors of identical slope, $\ell \in \mathbb{R}$), as shown in Equation (10). These operations are invertible using garblings and do not affect the underlying zonotope.

$$\kappa^t \sim \begin{bmatrix} \kappa^t & \begin{bmatrix} 0 \\ 0 \end{bmatrix} \end{bmatrix}; \tag{10a}$$

$$\kappa^t \sim \kappa^t \mathbf{P}; \tag{10b}$$

$$\begin{bmatrix} (1+\ell)\vec{v}_1 & \vec{v}_2 & \dots \end{bmatrix} \sim \begin{bmatrix} \vec{v}_1 & \ell\vec{v}_1 & \vec{v}_2 & \dots \end{bmatrix}. \tag{10c}$$

Based on this definition, block matrices cancel at an inverted sign ($\ell = -1$) if we allow negative columns, as shown in Equation (11), where $\mathbf{M}_1$ and $\mathbf{M}_2$ are some $2 \times n$ matrix.

$$\mathbf{M}_1 \sim \begin{bmatrix} \mathbf{M}_1 & \mathbf{M}_2 & -\mathbf{M}_2 \end{bmatrix} \tag{11}$$

3.1. Motivation and Operational Interpretation

The aim of this section is to provide a first intuition based on a visual example for the methodology that will be used in Section 3.2 to construct a distributive lattice of the reachable decision regions and its consistent valuation. We only consider binary variables $T^t = \{t, \bar{t}\}$ or the one-vs-rest encoding of others ($T^t = t \Leftrightarrow T = t$).

In the used example, the desired variable can be observed indirectly using the two variables V_1 and V_2. The visible variables are considered to be the output of the channels $T^t \xrightarrow{\kappa_1^t} V_1$, $T^t \xrightarrow{\kappa_2^t} V_2$ and $T^t \xrightarrow{\kappa_{12}^t} (V_1, V_2)$ and correspond to the zonotopes shown in Figure 5. We consider each reachable decision point (a pair of TPR and FPR) to represent a different notion of uncertainty about the state of the target variable. We want to attribute the reachable decision regions to each channel for constructing a lattice, as shown in Figure 6, with the following operational interpretation:

- *Synergy:* Corresponds to the partial contribution of $\kappa_{12}^t = T^t \to (V_1, V_2)$ and represents the decision region which is only accessible due to the (in-)dependence of both variables.
- *Joint:* The joint element $\kappa_1^t \vee \kappa_2^t = (T^t \to V_1) \vee (T^t \to V_2)$ corresponds to the joint under the Blackwell order and represents the decision region which is always accessible if the marginal distributions (V_1, T^t) and (V_2, T^t) can be obtained. Therefore, we say that its information shall be fully attributed to V_1 and V_2 such that is has no partial contribution. For binary target variables, this definition is equivalent to the notion of union information by Bertschinger et al. [10] and Griffith and Koch [11]. However, we extend the analysis beyond binary target variables with a different approach in Section 3.3.
- *Unique:* Corresponds to the partial contribution of $\kappa_1^t = T^t \to V_1$ or $\kappa_2^t = T^t \to V_2$ and represents the decision region that is lost when losing the variable. It only depends on their marginal distributions (V_1, T^t) and (V_2, T^t).
- *Shared:* Corresponds to the cumulative contribution of $\kappa_1^t \wedge \kappa_2^t = (T^t \to V_1) \wedge (T^t \to V_2)$ and represents the decision region which is lost when losing either V_1 or V_2. Since it only depends on the marginal distributions, we interpret it as being part of both variables. The shared decision region can be split in two components: the decision region that is part of both individual variables and the component that is part of the convex hull but neither individual one. The latter component only exists if both variables provide unique information.
- *Redundant:* The largest decision region $\kappa_1^t \sqcap \kappa_2^t = (T^t \to V_1) \sqcap (T^t \to V_2)$ which can be accessed from both V_1 and V_2. It corresponds to the meet under the Blackwell order and the part of shared information that can be represented by some random variable (pointwise extractable component of shared information). The redundant and shared regions are equal unless both variables provide some unique information.

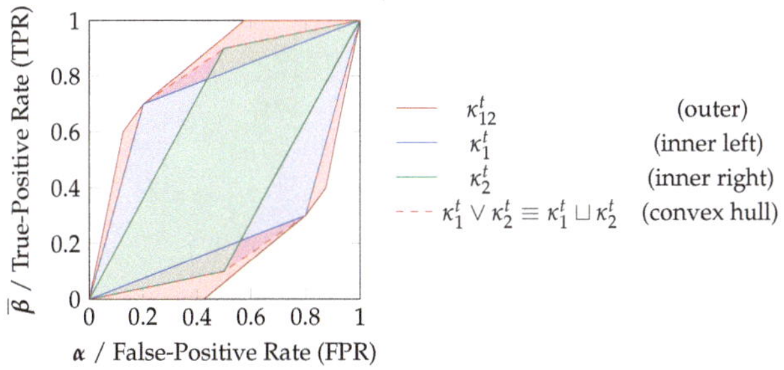

Figure 5. Relating the zonotope representations to TPR/FPR plots. The zonotopes correspond to the regions of a TPR/FPR plot that are reachable by some decision strategy. Regions outside of the zonotopes are known to be unreachable since the likelihood ratio test is optimal for binary decision problems. The convex hull of both zonotopes $\kappa_1^t \vee \kappa_2^t$ is the (unique) lower bound of any joint distribution under the Blackwell order.

Due to the invariance of re-ordering columns under the defined equivalence relation, κ^t represents a set of likelihood vectors. All cumulative and partial decision regions of Figure 6 can be constructed using a convex hull operator (joint) and matrix concatenations under the defined equivalence relation ($\sim$). For example, the shared decision region (meet) can be expressed through an inclusion–exclusion principle with the joint operator $\kappa_1^t \wedge \kappa_2^t \sim \begin{bmatrix} \kappa_1^t & \kappa_2^t & -\kappa_1^t \vee \kappa_2^t \end{bmatrix}$. This operator is not closed on channels since it introduces negative likelihood vectors. Therefore, we distinguish the notation between channels (κ^t) and atoms (α^t). These matrices α^t sum to one similar to channels but may contain negative columns. Their partial contributions $\alpha^{\delta t}$ sum to zero.

- The unique contribution of V_2: $\alpha^{\delta t} \sim \begin{bmatrix} (\kappa_1^t \vee \kappa_2^t) & -\kappa_1^t \end{bmatrix}$
- The shared cumulative region of V_1 and V_2: $\beta^t \sim \begin{bmatrix} \kappa_1^t & \kappa_2^t & -(\kappa_1^t \vee \kappa_2^t) \end{bmatrix} \sim \kappa_1^t \wedge \kappa_2^t$
- The shared partial contribution: $\beta^{\delta t} \sim \begin{bmatrix} \beta^t & -(\kappa_1^t \sqcap \kappa_2^t) \end{bmatrix}$
- Each cumulative region corresponds to the combination of partial contributions in its down-set. Notice that the partial contribution of the shared region is canceled by a section of each unique contribution due to an opposing sign:

$$\kappa_1^t \sim \begin{bmatrix} \alpha^{\delta t} & \beta^{\delta t} & (\kappa_1^t \sqcap \kappa_2^t) \end{bmatrix}$$

In Section 3.3, we demonstrate a valuation function f that can quantify all cumulative and partial atoms of this lattice while ensuring their non-negativity and consistency with the defined equivalence relation ($\sim$). We will refer to a more detailed example on the valuation of partial decision regions in Appendix C in the context of the following section.

Why does the decomposition of reachable decision regions as shown in Figure 6 provide a meaningful operational interpretation? Because combining the partial contributions of the up-set for a variable results in the decision region that becomes inaccessible when the variable is lost, while combining the partial contributions of the down-set results in the decision region that is accessible through the variable. For example, losing access to variable V_2 results in losing access to the decision regions provided uniquely by V_2 and its synergy with V_1 (the up-set on the lattice). Additionally, the cumulative component corresponds to the combination of all partial contributions in its down-set since opposing vectors cancel under the defined equivalence relation ($\sim$) such as the shared and unique contributions. Therefore, we define a consistent valuation of this lattice in Section 3.2 by quantifying decision regions based on their spanning vectors and highlight that the expected value for each $t \in \mathcal{T}$ corresponds to the definition of mutual information.

Sections 3.2 and 3.3 focus only on defining the meet and joint operators ($\wedge/\vee$) with their consistent valuation. To obtain the pointwise redundant and synergetic components for a PID, we can later add the corresponding channels when constructing the pointwise lattices $\mathbf{V} = \{V_1, V_2, (V_1, V_2), V_1 \sqcap V_2\}$ with the ordering of Figure 6 from the meet and joint operators.

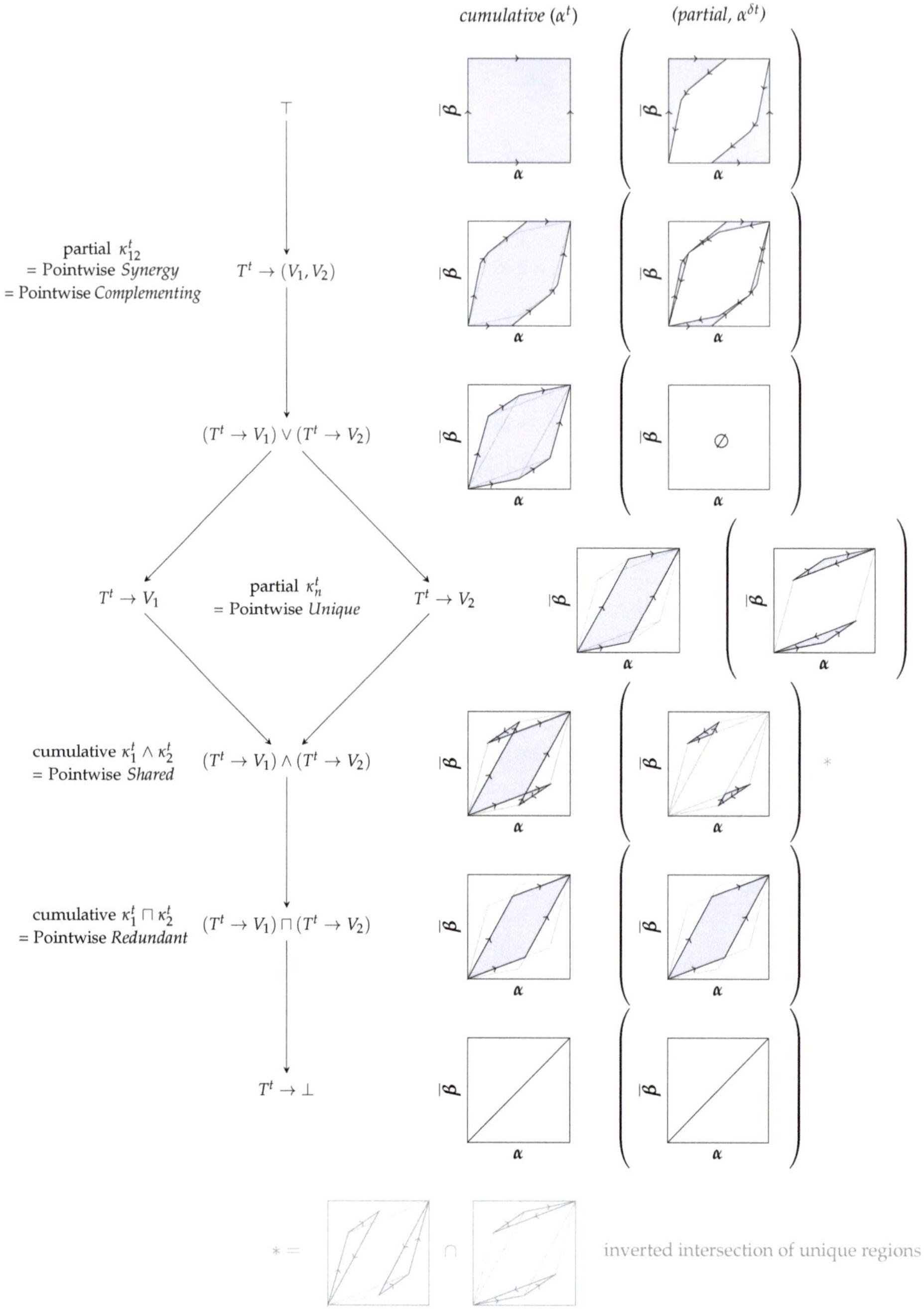

Figure 6. Decomposing the achievable decision regions for binary decision problems from an operational perspective. Each node is visualized by its cumulative and partial decision region. The partial decision region is shown within round brackets. The cumulative region corresponds to the matrix concatenation of the partial regions in its down-set under the defined equivalence relation. Three key elements are highlighted using a grey background.

3.2. Decomposition Lattice and Its Valuation

This section first defines the meet and joint operators ($\wedge$, $\vee$) and then constructs a consistent valuation for the resulting distributive lattice. For constructing a pointwise channel lattice based on the redundancy lattice, we notate the map of functions as shown in Equation (12) and consider the function $k^t(\mathbf{S}_i) = T^t \to \mathbf{S}_i = \kappa_i^t$ to obtain the pointwise channel κ_i^t of a source $\mathbf{S}_i$.

$$\begin{aligned} f\langle \mathbf{P} \rangle &= \{f(x) \mid x \in \mathbf{P}\}, \\ f\langle\langle \mathbf{P} \rangle\rangle &= \{f\langle \mathbf{x} \rangle \mid \mathbf{x} \in \mathbf{P}\}, \\ f\langle\langle\langle \mathbf{P} \rangle\rangle\rangle &= \{f\langle\langle \mathbf{x} \rangle\rangle \mid \mathbf{x} \in \mathbf{P}\}. \end{aligned} \tag{12}$$

The intersections shall correspond to some meet operation and the union to some joint operation on the pointwise channels, as shown in Equation (13), while maintaining the ordering relation of Williams and Beer [5]. This section aims to define suitable meet and joint operations together with a function for their consistent valuation. Each atom $\alpha^t, \beta^t \in \mathcal{B}^t(\mathbf{V})$ now represents an expression of channels κ^t with the operators $\vee/\wedge$, as shown in Appendix A. For example, the element $\{\mathbf{S}_{12}, \mathbf{S}_3\}$ is converted to the expression $(\kappa_1^t \vee \kappa_2^t) \wedge \kappa_3^t$.

$$\mathcal{B}^t(\mathbf{V}) = \bigwedge\langle \bigvee\langle\langle k^t\langle\langle\langle \mathcal{A}(\mathbf{V})\rangle\rangle\rangle \rangle\rangle \rangle. \tag{13}$$

As seen in Section 3.1, we want to define the joint for a set of channels to be equivalent to their convex hull, matching the Blackwell order. This also ensures that the joint operation is closed on channels.

$$\kappa_1^t \vee \kappa_2^t \equiv \kappa_1^t \sqcup \kappa_2^t \qquad \text{(joint is closed on channels)} \tag{14}$$

Since opposing vectors cancel under the defined equivalence relation, we can use a notion of the Möbius inverse to define the set of vectors spanning a partial decision region $\alpha^{\delta t}$ for an atom $\alpha^t \in \mathcal{B}^t(\mathbf{V})$, as shown in Equation (15), written as a recursive block matrix and using the strict down-set of the ordering based on the underlying redundancy lattice.

$$\alpha^{\delta t} \equiv \begin{bmatrix} \alpha^t & -[\beta^{\delta t} \mid \beta^t \in \dot{\downarrow}\alpha^t] \end{bmatrix} \tag{15}$$

The definition of the meet operator ($\wedge$) and the extension of the joint operator ($\vee$) from channels to atoms is now obtained from the constraint that the partial contribution for the joint of two incomparable atoms ($\alpha^t, \beta^t \in \mathcal{B}^t(\mathbf{V}), \alpha^t \vee \beta^t \not\sim \alpha^t$ and $\alpha^t \vee \beta^t \not\sim \beta^t$) shall be zero, as shown in Equation (16).

$$\alpha^t \vee \beta^t \not\sim \alpha^t \text{ and } \alpha^t \vee \beta^t \not\sim \beta^t \quad \Rightarrow \quad (\alpha^t \vee \beta^t)^{\delta t} \equiv \begin{bmatrix} 0 \\ 0 \end{bmatrix} \tag{16}$$

This creates the desired inclusion–exclusion principle and results in the equivalences of the meet for two and three atoms, as shown in Equation (17). Their resulting partial channels ($\alpha^{\delta t}$) correspond to the set of vectors spanning the desired unique and shared decision regions of Figure 6.

$$\alpha^t \wedge \beta^t \sim \begin{bmatrix} \alpha^t & \beta^t & -\alpha^t \vee \beta^t \end{bmatrix} \tag{17a}$$

$$\alpha^t \wedge (\beta^t \wedge \gamma^t) \sim \begin{bmatrix} \alpha^t & \beta^t & \gamma^t & -\alpha^t \vee \beta^t & -\alpha^t \vee \gamma^t & -\beta^t \vee \gamma^t & \alpha^t \vee \beta^t \vee \gamma^t \end{bmatrix} \tag{17b}$$

From their construction, the meet and joint operators provide a distributive lattice for a set of channels under the defined equivalence relation as shown in Appendix B by satisfying idempotency, commutativity, associativity, absorption and distributivity. This can be used to define a corresponding ordering relation (Equation (18)).

$$\alpha^t \preceq \beta^t \equiv \alpha^t \wedge \beta^t \sim \alpha^t \Leftrightarrow \alpha^t \vee \beta^t \sim \beta^t \tag{18}$$

To obtain a consistent valuation of this lattice, we consider a function $f(\alpha^t)$, as shown in Equation (19). First, this function has to be invariant under the defined equivalence relation, and second, it has to match the ordering of the constructed lattice.

$$f(\alpha^t) = \sum_{\vec{v}\in\alpha^t} r(\vec{v}) \quad \text{where } r \text{ is } \textit{convex} \text{ and satisfies} \quad r(\ell\vec{v}) = \ell r(\vec{v}) \text{ and } r\left(\left[\begin{smallmatrix}\ell\\ \ell\end{smallmatrix}\right]\right) = 0 \quad (19)$$

The function f shall apply a (convex) function $r(\vec{v})$ to each vector of the matrix of an atom $\vec{v} \in \alpha^t$. The function is invariant under the equivalence relation ($\sim$, Equation (10)):

- Zero vectors do not affect the quantification: $r\left(\left[\begin{smallmatrix}0\\ 0\end{smallmatrix}\right]\right) = 0$
- The structure of f ensures invariance under reordering columns: $f(\kappa^t) = f(\kappa^t \mathbf{P})$
- The property $r(\ell\vec{v}) = \ell r(\vec{v})$ with $\ell \in \mathbb{R}$ ensures invariance under splitting/merging columns of identical likelihood ratios:
  $f([(1+\ell)\vec{v}_1]) = (1+\ell)r(\vec{v}_1) = r(\vec{v}_1) + \ell r(\vec{v}_1) = f([\vec{v}_1 \quad \ell\vec{v}_1])$

The function f is a consistent valuation of the ordering relation ($\preceq$, Equation (18)) from the constructed lattice:

- The convexity of r ensures that the quantification $f(\alpha^t)$ is a valuation as shown in Appendix C: $\beta^t \preceq \alpha^t \Rightarrow f(\beta^t) \leq f(\alpha^t)$
- The function f provides a sum-rule: $f(\alpha^t \wedge \beta^t) = f([\alpha^t \quad \beta^t \quad -\alpha^t\vee\beta^t]) = f(\alpha^t) + f(\beta^t) - f(\alpha^t \vee \beta^t)$
- The function f quantifies the bottom element correctly: $f(\bot) = r\left(\left[\begin{smallmatrix}\ell\\ \ell\end{smallmatrix}\right]\right) = 0$

A parameterized function that forms a consistent lattice valuation with $0 \leq p \leq 1$ and that will be used in Section 3.3 is shown in Equation (20) (the convexity of r_p is shown in Appendix D).

$$f_p(\alpha^t) = \sum_{\vec{v}\in\alpha^t} r_p(\vec{v}) \quad (20a)$$

$$r_p(\vec{v}) = r_p\left(\left[\begin{smallmatrix}x\\ y\end{smallmatrix}\right]\right) = x\log\left(\frac{x}{px + (1-p)y}\right) \quad (20b)$$

This section demonstrated the construction of a distributive lattice and its consistent valuation, resulting in an algebra as shown in Equation (9).

3.3. Decomposing Mutual Information

This section demonstrates that mutual information is the expected value of a consistent valuation for the constructed pointwise lattices and discusses the resulting algebra. To show this, we define the parameter p and pointwise channel κ_i^t for the consistent valuation (Equation (20)) using a one-vs-rest encoding (Equation (21)).

$$\begin{aligned} p &= P_{(T=t)} && \text{(parameter)} \\ \kappa_i^t &= \begin{bmatrix} P_{(\mathbf{S}_i|T=t)} \\ P_{(\mathbf{S}_i|T\neq t)} \end{bmatrix} = \begin{bmatrix} x_1 & x_2 & \dots & x_m \\ y_1 & y_2 & \dots & y_m \end{bmatrix} && \text{(binary input channel)} \end{aligned} \quad (21)$$

The expected value of the resulting valuation in Equation (20) is equivalent to the definition of mutual information, as shown in Equation (22). Therefore, we can interpret mutual information as being the expected value of quantifying the reachable decision regions for each state of the target variable that represent a concept of pointwise uncertainty.

$$I(T;\mathbf{S}_i) = \sum_{s\in\mathcal{S}_i}\sum_{t\in\mathcal{T}} P_{(\mathbf{S}_i,T)}(s,t)\log(\frac{P_{(\mathbf{S}_i,T)}(s,t)}{P_{\mathbf{S}_i}(s)P_T(t)}) \tag{22a}$$

$$= \mathbb{E}_T\left[\sum_{s\in\mathcal{S}_i} \underbrace{P_{(\mathbf{S}_i|T=t)}(s)}_{x_j}\log\left(\frac{\overbrace{P_{(\mathbf{S}_i|T=t)}(s)}^{x_j}}{\underbrace{P_{(T=t)}}_{p}\underbrace{P_{(\mathbf{S}_i|T=t)}(s)}_{x_j}+\underbrace{(1-P_{(T=t)})}_{1-p}\underbrace{P_{(\mathbf{S}_i|T\neq t)}(s)}_{y_j}}\right)\right] \tag{22b}$$

The expected value for a set of consistent lattice valuations corresponds to a weighted sum such that the resulting lattice remains consistent. Therefore, we can combine the pointwise lattices to extend the definition of mutual information for meet and joint elements, which we will think of as intersections and unions. Let α represent an expression of sources with the operators $\vee$ and $\wedge$. Then, we can obtain its valuation from the pointwise lattices using the function $\hat{I}_T$, as shown in Equation (23). Notice that we do not define the operators for random variables but only use the notation for selecting the corresponding element on the underlying pointwise lattices. For example, we write $\alpha = (\mathbf{S}_{12} \wedge \mathbf{S}_3) \vee \mathbf{S}_4$ to refer to the pointwise atom $\alpha^t = (\kappa^t_{12} \wedge \kappa^t_3) \vee \kappa^t_4$ on each pointwise lattice.

The special case of atoms that consist of a single source corresponds by construction to the definition of mutual information. However, we propose normalizing the measure, as shown in Equation (23), to capture a degree of inclusion between zero and one. This is possible for discrete variables and will lead to an easier intuition for the later definition of bi-valuations and product spaces by ensuring the same output range for these measures. As a possible interpretation for the special role of the target variable, we like to think of T as the considered origin of information within the system, which then propagates through channels to other variables.

$$\begin{aligned}
\hat{I}_T(\alpha) &\equiv \frac{\mathbb{E}_T\left[f_{P_T(t)}(\alpha^t)\right]}{\mathbb{E}_T\left[f_{P_T(t)}(\top)\right]} &&= \frac{\mathbb{E}_T\left[f_{P_T(t)}(\alpha^t)\right]}{H(T)} \\
\hat{I}_T(T) &= 1 &&= \frac{H(T)}{H(T)} \\
\hat{I}_T(\mathbf{S}_i) &= \hat{I}_T(T\wedge\mathbf{S}_i) &&= \frac{I(T;\mathbf{S}_i)}{H(T)}
\end{aligned} \tag{23}$$

We obtain the following algebra with the bi-valuation $\hat{I}_T([\alpha;\ \beta])$ that quantifies a degree of inclusion from α within the context of β. We can think of $\hat{I}_T([\alpha;\ \beta])$ as asking how much of the information from β about T is shared with α.

$$\hat{I}_T(\alpha\vee\beta) = \hat{I}_T(\alpha) + \hat{I}_T(\beta) - \hat{I}_T(\alpha\wedge\beta) \qquad \text{(Sum rule)} \tag{24a}$$

$$\hat{I}_T([\alpha;\ \beta]) \equiv \frac{\hat{I}_T(\alpha\wedge\beta)}{\hat{I}_T(\beta)} \qquad \text{(Bi-Valuation)} \tag{24b}$$

$$\hat{I}_T([\alpha\vee\beta;\ \gamma]) = \hat{I}_T([\alpha;\ \gamma]) + \hat{I}_T([\beta;\ \gamma]) - \hat{I}_T([\alpha\wedge\beta;\ \gamma]) \qquad \text{(Conditioned sum rule)} \tag{24c}$$

$$\hat{I}_T([\beta\wedge\gamma;\ \alpha]) = \hat{I}_T([\gamma;\ \alpha\wedge\beta])\cdot\hat{I}_T([\beta;\ \alpha]) \qquad \text{(Product rule)} \tag{24d}$$

$$\hat{I}_T([\beta;\ \alpha\wedge\gamma]) = \frac{\hat{I}_T([\gamma;\ \alpha\wedge\beta])\cdot\hat{I}_T([\beta;\ \alpha])}{\hat{I}_T([\gamma;\ \alpha])} \qquad \text{(Bayes' Theorem)} \tag{24e}$$

Since the definitions satisfy an inclusion–exclusion principle, we obtain the interpretation of classical measures as proposed by Williams and Beer [5]: conditional mutual information $I(T;V_1 \mid V_2)$ measures the unique contribution of V_1 plus its synergy with V_2, and interaction information $I(T;V_1;V_2)$ measures the difference between synergy and shared information, which explains its possible negativity.

As highlighted by Knuth [13], the lattice product (the Cartesian product with ordering $(\alpha;\beta) \preceq (\tau;v) \Leftrightarrow \alpha \preceq \tau$ and $\beta \preceq v$) can be valuated using a product rule to maintain consistency with the ordering of the individual lattices. This creates an opportunity to define information product spaces for multiple reference variables. Since we normalized the measures, the valuation of the product space will also be normalized to the range from zero to one. The subscript notation $T_1 \times T_2$ shall indicate the product of the lattice constructed for T_1 with the product of the lattice constructed for T_2.

$$\hat{I}_{(T_1\times T_2)}((\alpha;\ \beta)) = \hat{I}_{T_1}(\alpha)\cdot\hat{I}_{T_2}(\beta) \qquad \text{(Valuation Product rule)} \qquad (25a)$$

$$\hat{I}_{(T_1\times T_2)}(([\alpha;\ \tau];\ [\beta;\ v])) = \hat{I}_{T_1}([\alpha;\ \beta])\cdot\hat{I}_{T_2}([\tau;v]) \qquad \text{(Bi-Valuation Product rule)} \qquad (25b)$$

The lattice product is distributive over the joint for disjoint elements [13], which leads to the equivalence in Equation (26). Unfortunately, it appears that only the bottom element is disjoint with other atoms in the constructed lattice.

$$\forall t : \alpha^t \wedge \beta^t \sim \bot \quad \Rightarrow \quad \hat{I}_{(T_1\times T_2)}((\alpha \vee \beta;\ \tau)) = \hat{I}_{(T_1\times T_2)}((\alpha;\ \tau) \vee (\beta;\ \tau)) \qquad (26)$$

Finally, we would like to provide an intuition for this approach based on possible operational scenarios:

1. Consider having characterized four radio links and obtained the conditional distributions $P_{V_1|T}$, $P_{(V_2,V_3)|T}$ and $P_{V_4|T}$. We are interested in their joint channel capacity; however, lack the required joint distribution. In this case, we can use their joint $\sup_{P_T(t)} \hat{I}_T(\mathbf{S}_1 \vee \mathbf{S}_{23} \vee \mathbf{S}_4)$ to obtain a (pointwise) lower bound on their joint channel capacity.
2. Consider having two datasets $\{T_1, V_1, V_2, V_3\}$ and $\{T_2, V_2, V_3, V_4\}$ that provide different types of labels (T_x) and associated features (V_y), where some events were recorded in both datasets. In such cases, one may choose to study the cases $T_1 \to (V_1, V_2, V_3)$, $T_2 \to (V_2, V_3, V_4)$ and $(T_1, T_2) \to (V_1, V_2, V_3, V_4)$ for events appearing in both datasets, which could then be combined into a product lattice $\hat{I}_{(T_1\times T_2\times(T_1,T_2))}$.

4. Applications

This section focuses on applications of the obtained measure from Section 3.3. We first apply the meet operator to the redundancy lattice for constructing a PID. Since an atom of the redundancy lattice $\alpha \in \mathcal{A}(\mathbf{V})$ corresponds to a set of sources for which the shared information shall be measured, we use the notation $\bigwedge \alpha$ to obtain an expression for the function $\hat{I}_T$. Section 4.2 additionally utilizes the properties of a Markov chain to demonstrate how the flow of partial information can be traced through system models.

4.1. Partial Information Decomposition

Based on Section 3.3, we can define a measure of shared information $\hat{I}(\alpha;T)$ for the elements of the redundancy lattice $\alpha \in \mathcal{A}(\mathbf{V})$ in the framework of Williams and Beer [5], as shown in Equation (27). The measure satisfies the three axioms of Williams and Beer [5] (commutativity from the equivalence relation and structure of f_p, monotonicity from being a lattice valuation and self-redundancy from removing the normalization), and the decomposition is non-negative since the joint channel κ_{12}^t is superior to the joint of two channels $\kappa_1^t \vee \kappa_2^t$ for all $t \in \mathcal{T}$. The partial contribution $\hat{I}^\delta(\alpha;T)$ corresponds to the expected value of the quantified partial decision regions $\alpha^{\delta t}$.

This provides the interpretation of Section 3.1, where combining the partial contributions of the up-set corresponds to the expected value of quantifying the decision regions that are lost when losing the variable, while combining the partial contributions of the down-set corresponds to the expected value of quantifying the accessible decision region from this variable. Additionally, we obtain a pointwise version of the property by Bertschinger et al. [10]: if a variable provides unique information, then there is a way to utilize this information for a reward function to some target variable state. Finally, it can be seen that taking the minimal quantification of the different decision regions as done by Williams and Beer [5] leads to a lack in distinguishing distinct reachable decision regions or, as phrased in the literature: a lack of distinguishing "the *same* information and the *same amount* of information" [6–9].

$$\forall \alpha \in \mathcal{A}(\mathbf{V}), \quad \hat{I}(\alpha; T) = \hat{I}_T\left(\bigwedge \alpha\right) \cdot H(T), \tag{27a}$$

$$\hat{I}^{\delta}(\alpha; T) = \hat{I}(\alpha; T) - \sum_{\beta \in \downarrow\alpha} \hat{I}^{\delta}(\beta; T) = \mathbb{E}_T\left[f_{P_T(t)}\left(\alpha^{\delta t}\right)\right] \tag{27b}$$

An identical definition of $\hat{I}(\alpha; T)$ can be obtained only based on the Blackwell order, as shown in Equation (28). Let $\alpha \in \mathcal{A}(\mathbf{V})$ be a set of sources and let T^t represent a binary target variable ($\mathcal{T}^t = \{t, \bar{t}\}$) such that $T^t = t \Leftrightarrow T = t$. We can expand the meet operator used in Equation (27a) using the sum-rule and utilize the distributivity for arriving at the joint of two channels, which matches the Blackwell order (Equation (28b)). We write $\mathbf{S}_i \sqcup_{T^t} \mathbf{S}_j$ to refer to the joint of $\mathbf{S}_i$ and $\mathbf{S}_j$ under the Blackwell order with respect to variable T^t. This results in the recursive definition of $i(\alpha; T^t)$ that corresponds to the definition of mutual information for a single source (Equation (28a)). This expansion of Equation (27a) is particularly helpful since it eliminates the operators $\wedge/\vee$ for a simplified implementation.

$$i(\{\mathbf{S}_i\}; T^t) = \sum_{s \in \mathcal{S}_i} P_{(\mathbf{S}_i|T^t=t)}(s) \log\left(\frac{P_{(\mathbf{S}_i|T^t=t)}(s)}{P_{(T^t=t)}P_{(\mathbf{S}_i|T^t=t)}(s) + (1 - P_{(T^t=t)})P_{(\mathbf{S}_i|T^t \neq t)}(s)}\right) \tag{28a}$$

$$i(\{\mathbf{S}_i\} \cup \beta; T^t) = i(\{\mathbf{S}_i\}; T^t) + i(\beta; T^t) - i(\{\mathbf{S}_i \sqcup_{T^t} \mathbf{S}_j \mid \mathbf{S}_j \in \beta\}; T^t) \tag{28b}$$

$$\hat{I}(\alpha; T) = \mathbb{E}_T\left[i(\alpha, T^t)\right] \tag{28c}$$

Our decomposition is equivalent to the measures of Bertschinger et al. [10], Griffith and Koch [11] and Williams and Beer [5] in two special cases:

- For a binary target variable $\mathcal{T} = \{t, \bar{t}\}$ with two observable variables V_1 and V_2, our approach is identical to Bertschinger et al. [10] and Griffith and Koch [11] since $\kappa_1 \sqcup \kappa_2 \sim \kappa_1^t \vee \kappa_2^t \sim \kappa_1^{\bar{t}} \vee \kappa_2^{\bar{t}}$. Beyond binary target variables, the resulting definitions differ due to the pointwise construction (see Appendix E).
- If from a pointwise perspective (T^t), some variable is Blackwell superior to the other (not necessarily the same each time), then our method is identical to Williams and Beer [5] since the defined meet operation will equal their minimum $\kappa_1^t \sqcup \kappa_2^t \sim \kappa_2^t \Rightarrow f_p(\kappa_1^t) \leq f_p(\kappa_2^t) \Rightarrow \min(f_p(\kappa_1^t), f_p(\kappa_2^t)) = f_p(\kappa_1^t \wedge \kappa_2^t) = f_p(\kappa_1^t)$ and equivalently for the function $i(\alpha, T^t)$.

A decomposition of typical examples can be found in Appendix E. We also provide an implementation of the PID based on our approach [18].

4.2. Information Flow Analysis

Due to the achieved inclusion–exclusion principle, the data processing inequality of mutual information and the achieved non-negativity of partial information for an arbitrary number of variables, it is possible to trace the flow of information through Markov chains. The measure $\hat{I}_T$ appears suitable for this analysis due to the chaining properties of the underlying pointwise channels that are quantified. The analysis can be applied among others for analyzing communication networks or designing data processing systems.

The flow of information in Markov chains has been studied by Niu and Quinn [19], who considered chaining individual variables $X_1 \rightarrow X_2 \rightarrow \ldots \rightarrow X_n$ and performed a decomposition on $\mathbf{V} = \{X_1, X_2, \ldots, X_n\}$. In contrast to this, we consider Markov chains that map sets of random variables from one step to the next. In this case, it is possible to perform an information decomposition at each step of the Markov chain and identify how the partial information components propagate from one set of variables to the next.

Let $T \rightarrow \mathbf{V} \rightarrow \mathbf{Q}$ be a Markov chain with the atoms $\alpha \in \mathcal{A}(\mathbf{V})$ and $\beta \in \mathcal{A}(\mathbf{Q})$, through which we trace the flow of partial information from α to β about T. We can measure the shared information between both atoms α and β, as shown in Equation (29a), to obtain how much information their cumulative components share $\hat{f}^{\cap\rightarrow\cap}(\alpha \rightarrow \beta; T)$. Similar to the PID, we remove the normalization for the self-redundancy axiom. To identify how much of the cumulative information of β is obtained from the partial information of α, we subtract the strict down-set of α on the lattice $(\mathcal{A}(\mathbf{V}), \preccurlyeq)$ as shown in Equation (29b) to obtain $\hat{f}^{\delta\rightarrow\cap}(\alpha \rightarrow \beta; T)$. To compute how much of the partial information of α is shared with the partial contribution of β, we similarly remove the flow from the partial information of α into the strict down-set of β on the lattice $(\mathcal{A}(\mathbf{Q}), \preccurlyeq)$, as shown in Equation (29c), to obtain $\hat{f}^{\delta\rightarrow\delta}(\alpha \rightarrow \beta; T)$. This can be used to trace the origin of information for each atom $\beta \in \mathcal{A}(\mathbf{Q})$ to the previous elements $\alpha \in \mathcal{A}(\mathbf{V})$.

The approach is not limited to one step and can be extended for tracing the flow through Markov chains of arbitrary length $\hat{f}^{\delta\rightarrow\delta\rightarrow\delta\,\cdots}(\alpha \rightarrow \beta \rightarrow \gamma\ \ldots; T)$. However, we only trace one step in this demonstration for simplicity.

$$\hat{f}^{\cap\rightarrow\cap}(\alpha \rightarrow \beta; T) = \hat{I}_T\left(\bigwedge \alpha \wedge \bigwedge \beta\right) \cdot H(T) \tag{29a}$$

$$\hat{f}^{\delta\rightarrow\cap}(\alpha \rightarrow \beta; T) = \hat{f}^{\cap\rightarrow\cap}(\alpha \rightarrow \beta; T) - \sum_{\gamma \in \downarrow \alpha} \hat{f}^{\delta\rightarrow\cap}(\gamma \rightarrow \beta; T) \tag{29b}$$

$$\hat{f}^{\delta\rightarrow\delta}(\alpha \rightarrow \beta; T) = \hat{f}^{\delta\rightarrow\cap}(\alpha \rightarrow \beta; T) - \sum_{\gamma \in \downarrow \beta} \hat{f}_T^{\delta\rightarrow\delta}(\alpha \rightarrow \gamma; T) \tag{29c}$$

We demonstrate the Information Flow Analysis using a full-adder as a small logic circuit with the input variables $\mathbf{V} = \{A, B, C_{\text{in}}\}$ and the output $\mathbf{T} = \{S, C_{\text{out}}\}$ as shown in Equation (30). Any ideal implementation of this computation results in the same channel from $\mathbf{V}$ to $\mathbf{T}$. Therefore, they create an identical flow of the partial information from $\mathbf{V}$ to the partial information of $\mathbf{T}$. However, the specific implementation will determine how (over which intermediate representations and paths) the partial information is transported.

$$\begin{aligned} S &= A \oplus B \oplus C_{\text{in}} \\ C_{\text{out}} &= A \cdot B + A \cdot C_{\text{in}} + B \cdot C_{\text{in}} \\ &= (A \cdot B) + C_{\text{in}} \cdot (A \oplus B)) \qquad \text{(typical implementation)} \\ T &= (S, C_{\text{out}}) \end{aligned} \tag{30}$$

To make the example more interesting, we consider the implementation of a noisy full-adder, as shown in Figure 7, which allows for bit-flips on wires. We indicate the probability of a bit-flip below each line and imagine this value correlates to the wire length and proximity to others. Now, changing the implementation or even the layout of the same circuit would have an impact on the overall channel.

To perform the analysis, we first have to define the target variable: What it is that we want to measure information about? In this case, we select the joint distribution of the desired computation output T as the target variable and define the noisy computation result to be $\hat{\mathbf{T}} = \{\hat{S}, \hat{C}_{\text{out}}\}$, as shown in Figure 7. We obtain both variables from their definition by assuming that the input variables $\mathbf{V}$ are independently and uniformly distributed and that bit-flips occurred independently. However, it is worth noting that noise dependencies can be modeled in the joint distribution. This fully characterizes the Markov chain shown in Equation (31).

$$T = (S, C_{\text{out}}) \rightarrow \mathbf{T} = \{S, C_{\text{out}}\} \rightarrow \mathbf{V} = \{A, B, C_{\text{in}}\} \rightarrow \mathbf{Q} = \{Q_1, Q_2, Q_3\} \rightarrow \mathbf{R} = \{R_1, R_2, R_3\} \rightarrow \hat{\mathbf{T}} = \{\hat{S}, \hat{C}_{\text{out}}\} \tag{31}$$

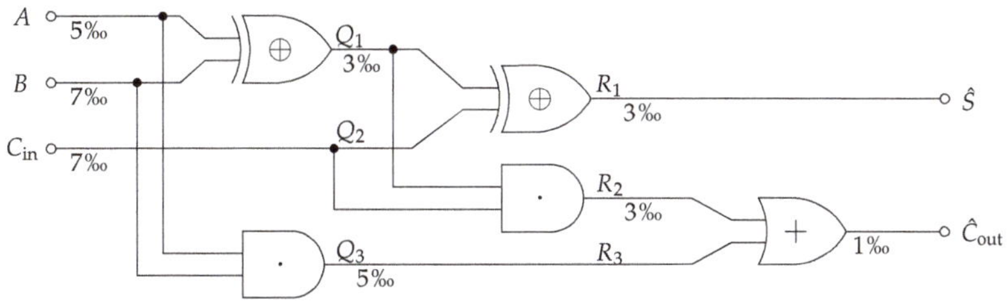

Figure 7. Noisy full-adder example for the Information Flow Analysis demonstration. The probability of a bit-flip is indicated below the wires. If a wire has two labels, the first label corresponds to the wire input and the second label to its output.

We group two variables at each stage to reduce the number of interactions in the visualization. The resulting information flow of the full-adder is shown as a Sankey diagram in Figure 8. Each bar corresponds to the mutual information of a stage in the Markov chain with the input T. The bars' colors indicate the partial information decomposition of Equation (27). The information flow over one step using Equation (29) is indicated by the width of a line between the partial contributions of two stages. To follow the flow of a particular component over more than one step—for example, to see how the shared information of $\mathbf{T}$ propagates to the shared information of $\hat{\mathbf{T}}$—the analysis can be performed by tracing multiple steps after extending Equation (29).

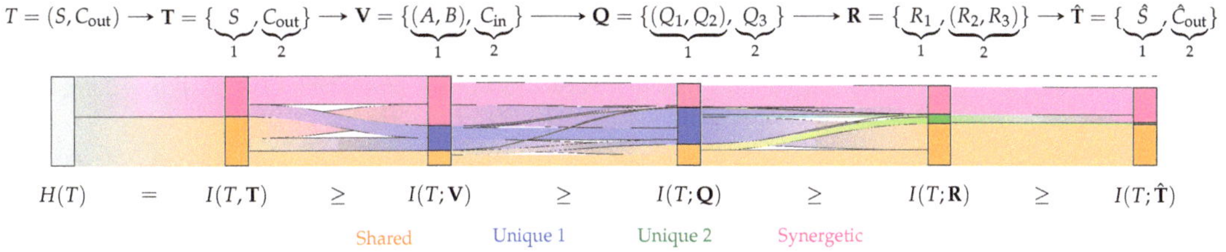

Figure 8. Sankey diagram of the Information Flow Analysis for the noisy full-adder in Figure 7. Each bar corresponds to one stage in the Markov chain, and its height corresponds to this stage's mutual information with the target T. Each bar is decomposed into the information that the considered variables provide shared (orange), unique (blue/green) or synergetic (pink) about the target. If a stage is represented by a single variable or joint distribution, no further decomposition is performed (gray). We trace the information between variables over one step using the sub-chains $T \to T \to \mathbf{T}$, $T \to \mathbf{T} \to \mathbf{V}$, $T \to \mathbf{V} \to \mathbf{Q}$, $T \to \mathbf{Q} \to \mathbf{R}$ and $T \to \mathbf{R} \to \hat{\mathbf{T}}$ using Equation (29). The resulting flows between each bar visualize how the partial information propagates for one step in the Markov chain. For following the flow of a particular partial component over more than one step in the Sankey diagram, Equation (29) can be extended.

The results (Figure 8) show that the decomposition does not attribute unique information to S or C_{out} about their own joint distribution. The reason for this is shown in Equation (32): both variables provide an equivalent channel for each state of their joint distribution and, thus, an equivalent uncertainty about each state of T. Phrased differently, both variables provide access to the identical decision regions for each state of their joint distribution and can therefore not provide unique information (no advantage for any reward function to any $t \in \mathcal{T}$). If this result feels counter-intuitive, we would also recommend the discussion of the two-bit-copy problem and identity axiom by Finn [9] (p. 16ff.) and Finn and Lizier [20]. The same effect can also be seen when viewing each variable in $\mathbf{V}$ individually (not shown in Figure 8), which causes neither of them to provide unique information on their own about the joint target distribution T.

$$\begin{aligned}(T^{(0,0)} \to C_{\text{out}}) \sim (T^{(0,0)} \to S) \sim \begin{bmatrix} 1 & 0 \\ 3/7 & 4/7 \end{bmatrix} \sim (T^{(1,1)} \to C_{\text{out}}) \sim (T^{(1,1)} \to S) \\ (T^{(0,1)} \to C_{\text{out}}) \sim (T^{(0,1)} \to S) \sim \begin{bmatrix} 1 & 0 \\ 1/5 & 4/5 \end{bmatrix} \sim (T^{(1,0)} \to C_{\text{out}}) \sim (T^{(1,0)} \to S)\end{aligned} \tag{32}$$

The Information Flow Analysis is particularly useful in practice since it can be performed on an arbitrary resolution of the system model to handle its complexity. For example, a small full-adder can be analyzed on the level of gates and wires represented by channels. However, the full-adder is itself a channel that can be used to analyze an n-bit adder on the level of full-adders.

Further applications of the Information Flow Analysis could include the identification of which inputs are most critical for the computational result and where information is being lost. It can also be explored if a notion of robustness in data processing systems could be meaningfully defined based on how much pointwise redundant or shared information of the input $\mathbf{V}$ can be traced to its output $\hat{\mathbf{T}}$. This might indicate a notion of robustness based on whether or not it is possible to compensate for the unavailability of input sources through a system modification.

Finally, the target variable does not have to be the desired computational outcome as has been done in the demonstration. When thinking about secure multi-party computations, it might be of interest to identify the flow of information from the perspective of some sensitive or private variable (T) to understand the impact of disclosing the final computation result. The possible applications of such an analysis are as diverse as those of information theory.

5. Discussion

We propose the interpretation that the reachable decision regions correspond to different notions of uncertainty about each state of the target variable and that mutual information corresponds to the expected value of quantifying these decision regions. This allows partial information to represent the expected value of quantifying partial decision regions (Equations (27) and (28)), which can be used to attribute mutual information to the visible variables and their interactions (pointwise redundant/shared/unique/synergetic). Since the proposed quantification results in the consistent valuation of a distributive lattice, it creates a novel algebra for mutual information with possible practical applications (Equations (24) and (25)). Finally, the approach allows for tracing information components through Markov chains (Equation (29)), which can be used to model and study a wide range of scenarios. The presented method is directly applicable to discrete and categorical source variables due to their equivalent construction for the reachable decision regions (zonotopes). However, we recommend that the target variable should be categorical since the measure does not consider a notion of distance between target states (achievable estimation proximity). This would be an interesting direction for future work due to its practical application for introducing semantic meaning to sets of variables. An intuitive example is a target variable with 256 states that is used to represent an 8-bit unsigned integer as the computation result. For this reason, we wonder if it is possible to introduce a notion of distance to the analysis such that the classical definition of mutual information becomes the special case for encoding categorical targets.

A recent work by Kolchinsky [21] removes the assumption that an inclusion–exclusion principle relates the intersection and union of information and demands their extractability. This has the disadvantage that a similar algebra or tracing of information would no longer be possible. We tried to address this point by distinguishing the *pointwise redundant* from the *pointwise shared* element and also obtain no inclusion–exclusion principle for the pointwise redundancy. We focus in this work on the pointwise shared element due to the resulting properties and operational interpretation from the accessibility and losses of reachable decision regions. Moreover, the relation between the used meet and joint operators provides consistent results from performing the decomposition using the meet operator on a redundancy lattice, as done in this work, or a decomposition using the joint operator on a synergy or loss lattice [22].

Further notions of redundancy and synergy can be studied within this framework if they are extractable, meaning they can be represented by some random variable. Depending on the desired interpretation, the representing variable can be constructed for T and added to the set of visible variables or can be constructed for each pointwise variable T^t and added to the pointwise lattices. We showed an example of the latter in Section 3.1 by adding the pointwise redundant element to the lattice, which we interpret as pointwise extractable components of shared information to quantify the decision regions that can be obtained from each source.

Since our approach satisfies the original axioms of Williams and Beer [5] and results in non-negative partial contributions for an arbitrary number of variables, it cannot satisfy the proposed identity axiom of Harder et al. [8]. This can also be seen by the decomposition examples in Appendix E (Table A2 and Figure A3). We do not consider this a limitation since all four axioms cannot be satisfied without obtaining negative partial information [23], which creates difficulties for interpreting results.

Finally, our approach does not appear to satisfy a target/left chain rule as proposed by Bertschinger et al. [7]. While our approach provides an algebra that can be used to handle multiple target variables, we think that further work on understanding the relations when decomposing with multiple target variables is needed. In particular, it would be helpful for the analysis of complex systems if the flow of already analyzed sub-chains could be reused and their interactions could be predicted.

6. Conclusions

We use the approach of Bertschinger et al. [10] and Griffith and Koch [11] to construct a pointwise partial information decomposition that provides non-negative results for an arbitrary number of variables and target states. The measure obtains an algebra from the resulting lattice structure and enables the analysis of complex multivariate systems in practice. To our knowledge, this is the first alternative to the original measure of Williams and Beer [5] that satisfies their three proposed axioms and results in a non-negative decomposition for an arbitrary number of variables.

Author Contributions: T.M. and C.R conceived the idea; T.M. prepared the original draft; C.R. reviewed and edited the draft. All authors have read and agreed to the published version of the manuscript.

Funding: This research was funded by the Swedish Civil Contingencies Agency (MSB) through the project RIOT grant number MSB 2018-12526.

Data Availability Statement: Not applicable.

Conflicts of Interest: The authors declare no conflict of interest. The funders had no role in the design of the study; in the collection, analyses, or interpretation of data; in the writing of the manuscript; or in the decision to publish the results.

Abbreviations

The following abbreviations are used:

PID	Partial Information Decomposition
ROC	Receiver Operating Characteristic
TPR	True-Positive Rate ($\overline{\beta}$)
FPR	False-Positive Rate (α)

We use the following notation conventions:

$T, \mathcal{T}, t, T^t$	T (upper case) represents the target variable with an event t (lower case) of its event space (calligraphic), $t \in \mathcal{T}$. T^t represents a pointwise (binary) target variable which takes state one if $T = t$ and state two if $T \neq t$ (T^t represents the one-vs-rest encoding of state t);
$\mathbf{V}, V_i, \mathcal{V}_i, v$	$\mathbf{V}$ represents a set of visible/observable/predictor variables V_i with $v \in \mathcal{V}_i$;
$\mathbf{S}_i, \mathcal{S}_i$	*sources* represent a set of visible variables, where the index i lists the contained visible variables, such as $\mathbf{S}_{12} = \{V_1, V_2\}$. The event $s \in \mathcal{S}_i$ corresponds to an event of the corresponding joint variable, e.g., (V_1, V_2).

We represent channels (κ, λ) as row stochastic matrices with the following indexing:

$\mathbf{P}$	represents a permutation matrix;
κ_i	represents a channel from the target to a source $T \xrightarrow{\kappa_i} \mathbf{S}_i$ using the joint distribution of the variables within the source, such as $T \xrightarrow{\kappa_{12}} (V_1, V_2)$;
κ_i^t	represents a pointwise channel from the target to a source $T^t \xrightarrow{\kappa_i^t} \mathbf{S}_i$, such as $T^t \xrightarrow{\kappa_{12}^t} (V_1, V_2)$;
$Z_{\kappa_i^t}$	binary input channels κ_i^t can be represented as (row) stochastic matrix, which contain a likelihood vector $\vec{v}_s = \begin{pmatrix} p(\mathbf{S}_i=s \mid T=t) \\ p(\mathbf{S}_i=s \mid T\neq t) \end{pmatrix}$ for each state $s \in \mathcal{S}_i$. $Z_{\kappa_i^t}$ represents the zonotope for this set of vectors;
$\kappa_1^t \vee \kappa_2^t$	represents the binary input channel corresponding to the convex hull of $Z_{\kappa_1^t}$ and $Z_{\kappa_2^t}$ (Blackwell order joint of binary input channels $\kappa_1^t \vee \kappa_2^t \equiv \kappa_1^t \sqcup \kappa_2^t$);
$\kappa_1^t \wedge \kappa_2^t$	represents the meet element for constructing a distributive lattice with the joint operator $\kappa_1^t \vee \kappa_2^t$;
$\kappa_1^t \sqcap \kappa_2^t$	represents the binary input channel corresponding to the intersection of $Z_{\kappa_1^t}$ and $Z_{\kappa_2^t}$ (Blackwell order meet of binary input channels);
α, β	*atoms* represent an expression of random variables with the operators ($\vee/\wedge$). In Sections 2.2 and 4, they represent sets of sources;
α^t, β^t	represent an expression of pointwise channels with the operators ($\vee/\wedge$);
$\alpha^{\delta t}, \beta^{\delta t}$	represent a partial pointwise channel corresponding to α^t.

We use the following convention for operations, functions and brackets:

$\mathcal{P}_1(\cdot)$	represents the power set without the empty set;
$\{V_1, V_2\}$	curly brackets with comma separation represent a set;
$[\, M_1 \; M_2 \,]$	square brackets without comma separation represent a matrix, and the listing of matrices in this manner represents their concatenation;
$q([\alpha; \beta])$	square brackets with semicolon separation are used to refer to the bi-valuation $b(\alpha, \beta)$ of a consistent lattice valuation $q(\alpha)$. In a similar manner to Knuth [13], we use the notation $q([\alpha; \beta]) \equiv b(\alpha, \beta)$;
$(\alpha; \beta)$	round brackets with semicolon separation represent an element of a Cartesian product $\mathbf{L}_1 \times \mathbf{L}_2$, where $\alpha \in \mathbf{L}_1$ and $\beta \in \mathbf{L}_2$;
$f\langle \mathbf{L} \rangle$	angled brackets indicate that a function f shall be mapped to each element of the set $\mathbf{L}$. We may nest this notation, such as $f\langle\langle \mathbf{L} \rangle\rangle$, to indicate a map to each element of the sets within $\mathbf{L}$;
$\boldsymbol{\alpha}$	False-Positive Rate, type I error;
$\overline{\boldsymbol{\beta}}$	True-Positive Rate, $1-$ type II error.

We distinguish between a *joint channel* $T \xrightarrow{\kappa_{12}} (V_1, V_2)$ and the *joint of two channels* $\kappa_1 \vee \kappa_2$. To avoid confusion, we write the first case as "joint channel (κ)" and the latter case as "joint of channels ($\kappa_i \vee \kappa_j$)" throughout this work.

Appendix A

The considered lattice relates the meet and joint elements ($\wedge/\vee$) through an inclusion–exclusion principle. Here, the partial contribution for the joint of any two incomparable elements ($\alpha^t, \beta^t \in \mathcal{B}^t(\mathbf{V}), \alpha^t \vee \beta^t \not\sim \alpha^t$ and $\alpha^t \vee \beta^t \not\sim \beta^t$) shall be zero, which is indicated using a gray font in Figure A1.

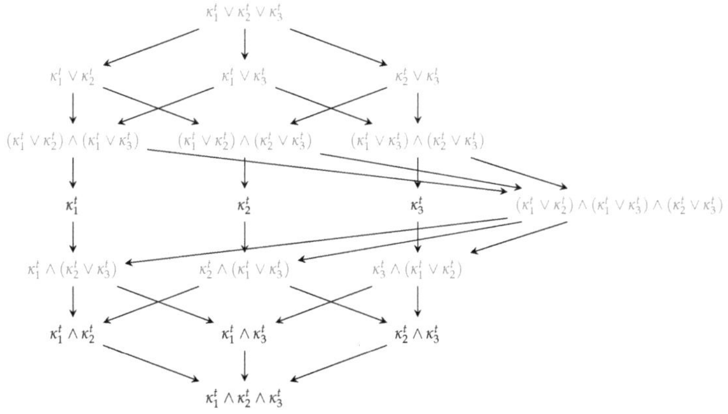

Figure A1. The considered lattice relating the meet and joint operators. The joint of any two incomparable elements ($\alpha^t, \beta^t \in \mathcal{B}^t(\mathbf{V}), \alpha^t \vee \beta^t \not\sim \alpha^t$ and $\alpha^t \vee \beta^t \not\sim \beta^t$) shall have no partial contribution to create an inclusion–exclusion principle between the operators and is highlighted using a gray font.

Appendix B

This section demonstrates that the defined meet and joint operators of Section 3.2 provide a distributive lattice under the defined equivalence relation ($\sim$, Equation (10)).

Lemma A1. *The meet and joint operators ($\wedge$, $\vee$) define a distributive lattice for a set of channels under the defined equivalence relation ($\sim$).*

Proof. The definitions of the meet and joint satisfy associativity, commutativity, idempotency, absorption and distributivity on channels under the defined equivalence relation:

1. *Idempotency:* $\kappa_1^t \vee \kappa_1^t \sim \kappa_1^t$ and $\kappa_1^t \wedge \kappa_1^t \sim \kappa_1^t$.

$$\begin{aligned} &\kappa_1^t \vee \kappa_1^t \sim \kappa_1^t \sqcup \kappa_1^t \sim \kappa_1^t; \\ &\kappa_1^t \wedge \kappa_1^t \sim \begin{bmatrix} \kappa_1^t & \kappa_1^t & -\kappa_1^t \vee \kappa_1^t \end{bmatrix} \sim \begin{bmatrix} \kappa_1^t & \kappa_1^t & -\kappa_1^t \end{bmatrix} \sim \kappa_1^t. \end{aligned}$$

2. *Commutativity:* $\kappa_1^t \vee \kappa_2^t \sim \kappa_2^t \vee \kappa_1^t$ and $\kappa_1^t \wedge \kappa_2^t \sim \kappa_2^t \wedge \kappa_1^t$.

$$\begin{aligned} &\kappa_1^t \vee \kappa_2^t \sim \kappa_1^t \sqcup \kappa_2^t \sim \kappa_2^t \sqcup \kappa_1^t \sim \kappa_2^t \vee \kappa_1^t; \\ &\kappa_1^t \wedge \kappa_2^t \sim \begin{bmatrix} \kappa_1^t & \kappa_2^t & -\kappa_1^t \vee \kappa_2^t \end{bmatrix} \sim \begin{bmatrix} \kappa_2^t & \kappa_1^t & -\kappa_2^t \vee \kappa_1^t \end{bmatrix} \sim \kappa_2^t \wedge \kappa_1^t. \end{aligned}$$

3. *Associativity:* $\kappa_1^t \vee (\kappa_2^t \vee \kappa_3^t) \sim (\kappa_1^t \vee \kappa_2^t) \vee \kappa_3^t$ and $\kappa_1^t \wedge (\kappa_2^t \wedge \kappa_3^t) \sim (\kappa_1^t \wedge \kappa_2^t) \wedge \kappa_3^t$.

$$\begin{aligned} \kappa_1^t \vee (\kappa_2^t \vee \kappa_3^t) &\sim \kappa_1^t \sqcup (\kappa_2^t \sqcup \kappa_3^t) \sim (\kappa_1^t \sqcup \kappa_2^t) \sqcup \kappa_3^t \sim (\kappa_1^t \vee \kappa_2^t) \vee \kappa_3^t; \\ \kappa_1^t \wedge (\kappa_2^t \wedge \kappa_3^t) &\sim \begin{bmatrix} \kappa_1^t & \kappa_2^t & \kappa_3^t & -\kappa_1^t \vee \kappa_2^t & -\kappa_1^t \vee \kappa_3^t & -\kappa_2^t \vee \kappa_3^t & \kappa_1^t \vee \kappa_2^t \vee \kappa_3^t \end{bmatrix} \\ &\sim \begin{bmatrix} \kappa_3^t & \kappa_2^t & \kappa_1^t & -\kappa_3^t \vee \kappa_2^t & -\kappa_3^t \vee \kappa_1^t & -\kappa_2^t \vee \kappa_1^t & \kappa_3^t \vee \kappa_2^t \vee \kappa_1^t \end{bmatrix} \\ &\sim \kappa_3^t \wedge (\kappa_2^t \wedge \kappa_1^t) \sim (\kappa_1^t \wedge \kappa_2^t) \wedge \kappa_3^t. \end{aligned}$$

4. *Absorption:* $\kappa_1^t \wedge (\kappa_1^t \vee \kappa_2^t) \sim \kappa_1^t$ and $\kappa_1^t \vee (\kappa_1^t \wedge \kappa_2^t) \sim \kappa_1^t$.

$$\begin{aligned} \kappa_1^t \wedge (\kappa_1^t \vee \kappa_2^t) &\sim \begin{bmatrix} \kappa_1^t & \kappa_1^t \vee \kappa_2^t & -\kappa_1^t \vee \kappa_1^t \vee \kappa_2^t \end{bmatrix} \\ &\sim \begin{bmatrix} \kappa_1^t & \kappa_1^t \vee \kappa_2^t & -\kappa_1^t \vee \kappa_2^t \end{bmatrix} \sim \kappa_1^t; \\ \kappa_1^t \vee (\kappa_1^t \wedge \kappa_2^t) &\sim \begin{bmatrix} \kappa_1^t & \kappa_1^t \wedge \kappa_2^t & -\kappa_1^t \wedge \kappa_1^t \wedge \kappa_2^t \end{bmatrix} \\ &\sim \begin{bmatrix} \kappa_1^t & \kappa_1^t \wedge \kappa_2^t & -\kappa_1^t \wedge \kappa_2^t \end{bmatrix} \sim \kappa_1^t. \end{aligned}$$

5. *Distributivity:* $\kappa_1^t \vee (\kappa_2^t \wedge \kappa_3^t) \sim (\kappa_1^t \vee \kappa_2^t) \wedge (\kappa_1^t \vee \kappa_3^t)$ and $\kappa_1^t \wedge (\kappa_2^t \vee \kappa_3^t) \sim (\kappa_1^t \wedge \kappa_2^t) \vee (\kappa_1^t \wedge \kappa_3^t)$.

$$
\begin{aligned}
\kappa_1^t \vee (\kappa_2^t \wedge \kappa_3^t) &\sim \left[\kappa_2^t \wedge \kappa_3^t \quad \kappa_1^t \quad -\kappa_1^t \wedge (\kappa_2^t \wedge \kappa_3^t)\right] \\
&\sim \left[\kappa_2^t \wedge \kappa_3^t \quad -\kappa_2^t \quad -\kappa_3^t \quad \kappa_1^t \vee \kappa_2^t \quad \kappa_1^t \vee \kappa_3^t \quad \kappa_2^t \vee \kappa_3^t \quad -\kappa_1^t \vee \kappa_2^t \vee \kappa_3^t\right] \\
&\sim \left[-\kappa_2^t \vee \kappa_3^t \quad \kappa_1^t \vee \kappa_2^t \quad \kappa_1^t \vee \kappa_3^t \quad \kappa_2^t \vee \kappa_3^t \quad -\kappa_1^t \vee \kappa_2^t \vee \kappa_3^t\right] \\
&\sim \left[\kappa_1^t \vee \kappa_2^t \quad \kappa_1^t \vee \kappa_3^t \quad -\kappa_1^t \vee \kappa_2^t \vee \kappa_3^t\right] \\
&\sim \left[\kappa_1^t \vee \kappa_2^t \quad \kappa_1^t \vee \kappa_3^t \quad -(\kappa_1^t \vee \kappa_2^t) \vee (\kappa_1^t \vee \kappa_3^t)\right] \\
&\sim (\kappa_1^t \vee \kappa_2^t) \wedge (\kappa_1^t \vee \kappa_3^t); \\
\kappa_1^t \wedge (\kappa_2^t \vee \kappa_3^t) &\sim \left[\kappa_2^t \vee \kappa_3^t \quad \kappa_1^t \quad -\kappa_1^t \vee (\kappa_2^t \vee \kappa_3^t)\right] \\
&\sim \left[\kappa_2^t \vee \kappa_3^t \quad -\kappa_2^t \quad -\kappa_3^t \quad \kappa_1^t \wedge \kappa_2^t \quad \kappa_1^t \wedge \kappa_3^t \quad \kappa_2^t \wedge \kappa_3^t \quad -\kappa_1^t \wedge \kappa_2^t \wedge \kappa_3^t\right] \\
&\sim \left[-\kappa_2^t \wedge \kappa_3^t \quad \kappa_1^t \wedge \kappa_2^t \quad \kappa_1^t \wedge \kappa_3^t \quad \kappa_2^t \wedge \kappa_3^t \quad -\kappa_1^t \wedge \kappa_2^t \wedge \kappa_3^t\right] \\
&\sim \left[\kappa_1^t \wedge \kappa_2^t \quad \kappa_1^t \wedge \kappa_3^t \quad -(\kappa_1^t \wedge \kappa_2^t) \wedge (\kappa_1^t \wedge \kappa_3^t)\right] \\
&\sim (\kappa_1^t \wedge \kappa_2^t) \vee (\kappa_1^t \wedge \kappa_3^t).
\end{aligned}
$$

□

Appendix C

This section demonstrates the quantification of a small example and proves that the function f of Equation (19) creates a *consistent valuation* $\alpha^t \wedge \beta^t \sim \beta^t \Rightarrow f(\beta^t) \leq f(\alpha^t)$ for the pointwise lattice $(\mathcal{B}^t(\mathbf{V}), \wedge, \vee)$.

The convexity of the function $r(\vec{v})$ results, in combination with the property that $r(\ell\vec{v}) = \ell r(\vec{v})$ with $\ell \in \mathbb{R}$, in a triangle inequality, as shown in Equation (A1). This ensures that Blackwell superior channels obtain a larger quantification result and thus the non-negativity of channels: $f(\kappa^t \sqcup \lambda^t) \geq f(\kappa^t) \geq f([\begin{smallmatrix}1\\1\end{smallmatrix}]) = 0$.

$$
\begin{aligned}
r(t\vec{v}_1 + (1-t)\vec{v}_2) &\leq tr(\vec{v}_1) + (1-t)r(\vec{v}_2) && \text{(convexity, } 0 \leq t \leq 1) \\
r(\vec{v}_1 + \vec{v}_2) &\leq r(\vec{v}_1) + r(\vec{v}_2) && \text{(using } t = 0.5 \text{ and } r(\ell\vec{v}) = \ell r(\vec{v}))
\end{aligned}
\tag{A1}
$$

To provide an intuition for the meet operator with a minimal example and highlight its relation to the intersection of zonotopes (redundant region), consider the two channels κ_1^t and κ_2^t of Equation (A2) and as visualized in Figure A2. To simplify the notation, we use the property $[((1+\ell)\vec{v}_1)] \sim [(\vec{v}_1) \ (\ell\vec{v}_1)]$ to differentiate the vectors $\vec{a}_2$ and $\vec{a}_3$ as well as $\vec{b}_1$ and $\vec{b}_2$.

$$
\begin{aligned}
\kappa_1^t &\sim \left[(\vec{a}_1) \quad (\vec{a}_2) \quad (\vec{a}_3)\right] \\
\kappa_2^t &\sim \left[(\vec{b}_1) \quad (\vec{b}_2) \quad (\vec{b}_3)\right] \\
\kappa_1^t \vee \kappa_2^t &\sim \left[(\vec{a}_1) \quad (\vec{a}_2 + \vec{b}_2) \quad (\vec{b}_3)\right]
\end{aligned}
\tag{A2}
$$

The resulting shared and redundant element is shown in Equation (A3). Due to the construction of the meet element through an inclusion–exclusion principle with the joint, the meet element always contains the vectors which span the redundant decision region as the first component.

$$
\begin{aligned}
\kappa_1^t \wedge \kappa_2^t &\sim \left[(\vec{b}_1) \quad (\vec{a}_3) \quad (\vec{b}_2) \quad (\vec{a}_2) \quad -(\vec{a}_2 + \vec{b}_2)\right] \\
\kappa_1^t \sqcap \kappa_2^t &\sim \left[(\vec{b}_1) \quad (\vec{a}_3)\right]
\end{aligned}
\tag{A3}
$$

The second component of the meet element corresponds to the decision region of the joint, which is not part of either individual channel. This component is non-negative due to the triangle inequality.

$$
0 \leq f(\kappa_1^t \wedge \kappa_2^t) - f(\kappa_1^t \sqcap \kappa_2^t) = r(\vec{a}_2) + r(\vec{b}_2) - r(\vec{a}_2 + \vec{b}_2) \tag{A4}
$$

The same argument applies to the meet for an arbitrary number of channels since the inclusion–exclusion principle with the joint elements ensures that the vectors spanning the redundant region are contained in the meet element, and the triangle inequality ensures non-negativity for the additional components.

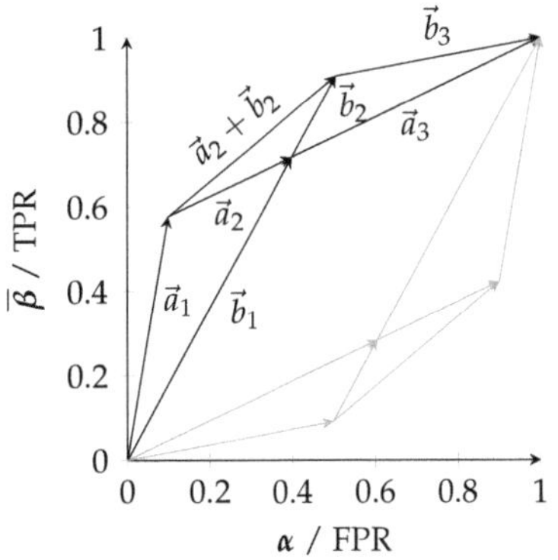

Figure A2. A minimal example to discuss the relation between the shared ($\kappa_1^t \wedge \kappa_2^t$) and redundant ($\kappa_1^t \sqcap \kappa_2^t$) decision regions. The channel κ_1^t consists of the vectors $\vec{a}_x$, and the channel κ_2^t consists of the vectors $\vec{b}_x$.

Lemma A2. *The function $f(\alpha^t)$ is a (consistent) valuation $\alpha^t \wedge \beta^t \sim \beta^t \Rightarrow f(\beta^t) \leq f(\alpha^t)$ on the pointwise lattice corresponding to $(\mathcal{B}^t(\mathbf{V}), \wedge, \vee)$, as visualized in Appendix A.*

Proof. Let $\mathbf{S}^t = \{\kappa_1^t, \ldots, \kappa_a^t\}$ represent a set of pointwise channels. The meet element ($\bigwedge_{\lambda^t \in \mathbf{S}^t} \lambda^t$) is constructed through an inclusion–exclusion principle with the joint (convex hull). This ensures that the set of vectors spanning the zonotope intersection ($\bigsqcap_{\lambda^t \in \mathbf{S}^t} \lambda^t$) is contained within the meet element. Additionally, the meet contains a second component that is ensured to be positive from the triangle inequality of r: $f(\bigwedge_{\lambda^t \in \mathbf{S}^t} \lambda^t) \geq f(\bigsqcap_{\lambda^t \in \mathbf{S}^t} \lambda^t)$. Since the joint operator is closed on channels and is distributive, we can introduce a channel to enforce a minimal redundant decision region between the channels: $f(\kappa_0^t) \leq f(\bigsqcap_{\lambda^t \in \mathbf{S}^t} \kappa_0^t \sqcup \lambda^t) \leq f(\bigwedge_{\lambda^t \in \mathbf{S}^t} \kappa_0^t \vee \lambda^t) = f(\kappa_0^t \vee \bigwedge_{\lambda^t \in \mathbf{S}^t} \lambda^t)$. Applying the sum-rule shows that $f(\kappa_0^t \wedge \bigwedge_{\lambda^t \in \mathbf{S}^t} \lambda^t) \leq f(\bigwedge_{\lambda^t \in \mathbf{S}^t} \lambda^t)$.

We again make use of the distributive property, which allows writing any expression α^t into a conjunctive normal form. Since the joint operator is closed for channels, any expression α^t can be represented as meet for a set of channels $\alpha^t \sim \bigwedge_{\lambda^t \in \{\kappa_{p_1}^t, \ldots, \kappa_{p_i}^t\}} \lambda^t$. This demonstrates that the obtained inequality of the meet operator on channels also applies to atoms $f(\alpha^t \wedge \beta^t) \leq f(\alpha^t)$, such that $\alpha^t \wedge \beta^t \sim \beta^t \Rightarrow f(\beta^t) \leq f(\alpha^t)$. □

Appendix D

The considered function $f_p(\kappa^t)$ of Section 3.2 takes the sum of a convex function. The Hessian matrix $\mathbf{H}_r$ of the function $r_p(x, y) = x \log_b \left(\frac{x}{px + (1-p)y} \right)$ is positive-semidefinite in the required domain (symmetric and its eigenvalues e_1 and e_2 are greater than or equal to zero for $x > 0$ and $b > 1$).

$$\begin{aligned}
\mathbf{H}_r &= \frac{1}{\log(b)} \begin{bmatrix} \frac{(p-1)^2 y^2}{x(px+(1-p)y)^2} & -\frac{(p-1)^2 y}{(px+(1-p)y)^2} \\ -\frac{(p-1)^2 y}{(px+(1-p)y)^2} & \frac{(p-1)^2 x}{(px+(1-p)y)^2} \end{bmatrix} \\
e_1 &= 0 \\
e_2 &= \frac{(p-1)^2 (x^2 + y^2)}{x \log(b) (px + (1-p)y)^2}
\end{aligned} \tag{A5}$$

Appendix E

We use the examples of Finn and Lizier [20] since they provided an extensive discussion of their motivation. We compare our decomposition results to $I_{\min}$ of Williams and Beer [5] and $I^{\pm}$ of Finn and Lizier [20]. Examples with two sources are additionally compared to I^{BROJA} of Bertschinger et al. [10] and Griffith and Koch [11]. We notate the results for shared information $S(V_1, V_2; T)$, unique information $U(V_x; T)$ and synergetic/complementing information $C(V_1, V_2; T)$. We use the implementation of $I_{\min}$, I^{BROJA} and $I^{\pm}$ provided by the `dit` Python package for discrete information theory [24].

Notice that our approach is identical to Williams and Beer [5] if one of the variables is pointwise (for each T^t, not necessarily the same one each time) Blackwell superior to another, and that our approach is equal to Bertschinger et al. [10] and Griffith and Koch [11] for two visible variables at a *binary* target variable.

We would like to highlight Table A1 for the difference in our approach to Williams and Beer [5]. This is an arbitrary example, where the variables V_1 and V_2 are not Blackwell superior to each other from the perspective of T^t, as visualized in Figure 6. For highlighting the difference in our approach to Bertschinger et al. [10] and Griffith and Koch [11], we require an example where the target variable is not binary, such as the two-bit copy example in Table A2.

It can be seen that our approach does not satisfy the identity axiom of Harder et al. [8]. This axiom demands the decomposition of the two-bit-copy example (Table A2) to both variables providing one bit unique information and demands negative partial contributions in the three-bit even-parity example (Figure A3) [8,20].

Table A1. Two incomparable channels (visualized in Section 3.1). The table highlights the difference in our approach to Williams and Beer [5] while being identical to Bertschinger et al. [10] since the target variable is binary.

(a) Distribution				**(b) Results**				
V_1	V_2	T	**Pr**	**Method**	$S(V_1, V_2; T)$	$U(V_1; T)$	$U(V_2; T)$	$C(V_1, V_2; T)$
0	0	0	0.0625	$\hat{I}_T \cdot H(T)$	0.1196	0.0272	0.0716	0.1205
0	0	1	0.3	$I_{\min}$ [5]	0.1468	0	0.0444	0.1477
1	0	0	0.0375	$I^{\pm}$ [20]	0.3214	−0.1746	−0.1302	0.3223
1	0	1	0.05	I^{BROJA} [10,11]	0.1196	0.0272	0.0716	0.1205
0	1	0	0.1875					
0	1	1	0.15					
1	1	0	0.2125					

Table A2. Two-bit-copy (TBC) example. The results of our approach differ from Bertschinger et al. [10] and Griffith and Koch [11] since the target variable is not binary.

(a) Distribution				**(b) Results**				
V_1	V_2	T	**Pr**	**Method**	$S(V_1, V_2; T)$	$U(V_1; T)$	$U(V_2; T)$	$C(V_1, V_2; T)$
0	0	0	1/4	$\hat{I}_T \cdot H(T)$	1	0	0	1
0	1	1	1/4	$I_{\min}$ [5]	1	0	0	1
1	0	2	1/4	$I^{\pm}$ [20]	1	0	0	1
1	1	3	1/4	I^{BROJA} [10,11]	0	1	1	0

V_1	V_2	V_3	T	Pr
0	0	0	0	1/4
0	1	1	1	1/4
1	0	1	2	1/4
1	1	0	3	1/4

(**a**)

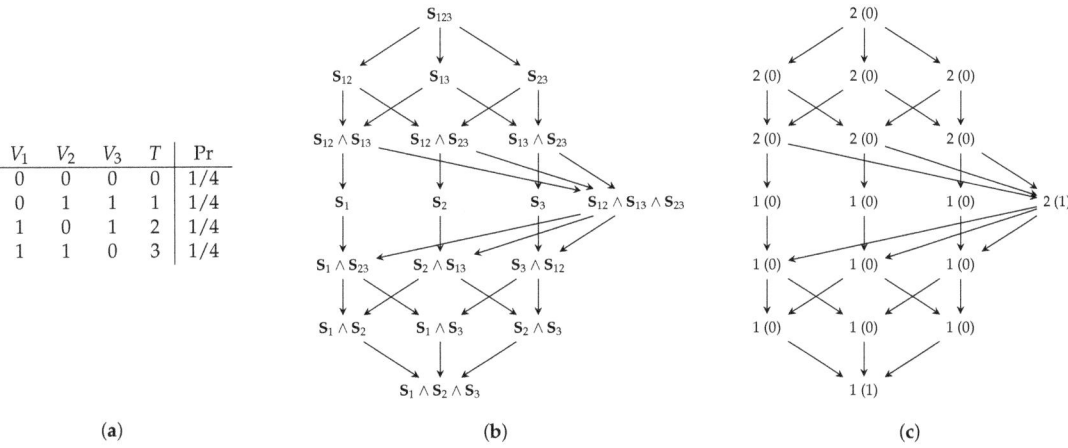

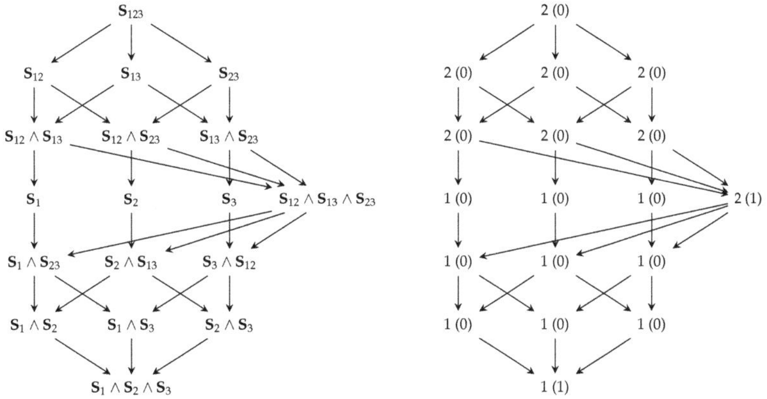

(**b**) (**c**)

Figure A3. Three-bit even-parity (Tbep) example. The results for $\hat{I}_T \cdot H(T)$, $I_{\min}$ and $I^{\pm}$ are identical. (**a**) Distribution. (**b**) Decomposition lattice. (**c**) Cumulative results (partial).

Table A3. XOR-gate (Xor) example. All compared measures provide the same results.

(a) Distribution				**(b) Results**				
V_1	V_2	T	Pr	**Method**	$S(V_1, V_2; T)$	$U(V_1; T)$	$U(V_2; T)$	$C(V_1, V_2; T)$
0	0	0	1/4	$\hat{I}_T \cdot H(T)$	0	0	0	1
0	1	1	1/4	$I_{\min}$ [5]	0	0	0	1
1	0	1	1/4	$I^{\pm}$ [20]	0	0	0	1
1	1	0	1/4	I^{BROJA} [10,11]	0	0	0	1

Table A4. Pointwise unique (PwUnq) example. Our approach provides the same results as Williams and Beer [5] and Bertschinger et al. [10].

(a) Distribution				**(b) Results**				
V_1	V_2	T	Pr	**Method**	$S(V_1, V_2; T)$	$U(V_1; T)$	$U(V_2; T)$	$C(V_1, V_2; T)$
0	1	0	1/4	$\hat{I}_T \cdot H(T)$	0.5	0	0	0.5
1	0	0	1/4	$I_{\min}$ [5]	0.5	0	0	0.5
0	2	1	1/4	$I^{\pm}$ [20]	0	0.5	0.5	0
2	0	1	1/4	I^{BROJA} [10,11]	0.5	0	0	0.5

Table A5. Redundant Error (RdnErr) example. Our approach provides the same results as Williams and Beer [5] and Bertschinger et al. [10].

(a) Distribution				**(b) Results**				
V_1	V_2	T	Pr	**Method**	$S(V_1, V_2; T)$	$U(V_1; T)$	$U(V_2; T)$	$C(V_1, V_2; T)$
0	0	0	3/8	$\hat{I}_T \cdot H(T)$	0.189	0.811	0	0
1	1	1	3/8	$I_{\min}$ [5]	0.189	0.811	0	0
0	1	0	1/8	$I^{\pm}$ [20]	1	0	−0.811	0.811
1	0	1	1/8	I^{BROJA} [10,11]	0.189	0.811	0	0

Table A6. Unique (Unq) example. Our approach provides the same results as Williams and Beer [5] and Bertschinger et al. [10].

(a) Distribution				(b) Results				
V_1	V_2	T	Pr	Method	$S(V_1, V_2; T)$	$U(V_1; T)$	$U(V_2; T)$	$C(V_1, V_2; T)$
0	0	0	1/4	$\hat{I}_T \cdot H(T)$	0	1	0	0
0	1	0	1/4	$I_{\min}$ [5]	0	1	0	0
1	0	1	1/4	$I^{\pm}$ [20]	1	0	−1	1
1	1	1	1/4	I^{BROJA} [10,11]	0	1	0	0

Table A7. And-gate (And) example. Our approach provides the same results as Williams and Beer [5] and Bertschinger et al. [10].

(a) Distribution				(b) Results				
V_1	V_2	T	Pr	Method	$S(V_1, V_2; T)$	$U(V_1; T)$	$U(V_2; T)$	$C(V_1, V_2; T)$
0	0	0	1/4	$\hat{I}_T \cdot H(T)$	0.311	0	0	0.5
0	1	0	1/4	$I_{\min}$ [5]	0.311	0	0	0.5
1	0	0	1/4	$I^{\pm}$ [20]	0.561	−0.25	−0.25	0.75
1	1	1	1/4	I^{BROJA} [10,11]	0.311	0	0	0.5

References

1. Lizier, J.T.; Bertschinger, N.; Jost, J.; Wibral, M. Information Decomposition of Target Effects from Multi-Source Interactions: Perspectives on Previous, Current and Future Work. *Entropy* **2018**, *20*, 307. [CrossRef] [PubMed]
2. Wibral, M.; Finn, C.; Wollstadt, P.; Lizier, J.T.; Priesemann, V. Quantifying Information Modification in Developing Neural Networks via Partial Information Decomposition. *Entropy* **2017**, *19*, 494. [CrossRef]
3. Rassouli, B.; Rosas, F.E.; Gündüz, D. Data Disclosure Under Perfect Sample Privacy. *IEEE Trans. Inf. Forensics Secur.* **2020**, *15*, 2012–2025. [CrossRef]
4. Rosas, F.E.; Mediano, P.A.M.; Rassouli, B.; Barrett, A.B. An operational information decomposition via synergistic disclosure. *J. Phys. Math. Theor.* **2020**, *53*, 485001. [CrossRef]
5. Williams, P.L.; Beer, R.D. Nonnegative Decomposition of Multivariate Information. *arXiv* **2010**, arXiv:1004.2515.
6. Griffith, V.; Chong, E.K.P.; James, R.G.; Ellison, C.J.; Crutchfield, J.P. Intersection Information Based on Common Randomness. *Entropy* **2014**, *16*, 1985–2000. [CrossRef]
7. Bertschinger, N.; Rauh, J.; Olbrich, E.; Jost, J. Shared Information—New Insights and Problems in Decomposing Information in Complex Systems. In *Proceedings of the European Conference on Complex Systems 2012*; Gilbert, T., Kirkilionis, M., Nicolis, G., Eds., Springer: Cham, Switzerland, 2013; pp. 251–269.
8. Harder, M.; Salge, C.; Polani, D. Bivariate measure of redundant information. *Phys. Rev. E* **2013**, *87*, 012130. [CrossRef] [PubMed]
9. Finn, C. A New Framework for Decomposing Multivariate Information. Ph.D. Thesis, University of Sydney, Sydney, NSW, Australia, 2019.
10. Bertschinger, N.; Rauh, J.; Olbrich, E.; Jost, J.; Ay, N. Quantifying Unique Information. *Entropy* **2014**, *16*, 2161–2183. [CrossRef]
11. Griffith, V.; Koch, C. Quantifying Synergistic Mutual Information. In *Guided Self-Organization: Inception*; Springer: Berlin/Heidelberg, Germany, 2014; pp. 159–190. [CrossRef]
12. Bertschinger, N.; Rauh, J. The Blackwell Relation Defines No Lattice. In Proceedings of the 2014 IEEE International Symposium on Information Theory, Honolulu, HI, USA, 29 June–4 July 2014; pp. 2479–2483. [CrossRef]
13. Knuth, K.H. Lattices and Their Consistent Quantification. *Ann. Der Phys.* **2019**, *531*, 1700370. [CrossRef]
14. Blackwell, D. Equivalent Comparisons of Experiments. In *The Annals of Mathematical Statistics*; Institute of Mathematical Statistics: Beachwood, OH, USA, 1953; pp. 265–272.
15. Fawcett, T. An introduction to ROC analysis. *Pattern Recognit. Lett.* **2006**, *27*, 861–874. [CrossRef]
16. Schechtman, E.; Schechtman, G. The relationship between Gini terminology and the ROC curve. *Metron* **2019**, *77*, 171–178. [CrossRef]
17. Neyman, J.; Pearson, E.S. IX. On the Problem of the Most Efficient Tests of Statistical Hypotheses. *Philos. Trans. R. Soc. Lond. Ser. Contain. Pap. Math. Phys. Character* **1933**, *231*, 289–337.
18. Mages, T.; Rohner, C. Implementation: PID Quantifying Reachable Decision Regions. 2023. Available online: https://github.com/uu-core/pid-quantifying-reachable-decision-regions (accessed on 1 May 2023).
19. Niu, X.; Quinn, C.J. Information Flow in Markov Chains. In Proceedings of the 2021 60th IEEE Conference on Decision and Control (CDC), Austin, TX, USA, 14–17 December 2021; pp. 3442–3447. [CrossRef]

20. Finn, C.; Lizier, J.T. Pointwise Partial Information Decomposition Using the Specificity and Ambiguity Lattices. *Entropy* **2018**, *20*, 297. [CrossRef] [PubMed]
21. Kolchinsky, A. A Novel Approach to the Partial Information Decomposition. *Entropy* **2022**, *24*, 403. [CrossRef]
22. Chicharro, D.; Panzeri, S. Synergy and Redundancy in Dual Decompositions of Mutual Information Gain and Information Loss. *Entropy* **2017**, *19*, 71. [CrossRef]
23. Rauh, J.; Bertschinger, N.; Olbrich, E.; Jost, J. Reconsidering Unique Information: Towards a Multivariate Information Decomposition. In Proceedings of the 2014 IEEE International Symposium on Information Theory, Honolulu, HI, USA, 29 June–4 July 2014; pp. 2232–2236. [CrossRef]
24. James, R.G.; Ellison, C.J.; Crutchfield, J.P. dit: A Python package for discrete information theory. *J. Open Source Softw.* **2018**, *3*, 738. [CrossRef]

entropy

MDPI

Article

Arrow Contraction and Expansion in Tropical Diagrams

Rostislav Matveev [1,*] and Jacobus W. Portegies [2,*]

1 Max Planck Institute for Mathematics in the Sciences, 04103 Leipzig, Germany
2 Department of Mathematics and Computer Science, Eindhoven University of Technology, 5612 AZ Eindhoven, The Netherlands
* Correspondence: matveev@mis.mpg.de (R.M.); j.w.portegies@tue.nl (J.W.P.)

Abstract: Arrow contraction applied to a tropical diagram of probability spaces is a modification of the diagram, replacing one of the morphisms with an isomorphism while preserving other parts of the diagram. It is related to the rate regions introduced by Ahlswede and Körner. In a companion article, we use arrow contraction to derive information about the shape of the entropic cone. Arrow expansion is the inverse operation to the arrow contraction.

Keywords: tropical probability; entropic cone

Citation: Matveev, R.; Portegies, J.W. Arrow Contraction and Expansion in Tropical Diagrams. *Entropy* **2023**, *25*, 1637. https://doi.org/10.3390/e25121637

Academic Editor: Daniel Chicharro

Received: 6 November 2023
Revised: 4 December 2023
Accepted: 6 December 2023
Published: 8 December 2023

1. Introduction

In [1], we have initiated the theory of *tropical probability spaces* for the systematic study of information optimization problems in information theory and artificial intelligence, such as those arising in robotics [2], neuroscience [3], artificial intelligence [4], variational autoencoders [5], information decomposition [6], and causal inference [7]. In [8], we applied the techniques to derive a dimension-reduction result for the entropic cone of four random variables.

Two of the main tools used for the latter are what we call *arrow contraction* and *arrow expansion*. They are formulated for tropical commutative diagrams of probability spaces. Tropical diagrams are points in the asymptotic cone of the metric space of commutative diagrams of probability spaces endowed with the asymptotic entropy distance. Arrows in diagrams of probability spaces are (equivalence classes of) measure-preserving maps.

Arrow contraction and expansion take a commutative diagram of probability spaces as input, modify it, but preserve important properties of the diagram. The precise results are formulated as Theorems 3 and 4 in the main text. Their formulation requires language, notation, and definitions that we review in Section 2.

However, to give an idea of the results in this paper, we now present two examples. For basic terminology and notations used in these examples below, the reader unfamiliar with them is referred either to Section 2 of the present article or in the introductory material in the article [9].

1.1. Two Examples

1.1.1. Arrow Contraction and Expansion in a Two-Fan

Suppose we are given a fan $\mathcal{Z} = (X \leftarrow Z \rightarrow Y)$, and we would like to complete it to a diamond

$$\mathcal{Z}_\diamond = \left(\begin{array}{ccccc} & & Z & & \\ X & \swarrow & & \searrow & Y \\ & \searrow & V & \swarrow & \end{array} \right) \tag{1}$$

such that the entropy of V, denoted by $[V]$, equals the mutual information $[X : Y]$ between X and Y, i.e., we would like to realize the mutual information between X and Y by a pair of reductions $X \to V$ and $Y \to V$. This is not always possible, not even approximately. The Gacs-Körner Theorem [10] describes when such exact realization of mutual information is possible.

Arrow contraction instead produces another fan $\mathcal{Z}' = (X \leftarrow Z' \to V)$, such that the reduction $Z' \to X$ is an isomorphism and the relative entropy $[X|V]$ of X given V equals $[X|Y]$. By collapsing this reduction, we obtain as a diagram just the reduction $X \to V$. If necessary, we can keep the original spaces Z and Y in the modified diagram obtaining the "broken diamond" diagram

$$\begin{array}{ccccc} & & Z & & \\ & \swarrow & & \searrow & \\ X & & & & Y \\ & \searrow & & & \\ & & V & & \end{array}$$

such that $[V] = [X : Y]$. Of course, no special technique is necessary to achieve this result since it is easy to find a reduction from a tropical space $[X]$ to another tropical probability space with the prespecified entropy, as long as the Shannon inequalities are not violated.

However, a similar operation becomes non-trivial and in fact impossible without passing to the tropical limit, if instead of a single space X, there is a more complex sub-diagram as in the example in the next subsection.

To explain how arrow expansion works, we start with the chain of reductions $Z \to X \to V$. Can we extend it to a diamond, as in (1), so that $[X : Y|V] = 0$? This is again not possible, in general. However, if we pass to tropical diagrams, then such an extension always exists.

1.1.2. One More Example of Arrow Expansion and Contraction

Consider a diagram presented in Figure 1. Such a diagram is called a $\mathbf{\Lambda}_3$-diagram. We would like to find a reduction $X \to V$ so that $[\mathcal{X}|U] = [\mathcal{X}|V]$. It is not possible to achieve this within the realm of diagrams of classical probability spaces. But once we pass to the tropical limit, the reduction $[X] \to [V]$ can be found by contracting and then collapsing the arrow $[Z] \to [X]$, as shown in Figure 1.

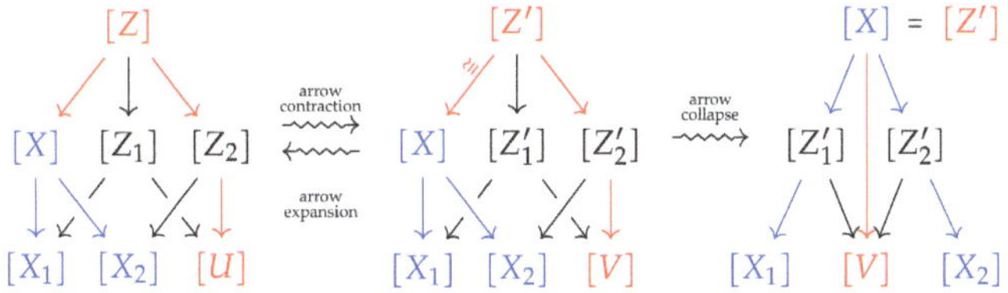

Figure 1. Arrow contraction and expansion in a $\mathbf{\Lambda}_3$-diagram. The fan $([X] \leftarrow [Z] \to [U])$ (shown in red in the Figure) is admissible. Spaces $[Z_1]$, $[Z_2]$ and $[Z]$ belong to the co-ideal $\lfloor U \rfloor$. After the operation the part of the diagram shown in blue in the Figure is left unmodified.

Arrow contraction is closely related to the Shannon channel coding theorem. This is perhaps most obvious from the proof. Furthermore, arrow contraction has connections with rate regions, as introduced by Ahlswede and Körner, see [11,12]. These results by Ahlswede and Körner were applied by [13], resulting in a new non-Shannon information inequality. Moreover, in [13], a new proof was given of the results; this new proof is similar to the proof of the arrow contraction result in the present paper.

The main contribution of our work lies in the fact that we prove a much stronger preservation of properties of the diagram under arrow contraction.

2. Preliminaries

2.1. Probability Spaces and Their Diagrams

Our main objects of study will be *commutative diagrams of probability spaces*. A *finite probability space* X is a set with a probability measure on it, supported on a finite set. We denote by $|X|$ the cardinality of the support of the measure. The statement $x \in X$ means that point x is an atom with positive weight in X. For details see [1,9,14].

Examples of commutative diagrams of probability spaces are shown in Figure 2. The objects in such diagrams are finite probability spaces and morphisms are equivalence classes of measure-preserving maps. Two such maps are considered to be equivalent if they coincide on a set of full measurements. To record the combinatorial structure of a commutative diagram, i.e., the arrangement of spaces and morphisms, we use *indexing categories*, which are finite poset categories satisfying an additional property, which we describe below.

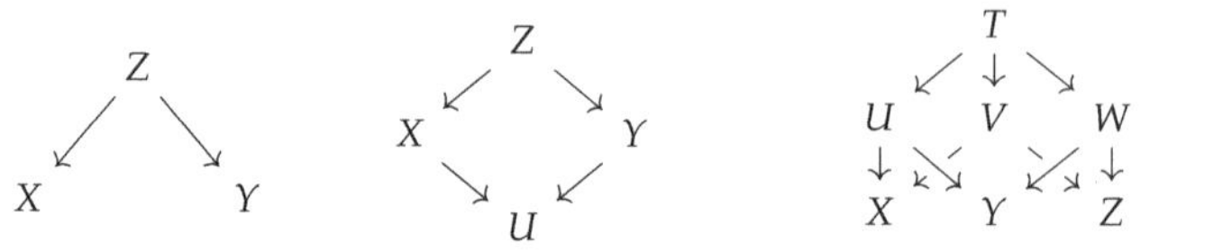

1. A fan 2. A diamond diagram 3. Full diagram on 3 spaces

Figure 2. Examples of diagrams of probability spaces.

2.1.1. Indexing Categories

A *poset category* is a finite category such that there is at most one morphism between any two objects either way.

For a pair of objects k, l in a poset category $\mathbf{G} = \{i; \gamma_{ij}\}$, such that there is a morphism γ_{kl} in $\mathbf{G}$, we call k an ancestor of l and l a descendant of k. The set of all ancestors of an object k together with all the morphisms between them is itself a poset category and will be called a *co-ideal* generated by k and denoted by $\lfloor k \rfloor$. Co-ideals are also sometimes called *filters*. Similarly, a poset category consisting of all descendants of $k \in \mathbf{G}$ and morphisms between them will be called an *ideal* generated by k and denoted $\lceil k \rceil$.

An *indexing category* $\mathbf{G} = \{i; \gamma_{ij}\}$ used for indexing diagrams is a poset category satisfying the following additional property: for any pair of objects $i_1, i_2 \in \mathbf{G}$ the the intersection of co-ideals is also a co-ideal generated by some object $i_3 \in \mathbf{G}$,

$$\lfloor i_1 \rfloor \cap \lfloor i_2 \rfloor = \lfloor i_3 \rfloor$$

In other words, for any pair of objects $i_1, i_2 \in \mathbf{G}$ there exists a *least common ancestor* i_3, i.e., i_3 is an ancestor to both i_1 and i_2 and any other common ancestor is also an ancestor of i_3. Any indexing category is *initial*, i.e., there is a (necessarily unique) *initial* object $\hat{\imath}$ in it, which is the ancestor of any other object in $\mathbf{G}$, in other words $\mathbf{G} = \lceil \hat{\imath} \rceil$.

A *fan* in a category is a pair of morphisms with the same domain. Such a diagram is also called a *span* in some literature on Category Theory. A fan $(i \leftarrow k \rightarrow j)$ is called *minimal*, if for any other fan $(i \leftarrow l \rightarrow j)$ included in a commutative diagram

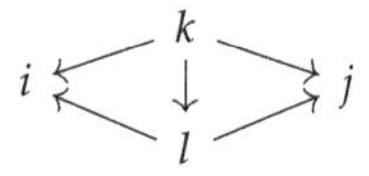

the vertical morphism $(k \rightarrow l)$ must be an isomorphism. Any indexing category also satisfies the property that, for any pair of objects in it, there exists a unique minimal fan with target objects of the given ones.

This terminology will also be applied to diagrams of probability spaces indexed by $\mathbf{G}$. Thus, given a space X in a $\mathbf{G}$-diagram, we can talk about its ancestors, descendants, co-ideal $\lfloor X \rfloor$, and ideal $\lceil X \rceil$. We use square brackets to denote tropical diagrams and spaces in them. For the (co-)ideals in tropical diagrams, in order to unclutter notations, we will write

$$\lfloor X \rfloor := \lfloor [X] \rfloor \quad \text{and} \quad \lceil X \rceil := \lceil [X] \rceil$$

2.1.2. Diagrams

For an indexing category $\mathbf{G} = \{i; \gamma_{ij}\}$ and a category $\mathbf{Cat}$, a commutative $\mathbf{G}$-diagram $\mathcal{X} = \{X_i; \chi_{ij}\}$ is a functor $\mathcal{X} : \mathbf{G} \to \mathbf{Cat}$. A diagram $\mathcal{X}$ is called *minimal* if it maps minimal fans in $\mathbf{G}$ to minimal fans in $\mathbf{Cat}$.

A *constant* $\mathbf{G}$*-diagram* denoted $X^{\mathbf{G}}$ is a diagram where all the objects equal to X, and all morphisms are identities.

Important examples of indexing categories are a two-fan, a diamond category, a full category $\mathbf{\Lambda}_n$ on n spaces, chains $\mathbf{C}_n$. For detailed descriptions and more examples, the reader is referred to the articles cited at the beginning of this section.

2.2. Tropical Diagrams

2.2.1. Intrinsic Entropy Distance

For a fixed indexing category $\mathbf{G}$, the space of commutative $\mathbf{G}$-diagrams will be denoted by $\mathbf{Prob}\langle\mathbf{G}\rangle$. Evaluating entropy on every space in a $\mathbf{G}$ diagram gives a map

$$\mathsf{Ent}_* : \mathbf{Prob}\langle\mathbf{G}\rangle \to \mathbb{R}^{\mathbf{G}}$$

where the target space $\mathbb{R}^{\mathbf{G}}$ is the space of real-valued functions on objects of $\mathbf{G}$. We endow this space with the ℓ^1-norm. For a fan $\mathcal{F} = (\mathcal{X} \leftarrow \mathcal{Z} \to \mathcal{Y})$ of $\mathbf{G}$-diagrams we define the entropy distance between its terminal objects by

$$\mathrm{kd}(\mathcal{F}) := \|\mathsf{Ent}_* \mathcal{Z} - \mathsf{Ent}_* \mathcal{X}\|_1 + \|\mathsf{Ent}_* \mathcal{Z} - \mathsf{Ent}_* \mathcal{Y}\|_1$$

and the intrinsic entropy distance between two arbitrary $\mathbf{G}$-diagrams by

$$\mathbf{k}(\mathcal{X},\mathcal{Y}) := \inf\{\mathrm{kd}(\mathcal{F}) : \mathcal{F} = (\mathcal{X} \leftarrow \mathcal{Z} \to \mathcal{Y})\}$$

This intrinsic version of the entropy distance was introduced in [15,16]. The triangle inequality for $\mathbf{k}$ and various other properties are discussed in [1].

In the same article, a useful estimate for the intrinsic entropy distance called the Slicing Lemma is also proven. The following corollary ([1], Corollary 3.10(1)) of the Slicing Lemma will be used in the next section.

Proposition 1. *Let* $\mathbf{G}$ *be an indexing category,* $\mathcal{X},\mathcal{Y} \in \mathbf{Prob}\langle\mathbf{G}\rangle$ *and* $U \in \mathbf{Prob}$ *included in a pair of two fans*

$$\mathcal{X} \leftarrow \tilde{\mathcal{X}} \to U^{\mathbf{G}} \qquad U^{\mathbf{G}} \leftarrow \tilde{\mathcal{Y}} \to \mathcal{Y}$$

Then

$$\mathbf{k}(\mathcal{X},\mathcal{Y}) \le \int_U \mathbf{k}(\mathcal{X}|u,\mathcal{Y}|u)\, dp_U(u) + 2\cdot [\![\mathbf{G}]\!] \cdot \mathsf{Ent}(U)$$

2.2.2. Tropical Diagrams

Points in the asymptotic cone of $(\mathbf{Prob}\langle\mathbf{G}\rangle, \mathbf{k})$ are called tropical $\mathbf{G}$-diagrams and the space of all tropical $\mathbf{G}$-diagrams, denoted $\mathbf{Prob}[\mathbf{G}]$, is endowed with the *asymptotic entropy distance*. We explain this now in more detail, and a more extensive description can be found in [14].

To describe points in $\mathbf{Prob}[\mathbf{G}]$ we consider *quasi-linear* sequences $\bar{\mathcal{X}} := (\mathcal{X}(n) : n \in \mathbb{N})$ of $\mathbf{G}$-diagrams. That is, we fix a "slowly growing" increasing function $\varphi : \mathbb{R}_{\ge 0} \to \mathbb{R}$ satisfying

$$t \cdot \int_t^\infty \frac{\varphi(t)}{t^2}\, dt \le D_\varphi \cdot \varphi(t)$$

for some constant $D_\varphi > 0$ and any $t > 1$. We call a sequence $\bar{\mathcal{X}} := (\mathcal{X}(n) : n \in \mathbb{N})$ φ-quasi-linear if it satisfies the bound for all $m, n \in \mathbb{N}$

$$\boldsymbol{\kappa}\big(\mathcal{X}(n+m), \mathcal{X}(n) \otimes \mathcal{X}(m)\big) \le C \cdot \varphi(n+m)$$

We have shown in [14] that the space $\mathbf{Prob}[G]$ does not depend on the choice of function φ as long as it is not zero. The space of all such sequences is endowed with the *asymptotic entropy distance* defined by

$$\boldsymbol{\kappa}(\bar{\mathcal{X}},\bar{\mathcal{Y}}) := \lim_{n\to\infty}\frac{1}{n}\mathbf{k}\big(\mathcal{X}(n),\mathcal{Y}(n)\big)$$

A tropical diagram $[\mathcal{X}]$ is defined to be an equivalence class of such sequences, where two sequences $\bar{\mathcal{X}}$ and $\bar{\mathcal{Y}}$ are equivalent if $\boldsymbol{\kappa}(\bar{\mathcal{X}},\bar{\mathcal{Y}}) = 0$. The space $\mathbf{Prob}[\mathbf{G}]$ carries the asymptotic entropy distance and has the structure of a $\mathbb{R}_{\geq 0}$-semi-module—one can take linear combinations with non-negative coefficients of tropical diagrams. The linear entropy functional $\mathsf{Ent}_* : \mathbf{Prob}[\mathbf{G}] \to \mathbb{R}^{\mathbf{G}}$ is defined by

$$\mathsf{Ent}_*[\mathcal{X}] := \lim_{n\to\infty}\frac{1}{n}\mathsf{Ent}_*\,\mathcal{X}(n)$$

A detailed discussion about tropical diagrams can be found in [14]. In the cited article, we show that the space $\mathbf{Prob}[\mathbf{G}]$ is metrically complete and isometrically isomorphic to a closed convex cone in some Banach space.

For $\mathbf{G} = \mathbf{C}_k$ a *chain category*, containing k objects $\{1,\dots,k\}$ and unique morphism $i \to j$ for every pair $i \geq j$, we have shown in [14] that the space $\mathbf{Prob}[\mathbf{C}_k]$ is isomorphic to the following cone in $(\mathbb{R}^k, \|\cdot\|_1)$

$$\mathbf{Prob}[\mathbf{C}_k] \cong \left\{\begin{pmatrix} x_1 \\ \vdots \\ x_k \end{pmatrix} : 0 \leq x_1 \leq \cdots \leq x_k\right\}$$

The isomorphism is given by the entropy function. Thus, we can identify tropical probability spaces (elements in $\mathbf{Prob}[\mathbf{C}_1]$) with non-negative numbers via entropy. We will simply write $[X]$ to mean the entropy of the space $[X]$. Along these lines, we also adopt the notations $[X|Y]$, $[X:Y]$ and $[X:Y|Z]$ for the conditional entropy and mutual information for the tropical spaces included in some diagrams.

2.3. *Asymptotic Equipartition Property for Diagrams*

2.3.1. Homogeneous Diagrams

A $\mathbf{G}$-diagram $\mathcal{X}$ is called *homogeneous* if the automorphism group $\mathrm{Aut}(\mathcal{X})$ acts transitively on every space in $\mathcal{X}$. Homogeneous probability spaces are uniform. For more complex indexing categories, this simple description is not sufficient.

2.3.2. Tropical Homogeneous Diagrams

The subcategory of all homogeneous $\mathbf{G}$-diagrams will be denoted $\mathbf{Prob}\langle\mathbf{G}\rangle_{\mathsf{h}}$ and we write $\mathbf{Prob}\langle\mathbf{G}\rangle_{\mathsf{h,m}}$ for the category of minimal homogeneous $\mathbf{G}$-diagrams. These spaces are invariant under the tensor product. Thus, they are metric Abelian monoids.

Passing to the tropical limit, we obtain spaces of tropical (minimal) homogeneous diagrams that we denote $\mathbf{Prob}[\mathbf{G}]_{\mathsf{h}}$ and $\mathbf{Prob}[\mathbf{G}]_{\mathsf{h,m}}$.

2.3.3. Asymptotic Equipartition Property

In [1] the following theorem is proven

Theorem 1. *Suppose $\mathcal{X} \in \mathbf{Prob}\langle\mathbf{G}\rangle$ is a $\mathbf{G}$-diagram of probability spaces for some fixed indexing category $\mathbf{G}$. Then, there exists a sequence $\bar{\mathcal{H}} = (\mathcal{H}_n)_{n=0}^{\infty}$ of homogeneous $\mathbf{G}$-diagrams such that*

$$\frac{1}{n}\mathbf{k}(\mathcal{X}^n,\mathcal{H}_n) \leq C(|X_0|,[\![\mathbf{G}]\!])\cdot\sqrt{\frac{\ln^3 n}{n}} \tag{2}$$

where $C(|X_0|,[\![\mathbf{G}]\!])$ is a constant only depending on $|X_0|$ and $[\![\mathbf{G}]\!]$.

The approximating sequence of homogeneous diagrams is evidently quasi-linear with the defect bounded by the admissible function

$$\varphi(t) := 2C(|X_0|, [\![\mathbf{G}]\!]) \cdot t^{3/4} \geq 2C(|X_0|, [\![\mathbf{G}]\!]) \cdot t^{1/2} \cdot \ln^{3/2} t$$

Thus, Theorem 1 above states that $\mathsf{L}(\mathbf{Prob}\langle\mathbf{G}\rangle) \subset \mathbf{Prob}[\mathbf{G}]_{\mathsf{h}}$. On the other hand, we have shown in [14] that the space of linear sequences $\mathsf{L}(\mathbf{Prob}\langle\mathbf{G}\rangle)$ is dense in $\mathbf{Prob}[\mathbf{G}]$. Combining the two statements, we obtain the following theorem.

Theorem 2. *For any indexing category* $\mathbf{G}$*, the space* $\mathbf{Prob}[\mathbf{G}]_{\mathsf{h}}$ *is dense in* $\mathbf{Prob}[\mathbf{G}]$*. Similarly, the space* $\mathbf{Prob}[\mathbf{G}]_{\mathsf{h,m}}$ *is dense in* $\mathbf{Prob}[\mathbf{G}]_{\mathsf{m}}$*.*

It is possible that the spaces $\mathbf{Prob}[\mathbf{G}]_{\mathsf{h}}$ and $\mathbf{Prob}[\mathbf{G}]$ coincide. At this time, we have neither a proof nor a counterexample to this conjecture.

2.4. Conditioning in Tropical Diagrams

For a tropical $\mathbf{G}$-diagram $[\mathcal{X}]$ containing a space $[U]$ we defined a conditioned diagram $[\mathcal{X}|U]$. It can be understood as the tropical limit of the sequence $(\mathcal{X}(n)|u_n)$, where $(\mathcal{X}(n))$ is the homogeneous approximation of $[\mathcal{X}]$, $U(n)$ is the space in $\mathcal{X}(n)$ that corresponds to $[U]$ under combinatorial isomorphism and u_n is any atom in $U(n)$.

We have shown in [9] that operation of conditioning is Lipschitz-continuous with respect to the asymptotic entropy distance.

3. Arrow Contraction

3.1. Arrow Collapse, Arrow Contraction, and Arrow Expansion

3.1.1. Prime Morphisms

A morphism $\gamma_{ij} : i \to j$ in an indexing category $\mathbf{G} = \{i; \gamma_{ij}\}$ will be called *prime* if it cannot be factored into a composition of two non-identity morphisms in $\mathbf{G}$. A morphism in a $\mathbf{G}$-diagram indexed by a prime morphism in $\mathbf{G}$ will also be called *prime*.

3.1.2. Arrow Collapse

Suppose $\mathcal{Z}$ is a $\mathbf{G}$-diagram such that for some pair $i, j \in \mathbf{G}$, the prime morphism $\zeta_{ij} : Z_i \to Z_j$ is an isomorphism. *Arrow collapse* applied to $\mathcal{Z}$ results in a new diagram $\mathcal{Z}'$ obtained from $\mathcal{Z}$ by identifying Z_i and Z_j via the isomorphism ζ_{ij}. The combinatorial type of $\mathcal{Z}'$ is different from that of $\mathcal{Z}$. The spaces Z_i and Z_j are replaced by a single space, and the new space will inherit all the morphisms in $\mathcal{Z}$ with targets and domains Z_i and Z_j.

3.1.3. Arrow Contraction and Expansion

Arrow contraction and expansion are two operations on tropical $\mathbf{G}$-diagrams. Roughly speaking, arrow contraction applied to a tropical $\mathbf{G}$-diagram $[\mathcal{Z}]$ results in another tropical $\mathbf{G}$-diagram $[\mathcal{Z}']$ such that one of the arrows becomes an isomorphism, while some parts of the diagram are not modified. Arrow expansion is an inverse operation to arrow contraction.

3.1.4. Admissible and Reduced Sub-Fans

An *admissible fan* in a $\mathbf{G}$-diagram $\mathcal{Z}$ is a minimal fan $X \leftarrow Z \to U$, such that Z is the initial space of $\mathcal{Z}$ and any space in $\mathcal{Z}$ belongs either to the co-ideal $\lceil X \rceil$ or ideal $\lfloor U \rfloor$. For example, in the left-most diagram of Figure 1, the fan $X \leftarrow Z \to U$ is admissible, while $X_1 \leftarrow Z_1 \to U$ or $X \leftarrow Z \to Z_2$ are not.

An admissible fan $X \leftarrow Z \to U$ in a diagram will be called *reduced* if the morphism $Z \to X$ is an isomorphism.

3.2. The Contraction Theorem

Our aim is to prove the following theorem.

Theorem 3. *Let* $([X] \leftarrow [Z] \rightarrow [U])$ *be an admissible fan in some tropical* **G***-diagram* $[\mathcal{Z}]$. *Then for every* $\varepsilon > 0$ *there exists a* **G***-diagram* $[\mathcal{Z}']$ *containing an admissible fan* $([X'] \leftarrow [Z'] \rightarrow [U'])$, *corresponding to the original admissible fan through the combinatorial isomorphism, such that, with the notations* $\mathcal{X} = \lceil X \rceil$ *and* $\mathcal{X}' = \lceil X' \rceil$, *the diagram* $[\mathcal{Z}']$ *satisfies*

(i) $\boldsymbol{\kappa}([\mathcal{X}'|U'], [\mathcal{X}|U]) \leq \varepsilon$
(ii) $\boldsymbol{\kappa}(\mathcal{X}', \mathcal{X}) \leq \varepsilon$
(iii) $[Z'|X'] \leq \varepsilon$

It is not clear that constructing diagrams $\mathcal{Z}'$ as in the theorem above for a sequence of values of parameter ε decreasing to 0, we can obtain a convergent sequence in **Prob**$[\mathbf{G}]$ with the limiting diagram satisfying conclusions of the theorem with $\varepsilon = 0$. If **Prob**$[\mathbf{G}]$ were a locally compact space, which is an open question at the moment. The convergence would be guaranteed, and then ε in the theorem above could be replaced by 0.

The proof of Theorem 3 is based on the following proposition, which will be proven in Section 5.

Proposition 2. *Let* $(X_0 \leftarrow Z_0 \rightarrow U)$ *be an admissible fan in some* homogeneous **G***-diagram of probability spaces* $\mathcal{Z}$. *Then there exists a* **G***-diagram* $\mathcal{Z}'$ *containing the admissible fan* $(X_0' \leftarrow Z_0' \rightarrow U')$ *such that, with the notations* $\mathcal{X} := \lceil X_0 \rceil$ *and* $\mathcal{X}' := \lceil X_0' \rceil$, *it holds that*

(1) $\mathcal{X}|u = \mathcal{X}'|u'$ *for any* $u \in U$ *and* $u' \in U'$.
(2) $\boldsymbol{\kappa}(\mathcal{X}, \mathcal{X}') \leq \mathbf{k}(\mathcal{X}, \mathcal{X}') \leq 20 \cdot [\![\mathbf{G}]\!]$
(3) $[Z_0'|X_0'] \leq 4 \ln \ln |X_0|$

Proof of Theorem 3. First, we assume that $[\mathcal{Z}]$ is a homogeneous tropical diagram. It means that it can be represented by a quasi-linear sequence $(\mathcal{Z}(n))_{n \in \mathbb{N}_0}$ of homogeneous diagrams, with defect of the sequence bounded by the function $\varphi(t) := C \cdot t^{3/4}$ for some $C \geq 0$. This means that for any $m, n \in \mathbb{N}$

$$\boldsymbol{\kappa}(\mathcal{Z}(m) \otimes \mathcal{Z}(n), \mathcal{Z}(m+n)) \leq \varphi(m+n)$$
$$\boldsymbol{\kappa}(\mathcal{Z}^m(n), \mathcal{Z}(m \cdot n)) \leq D_\varphi \cdot m \cdot \varphi(n)$$

where D_φ is some constant depending on φ, see [14].

Fix a number $n \in \mathbb{N}$ and apply Proposition 2 to the *homogeneous* diagram $\mathcal{Z}(n)$, containing the admissible fan $X_0(n) \leftarrow Z_0(n) \rightarrow U(n)$ and sub-diagram $\mathcal{X}(n) = \lceil X_0(n) \rceil$. As a result, we obtain a diagram $\mathcal{Z}''$ containing the fan $X_0'' \leftarrow Z_0'' \rightarrow U''$ and the sub-diagram $\mathcal{X}'' = \lceil X_0'' \rceil$, such that

$$\begin{aligned} &\mathcal{X}''|u'' = \mathcal{X}(n)|u \qquad \text{for any } u'' \in U'' \text{ and } u \in U(n) \\ &\boldsymbol{\kappa}(\mathcal{X}'', \mathcal{X}(n)) \leq 20[\![\mathbf{G}]\!] \\ &[Z_0''|X_0''] \leq 4 \ln \ln |X_0(n)| \end{aligned} \tag{3}$$

Recall that for a diagram $\mathcal{A}$ of probability spaces, we denote by $\overrightarrow{\mathcal{A}}$ the tropical diagram represented by the linear sequence $(\mathcal{A}^k : k \in \mathbb{N}_0)$. As an element of a closed convex cone **Prob**$[\mathbf{G}]$, it can be scaled by an arbitrary non-negative real number; see, for instance, Section 2.3.5 in [14]. For example, $\frac{1}{n}\overrightarrow{\mathcal{A}}$ is represented by the sequence $(\mathcal{A}^{\lfloor \frac{k}{n} \rfloor} : k \in \mathbb{N}_0)$.

Define the two tropical diagrams

$$[\mathcal{Z}'] := \frac{1}{n}\overrightarrow{\mathcal{Z}''}$$
$$[\tilde{\mathcal{Z}}] := \frac{1}{n}\overrightarrow{\mathcal{Z}(n)}$$

Since $\mathcal{X}''|u''$ does not depend on u'' and $\mathcal{X}(n)|u$ does not depend on u we have $[\mathcal{X}'|U'] = (1/n)\cdot\overrightarrow{(\mathcal{X}''|u'')}$ and $[\tilde{\mathcal{X}}|\tilde{U}] = (1/n)\cdot\overrightarrow{(\mathcal{X}(n)|u)}$. From (3), we obtain

$$
\begin{aligned}
[\mathcal{X}'|U'] &= [\tilde{\mathcal{X}}|\tilde{U}] \\
\boldsymbol{\kappa}\big([\mathcal{X}'],[\tilde{\mathcal{X}}]\big) &\le \frac{20[\![\mathbf{G}]\!]}{n} \\
[Z_0'|X_0'] &\le \frac{4\ln\ln|X_0(n)|}{n}
\end{aligned}
\tag{4}
$$

The distance between $[\tilde{\mathcal{Z}}]$ and $[\mathcal{Z}]$ can be bounded as follows

$$
\begin{aligned}
\boldsymbol{\kappa}\big([\tilde{\mathcal{Z}}],[\mathcal{Z}]\big) &= \frac{1}{n}\boldsymbol{\kappa}\big(\overrightarrow{\mathcal{Z}(n)}, n\cdot[\mathcal{Z}]\big) = \frac{1}{n}\lim_{m\to\infty}\frac{1}{m}\boldsymbol{\kappa}\big(\mathcal{Z}^m(n),\mathcal{Z}(m\cdot n)\big) \\
&\le \frac{1}{n}D_\varphi\cdot\varphi(n)
\end{aligned}
\tag{5}
$$

This also implies

$$
\boldsymbol{\kappa}\big([\tilde{\mathcal{X}}],[\mathcal{X}]\big) \le \frac{1}{n}D_\varphi\cdot\varphi(n) \tag{6}
$$

Since conditioning is a Lipschitz-continuous operation with Lipschitz constant 2, we also have

$$
\boldsymbol{\kappa}\big([\tilde{\mathcal{X}}|\tilde{U}],[\mathcal{X}|U]\big) \le \frac{2}{n}D_\varphi\cdot\varphi(n) \tag{7}
$$

Combining the estimates in (4)–(7) we obtain

$$
\begin{aligned}
\boldsymbol{\kappa}\big([\mathcal{X}'|U'],[\mathcal{X}|U]\big) &\le 2D_\varphi\cdot\frac{\varphi(n)}{n} \\
\boldsymbol{\kappa}\big([\mathcal{X}'],[\mathcal{X}]\big) &\le \frac{20[\![\mathbf{G}]\!]}{n} + D_\varphi\frac{\varphi(n)}{n} \\
[Z_0'|X_0'] &\le \frac{4\ln\ln|X_0(n)|}{n} + 2D_\varphi\frac{\varphi(n)}{n}
\end{aligned}
$$

Please note that $|X_0(n)|$ grows at most exponentially (it is bounded by $\mathbf{e}^{n([X_0]+C)}$ for some C) and φ is a strictly sub-linear function. Thus, by choosing sufficiently large n depending on the given $\varepsilon > 0$, we obtain $[\mathcal{Z}']$, satisfying conclusions of the theorem for homogeneous $[\mathcal{Z}]$.

To prove the theorem in full generality, observe that all the quantities on the right-hand side of the inequalities are Lipschitz-continuous. Since $\mathbf{Prob}[\mathbf{G}]_\mathsf{h}$ is dense in $\mathbf{Prob}[\mathbf{G}]$ the theorem extends to any $[\mathcal{Z}]$ by first approximating it with any precision by a homogeneous configuration and applying the argument above. □

3.3. The Expansion Theorem

The following theorem is complementary to Theorem 3. The expansion applied to a diagram containing a reduced admissible fan produces a diagram with an admissible fan, such that the contraction of it is the original diagram. Thus, arrow expansion is a right inverse of the arrow contraction operation.

In general, contraction erases some information stored in the diagram, so there are many right inverses. We prove the theorem below by providing a simple construction of one such right inverse.

Theorem 4. *Let $([X] \leftarrow [Z'] \rightarrow [U'])$ be a reduced admissible fan in some tropical* **G***-diagram $[\mathcal{Z}']$ and $\lambda > 0$. Let $[\mathcal{X}] := [X]$. Then there exists a* **G***-diagram $[\mathcal{Z}]$ containing the copy of $[\mathcal{X}]$, such that the corresponding admissible fan $([X] \leftarrow [Z] \rightarrow [U])$ has $[Z|X] = \lambda$ and $[\mathcal{X}|U] = [\mathcal{X}|U']$.*

Proof. Let $[W]$ be a tropical probability space with entropy equal to λ. For any reduction of tropical spaces $[A] \rightarrow [B]$, there are natural reductions

$$\begin{gathered}([A]+[W]) \to ([B]+[W]) \\ ([A]+[W]) \to [W]\end{gathered}$$

We construct the diagram $[\mathcal{Z}]$ by replacing every space $[V]$ in the ideal $\lfloor U' \rfloor$ with $[U]+[W]$. Every morphism $[V_1] \to [V_2]$ within $\lfloor U' \rfloor$ is replaced by

$$([V_1]+[W]) \to ([V_2]+[W])$$

And any morphism from $[V]$ in $\lfloor U' \rfloor$ to a space $[Y]$ in $\lceil X \rceil$ is replaced by a composition

$$([V]+[W]) \to [V] \to [Y]$$

Clearly, the resulting diagram satisfies the conclusion of the theorem. □

The rest of the article is devoted to the development of the necessary tools and the proof of Proposition 2.

4. Local Estimate

In this section, we derive a bound, very similar to Fano's inequality, on the intrinsic entropic distance between two diagrams of probability spaces with the same underlying diagram of sets. The bound will be in terms of the total variation distance between two distributions corresponding to the diagrams of probability spaces. It will be used in the next section to prove Proposition 2.

4.1. Distributions

4.1.1. Distributions on Sets

For a finite set S we denote by ΔS the collection of all probability distributions on S and by $\|\pi_1 - \pi_2\|_1$ we denote the total variation distance between $\pi_1, \pi_2 \in \Delta S$.

4.1.2. Distributions on Diagrams of Sets

Let **Set** denote the category of finite sets and surjective maps. For an indexing category **G**, we denote by **Set**⟨**G**⟩ the category of **G**-diagrams in **Set**. That is, objects in **Set**⟨**G**⟩ are commutative diagrams of sets indexed by the category **G**, the spaces in such a diagram are finite sets, and arrows represent surjective maps, subject to commutativity relations.

For a diagram of sets $\mathcal{S} = \{S_i; \sigma_{ij}\}$ we define the *space of distributions on the diagram* $\mathcal{S}$ by

$$\Delta\mathcal{S} := \left\{(\pi_i) \in \prod_i \Delta S_i : (\sigma_{ij})_* \pi_i = \pi_j\right\}$$

where $f_* : \Delta S \to \Delta S'$ is the affine map induced by a surjective map $f : S \to S'$. If S_0 is the initial space of $\mathcal{S}$, then there is an isomorphism

$$\begin{gathered}\Delta S_0 \overset{\cong}{\leftrightarrow} \Delta\mathcal{S} \\ \Delta S_0 \ni \pi_0 \mapsto \{(\sigma_{0i})_* \pi_0\} \in \Delta\mathcal{S} \\ \Delta S_0 \ni \pi_0 \leftarrow\!\shortmid \{\pi_i\} \in \Delta\end{gathered} \tag{8}$$

Using the isomorphism (8) we define total variation distance between two distributions $\pi, \pi' \in \Delta\mathcal{S}$ as

$$\|\pi - \pi'\|_1 := \|\pi_0 - \pi_0'\|_1$$

Given a **G**-diagram of sets $\mathcal{S} = \{S_i; \sigma_{ij}\}$ and an element $\pi \in \Delta\mathcal{S}$ we can construct a **G**-diagram of probability spaces $(\mathcal{S}, \pi) := \{(S_i, \pi_i); \sigma_{ij}\}$.

Below, we give the estimate of the entropy distance between two **G**-diagrams of probability spaces $(\mathcal{S}, \pi)$ and $(\mathcal{S}, \pi')$ in terms of the total variation distance $\|\pi - \pi'\|$ between distributions.

4.2. The Estimate

The upper bound on the entropy distance, which we derive below, has two summands. One is linear in the total variation distance with the slope proportional to the log-cardinality of S_0. The second one is super-linear in the total variation distance, but it does not depend on $\mathcal{S}$. So, we have the following interesting observation: of course, the super-linear summand always dominates the linear one locally. However, as the cardinality of $\mathcal{S}$ becomes large, it is the linear summand that starts playing the main role. This will be the case when we apply the bound in the next section.

For $\alpha \in [0,1]$ consider a binary probability space with the weight of one of the atoms equal to α

$$\mathbb{B}_\alpha := \big(\{\square, \blacksquare\};\ p(\square) = 1-\alpha,\ p(\blacksquare) = \alpha\big)$$

Proposition 3. *For an indexing category* $\mathbf{G}$*, consider a* $\mathbf{G}$*-diagram of sets* $\mathcal{S} = \{S_i, \sigma_{ij}\} \in \mathbf{Set}\langle\mathbf{G}\rangle$*. Let* $\pi, \pi' \in \Delta\mathcal{S}$ *be two probability distributions on* $\mathcal{S}$*. Denote* $\mathcal{X} := (\mathcal{S}, \pi)$*,* $\mathcal{Y} := (\mathcal{S}, \pi')$ *and* $\alpha := \frac{1}{2}\|\pi - \pi'\|_1$*. Then*

$$\mathbf{k}(\mathcal{X}, \mathcal{Y}) \le 2[\![\mathbf{G}]\!]\big(\alpha \cdot \ln|S_0| + \mathsf{Ent}(\mathbb{B}_\alpha)\big)$$

Proof. To prove the local estimate, we decompose both π and π' into a convex combination of a common part $\hat{\pi}$ and rests π^+ and π'^+. The coupling between the common parts gives no contribution to the distance and the worst possible estimate on the other parts is still enough to obtain the bound in the lemma, using Proposition 1.

Let S_0 be the initial set in the diagram $\mathcal{S}$. We will need the following obvious rough estimate of the entropy distance that holds for any $\pi, \pi' \in \Delta\mathcal{S}$:

$$\mathbf{k}(\mathcal{X}, \mathcal{Y}) \le 2[\![\mathbf{G}]\!] \cdot \ln|S_0| \tag{9}$$

It can be obtained by taking a tensor product for the coupling between $\mathcal{X}$ and $\mathcal{Y}$.

Our goal now is to write π and π' as the convex combination of three other distributions $\hat{\pi}$, π^+ and π'^+ as in

$$\pi = (1-\alpha) \cdot \hat{\pi} + \alpha \cdot \pi^+$$
$$\pi' = (1-\alpha) \cdot \hat{\pi} + \alpha \cdot \pi'^+$$

with the smallest possible $\alpha \in [0,1]$.

We could do it the following way. Let π_0 and π'_0 be the distributions on S_0 that correspond to π and π' under isomorphisms (8). Let $\alpha := \frac{1}{2}\|\pi - \pi'\|_1$. If $\alpha = 1$ then the proposition follows from the rough estimate (9), so from now on, we assume that $\alpha < 1$. Define three probability distributions $\hat{\pi}_0$, π_0^+ and $\pi_0'^+$ on S_0 by setting for every $x \in S_0$

$$\hat{\pi}_0(x) := \frac{1}{1-\alpha} \min\{\pi_0(x), \pi'_0(x)\}$$
$$\pi_0^+ := \frac{1}{\alpha}\big(\pi_0 - (1-\alpha)\hat{\pi}_0\big)$$
$$\pi_0'^+ := \frac{1}{\alpha}\big(\pi'_0 - (1-\alpha)\hat{\pi}_0\big)$$

Denote by $\hat{\pi}, \pi^+, \pi'^+ \in \Delta\mathcal{S}$ the distributions corresponding to $\hat{\pi}_0, \pi_0^+, \pi_0'^+ \in \Delta S_0$ under isomorphism (8). Thus, we have

$$\pi = (1-\alpha)\hat{\pi} + \alpha \cdot \pi^+$$
$$\pi' = (1-\alpha)\hat{\pi} + \alpha \cdot \pi'^+$$

Now, we construct two fans of **G**-diagrams

$$\mathcal{X} \leftarrow \tilde{\mathcal{X}} \rightarrow \mathbb{B}_\alpha \qquad \mathbb{B}_\alpha \leftarrow \tilde{\mathcal{Y}} \rightarrow \mathcal{Y} \tag{10}$$

by setting

$$\tilde{X}_i := \Big(S_i \times \mathbb{B}_\alpha;\ \tilde{\pi}_i(s,\square) = (1-\alpha)\hat{\pi}_i(s),\ \tilde{\pi}_i(s,\blacksquare) = \alpha\cdot\pi_i^+(s)\Big)$$
$$\tilde{Y}_i := \Big(S_i \times \mathbb{B}_\alpha;\ \tilde{\pi}_i'(s,\square) = (1-\alpha)\hat{\pi}_i(s),\ \tilde{\pi}_i'(s,\blacksquare) = \alpha\cdot\pi_i'^+(s)\Big)$$

and

$$\tilde{\mathcal{X}} := \{\tilde{X}_i;\ \sigma_{ij}\times\mathbf{id}\}$$
$$\tilde{\mathcal{Y}} := \{\tilde{Y}_i;\ \sigma_{ij}\times\mathbf{id}\}$$

The reduction in the fans in (10) is given by coordinate projections. Note that the following isomorphisms hold

$$\mathcal{X}|\square \cong (\mathcal{S},\hat{\pi})$$
$$\mathcal{X}|\blacksquare \cong (\mathcal{S},\pi^+)$$
$$\mathcal{Y}|\square \cong (\mathcal{S},\hat{\pi}) \cong \mathcal{X}|\square$$
$$\mathcal{Y}|\blacksquare \cong (\mathcal{S},\pi'^+)$$

Now we apply Proposition 1 along with the rough estimate in (9) to obtain the desired inequality

$$\begin{aligned}\mathbf{k}(\mathcal{X},\mathcal{Y}) &\le (1-\alpha)\,\mathbf{k}(\mathcal{X}|\square,\mathcal{Y}|\square) + \alpha\cdot\mathbf{k}(\mathcal{X}|\blacksquare,\mathcal{Y}|\blacksquare)\\ &\quad+\sum_i\big[\,\mathsf{Ent}(\mathbb{B}_\alpha|X_i)+\mathsf{Ent}(\mathbb{B}_\alpha|Y_i)\big]\\ &\le 2[\![\mathbf{G}]\!]\big(\alpha\cdot\ln|S_0| + \mathsf{Ent}(\mathbb{B}_\alpha)\big)\end{aligned}$$

□

5. Proof of Proposition 2

In this section, we prove Proposition 2, which is shown below verbatim. The proof consists of the construction in Section 5.1 and estimates in Propositions 5 and 6.

5.1. The Construction

In this section, we fix an indexing category **G**, a minimal **G**-diagram of probability spaces $\mathcal{Z}$ with an admissible sub-fan $X_0 \leftarrow Z_0 \rightarrow U$. We denote $\mathcal{X} := \lceil X_0 \rceil$ and by **H** we denote the combinatorial type of $\mathcal{X} = \{X_i;\chi_{ij}\}$.

Instead of diagram $\mathcal{Z}$, we consider an extended diagram, which is a two-fan of **H**-diagrams

$$\mathcal{X} \xleftarrow{\pi_1} \mathcal{Y} \rightarrow U^{\mathbf{H}} \tag{11}$$

where $\mathcal{Y} = \{Y_i; v_{ij}\}$ consists of those spaces in $\mathcal{Z}$, which are initial spaces of two fans with feet in U and in some space in $\mathcal{X}$. That is for every $i \in \mathbf{H}$ the space Y_i is defined to be the initial space in the minimal fan $X_i \leftarrow Y_i \rightarrow U$ in $\mathcal{Z}$. It may happen that for some pair of indices $i_1, i_2 \in \mathbf{H}$ the initial spaces of the fans with one feet U and the other X_{i_1} and X_{i_2} coincide in $\mathcal{Z}$. In $\mathcal{Y}$, however, they will be treated as separate spaces so that the combinatorial type of $\mathcal{Y}$ is $\mathbf{H}$. Starting with the diagram in (11) one can recover $\mathcal{Z}$ by collapsing all the isomorphism arrows. The initial space of $\mathcal{Y}$ will be denoted Y_0.

We would like to construct a new fan $\mathcal{X}' \overset{\pi_1'}{\leftarrow} \mathcal{Y}' \to V^{\mathbf{H}}$, such that

$$\begin{cases} \mathcal{X}|u = \mathcal{X}'|v & \text{for any } u \in U \text{ and } v \in V \\ \mathbf{k}(\mathcal{X}', \mathcal{X}) \leq 20[\![\mathbf{G}]\!] \\ [Y_0'|X_0'] \leq 4 \ln\ln|X_0| \end{cases} \tag{12}$$

Once this goal is achieved, we collapse all the isomorphisms to obtain $\mathbf{G}$-diagram satisfying conditions in the conclusion of Proposition 2.

We start with a general description of the idea behind the construction, followed by a detailed argument. To introduce the new space V we take its points to be N atoms in $u_1, \dots, u_N \in U$. Ideally, we would like to choose the atoms in such a way that $X_0|u_n$ are disjoint and cover the whole of X_0. It is not always possible to achieve this exactly. However, when $|X_0|$ is large, N is taken slightly larger than $\mathbf{e}^{[X_0:U]}$, and $u_1, \dots, u_N$ are chosen at random, then with high probability the spaces $X_0|u_n$ will overlap only little and will cover most of X_0. The details of the construction follow.

We fix $N \in \mathbb{N}$ and construct several new diagrams. For each of the new diagrams, we provide a verbal and formal description.

- The space U^N. Points in it are independent samples of length N of points in U.
- The space $V_N = (\{1, \dots, N\}, \mathsf{unif})$. A point $n \in V_N$ should be interpreted as a choice of index in a sample $\bar{u} \in U^N$.
- The $\mathbf{H}$-diagram $\mathcal{A}$, where

$$\begin{aligned} \mathcal{A} &= \{A_i; \alpha_{ij}\} \\ A_i &= (\{(x, n, \bar{u}) : x \in X_i|u_n\}, \mathsf{unif}) \\ \alpha_{ij} &= (\chi_{ij}, \mathrm{Id}, \mathrm{Id}) \end{aligned}$$

  A point $(x, n, \bar{u})$ in A_i corresponds to the choice of a sample $\bar{u} \in U^N$, an independent choice of a member of the sample u_n and a point $x \in X_i|u_n$. Recall that the original diagram $\mathcal{Z}$ was assumed to be homogeneous and, in particular, the distribution on $X_i|u_n$ is uniform. Due to the assumption on homogeneity of $\mathcal{Z}$, the space $X_i|u$ does not depend on $u \in U$. Since V_N is also equipped with the uniform distribution, it follows that the distribution on A_i will also be uniform.
- The $\mathbf{H}$-diagram $\mathcal{B}$, where

$$\begin{aligned} \mathcal{B} &= \{B_i; \beta_{ij}\} \\ B_i &= \left(\left\{(x, \bar{u}) : x \in \bigcup_{n=1}^{N} X_i|u_n\right\}, p_{B_i}\right) \\ \beta_{ij} &= (\chi_{ij}, \mathrm{Id}) \end{aligned}$$

  A point $(x, \bar{u}) \in B_i$ is the choice of a sample $\bar{u} \in U^N$ and a point x in one of the fibers $X_i|u_n$, $n = 1, \dots, N$. The distribution p_{B_i} on B_i is chosen so that the natural projection $A_i \to B_i$ is the reduction of probability spaces. Given a sample $\bar{u}$, if the fibers $X_i|u_n$ are not disjoint, then the distribution on $B_i|\bar{u}$ need not to be uniform. Below, we will give an explicit description of $p_{\mathcal{B}}$ and study the dependence of $p_{\mathcal{B}}(\,\cdot\,|\bar{u})$ on the sample $\bar{u} \in U^N$.

These diagrams can be organized into a minimal diamond diagram of $\mathbf{H}$-diagrams, where reductions are obvious projections.

$$
\begin{array}{ccccc}
 & & \mathcal{A} & & \\
 & \swarrow & & \searrow & \\
\mathcal{B} & & & & V_N \otimes U^N \\
 & \searrow & & \swarrow & \\
 & & U^N & &
\end{array}
\tag{13}
$$

To describe the probability distribution on $\mathcal{B}$, first we define several relevant quantities:

$$
\begin{aligned}
\rho &:= \frac{|X_0|u|}{|X_0|} = \mathbf{e}^{-[X_0:U]} \\
N(x,\bar{u}) &:= \left|\{n \in V_N : x \in X_0|u_n\}\right| \\
\nu(x,\bar{u}) &:= \frac{N(x,\bar{u})}{N} = p_{V_N}\{n \in V_N : x \in X_0|u_n\}
\end{aligned}
\tag{14}
$$

Recall that the distribution $p_{\mathcal{B}}$ is completely determined by the distribution p_{B_0} on the initial space of $\mathcal{B}$ via isomorphism (8). From homogeneity of $\mathcal{Z}$ it follows that distributions on both A_0 and $A|_{\bar{u}}$ are uniform. Therefore

$$
p_{B_0}(x|\bar{u}) := \frac{\nu(x,\bar{u})}{\rho \cdot |X_0|}
\tag{15}
$$

The desired fan $(\mathcal{X}' \leftarrow \mathcal{Y}' \rightarrow V^{\mathbf{H}})$ mentioned in the beginning of the section is obtained from the top fan in the diagram in (13) by conditioning on $\bar{u} \in U^N$. We will show later that for an appropriate choice of N and for most choices of $\bar{u}$, the fan we obtain in this way has the required properties.

First, we would like to make the following observations. Fix an arbitrary $\bar{u} \in U^N$. Then:

(1) The underlying set of the probability space $B_0|\bar{u} = X_0|\bar{u}$ is $\underline{X}_0$.
(2) The diagrams

$$
\begin{aligned}
\mathcal{Y}'_{\bar{u}} &:= \mathcal{A}|\bar{u} \\
\mathcal{X}'_{\bar{u}} &:= \mathcal{B}|\bar{u}
\end{aligned}
$$

are included in a two-fan of $\mathbf{H}$-diagrams

$$
\mathcal{X}'_{\bar{u}} \leftarrow \mathcal{Y}'_{\bar{u}} \rightarrow V_N
$$

which is obtained by conditioning the top fan in the diagram in (13).
The very important observation is that diagrams $\mathcal{X}'_{\bar{u}}|n$ and $\mathcal{X}|u$ are isomorphic for any choice of $n \in V_N$ and $u \in U$. The isomorphism is the composition of the following sequence of isomorphisms

$$
\mathcal{X}'_{\bar{u}}|n \rightarrow \mathcal{B}|(\bar{u},n) \rightarrow \mathcal{A}|(\bar{u},n) \rightarrow \mathcal{X}|u_n \rightarrow \mathcal{X}|u
$$

where the first isomorphism follows from the definition of $\mathcal{X}'_{\bar{u}}$, the second—from minimality of the fan $\mathcal{B} \leftarrow \mathcal{A} \rightarrow V_N$, the third—from the definition of $\mathcal{A}$ and the fourth—from the homogeneity of $\mathcal{Z}$.

5.2. The Estimates

We now claim and prove that one could choose a number N and $\bar{u}$ in U^N such that

(1) $\mathbf{k}(\mathcal{X}'_{\bar{u}}, \mathcal{X}) \leq 20[\![\mathbf{H}]\!]$.
(2) $[Y'_{\bar{u},0}|X'_{\bar{u},0}] \leq 4 \ln\ln |X_0|$, where $Y'_{\bar{u},0}$ and $X'_{\bar{u},0}$ are initial spaces in $\mathcal{X}'_{\bar{u}}$ and $\mathcal{Y}'_{\bar{u}}$, respectively.

5.2.1. Total Variation and Entropic Distance Estimates

If we fix some $x_0 \in X_0$, then $\nu = \nu(x_0, \cdot)$ is a scaled binomially distributed random variable with parameters N and ρ, which means that $N \cdot \nu \sim \text{Bin}(N, \rho)$.

First, we state the following bounds on the tails of a binomial distribution.

Lemma 1. *Let ν be a scaled binomial random variable with parameters N and ρ, then*

(i) for any $t \in [0,1]$ holds

$$\mathbb{P}\{|\nu - \rho| > \rho \cdot t\} \leq 2 \cdot \mathbf{e}^{-\frac{1}{3} \cdot N \cdot \rho \cdot t^2}$$

(ii) for any $t \in [0,2]$ holds

$$\mathbb{P}\left\{\frac{\nu}{\rho} \ln \frac{\nu}{\rho} > t\right\} \leq \mathbf{e}^{-\frac{1}{12} \cdot N \cdot \rho \cdot t^2}$$

The proof of Lemma 1 can be found at the end of this section.

Below we use the notation $\mathbb{P} := p_{U^N}$ for the probability distribution on U^N. For a pair of complete diagrams $\mathcal{C}, \mathcal{C}'$ with the same underlying diagram of sets and with initial spaces C_0, C_0', we will write $\alpha(\mathcal{C}, \mathcal{C}')$ for the halved total variation distance between their distributions

$$\alpha(\mathcal{C}, \mathcal{C}') := \frac{1}{2} \left\| p_{C_0} - p_{C_0'} \right\|_1$$

Proposition 4. *In the settings above, for $t \in [0,1]$, the following inequality holds*

$$\mathbb{P}\{\bar{u} \in U^N : 2\alpha(\mathcal{X}_{\bar{u}}', \mathcal{X}) > t\} \leq 2|X_0| \cdot \mathbf{e}^{-\frac{1}{3} N \cdot \rho \cdot t^2}$$

Proof. Recall that by definition $\mathcal{X}_{\bar{u}}' = \mathcal{B}|\bar{u}$. We use Equation (15) to expand the left-hand side of the inequality as follows

$$\begin{aligned}
\mathbb{P}\{\bar{u} \in U^N : 2\alpha(\mathcal{B}|\bar{u}, \mathcal{X}) > t\} &= \mathbb{P}\left\{\bar{u} \in U^N : \sum_{x \in X_0} \left| \frac{\nu(x, \bar{u})}{\rho \cdot |X_0|} - \frac{1}{|X_0|} \right| > t\right\} \\
&= \mathbb{P}\left\{\bar{u} \in U^N : \sum_{x \in X_0} |\nu(x, \bar{u}) - \rho| > \rho \cdot |X_0| \cdot t\right\} \\
&\leq \mathbb{P}\{\bar{u} \in U^N : \text{there exists } x_0 \text{ such that } |\nu(x_0, \bar{u}) - \rho| > \rho \cdot t\} \\
&\leq \sum_{x \in X_0} \mathbb{P}\{\bar{u} \in U^N : |\nu(x, \bar{u}) - \rho| > \rho \cdot t\}
\end{aligned}$$

Since by homogeneity of the original diagram, all the summands are the same, we can fix some $x_0 \in X_0$ and estimate further:

$$\mathbb{P}\{\bar{u} \in U^N : 2\alpha(\mathcal{B}|\bar{u}, \mathcal{X}) > t\} \leq |X_0| \cdot \mathbb{P}\{\bar{u} \in U^N : |\nu(x_0, \bar{u}) - \rho| > \rho \cdot t\}$$

Applying Lemma 1(i), we obtain the required inequality. □

In the propositions below we assume that $|X_0|$ is sufficiently large (larger than $\mathbf{e}^{20}$).

Proposition 5. *In the settings above and for any $\frac{10}{\ln |X_0|} \leq t \leq 1$ holds:*

$$\mathbb{P}\{\bar{u} \in U^N : \mathbf{k}(\mathcal{X}_{\bar{u}}', \mathcal{X}) > t(2 \cdot [\![\mathbf{G}]\!] \cdot \ln |X_0|)\} \leq 2|X_0| \cdot \mathbf{e}^{-\frac{1}{3} N \cdot \rho \cdot t^2}$$

Proof. We will use local estimate, Proposition 3, to bound the entropy distance and then apply Proposition 4. To simplify notations, we will write simply α for $\alpha(\mathcal{X}'_{\bar{u}},\mathcal{X}) = \alpha(\mathcal{B}|\bar{u},\mathcal{X})$.

$$\begin{aligned}
&\mathbb{P}\{\bar{u} \in U^N : \mathbf{k}(\mathcal{B}|\bar{u},\mathcal{X}) > (2\cdot[\![\mathbf{G}]\!]\cdot \ln|X_0|)t\} \\
&\le \mathbb{P}\{\bar{u} \in U^N : 2\cdot[\![\mathbf{G}]\!](\alpha\cdot\ln|X_0| + \mathsf{Ent}(\Lambda_\alpha)) > (2\cdot[\![\mathbf{G}]\!]\cdot\ln|X_0|)t\} \\
&\le \mathbb{P}\{\bar{u} \in U^N : \alpha + \mathsf{Ent}(\Lambda_\alpha)/\ln|X_0| > t\}
\end{aligned}$$

Please note that in the chosen regime, $t \ge 10/\ln|X_0|$, the first summand in the right-hand side of the inequality is larger than the second, i.e., $\alpha \ge \mathsf{Ent}(\Lambda_\alpha)/\ln|X_0|$ and therefore we can write

$$\begin{aligned}
&\mathbb{P}\{\bar{u} \in U^N : \mathbf{k}(\mathcal{B}|\bar{u},\mathcal{X}) > (2\cdot[\![\mathbf{G}]\!]\cdot\ln|X_0|)t\} \\
&\le \mathbb{P}\{\bar{u} \in U^N : 2\alpha > t\} \\
&\le 2|X_0|\cdot \mathbf{e}^{-\frac{1}{3}N\cdot\rho\cdot t^2}
\end{aligned}$$

□

5.2.2. The "Height" Estimate

Recall that for given $N \in \mathbb{N}$ and $\bar{u} \in U^N$ we have constructed a two-fan of **H**-diagrams

$$\mathcal{X}'_{\bar{u}} \leftarrow \mathcal{Y}'_{\bar{u}} \rightarrow V_N^{\mathbf{H}}$$

We will now estimate the length of the arrow $Y'_{\bar{u},0} \rightarrow X'_{\bar{u},0}$.

Proposition 6. *In the settings above and for* $t \in [0,2]$

$$\mathbb{P}\{\bar{u} \in U^N : [Y'_{\bar{u},0}|X'_{\bar{u},0}] > \ln(N\cdot\rho) + t\} \le |X_0|\cdot \mathbf{e}^{-\frac{1}{12}N\cdot\rho\cdot t^2}$$

Proof. First, we observe that the fiber of the reduction $Y'_{\bar{u},0} \rightarrow X'_{\bar{u},0}$ over a point $x \in X'_{\bar{u},0}$ is a homogeneous probability space of cardinality equal to $N(x,\bar{u})$, therefore its entropy is $\ln N(x,\bar{u})$.

$$\begin{aligned}
&\mathbb{P}\{\bar{u} \in U^N : [Y'_{\bar{u},0}|X'_{\bar{u},0}] > \ln(N\cdot\rho) + t\} \\
&\mathbb{P}\left\{\bar{u} \in U^N : \int_{X'_{\bar{u},0}} [Y'_{\bar{u},0}|x]\, dp_{X'_{\bar{u},0}}(x) > \ln(N\cdot\rho) + t\right\} \\
&= \mathbb{P}\left\{\bar{u} \in U^N : \sum_{x\in X_0} \frac{\nu(x,\bar{u})}{\rho\cdot|X_0|} \ln\left(N\cdot\nu(x,\bar{u})\right) > \ln(N\cdot\rho) + t\right\} \\
&\le \mathbb{P}\left\{\bar{u} \in U^N : \sum_{x\in X_0} \frac{\nu(x,\bar{u})}{\rho\cdot|X_0|} \ln\left(\frac{\nu(x,\bar{u})}{\rho}\right) > t\right\} \\
&\le |X_0|\cdot\mathbb{P}\left\{\bar{u} \in U^N : \frac{\nu(x_0,\bar{u})}{\rho} \ln\left(\frac{\nu(x_0,\bar{u})}{\rho}\right) > t\right\} \\
&\le |X_0|\cdot \mathbf{e}^{-\frac{1}{12}N\cdot\rho\cdot t^2}
\end{aligned}$$

The last inequality above follows from Lemma 1 (ii). □

5.3. Proof of Proposition 2

Let $\mathcal{X}'_{\bar{u}} \leftarrow \mathcal{Y}'_{\bar{u}} \rightarrow V_N$ be the fan constructed in Section 5.1. The construction is parameterized by number N and atom $\bar{u} \in U^N$. Below, we will choose a particular value for N and apply estimates in Propositions 5 and 6 with particular choice of parameter t to show that there is $\bar{u} \in U^N$, so that the fan satisfies the conclusions of Proposition 2.

Let

$$N := \ln^3 |X_0| \cdot \rho^{-1} = \ln^3 |X_0| \cdot \mathbf{e}^{[X_0:U]}$$
$$t := \frac{10}{\ln |X_0|}$$

With these choices of N and t, Proposition 5 implies

$$\mathbb{P}\{\bar{u} \in U^N : \mathbf{k}(\mathcal{X}'_{\bar{u}}, \mathcal{X}) > 20[\![\mathbf{G}]\!]\} \leq \frac{1}{4}$$

while Proposition 6 gives

$$\mathbb{P}\{\bar{u} \in U^N : [Y'_{\bar{u},0}|X'_{\bar{u},0}] > 4 \ln \ln |X_0|\} \leq \frac{1}{4}$$

Therefore, there is a choice of $\bar{u}$ such that the fan

$$(\mathcal{X}' \leftarrow \mathcal{Y}' \rightarrow V) := (\mathcal{X}'_{\bar{u},0} \leftarrow \mathcal{Y}'_{\bar{u},0} \rightarrow V_N)$$

satisfies conditions in (12). As we have explained at the beginning of Section 5.1, by collapsing isomorphism arrows, we obtain **G**-diagram $\mathcal{Z}'$ satisfying conclusions of Proposition 2.

5.4. *Proof of Lemma 1*

The Chernoff bound for the tail of a binomially distributed random variable $X \sim \text{Bin}(N, \rho)$ asserts that for any $0 \leq \delta \leq 1$ holds

$$\mathbb{P}\{X < (1-\delta)N \cdot \rho\} \leq \mathbf{e}^{-\frac{1}{2}\delta^2 N \cdot \rho}$$
$$\mathbb{P}\{X > (1+\delta)N \cdot \rho\} \leq \mathbf{e}^{-\frac{1}{3}\delta^2 N \cdot \rho}$$

Applying the bound for the upper and lower tail for the binomially distributed random variable $N \cdot \nu$, we obtain the inequality in (i).

The second assertion follows from the following estimate

$$\mathbb{P}\left\{\frac{\nu}{\rho} \ln \frac{\nu}{\rho} > t\right\} \leq \mathbb{P}\left\{\frac{\nu}{\rho}\left(\frac{\nu}{\rho} - 1\right) > t\right\}$$
$$= \mathbb{P}\left\{\nu > \rho \cdot \left(\frac{\sqrt{1+4t} - 1}{2} + 1\right)\right\}$$

For $0 \leq t \leq 2$ we have $\sqrt{1+4t} - 1 \geq t$, therefore

$$\mathbb{P}\left\{\frac{\nu}{\rho} \ln \frac{\nu}{\rho} > t\right\} \leq \mathbb{P}\left\{\nu > \rho \cdot \left(\frac{t}{2} + 1\right)\right\}$$

By the Chernoff bound, we have

$$\mathbb{P}\left\{\frac{\nu}{\rho} \ln \frac{\nu}{\rho} > t\right\} \leq \mathbf{e}^{-\frac{1}{12} N \cdot \rho \cdot t^2}$$

Author Contributions: Investigation, R.M. and J.W.P. All authors have read and agreed to the published version of the manuscript.

Funding: pen Access funding was provided by the Max Planck Society.

Institutional Review Board Statement: Not applicable.

Data Availability Statement: No new data were created or analyzed in this study. Data sharing is not applicable to this article.

Conflicts of Interest: The authors declare no conflict of interest.

References

1. Matveev, R.; Portegies, J.W. Asymptotic dependency structure of multiple signals. *Inf. Geom.* **2018**, *1*, 237–285. [CrossRef]
2. Ay, N.; Bertschinger, N.; Der, R.; Güttler, F.; Olbrich, E. Predictive information and explorative behavior of autonomous robots. *Eur. Phys. J. B* **2008**, *63*, 329–339. [CrossRef]
3. Friston, K. The free-energy principle: A rough guide to the brain? *Trends Cogn. Sci.* **2009**, *13*, 293–301. [CrossRef] [PubMed]
4. Van Dijk, S.G.; Polani, D. Informational constraints-driven organization in goal-directed behavior. *Adv. Complex Syst.* **2013**, *16*, 1350016. [CrossRef]
5. Kingma, D.P.; Welling, M. Auto-encoding variational Bayes. *arXiv* **2013**, arXiv:1312.6114.
6. Bertschinger, N.; Rauh, J.; Olbrich, E.; Jost, J.; Ay, N. Quantifying unique information. *Entropy* **2014**, *16*, 2161–2183. [CrossRef]
7. Steudel, B.; Ay, N. Information-theoretic inference of common ancestors. *Entropy* **2015**, *17*, 2304–2327. [CrossRef]
8. Matveev, R.; Portegies, J.W. Tropical probability theory and an application to the entropic cone. *Kybernetika* **2020**, *56*, 1133–1153. [CrossRef]
9. Matveev, R.; Portegies, J.W. Conditioning in tropical probability theory. *Entropy* **2023**, *25*, 1641.
10. Gács, P.; Körner, J. Common information is far less than mutual information. *Probl. Control Inf. Theory* **1973**, *2*, 149–162.
11. Ahlswede, R.; Körner, J. On the connection between the entropies of input and output distributions of discrete memoryless channels. In Proceedings of the Fifth Conference on Probability Theory, Brasov, Romania, 1–6 September 1974.
12. Ahlswede, R.; Körner, J. *Appendix: On Common Information and Related Characteristics of Correlated Information Sources*; Springer: Berlin/Heidelberg, Germany, 2006; pp. 664–677.
13. Makarychev, K.; Makarychev, Y.; Romashchenko, A.; Vereshchagin, N. A new class of non-Shannon-type inequalities for entropies. *Commun. Inf. Syst.* **2002**, *2*, 147–166. [CrossRef]
14. Matveev, R.; Portegies, J.W. Tropical diagrams of probability spaces. *Inf. Geom.* **2020**, *3*, 61–88. [CrossRef]
15. Kovačević, M.; Stanojević, I.; Šenk, V. On the hardness of entropy minimization and related problems. In Proceedings of the 2012 IEEE Information Theory Workshop, Lausanne, Switzerland, 3–7 September 2012; pp. 512–516.
16. Vidyasagar, M. A metric between probability distributions on finite sets of different cardinalities and applications to order reduction. *IEEE Trans. Autom. Control* **2012**, *57*, 2464–2477. [CrossRef]

entropy

MDPI

Article

Conditioning in Tropical Probability Theory

Rostislav Matveev [1,*] and Jacobus W. Portegies [2,*]

1 Max Planck Institute for Mathematics in the Sciences, 04103 Leipzig, Germany
2 Department of Mathematics and Computer Science, Eindhoven University of Technology, 5600 MB Eindhoven, The Netherlands
* Correspondence: matveev@mis.mpg.de (R.M.); j.w.portegies@tue.nl (J.W.P.)

Abstract: We define a natural operation of conditioning of tropical diagrams of probability spaces and show that it is Lipschitz continuous with respect to the asymptotic entropy distance.

Keywords: tropical probability

1. Introduction

In [1,2], we have initiated the study of tropical probability spaces and their diagrams. In [1], we endowed (commutative) diagrams of probability spaces with the intrinsic entropy distance and, in [2], we defined tropical diagrams as points in the asymptotic cone of the metric space. They are represented by certain sequences of diagrams of probability spaces.

We expect that tropical diagrams will be helpful in the study of information optimization problems, such as the ones considered in [3–8], and we have indeed applied them to derive a dimension-reduction result for the shape of the entropic cone in [9].

In this present article, we introduce the notion of conditioning on a space in a tropical diagram and show that the operation is Lipschitz continuous with respect to the asymptotic entropy distance.

It is a rather technical result, and we have, therefore, decided to treat it in this separate article, but it is an important ingredient in the theory and, in particular, we need it for the dimension-reduction result mentioned before.

Given a tuple of finite-valued random variables $(\mathsf{X}_i)_{i=1}^n$ and a random variable Y, one may "condition" the collection (X_i) on Y. The result of this operation is a family of n-tuples of random variables denoted $(\mathsf{X}_i|\mathsf{Y})_{i=1}^n$ parameterized by those values of Y that have positive probability. Each tuple of random variables in this family is defined on a separate probability space.

When passing to the tropical setting, the situation is different in the sense that when we condition a tropical diagram $[\mathcal{X}]$ on a space $[Y]$, the result is again a tropical diagram $[\mathcal{X}|Y]$ rather than a family. After recalling some preliminaries in Section 2, we describe the operation of conditioning and prove that the result depends in a Lipschitz way on the original diagram in Section 3.

Citation: Matveev, R.; Portegies, J.W. Conditioning in Tropical Probability Theory. *Entropy* **2023**, *25*, 1641. https://doi.org/10.3390/e25121641

Academic Editor: Daniel Chicharro

Received: 6 November 2023
Revised: 4 December 2023
Accepted: 7 December 2023
Published: 9 December 2023

2. Preliminaries

Our main objects of study are commutative diagrams of probability spaces and their tropical counterparts. In this section, we recall briefly the main definitions and results.

2.1. Probability Spaces and Their Diagrams

2.1.1. Probability Spaces

By a *finite probability space,* we mean a set with a probability measure that has finite support. A *reduction* from one probability space to another is an equivalence class of measure-preserving maps. Two maps are equivalent if they coincide on a set of full measures. We call a point x in a probability space $X = (\underline{X}, p)$ an *atom* if it has positive weight, and we write $x \in X$ to mean x is an atom in X (as opposed to $x \in \underline{X}$ for points in the underlying set). For a probability space X, we denote by $|X|$ the cardinality of the support of the probability measure.

2.1.2. Indexing Categories

To record the combinatorial structure of commutative diagrams of probability spaces and reductions, we use an object that we call an *indexing category*. By an indexing category, we mean a finite category $\mathbf{G}$ such that for any pair of objects $i, j \in \mathbf{G}$, there is at most one morphism between them either way. In addition, we will assume it satisfies one additional property that we will describe after introducing some terminology. For a pair of objects $i, j \in \mathbf{G}$ such that there is a morphism $\gamma_{ij} : i \to j$, object i will be called an *ancestor* of j and object j will be called a *descendant* of i. The subcategory of all descendants of an object $i \in \mathbf{G}$ is called an *ideal* generated by i and will be denoted $\lceil i \rceil$, while we will call the subcategory consisting of all ancestors of i together with all the morphisms in it a *co-ideal* generated by i and denote it by $\lfloor i \rfloor$. (The term *filter* is also used for a co-ideal in the literature about lattices).

The additional property that an indexing category has to satisfy is that for any pair of objects $i, j \in \mathbf{G}$, there exists a *minimal common ancestor* $\hat{\imath}$, and $\hat{\imath}$ is an ancestor for both i and j and any other ancestor of them both is also an ancestor of $\hat{\imath}$; in other words, $\mathbf{G}$ is an upper semi-lattice.

An equivalent formulation of the property above is the following: the intersection of the co-ideals generated by two objects $i, j \in \mathbf{G}$ is also a co-ideal generated by some object $\hat{\imath} \in \mathbf{G}$.

Any indexing category $\mathbf{G}$ is necessarily *initial*, which means that there exists an *initial object*, that is an object i_0 such that $\mathbf{G} = \lceil i_0 \rceil$.

A *fan* in a category is a pair of morphisms with the same domain. A fan $(i \leftarrow k \to j)$ is called *minimal* if for any other fan $(i \leftarrow l \to j)$ included in a commutative diagram

$$\begin{array}{ccccc} & \swarrow & k & \searrow & \\ i & & \downarrow & & j \\ & \nwarrow & l & \nearrow & \end{array},$$

the vertical arrow must be an isomorphism; in other words, k is a minimal common ancestor of i and j.

For any pair of objects i, j in an indexing category $\mathbf{G}$, there exists a unique minimal fan $(i \leftarrow \hat{\imath} \to j)$ in $\mathbf{G}$.

2.1.3. Diagrams

We denote by **Prob** the category of finite probability spaces and reductions, i.e., the equivalence classes of measure-preserving maps. For an indexing category $\mathbf{G} = \{i; \gamma_{ij}\}$, a $\mathbf{G}$-diagram is a functor $\mathcal{X} : \mathbf{G} \to \mathbf{Prob}$. A reduction f from one $\mathbf{G}$-diagram $\mathcal{X} = \{X_i; \chi_{ij}\}$ to another $\mathcal{Y} = \{Y_i; \upsilon_{ij}\}$ is a natural transformation between the functors. It amounts to a collection of reductions $f_i : X_i \to Y_i$, such that the big diagram consisting of all spaces X_i, Y_i and all morphisms χ_{ij}, υ_{ij} and f_i is commutative. The category of $\mathbf{G}$-diagrams and reductions will be denoted as $\mathbf{Prob}\langle\mathbf{G}\rangle$. The construction of diagrams could be iterated; thus, we can consider $\mathbf{H}$-diagrams of $\mathbf{G}$-diagrams and denote the corresponding category $\mathbf{Prob}\langle\mathbf{G}\rangle\langle\mathbf{H}\rangle = \mathbf{Prob}\langle\mathbf{G},\mathbf{H}\rangle$. Every $\mathbf{H}$-diagram of a $\mathbf{G}$-diagram can also be considered as $\mathbf{G}$-diagrams of $\mathbf{H}$-diagrams; thus, there is a natural equivalence of categories $\mathbf{Prob}\langle\mathbf{G},\mathbf{H}\rangle \cong \mathbf{Prob}\langle\mathbf{H},\mathbf{G}\rangle$.

A $\mathbf{G}$-diagram $\mathcal{X}$ will be called *minimal* if it maps minimal fans in $\mathbf{G}$ to minimal fans in the target category. The subspace of all minimal $\mathbf{G}$-diagrams will be denoted $\mathbf{Prob}\langle\mathbf{G}\rangle_{\mathrm{m}}$. In [1], we have shown that for any fan in **Prob** or in $\mathbf{Prob}\langle\mathbf{G}\rangle$, its minimization exists and is unique up to isomorphism.

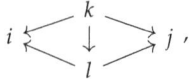

2.1.4. Tensor Product

The tensor product of two probability spaces $X = (\underline{X}, p)$ and $Y = (\underline{Y}, q)$ is their independent product $X \otimes Y := (\underline{X} \times \underline{Y}, p \otimes q)$. For two **G**-diagrams $\mathcal{X} = \{X_i; \chi_{ij}\}$ and $\mathcal{Y} = \{Y_i; v_{ij}\}$, we define their tensor product to be $\mathcal{X} \otimes \mathcal{Y} = \{X_i \otimes \mathcal{Y}; \chi_{ij} \times v_{ij}\}$.

2.1.5. Constant Diagrams

Given an indexing category **G** and a probability space, we can form a *constant* diagram $X^{\mathbf{G}}$ that has all spaces equal to X and all reductions equal to the identity isomorphism. Sometimes, when such a constant diagram is included in a diagram with other **G**-diagrams (such as, for example, a reduction $\mathcal{X} \to X^{\mathbf{G}}$), we will write simply X in place of $X^{\mathbf{G}}$.

2.1.6. Entropy

Evaluating entropy on every space in a **G**-diagram, we obtain a tuple of non-negative numbers indexed by objects in **G**; thus, entropy gives a map

$$\mathsf{Ent}_* : \mathbf{Prob}\langle \mathbf{G} \rangle \to \mathbb{R}^{\mathbf{G}},$$

where the target space $\mathbb{R}^{\mathbf{G}}$ is a space of real-valued functions on the set of objects in **G** endowed with the ℓ^1-norm. Entropy is a homomorphism in that it satisfies

$$\mathsf{Ent}_*(\mathcal{X} \otimes \mathcal{Y}) = \mathsf{Ent}_*(\mathcal{X}) + \mathsf{Ent}_*(\mathcal{Y}).$$

2.1.7. Entropy Distance

Let **G** be an indexing category and $\mathcal{K} = (\mathcal{X} \leftarrow \mathcal{Z} \to \mathcal{Y})$ be a fan of **G**-diagrams. We define the *entropy distance* as

$$\mathrm{kd}(\mathcal{K}) := \|\mathsf{Ent}_* \mathcal{Z} - \mathsf{Ent}_* \mathcal{X}\|_1 + \|\mathsf{Ent}_* \mathcal{Z} - \mathsf{Ent}_* \mathcal{Y}\|_1.$$

The *intrinsic entropy distance* between two **G**-diagrams is defined to be the infimal entropy distance of all fans with terminal diagrams $\mathcal{X}$ and $\mathcal{Y}$:

$$\mathbf{k}(\mathcal{X}, \mathcal{Y}) := \inf\{\mathrm{kd}(\mathcal{K}) : \mathcal{K} = (\mathcal{X} \leftarrow \mathcal{Z} \to \mathcal{Y})\}.$$

The intrinsic entropy distance was introduced in [10,11] for probability spaces.

In [1], it is shown that the infimum is attained, that the optimal fan is minimal, that $\mathbf{k}$ is a pseudo-distance, which vanishes if, and only if, $\mathcal{X}$ and $\mathcal{Y}$ are isomorphic, and that Ent_* is a 1-Lipschitz linear functional with respect to $\mathbf{k}$.

2.2. Diagrams of Sets, Distributions, and Empirical Reductions

2.2.1. Distributions on Sets

For a set S, we denote by ΔS the collection of all finitely-supported probability distributions on S. For a pair of distributions $\pi_1, \pi_2 \in \Delta S$, we denote by $\|\pi_1 - \pi_2\|_1$ the *total variation distance* between them.

For a map $f : S \to S'$ between two sets, we denote by $f_* : \Delta S \to \Delta S'$ the induced affine map (the map-preserving convex combinations).

For $n \in \mathbb{N}$, we define the *empirical map* $\mathbf{q} : S^n \to \Delta S$ by the assignment below. For $\bar{s} = (s_1, \ldots, s_n) \in S^n$ and $A \subset S$, we define

$$\mathbf{q}(\bar{s})(A) := \frac{1}{n} \cdot \left|\{k : s_k \in A\}\right|.$$

For a finite probability space $X = (S, p)$, the *empirical distribution* on ΔX is the push-forward $\tau_n := \mathbf{q}_* p^{\otimes n}$. Thus,

$$\mathbf{q} : X^n \to (\Delta X, \tau_n)$$

is a reduction of finite probability spaces. The construction of empirical reduction is functorial, which is for a reduction between two probability spaces $f: X \to Y$, the diagram of the reductions

$$\begin{array}{ccc} X^n & \xrightarrow{f^n} & Y^n \\ \downarrow\mathfrak{q} & & \downarrow\mathfrak{q} \\ (\Delta X, \tau_n) & \xrightarrow{f_*} & (\Delta Y, \tau_n) \end{array}$$

commutes.

2.2.2. Distributions on Diagrams of Sets

Let **Set** denote the category of sets and surjective maps. For an indexing category **G**, we denote by **Set**⟨**G**⟩ the category of **G**-diagrams in **Set**. The objects in **Set**⟨**G**⟩ are commutative diagrams of sets indexed by **G**, and the spaces in such a diagram are sets, where the arrows represent surjective maps, subject to commutativity relations.

For a diagram of sets $\mathcal{S} = \{S_i; \sigma_{ij}\}$, we define the *space of distributions on the diagram* $\mathcal{S}$ by

$$\Delta\mathcal{S} := \left\{(\pi_i) \in \prod_i \Delta S_i : (\sigma_{ij})_* \pi_i = \pi_j\right\}.$$

If S_0 is the initial set of $\mathcal{S}$, then there is an isomorphism of

$$\begin{aligned} \Delta S_0 &\overset{\cong}{\leftrightarrow} \Delta\mathcal{S} \\ \Delta S_0 \ni \pi_0 &\mapsto \{(\sigma_{0i})_* \pi_0\} \in \Delta\mathcal{S} \\ \Delta S_0 \ni \pi_0 &\leftarrow \{\pi_i\} \in \Delta\mathcal{S}. \end{aligned} \tag{1}$$

Given a **G**-diagram of sets $\mathcal{S} = \{S_i; \sigma_{ij}\}$ and an element $\pi \in \Delta\mathcal{S}$, we can construct a **G**-diagram of probability spaces $(\mathcal{S}, \pi) := \{(S_i, \pi_i); \sigma_{ij}\}$. Note that any diagram $\mathcal{X}$ of probability spaces has this form.

2.3. Conditioning

Consider a **G**-diagram of probability spaces $\mathcal{X} = (\mathcal{S}, \pi)$, where $\mathcal{S}$ is a diagram of sets and $\pi \in \Delta\mathcal{S}$. Let $X_0 = (S_0, \pi_0)$ be the initial space in $\mathcal{X}$ and $U := X_i$ be another space in $\mathcal{X}$. Since S_0 is initial, there is a map $\sigma_{0,i}: S_0 \to S_i$. Fix an atom $u \in U$ and define the conditioned distribution $\pi_0(\cdot|u)$ on S_0 as the distribution supported in $\sigma_{0,i}^{-1}(u)$ and for every $s \in \sigma_{0,i}^{-1}(u)$ defined by

$$\pi_0(s|u) := \frac{\pi_0(s)}{\pi_0(\sigma_{0,i}^{-1}(u))}.$$

Let $\pi(\cdot|u) \in \Delta\mathcal{S}$ be the distribution corresponding to $\pi_0(\cdot|u)$ under the isomorphism in (1). We define the *conditioned* **G**-diagram as $\mathcal{X}|u := (\mathcal{S}, \pi(\cdot|u))$.

2.4. The Slicing Lemma

In [1], we prove the so-called Slicing Lemma that allows us to estimate the intrinsic entropy distance between two diagrams in terms of distances between conditioned diagrams. Among the corollaries of the Slicing Lemma is the following inequality.

Proposition 1. *Let* $(\mathcal{X} \leftarrow \hat{\mathcal{X}} \to U^{\mathbf{G}}) \in \mathbf{Prob}\langle\mathbf{G}, \Lambda_2\rangle$ *be a fan of* **G***-diagrams of probability spaces and* $\mathcal{Y} \in \mathbf{Prob}\langle\mathbf{G}\rangle$ *be another diagram. Then,*

$$\mathbf{k}(\mathcal{X}, \mathcal{Y}) \le \int_U \mathbf{k}(\mathcal{X}|u, \mathcal{Y})\, dp(u) + 2[\![\mathbf{G}]\!] \cdot \mathsf{Ent}\, U.$$

The fan in the assumption of the proposition above can often be constructed in the following manner. Suppose $\mathcal{X}$ is a **G**-diagram and $U := X_\iota$ is a space in it for some $\iota \in \mathbf{G}$. We can construct a fan $(\mathcal{X} \overset{f}{\leftarrow} \hat{\mathcal{X}} \overset{g}{\to} U^{\mathbf{G}}) \in \mathbf{Prob}\langle\mathbf{G}, \Lambda_2\rangle$ by assigning $\hat{X}_i$ to be the initial space of the (unique) minimal fan in $\mathcal{X}$ with terminal spaces X_i and U and f_i and g_i to be left and right reductions in that fan for any $i \in \mathbf{G}$.

2.5. Tropical Diagrams

A detailed discussion of the topics in this section can be found in [2].

The asymptotic entropy distance between two diagrams of the same combinatorial type is defined by

$$\boldsymbol{\kappa}(\mathcal{X},\mathcal{Y}) := \lim \frac{1}{n}\mathbf{k}(\mathcal{X}^n,\mathcal{Y}^n).$$

A tropical $\mathbf{G}$-diagram is an equivalence class of certain sequences of $\mathbf{G}$-diagrams of probability spaces. Below, we describe the type of sequences and the equivalence relation.

A function $\varphi : \mathbb{R} \geq 1 \to \mathbb{R} \geq 0$ is called an *admissible function* if φ is non-decreasing and there is a constant D_φ, such that for any $t \geq 1$:

$$t \cdot \int_t^\infty \frac{\varphi(s)}{s^2}\, ds \leq D_\varphi \cdot \varphi(t).$$

An example of an admissible function will be $\varphi(t) = t^\alpha$ for $\alpha \in [0,1)$.

A sequence $\bar{\mathcal{X}} = (\mathcal{X}(n) : n \in \mathbb{N}_0)$ of diagrams of probability spaces will be called *quasi-linear* with the *defect* bounded by an admissible function φ if for some $C > 0$ and all $m, n \in \mathbb{N}$, it satisfies

$$\boldsymbol{\kappa}\big(\mathcal{X}(n+m), \mathcal{X}(n) \otimes \mathcal{X}(m)\big) \leq C \cdot \varphi(n+m).$$

For example for a diagram $\mathcal{X}$, the sequence $\overrightarrow{\mathcal{X}} := (\mathcal{X}^n : n \in \mathbb{N}_0)$ is φ-quasi-linear for $\varphi \equiv 0$ (and for any admissible φ). Sequences with zero defect are called *linear*, and the space of all linear sequences in $\mathbf{Prob}\langle\mathbf{G}\rangle$ is denoted by $\mathsf{L}(\mathbf{Prob}\langle\mathbf{G}\rangle)$.

The asymptotic entropic distance between two φ-quasi-linear sequences $\bar{\mathcal{X}} = \big(\mathcal{X}(n) : n \in \mathbb{N}_0\big)$ and $\bar{\mathcal{Y}} = \big(\mathcal{Y}(n) : n \in \mathbb{N}_0\big)$ is defined to be

$$\boldsymbol{\kappa}(\bar{\mathcal{X}},\bar{\mathcal{Y}}) := \lim_{n\to\infty} \frac{1}{n}\mathbf{k}(\mathcal{X}(n),\mathcal{Y}(n)),$$

and the sequences are called *asymptotically equivalent* if $\boldsymbol{\kappa}(\bar{\mathcal{X}},\bar{\mathcal{Y}}) = 0$. An equivalence class of a sequence $\bar{\mathcal{X}}$ will be denoted as $[\mathcal{X}]$, and the totality of all the classes as $\mathbf{Prob}[\mathbf{G}]$. We have shown in [2] that the space of equivalence classes of φ-quasi-linear sequences does not depend on the choice of a non-zero admissible function φ.

The sum of two such equivalence classes is defined to be the equivalence class of the sequence obtained by tensor-multiplying representative sequences of the summands term-wise. In addition, there is a doubly transitive action of $\mathbb{R}_{\geq 0}$ on $\mathbf{Prob}[\mathbf{G}]$. In [2], the following theorem is proven.

Theorem 1. *Let* $\mathbf{G}$ *be an indexing category. Then:*

1. *The space* $\mathbf{Prob}[\mathbf{G}]$ *does not depend on the choice of a positive admissible function* φ *up to isometry.*
2. *The space* $\mathbf{Prob}[\mathbf{G}]$ *is metrically complete.*
3. *The map* $\mathcal{X} \mapsto \overrightarrow{\mathcal{X}}$ *is a* $\boldsymbol{\kappa}$-$\boldsymbol{\kappa}$*-isometric embedding. The space of linear sequences, i.e., the image of the map above, is dense in* $\mathbf{Prob}[\mathbf{G}]$.
4. *There is a distance-preserving homomorphism from* $\mathbf{Prob}[\mathbf{G}]$ *into a Banach space B, whose image is a closed convex cone in B.*
5. *The entropy functional*

$$\mathsf{Ent}_* : \mathbf{Prob}[\mathbf{G}] \to \mathbb{R}^{\mathbf{G}}$$
$$[(\mathcal{X}(n))_{n\in\mathbb{N}_0}] \mapsto \lim_{n\to\infty} \frac{1}{n} \mathsf{Ent}_* \mathcal{X}(n)$$

is a well-defined 1-Lipschitz linear map.

2.6. Asymptotic Equipartition Property for Diagrams

Among all **G**-diagrams, there is a special class of maximally symmetric ones. We call such diagrams *homogeneous*; see below for the definition. Homogeneous diagrams come in very handy in many considerations, because their structure is easier to describe than that of general diagrams. We show below that among the tropical diagrams, those that have homogeneous representatives are dense. It means, in particular, that when considering continuous functionals in the space of diagrams, it suffices to only study them in the space of all homogeneous diagrams.

2.6.1. Homogeneous Diagrams

A **G**-diagram $\mathcal{X}$ is called *homogeneous* if the automorphism group $\mathrm{Aut}(\mathcal{X})$ acts transitively on every space in $\mathcal{X}$, by which we mean that the action is transitive on the support of the probability measure. Homogeneous probability spaces are isomorphic to uniform spaces. For more complex indexing categories, this simple description is not sufficient.

2.6.2. Tropical Homogeneous Diagrams

The subcategory of all homogeneous **G**-diagrams will be denoted $\mathbf{Prob}\langle\mathbf{G}\rangle_{\mathsf{h}}$, and we write $\mathbf{Prob}\langle\mathbf{G}\rangle_{\mathsf{h,m}}$ for the category of minimal homogeneous **G**-diagrams. These spaces are invariant under the tensor product; thus, they are metric Abelian monoids, and the general "tropicalization" described in [2] can be performed. Passing to the tropical limit, we obtain spaces of tropical (minimal) homogeneous diagrams, which we denote by $\mathbf{Prob}[\mathbf{G}]_{\mathsf{h}}$ and $\mathbf{Prob}[\mathbf{G}]_{\mathsf{h,m}}$, respectively.

2.6.3. Asymptotic Equipartition Property

For an indexing category **G**, denote by $[\![G]\!]$ the number of objects in **G**. In [1], the following theorem is proven.

Theorem 2. *Suppose $\mathcal{X} \in \mathbf{Prob}\langle\mathbf{G}\rangle$ is a **G**-diagram of probability spaces for some fixed indexing category **G**. Then, there exists a sequence $\bar{\mathcal{H}} = (\mathcal{H}_n)_{n=0}^{\infty}$ of homogeneous **G**-diagrams, such that*

$$\frac{1}{n}\mathbf{k}(\mathcal{X}^n, \mathcal{H}_n) \leq \mathrm{C}(|X_0|, [\![\mathbf{G}]\!]) \cdot \sqrt{\frac{\ln^3 n}{n}}, \tag{2}$$

where $\mathrm{C}(|X_0|, [\![\mathbf{G}]\!])$ is a constant only depending on $|X_0|$ and $[\![\mathbf{G}]\!]$.

The approximating sequence of homogeneous diagrams is evidently quasi-linear with the defect bounded by the admissible function

$$\varphi(t) := 2C(|X_0|, [\![\mathbf{G}]\!]) \cdot t^{3/4} \geq 2C(|X_0|, [\![\mathbf{G}]\!]) \cdot t^{1/2} \cdot \ln^{3/2} t.$$

Thus, Theorem 2 above states that $\mathsf{L}(\mathbf{Prob}\langle\mathbf{G}\rangle) \subset \mathbf{Prob}[\mathbf{G}]_{\mathsf{h}}$. On the other hand, we have shown in [2] that the space of linear sequences $\mathsf{L}(\mathbf{Prob}\langle\mathbf{G}\rangle)$ is dense in $\mathbf{Prob}[\mathbf{G}]$. Combining the two statements, we obtain the following theorem.

Theorem 3. *For any indexing category **G**, the space $\mathbf{Prob}[\mathbf{G}]_{\mathsf{h}}$ is dense in $\mathbf{Prob}[\mathbf{G}]$. Similarly, the space $\mathbf{Prob}[\mathbf{G}]_{\mathsf{h,m}}$ is dense in $\mathbf{Prob}[\mathbf{G}]_{\mathsf{m}}$.*

3. Conditioning of Tropical Diagrams

3.1. Motivation

Let $\mathcal{X} \in \mathbf{Prob}\langle\mathbf{G}\rangle$ be a **G**-diagram of probability spaces containing probability space $U = X_{i_0}$ indexed by an object $i_0 \in \mathbf{G}$.

Given an atom $u \in U$, we can define a conditioned diagram $\mathcal{X}|u$. If the diagram $\mathcal{X}$ is homogeneous, then the isomorphism class of $\mathcal{X}|u$ is independent of u, so that $(\mathcal{X}|u : u \in U)$ is a constant family. On the other hand, we have shown that the power of any diagram can be approximated by homogeneous diagrams, thus suggesting that in the tropical setting $\mathcal{X}|U$ should be a well-defined tropical diagram, rather than a family. Below, we give a definition of the tropical conditioning operation and prove its consistency.

3.2. Classical-Tropical Conditioning

Here, we define the operation of conditioning of the classical diagram, such that the result is a tropical diagram. Let $\mathcal{X}$ be a $\mathbf{G}$-diagram of probability spaces and U be a space in $\mathcal{X}$. We define the conditioning map

$$[\cdot|\cdot] : \mathbf{Prob}\langle\mathbf{G}\rangle \to \mathbf{Prob}[\mathbf{G}]$$

by conditioning $\mathcal{X}$ by $u \in U$ and averaging the corresponding tropical diagrams:

$$[\mathcal{X}|U] := \int_{u \in U} \overrightarrow{(\mathcal{X}|u)}\, dp_U(u),$$

where $\overrightarrow{(\mathcal{X}|u)}$ is the tropical diagram represented by a linear sequence generated by $\mathcal{X}|u$; see Section 2.5. Note that the integral on the right-hand side is just a finite convex combination of tropical diagrams. Expanding all the definitions, we will obtain for $[\mathcal{Y}] := [\mathcal{X}|U]$, the representative sequence

$$\mathcal{Y}(n) = \bigotimes_{u \in U} (\mathcal{X}|u)^{\lfloor n \cdot p(u) \rfloor}.$$

3.3. Properties

3.3.1. Conditioning of Homogeneous Diagrams

If the diagram $\mathcal{X}$ is *homogeneous*, then for any atom $u \in U$, with a positive weight,

$$[\mathcal{X}|U] \overset{\vee}{=} \overrightarrow{(\mathcal{X}|u)}.$$

3.3.2. Entropy

By definition, the conditioned entropy is

$$\mathsf{Ent}_*(\mathcal{X}|U) := \int_U \mathsf{Ent}_*(\mathcal{X}|u)\, dp_U(u).$$

Now that $[\mathcal{X}|U]$ is a tropical diagram, the expression $\mathsf{Ent}_*(\mathcal{X}|U)$ can be interpreted in two, a priori different, ways: by the formula above and as the entropy of the object introduced in the previous subsection. Fortunately, the numeric value of it does not depend on the interpretation since the entropy is a linear functional on $\mathbf{Prob}[\mathbf{G}]$.

3.3.3. Additivity

If $\mathcal{X}$ and $\mathcal{Y}$ are two $\mathbf{G}$-diagrams with $U := X_\iota$, $V := Y_\iota$ for some $\iota \in \mathbf{G}$, then

$$[(\mathcal{X} \otimes \mathcal{Y})|(U \otimes V)] = [\mathcal{X}|U] + [\mathcal{Y}|V].$$

Proof.

$$\begin{aligned}
[(\mathcal{X}\otimes\mathcal{Y})|(U \otimes V)] &= \int_{U\otimes V} \overrightarrow{(\mathcal{X} \otimes \mathcal{Y})|(u,v)}\, dp(u)\, dp(v) \\
&= \int_{U\otimes V} (\overrightarrow{\mathcal{X}|u} + \overrightarrow{\mathcal{Y}|v})\, dp(u)\, dp(v) = \int_U \overrightarrow{\mathcal{X}|u}\, dp(u) + \int_V \overrightarrow{\mathcal{Y}|v}\, dp(v) \\
&= [\mathcal{X}|U] + [\mathcal{Y}|V]
\end{aligned}$$

□

3.3.4. Homogeneity

It follows that for any diagram $\mathcal{X}$, a space U in $\mathcal{X}$ and $n \in \mathbb{N}_0$ holds

$$[\mathcal{X}^n | U^n] = n \cdot [\mathcal{X} | U].$$

3.4. Continuity and Lipschitz Property

Proposition 2. *Let* $\mathbf{G}$ *be an indexing category,* $\mathcal{X}, \mathcal{Y} \in \mathbf{Prob}\langle\mathbf{G}\rangle$ *be two* $\mathbf{G}$ *diagrams, and* $U := X_\iota$ *and* $V := Y_\iota$ *be two spaces in* $\mathcal{X}$ *and* $\mathcal{Y}$*, respectively, indexed by some* $\iota \in \mathbf{G}$*. Then,*

$$\boldsymbol{\kappa}\Big([\mathcal{X}|U], [\mathcal{Y}|V]\Big) \le (2 \cdot [\![\mathbf{G}]\!] + 1) \cdot \mathbf{k}(\mathcal{X}, \mathcal{Y}).$$

Using the homogeneity property of conditioning, Section 3.3.4, we can obtain the following stronger inequality.

Corollary 1. *In the setting of Proposition 2, the following holds:*

$$\boldsymbol{\kappa}\Big([\mathcal{X}|U], [\mathcal{Y}|V]\Big) \le (2 \cdot [\![\mathbf{G}]\!] + 1) \cdot \boldsymbol{\kappa}(\mathcal{X}, \mathcal{Y}).$$

Before we prove Proposition 2, we will need some preparatory lemmas.

Lemma 1. *Let* $\mathcal{A}$ *be a* $\mathbf{G}$*-diagram of probability spaces and* E *be a space in it. Let* $\mathbf{q} : E^n \to (\Delta E, \tau_n)$ *be the empirical reduction. Then, for any* $n \in \mathbb{N}$ *and any* $\bar{e}, \bar{e}' \in, E^n$

$$\mathbf{k}(\mathcal{A}^n|\bar{e}, \mathcal{A}^n|\bar{e}') \le n \cdot \| \mathsf{Ent}_*(\mathcal{A}) \|_1 \cdot \| \mathbf{q}(\bar{e}) - \mathbf{q}(\bar{e}') \|_1.$$

Proof. To prove the lemma, we construct a coupling between $\mathcal{A}^n|\bar{e}$ and $\mathcal{A}^n|\bar{e}'$ in the following manner. Note that there exists a permutation $\sigma \in S_n$, such that

$$\left|\{i : e_i \ne e'_{\sigma i}\}\right| = \frac{n}{2} \cdot \| \mathbf{q}(\bar{e}) - \mathbf{q}(\bar{e}') \|_1.$$

Let

$$I = \{i : e_i = e'_{\sigma i}\}$$
$$\bar{I} = \{i : e_i \ne e'_{\sigma i}\}.$$

Using that $|\bar{I}| = \frac{n}{2} \cdot \| \mathbf{q}(\bar{e}) - \mathbf{q}(\bar{e}') \|_1$, we can estimate

$$\begin{aligned}
\mathbf{k}\left(\mathcal{A}^n|\bar{e}, \mathcal{A}^n|\bar{e}'\right) &= \mathbf{k}\left(\bigotimes_{i=1}^{n}(\mathcal{A}|e_i), \bigotimes_{i=1}^{n}(\mathcal{A}|e'_{\sigma i})\right) \\
&\le \sum_{i \in I} \mathrm{kd}(\mathcal{A}|e_i \overset{=}{\longleftrightarrow} \mathcal{A}|e'_{\sigma i}) + \sum_{i \in \bar{I}} \mathrm{kd}(\mathcal{A}|e_i \overset{\otimes}{\longleftrightarrow} \mathcal{A}|e'_{\sigma i}) \\
&\le n \cdot \| \mathsf{Ent}_*(\mathcal{A}) \|_1 \cdot \| \mathbf{q}(\bar{e}) - \mathbf{q}(\bar{e}') \|_1,
\end{aligned}$$

where $\mathcal{A} \overset{=}{\leftrightarrow} \mathcal{B}$ denotes the isomorphism coupling of two naturally isomorphic diagrams, while $\mathcal{A} \overset{\otimes}{\leftrightarrow} \mathcal{B}$ denotes the "independence" coupling. □

Lemma 2. *Let* $\mathcal{A}$ *be a* $\mathbf{G}$*-diagram of probability spaces and* E *be a space in* $\mathcal{A}$*. Then,*

$$\int_{E^n} \mathbf{k}(\mathcal{A}^n, \mathcal{A}^n|\bar{e})\, dp(\bar{e}) \le 2n \cdot [\![\mathbf{G}]\!] \cdot \mathsf{Ent}(E) + o(n).$$

Proof. First, we apply Proposition 1 slicing the first argument:

$$\int_{E^n} \mathbf{k}(\mathcal{A}^n, \mathcal{A}^n|\bar{e})\, dp(\bar{e}) \\ \leq \int_{E^n} \int_{E^n} \mathbf{k}(\mathcal{A}^n|\bar{e}', \mathcal{A}^n|\bar{e})\, dp(\bar{e}')\, dp(\bar{e}) + 2n \cdot [\![\mathbf{G}]\!] \cdot \mathsf{Ent}(E).$$

We will argue now that the double integral on the right-hand side grows sub-linearly with n. We estimate the double integral by applying Lemma 1 to the integrand

$$\int_{E^n} \int_{E^n} \mathbf{k}(\mathcal{A}^n|\bar{e}', \mathcal{A}^n|\bar{e})\, dp(\bar{e}')\, dp(\bar{e}) \\ \leq \int_{E^n} \int_{E^n} n \cdot [\![\mathbf{G}]\!] \cdot |\,\mathsf{Ent}_*(\mathcal{A})|_1 \cdot |\mathbf{q}(\bar{e}) - \mathbf{q}(\bar{e}')|_1\, dp(\bar{e}')\, dp(\bar{e}) \\ = n \cdot [\![\mathbf{G}]\!] \cdot |\,\mathsf{Ent}_*(\mathcal{A})|_1 \cdot \int_{\Delta E} \int_{\Delta E} |\pi - \pi'|_1\, d\tau_n(\pi)\, d\tau_n(\pi') = o(n),$$

where the convergence to zero of the last double integral follows from Sanov's theorem. □

Corollary 2. *Let $\mathcal{A}$ be a* **G**-*diagram and E a probability space included in $\mathcal{A}$. Then,*

$$\boldsymbol{\kappa}\Big(\vec{\mathcal{A}}, [\mathcal{A}|E]\Big) \leq 2[\![\mathbf{G}]\!] \cdot \mathsf{Ent}(E).$$

Proof. Let $n \in \mathbb{N}$. Then,

$$\begin{aligned} \boldsymbol{\kappa}\Big(\vec{\mathcal{A}}, [\mathcal{A}|E]\Big) &= \frac{1}{n}\boldsymbol{\kappa}\Big(\overrightarrow{\mathcal{A}^n}, [\mathcal{A}^n|E^n]\Big) \\ &= \frac{1}{n}\boldsymbol{\kappa}\Big(\overrightarrow{\mathcal{A}^n}, \int_{E^n} \overrightarrow{\mathcal{A}^n|\bar{e}}\, dp(\bar{e})\Big) \\ &\leq \frac{1}{n}\int_{E^n} \boldsymbol{\kappa}\Big(\overrightarrow{\mathcal{A}^n}, \overrightarrow{\mathcal{A}^n|\bar{e}}\Big)\, dp(\bar{e}) \\ &= \frac{1}{n}\int_{E^n} \boldsymbol{\kappa}(\mathcal{A}^n, \mathcal{A}^n|\bar{e})\, dp(\bar{e}) \\ &\leq 2 \cdot [\![\mathbf{G}]\!] \cdot \mathsf{Ent}(E) + o(n^0), \end{aligned}$$

where we used Lemma 2 and the fact that $\boldsymbol{\kappa} \leq \mathbf{k}$ in the last line. We finish the proof by taking the limit $n \to \infty$. □

Proof of Proposition 2. We start with a note on general terminology: a reduction $f : A \to B$ of probability spaces can also be considered as a fan $\mathcal{F} := (A \xleftarrow{=} A \xrightarrow{f} B)$. Then, the entropy distance of f is

$$\mathrm{kd}(f) := \mathrm{kd}(\mathcal{F}) = \mathsf{Ent}\, A - \mathsf{Ent}\, B.$$

If the reduction f is a part of a bigger diagram containing also space U, then the following inequality holds:

$$\int_U \mathrm{kd}(f|u)\, dp(u) \leq \mathrm{kd}(f).$$

Let $\mathcal{K} \in \mathbf{Prob}\langle \mathbf{G}, \mathbf{\Lambda}_2 \rangle$

$$\mathcal{K} = \Big(\mathcal{X} \xleftarrow{f} \mathcal{Z} \xrightarrow{g} \mathcal{Y} \Big) \in \mathbf{Prob}\langle \mathbf{G}, \mathbf{\Lambda}_2 \rangle = \mathbf{Prob}\langle \mathbf{\Lambda}_2, \mathbf{G} \rangle$$

be an optimal coupling between $\mathcal{X}$ and $\mathcal{Y}$. It can also be viewed as a **G**-diagram of two fans, $\mathcal{K} = \{\mathcal{K}_i\}_{i \in \mathbf{G}}$, each of which is a minimal coupling between X_i and Y_i. Among them is the minimal fan $\mathcal{W} := \mathcal{K}_\iota = (U \xleftarrow{f_\iota} W \xrightarrow{g_\iota} V)$.

We use the triangle inequality to bound the distance $\boldsymbol{\kappa}\Big([\mathcal{X}|U],[\mathcal{Y}|V]\Big)$ by four summands as follows:

$$\begin{aligned}\boldsymbol{\kappa}\Big([\mathcal{X}|U],[\mathcal{Y}|V]\Big) \leq &\boldsymbol{\kappa}\Big([\mathcal{X}|U],[\mathcal{Z}|U]\Big)+\boldsymbol{\kappa}\Big([\mathcal{Z}|U],[\mathcal{Z}|W]\Big)+\\ &\boldsymbol{\kappa}\Big([\mathcal{Z}|W],[\mathcal{Z}|V]\Big)+\boldsymbol{\kappa}\Big([\mathcal{Z}|V],[\mathcal{Y}|V]\Big).\end{aligned}$$

We will estimate each of the four summands separately. The bound for the first one is as follows:

$$\begin{aligned}\boldsymbol{\kappa}\Big([\mathcal{X}|U],[\mathcal{Z}|U]\Big) &= \boldsymbol{\kappa}\Big(\int_U \overrightarrow{\mathcal{X}|u}\,dp(u), \int_U \overrightarrow{\mathcal{Z}|u}\,dp(u)\Big)\\ &\leq \int_U \boldsymbol{\kappa}\Big(\overrightarrow{\mathcal{X}|u}, \overrightarrow{\mathcal{Z}|u}\Big)\,dp(u) = \int_U \boldsymbol{\kappa}(\mathcal{X}|u, \mathcal{Z}|u)\,dp(u)\\ &\leq \int_U \mathbf{k}(\mathcal{X}|u, \mathcal{Z}|u)\,dp(u) \leq \int_U \mathrm{kd}(f|u)\,dp(u)\\ &\leq \sum_{i\in\mathbf{G}}\int_U \mathrm{kd}(f_i|u)\,dp(u) = \sum_{i\in\mathbf{G}}\mathrm{kd}(f_i) = \mathrm{kd}(f).\end{aligned}$$

An analogous calculation shows that

$$\boldsymbol{\kappa}\Big([\mathcal{Z}|V],[\mathcal{Y}|V]\Big) \leq \mathrm{kd}(g).$$

To bound the second summand, we will use Corollary 2:

$$\begin{aligned}\boldsymbol{\kappa}\Big([\mathcal{Z}|U],[\mathcal{Z}|W]\Big) &= \boldsymbol{\kappa}\Big(\int_U \overrightarrow{\mathcal{Z}|u}\,dp(u), \int_W \overrightarrow{\mathcal{Z}|w}\,dp(w)\Big)\\ &= \boldsymbol{\kappa}\Big(\int_U \overrightarrow{\mathcal{Z}|u}\,dp(u), \int_U\int_{W|u} \overrightarrow{\mathcal{Z}|w}\,dp(w|u)\,dp(u)\Big)\\ &\leq \int_U \boldsymbol{\kappa}\Big(\overrightarrow{\mathcal{Z}|u}, \int_{W|u} \overrightarrow{\mathcal{Z}|w}\,dp(w|u)\Big)\,dp(u).\end{aligned}$$

We will now use Corollary 2 with $\mathcal{A} = \mathcal{Z}|u$ and $E = W|u$ to estimate the integrand. Then,

$$\begin{aligned}\boldsymbol{\kappa}\Big([\mathcal{Z}|U],[\mathcal{Z}|W]\Big) &= \int_U \boldsymbol{\kappa}\Big(\overrightarrow{\mathcal{Z}|u}, \int_{W|u} \overrightarrow{\mathcal{Z}|w}\,dp(w|u)\Big)\,dp(u)\\ &\leq 2[\![\mathbf{G}]\!]\cdot \int_U \mathsf{Ent}(W|u)\,dp(u)\\ &\leq 2[\![\mathbf{G}]\!]\cdot \mathsf{Ent}(W|U) \leq 2[\![\mathbf{G}]\!]\cdot \mathrm{kd}(f).\end{aligned}$$

Similarly,

$$\boldsymbol{\kappa}\Big([\mathcal{Z}|W],[\mathcal{Z}|V]\Big) \leq 2[\![\mathbf{G}]\!]\cdot \mathrm{kd}(g).$$

Combining the estimates, we obtain

$$\boldsymbol{\kappa}\Big([\mathcal{X}|U],[\mathcal{Y}|V]\Big) \leq (2[\![\mathbf{G}]\!]+1)\cdot(\mathrm{kd}\,(f)+\mathrm{kd}(g)) = (2[\![\mathbf{G}]\!]+1)\cdot\mathbf{k}(\mathcal{X},\mathcal{Y}).$$

□

3.5. Tropical Conditioning

Let $[\mathcal{X}]$ be a tropical **G**-diagram and $[U] = [X_\iota]$ for some $\iota \in \mathbf{G}$. Choose a representative $(\mathcal{X}(n))_{n\in\mathbb{N}_0}$ and denote $u(n) := X_\iota(n)$. We define now a conditioned diagram $[\mathcal{X}|U]$ by the following limit:

$$[\mathcal{X}|U] := \lim_{n\to\infty}\frac{1}{n}[\mathcal{X}(n)|U(n)].$$

Proposition 1 guarantees that the limit exists and is independent of the choice of representative. For a fixed $\iota \in \mathbf{G}$, the conditioning is a linear Lipschitz map of

$$[\cdot \mid \cdot_\iota] : \mathbf{Prob}[\mathbf{G}] \to \mathbf{Prob}[\mathbf{G}].$$

Author Contributions: Investigation, R.M. and J.W.P. All authors have read and agreed to the published version of the manuscript.

Funding: Open Access funding was provided by the Max Planck Society.

Data Availability Statement: No new data were created or analyzed in this study. Data sharing is not applicable to this article.

Conflicts of Interest: The authors declare no conflict of interest.

References

1. Matveev, R.; Portegies, J.W. Asymptotic dependency structure of multiple signals. *Inf. Geom.* **2018**, *1*, 237–285. [CrossRef]
2. Matveev, R.; Portegies, J.W. Tropical diagrams of probability spaces. *Inf. Geom.* **2020**, *3*, 61–88. [CrossRef]
3. Ay, N.; Bertschinger, N.; Der, R.; Güttler, F.; Olbrich, E. Predictive information and explorative behavior of autonomous robots. *Eur. Phys. J. B* **2008**, *63*, 329–339. [CrossRef]
4. Bertschinger, N.; Rauh, J.; Olbrich, E.; Jost, J.; Ay, N. Quantifying unique information. *Entropy* **2014**, *16*, 2161–2183. [CrossRef]
5. Friston, K. The free-energy principle: A rough guide to the brain? *Trends Cogn. Sci.* **2009**, *13*, 293–301. [CrossRef] [PubMed]
6. Kingma, D.P.; Welling, M. Auto-encoding variational Bayes. *arXiv* **2013**, arXiv:1312.6114.
7. Steudel, B.; Ay, N. Information-theoretic inference of common ancestors. *Entropy* **2015**, *17*, 2304–2327. [CrossRef]
8. Dijk, S.G.V.; Polani, D. Informational constraints-driven organization in goal-directed behavior. *Adv. Complex Syst.* **2013**, *16*, 1350016. [CrossRef]
9. Matveev, R.; Portegies, J.W. Tropical probability theory and an application to the entropic cone. *Kybernetika* **2020**, *56*, 1133–1153. [CrossRef]
10. Kovačević, M.; Stanojević, I.; Šenk, V. On the hardness of entropy minimization and related problems. In Proceedings of the 2012 IEEE Information Theory Workshop, Lausanne, Switzerland, 3–7 September 2012; pp. 512–516.
11. Vidyasagar, M. A metric between probability distributions on finite sets of different cardinalities and applications to order reduction. *IEEE Trans. Autom. Control* **2012**, *57*, 2464–2477. [CrossRef]

entropy

MDPI

Article

A Measure of Synergy Based on Union Information

André F. C. Gomes * and Mário A. T. Figueiredo

Instituto de Telecomunicações and LUMLIS (Lisbon ELLIS Unit), Instituto Superior Técnico, Universidade de Lisboa, 1049-001 Lisboa, Portugal; mario.figueiredo@tecnico.ulisboa.pt
* Correspondence: andrefcgomes@tecnico.ulisboa.pt

Abstract: The *partial information decomposition* (PID) framework is concerned with decomposing the information that a set of (two or more) random variables (the sources) has about another variable (the target) into three types of information: unique, redundant, and synergistic. Classical information theory alone does not provide a unique way to decompose information in this manner and additional assumptions have to be made. One often overlooked way to achieve this decomposition is using a so-called measure of union information—which quantifies the information that is present in at least one of the sources—from which a synergy measure stems. In this paper, we introduce a new measure of union information based on adopting a communication channel perspective, compare it with existing measures, and study some of its properties. We also include a comprehensive critical review of characterizations of union information and synergy measures that have been proposed in the literature.

Keywords: information theory; partial information decomposition; union information; synergy; communication channels

1. Introduction

Williams and Beer [1] introduced the *partial information decomposition* (PID) framework as a way to characterize, or analyze, the information that a set of random variables (often called *sources*) has about another variable (referred to as the *target*). PID is a useful tool for gathering insights and analyzing the way information is stored, modified, and transmitted within complex systems [2,3]. It has been applied in several areas such as cryptography [4] and neuroscience [5,6], with many other potential use cases, such as in studying information flows in gene regulatory networks [7], neural coding [8], financial markets [9], and network design [10,11].

Consider the simplest case, a three-variable joint distribution $p(y_1, y_2, t)$ describing three random variables: two so-called sources, Y_1 and Y_2, and a target T. Notice that, despite what the names *sources* and *target* might suggest, there is no directionality (causal or otherwise) assumption. The goal of PID is to *decompose* the information that the sources $Y = (Y_1, Y_2)$ have about T into the sum of four non-negative quantities: the information that is present in both Y_1 and Y_2, known as *redundant* information, R; the information that only Y_1 (respectively Y_2) has about T, known as *unique* information, U_1 (respectively U_2); and the *synergistic* information, S, that is present in the pair (Y_1, Y_2) but not in Y_1 or Y_2 alone. In this case with two variables, the goal is, thus, to write

$$I(T;Y) = R + U_1 + U_2 + S, \tag{1}$$

where $I(T;Y)$ is the mutual information between T and Y [12]. The redundant information R, because it is present in both Y_1 and Y_2, is also referred to as *intersection* information and denoted as $I_\cap$. Finally, $I_\cup$ refers to *union* information, i.e., the amount of information provided by at least one of the sources; in the case of two sources, $I_\cup = U_1 + U_2 + R$, thus $S = I(T;Y) - I_\cup$.

Citation: Gomes, A.F.C.; Figueiredo, M.A.T. A Measure of Synergy Based on Union Information. *Entropy* **2024**, *26*, 271. https://doi.org/10.3390/e26030271

Academic Editor: Daniel Chicharro

Received: 16 January 2024
Revised: 8 March 2024
Accepted: 16 March 2024
Published: 19 March 2024

Because unique information and redundancy satisfy the relationship $U_i = I(T;Y_i) - R$ (for $i \in \{1,2\}$), it turns out that defining how to compute one of these quantities (R, U_i, or S) is enough to fully determine the others [1]. Williams and Beer [1] suggested a set of axioms that a measure of redundancy should satisfy, and proposed a measure of their own. Those axioms became well known as the Williams–Beer axioms, although the measure they proposed has subsequently been criticized for not capturing informational content, but only information *size* [13]. It is worth noting that as the number of variables grows the number of terms appearing in the PID of $I(T;Y)$ grows super-exponentially [14].

Stimulated by that initial work, other measures of information and other sets of axioms for information decomposition have been introduced; see, for example, the work by Bertschinger et al. [15], Griffith and Koch [16], and James et al. [17], for different measures of redundant, unique, and synergistic information. There is no consensus about what axioms any measure should satisfy or whether a given measure *captures the information* that it should capture, except for the Williams–Beer axioms. Today, there is still debate about what axioms different measures of information should satisfy, and there is no general agreement on what is an appropriate PID [17–21].

Most PID measures that have been suggested thus far are either measures of redundant information, e.g., [1,13,21–26], or measures of unique information, e.g., [15,17]. Alternatively, it is possible to define the *union information* of a set of sources as the amount of information provided by at least one of those sources. Synergy is then defined as the difference between the total information and union information [22].

In this paper, we introduce a new measure of union information based on the information channel perspective that we already pursued in earlier work [26] and study some of its properties. The resulting measure leads to a novel information decomposition that is particularly suited for analyzing how information is distributed in channels.

The rest of the paper is organized as follows. A final subsection of this section introduces the notation used throughout the paper. In Section 2, we recall some properties of PID and take a look at how the degradation measure for redundant information introduced by Kolchinsky [22] decomposes information in bivariate systems, while also pointing out some drawbacks of that measure. Section 3 presents the motivation for our proposed measure, its operational interpretation, its multivariate definition, as well as some of its drawbacks. In Section 4, we propose an extension of the Williams–Beer axioms for measures of union information and show that our proposed measure satisfies those axioms. We review all properties that have been proposed both for measures of union information and synergy, and either accept or reject them. We also compare different measures of synergy and relate them, whenever possible. Finally, Section 5 presents concluding remarks and suggestions for future work.

Notation

For two discrete random variables $X \in \mathcal{X}$ and $Z \in \mathcal{Z}$, their Shannon mutual information $I(X;Z)$ is given by $I(X;Z) = I(Z;X) = H(X) - H(X|Z) = H(Z) - H(Z|X)$, where $H(X) = -\sum_{x\in\mathcal{X}} p(x)\log p(x)$ and $H(X|Z) = -\sum_{x\in\mathcal{X}}\sum_{z\in\mathcal{X}} p(x,z)\log p(x|z)$ are the entropy and conditional entropy, respectively [12]. The conditional distribution $p(z|x)$ corresponds, in an information-theoretical perspective, to a discrete memoryless channel with a channel matrix K, i.e., such that $K[x,z] = p(z|x)$ [12]. This matrix is row-stochastic: $K[x,z] \geq 0$, for any $x \in \mathcal{X}$ and $z \in \mathcal{Z}$, and $\sum_{z\in\mathcal{Z}} K[x,z] = 1$, for any x.

Given a set of n discrete random variables (sources), $Y_1 \in \mathcal{Y}_1, \ldots, Y_n \in \mathcal{Y}_n$, and a discrete random variable $T \in \mathcal{T}$ (target) with joint distribution (probability mass function) $p(y_1, \ldots, y_n, t)$, we consider the channels $K^{(i)}$ between T and each Y_i, that is, each $K^{(i)}$ is a $|\mathcal{T}| \times |\mathcal{Y}_i|$ row-stochastic matrix with the conditional distribution $p(y_i|t)$. For a vector y, y_{-i} refers to the same vector without the ith component.

We say that three random variables, say X, Y, Z, form a Markov chain (which we denote by $X - Y - Z$ or by $X \perp Z \mid Y$) if X and Z are conditionally independent, given Y.

2. Background

2.1. PID Based of Channel Orders

In its current versions, PID is agnostic to causality in the sense that, like mutual information, it is an undirected measure, i.e., $I(T;Y) = I(Y;T)$. Some measures indirectly presuppose some kind of directionality to perform PID. Take, for instance, the redundancy measure introduced by Kolchinsky [22], based on the so-called degradation order $\preceq_d$ between communication channels (see recent work by Kolchinsky [22] and Gomes and Figueiredo [26] for definitions):

$$I_\cap^{\mathrm{d}}(Y_1, Y_2, \ldots, Y_m \to T) := \sup_{K^Q:\, K^Q \preceq_d K^{(i)},\, i \in \{1,\ldots,m\}} I(Q;T). \tag{2}$$

In the above equation, Q is the output of the channel $T \to Q$, which we also denote as K^Q. When computing the information shared by the m sources, $I_\cap^{\mathrm{d}}(Y_1, Y_2, \ldots, Y_m \to T)$, the perspective is that there is a channel with a single input T and m outputs $Y_1, \ldots, Y_m$. This definition of $I_\cap^{\mathrm{d}}$ corresponds to the mutual information of the most informative channel, under the constraint that this channel is dominated (in the degradation order $\preceq_d$ sense) by all channels $K^{(1)}, \ldots, K^{(m)}$. Since mutual information was originally introduced to formalize the capacity of communication channels, it is not surprising that measures that presuppose channel directionality are found useful in this context. For instance, the work of James et al. [27] concluded that only if one assumes the directionality $T \to Y_i$ does one obtain a valid PID from a secret key agreement rate, which supports the approach of assuming this directionality perspective.

Although it is not guaranteed that the structure of the joint distribution $p(y_1, \ldots, y_n, t)$ is compatible with the causal model of a single input and multiple output channels (which implies that the sources are conditionally independent, given T), one may always compute such measures, which have interesting and relevant operational interpretations. In the context of PID, where the goal is to study how information is decomposed, such measures provide an excellent starting point. Although it is not guaranteed that there is actually a channel (or a direction) from T to Y_i, we can characterize how information about T is spread through the sources. In the case of the degradation order, $I_\cap^{\mathrm{d}}$ provides insight about the maximum information obtained about T if any Y_i is observed.

Arguably, the most common scenario in PID is finding out something about the structure of the information the variables $Y_1, \ldots, Y_n$ have about T. In a particular system of variables characterized by its joint distribution, we do not make causal assumptions, so we can adopt the perspective that the variables Y_i are functions of T, hence obtaining the channel structure. Although this channel structure may not be *faithful* [28] to the conditional independence properties implied by $p(y_1, \ldots, y_n, t)$, this channel perspective allows for decomposition of $I(Y;T)$ and for drawing conclusions about the inner structure of the information that Y has about T. Some distributions, however, *cannot* have this causal structure. Take, for instance, the distribution generated by $T = Y_1$ xor Y_2, where Y_1 and Y_2 are two equiprobable and independent binary random variables. We will call this distribution XOR. For this well-known distribution, we have $Y_1 \perp Y_2$ and $Y_1 \not\perp Y_2 \mid T$, whereas the implied channel distribution that $I_\cap^{\mathrm{d}}$ assumes yields the exact opposite dependencies, that is, $Y_1 \not\perp Y_2$ and $Y_1 \perp Y_2 | T$; see Figure 1 for more insight.

Consider the computation of $I_\cap^{\mathrm{d}}(Y_1, Y_2 \to T)$ for the XOR distribution. This measure argues that, since

$$K^{(1)} = K^{(2)} = \begin{bmatrix} 0.5 & 0.5 \\ 0.5 & 0.5 \end{bmatrix},$$

then a solution to $I_\cap^{\mathrm{d}}(Y_1, Y_2 \to T)$ is given by the channel $K^Q = K^{(1)}$ and redundancy is computed as $I(Q;T)$, yielding 0 bits of redundancy, and consequently 1 bit of synergy (as computed from (1)). Under this channel perspective (as in Figure 1b), $I_\cap^{\mathrm{d}}$ is not concerned with, for example, $p(Y_1|T, Y_2)$ or $p(Y_1, Y_2)$. If all that is needed to compute redundancy is $p(T)$, $K^{(1)}$, and $K^{(2)}$, this would lead to the wrong conclusion that the outcome

$(Y_1, Y_2, T) = (0,0,1)$ has non-null probability, which it does not. With this, we do not mean that $I_\cap^d$ is an incomplete or incorrect measure to perform PID, we are using its insights to point us in a different direction.

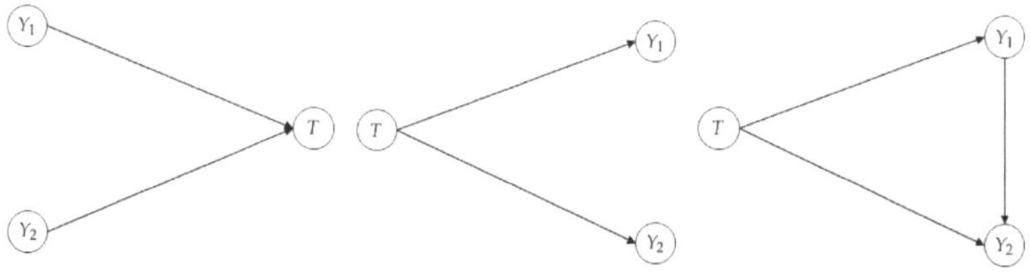

Figure 1. (**a**) Assuming faithfulness [28], this is the only three-variable directed acyclic graph (DAG) that satisfies $Y_1 \perp Y_2$ and $Y_1 \not\perp Y_2|T$, in general [28]. (**b**) The DAG that is "implied" by the perspective of $I_\cap^d$. (**c**) A DAG that can generate the XOR distribution, but does not satisfy the dependencies implied by $T = Y_1$ xor Y_2. In fact, any DAG that is in the same Markov equivalence class as (**c**) can generate the XOR distribution (or any other joint distribution), but none satisfy the earlier dependencies, assuming faithfulness.

2.2. Motivation for a New PID

At this point, the most often used approaches to PID are based on redundancy measures. Usually, these are in one of the two following classes:

- Measures that are not concerned with information content, only *information size*, which makes them easy to compute even for distributions with many variables, but at the cost that the resulting decompositions may not give realistic insights into the system, precisely because they are not sensitive to informational content. Examples are $I_\cap^{\text{WB}}$ [1] or $I_\cap^{\text{MMI}}$ [23], and applications of these can be found in [29–32].
- Measures that satisfy the Blackwell property—which arguably do measure information content—but are insensitive to changes in the sources' distributions $p(y_1, \ldots, y_n) = \sum_t p(y_1, \ldots, y_n, t)$ (as long as $p(T), K^{(1)}, \ldots, K^{(n)}$ remain the same). Examples are $I_\cap^d$ [22] (see Equation (2)) or $I_\cap^{\text{BROJA}}$ [15]. It should be noted that $I_\cap^{\text{BROJA}}$ is only defined for the bivariate case, that is, for distributions with at most two sources, described by $p(y_1, y_2, t)$. Applications of these can be found in [33–35].

Particularly, $I_\cap^d$ and $I_\cap^{\text{BROJA}}$ satisfy the so-called (*) assumption [15], which argues that redundant and unique information should only depend on the marginal distribution of the target $p(T)$ and on the conditional distributions of the sources given the target, that is, on the stochastic matrices $K^{(i)}$. James et al. [17] (Section 4) and Ince [21] (Section 5) provide great arguments as to why the (*) assumption should not hold in general, and we agree with them.

Towards motivating a new PID, let us look at how $I_\cap^d$ decomposes information in the bivariate case. Any measure that is based on a preorder between channels and which satisfies Kolchinsky's axioms yields similar decompositions [26], thus there is no loss of generality in focusing on $I_\cap^d$. We next analyze three different cases.

- Case 1: There is an ordering between the channels, that is, w.l.o.g., $K^{(2)} \preceq_d K^{(1)}$. This means that $I(Y_2; T) \leq I(Y_1; T)$ and the decomposition (as in (1)) is given by $R = I(Y_2; T)$, $U_2 = 0$, $U_1 = I(Y_1; T) - I(Y_2; T)$, and $S = I(Y; T) - I(Y_1; T)$. Moreover, if $K^{(1)} \not\preceq_d K^{(2)}$, then $S = 0$.

  As an example, consider the leftmost distribution in Table 1, which satisfies $T = Y_1$. In this case,
$$K^{(1)} = \begin{bmatrix} 1 & 0 \\ 0 & 1 \end{bmatrix} \succeq_d K^{(2)} = \begin{bmatrix} 0.5 & 0.5 \\ 0.5 & 0.5 \end{bmatrix},$$
  yielding $R = 0$, $U_1 = 1$, $U_2 = 0$, and $S = 0$, as expected, because $T = Y_1$.

Table 1. Three joint distributions $p(yt, y_2, y_2)$ used to exemplify the three cases. Left: joint distribution satisfying $T = Y_1$. Middle: distribution satisfying $T = (Y_1, Y_2)$, known as the COPY distribution. Right: the so-called BOOM distribution (see text).

t	y_1	y_2	$p(t, y_1, y_2)$	t	y_1	y_2	$p(t, y_1, y_2)$	t	y_1	y_2	$p(t, y_1, y_2)$
0	0	0	1/4	(0,0)	0	0	1/4	0	0	2	1/6
0	0	1	1/4	(0,1)	0	1	1/4	1	0	0	1/6
1	1	0	1/4	(1,0)	1	0	1/4	1	1	2	1/6
1	1	1	1/4	(1,1)	1	1	1/4	2	0	0	1/6
								2	2	0	1/6
								2	2	1	1/6

- Case 2: There is no ordering between the channels and the solution of $I_\cap^{\mathrm{d}}(Y_1, Y_2 \to T)$ is a trivial channel, in the sense that it has no information about T. The decomposition is given by $R = 0$, $U_2 = I(Y_2; T)$, $U_1 = I(Y_1; T)$, and $S = I(Y; T) - I(Y_1; T) - I(Y_2; T)$, which may lead to a negative value of synergy. An example of this is provided later. As an example, consider the COPY distribution with Y_1 and Y_2 i.i.d. Bernoulli variables with parameter 0.5, shown in the center of Table 1. In this case, channels $K^{(1)}$ and $K^{(2)}$ have the forms
$$K^{(1)} = \begin{bmatrix} 1 & 0 \\ 1 & 0 \\ 0 & 1 \\ 0 & 1 \end{bmatrix}, \quad K^{(2)} = \begin{bmatrix} 1 & 0 \\ 0 & 1 \\ 1 & 0 \\ 0 & 1 \end{bmatrix},$$
with no degradation order between them. This yields $R = 0$, $U_1 = U_2 = 1$, and $S = 0$.
- Case 3: There is no ordering between the channels and $I_\cap^{\mathrm{d}}(Y_1, Y_2 \to T)$ is achieved by a nontrivial channel K^Q. The decomposition is given by $R = I(Q; T)$, $U_2 = I(Y_2; T) - I(Q; T)$, $U_1 = I(Y_1; T) - I(Q; T)$, and $S = I(Y; T) + I(Q; T) - I(Y_1; T) - I(Y_2; T)$.
As an example, consider the BOOM distribution [17], shown on the right-hand side of Table 1. In this case, channels $K^{(1)}$ and $K^{(2)}$ are
$$K^{(1)} = \begin{bmatrix} 1 & 0 & 0 \\ 1/2 & 1/2 & 0 \\ 1/3 & 0 & 2/3 \end{bmatrix}, \quad K^{(2)} = \begin{bmatrix} 0 & 0 & 1 \\ 1/2 & 0 & 1/2 \\ 2/3 & 1/3 & 0 \end{bmatrix},$$
and there is no degradation order between them. However, there is a nontrivial channel K^Q that is dominated by both $K^{(1)}$ and $K^{(2)}$ that maximizes $I(Q; T)$. One of its versions is
$$K^Q = \begin{bmatrix} 0 & 1 & 0 \\ 0 & 3/4 & 1/4 \\ 1/3 & 1/3 & 1/3 \end{bmatrix},$$
yielding $R \approx 0.322$, $U_1 = U_2 \approx 0.345$, and $S \approx 0.114$.

This class of approaches has some limitations, as is the case for all PID measures. In the bivariate case, the definition of synergy S from a measure of redundant information is the completing term such that $I(Y; T) = S + R + U_1 + U_2$ holds. The definition of $I_\cap^{\mathrm{d}}$ supports the argument that if $K^{(2)} \preceq_d K^{(1)}$ and $K^{(1)} \npreceq_d K^{(2)}$, then there is no synergy. This makes intuitive sense because, in this case, $T - Y_1 - Y_2$ is a Markov chain (see Section 1 for the definition), consequently, $I(Y; T) = I(Y_1; T)$, that is, Y_1 has the same information about T as the pair $Y = (Y_1, Y_2)$.

If there is no $\preceq_d$ ordering between the channels, as in the COPY distribution (Table 1, middle), the situation is more complicated. We saw that the decomposition for this distribution yields $R = 0$, $U_1 = U_2 = 1$, and $S = 0$. However, suppose we change the distribution such that $T = (1, 1)$ has probability 0 and the other outcomes have probability 1/3. For example, consider the distribution in Table 2. For this distribution, we have $I(Y; T) \approx 1.585$. Intuitively, we would expect that $I(Y; T)$ would be decomposed as

$R = 0$, $U_1 = U_2 = I(Y;T)/2$, and $S = 0$, just as before, so that the proportions $U_i/I(Y;T)$, for $i \in \{1,2\}$, in both distributions remain the same, whereas redundancy and synergy would remain zero. That is, we do not expect that removing one of the outcomes while maintaining the remaining outcomes equiprobable would change the types of information in the system. However, if we perform this and compute the decomposition yielded by $I_\cap^{\mathrm{d}}$, we obtain $R = 0$, $U_1 = U_2 = 0.918 \neq I(Y;T)/2$, and $S = -0.251$, i.e., a negative synergy, arguably meaningless.

Table 2. Tweaked COPY distribution, now without the outcome $(T, Y_1, Y_2) = ((1,1),1,1)$.

T	Y_1	Y_2	$p(t, y_1, y_2)$
(0,0)	0	0	1/3
(0,1)	0	1	1/3
(1,0)	1	0	1/3

There are still many open questions in PID. One of those questions is: Should measures of redundant information be used to measure synergy, given that they compute it as the completing term in Equation (1). We agree that using a measure of redundant information to compute the synergy in this way may not be appropriate, especially because the *inclusion–exclusion principle* (IEP) should not necessarily hold in the context of PID; see [22] for comments on the IEP.

With these motivations, we propose a measure of union information for PID that shares with $I_\cap^{\mathrm{d}}$ the implicit view of channels. However, unlike $I_\cap^{\mathrm{d}}$ and $I_\cap^{\mathrm{BROJA}}$—which satisfy the (*) assumption, and thus, are not concerned with the conditional dependencies in $p(y_i|t, y_{-i})$—our measure defines synergy as the information that cannot be computed from $p(y_i|t)$, but can be computed from $p(y_i|t, y_{-i})$. That is, we propose that synergy be computed as the information that is not captured by assuming conditional independence of the sources, given the target.

3. A New Measure of Union Information

3.1. Motivation and Bivariate Definition

Consider a distribution $p(y_1, y_2, t)$ and suppose there are two agents, agent 1 and agent 2, whose goal is to reduce their uncertainty about T by observing Y_1 and Y_2, respectively. Suppose also that the agents know $p(t)$, and that agent i has access to its channel distribution $p(y_i|t)$. Many PID measures make this same assumption, including $I_\cap^{\mathrm{d}}$. When agent i works alone to reduce the uncertainty about T, since it has access to $p(t)$ and $p(y_i|t)$, it also knows $p(y_i)$ and $p(y_i, t)$, which allows it to compute $I(Y_i; T)$: the amount of uncertainty reduction about T achieved by observing Y_i.

Now, if the agents can work together, that is, if they have access to $Y = (Y_1, Y_2)$, then they can compute $I(Y;T)$, because they have access to $p(y_1, y_2|t)$ and $p(t)$. On the other hand, if the agents are not able to work together (in the sense that they are not able to observe Y together, but only Y_1 and Y_2, separately) yet can communicate, then they can construct a different distribution q given by $q(y_1, y_2, t) := p(t)p(y_1|t)p(y_2|t)$, i.e., a distribution under which Y_1 and Y_2 are conditionally independent given T, but have the same marginal $p(t)$ and the same individual conditionals $p(y_1|t)$ and $p(y_2|t)$.

The form of q in the previous paragraph should be contrasted with the following factorization of p, which entails no conditional independence assumption:

$p(y_1, y_2, t) = p(t)p(y_1|t)p(y_2|t, y_1)$. In this sense, we would propose to define union information, for the bivariate case, as follows:

$$\begin{aligned} I_\cup(Y_1 \to T) &= I_q(Y_1;T) = I_p(Y_1;T), \\ I_\cup(Y_2 \to T) &= I_q(Y_2;T) = I_p(Y_2;T), \\ I_\cup(Y_1, Y_2 \to T) &= I_q(Y;T), \\ I_\cup((Y_1, Y_2) \to T) &= I_p(Y;T), \end{aligned} \tag{3}$$

where the subscript refers to the distribution under which the mutual information is computed. From this point forward, the absence of a subscript means that the computation is performed under the true distribution p. As we will see, this is not yet the final definition, for reasons to be addressed below.

Using the definition of synergy derived from a measure of union information [22], for the bivariate case we have

$$S(Y_1, Y_2 \to T) := I(Y;T) - I_\cup(Y_1, Y_2 \to T). \tag{4}$$

Synergy is often posited as *the difference between the whole and the union of the parts*. For our measure of union information, the 'union of the parts' corresponds to the reduction in uncertainty about T—under q—that agents 1 and 2 can obtain by sharing their conditional distributions. Interestingly, there are cases where the union of the parts is better than the whole, in the sense that $I_\cup(Y_1, Y_2 \to T) > I(Y;T)$. An example of this is given by the *Adapted ReducedOR* distribution, originally introduced by Ince [21] and adapted by James et al. [17], which is shown in the left-hand side of Table 3, where $r \in [0, 1]$. This distribution is such that $I_q(Y;T)$ does not depend on r ($I_q(Y;T) \approx 0.549$), since neither $p(t)$ nor $p(y_1|t)$ and $p(y_2|t)$ depend on r; consequently, $q(t, y_1, y_2)$ also does not depend on r, as shown in the right-hand side of Table 3.

Table 3. Left: The *Adapted Reduced OR* distribution, where $r \in [0, 1]$. Right: The corresponding distribution $q(t, y_1, y_2) = p(t)p(y_1|t)p(y_2|t)$.

t	y_1	y_2	$p(t, y_1, y_2)$	t	y_1	y_2	$q(t, y_1, y_2)$
0	0	0	1/2	0	0	0	1/2
1	0	0	r/4	1	0	0	1/8
1	1	0	(1 − r)/4	1	1	0	1/8
1	0	1	(1 − r)/4	1	0	1	1/8
1	1	1	r/4	1	1	1	1/8

It can be easily shown that if $r > 0.5$, then $I_q(Y;T) > I(Y;T)$, which implies that synergy, if defined as in (4), could be negative. How do we interpret the fact that there exist distributions such that $I_q(Y;T) > I(Y;T)$? This means that under distribution q, which assumes Y_1 and Y_2 are conditionally independent given T, Y_1 and Y_2 reduce the uncertainty about T more than in the original distribution. Arguably, the parts working independently and achieving better results than the whole should mean there is no synergy, as opposed to negative synergy.

The observations in the previous paragraphs motivate our definition of a new measure of union information as

$$I_\cup^{\text{CI}}(Y_1, Y_2 \to T) := \min\{I(Y;T), I_q(Y;T)\}, \tag{5}$$

with the superscript CI standing for *conditional independence*, yielding a non-negative synergy:

$$S^{\text{CI}}(Y_1, Y_2 \to T) = I(Y;T) - I_\cup^{\text{CI}}(Y_1, Y_2 \to T) = \max\{0, I(Y;T) - I_q(Y;T)\}. \tag{6}$$

Note that for the bivariate case we have zero synergy if $p(t, y_2, y_2)$ is such that $Y_1 \perp_p Y_2 | T$, that is, if the outputs are indeed conditionally independent given T. Moreover, $I_\cup^{\text{CI}}$ satisfies the monotonicity axiom from the extension of the Williams–Beer axioms to measures of union information (to be mentioned in Section 4.1), which further supports this definition. For the bivariate source case, the decomposition of $I(Y;T)$ derived from a measure of union information is given by

$$\begin{cases} I_\cup(Y_1) = I(Y_1;T) = U_1 + R \\ I_\cup(Y_2) = I(Y_2;T) = U_2 + R \\ I_\cup(Y_1, Y_2) = U_1 + U_2 + R \\ I_\cup(Y_{12}) = I(Y_{12};T) = U_1 + U_2 + R + S \end{cases} \iff \begin{cases} S = I(Y;T) - I_\cup(Y_1, Y_2) \\ U_1 = I_\cup(Y_1, Y_2) - I(Y_2;T) \\ U_2 = I_\cup(Y_1, Y_2) - I(Y_1;T) \\ R = I(Y_1;T) - U_1 = I(Y_2;T) - U_2 \end{cases}.$$

3.2. Operational Interpretation

For the bivariate case, if Y_1 and Y_2 are conditionally independent given T (Figure 1b), then $p(y_1|t)$ and $p(y_2|t)$ (and $p(t)$) suffice to reconstruct the original joint distribution $p(y_1, y_2, t)$, which means the union of the parts is enough to reconstruct the whole, i.e., there is no synergy between Y_1 and Y_2. Conversely, a distribution generated by the DAG in Figure 1c does not satisfy conditional independence (given T), hence we expect positive synergy, as is the case for the XOR distribution, and indeed our measure yields 1 bit of synergy for this distribution. These two cases motivate the operational interpretation of our measure of synergy: it is the amount of information that is not captured by assuming conditional independence of the sources (given the target).

Recall, however, that some distributions are such that $I_q(Y;T) > I_p(Y;T)$, i.e., such that the union of the parts 'outperforms' the whole. What does this mean? It means that under q, Y_1 and Y_2 have more information about T than under p: the constructed distribution q, which drops the conditional dependence of Y_1 and Y_2 given T, reduces the uncertainty that Y has about T more than the original distribution p. In some cases, this may happen because the support of q is larger than that of p, which may lead to a reduction in uncertainty under q that cannot be achieved under p. In these cases, since we are decomposing $I_p(Y;T)$, we revert to saying that the union information that a set of variables has about T is equal to $I_p(Y;T)$, so that our measure satisfies the monotonicity axiom (later introduced in Definition 2). We will comment on this compromise between satisfying the monotonicity axiom and ignoring dependencies later.

3.3. General (Multivariate) Definition

To extend the proposed measure to an arbitrary number $n \geq 2$ of sources, we briefly recall the synergy lattice [18,36] and the union information semi-lattice [36]. For $n = 3$, these two lattices are shown in Figure 2. For the sake of brevity, we will not address the construction of the lattices or the different orders between sources. We refer the reader to the work of Gutknecht et al. [36] for an excellent overview of the different lattices, the orders between sources, and the construction of different PID measures.

In the following, we use the term *source* to mean a subset of the variables $\{Y_1, \ldots, Y_n\}$, or a set of such subsets, we drop the curly brackets for clarity and refer to the different variables by their indices, as is common in most works on PID. The decomposition resulting from a measure of union information is not as direct to obtain as one obtained from a measure of redundant information, as the solution for the information atoms is not a Möbius inversion [14]. One must first construct the measure of synergy for source α by writing

$$S^{\text{CI}}(\alpha \to T) = I(Y;T) - I_\cup^{\text{CI}}(\alpha \to T), \tag{7}$$

which is the generalization of (6) for an arbitrary *source* α. In the remainder of this paper, we will often omit "$\to T$" from the notation (unless it is explicitly needed), with the understanding that the target variable is always referred to as T. Also for simplicity, in the following, we identify the different agents that have access to different distributions as the distributions they have access to.

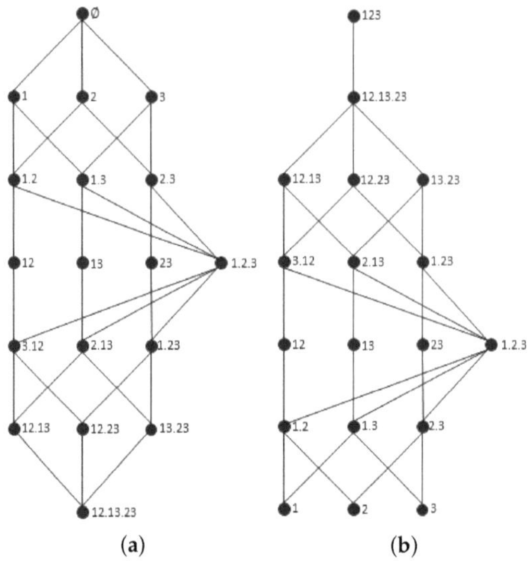

Figure 2. Trivariate distribution lattices and their respective ordering of sources. Left (**a**): synergy lattice [18]. Right (**b**): union information semi-lattice [36].

It is fairly simple to extend the proposed measure to an arbitrary number of sources, as illustrated in the following two examples.

Example 1. *To compute* $I_\cup^{CI}((Y_1, Y_2), Y_3)$*, agent* (Y_1, Y_2) *knows* $p(y_1, y_2|t)$*, thus it can also compute, by marginalization,* $p(y_1|t)$ *and* $p(y_2|t)$*. On the other hand, agent* Y_3 *only knows* $p(y_3|t)$*. Recall that both agents also have access to* $p(t)$*. By sharing their conditionals, the agents can compute* $q_1(y_1, y_2, y_3, t) := p(t)p(y_1, y_2|t)p(y_3|t)$*, and also* $q_2(y_1, y_2, y_3, t) := p(t)p(y_1|t)p(y_2|t)p(y_3|t)$*. After this, they may choose whichever distribution has the highest information about* T*, while still holding the view that any information gain larger than* $I(Y;T)$ *must be disregarded. Consequently, we write*

$$I_\cup^{CI}((Y_1, Y_2), Y_3) = \min\Big\{I(Y;T), \max\big\{I_{q_1}(Y;T), I_{q_2}(Y;T)\big\}\Big\}.$$

Example 2. *Slightly more complicated is the computation of* $I_\cup^{CI}((Y_1, Y_2), (Y_1, Y_3), (Y_2, Y_3))$*. In this case, the three agents may compute four different distributions, two of which are the same* q_1 *and* q_2 *defined in the previous paragraph, and the other two are* $q_3(y_1, y_2, y_3, t) := p(t)p(y_1, y_3|t)p(y_2|t)$*, and* $q_4(y_1, y_2, y_3, t) := p(t)p(y_1|t)p(y_2, y_3|t)$*.*

Given these insights, we propose the following measure of union information.

Definition 1. *Let* $A_1, \ldots, A_m$ *be an arbitrary collection of* $m \geq 1$ *sources (recall sources may be subsets of variables). Assume that no source is a subset of another source and no source is a deterministic function of other sources (if there is, remove it). We define*

$$I_\cup^{CI}(A_1, \ldots, A_m \to T) = \min\Big\{I(A;T), \max_{q \in Q} I_q(A;T)\Big\},$$

where $A = \bigcup_{i=1}^{m} A_i$ *and* Q *is the set of all different distributions that the* m *agents can construct by combining their conditional distributions and marginalizations thereof.*

For instance, in Example 1 above, $A = \{Y_1, Y_2\} \cup \{Y_3\} = \{Y_1, Y_2, Y_3\}$; in Example 2, $A = \{Y_1, Y_2\} \cup \{Y_1, Y_3\} \cup \{Y_2, Y_3\} = \{Y_1, Y_2, Y_3\}$. In Example 1, $\mathcal{Q} = \{q_1, q_2\}$, whereas in Example 2, $\mathcal{Q} = \{q_1, q_2, q_3, q_4\}$. We now justify the conditions in Definition 1 and the fact that they do not entail any loss of generality.

- The condition that no source is a subset of another source (which also excludes the case where two sources are the same) implies no loss of generality: if one source is a subset of another, say $A_i \subseteq A_j$, then A_i may be removed without affecting either A or $\mathcal{Q}$, thus yielding the same value for $I_\cup^{\mathrm{CI}}$. The removal of source A_i is also performed for measures of intersection information, but under the opposite condition: whenever $A_j \subseteq A_i$.
- The condition that no source is a deterministic function of other sources is slightly more nuanced. In our perspective, an intuitive and desired property of measures of both union and synergistic information is that their value should not change whenever one adds a source that is a deterministic function of sources that are already considered. We provide arguments in favor of this property in Section 4.2.1. This property may not be satisfied by computing $I_\cup^{\mathrm{CI}}$ without previously excluding such sources. For instance, consider $p(t, y_1, y_2, y_3)$, where Y_1 and Y_2 are two i.i.d. random variables following a Bernoulli distribution with parameter 0.5, $Y_3 = Y_2$ (that is, Y_3 is deterministic function of Y_2), and $T = Y_1$ AND Y_2. Computing $I_\cup^{\mathrm{CI}}(Y_1, Y_2, Y_3)$ without excluding Y_3 (or Y_2) yields $I_\cup^{\mathrm{CI}}(Y_1, Y_2, Y_3) = I_q(Y_1, Y_2, Y_3; T) \approx 0.6810$ and $I_\cup^{\mathrm{CI}}(Y_1, Y_2) = I_q(Y_1, Y_2; T) \approx 0.5409$. This issue is resolved by removing deterministic sources before computing $I_\cup^{\mathrm{CI}}$.

We conclude this section by commenting on the monotonicity of our measure. Suppose we wish to compute the union information of sources $\{(Y_1, Y_2), Y_3\}$ and $\{Y_1, Y_2, Y_3\}$. PID theory demands that $I_\cup^{\mathrm{CI}}((Y_1, Y_2), Y_3) \geq I_\cup^{\mathrm{CI}}(Y_1, Y_2, Y_3)$ (monotonicity of union information). Recall our motivation for $I_\cup^{\mathrm{CI}}((Y_1, Y_2), Y_3)$: there are two agents, the first has access to $p(y_1, y_2|t)$ and the second to $p(y_3|t)$. The two agents assume conditional independence of their variables and construct $q'(y_1, y_2, y_3, t) = p(t)p(y_1, y_2|t)p(y_3|t)$. The story is similar for the computation of $I_\cup^{\mathrm{CI}}(Y_1, Y_2, Y_3)$, in which case we have three agents that construct $q''(y_1, y_2, y_3, t) = p(t)p(y_1|t)p(y_2|t)p(y_3|t)$. Now, it may be the case that $I_{q'}(Y; T) < I_{q''}(Y; T)$; considering only these two distributions would yield $I_\cup^{\mathrm{CI}}((Y_1, Y_2), Y_3) < I_\cup^{\mathrm{CI}}(Y_1, Y_2, Y_3)$, contradicting monotonicity for measures of union information. To overcome this issue, for the computation of $I_\cup^{\mathrm{CI}}((Y_1, Y_2), Y_3)$—and other sources in general—the agent that has access to $p(y_1, y_2|t)$ must be allowed to disregard the conditional dependence of Y_1 and Y_2 on T, even if it holds in the original distribution p.

4. Properties of Measures of Union Information and Synergy

4.1. Extension of the Williams–Beer Axioms for Measures of Union Information

As Gutknecht et al. [36] rightfully notice, the so-called Williams–Beer axioms [1] can actually be derived from parthood distribution functions and the consistency equation [36]. Consequently, they are not really axioms but consequences of the PID framework. As far as we know, there has been no proposal in the literature for the equivalent of the Williams–Beer axioms (which refer to measures of redundant information) for measures of union information. In the following, we extend the Williams–Beer axioms to measures of union information and show that the proposed $I_\cup^{\mathrm{CI}}$ satisfies these axioms. Although we just argued against calling them axioms, we keep the designation *Williams–Beer axioms* because of its popularity. Although the following definition is not in the formulation of Gutknecht et al. [14], we suggest formally defining union information from the formulation of parthood functions as

$$I_\cup(Y_1, \ldots, Y_m; T) = \sum_{\exists i: f(Y_i)=1} \Pi(f), \tag{8}$$

where f refers to a parthood function and $\Pi(f)$ is the information atom associated with the parthood function f. Given this formulation, the following properties must hold.

Definition 2. *Let $A_1, \ldots, A_m$ be an arbitrary number $m \geq 2$ of sources. A measure of union information $I_\cup$ is said to satisfy the Williams–Beer axioms for union information measures if it satisfies:*

1. *Symmetry: $I_\cup$ is symmetric in the A_i's.*
2. *Self-redundancy: $I_\cup(A_i) = I(A_i; T)$.*
3. *Monotonicity: $I_\cup(A_1, \ldots, A_{m-1}, A_m) \geq I_\cup(A_1, \ldots, A_{m-1})$.*
4. *Equality for monotonicity: $A_m \subseteq A_{m-1} \Rightarrow I_\cup(A_1, \ldots, A_{m-1}, A_m) = I_\cup(A_1, \ldots, A_{m-1})$.*

Theorem 1. *$I_\cup^{CI}$ satisfies the Williams–Beer axioms for measures of union information given in Definition 2.*

Proof. We address each of the axioms in turn.

1. Symmetry follows from the symmetry of mutual information, which in turn is a consequence of the well-known symmetry of joint entropy.
2. Self-redundancy follows from the fact that agent i has access to $p(A_i|T)$ and $p(T)$, which means that $p(A_i, T)$ is one of the distributions in the set $\mathcal{Q}$, which implies that $I_\cup(A_i) = I(A_i; T)$.
3. To show that monotonicity holds, begin by noting that
$$I\left(\bigcup_{i=1}^{m} A_i; T\right) \geq I\left(\bigcup_{i=1}^{m-1} A_i; T\right),$$
due to the monotonicity of mutual information. Let $\mathcal{Q}_m$ be the set of distributions that the sources $A_1, \ldots, A_m$ can construct and $\mathcal{Q}_{m-1}$ that which the sources $A_1, \ldots, A_{m-1}$ can construct. Since $\mathcal{Q}_{m-1} \subseteq \mathcal{Q}_m$, it is clear that
$$\max_{q \in \mathcal{Q}_m} I_q\left(\bigcup_{i=1}^{m} A_i; T\right) \geq \max_{q \in \mathcal{Q}_{m-1}} I_q\left(\bigcup_{i=1}^{m-1} A_i; T\right).$$
Consequently,
$$\min\left\{I\left(\bigcup_{i=1}^{m} A_i; T\right), \max_{q \in \mathcal{Q}_m} I_q\left(\bigcup_{i=1}^{m} A_i; T\right)\right\} \geq \min\left\{I\left(\bigcup_{i=1}^{m-1} A_i; T\right), \max_{q \in \mathcal{Q}_{m-1}} I_q\left(\bigcup_{i=1}^{m-1} A_i; T\right)\right\},$$
which means monotonicity holds.
4. Finally, the proof of equality for monotonicity is the same that was used above to show that the assumption that no source is a subset of another source entails no loss of generality. If $A_m \subseteq A_{m-1}$, then the presence of A_m is irrelevant: $A = \bigcup_{i=1}^{m} A_i = \bigcup_{i=1}^{m-1} A_i$ and $\mathcal{Q}_m = \mathcal{Q}_{m-1}$, which implies that $I_\cup(A_1, \ldots, A_{m-1}, A_m) = I_\cup(A_1, \ldots, A_{m-1})$.

□

4.2. *Review of Suggested Properties: Griffith and Koch [16]*

We now review properties of measures of union information and synergy that have been suggested in the literature in chronological order. The first set of properties was suggested by Griffith and Koch [16], with the first two being the following.

- *Duplicating a predictor does not change synergistic information*; formally,
$$S(A_1, \ldots, A_m \to T) = S(A_1, \ldots, A_m, A_{m+1} \to T),$$
where $A_{m+1} = A_i$, for some $i = 1, \ldots, m$. Griffith and Koch [16] show that this property holds if the equality for monotonicity property holds for the "corresponding" measure

of union information ("corresponding" in the sense of Equation (7)). As shown in the previous subsection, $I_{\cup}^{\mathrm{CI}}$ satisfies this property, and so does the corresponding synergy S^{CI}.

- *Adding a new predictor can decrease synergy*, which is a weak statement. We suggest a stronger property: *Following the monotonicity property, adding a new predictor cannot increase synergy*, which is formally written as

$$S(A_1, \dots, A_m \to T) \geq S(A_1, \dots, A_m, A_{m+1} \to T).$$

This property simply follows from monotonicity for the corresponding measure of union information, which we proved above holds for $I_{\cup}^{\mathrm{CI}}$.

The next properties for any measure of union information were also suggested by Griffith and Koch [16]:

1. Global positivity: $I_{\cup}(A_1, \dots, A_m) \geq 0$.
2. Self-redundancy: $I_{\cup}(A_i) = I(A_i; T)$.
3. Symmetry: $I_{\cup}(A_1, \dots, A_m)$ is invariant under permutations of $A_1, \dots, A_m$.
4. Stronger monotonicity: $I_{\cup}(A_1, \dots, A_m) \leq I_{\cup}(A_1, \dots, A_m, A_{m+1})$, with equality if there is some A_i such that $H(A_{m+1}|A_i) = 0$.
5. Target monotonicity: for any (discrete) random variables T and Z, $I_{\cup}(A_1, \dots, A_m \to T) \leq I_{\cup}(A_1, \dots, A_m \to (T, Z))$.
6. Weak local positivity: for $n = 2$ the derived partial informations are non-negative. This is equivalent to

$$\max\left\{I(Y_1; T), I(Y_2; T)\right\} \leq I_{\cup}(Y_1, Y_2) \leq I(Y; T).$$

7. Strong identity: $I_{\cup}(T \to T) = H(T)$.

We argued before that self-redundancy and symmetry are properties that follow trivially from a well-defined measure of union information [36]. In the following, we discuss in more detail properties 4 and 5, and return to the global positivity property later.

4.2.1. Stronger Monotonicity

Property 4 in the above list was originally called monotonicity by Griffith and Koch [16]; we changed its name because we had already defined monotonicity in Definition 2, a weaker condition than stronger monotonicity. The proposed inequality clearly follows from the monotonicity of union information (the third Williams–Beer axiom). Now, if there is some A_i such that $H(A_{m+1}|A_i) = 0$ (equivalently, if A_{m+1} is a deterministic function of A_i), Griffith and Koch [16] suggest that we must have equality. Recall Axiom 4 (equality for monotonicity) in the extension of the WB axioms (Definition 2). It states that equality must hold if $A_m \subseteq A_{m-1}$. In this context, A_m and A_{m-1} are sets of random variables, for example, $A_m = \{Y_1, Y_2\}$ and $A_{m-1} = \{Y_1, Y_2, Y_3\}$. There is a different point of view we may take. The only way that A_m is a subset of A_{m-1} is if A_m, when viewed as a random vector (in this case, write $A_m = (Y_1, Y_2)$ and $A_{m-1} = (Y_1, Y_2, Y_3)$), is a subvector of A_{m-1}. A subvector of a random vector is a deterministic function, and no information gain can come from applying a deterministic function to a random vector. As such, there is no information gain when one considers A_m, a function of A_{m-1}, if one already has access to A_{m-1}. Griffith and Koch [16] argue similarly, there is no information gain by considering A_{m+1}—a function of A_i—in addition to A_i. In conclusion, considering the 'equality for monotonicity' strictly through a set-inclusion perspective, stronger monotonicity does not follow. On the other hand, extending the idea of set inclusion to the more general context of functions of random variables, then stronger monotonicity follows, because $\{A_{m+1}\} = \{f(A_i)\}$ is a subset of $\{A_i\}$, hence there is no information gain by considering $A_{m+1} = f(A_i)$ in addition to A_i. As such, we obtain $I_{\cup}(A_1, \dots, A_m) = I_{\cup}(A_1, \dots, A_m, A_{m+1})$. Consequently, it is clear that stronger monotonicity must hold for any measure of union information. We, thus, argue in favor of extending the concept of subset inclusion of property 4 in Definition 2 to include the concept of deterministic functions.

4.2.2. Target Monotonicity

Let us move on to target monotonicity, which we argue should not hold in general. This precise same property was suggested, but for a measure of redundant information, by Bertschinger et al. [19]; they argue that a measure of redundant information should satisfy

$$I_{\cap}(A_1, \ldots, A_m \to T) \leq I_{\cap}(A_1, \ldots, A_m \to (T, Z)),$$

for any discrete random variable Z, as they argue that this property *'captures the intuition that if $A_1, \ldots, A_m$ share some information about T, then at least the same amount of information is available to reduce the uncertainty about the joint outcome of (T, Z)'*. Since most PID approaches have been built upon measures of redundant information, it is simpler to refute this property. Consider $I_{\cap}^{\text{d}}$, which we argue is one of the most well-motivated and accepted measures of redundant information (as defined in (2)): it satisfies the WB axioms, it is based on the famous Blackwell channel preorder—thus inheriting a well-defined and rigorous operation interpretation—it is based on channels, just as $I(X;T)$ was originally motivated based on channels, and is defined for any number of input variables, which is more than most PID measures can accomplish. Consider also the distribution presented in Table 4, which satisfies $T = Y_1$ AND Y_2 and $Z = (Y_1, Y_2)$.

Table 4. Counter-example distribution for target monotonicity.

T	Z	Y_1	Y_2	$p(t,z,y_1,y_2)$
0	(0,0)	0	0	1/4
0	(0,1)	0	1	1/4
0	(1,0)	1	0	1/4
1	(1,1)	1	1	1/4

From a game theory perspective, since neither agent (Y_1 or Y_2) has an advantage when predicting T (because the channels that each agent has access to have the same conditional distributions), neither agent has any unique information. Moreover, redundancy—as computed by $I_{\cap}^{\text{d}}(Y_1, Y_2 \to T)$—evaluates to approximately 0.311. However, when considering the pair (T, Z), the structure that was present in T is now destroyed, in the sense that now there is no degradation order between the channels that each agent has access to. Note that $p((t,z), y_1, y_2)$ is a relabeling of the COPY distribution. As such, $I_{\cap}^{\text{d}}(Y_1, Y_2 \to (T, Z)) = 0 < I_{\cap}^{\text{d}}(Y_1, Y_2 \to T)$, contradicting the property proposed by Bertschinger et al. [19].

For a similar reason, we believe that this property should not hold for a general measure of union information, even if the measure satisfies the extension of the Williams–Beer axioms, as our proposed measure does. For instance, consider the distribution presented in Table 5.

Table 5. Counter-example distribution for target monotonicity.

T	Z	Y_1	Y_2	$p(t,z,y_1,y_2)$
0	0	1	0	0.419
1	1	2	1	0.203
2	1	3	0	0.007
0	0	3	1	0.346
2	2	4	4	0.025

This distribution yields $I_{\cup}^{\mathrm{CI}}(Y_1, Y_2 \to T) \approx 0.91 > 0.90 \approx I_{\cup}^{\mathrm{CI}}(Y_1, Y_2 \to (T, Z))$, meaning target monotonicity does not hold. This happens because although $I_p(Y;T) \leq I_p(Y;T,Z)$, it is not necessarily true that $I_q(Y;T) \leq I_q(Y;T,Z)$. The union information measure derived from the degradation order between channels, defined as the 'dual' of (2), also agrees with our conclusion [22]. For the distribution in Table 4 we have $I_{\cup}^{\mathrm{d}}(Y_1, Y_2 \to T) \approx 0.331 > 0 = I_{\cup}^{\mathrm{d}}(Y_1, Y_2 \to (T, Z))$, for the same reason as above: considering (T, Z) as the target variable destroys the structure present in T. We agree with the remaining properties suggested by Griffith and Koch [16] and we will address those later.

4.3. Review of Suggested Properties: Quax et al. [37]

Moving on to additional properties, Quax et al. [37] suggest the following properties for a measure of synergy:

1. Non-negativity: $S(A_1, \ldots, A_m \to T) \geq 0$.
2. Upper-bounded by mutual information: $S(Y \to T) \leq I(Y;T)$.
3. Weak symmetry: $S(A_1, \ldots, A_m \to T)$ is invariant under any reordering of $A_1, \ldots, A_m$.
4. Zero synergy about a single variable: $S(Y_i \to T) = 0$ for any $i \in \{1, \ldots, n\}$.
5. Zero synergy in a single variable: $S(Y \to Y_i) = 0$ for any $i \in \{1, \ldots, n\}$.

Let us comment on the proposed 'zero synergy' properties (4 and 5) under the context of PID. Property 4 seems to have been proposed with the rationale that synergy can only exist for at least two sources, which intuitively makes sense, as synergy is often defined as 'the information that is present in the pair, but that is not retrievable from any individual variable'. However, because of the way a synergy-based PID is constructed—or weak-synergy, as Gutknecht et al. [36] call it—synergy must be defined as in (7), so that, for example, in the bivariate case, $S(Y_1 \to T) := I(Y;T) - I_{\cup}(Y_1 \to T) = I(Y_2; T|Y_1)$, because of self-redundancy of union information and the chain rule of mutual information [12], and since $I(Y_2; T|Y_1)$ is in general larger than 0, we reject the property 'zero synergy about a single variable'. We note that our rejection of this property is based on the PID perspective. There may be other areas of research where it makes sense to demand that any (single) random variable alone has no synergy about any target, but under the PID framework, this must not happen, particularly so that we obtain a valid information decomposition.

Property 5, 'zero synergy in a single variable', on the other hand, must hold because of self-redundancy. That is because, for any $i \in \{1, \ldots, n\}$, $S(Y \to Y_i) := I(Y;Y_i) - I_{\cup}(Y \to Y_i) = I(Y_i;Y_i) - I(Y;Y_i) = H(Y_i) - H(Y_i) = 0$.

4.4. Review of Suggested Properties: Rosas et al. [38]

Based on the proposals of Griffith et al. [24], Rosas et al. [38] suggested the following properties for a measure of synergy:

- Target data processing inequality: if $Y - T_1 - T_2$ is a Markov chain, then $S(Y \to T_1) \geq S(Y \to T_2)$.
- Channel convexity: $S(Y \to T)$ is a convex function of $P(T|Y)$ for a given $P(Y)$.

We argue that a principled measure of synergy does not need to satisfy these properties (in general). Consider the distribution presented in Table 6, in which T_1 is a relabeling of the COPY distribution and $T_2 = Y_1$ xor Y_2.

Table 6. $T_1 =$ COPY, $T_2 =$ XOR.

T_2	T_1	Y_1	Y_2	$p(t_2, t_1, y_1, y_2)$
0	0	0	0	1/4
1	1	0	1	1/4
1	2	1	0	1/4
0	3	1	1	1/4

Start by noting that since T_2 is a deterministic function of T_1, then $Y - T_1 - T_2$ is a Markov chain. Since $Y_1 \perp Y_2|T_1$, our measure $S^{\text{CI}}(Y_1, Y_2 \to T_1) = I(Y; T_1) - I_{\cup}^{\text{CI}}(Y_1, Y_2 \to T_1) = 0$ leads to zero synergy. On the other hand, $S^{\text{CI}}(Y_1, Y_2 \to T_2) = 1$, contradicting the first property suggested by Rosas et al. [38]. This happens because $Y_1 \not\perp_p Y_2|T_2$, so synergy is positive. The loss of conditional independence of the inputs (given the target) when one goes from considering the target T_1 to T_2 is the reason why synergy increases. It can be easily seen that S^d, the measure of synergy derived from Kolchinsky's proposed union information measure $I_{\cup}^d$ [22], agrees with this. A simpler way to see this is by noticing that the XOR distribution must yield 1 bit of synergistic information, and many PID measures do not yield 1 bit of synergistic information for the COPY distribution.

The second suggested property argues that synergy should be a convex function of $P(T|Y)$, for fixed $P(Y)$. Our measure of synergy does not satisfy this property, even though it is derived from a measure of union information that satisfies the extension of the WB axioms. For instance, consider the XOR distribution with one extra outcome. We introduce it in Table 7 and parameterize it using $r = p(T = 0|Y = (0,0)) \in [0, 1]$. Notice that this modification does not affect $P(Y)$.

Table 7. Adapted XOR distribution.

T	Y_1	Y_2	$p(t, y_1, y_2)$
0	0	0	$r/4$
1	0	0	$(1-r)/4$
1	1	0	$1/4$
1	0	1	$1/4$
0	1	1	$1/4$

Synergy, as measured by $S^{\text{CI}}(Y_1, Y_2 \to T)$, is maximized when r equals 1 (the distribution becomes the standard XOR) and minimized when r equals 0. We do not see an immediate reason as to why a general synergy function should be convex in $p(t|y)$, or why it should have a unique minimizer as a function of r. Recall that a function S is convex if $\forall t \in [0,1], \forall x_1, x_2 \in D$, we have

$$S(tx_1 + (1-t)x_2) \leq tS(x_1) + (1-t)S(x_2).$$

In the following, we slightly abuse the notation of the input variables of a synergy function. Our synergy measure S^{CI}, when considered as a function of r, does not satisfy this inequality. For the adapted XOR distribution, take $t = 0.5$, $x_1 = 0$, and $x_2 = 0.5$. We have

$$S^{\text{CI}}(0.5 \times 0 + 0.5 \times 0.5) = S^{\text{CI}}(0.25) \approx 0.552$$

and

$$0.5 \times S^{\text{CI}}(0) + 0.5 \times S^{\text{CI}}(0.5) \approx 0.5 \times 0.270 + 0.5 \times 0.610 \approx 0.440,$$

contradicting the property of channel convexity. S^{d} agrees with this. We slightly change $p(y)$ in the above distribution to obtain a new distribution, which we present in Table 8.

This distribution does not satisfy the convexity inequality, since

$$S^{\text{d}}(0.5 \times 0 + 0.5 \times 0.5) \approx 0.338 > 0.3095 \approx 0.5S^{\text{d}}(0) + 0.5S^{\text{d}}(0.5).$$

This can be easily seen since $K^{(1)} = K^{(2)}$ for any $r \in [0,1]$, hence we may choose $K^{\text{Q}} = K^{(1)}$ to compute $S^{\text{d}} = I(Y;T) - I(Q;T)$, which is not convex for this particular distribution. To conclude this section, we present a plot of $S^{\text{CI}}(Y_1, Y_2)$ and $S^{\text{d}}(Y_1, Y_2)$ as a function of r in Figure 3, for the distribution presented in Table 7.

Table 8. Adapted XOR distribution v2.

T	Y_1	Y_2	$p(t, y_1, y_2)$
0	0	0	$r/10$
1	0	0	$(1-r)/10$
1	1	0	4/10
1	0	1	4/10
0	1	1	1/10

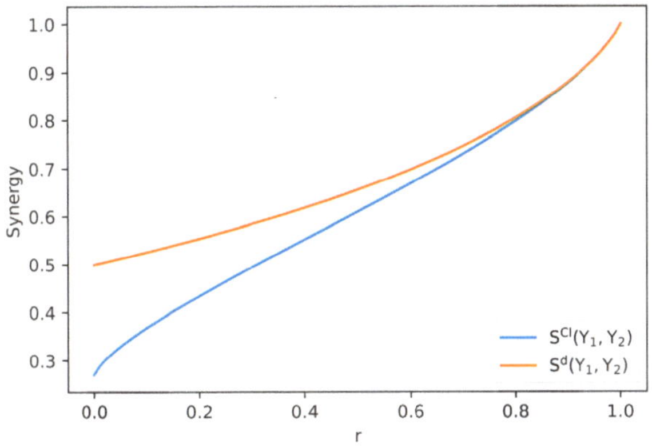

Figure 3. Computation of S^{CI} and S^d as functions of $r = p(T = 0|Y = (0,0))$ for the distribution presented in Table 8. As we showed for this distribution, S^{CI} is not a convex function of r.

With this we do not mean that these properties should not hold for an arbitrary PID. We are simply showing that some properties must be satisfied in the context of PID (such as the WB axioms), whereas other properties are not necessary for PID (such as the previous two properties).

4.5. Relationship with the Extended Williams–Beer Axioms

We now prove which of the introduced properties are implied by the extension of the Williams–Beer axioms for measures of union information. In what follows, assume that the goal is to decompose the information present in the distribution $p(y,t) = p(y_1, \ldots, y_n, t)$.

Theorem 2. *Let $I_\cup$ be a measure of union information that satisfies the extension of the Williams–Beer axioms (symmetry, self-redundancy, monotonicity, and equality for monotonicity) for measures of union information as in Definition (2). Then, $I_\cup$ also satisfies the following properties of Griffith and Koch [16]: global positivity, weak local positivity, strong identity, "duplicating a predictor does not change synergistic information", and "adding a new predictor cannot increase synergy".*

Proof. We argued before that the last two properties follow from the definition of a measure of union information. Global positivity is a direct consequence of monotonicity and the non-negativity of mutual information: $I_\cup(A_1, \ldots, A_m) \geq I_\cup(A_1) = I(A_1; T) \geq 0$.

Weak local positivity holds because monotonicity and self-redundancy imply that $I_\cup(Y_1, Y_2) \geq I_\cup(Y_1) = I(Y_1; T)$, as well as $I_\cup(Y_1, Y_2) \geq I(Y_2; T)$, hence $\max\{I(Y_1; T), I(Y_2; T)\} \leq I_\cup(Y_1, Y_2)$. Moreover, $I_\cup(Y_1, Y_2) \leq I_\cup(Y_1, Y_2, Y_{12}) = I_\cup(Y_{12}) = I(Y; T)$.

Strong identity follows trivially from self-redundancy, since $I_\cup(T \rightarrow T) = I(T; T) = H(T)$. $\square$

Theorem 3. *Consider a measure of union information that satisfies the conditions of Theorem 2. If synergy is defined as in Equation (7), it satisfies the following properties of [37]: non-negativity, upper-bounded by mutual information, weak symmetry, and zero synergy in a single variable.*

Proof. Non-negativity of synergy and upper-bounded by mutual information follow from the definition of synergy and from the fact that for whichever source $(A_1, \ldots, A_m)$, with $m \geq 1$, we have that $I_\cup(A_1, \ldots, A_m \to T) \leq I(Y; T)$.

Weak symmetry follows trivially from the fact that both $I(Y; T)$ and $I_\cup(A_1, \ldots, A_m \to T)$ are symmetric in the relevant arguments.

Finally, zero synergy in a single variable follows from self-redundancy together with the definition of synergy, as shown above. □

5. Previous Measures of Union Information and Synergy

We now review other measures of union information and synergy proposed in the literature. For the sake of brevity, we will not recall all their definitions, only some important conclusions. We suggest the interested reader consult the bibliography for more information.

5.1. Qualitative Comparison

Griffith and Koch [16] review three previous measures of synergy:

- S^{WB}, derived from $I_\cap^{\text{WB}}$, the original redundancy measure proposed by Williams and Beer [1], using the IEP;
- the *whole-minus-sum* (WMS) synergy, S^{WMS};
- the *correlational importance* synergy, $S^{\Delta I}$.

These synergies can be interpreted as resulting directly from measures of union information; that is, they are explicitly written as $S(\alpha \to T) = I(Y; T) - I_\cup(\alpha \to T)$, where $I_\cup$ may not necessarily satisfy our intuitions of a measure of union information, as in Definition 2, except for $S^{\Delta I}$, which has the form of a Kullback–Leibler divergence.

Griffith and Koch [16] argue that S^{WB} *overestimates* synergy, which is not a surprise, as many authors criticized $I_\cap^{\text{WB}}$ for not measuring informational content, only informational values [13]. The WMS synergy, on the other hand, which can be written as a difference of total correlations, can be shown to be equal to the difference between synergy and redundancy for $n = 2$, which is not what is desired in a measure of synergy. For $n > 2$, the authors show that the problem becomes even more exacerbated: S^{WMS} equals synergy minus the redundancy *counted multiple times*, which is why the authors argue that S^{WMS} *underestimates* synergy. Correlational importance, $S^{\Delta I}$, is known to be larger than $I(Y; T)$ for some distributions, excluding it from being an appropriately interpretable measure of synergy.

Faced with these limitations, Griffith and Koch [16] introduce their measure of union information, which they define as

$$I_\cup^{\text{VK}}(A_1, \ldots, A_m \to T) := \min_{p^*} I_{p^*}\left(\bigcup_{i=1}^{m} A_i; T\right) \quad \text{s.t. } p^*(A_i, T) = p(A_i, T), i = 1, \ldots, m, \tag{9}$$

where the minimization is over joint distributions of $A_1, \ldots, A_m, T$, alongside the derived measure of synergy $S^{\text{VK}}(\alpha \to T) = I(Y; T) - I_\cup^{\text{VK}}(\alpha \to T)$. This measure quantifies union information as the least amount of information that source α has about T when the source–target marginals (as determined by α) are fixed by p. Griffith and Koch [16] also established the following inequalities for the synergistic measures they reviewed:

$$\max\left\{0, S^{\text{WMS}}(\alpha \to T)\right\} \leq S^{\text{VK}}(\alpha \to T) \leq S^{\text{WB}}(\alpha \to T) \leq I\left(\bigcup_{i=1}^{m} A_i; T\right), \tag{10}$$

where $\alpha = (A_1, \ldots, A_m)$. At the time, Griffith and Koch [16] did not provide a way to analytically compute their measure. Later, Kolchinsky [22] showed that the measure of union information derived from the degradation order, $I_{\cup}^{\mathrm{d}}$, is equivalent to $I_{\cup}^{\mathrm{VK}}$, and provided a way to compute it. For this reason, we will only consider $I_{\cup}^{\mathrm{d}}$.

After the work of Griffith and Koch [16] in 2014, we are aware of only three other suggested measures of synergy:

- S^{MSRV}, proposed by Quax et al. [37], where MSRV stands for *maximally synergistic random variable;*
- *synergistic disclosure*, S^{SD}, proposed by Rosas et al. [38];
- S^d, proposed by Kolchinsky [22].

The first two proposals do not define synergy via a measure of union information. They define synergy through an auxiliary random variable, Z, which has positive information about the whole—that is, $I(Z;Y) > 0$—but no information about any of the parts—that is, $I(Z;Y_i) = 0, i = 1, \ldots, n$. While this property has an appealing operational interpretation, we believe that it is too restrictive; that is, we believe that information *can* be synergistic, even if it provides some positive information about some part of Y.

The authors of S^{MSRV} show that their proposed measure is incompatible with PID and that it cannot be computed for all distributions, as it requires the ability to compute orthogonal random variables, which is not always possible [37]. A counter-intuitive example for the value of this measure can be seen for the AND distribution, defined by $T = Y_1$ AND Y_2, with Y_1 and Y_2 i.i.d. taking values in $\{0,1\}$ with equal probability. In this case, $S^{\mathrm{MSRV}} = 0.5$, a value that we argue is too large, because whenever Y_1 (respectively Y_2) is 0, then T does not depend on Y_2 (respectively Y_1) (which happens with probability 0.75). Consequently, $S^{\mathrm{MSRV}}/I(Y;T) \approx 0.5/0.811 \approx 0.617$ may be too large of a synergy ratio for this distribution. As the authors note, the only other measure that agrees with S^{MSRV} for the AND distribution is S^{WB}, which Griffith and Koch [16] argued also overestimates synergy.

Concerning S^{SD}, we do not have any criticism, except for the one already pointed out by Gutknecht et al. [36]: they note that the resulting decomposition from S^{SD} is not a standard PID, in the sense that it does not satisfy a consistency equation (see [36] for more details), which implies that '... the atoms cannot be interpreted in terms of parthood relations with respect to mutual information terms .... For example, we do not obtain any atoms interpretable as unique or redundant information in the case of two sources' [36]. Gutknecht et al. [36] suggest a very simple modification to the measure so that it satisfies the consistency equation.

For the AND distribution, S^{SD} evaluates to approximately 0.311, as does S^{d}, whereas our measure yields $S^{\mathrm{CI}} \approx 0.270$, as the information that the parts cannot obtain when they combine their marginals, under distribution q. This shows that these four measures are not equivalent.

5.2. Quantitative Comparison

Griffith and Koch [16] applied the synergy measures they reviewed to other distributions. We show their results below in Table 9 and compare them with the synergy resulting from our measure of union information, S^{CI}, with the measure of Rosas et al. [38], S^{SD}, and that of Kolchinsky [22], S^{d}. Since the code for the computation of S^{MSRV} is no longer available online, we do not present it.

We already saw the definition of the AND, COPY, and XOR distributions. The XORDUPLICATE and ANDDUPLICATE are built from the XOR and the AND distributions by inserting a duplicate source variable $Y_3 = Y_2$. The goal is to test if the presence of a duplicate predictor impacts the different synergy measures. The definitions of the remaining distributions are presented in Appendix A. Some of these are trivariate, and for those we compute synergy as

$$S(Y_1, Y_2, Y_3 \to T) = I(Y_1, Y_2, Y_3; T) - I_{\cup}(Y_1, Y_2, Y_3 \to T), \quad (11)$$

unless the synergy measure is directly defined (as opposed to being defined via a union information measure). We now comment on the results. It should be noted that Kolchinsky [22] suggested that unique information U_1 and U_2 should be computed from measures of redundant information, and excluded information E_1 and E_2 should be computed from measures of union information, as in our case. However, since we will only present the decompositions for the bivariate case and in this case $E_1 = U_2$ and $E_2 = U_1$, we present the results considering unique information, as is mostly performed in the literature.

Table 9. Application of the measures reviewed in Griffith and Koch [16] (S^{WB}, S^{WMS}, and $S^{\Delta I}$), S^{SD} introduced by Rosas et al. [38], S^{d} introduced by Kolchinsky [22], and our measure of synergy S^{CI} to different distributions. The bottom four distributions are trivariate. We write DNF to mean that a specific computation did not finish within 10 min.

Example	S^{WB}	S^{WMS}	$S^{\Delta I}$	S^{d}	S^{SD}	S^{CI}
XOR	1	1	1	1	1	1
AND	0.5	0.189	0.104	0.5	0.311	0.270
COPY	1	0	0	0	1	0
RDNXOR	1	0	1	1	1	1
RDNUNQXOR	2	0	1	1	DNF	1
XORDUPLICATE	1	1	1	1	1	1
ANDDUPLICATE	0.5	-0.123	0.038	0.5	0.311	0.270
XORLOSES	0	0	0	0	0	0
XORMULTICOAL	1	1	1	1	DNF	1

- XOR yields $I(Y;T) = 1$. The XOR distribution is the hallmark of synergy. Indeed, the only solution of (1) is $(S, R, U_1, U_2) = (1, 0, 0, 0)$, and all of the above measures yield 1 bit of synergy.
- AND yields $I(Y;T) \approx 0.811$. Unlike XOR, there are multiple solutions for (1), and none is universally agreed upon, since different information measures capture different concepts of information.
- COPY yields $I(Y;T) = 2$. Most PID measures argue one of two different possibilities for this distribution. They suggest that the solution is either $(S, R, U_1, U_2) = (1, 1, 0, 0)$ or $(0, 0, 1, 1)$. Our measure suggests that all information flows uniquely from each source.
- RDNXOR yields $I(Y;T) = 2$. In words, this distribution is the concatenation of two XOR 'blocks', each of which has its own symbols, and not allowing the two blocks to mix. That is, both Y_1 and Y_2 can determine in which XOR block the resulting value T will be—which intuitively means that they both have this information, meaning it is redundant—but neither Y_1 nor Y_2 have information about the outcome of the XOR operation—as is expected in the XOR distribution—which intuitively means that such information must be synergistic. All measures except S^{WMS} agree with this.
- RDNUNQXOR yields $I(Y;T) = 4$. According to Griffith and Koch [16], it was constructed to carry 1 bit of each information type. Although the solution is not unique, it must satisfy $U_1 = U_2$. Indeed, our measure yields the solution $(S, R, U_1, U_2) = (1, 1, 1, 1)$, like most measures except S^{WB} and S^{WMS}. This confirms the intuition by Griffith and Koch [16] that S^{WB} and S^{WMS} overestimate and underestimate synergy, respectively. In fact, in the decomposition resulting from S^{WB}, there are 2 bits of synergy and 2 bits of redundancy, which we argue cannot be the case, as this would imply that $U_1 = U_2 = 0$, and given the construction of this distribution, it is clear that there is some unique information since, unlike in RDNXOR, the XOR blocks are allowed to mix, thus $(T, Y_1, Y_2) = (1, 0, 1)$ is a possible outcome, but so is $(T, Y_1, Y_2) = (2, 0, 2)$. That is not the case with RDNXOR. On the other hand, S^{WMS} yields zero synergy and redundancy, with U_1 and U_2 each evaluating to 2 bits. Since this distribution is a mix of blocks satisfying a relation of the form $T = Y_1$ xor Y_2, we argue that there must be some non-null amount of synergy, which is why we claim that S^{WMS} is not valid.

- XORDUPLICATE yields $I(Y;T) = 1$. All measures correctly identify that the duplication of a source should not change synergy, at least for this particular distribution.
- ANDDUPLICATE yields $I(Y;T) \approx 0.811$. Unlike in the previous example, both S^{WMS} and $S^{\Delta I}$ yield a change in their synergy value. This is a shortcoming, since duplicating a source should not increase either synergy or union information. The other measures are not affected by the duplication of a source.
- XORLOSES yields $I(Y;T) = 1$. Its distribution is the same as XOR but with a new source Y_3 satisfying $T = Y_3$. As such, since Y_3 uniquely determines T, we expect no synergy. All measures agree with this.
- XORMULTICOAL yields $I(Y;T) = 1$. Its distribution is such that any pair (Y_i, Y_j), $i, j = 1,2,3, i \neq j$ is able to determine T with no uncertainty. All measures agree that the information present in this distribution is purely synergistic.

From these results, we agree with Griffith and Koch [16] that S^{WB}, S^{WMS}, and $S^{\Delta I}$ are not good measures of synergy: they do not satisfy many of our intuitions and overestimate synergy, not being invariant to duplicate sources or taking negative values. For these reasons, and those presented in Section 5, we reject those measures of synergy. In the next section, we comment on the remaining measures S^{d}, S^{SD}, and S^{CI}.

5.3. Relation to Other PID Measures

Kolchinsky [22] introduced $I_{\cup}^{\text{d}}$ and showed that this measure is equivalent to $I_{\cup}^{\text{VK}}$ [16] and to $I_{\cup}^{\text{BROJA}}$ [15], in the sense that the three of them achieve the same optimum value [22]. The multivariate extension of $I_{\cup}^{\text{BROJA}}$ was proposed by Griffith and Koch [16], defined as

$$I_{\cup}^{\text{BROJA}}(A_1, \ldots, A_m \to T) := \min_{\tilde{A}_1, \ldots, \tilde{A}_m} I(\tilde{A}_1, \ldots, \tilde{A}_m; T) \text{ such that } \forall i \;\; P(\tilde{A}_i, T) = P(A_i, T),$$

which we present because it makes it clear what conditions are enforced upon the marginals. There is a relation between $I_{\cup}^{\text{BROJA}}(A_1, \ldots, A_m) = I_{\cup}^{\text{d}}(A_1, \ldots, A_m)$ and $I_{\cup}^{\text{CI}}(A_1, \ldots, A_m)$ whenever the sources $A_1, \ldots A_m$ are singletons. In this case, and only in this case, the set $\mathcal{Q}$ involved in the computation of $I_{\cup}^{\text{CI}}(A_1, \ldots, A_m)$ has only one element: $q(t, a_1, \ldots, a_m) = p(t)p(a_1|t) \ldots p(a_m|t)$. Since this distribution, as well as the original distribution p, are both admissible points in $I_{\cup}^{\text{d}}$, we have that $I_{\cup}^{\text{d}} \leq I_{\cup}^{\text{CI}}$, which implies that $S^{\text{d}} \geq S^{\text{CI}}$. On the other hand, if there is at least one source $A_1, \ldots, A_m$ that is not a singleton, the measures are not trivially comparable. For example, suppose we wish to compute $I_{\cup}((Y_1, Y_2), (Y_2, Y_3))$. We know that the solution of $I_{\cup}^{\text{d}}((Y_1, Y_2), (Y_2, Y_3))$ is a distribution p^* whose marginals $p^*(y_1, y_2, t)$ and $p^*(y_2, y_3, t)$ must coincide with the marginals under the original p. However, in the computation of $I_{\cup}^{\text{CI}}((Y_1, Y_2), (Y_2, Y_3))$, it may be the case that the solution p^* of $I_{\cup}^{\text{d}}((Y_1, Y_2), (Y_2, Y_3))$ is not in the set $\mathcal{Q}$, involved in the computation of $I_{\cup}^{\text{CI}}$, and it achieves a lower mutual information with T. That is, it might be the case that $I_{p^*}(Y;T) < I_q(Y;T)$, for all $q \in \mathcal{Q}$. In such a case, we would have $I_{\cup}^{\text{d}} > I_{\cup}^{\text{CI}}$.

It is convenient to be able to upper-bound certain measures with other measures. For example, Gomes and Figueiredo [26] (see that paper for the definitions of these measures) showed that for any source $(A_1, \ldots, A_m), m \geq 1$,

$$I_{\cap}^{\text{d}}(A_1, \ldots, A_m) \leq I_{\cap}^{\text{ln}}(A_1, \ldots, A_m) \leq I_{\cap}^{\text{mc}}(A_1, \ldots, A_m).$$

However, we argue that the inability to draw such strong conclusions (or bounds) is a positive aspect of PID. This is because there are many different ways to define the information (be it redundant, unique, union, etc.) that one wishes to capture. If one could trivially relate all measures, it would mean that it would be possible to know *a priori* how those measures would behave. Consequently, this would imply the absence of variability/freedom in how to measure different information concepts, as those measures would capture, non-equivalent but similar types of information, as they would all be ordered. It is precisely because one cannot order different measures of information trivially that PID provides a rich and complex framework to distinguish different types of information, although we believe that PID is still in its infancy.

James et al. [17] introduced a measure of unique information, which we recall now. In the bivariate case—i.e., consider $p(y_1, y_2, t)$—let q be the maximum entropy distribution that preserves the marginals $p(y_1, t)$ and $p(y_2, t)$, and let r be the maximum entropy distribution that preserves the marginals $p(y_1, t)$, $p(y_2, t)$, and $p(y_1, y_2)$. Although there is no closed form for r, which has to be computed using an iterative algorithm [39], it may be shown that the solution for q is $q(y_1, y_2, t) = p(t)p(y_1|t)p(y_2|t)$ (see, e.g., [17]). This is the same distribution q that we consider for the bivariate decomposition (3). James et al. [17] suggest defining unique information U_i as the least change (in sources–target mutual information) that involves the addition of the (Y_i, T) marginal constraint, that is,

$$U_1 = \min\{I_q(Y_1; T|Y_2), I_r(Y_1; T|Y_2)\}, \tag{12}$$

and analogously for U_2. They show that their measure yields a non-negative decomposition for the bivariate case. Since $I(Y_1; T|Y_2) = S + U_1$, some algebra leads to

$$S^{\text{dep}} = I(Y; T) - \min\{I_q(Y; T), I_r(Y; T)\}, \tag{13}$$

where S^{dep} is the synergy resulting from the decomposition of James et al. [17] in the bivariate case. Recall that our measure of synergy for the bivariate case is given by

$$S^{\text{CI}} = I(Y; T) - \min\{I_q(Y; T), I_p(Y; T)\}. \tag{14}$$

The similarity is striking. Computing S^{dep} for the bivariate distributions in Table 9 shows that it coincides with the decomposition given by our measure, although this is not the case in general. We could not obtain S^{dep} for the RDNUNQXOR distribution because the algorithm that computes r did not finish in the allotted time of 10 min. James et al. [17] showed that for whichever bivariate distribution $I_r(Y; T) \leq I_p(Y; T)$; therefore, for the bivariate case we have $S^{\text{CI}} \leq S^{\text{dep}}$. Unfortunately, the measure of unique information proposed by James et al. [17], unlike the usual proposals of intersection or union information, does not allow for the computation of the partial information atoms in the complete redundancy lattice if $n > 2$. The authors also comment that it is not clear if their measure satisfies monotonicity when $n > 2$. Naturally, our measure is not the same as S^{dep}, so it does not retain the operational interpretation of unique information U_i being the least amount that influences $I(Y; T)$ when the marginal constraint (Y_i, T) is added to the resulting maximum entropy distributions. Given the form of S^{dep}, one could define $I_{\cup}^{\text{dep}} := \min\{I_q(Y; T), I_r(Y; T)\}$ and study its properties. Clearly, it does not satisfy the self-redundancy axiom, but we wonder if it could be adjusted so that it satisfies all of the proposed axioms. The $n = 2$ decomposition retains the operational interpretation of the original measure, but it is not clear whether this is true for $n > 2$. For the latter case, the maximum entropy distributions that we wrote as q and r have different definitions [17]. We leave this for future work.

6. Conclusions and Future Work

In this paper, we introduced a new measure of *union information* for the *partial information decomposition* (PID) framework, based on the channel perspective, which quantifies synergy as the information that is beyond conditional independence of the sources, given the target. This measure has a clear interpretation and is very easy to compute, unlike most measures of union information or synergy, which require solving an optimization problem. The main contributions and conclusions of the paper can be summarized as follows.

- We introduced new measures of union information and synergy for the PID framework, which thus far was mainly developed based on measures of redundant or unique information. We provided its operational interpretation and defined it for an arbitrary number of sources.

- We proposed an extension of the Williams–Beer axioms for measures of union information and showed our proposed measure satisfies them.
- We reviewed, commented on, and rejected some of the previously proposed properties for measures of union information and synergy in the literature.
- We showed that measures of union information that satisfy the extension of the Williams–Beer axioms necessarily satisfy a few other appealing properties, as well as the derived measures of synergy.
- We reviewed previous measures of union information and synergy, critiqued them, and compared them with our proposed measure.
- The proposed conditional independence measure is very simple to compute.
- We provide code for the computation of our measure for the bivariate case and for source $\{\{Y_1\},\{Y_2\},\{Y_3\}\}$ in the trivariate case.

Finally, we believe this paper opens several avenues for future research, thus we point out several directions to be pursued in upcoming work:

- We saw that the synergy yielded by the measure of James et al. [17] is given by $S^{\text{dep}} = I(Y;T) - \min\{I_q(Y;T), I_r(Y;T)\}$. Given its analytical expression, one could start by defining a measure of union information as $I_\cup(Y_1, Y_2 \to T) = \min\{I_q(Y;T), I_r(Y;T)\}$, possibly tweak it so it satisfies the WB axioms, study its properties, and possibly extend it to the multivariate case.
- Our proposed measure may ignore conditional dependencies that are present in p in favor of maximizing mutual information, as we commented in Section 3.3. This is a compromise so that the measure satisfies monotonicity. We believe this is a potential drawback of our measure, and we suggest the investigation of a measure similar to ours, but that does not ignore conditional dependencies that it has access to.
- Extending this measure for absolutely continuous random variables.
- Implementing our measure in the `dit` package [40].
- This paper reviewed measures of union information and synergy, as well as properties that were suggested throughout the literature. Sometimes this was by providing examples where the suggested properties fail, and other times simply by commenting. We suggest performing something similar for measures of redundant information.

7. Code Availability

The code is publicly available at https://github.com/andrefcorreiagomes/CIsynergy/ and requires the `dit` package [40] (accessed on 12 January 2024).

Author Contributions: Conceptualization, A.F.C.G. and M.A.T.F.; Software, A.F.C.G.; Validation, M.A.T.F.; Formal analysis, A.F.C.G.; Writing—original draft, A.F.C.G.; Writing—review & editing, M.A.T.F.; Supervision, M.A.T.F. All authors have read and agreed to the published version of the manuscript.

Funding: This research was partially funded by: FCT—*Fundação para a Ciência e a Tecnologia*, under grants number SFRH/BD/145472/2019 and UIDB/50008/2020; Instituto de Telecomunicações; Portuguese Recovery and Resilience Plan, through project C645008882-00000055 (NextGenAI, CenterforResponsibleAI).

Institutional Review Board Statement: Not applicable.

Data Availability Statement: Data is contained within the article.

Conflicts of Interest: The authors declare no conflicts of interest.

Appendix A

In this appendix, we present the remaining distributions for which we computed different measures of synergy. For these distributions each outcome has the same probability, so we do not present their probabilities.

Table A1. RDNXOR (left), XORLOSES (center), and XORMULTICOAL (right).

T	Y_1	Y_2	T	Y_1	Y_2	Y_3	T	Y_1	Y_2	Y_3
0	0	0	0	0	0	0	0	0	0	0
1	0	1	1	0	1	1	0	1	1	1
1	1	0	1	1	0	1	0	2	2	2
0	1	1	0	1	1	0	0	3	3	3
2	2	2					1	2	1	0
3	2	3					1	3	0	1
3	3	2					1	0	3	2
2	3	3					1	1	2	3

Table A2. RDNUNQXOR.

T	Y_1	Y_2	T	Y_1	Y_2
0	0	0	8	4	4
1	0	1	9	4	5
1	1	0	9	5	4
0	1	1	8	5	5
2	0	2	10	4	6
3	0	3	11	4	7
3	1	2	11	5	6
2	1	3	10	5	7
4	2	0	12	6	4
5	2	1	13	6	5
5	3	0	13	7	4
4	3	1	12	7	5
6	2	2	14	6	6
7	2	3	15	6	7
7	3	2	15	7	6
6	3	3	14	7	7

References

1. Williams, P.; Beer, R. Nonnegative decomposition of multivariate information. *arXiv* **2010**, arXiv:1004.2515.
2. Lizier, J.; Flecker, B.; Williams, P. Towards a synergy-based approach to measuring information modification. In Proceedings of the 2013 IEEE Symposium on Artificial Life (ALIFE), Singapore, 15–19 April 2013; pp. 43–51.
3. Wibral, M.; Finn, C.; Wollstadt, P.; Lizier, J.T.; Priesemann, V. Quantifying information modification in developing neural networks via partial information decomposition. *Entropy* **2017**, *19*, 494. [CrossRef]
4. Rauh, J. Secret sharing and shared information. *Entropy* **2017**, *19*, 601. [CrossRef]
5. Luppi, A.I.; Craig, M.M.; Pappas, I.; Finoia, P.; Williams, G.B.; Allanson, J.; Pickard, J.D.; Owen, A.M.; Naci, L.; Menon, D.K.; et al. Consciousness-specific dynamic interactions of brain integration and functional diversity. *Nat. Commun.* **2019**, *10*, 4616. [CrossRef]
6. Varley, T.F.; Pope, M.; Faskowitz, J.; Sporns, O. Multivariate information theory uncovers synergistic subsystems of the human cerebral cortex. *Commun. Biol.* **2023**, *6*, 451. [CrossRef]
7. Chan, T.E.; Stumpf, M.P.; Babtie, A.C. Gene regulatory network inference from single-cell data using multivariate information measures. *Cell Syst.* **2017**, *5*, 251–267. [CrossRef]
8. Faber, S.; Timme, N.; Beggs, J.; Newman, E. Computation is concentrated in rich clubs of local cortical networks. *Netw. Neurosci.* **2019**, *3*, 384–404. [CrossRef] [PubMed]
9. James, R.; Ayala, B.; Zakirov, B.; Crutchfield, J. Modes of information flow. *arXiv* **2018**, arXiv:1808.06723.
10. Ehrlich, D.A.; Schneider, A.C.; Priesemann, V.; Wibral, M.; Makkeh, A. A Measure of the Complexity of Neural Representations based on Partial Information Decomposition. *arXiv* **2022**, arXiv:2209.10438.
11. Tokui, S.; Sato, I. Disentanglement analysis with partial information decomposition. *arXiv* **2021**, arXiv:2108.13753.
12. Cover, T.; Thomas, J. *Elements of Information Theory*; John Wiley & Sons: Hoboken, NJ, USA, 1999.

13. Harder, M.; Salge, C.; Polani, D. Bivariate measure of redundant information. *Phys. Rev. E* **2013**, *87*, 012130. [CrossRef] [PubMed]
14. Gutknecht, A.; Wibral, M.; Makkeh, A. Bits and pieces: Understanding information decomposition from part-whole relationships and formal logic. *Proc. R. Soc. A* **2021**, *477*, 20210110. [CrossRef] [PubMed]
15. Bertschinger, N.; Rauh, J.; Olbrich, E.; Jost, J.; Ay, N. Quantifying unique information. *Entropy* **2014**, *16*, 2161–2183. [CrossRef]
16. Griffith, V.; Koch, C. Quantifying synergistic mutual information. In *Guided Self-Organization: Inception*; Springer: Berlin/Heidelberg, Germany, 2014; pp. 159–190.
17. James, R.; Emenheiser, J.; Crutchfield, J. Unique information via dependency constraints. *J. Phys. Math. Theor.* **2018**, *52*, 014002. [CrossRef]
18. Chicharro, D.; Panzeri, S. Synergy and redundancy in dual decompositions of mutual information gain and information loss. *Entropy* **2017**, *19*, 71. [CrossRef]
19. Bertschinger, N.; Rauh, J.; Olbrich, E.; Jost, J. Shared information—New insights and problems in decomposing information in complex systems. In *Proceedings of the European Conference on Complex Systems 2012*; Springer: Berlin/Heidelberg, Germany, 2013, pp. 251–269.
20. Rauh, J.; Banerjee, P.; Olbrich, E.; Jost, J.; Bertschinger, N.; Wolpert, D. Coarse-graining and the Blackwell order. *Entropy* **2017**, *19*, 527. [CrossRef]
21. Ince, R. Measuring multivariate redundant information with pointwise common change in surprisal. *Entropy* **2017**, *19*, 318. [CrossRef]
22. Kolchinsky, A. A Novel Approach to the Partial Information Decomposition. *Entropy* **2022**, *24*, 403. [CrossRef]
23. Barrett, A. Exploration of synergistic and redundant information sharing in static and dynamical Gaussian systems. *Phys. Rev. E* **2015**, *91*, 052802. [CrossRef]
24. Griffith, V.; Chong, E.; James, R.; Ellison, C.; Crutchfield, J. Intersection information based on common randomness. *Entropy* **2014**, *16*, 1985–2000. [CrossRef]
25. Griffith, V.; Ho, T. Quantifying redundant information in predicting a target random variable. *Entropy* **2015**, *17*, 4644–4653. [CrossRef]
26. Gomes, A.F.; Figueiredo, M.A. Orders between Channels and Implications for Partial Information Decomposition. *Entropy* **2023**, *25*, 975. [CrossRef] [PubMed]
27. James, R.G.; Emenheiser, J.; Crutchfield, J.P. Unique information and secret key agreement. *Entropy* **2018**, *21*, 12. [CrossRef] [PubMed]
28. Pearl, J. *Causality*; Cambridge University Press: Cambridge, UK, 2009.
29. Colenbier, N.; Van de Steen, F.; Uddin, L.Q.; Poldrack, R.A.; Calhoun, V.D.; Marinazzo, D. Disambiguating the role of blood flow and global signal with partial information decomposition. *NeuroImage* **2020**, *213*, 116699. [CrossRef] [PubMed]
30. Sherrill, S.P.; Timme, N.M.; Beggs, J.M.; Newman, E.L. Partial information decomposition reveals that synergistic neural integration is greater downstream of recurrent information flow in organotypic cortical cultures. *PLoS Comput. Biol.* **2021**, *17*, e1009196. [CrossRef] [PubMed]
31. Sherrill, S.P.; Timme, N.M.; Beggs, J.M.; Newman, E.L. Correlated activity favors synergistic processing in local cortical networks in vitro at synaptically relevant timescales. *Netw. Neurosci.* **2020**, *4*, 678–697. [CrossRef] [PubMed]
32. Proca, A.M.; Rosas, F.E.; Luppi, A.I.; Bor, D.; Crosby, M.; Mediano, P.A. Synergistic information supports modality integration and flexible learning in neural networks solving multiple tasks. *arXiv* **2022**, arXiv:2210.02996.
33. Kay, J.W.; Schulz, J.M.; Phillips, W.A. A comparison of partial information decompositions using data from real and simulated layer 5b pyramidal cells. *Entropy* **2022**, *24*, 1021. [CrossRef]
34. Liang, P.P.; Cheng, Y.; Fan, X.; Ling, C.K.; Nie, S.; Chen, R.; Deng, Z.; Mahmood, F.; Salakhutdinov, R.; Morency, L.P. Quantifying & modeling feature interactions: An information decomposition framework. *arXiv* **2023**, arXiv:2302.12247.
35. Hamman, F.; Dutta, S. Demystifying Local and Global Fairness Trade-offs in Federated Learning Using Partial Information Decomposition. *arXiv* **2023**, arXiv:2307.11333.
36. Gutknecht, A.J.; Makkeh, A.; Wibral, M. From Babel to Boole: The Logical Organization of Information Decompositions. *arXiv* **2023**, arXiv:2306.00734.
37. Quax, R.; Har-Shemesh, O.; Sloot, P.M. Quantifying synergistic information using intermediate stochastic variables. *Entropy* **2017**, *19*, 85. [CrossRef]
38. Rosas, F.E.; Mediano, P.A.; Rassouli, B.; Barrett, A.B. An operational information decomposition via synergistic disclosure. *J. Phys. A Math. Theor.* **2020**, *53*, 485001. [CrossRef]
39. Krippendorff, K. Ross Ashby's information theory: A bit of history, some solutions to problems, and what we face today. *Int. J. Gen. Syst.* **2009**, *38*, 189–212. [CrossRef]
40. James, R.; Ellison, C.; Crutchfield, J. "dit": A Python package for discrete information theory. *J. Open Source Softw.* **2018**, *3*, 738. [CrossRef]

entropy

MDPI

Article

Non-Negative Decomposition of Multivariate Information: From Minimum to Blackwell-Specific Information

Tobias Mages *, Elli Anastasiadi and Christian Rohner

Department of Information Technology, Uppsala University, 752 36 Uppsala, Sweden
* Correspondence: tobias.mages@it.uu.se

Abstract: Partial information decompositions (PIDs) aim to categorize how a set of source variables provides information about a target variable redundantly, uniquely, or synergetically. The original proposal for such an analysis used a lattice-based approach and gained significant attention. However, finding a suitable underlying decomposition measure is still an open research question at an arbitrary number of discrete random variables. This work proposes a solution with a non-negative PID that satisfies an inclusion–exclusion relation for any f-information measure. The decomposition is constructed from a pointwise perspective of the target variable to take advantage of the equivalence between the Blackwell and zonogon order in this setting. Zonogons are the Neyman–Pearson region for an indicator variable of each target state, and f-information is the expected value of quantifying its boundary. We prove that the proposed decomposition satisfies the desired axioms and guarantees non-negative partial information results. Moreover, we demonstrate how the obtained decomposition can be transformed between different decomposition lattices and that it directly provides a non-negative decomposition of Rényi-information at a transformed inclusion–exclusion relation. Finally, we highlight that the decomposition behaves differently depending on the information measure used and how it can be used for tracing partial information flows through Markov chains.

Keywords: partial information decomposition; redundancy; synergy; information flow analysis; f-information; Rényi-information

Citation: Mages, T.; Anastasiadi, E.; Rohner, C. Non-Negative Decomposition of Multivariate Information: From Minimum to Blackwell-Specific Information. *Entropy* **2024**, *26*, 424. https://doi.org/10.3390/e26050424

Academic Editor: Daniel Chicharro

Received: 5 March 2024
Revised: 6 May 2024
Accepted: 11 May 2024
Published: 15 May 2024

1. Introduction

From computer science to neuroscience, we can find the following problem: We would like to know information about a random variable T, called the target, which we cannot observe directly. However, we can obtain information about the target indirectly from another set of variables $\mathbf{V} = \{V_1, \ldots, V_n\}$. We can use information measures to quantify how much information any set of variables provides about the target. When doing so, we can identify the concept of *redundancy*: For example, if we have two identical variables $V_1 = V_2$, then we can use one variable to predict the other and, thus, anything that this other variable can predict. Similarly, we can identify the concept of *synergy*: For example, if we have two independent variables and a target that corresponds to their XOR operation $T = (V_1 \text{ XOR } V_2)$, then both variables provide no advantage on their own for predicting the state of T, yet their combination fully determines it. Williams and Beer [1] suggested that it is possible to characterize information as visualized by the Venn diagram for two variables $\mathbf{V} = \{V_1, V_2\}$ in Figure 1a. This decomposition attributes the total information about the target to being redundant, synergetic, or unique to a particular variable. As indicated in Figure 1a by $I(\cdot, T)$, we can quantify three of the areas using information measures. However, this is insufficient to determine the four partial areas that represent the individual contributions. This causes the necessity to extend an information measure to either quantify the amount of redundancy or synergy between a set of variables.

Williams and Beer [1] first proposed a framework for Partial Information Decompositions (PIDs) and found favor by the community [2]. However, the proposed measure of redundancy was criticized for not distinguishing, "the *same* information and the *same amount* of information" [3–6]. The proposal of Williams and Beer [1] focused specifically on mutual information. This work additionally studies the decomposition of any f-information or Rényi-information at discrete random variables. They have significance, among others, in parameter estimations, high-dimensional statistics, hypothesis testing, channel coding, data compression, and privacy analyses [7,8].

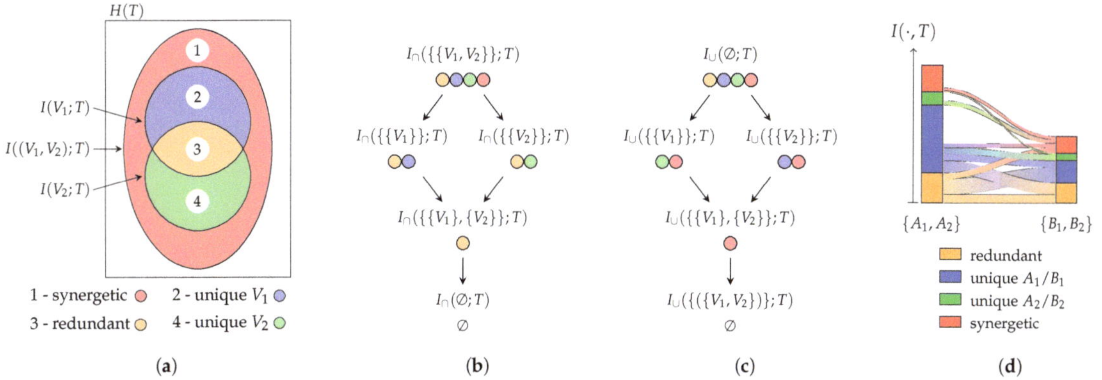

Figure 1. Partial information decomposition representations at two variables $\mathbf{V} = \{V_1, V_2\}$. (**a**) Desired set-theoretic analogy: Visualization of the desired intuition for multivariate information as a Venn diagram. (**b**) Representation as redundancy lattice, where the redundancy measure $I_\cap$ quantifies the information that is contained in all of its provided variables (inside their intersection). The ordering represents the expected subset relation of redundancy. (**c**) Representation as synergy lattice, where the loss measure $I_\cup$ quantifies the information that is contained in neither of its provided variables (outside their union). (**d**) Information flow visualization: When having two partial information decompositions with respect to the same target variable, we can study how the partial information of one decomposition propagates into the next. We refer to this as information flow analysis of a Markov chain such as $T \to (A_1, A_2) \to (B_1, B_2)$.

1.1. Related Work

Most of the literature focuses on the decomposition of mutual information. Here, many alternative measures have been proposed, but cannot fully replace the original measure of Williams and Beer [1] since they do not provide non-negative results for any $|\mathbf{V}|$: The special case of bivariate partial information decompositions ($|\mathbf{V}| = 2$) has been well studied, and several non-negative decompositions for the framework of Williams and Beer [1] are known [5,9–12]. However, each of these decompositions provides negative partial information for $|\mathbf{V}| > 2$. Further research [13–15] specifically aimed to define decompositions of mutual information for an arbitrary number of observable variables, but similarly obtained negative partial contributions and the resulting difficulty of interpreting their results. Griffith et al. [3] studied the decomposition of zero-error information and obtained negative partial contributions. Kolchinsky [16] proposed a decomposition framework for an arbitrary number of observable variables that is applicable beyond Shannon information theory, however, where the partial contributions do not sum to the total amount.

In this work, we propose a decomposition measure for replacing the one presented by Williams and Beer [1] while maintaining its desired properties. To achieve this, we combine several concepts from the literature: We use the Blackwell order, a preorder of information channels, for the decomposition and for deriving its operational interpretation, similar to Bertschinger et al. [9] and Kolchinsky [16]. We use its special case for binary input channels, the zonogon order studied by Bertschinger and Rauh [17], to achieve non-negativity at an arbitrary number of variables and provide it with a practical meaning by highlighting its equivalence to the Neyman–Pearson (decision) region. To utilize this special case for a general decomposition, we use the concept of a target pointwise decomposition as demonstrated by Williams and Beer [1] and related to Lizier et al. [18], Finn and Lizier [13], and Ince [14]. Specifically, we use Neyman–Pearson regions of an indicator variable for each target state to define distinct information and quantify pointwise information from its boundary. This allows for the non-negative decomposition of an arbitrary number of variables, where the source and target variables can have an arbitrary finite number of states. Finally, we apply the concepts from measuring on lattices, discussed by Knuth [19], to transform a non-negative decomposition with an inclusion–exclusion relation from one information measure to another while maintaining the decomposition properties.

Remark 1. *We use the term "target pointwise" or simply "pointwise" within this work to refer to the analysis of each target state individually. This differs from [13,14,18], who use the latter term for the analysis of all joint source–target realizations.*

1.2. Contributions

In a recent work [20], we presented a decomposition of mutual information on the redundancy lattice (Figure 1b). This work aims to simplify, generalize, and extend these ideas to make the following contributions to the area of partial information decompositions:

- We propose a representation of distinct uncertainty and distinct information, which is used to demonstrate the unexpected behavior of the measure by Williams and Beer [1] (Sections 2.2 and 3.1).
- We propose a non-negative decomposition for any f-information measure at an arbitrary number of discrete random variables that satisfies an inclusion–exclusion relation and provides a meaningful operational interpretation (Sections 3.2, 3.3 and 3.5). The decomposition satisfies the original axioms of Williams and Beer [1] (Theorems 3 and 4) and obtains different properties from different information measures (Section 4).
- We demonstrate several transformations of the proposed decomposition: (i) We transform the cumulative measure between different decomposition lattices (Section 3.4). (ii) We demonstrate that the non-negative decomposition of f-information directly provides a non-negative decomposition of Rényi- and Bhattacharyya-information at a transformed inclusion–exclusion relation (Section 3.6).

2. Background

This section aims to provide the required background information and introduce the notation used. Section 2.1 discusses the Blackwell order and its special case at binary targets, the zonogon order, which will be used for operational interpretations and the representation of f-information for its decomposition. Section 2.2 discusses the PID framework of Williams and Beer [1] and the relation between a decomposition based on the redundancy lattice and one based on the synergy lattice. We also demonstrate the unintuitive behavior of the original decomposition measure, which will be resolved by our proposal in Section 3. Section 2.3 provides the considered definitions of f-information, Rényi-information, and Bhattacharyya-information for the later demonstration of transforming decomposition results between measures.

Notation 1 (Random variables and their distribution)**.** *We use the notation T (upper case) to represent a random variable, ranging over the event space $\mathcal{T}$ (calligraphic) containing events $t \in \mathcal{T}$ (lower case) and use the notation P_T (P with subscript) to indicate its probability distribution. The same convention applies to other variables, such as a random variable S with events $s \in \mathcal{S}$ and distribution P_S. We indicate the outer product of two probability distributions as $P_S \otimes P_T$, which assigns the product of their marginals $P_S(s) \cdot P_T(t)$ to each event (s,t) of the Cartesian product $\mathcal{S} \times \mathcal{T}$. Unless stated otherwise, we use the notation T, S, and V to represent random variables throughout this work.*

2.1. Blackwell and Zonogon Order

Definition 1 (Channel). *A channel $\mu = T \to S$ from $\mathcal{T}$ to $\mathcal{S}$ represents a garbling of the input variable T, which results in variable S. Within this work, we represent an information channel μ as a (row) stochastic matrix, where each element is non-negative, and all rows sum to one.*

For the context of this work, we consider a variable S to be the observation of the output from an information channel $T \to S$ from the target variable T, such that the corresponding channel can be obtained from their conditional probability distribution, as shown in Equation (1) where $\mathcal{T} = \{t_1, \ldots, t_n\}$ and $\mathcal{S} = \{s_1, \ldots, s_m\}$.

$$\mu = (T \to S) = P_{(S|T)} = \begin{bmatrix} p(s_1 \mid t_1) & \ldots & p(s_m \mid t_1) \\ \vdots & \ddots & \vdots \\ p(s_1 \mid t_n) & \ldots & p(s_m \mid t_n) \end{bmatrix} \tag{1}$$

Notation 2 (Binary input channels). *Throughout this work, we reserve the symbol κ for binary input channels, meaning κ signals a stochastic matrix of dimension $2 \times m$. We use the notation $\vec{v} \in \kappa$ to indicate a column of this matrix.*

Definition 2 (More informative [17,21]). *An information channel $\mu_1 = T \to S_1$ is more informative than another channel $\mu_2 = T \to S_2$ if—for any decision problem involving a set of actions $a \in \Omega$ and a reward function $u : (\Omega, \mathcal{T}) \to \mathbb{R}$ that depends on the chosen action and state of the variable T—an agent with access to S_1 can always achieve an expected reward at least as high as another agent with access to S_2.*

Definition 3 (Blackwell order [17,21]). *The Blackwell order is a preorder of channels. A channel μ_1 is Blackwell superior to channel μ_2, if we can pass its output through a second channel λ to obtain an equivalent channel to μ_2, as shown in Equation (2).*

$$\mu_2 \sqsubseteq \mu_1 \iff \mu_2 = \mu_1 \cdot \lambda \qquad \textit{for some stochastic matrix } \lambda \tag{2}$$

Blackwell [21] showed that a channel is more informative if and only if it is Blackwell superior. Bertschinger and Rauh [17] showed that the Blackwell order does not form a lattice for channels $\mu = T \to S$ if $|\mathcal{T}| > 2$ since the ordering does not provide unique meet and join elements. However, binary target variables $|\mathcal{T}| = 2$ are a special case where the Blackwell order is equivalent to the zonogon order (discussed next) and does form a lattice [17].

Definition 4 (Zonogon [17]). *The zonogon $Z(\kappa)$ of a binary input channel $\kappa = T \to S$ is defined using the Minkowski sum from the collection of vector segments as shown in Equation (3). The zonogon $Z(\kappa)$ can similarly be defined as the image of the unit cube $[0,1]^{|\mathcal{S}|}$ under the linear map of κ.*

$$Z(\kappa) := \left\{ \sum_i x_i \vec{v}_i \ : \ 0 \leq x_i \leq 1, \vec{v}_i \in \kappa \right\} = \left\{ \kappa a \ : \ a \in [0,1]^{|\mathcal{S}|} \right\} \tag{3}$$

The zonogon $Z(\kappa)$ is a centrally symmetric convex polygon, and the set of vectors $\vec{v}_i \in \kappa$ spans its perimeter. Figure 2 shows an example of a binary input channel and its corresponding zonogon.

Definition 5 (Zonogon sum). *The addition of two zonogons corresponds to their Minkowski sum as shown in Equation (4).*

$$Z(\kappa_1) + Z(\kappa_2) := \{a + b \ : \ a \in Z(\kappa_1), b \in Z(\kappa_2)\} = Z(\begin{bmatrix}\kappa_1 & \kappa_2\end{bmatrix}) \tag{4}$$

Definition 6 (Zonogon order [17]). *A zonogon $Z(\kappa_1)$ is zonogon superior to another $Z(\kappa_2)$ if and only if $Z(\kappa_2) \subseteq Z(\kappa_1)$.*

Bertschinger and Rauh [17] showed that, for binary input channels, the zonogon order is equivalent to the Blackwell order and forms a lattice (Equation (5)). In the remaining work, we will only discuss binary input channels, such that the orderings of Definitions 2, 3, and 6 are equivalent and can be thought of as zonogons with a subset relation.

$$\kappa_1 \sqsubseteq \kappa_2 \iff Z(\kappa_1) \subseteq Z(\kappa_2) \tag{5}$$

To obtain an interpretation of what a channel zonogon $Z(\kappa)$ represents, we can consider a binary decision problem by aiming to predict the state $t \in \mathcal{T}$ of a *binary* target variable T using the output of channel $\kappa = T \rightarrow S$. Any decision strategy $\lambda \in [0,1]^{|\mathcal{S}| \times 2}$ for obtaining a binary prediction $\hat{T}$ can be fully characterized by its resulting pair of True-Positive Rate (TPR) and False-Positive Rate (FPR), as shown in Equation (6):

$$\kappa \cdot \lambda = (T \rightarrow S \rightarrow \hat{T}) = P_{(\hat{T}|T)} = \begin{bmatrix} p(\hat{T} = t \mid T = t) & p(\hat{T} \neq t \mid T = t) \\ p(\hat{T} = t \mid T \neq t) & p(\hat{T} \neq t \mid T \neq t) \end{bmatrix} = \begin{bmatrix} \text{TPR} & 1 - \text{TPR} \\ \text{FPR} & 1 - \text{FPR} \end{bmatrix} \tag{6}$$

Therefore, a channel zonogon $Z(\kappa)$ provides the set of all achievable (TPR,FPR)-pairs for a given channel κ [20,22]. This can also be seen from Equation (3), where the unit cube $a \in [0,1]^{|\mathcal{S}|}$ represents all possible first columns of the decision strategy λ. The first column of λ fully determines the second since each row has to sum to one. As a result, κa provides the (TPR,FPR)-pair for the decision strategy $\lambda = \begin{bmatrix} a & (1-a) \end{bmatrix}$ and the definition of Equation (3) for all achievable (TPR,FPR)-pairs for predicting the state of a binary target variable. Since this will be helpful for operational interpretations, we label the axis of zonogon plots accordingly, as shown in Figure 2. The zonogon ([17], p. 2480) is the Neyman–Pearson region ([7], p. 231).

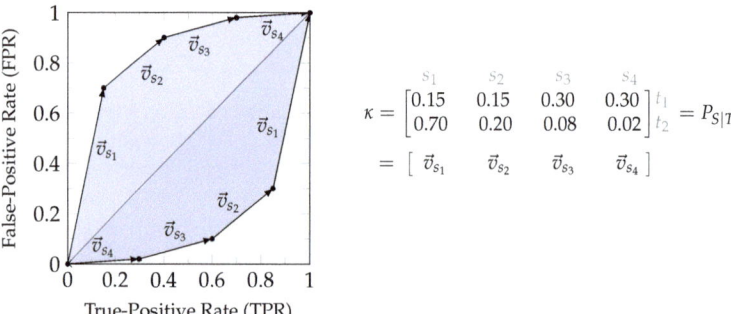

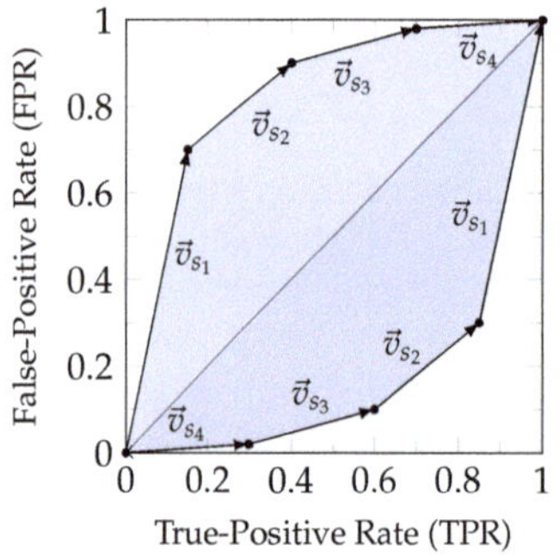

$$\kappa = \begin{array}{c} \begin{matrix} s_1 & s_2 & s_3 & s_4 \end{matrix} \\ \begin{bmatrix} 0.15 & 0.15 & 0.30 & 0.30 \\ 0.70 & 0.20 & 0.08 & 0.02 \end{bmatrix} \begin{matrix} t_1 \\ t_2 \end{matrix} \end{array} = P_{S|T}$$
$$= \begin{bmatrix} \vec{v}_{s_1} & \vec{v}_{s_2} & \vec{v}_{s_3} & \vec{v}_{s_4} \end{bmatrix}$$

Figure 2. An example zonogon (blue) for a binary input channel κ from $\mathcal{T} = \{t_1, t_2\}$ to $\mathcal{S} = \{s_1, s_2, s_3, s_4\}$. The zonogon is the Neyman–Pearson region, and its perimeter corresponds to the vectors $\vec{v}_{s_i} \in \kappa$ sorted by an increasing/decreasing slope for the lower/upper half, which results from the likelihood ratio test. The zonogon, thus, represents the achievable (TPR,FPR)-pairs for predicting T while knowing S.

Definition 7 (Neyman–Pearson region [7] and decision regions). *The Neyman–Pearson region for a binary decision problem is the set of achievable (TPR,FPR)-pairs and can be visualized as shown in Figure 2. The Neyman–Pearson regions underlie the zonogon order, and their boundary can be obtained from the likelihood-ratio test. We refer to subsets of the Neyman–Pearson region as reachable decision regions, or simply decision regions, and the boundary as the zonogon perimeter.*

Remark 2. *Due to the zonogon symmetry, the diagram labels can be swapped (FPR x-axis/TPR y-axis), which changes the interpretation to aiming at a prediction for $T \neq t$.*

Notation 3 (Channel lattice). *We use the notation $\kappa_1 \sqcap \kappa_2$ for the meet element of binary input channels under the Blackwell order and $\kappa_1 \sqcup \kappa_2$ for their join element. We use the notation $\top_{BW} = \begin{bmatrix} 1 & 0 \\ 0 & 1 \end{bmatrix}$ for the top element of binary input channels under the Blackwell order and $\perp_{BW} = \begin{bmatrix} 1 \\ 1 \end{bmatrix}$ for the bottom element.*

For binary input channels, the meet element of the Blackwell order corresponds to the zonogon intersection $Z(\kappa_1 \sqcap \kappa_2) = Z(\kappa_1) \cap Z(\kappa_2)$ and the join element of the Blackwell order corresponds to the convex hull of their union $Z(\kappa_1 \sqcup \kappa_2) = \text{Conv}(Z(\kappa_1) \cup Z(\kappa_2))$. Equation (7) describes this for an arbitrary number of channels.

$$Z\left(\bigsqcap_{\kappa \in \mathbf{A}} \kappa\right) = \bigcap_{\kappa \in \mathbf{A}} Z(\kappa) \quad \text{and} \quad Z\left(\bigsqcup_{\kappa \in \mathbf{A}} \kappa\right) = \text{Conv}\left(\bigcup_{\kappa \in \mathbf{A}} Z(\kappa)\right) \tag{7}$$

Example 1. *The remaining work only analyzes indicator variables, so we only need to consider the case $|\mathcal{T}| = 2$ where all presented ordering relations of this section are equivalent and form a lattice.*

Figure 3a visualizes a channel $T \xrightarrow{\kappa} S$ with $|\mathcal{S}| = 3$. We can use the observations of S for making a prediction $\hat{T}$ about T. For example, we predict that T is in its first state with probability w_1 if S is in its first state, with probability w_2 if S is in its second state, and with probability w_3 if S is in its third state. These randomized decision strategies can be noted as stochastic matrix λ shown in Figure 3a. The resulting TPR and FPR of this decision strategy is obtained from the weighted sum of these parameters (w_1, w_2, and w_3) with the vectors in κ. Each decision strategy corresponds to a point within the zonogon, since the probabilities are constrained by $w_1, w_2, w_3 \in [0,1]$ and the resulting zonogon is the Neyman–Pearson region.

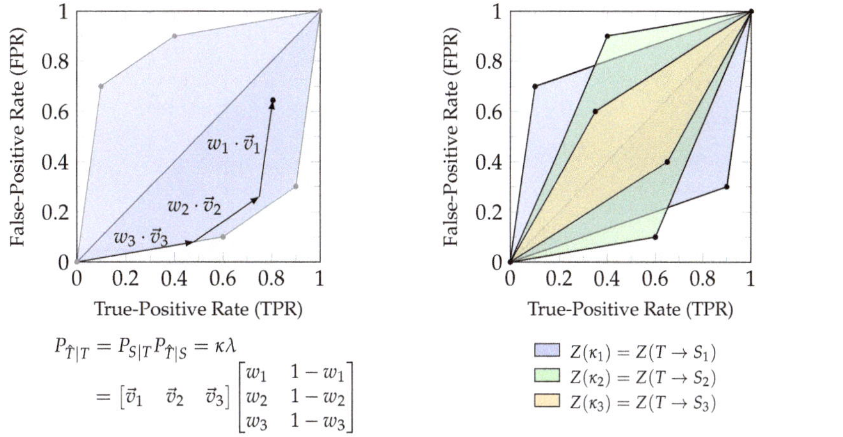

(**a**) Reachable decision regions (**b**) Channel orderings

Figure 3. Visualizations for Example 1 where $|\mathcal{T}| = 2$. (**a**) A randomized decision strategy for predictions based on $T \xrightarrow{\kappa} S$ can be represented by a $|\mathcal{S}| \times 2$ stochastic matrix λ. The first column of this decision matrix provides the weights for summing the columns of channel κ to determine the resulting prediction performance (TPR, FPR). Any decision strategy corresponds to a point in the zonogon. (**b**) All presented ordering relations in Section 2.1 are equivalent at binary targets and correspond to the subset relation of the visualized zonogons. The variable S_3 is less informative than both S_1 and S_2 with respect to T, and the variables S_1 and S_2 are incomparable. The shown channel in (a) is the Blackwell join of κ_1 and κ_2 in (**b**).

Figure 3b visualizes an example for the discussed ordering relations, where all observable variables have two states: $|S_i| = 2$ where $i \in \{1,2,3\}$. The zonogon/Neyman–Pearson region corresponding to variable S_3 is fully contained within the others ($Z(\kappa_3) \subseteq Z(\kappa_1)$ and $Z(\kappa_3) \subseteq Z(\kappa_2)$). Therefore, we can say that S_3 is Blackwell inferior (Definition 3) and less informative (Definition 2) than S_1 and S_2 about T. Practically, this means that we can construct an equivalent variable to S_3 by garbling S_1 or S_2 and that, for any sequence of actions based on S_3 and any reward function with dependence on T, we can achieve an expected reward at least as a high by acting based on S_1 or S_2 instead. The variables S_1 and S_2 are incomparable to the zonogon order, Blackwell order, and informativity order, since the Neyman–Pearson region of one is not fully contained in the other.

The zonogon shown in Figure 3a corresponds to the join under the zonogon order, Blackwell order, and informativity order of S_1 and S_2 in Figure 3b about T. For binary targets, this distribution can directly be obtained from the convex hull of their Neyman–Pearson regions and corresponds to a valid joint distribution for (T, S_1, S_2). All other joint distributions are either equivalent or superior to it. When doing this on indicator variables for $|\mathcal{T}| > 2$, then the obtained joint distributions for each $t \in \mathcal{T}$ may not combine into a specific valid overall joint distribution.

2.2. Partial Information Decomposition

The commonly used framework for PIDs was introduced by Williams and Beer [1]. A PID is computed with respect to a particular random variable that we would like to know information *about*, called the target, and tries to identify *from* which variables that we have access to, called visible variables, we obtain this information. Therefore, this section considers sets of variables that represent their joint distribution.

Notation 4. *Throughout this work, we use the notation T for the target variable and $\mathbf{V} = \{V_1, \ldots, V_n\}$ for the set of visible variables. We use the notation $\mathcal{P}(\mathbf{V})$ for the power set of $\mathbf{V}$ and $\mathcal{P}_1(\mathbf{V}) = \mathcal{P}(\mathbf{V}) \setminus \emptyset$ for its power set without the empty set.*

Definition 8 (Sources, atoms [1]).

- *A source $\mathbf{S}_i \in \mathcal{P}_1(\mathbf{V})$ is a non-empty set of visible variables.*
- *An atom $\alpha \in \mathcal{A}(\mathbf{V})$ is a set of sources constructed by Equation (8).*

$$\mathcal{A}(\mathbf{V}) = \{\alpha \in \mathcal{P}(\mathcal{P}_1(\mathbf{V})) \; : \; \forall \mathbf{S}_a, \mathbf{S}_b \in \alpha, \mathbf{S}_a \not\subset \mathbf{S}_b\}, \tag{8}$$

The filter used for obtaining the set of atoms (Equation (8)) removes sets that would be equivalent to other elements. This is required for obtaining a lattice from the following two ordering relations:

Definition 9 (Redundancy/gain lattice [1]). *The redundancy lattice $(\mathcal{A}(\mathbf{V}), \preccurlyeq)$ is obtained by applying the ordering relation of Equation (9) to all atoms $\alpha, \beta \in \mathcal{A}(\mathbf{V})$.*

$$\alpha \preccurlyeq \beta \iff \forall \mathbf{S}_b \in \beta, \exists \mathbf{S}_a \in \alpha, \mathbf{S}_a \subseteq \mathbf{S}_b \tag{9}$$

The redundancy lattice for three visible variables is visualized in Figure 4a. On this lattice, we can think of an atom as representing the information that can be obtained from all of its sources about the target T (their redundancy or informational intersection). For example, the atom $\alpha = \{\{V_1, V_2\}, \{V_1, V_3\}\}$ represents on the redundancy lattice the information that is contained in both (V_1, V_2) and (V_1, V_3) about T. Since both sources in α provide the information of V_1, their redundancy contains at least this information, and the atom $\beta = \{\{V_1\}\}$ is considered its predecessor. Therefore, the ordering indicates an informational subset relation for the redundancy of atoms, and the information that is represented by an atom increases as we move up. The up-set of an atom α on the redundancy lattice indicates the information that is lost when losing all of its sources. Considering the example from above, if we lose access to $\{V_1 \text{ (or) } V_2\}$ and $\{V_1 \text{ (or) } V_3\}$, then we lose access to all atoms in the up-set of $\alpha = \{\{V_1, V_2\}, \{V_1, V_3\}\}$.

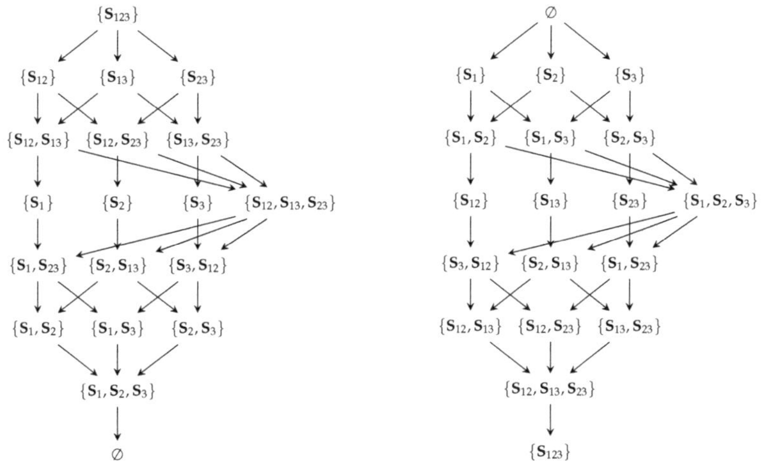

Figure 4. For the visualization, we abbreviated the notation by indicating the contained visible variable as the index of the source, for example $\mathbf{S}_{12} = \{V_1, V_2\}$ to represent their joint distribution: (**a**) A redundancy/gain lattice $(\mathcal{A}(\{V_1, V_2, V_3\}), \preccurlyeq)$ based on the ordering of Equation (9) quantifies information present in all sources. The redundancy of all sources within an atom increases while moving up on the redundancy lattice. (**b**) A synergy/loss lattice $(\mathcal{A}(\{V_1, V_2, V_3\}), \preceq)$ based on the ordering of Equation (10) quantifies information present in neither source. On the synergy lattice, the information that is obtained from neither source of an atom increases while moving up.

Definition 10 (Synergy/loss lattice [23])**.** *The synergy lattice* $(\mathcal{A}(\mathbf{V}), \preceq)$ *is obtained by applying the ordering relation of Equation (10) to all atoms* $\alpha, \beta \in \mathcal{A}(\mathbf{V})$.

$$\alpha \preceq \beta \iff \forall \mathbf{S}_b \in \beta, \exists \mathbf{S}_a \in \alpha, \mathbf{S}_b \subseteq \mathbf{S}_a \tag{10}$$

The synergy lattice for three visible variables is visualized in Figure 4b. On this lattice, we can think of an atom as representing the information that is contained in neither of its sources (information outside their union). For example, the atom $\alpha = \{\{V_1, V_2\}, \{V_1, V_3\}\}$ represents on the synergy lattice the information that is obtained from neither (V_1, V_2) nor (V_1, V_3) about T. The ordering again indicates their expected subset relation: the information that is obtained from neither $\{V_1$ (and) $V_2\}$ nor $\{V_1$ (and) $V_3\}$ is fully contained in the information that cannot be obtained from $\beta = \{\{V_1\}\}$, and thus, α is a predecessor of β.

With an intuition for both ordering relations in mind, we can see how the filter in the construction of atoms (Equation (8)) removes sets that would be equivalent to another atom: the set $\{\{V_1, V_2\}, \{V_1\}\}$ is removed from the power set of sources since it would be equivalent to the atom $\{\{V_1\}\}$ under the ordering of the redundancy lattice and equivalent to the atom $\{\{V_1, V_2\}\}$ under the ordering of the synergy lattice. Using Definition 11, one can similarly define the atoms of the decomposition lattices from the power set of sources without the equivalence relation.

Definition 11. *We define equivalence relations for sets of sources under the redundancy and synergy order:*

$$\textit{Redundancy order:} \quad (\alpha \simeq \beta) \iff (\alpha \preccurlyeq \beta \text{ and } \beta \preccurlyeq \alpha) \tag{11a}$$

$$\textit{Synergy order:} \quad (\alpha \cong \beta) \iff (\alpha \preceq \beta \text{ and } \beta \preceq \alpha) \tag{11b}$$

We use the notation $\mathbf{A}\ \{\cong\}\ \mathbf{B}$ *to indicate that two sets of atoms are equal when comparing their contained atoms with respect to equivalence under the synergy order.*

Notation 5 (Redundancy/synergy lattices). *We use the notation* $(\mathcal{A}(V), \curlyvee, \curlywedge)$ *for the join and meet operators on the redundancy lattice, and* $(\mathcal{A}(V), \vee, \wedge)$ *for the join and meet operators on the synergy lattice. We use the notation* $\top_{RL} = \{\mathbf{V}\}$ *for the top and* $\bot_{RL} = \emptyset$ *for the bottom atom on the redundancy lattice, and* $\top_{SL} = \emptyset$ *and* $\bot_{SL} = \{\mathbf{V}\}$ *for the top and bottom atom on the synergy lattice. For an atom* α *on the redundancy lattice, we use the notation* $\downarrow_R \alpha$ *for its down-set,* $\dot{\downarrow}_R \alpha$ *for its strict down-set,* $\uparrow_R \alpha$ *for its up-set,* $\dot{\uparrow}_R \alpha$ *for its strict up-set, and* α^{-R} *for its cover set. For an atom* α *on the synergy lattice, we use the notation* $\downarrow_S \alpha$ *for its down-set,* $\dot{\downarrow}_S \alpha$ *for its strict down-set,* $\uparrow_S \alpha$ *for its up-set,* $\dot{\uparrow}_S \alpha$ *for its strict up-set, and* α^{-S} *for its cover set.*

For convenience, Table 1 provides a summary of the notation used.

Table 1. Summary of the notation used for the redundancy and synergy lattice.

	Redundancy Order	Synergy Order
Ordering/equivalence	$\preccurlyeq$ / $\simeq$	$\preceq$ / $\cong$
Join/meet	$\curlyvee$ / $\curlywedge$	$\vee$ / $\wedge$
Up-set/strict up-set	$\uparrow_R$ / $\dot{\uparrow}_R$	$\uparrow_S$ / $\dot{\uparrow}_S$
Down-set/strict down-set	$\downarrow_R$ / $\dot{\downarrow}_R$	$\downarrow_S$ / $\dot{\downarrow}_S$
Cover-set	α^{-R}	α^{-S}
Top/bottom	$\top_{\mathrm{RL}} = \{\mathbf{V}\}$ / $\bot_{\mathrm{RL}} = \emptyset$	$\top_{\mathrm{SL}} = \emptyset$ / $\bot_{\mathrm{SL}} = \{\mathbf{V}\}$

The redundant, unique, or synergetic information (partial contributions) can be calculated based on either lattice. They are obtained by quantifying each atom of the redundancy or synergy lattice with a cumulative measure that increases as we move up in the lattice. The partial contributions are then obtained in a second step from a Möbius inverse.

Definition 12 ([Cumulative] redundancy measure [1]). *A redundancy measure* $I_\cap(\alpha; T)$ *is a function that assigns a real value to each atom of the redundancy lattice. It is interpreted as a cumulative information measure that quantifies the redundancy between all sources* $\mathbf{S} \in \alpha$ *of an atom* $\alpha \in \mathcal{A}(\mathbf{V})$ *about the target* T*.*

Definition 13 ([Cumulative] loss measure [23]). *A loss measure* $I_\cup(\alpha; T)$ *is a function that assigns a real value to each atom of the synergy lattice. It is interpreted as a cumulative measure that quantifies the information about* T *that is provided by neither of the sources* $\mathbf{S} \in \alpha$ *of an atom* $\alpha \in \mathcal{A}(\mathbf{V})$*.*

To ensure that a redundancy measure actually captures the desired concept of redundancy, Williams and Beer [1] defined three axioms that a measure $I_\cap$ should satisfy. For the synergy lattice, we consider the equivalent axioms discussed by Chicharro and Panzeri [23]:

Axiom 1 (Commutativity [1,23]). *Invariance in the order of sources (*σ *permuting the order of indices):*

$$I_\cap(\{\mathbf{S}_1, \ldots, \mathbf{S}_i\}; T) = I_\cap(\{\mathbf{S}_{\sigma(1)}, \ldots, \mathbf{S}_{\sigma(i)}\}; T)$$
$$I_\cup(\{\mathbf{S}_1, \ldots, \mathbf{S}_i\}; T) = I_\cup(\{\mathbf{S}_{\sigma(1)}, \ldots, \mathbf{S}_{\sigma(i)}\}; T)$$

Axiom 2 (Monotonicity [1,23]). *Additional sources can only decrease redundant information. Additional sources can only decrease the information that is in neither source.*

$$I_\cap(\{\mathbf{S}_1, \ldots, \mathbf{S}_{i-1}\}; T) \geq I_\cap(\{\mathbf{S}_1, \ldots, \mathbf{S}_i\}; T)$$
$$I_\cup(\{\mathbf{S}_1, \ldots, \mathbf{S}_{i-1}\}; T) \geq I_\cup(\{\mathbf{S}_1, \ldots, \mathbf{S}_i\}; T)$$

Axiom 3 (Self-redundancy [1,23]). *For a single source, redundancy equals mutual information. For a single source, the information loss equals the difference between the total available mutual information and the mutual information of the considered source with the target.*

$$I_\cap(\{\mathbf{S}_i\};T) = I(\mathbf{S}_i;T) \quad \textit{and} \quad I_\cup(\{\mathbf{S}_i\};T) = I(\mathbf{V};T) - I(\mathbf{S}_i;T)$$

The first axiom states that an atom's redundancy and information loss should not depend on the order of its sources. The second axiom states that adding sources to an atom can only decrease the redundancy of all sources (redundancy lattice) and decrease the information from neither source (synergy lattice). The third axiom binds the measures to be consistent with mutual information and ensures that the bottom element of both lattices is quantified to zero.

Once a lattice with the corresponding cumulative measure ($I_\cap/I_\cup$) is defined, we can use the Möbius inverse to compute the partial contribution of each atom. This partial information can be visualized as the partial area in a Venn diagram (see Figure 1a) and corresponds to the desired redundant, unique, and synergetic contributions. However, the same atom represents different partial contributions on each lattice: As visualized for the case of two visible variables in Figure 1, the unique information of variable V_1 is represented by $\alpha = \{\{V_1\}\}$ on the redundancy lattice and by $\beta = \{\{V_2\}\}$ on the synergy lattice.

Definition 14 (Partial information [1,23]). *Partial information $\Delta I_\cap(\alpha;T)$ and $\Delta I_\cup(\alpha;T)$ corresponds to the Möbius inverse of its corresponding cumulative measure on the respective lattice.*

$$\textit{Redundancy lattice:} \qquad \Delta I_\cap(\alpha;T) = I_\cap(\alpha;T) - \sum_{\beta \in \downarrow_R \alpha} \Delta I_\cap(\beta;T), \tag{12a}$$

$$\textit{Synergy lattice:} \qquad \Delta I_\cup(\alpha;T) = I_\cup(\alpha;T) - \sum_{\beta \in \downarrow_S \alpha} \Delta I_\cup(\beta;T). \tag{12b}$$

Remark 3. *Using the Möbius inverse for defining partial information enforces an inclusion–exclusion relation in that all partial information contributions have to sum to the corresponding cumulative measure. Kolchinsky [16] argues that an inclusion–exclusion relation should not be expected to hold for PIDs and proposes an alternative decomposition framework. In this case, the sum of partial contributions (unique/redundant/synergetic information) is no longer expected to sum to the total amount $I(\mathbf{V};T)$.*

Property 1 (Local positivity, non-negativity [1]). *A partial information decomposition satisfies non-negativity or local positivity if its partial information contributions are always non-negative, as shown in Equation (13).*

$$\forall \alpha \in \mathcal{A}(V). \qquad \Delta I_\cap(\alpha;T) \geq 0 \qquad \textit{or} \qquad \Delta I_\cup(\alpha;T) \geq 0 \tag{13}$$

The non-negativity property is important if we assume an inclusion–exclusion relation since it states that the unique, redundant, or synergetic information cannot be negative. If an atom α provides a negative partial contribution in the framework of Williams and Beer [1], then this may indicate that we over-counted some information in its down-set.

Remark 4. *Several additional axioms and properties have been suggested since the original proposal of Williams and Beer [1], such as target monotonicity and the target chain rule [4]. However, this work will only consider the axioms and properties of Williams and Beer [1]. To the best of our knowledge, no other measure since the original proposal (discussed below) has been able to satisfy these properties for an arbitrary number of visible variables while ensuring an inclusion–exclusion relation for their partial contributions.*

It is possible to convert between both representations due to a lattice duality:

Definition 15 (Lattice duality and dual-decompositions [23]). *Let $C = (\mathcal{A}(\mathbf{V})\backslash\{\perp_{RL}\}, \preccurlyeq)$ be a redundancy lattice with associated measure $I_\cap$, and let $D = (\mathcal{A}(\mathbf{V})\backslash\{\perp_{SL}\}, \preceq)$ be a synergy lattice with measure $I_\cup$; then, the two decompositions are said to be dual if and only if the down-set on one lattice corresponds to the up-set in the other, as shown in Equation (14).*

$$\forall\alpha \in C, \exists\beta \in D : \Delta I_\cap(\alpha; T) = \Delta I_\cup(\beta; T) \tag{14a}$$
$$\forall\alpha \in D, \exists\beta \in C : \Delta I_\cup(\alpha; T) = \Delta I_\cap(\beta; T) \tag{14b}$$
$$\forall\alpha \in C, \exists\beta \in D : \quad I_\cap(\alpha; T) = \sum_{\gamma \in \downarrow_R \alpha} \Delta I_\cap(\gamma; T) = \sum_{\gamma \in \uparrow_S \beta} \Delta I_\cup(\gamma; T) \tag{14c}$$
$$\forall\alpha \in D, \exists\beta \in C : \quad I_\cup(\alpha; T) = \sum_{\gamma \in \downarrow_S \alpha} \Delta I_\cup(\gamma; T) = \sum_{\gamma \in \uparrow_R \beta} \Delta I_\cap(\gamma; T) \tag{14d}$$
$$I_\cap(\perp_{RL}; T) = I_\cup(\perp_{SL}; T) = 0 = \Delta I_\cap(\perp_{RL}; T) = \Delta I_\cup(\perp_{SL}; T) \tag{14e}$$

Williams and Beer [1] proposed $I_\cap^{\min}$, as shown in Equation (15), to be used as a measure of redundancy and demonstrated that it satisfies the three required axioms and local positivity. They define redundancy (Equation (15b)) as the expected value of the minimum *specific information* (Equation (15a)).

Remark 5. *Throughout this work, we use the term "target pointwise information" or simply "pointwise information" to refer to "specific information". This shall avoid confusion when naming their corresponding binary input channels in Section 3.*

$$I(\mathbf{S}_i; T = t) = \sum_{s \in \mathcal{S}_i} p(s \mid t) \left[\log\left(\frac{1}{p(t)}\right) - \log\left(\frac{1}{p(t \mid s)}\right) \right] \tag{15a}$$
$$I_\cap^{\min}(\mathbf{S}_1, \ldots, \mathbf{S}_k; T) = \sum_{t \in \mathcal{T}} p(t) \min_{i \in 1..k} I(\mathbf{S}_i; T = t). \tag{15b}$$

To the best of our knowledge, this measure is the only existing non-negative decomposition that satisfies all three axioms listed above for an arbitrary number of visible variables while providing an inclusion–exclusion relation of partial information.

However, the measure $I_\cap^{\min}$ could be criticized for not providing a notion of distinct information due to its use of a pointwise minimum (for each $t \in \mathcal{T}$) over the sources. This leads to the question of distinguishing "the *same* information and the *same amount* of information" [3–6]. We can use the definition through a pointwise minimum (Equation (15)) to construct examples of unexpected behavior: consider, for example, a uniform binary target variable T and two visible variables as the output of the channels visualized in Figure 5. The channels are constructed to be equivalent for both target states and provide access to distinct decision regions while ensuring constant pointwise information $\forall t \in \mathcal{T}$: $I(V_x, T = t) = 0.2$.

Even though our ability to predict the target variable significantly depends on which of the two indicated channel outputs we observe (blue or green in Figure 5, incomparable informativity based on Definition 2), the measure $I_\cap^{\min}$ concludes full redundancy between them $I(V_1; T) = I_\cap^{\min}(\{V_1, V_2\}; T) = I(V_2, T) = 0.2$. We think this behavior is undesired and, as discussed in the literature, caused by an underlying lack of distinguishing the *same* information. To resolve this issue, we will present a representation of f-information in Section 3.1, which allows the use of all (TPR,FPR)-pairs for each state of the target variable to represent a distinct notion of uncertainty.

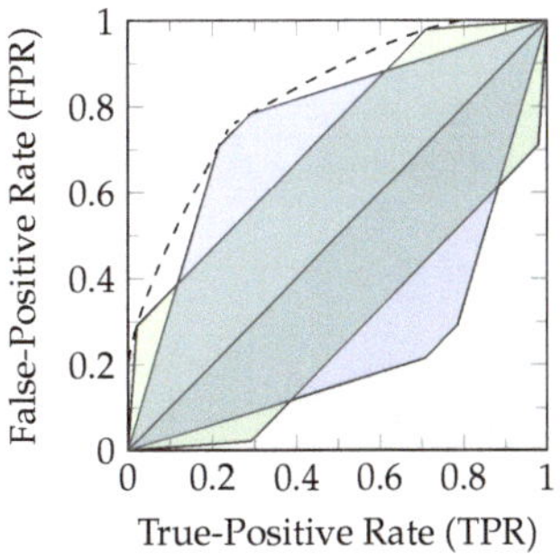

$$\kappa(x,y) = \begin{bmatrix} x & 1-x-y & y \\ y & 1-x-y & x \end{bmatrix}, \text{ where } x \leq y.$$

$$I(V_1;T) = I_\cap^{\min}(\{V_1,V_2\};T) = I(V_2,T) = 0.2$$

Figure 5. Example of the unexpected behavior of $I_\cap^{\min}$: the dashed isoline indicates the pairs (x,y) for which channel $\kappa(x,y) = T \to V_i$ results in pointwise information $\forall t \in \mathcal{T} : I(V_i, T=t) = 0.2$ for a uniform binary target variable. Even though observing the output of both indicated example channels (blue/green) provides significantly different abilities for predicting the target variable state, the measure $I_\cap^{\min}$ indicates full redundancy.

2.3. *Information Measures*

This section discusses two generalizations of mutual information at discrete random variables based on f-divergences and Rényi-divergences [24,25]. While mutual information has interpretational significance in channel coding and data compression, other f-divergences have their significance in parameter estimations, high-dimensional statistics, and hypothesis testing ([7], p. 88), while Rényi-divergences can be found among others in privacy analysis [8]. Finally, we introduce Bhattacharyya information for demonstrating that it is possible to chain decomposition transformations in Section 3.6. All definitions in this section only consider the case of discrete random variables (which is what we need for the context of this work).

Definition 16 (f-divergence [24]). *Let $f : (0,\infty) \to \mathbb{R}$ be a function that satisfies the following three properties:*

- *f is convex;*
- *$f(1) = 0$;*
- *$f(z)$ is finite for all $z > 0$.*

By convention, we understand that $f(0) = \lim_{z\to 0^+} f(z)$ and $0f(\frac{0}{0}) = 0$. For any such function f and two discrete probability distributions P and Q over the event space $\mathcal{X}$, the f-divergence for discrete random variables is defined as shown in Equation (16).

$$D_f(P \parallel Q) := \sum_{x\in\mathcal{X}} Q(x) f\left(\frac{P(x)}{Q(x)}\right) = \mathbb{E}_Q\left[f\left(\frac{P(X)}{Q(X)}\right)\right] \tag{16}$$

Notation 6. *Throughout this work, we reserve the name f for functions that satisfy the required properties for an f-divergence of Definition 16.*

An f-divergence quantifies a notion of dissimilarity between two probability distributions P and Q. Key properties of f-divergences are their non-negativity, their invariance under bijective transformations, and them satisfying a data-processing inequality ([7], p. 89). A list of commonly used f-divergences is shown in Table 2. Notably, the continuation for $a = 1$ of both the Hellinger- and α-divergence results in the KL-divergence [26].

The generator function of an f-divergence is not unique since $D_{f(z)} = D_{f(z)+c(z-1)}$ for a real constant $c \in \mathbb{R}$ ([7], p. 90f). As a result, the considered α-divergence is a linear scaling of the Hellinger divergence ($D_{\mathrm{H}_a} = a \cdot D_{\alpha=a}$), as shown in Equation (17).

$$\frac{z^a - 1}{a-1} + c(z-1) = a \cdot \frac{z^a - 1 - a(z-1)}{a(a-1)} \qquad \text{for } c = -\frac{a}{a-1} \tag{17}$$

Table 2. Commonly used functions for f-divergences.

Notation	Name	Generator Function
D_{KL}	Kullback-Leiber (KL)-divergence	$f(z) = z \log z$
D_{TV}	Total Variation (TV)	$f(z) = \frac{1}{2}\lvert z-1\rvert$
D_{χ^2}	χ^2-divergence	$f(z) = (z-1)^2$
D_{H^2}	Squared Hellinger distance	$f(z) = (1-\sqrt{z})^2$
D_{LC}	Le Cam distance	$f(z) = \frac{1-z}{2z+2}$
D_{JS}	Jensen–Shannon divergence	$f(z) = z \log \frac{2z}{z+1} + \log \frac{2}{z+1}$
D_{H_a}	Hellinger-divergence with $a \in (0,1) \cup (1,\infty)$	$f(z) = \frac{z^a-1}{a-1}$
$D_{\alpha=a}$	α-divergence with $a \in (0,1) \cup (1,\infty)$	$f(z) = \frac{z^a-1-a(z-1)}{a(a-1)}$

Definition 17 (f-information [7])**.** *An f-information is defined based on an f-divergence from the joint distribution of two discrete random variables and the product of their marginals, as shown in Equation (18).*

$$\begin{aligned} I_f(S;T) &:= D_f\Big(P_{(S,T)} \parallel P_S \otimes P_T\Big) \\ &= \sum_{(s,t)\in\mathcal{S}\times\mathcal{T}} P_S(s)\cdot P_T(t)\cdot f\left(\frac{P_{(S,T)}(s,t)}{P_S(s)\cdot P_T(t)}\right) \\ &= \sum_{t\in\mathcal{T}} P_T(t)\left[\sum_{s\in\mathcal{S}} P_S(s)\cdot f\left(\frac{P_{S|T}(s\mid t)}{P_S(s)}\right)\right] \end{aligned} \tag{18}$$

Definition 18 (f-entropy)**.** *A notion of f-entropy for a discrete random variable is obtained from the self-information of a variable $H_f(T) := I_f(T;T)$.*

Notation 7. *Using the KL-divergence results in the definition of mutual information and Shannon entropy. Therefore, we use the notation I_{KL} for mutual information (KL-information) and H_{KL} (KL entropy) for the Shannon entropy.*

The remaining part of this section will define Rényi- and Bhattacharyya-information to highlight that they can be represented as an invertible transformation of Hellinger-information. This will be used in Section 3.6 to transform the decomposition of Hellinger-information to a decomposition of Rényi- and Bhattacharyya-information.

Remark 6. *We could similarly choose to represent Rényi-divergence as a transformation of the α-divergence. A liner scaling of the considered f-divergence will, however, not affect our later results (see Section 3.6).*

Definition 19 (Rényi divergence [25])**.** *Let P and Q be two discrete probability distributions over the event space $\mathcal{X}$, then Rényi-divergence R_a is defined as shown in Equation (19) for $a \in (0,1) \cup (1,\infty)$, and extended to $a \in \{0,1,\infty\}$ by continuation.*

$$\begin{aligned} R_a(P \parallel Q) &:= \frac{1}{a-1}\log\left(\mathbb{E}_Q\left[\left(\frac{P(X)}{Q(X)}\right)^a\right]\right) \\ &= \frac{1}{a-1}\log\left(1+(a-1)\mathbb{E}_Q\left[\frac{\left(\frac{P(X)}{Q(X)}\right)^a - 1}{a-1}\right]\right) \\ &= \frac{1}{a-1}\log(1+(a-1)D_{H_a}(P \parallel Q)) \end{aligned} \tag{19}$$

Notably, the continuation of Rényi-divergence for $a = 1$ also equals the KL-divergence ([7], p. 116). Rényi-divergence can be expressed as an invertible transformation of the Hellinger-divergence (D_{H_a}; see Equation (19)) [26].

Definition 20 (Rényi-information [7]). *Rényi-information is defined equivalent to f-information as shown in Equation (20) and corresponds to an invertible transformation of Hellinger-information (I_{H_a}).*

$$\begin{aligned} I_{R_a}(S;T) &:= R_a\left(P_{(S;T)} \parallel P_S \otimes P_T\right) \\ &= \frac{1}{a-1}\log(1+(a-1)I_{H_a}(S;T)) \end{aligned} \tag{20}$$

Finally, we consider the Bhattacharyya distance (Definition 21), which is equivalent to a linear scaling from a special case of Rényi-divergence (Equation (21)) [26]. It is applied, among others, in signal processing [27] and coding theory [28]. The corresponding information measure (Equation (22)) is like its distance, the scaling of a special case of Rényi-information.

Definition 21 (Bhattacharyya distance [29]). *Let P and Q be two discrete probability distributions over the event space $\mathcal{X}$, then the Bhattacharyya distance is defined as shown in Equation (21).*

$$\begin{aligned} B(P \parallel Q) &:= -\log\left(\sum_{x\in\mathcal{X}} \sqrt{P(x)Q(x)}\right) \\ &= -\log\left(\sum_{x\in\mathcal{X}} Q(x)\sqrt{\frac{P(x)}{Q(x)}}\right) \\ &= -\log\left(1 - 0.5\cdot\mathbb{E}_Q\left[\frac{\left(\frac{P(X)}{Q(X)}\right)^{0.5}-1}{0.5-1}\right]\right) \\ &= -\log(1-0.5\cdot D_{H_{0.5}}(P \parallel Q)) \\ &= 0.5\cdot R_{0.5}(P \parallel Q) \end{aligned} \tag{21}$$

Definition 22 (Bhattacharyya-information). *Bhattacharyya-information is defined equivalent to f-information as shown in Equation (22).*

$$I_B(S;T) := B\left(P_{(S,T)} \parallel P_S \otimes P_T\right) = 0.5\cdot I_{R_{0.5}}(S;T) \tag{22}$$

Example 2. *Consider the channel $T \xrightarrow{\kappa} S$ with $\mathcal{T} = \{t_1, t_2\}$ and $\mathcal{S} = \{s_1, s_2\}$. While it will be discussed in more detail in Section 3.1, Equation (23) already indicates that f-information can be interpreted as the expected value of quantifying the boundary of the Neyman–Pearson region for an indicator variable of each target state $t \in \mathcal{T}$. Each state of a source variable $s \in \mathcal{S}$ corresponds to one side/edge of this boundary as discussed in Section 2.1 and visualized in Figure 2. Therefore, the sum over $s \in \mathcal{S}$ corresponds to the sum of quantifying each edge of the zonogon by some function, which is only parameterized by the distribution of the indicator variable for t. This function satisfies a triangle inequality (Corollary A1), and the total boundary is non-negative (Theorem 2 discussed later). Therefore, we can vaguely think of pointwise f-information as quantifying the length of the boundary of the Neyman–Pearson region or zonogon perimeter to give an oversimplified intuition.*

$$I_f(S;T) = \sum_{t\in\mathcal{T}} P_T(t) \underbrace{\left[\sum_{s\in\mathcal{S}} \overbrace{P_S(s)\cdot f\left(\frac{P_{S|T}(s\mid t)}{P_S(s)}\right)}^{\text{quantifies each zonogon edge}}\right]}_{\text{pointwise information of an indicator variable } T=t} \tag{23}$$

Below is a stepwise computation of χ^2-information ($f(z) = (z-1)^2$) on a small example from this interpretation for the setting of Equation (24).

$$\kappa = P_{S|T} = \begin{bmatrix} p(S=s_1 \mid T=t_1) & p(S=s_2 \mid T=t_1) \\ p(S=s_1 \mid T=t_2) & p(S=s_2 \mid T=t_2) \end{bmatrix} = \begin{bmatrix} 0.8 & 0.2 \\ 0.35 & 0.65 \end{bmatrix} \tag{24a}$$

$$P_T = \begin{bmatrix} p(T=t_1) & p(T=t_2) \end{bmatrix} = \begin{bmatrix} 0.4 & 0.6 \end{bmatrix} \tag{24b}$$

Since $|\mathcal{T}| = 2$, we compute the pointwise information for two indicator variables as shown in Figure 6. Since each state $s \in \mathcal{S}$ corresponds to one edge of the zonogon, we compute them individually. Notice that the quantification of each vector v_{s_i} can be expressed as a function that is only parameterized by the distribution of the indicator variable. The total zonogon perimeter is quantified as the sum of each of its edges, which equals pointwise information. In this particular case, we obtain 0.292653 for the total boundary on the indicator of t_1 and 0.130068 for the total boundary on the indicator of t_2. The expected information corresponds to the expected value of these pointwise quantifications and provides the final result (Equation (25)).

$$I_{\chi^2}(S;T) = p(T=t_1) \cdot 0.292653 + p(T=t_2) \cdot 0.130068 = 0.195102 \tag{25}$$

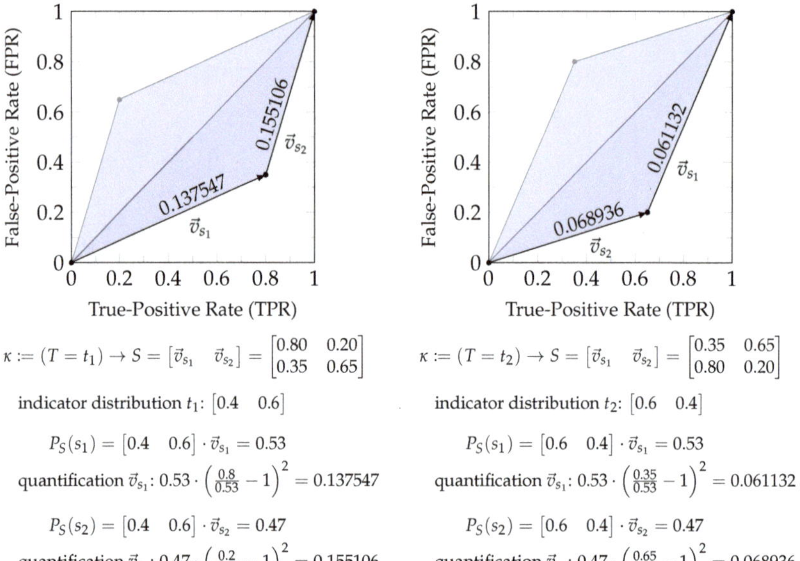

$\kappa := (T=t_1) \to S = \begin{bmatrix} \vec{v}_{s_1} & \vec{v}_{s_2} \end{bmatrix} = \begin{bmatrix} 0.80 & 0.20 \\ 0.35 & 0.65 \end{bmatrix}$

indicator distribution t_1: $\begin{bmatrix} 0.4 & 0.6 \end{bmatrix}$

$P_S(s_1) = \begin{bmatrix} 0.4 & 0.6 \end{bmatrix} \cdot \vec{v}_{s_1} = 0.53$

quantification $\vec{v}_{s_1}$: $0.53 \cdot \left(\frac{0.8}{0.53} - 1\right)^2 = 0.137547$

$P_S(s_2) = \begin{bmatrix} 0.4 & 0.6 \end{bmatrix} \cdot \vec{v}_{s_2} = 0.47$

quantification $\vec{v}_{s_2}$: $0.47 \cdot \left(\frac{0.2}{0.47} - 1\right)^2 = 0.155106$

total pointwise χ^2-information of t_1:

$0.137547 + 0.155106 = 0.292653$

(**a**) Pointwise information of indicator $T = t_1$

$\kappa := (T=t_2) \to S = \begin{bmatrix} \vec{v}_{s_1} & \vec{v}_{s_2} \end{bmatrix} = \begin{bmatrix} 0.35 & 0.65 \\ 0.80 & 0.20 \end{bmatrix}$

indicator distribution t_2: $\begin{bmatrix} 0.6 & 0.4 \end{bmatrix}$

$P_S(s_1) = \begin{bmatrix} 0.6 & 0.4 \end{bmatrix} \cdot \vec{v}_{s_1} = 0.53$

quantification $\vec{v}_{s_1}$: $0.53 \cdot \left(\frac{0.35}{0.53} - 1\right)^2 = 0.061132$

$P_S(s_2) = \begin{bmatrix} 0.6 & 0.4 \end{bmatrix} \cdot \vec{v}_{s_2} = 0.47$

quantification $\vec{v}_{s_2}$: $0.47 \cdot \left(\frac{0.65}{0.47} - 1\right)^2 = 0.068936$

total pointwise χ^2-information of t_2:

$0.061132 + 0.068936 = 0.130068$

(**b**) Pointwise information of indicator $T = t_2$

Figure 6. This example visualizes the computation of χ^2-information by indicating its results on the representation of zonogons of an indicator variable. (**a**) For the pointwise information of t_1, both vectors of the zonogon perimeter are quantified to the sum 0.292653. (**b**) For the pointwise information of t_2, both vectors of the zonogon perimeter are quantified to the sum of 0.130068. The final χ^2-information is their expected value $I_{\chi^2}(S;T) = 0.4 \cdot 0.292653 + 0.6 \cdot 0.130068 = 0.195102$.

3. Decomposition Methodology

To construct a partial information decomposition in the framework of Williams and Beer [1], we only have to define a cumulative redundancy measure ($I_\cap$) or cumulative loss measure ($I_\cup$). However, doing this requires a meaningful definition of when information is the *same*. Therefore, Section 3.1 presents an interpretation of f-information that enables a representation of distinct information. Specifically, we demonstrate that pointwise f-information for a target state $t \in \mathcal{T}$ corresponds to the Neyman–Pearson region of its indicator variable, which is quantified by its boundary (zonogon perimeter). This allows for the interpretation that each distinct (TPR,FPR)-pair for predicting a state of the target variable provides a distinct notion of uncertainty. This interpretation of f-information is used in Section 3.2 to construct a partial information decomposition on the synergy lattice under the Blackwell order for each state $t \in \mathcal{T}$ individually. These individual decompositions are then combined into the final result. Therefore, we decompose specific information based on the Blackwell order rather than using its minimum, like Williams and Beer [1]. The resulting operational interpretation is discussed in Section 3.3. Section 3.4 studies the relation between decomposition lattices to derive the dual-decomposition of any f-information on the redundancy lattice in the following Section 3.5 and prove its correctness. We use the obtained decomposition for any f-information in Section 3.6 to transform a Hellinger-information decomposition into a Rényi-information decomposition while maintaining its non-negativity and an inclusion–exclusion relation. To achieve the desired axioms and properties, we combine different aspects of the existing literature:

- Like Bertschinger et al. [9] and Kolchinsky [16], we base the decomposition on the Blackwell order and use this to obtain the operational interpretation of the decomposition.
- Like Williams and Beer [1] and related to Lizier et al. [18], Finn and Lizier [13], and Ince [14], we perform a decomposition from a pointwise perspective, but only for the target variable.
- In a similar manner to how Finn and Lizier [13] used probability mass exclusion to differentiate distinct information, we use Neyman–Pearson regions for each state of a target variable to differentiate distinct information.
- We propose applying the concepts about lattice re-graduations discussed by Knuth [19] to PIDs to transform the decomposition of one information measure to another while maintaining its consistency.

We extend Axiom 3 of Williams and Beer [1] as shown below, to allow binding any information measure to the decomposition.

Axiom 3* (Self-redundancy). *For a single source, redundancy $I_{\cap,*}$ and information loss $I_{\cup,*}$ correspond to information measure I_* as shown below:*

$$I_{\cap,*}(\{\mathbf{S}_i\};T) = I_*(\mathbf{S}_i;T) \quad \text{and} \quad I_{\cup,*}(\{\mathbf{S}_i\};T) = I_*(\mathbf{V};T) - I_*(\mathbf{S}_i;T) \tag{26}$$

3.1. Representing f-Information

We begin with an interpretation of f-information, for which we define a pointwise (indicator) variable $\pi(T,t)$ that represents one state of the target variable (Equation (27a)) and construct its pointwise information channel (Definition 23). Then, we define a function r_f based on the generator function of an f-divergence for quantifying (half) the zonogon perimeter of each pointwise information channel (see Figure 2). These perimeter quantifications are pointwise f-information.

Definition 23 ([Target] pointwise binary input channel). *We define a target pointwise binary input channel $\kappa(\mathbf{S},T,t)$ from one state of the target variable $t \in \mathcal{T}$ to an information source $\mathbf{S}$ with event space $\mathcal{S} = \{s_1,\dots,s_m\}$ as shown in Equation (27b).*

$$\pi(T,t) := \begin{cases} 1 & \text{if } T = t \\ 0 & \text{otherwise} \end{cases} \tag{27a}$$

$$\kappa(\mathbf{S},T,t) := \pi(T,t) \to \mathbf{S} = \begin{bmatrix} p(S=s_1 \mid T=t) & \dots & p(S=s_m \mid T=t) \\ p(S=s_1 \mid T\neq t) & \dots & p(S=s_m \mid T\neq t) \end{bmatrix} \tag{27b}$$

Definition 24 ([Target] pointwise f-information).

- *We define a function r_f as shown in Equation (28a) to quantify a vector, where $0 \leq p, x, y \leq 1$.*
- *We define a target pointwise f-information function i_f, as shown in Equation (28b), to quantify half the zonogon perimeter for the corresponding pointwise channel $Z(\kappa(\mathbf{S}, T, t))$.*

$$r_f(p, \left[\begin{smallmatrix} x \\ y \end{smallmatrix}\right]) := (px + (1-p)y) \cdot f\left(\frac{x}{px + (1-p)y}\right) \tag{28a}$$

$$i_f(p, \kappa) := \sum_{\vec{v} \in \kappa} r_f(p, \vec{v}) \tag{28b}$$

Theorem 1 (Properties of r_f). *For a constant $0 \leq p \leq 1$, (1) the function $r_f(p, \vec{v})$ is convex in $\vec{v}$, (2) scales linearly in $\vec{v}$, (3) satisfies a triangle inequality in $\vec{v}$, (4) quantifies any vector of slope one to zero, and (5) quantifies the zero vector to zero.*

Proof.

1. The convexity of $r_f(p, \vec{v})$ in $\vec{v}$ is shown separately in Lemma A1 of Appendix A.
2. That $r_f(p, \ell\vec{v}) = \ell r_f(p, \vec{v})$ scales linearly in $\vec{v}$ can directly be seen from Equation (28a).
3. The triangle inequality of $r_f(p, \vec{v})$ in $\vec{v}$ is shown separately in Corollary A1 of Appendix A.
4. A vector of slope one is quantified to zero $r_f(p, \left[\begin{smallmatrix} \ell \\ \ell \end{smallmatrix}\right]) = \ell \cdot f(1) = 0$, since $f(1) = 0$ is a requirement on the generator function of an f-divergence (Definition 16).
5. The zero vector is quantified to zero $r_f(p, \left[\begin{smallmatrix} 0 \\ 0 \end{smallmatrix}\right]) = 0 \cdot f(\frac{0}{0}) = 0$ by the convention of generator functions for an f-divergence (Definition 16).

□

The function r_f provides the following properties to the pointwise information measure i_f.

Theorem 2 (Properties of i_f). *The pointwise information measure i_f (1) maintains the ordering relation of the Blackwell order for binary input channels and (2) is non-negative.*

Proof.

1. That the function r_f maintains the ordering relation of the Blackwell order on binary input channels is shown separately in Lemma A2 of Appendix A (Equation (29a)).
2. The bottom element $\perp_{\text{BW}} = \left[\begin{smallmatrix} 1 \\ 1 \end{smallmatrix}\right]$ consists of a single vector of slope one, which is quantified to zero by Theorem 1 (Equation (29b)). The combination with Equation (29a) ensures the non-negativity.

$$\kappa_1 \sqsubseteq \kappa_2 \Longrightarrow i_f(p, \kappa_1) \leq i_f(p, \kappa_2), \tag{29a}$$

$$i_f(p, \perp_{\text{BW}}) = 0. \tag{29b}$$

□

An f-information corresponds to the expected value of the target pointwise f-information function defined above (Equation (30)). As a result, we can interpret f-information as the expected value of quantifying (half) the zonogon perimeters for the target pointwise channels $\kappa(\mathbf{S}, T, t)$.

$$
\begin{aligned}
I_f(\mathbf{S}; T) &= \sum_{t \in \mathcal{T}} P_T(t) \cdot i_f(P_T(t), \kappa(\mathbf{S}, T, t)) \\
&= \sum_{t \in \mathcal{T}} P_T(t) \cdot \left[\sum_{\vec{v} \in \kappa(\mathbf{S},T,t)} r_f(P_T(t), \vec{v}) \right] \\
&= \sum_{t \in \mathcal{T}} P_T(t) \cdot \left[\sum_{s \in \mathcal{S}} P_S(s) \cdot f\left(\frac{P_{S|T}(s \mid t)}{P_S(s)} \right) \right]
\end{aligned} \tag{30}
$$

3.2. Decomposing f-Information on the Synergy Lattice

With the representation of Section 3.1 in mind, we can define a non-negative partial information decomposition for a set of visible variables $\mathbf{V} = \{V_1, \ldots, V_n\}$ about a target variable T for any f-information. The decomposition is performed from a pointwise perspective, which means that we decompose the pointwise measure i_f on the synergy lattice $(\mathcal{A}(\mathbf{V}), \preceq)$ for each $t \in \mathcal{T}$. The pointwise synergy lattices are then combined using a weighted sum to obtain the decomposition of I_f.

We map each atom of the synergy lattice to the join of pointwise channels for its contained sources.

Definition 25 (From atoms to channels). *We define the channel corresponding to an atom $\alpha \in \mathcal{A}(\mathbf{V})$ as shown in Equation (31).*

$$
\kappa_{\sqcup}(\alpha, T, t) := \begin{cases} \bot_{BW} & \text{if } \alpha = \emptyset \\ \bigsqcup_{\mathbf{S} \in \alpha} \kappa(\mathbf{S}, T, t)) & \text{otherwise} \end{cases} \tag{31}
$$

Lemma 1. *For any set of sources $\alpha, \beta \in \mathcal{P}(\mathcal{P}_1(\mathbf{V}))$ and target variable T with state $t \in \mathcal{T}$, the function $\kappa_{\sqcup}$ maintains the ordering of the synergy lattice under the Blackwell order as shown in Equation (32).*

$$
\alpha \preceq \beta \Longrightarrow \kappa_{\sqcup}(\beta, T, t) \sqsubseteq \kappa_{\sqcup}(\alpha, T, t) \tag{32}
$$

Lemma 1 is shown separately in Appendix C. The mapping from Definition 25 provides a lattice that can be quantified using pointwise f-information to construct a cumulative loss measure for its decomposition using the Möbius inverse.

Definition 26 ([Target] pointwise cumulative and partial loss measures). *We define the target pointwise cumulative and partial loss functions as shown in Equations (33a) and (33b).*

$$
i_{\cup,f}(\alpha, T, t) := i_f(P_T(t), \kappa(\mathbf{V}, T, t)) - i_f(P_T(t), \kappa_{\sqcup}(\alpha, T, t)) \tag{33a}
$$

$$
\Delta i_{\cup,f}(\alpha, T, t) := i_{\cup,f}(\alpha, T, t) - \sum_{\beta \in \dot{\downarrow}_S \alpha} \Delta i_{\cup,f}(\beta, T, t) \tag{33b}
$$

The combined cumulative and partial measures are the expected value of their corresponding pointwise measures. This corresponds to combining the pointwise decomposition lattices by a weighted sum.

Definition 27 (Combined cumulative and partial loss measures). *The cumulative loss measure $I_{\cup,f}$ is defined by Equation* (34) *and the decomposition result $\Delta I_{\cup,f}$ by Equation* (35).

$$
I_{\cup,f}(\alpha; T) := \sum_{t \in \mathcal{T}} P_T(t) \cdot i_{\cup,f}(\alpha, T, t) \tag{34}
$$

$$
\begin{aligned}
\Delta I_{\cup,f}(\alpha;T) &:= \sum_{t\in\mathcal{T}} P_T(t)\cdot\Delta i_{\cup,f}(\alpha,T,t) \\
&= I_{\cup,f}(\alpha;T) - \sum_{\beta\in\downarrow_S\alpha} \Delta I_{\cup,f}(\beta;T)
\end{aligned} \tag{35}
$$

Theorem 3. *The presented definitions for the pointwise and expected loss measures ($i_{\cup,f}$ and $I_{\cup,f}$) provide a non-negative PID on the synergy lattice with an inclusion–exclusion relation that satisfies Axioms 1, 2, and 3* for any f-information measure.*

Proof.

- **Axiom 1**: The measure $i_{\cup,f}$ (Equation (33a)) is invariant to permuting the order of sources in α, since the join operator of the zonogon order ($\bigsqcup_{\mathbf{S}\in\alpha}$) is. Therefore, also $I_{\cup,f}$ satisfies Axiom 1.
- **Axiom 2**: The monotonicity of both $i_{\cup,f}$ and $I_{\cup,f}$ on the synergy lattice is shown separately as Corollary A2 in Appendix C.
- **Axiom 3***: For a single source, $i_{\cup,f}$ equals the pointwise information loss by definition (see Equations (26), (28b), and (33a)). Therefore, $I_{\cup,f}$ satisfies Axiom 3*.
- **Non-negativity**: The non-negativity of $\Delta i_{\cup,f}$ and $\Delta I_{\cup,f}$ is shown separately as Lemma A8 in Appendix C.

□

3.3. Operational Interpretation

From a pointwise perspective ($|\mathcal{T}| = 2$), there always exists a dependency between the sources for which the synergy of this state becomes zero. This dependence corresponds, by definition, to the join of their channels. This is helpful for the operational interpretation in the following paragraph since, individually, each pointwise synergy becomes fully volatile to the dependence between the sources. There may not exist a dependency between the sources for which the expected synergy becomes zero for $|\mathcal{T}| > 2$. However, each decision region that is quantified as synergetic becomes inaccessible at some dependence between the sources.

The decomposition obtains the operational interpretation that, if a variable provides pointwise unique information, then there exists a unique decision region for some $t \in \mathcal{T}$ that this variable provides access to. Moreover, if a set of variables provides synergetic information, then a decision region for some $t \in \mathcal{T}$ may become inaccessible if the dependence between the variables changes. Due to the equivalence of the zonogon and Blackwell order for binary input variables, these interpretations can also be transferred to a set of actions $a \in \Omega$ and a *pointwise* reward function $u(a, \pi(T,t))$, which only depends on one state of the target variable $\pi(T,t)$ (see Section 2.1): If a variable provides unique information, then it provides an advantage for some set of actions and pointwise reward function, while synergy indicates that the advantage for some pointwise reward function is based on the dependence between variables.

The implication of the interpretation does not hold in the other direction, which we will also highlight in the example of $I_{\cup,\mathrm{TV}}$ in Section 4.1. Finally, the definition of the Blackwell order through the chaining of channels (Equation (2)) highlights its suitability for tracing the flows of information in Markov chains (see Section 4.2).

Remark 7. *The operational interpretation can be strengthened further such that the implication between accessible regions and partial information holds in both directions by revising Lemmas A1 and A2 with a strictly convex generator function to obtain* $\kappa_1 \sqsubset \kappa_2 \implies i_f(p,\kappa_1) < i_f(p,\kappa_2)$.

3.4. Decomposition Duality

A non-negative decomposition on the synergy lattice raises the question about its dual-decomposition on the redundancy lattice. Unfortunately, the definition of decomposition duality (Definition 15 [23]) does not specify the mapping between atoms to easily construct dual-decompositions. Therefore, this section discusses how the redundancy and synergy lattice are related by identifying operators that transform one lattice into the other. This transformation can then be used to refine the definition of decomposition duality and, correspondingly, transforms the cumulative measure between lattices.

Definition 28. *We define two functions: The function* $\Xi : \mathcal{P}(\mathcal{P}_1(\mathbf{V})) \to \mathcal{P}(\mathcal{P}_1(\mathbf{V}))$ *provides the atom with complement sources, and the function* $\Psi : \mathcal{P}(\mathcal{P}_1(\mathbf{V})) \to \mathcal{P}(\mathcal{P}_1(\mathbf{V}))$ *is the n-ary Cartesian product. We indicate the i-th source of an atom as* $\alpha[i]$ *and indicate some variable within the i-th source as* x_i*.*

$$\Xi(\alpha) := \begin{cases} \emptyset & \text{if } \alpha = \{\mathbf{V}\} \\ \{\mathbf{V}\} & \text{if } \alpha = \emptyset \\ \{\mathbf{V} \setminus \{\mathbf{S}\} \ : \ \mathbf{S} \in \alpha\} & \text{otherwise} \end{cases}$$
$$\Psi(\alpha) := \begin{cases} \{\emptyset\} & \text{if } \alpha = \emptyset \\ \{\{x_1, \dots, x_m\} \ : \ x_1 \in \alpha[1], \cdots, x_m \in \alpha[m]\} & \text{otherwise, where } m = |\alpha| \end{cases} \tag{36}$$

Example 3. *For an example of these functions, let* $\mathbf{V} = \{V_1, V_2, V_3, V_4\}$ *and* $\alpha = \{\{V_1\}, \{V_2, V_3\}\}$*:*

$$\begin{aligned}
\Xi(\alpha) &= \{\{\{V_2, V_3, V_4\}, \{V_1, V_4\}\}\} \\
\Xi(\Xi(\alpha)) &= \{\{V_1\}, \{V_2, V_3\}\} = \alpha \\
\Psi(\alpha) &= \{\{V_1, V_2\}, \{V_1, V_3\}\} \\
\Psi(\Psi(\alpha)) &= \{\{V_1\}, \{V_1, V_3\}, \{V_2, V_1\}, \{V_2, V_3\}\} \\
&\simeq \{\{V_1\}, \{V_2, V_1\}, \{V_2, V_3\}\} && (\text{since } \{V_1\} \subseteq \{V_1, V_3\}) \\
&\simeq \{\{V_1\}, \{V_2, V_3\}\} \simeq \alpha && (\text{since } \{V_1\} \subseteq \{V_2, V_1\}) \\
\Xi(\Psi(\Psi(\alpha))) &= \{\{V_2, V_3, V_4\}, \{V_2, V_4\}, \{V_3, V_4\}, \{V_1, V_4\}\} \\
&\cong \{\{V_2, V_3, V_4\}, \{V_3, V_4\}, \{V_1, V_4\}\} && (\text{since } \{V_2, V_4\} \subseteq \{V_2, V_3, V_4\}) \\
&\cong \{\{V_2, V_3, V_4\}, \{V_1, V_4\}\} \cong \Xi(\alpha) && (\text{since } \{V_3, V_4\} \subseteq \{V_2, V_3, V_4\})
\end{aligned}$$

Lemma 2. *The function* $\Psi(\cdot)$ *is a bijection on the redundancy lattice without the bottom element* ($\emptyset$) *that reverses its order. Let* $\alpha, \beta \in \mathcal{A}(\mathbf{V}) \setminus \{\bot_{RL}\}$*:*

1. $\Psi(\Psi(\alpha)) \simeq \alpha$
2. $\alpha \preccurlyeq \beta \Longleftrightarrow \Psi(\beta) \preccurlyeq \Psi(\alpha)$

Lemma 3. *The function* $\Xi(\cdot)$ *is a bijection that maintains the ordering of atoms between the redundancy and synergy order. Let* $\alpha, \beta \in \mathcal{A}(\mathbf{V})$*:*

1. $\alpha = \Xi(\Xi(\alpha))$
2. $\alpha \preccurlyeq \beta \Longleftrightarrow \Xi(\alpha) \preceq \Xi(\beta)$

The proofs of Lemmas 2 and 3 are given separately in Appendix D.

Corollary 1. *Without bottom elements, the redundancy* $(\mathcal{A}(\mathbf{V}) \setminus \{\bot_{RL}\}, \preccurlyeq)$ *and synergy lattice* $(\mathcal{A}(\mathbf{V}) \setminus \{\bot_{SL}\}, \preceq)$ *are related, as shown below with* $\alpha, \beta \in \mathcal{A}(\mathbf{V}) \setminus \{\bot_{RL}\}$*:*

$$\alpha \preccurlyeq \beta \Longleftrightarrow \Xi(\Psi(\beta)) \preceq \Xi(\Psi(\alpha)) \tag{37a}$$
$$\Xi(\Psi(\alpha \curlywedge \beta)) \cong \Xi(\Psi(\alpha)) \vee \Xi(\Psi(\beta)) \tag{37b}$$
$$\Xi(\Psi(\alpha \curlyvee \beta)) \cong \Xi(\Psi(\alpha)) \wedge \Xi(\Psi(\beta)) \tag{37c}$$
$$\{\Xi(\Psi(\beta)) \ : \ \beta \in \downarrow_R \alpha\} \ \{\cong\} \ \uparrow_S \Xi(\Psi(\alpha)) \tag{37d}$$
$$\{\Xi(\Psi(\beta)) \ : \ \beta \in \uparrow_R \alpha\} \ \{\cong\} \ \downarrow_S \Xi(\Psi(\alpha)) \tag{37e}$$

Proof. Follows directly from Lemma 2 and 3. □

Figure 7 visualizes the relations from the introduced operators to provide an intuition. Applying the function Ψ to all atoms is equal to reversing the redundancy order, while applying the function Ξ to all atoms is equal to swapping the ordering relation used (synergy/redundancy order).

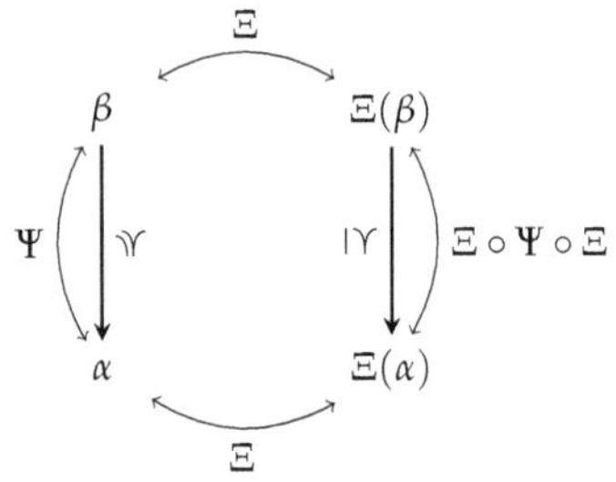

Figure 7. Visualization of the functions Ψ and Ξ: The application of function Ψ is equal to reversing the redundancy order, and the application of function Ξ is equal to swapping the ordering relation used between the redundancy and synergy lattice.

With these definitions in place, we can refine the definition of decomposition duality:

Lemma 4 (Decomposition duality). *A redundancy- and synergy-based information decomposition is pointwise dual if, for all $\alpha \in \mathcal{A}(\mathbf{V}) \setminus \{\bot_{RL}\}$:*

$$\begin{aligned} \Delta i_{\cap,f}(\alpha, T, t) &= \Delta i_{\cup,f}(\Xi(\Psi(\alpha)), T, t) \\ \Delta i_{\cap,f}(\bot_{RL}, T, t) &= 0 = \Delta i_{\cup,f}(\bot_{SL}, T, t) \end{aligned} \tag{38}$$

A redundancy- and synergy-based information decomposition is dual if, for all $\alpha \in \mathcal{A}(\mathbf{V}) \setminus \{\bot_{RL}\}$:

$$\begin{aligned} \Delta I_{\cap,f}(\alpha; T) &= \Delta I_{\cup,f}(\Xi(\Psi(\alpha)); T) \\ \Delta I_{\cap,f}(\bot_{RL}; T) &= 0 = \Delta I_{\cup,f}(\bot_{SL}; T) \end{aligned} \tag{39}$$

The proof of Lemma 4 is shown separately in Appendix D. To convert a decomposition from the synergy lattice into its dual-decomposition on to the redundancy lattice, the following relation is particularly useful. It states that, on the synergy lattice, all atoms are either in the up-set of $\Xi(\Psi(\alpha))$ or in the down-set of an atom that corresponds to an individual source within α.

Lemma 5. *For $\alpha \in \mathcal{A}(\mathbf{V}) \setminus \{\bot_{RL}\}$:*

$$\mathcal{A}(\mathbf{V}) \setminus \uparrow_S \Xi(\Psi(\alpha)) = \bigcup_{\mathbf{S}_a \in \alpha} \downarrow_S \{\mathbf{S}_a\} \tag{40}$$

Proof. When expanding the definition of up- and down-sets, it can directly be seen from Lemma A9 that both sets provide an exclusive partitioning of all atoms.

$$\begin{aligned} \uparrow_S \Xi(\Psi(\alpha)) &= \{\beta \in \mathcal{A}(\mathbf{V}) \ : \ (\Xi(\Psi(\alpha)) \preceq \beta)\} \\ \bigcup_{\mathbf{S}_a \in \alpha} \downarrow_S \{\mathbf{S}_a\} &= \{\beta \in \mathcal{A}(\mathbf{V}) \ : \ (\exists \mathbf{S}_a \in \alpha . \, \beta \preceq \{\mathbf{S}_a\})\} \\ (\Xi(\Psi(\alpha)) \preceq \beta) &\iff \neg(\exists \mathbf{S}_a \in \alpha . \, \beta \preceq \{\mathbf{S}_a\}) \qquad \text{(by Lemma A9)} \end{aligned} \tag{41}$$

□

Figure 8 summarizes and visualizes the required relations for the following transformation of the cumulative measure: (i) The bottom elements of all lattices are mapped to each other and quantified to zero. (ii) The function Ψ reverses the redundancy lattice ($\beta \simeq \Psi(\alpha)$ such that $\alpha \simeq \Psi(\beta)$) to relate the down-set of α to the up-set of β while ignoring the bottom element. The function Ξ captures the relation between both orderings ($\alpha' \cong \Xi(\beta)$ such that $\beta \simeq \Xi(\alpha')$), to relate the up-set of β on the redundancy lattice to the up-set of α' on the synergy lattice. This provides the desired mapping from the down-set of α on the redundancy lattice to the up-set of α' on the synergy lattice for duality. Alternatively, we could first transform the down-set of α on the redundancy to the down-set of $\beta' = \Xi(\alpha)$ on the synergy lattice, then reverse the synergy order and obtain the same result. (iii) Lemma 5 states that all atoms on the synergy lattice are either in the up-set of $\Xi(\Psi(\alpha))$ or in the down-set of $\{\mathbf{S}_a\}$ with $\mathbf{S}_a \in \alpha$. The example $\alpha = \{\mathbf{S}_3, \mathbf{S}_{12}\}$ is visualized in Figure 8, and we encourage the reader to view another example such as $\alpha = \{\mathbf{S}_{13}\} \xrightarrow{\Psi} \{\mathbf{S}_1, \mathbf{S}_3\} \xrightarrow{\Xi} \{\mathbf{S}_{12}, \mathbf{S}_{23}\}$.

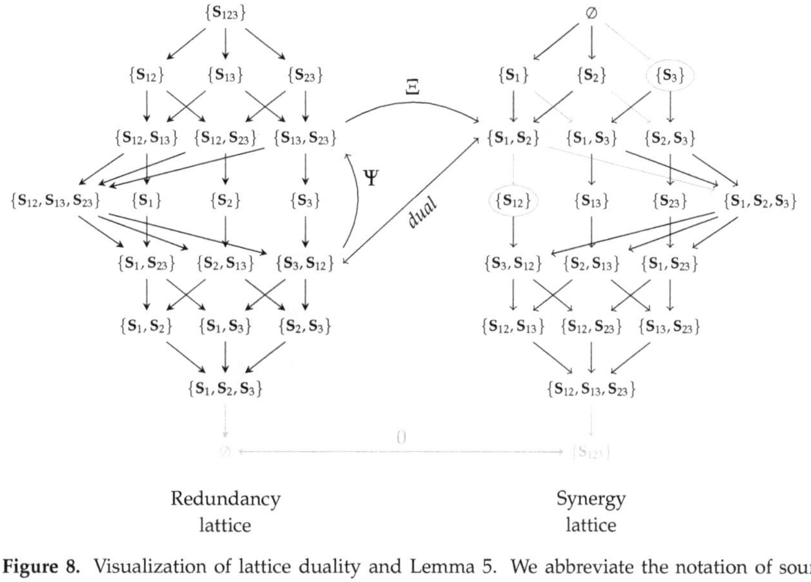

Figure 8. Visualization of lattice duality and Lemma 5. We abbreviate the notation of sources within this figure by listing the contained visible variables as source index ($\mathbf{S}_{12} = \{V_1, V_2\}$). (i) All bottom elements are mapped to each other and quantified to zero. (ii) To identify the dual for $\alpha = \{\mathbf{S}_3, \mathbf{S}_{12}\}$ from the redundancy lattice, we first apply the transformation $\Psi(\alpha) \simeq \{\mathbf{S}_{13}, \mathbf{S}_{23}\}$ and, then, $\Xi(\Psi(\alpha)) \cong \{\mathbf{S}_1, \mathbf{S}_2\}$. (iii) Ignoring the bottom elements, the down-set of α on the redundancy lattice corresponds to the up-set of $\Xi(\Psi(\alpha))$ on the synergy lattice for duality (gray areas). (iv) Lemma 5 states that, on the synergy lattice, exactly those atoms that are not in the up-set of $\Xi(\Psi(\{\mathbf{S}_3, \mathbf{S}_{12}\}))$ must be in the down-set of either $\{\mathbf{S}_3\}$ or $\{\mathbf{S}_{12}\}$.

With these relations in place, we can construct dual-decompositions and prove their correctness.

Lemma 6. *The pointwise dual-decomposition for the redundancy lattice of a loss measure on the synergy lattice is defined by:*

$$i_{\cap,f}(\alpha, T, t) := \begin{cases} 0 & \text{if } \alpha = \emptyset \\ i_{\cup,f}(\top_{SL}, T, t) - \sum_{\beta \in \mathcal{P}_1(\alpha)} (-1)^{|\beta|-1} i_{\cup,f}(\beta, T, t) & \text{otherwise} \end{cases} \tag{42}$$

The proof of Lemma 6 is shown separately in Appendix D. This section discussed the relation between four decomposition lattices, which are the redundancy and synergy lattice, as well as their reversed counterparts. Additionally, we demonstrated how this relation can be used to transform a cumulative decomposition measure between them. Decomposition duality enforces each lattice to be consistent with its set-theoretic interpretation. The function Ψ corresponds to taking the set-theoretic complement on the redundancy lattice and, thus, reflects on the cumulative measure by subtracting it from the top atom. The function Ξ corresponds to the relation between the union and intersection and, thus, introduces an inclusion–exclusion principle between their cumulative measures.

3.5. Decomposing f-Information on the Redundancy Lattice

Using the results from Section 3.4, we can now convert the decomposition of Section 3.2 to the redundancy lattice. The conversion can be applied to both the expected or pointwise measure. The partial contributions ($\Delta i_{\sqcap,f}$ and $\Delta I_{\sqcap,f}$) are obtained from the Möbius inverse.

Lemma 7 (Dual-decomposition on the redundancy lattice)**.** *The definitions of Equation (43) correspond to the dual-decomposition of Definition 26.*

$$i_{\sqcap,f}(\alpha,T,t) = \begin{cases} 0 & \text{if } \alpha = \emptyset \\ \sum_{\beta\in\mathcal{P}_1(\alpha)}(-1)^{|\beta|-1} i_f(P_T(t),\kappa_{\sqcup}(\beta,T,t)) & \text{otherwise} \end{cases} \tag{43a}$$

$$I_{\sqcap,f}(\alpha;T) = \sum_{t\in\mathcal{T}} P_T(t)\cdot i_{\sqcap,f}(\alpha,T,t) = I_f(\mathbf{V};T) - \sum_{\beta\in\mathcal{P}_1(\alpha)} (-1)^{|\beta|-1} I_{\sqcup,f}(\beta;T) \tag{43b}$$

Proof. The duality of the pointwise measure is obtained from Lemma 6 and Definition 26. The duality of the pointwise measure implies the duality of the combined measure. □

The function $i_f(P_T(t),\kappa_{\sqcup}(\alpha,T,t))$ quantifies the convex hull/blackwell join of the Neyman–Pearson regions of its sources and represents a notion of pointwise union information about the target state $t\in\mathcal{T}$. It is used in Equation (33a) to define a pointwise loss measure for the synergy lattice by subtracting it from the total information. As expected, we can see that the corresponding dual-decomposition on the redundancy lattice enforces an inclusion–exclusion relation between our notions of pointwise union information ($i_f(P_T(t),\kappa_{\sqcup}(\alpha,T,t))$) and pointwise intersection information ($i_{\sqcap,f}(\alpha,T,t)$).

Theorem 4. *The dual-decomposition as defined by Equation (43) provides a non-negative PID, which satisfies an inclusion–exclusion relation and the axioms of Williams and Beer [1] on the redundancy lattice for any f-information.*

Proof.

- **Axiom 1**: The measure $i_{\sqcap,f}$ is invariant to permuting the order of sources in α, since the join operator of the zonogon order ($\bigsqcup_{\mathbf{S}\in\alpha}$) is. Therefore, also, $I_{\sqcap,f}$ satisfies Axiom 1.
- **Non-negativity**: The non-negativity of $\Delta i_{\sqcap,f}$ is obtained from Lemma 7 and Theorem 3 as shown in Equation (44). The non-negativity of the pointwise measure implies the non-negativity of the combined measure $\Delta I_{\sqcap,f}$.

$$\forall\alpha\in\mathcal{A}(\mathbf{V}).\qquad \Delta i_{\sqcap,f}(\alpha,T,t) = \begin{cases} 0 & \geq 0 \quad \text{if } \alpha = \bot_{\text{RL}} \\ \Delta i_{\sqcup,f}(\Xi(\Phi(\alpha)),T,t) & \geq 0 \quad \text{otherwise} \end{cases} \tag{44}$$

- **Axiom 2**: Since the cumulative measures $i_{\sqcap,f}$ and $I_{\sqcap,f}$ correspond to the sum of partial contributions in their down-set, the non-negativity of partial information implies the monotonicity of the cumulative measures.
- **Axiom 3***: For a single source, $I_{\sqcap,f}$ equals f-information by definition (see Equation (30)). Therefore, $I_{\sqcap,f}$ satisfies Axiom 3*.

□

The operational interpretation of Section 3.3 is maintained since the partial contributions are identical between both lattices.

Remark 8. *The definitions of Equations (34) and (43) satisfy the desired property of Bertschinger et al. [9], who argued that any sensible measure for unique and redundant information should only depend on the marginal distribution of sources.*

Remark 9. *As discussed before [20], it is possible to further split redundancy into two components for extracting the pointwise meet under the Blackwell order (zonogon intersection, first component). The second component of redundancy as defined above contains decision regions that are part of the convex hull, but not the individual channel zonogons (discussed as shared information in [20]). By combining Equation (43) and Lemma A7, we obtain that both components of this split for redundancy are non-negative.*

3.6. Decomposing Rényi-Information

Since Rényi-information is an invertible transformation of Hellinger-information and α-information, we argue that their decompositions should be consistent. We propose to view the decomposition of Rényi-information as a transformation from an f-information and demonstrate the approach by transferring the Hellinger-information decomposition to a Rényi-information decomposition. Then, we demonstrate that the result is invariant to a linear scaling of the considered f-information, such that the transformation from α-information provides identical results. The obtained Rényi-information decomposition is non-negative and satisfies the three axioms proposed by Williams and Beer [1] (see below). However, its inclusion–exclusion relation is based on a transformed addition operator. For transforming the decomposition, we consider Rényi-information to be a re-graduation of Hellinger-information, as shown in Equation (45).

$$v_a(z) := \frac{1}{a-1}\log(1+(a-1)z) \tag{45a}$$

$$I_{\mathrm{R}_a}(\mathbf{S};T) = v_a(I_{\mathrm{H}_a}(\mathbf{S};T)) \tag{45b}$$

To maintain consistency when transforming the measure, we also have to transform its operators ([19], p. 6 ff.):

Definition 29 (Addition of Rényi-information). *We define the addition of Rényi-information $\oplus_a$ with its corresponding inverse function $\ominus_a$ by Equation (46).*

$$x \oplus_a y := v_a(v_a^{-1}(x) + v_a^{-1}(y)) = \frac{\log\left(e^{(a-1)x} + e^{(a-1)y} - 1\right)}{a-1} \tag{46a}$$

$$x \ominus_a y := v_a(v_a^{-1}(x) - v_a^{-1}(y)) = \frac{\log\left(e^{(a-1)x} - e^{(a-1)y} + 1\right)}{a-1} \tag{46b}$$

To transform a decomposition of the synergy lattice, we define the cumulative loss measures as shown in Equation (47) and use the transformed operators when computing the Möbius inverse (Equation (48a)) to maintain consistency in the results (Equation (48b)).

Definition 30. *The cumulative and partial Rényi-information loss measures are defined as transformations of the cumulative and partial Hellinger-information loss measures, as shown in Equations (47) and (48).*

$$I_{\cup,R_a}(\alpha;T) := v_a(I_{\cup,H_a}(\alpha;T)) \tag{47}$$

$$\Delta I_{\cup,R_a}(\alpha;T) := I_{\cup,R_a}(\alpha;T) \ominus_a \sum_{\beta\in\downarrow_S\alpha} \Delta I_{\cup,R_a}(\beta;T) \qquad \textit{where: } + := \oplus_a \tag{48a}$$

$$= v_a(\Delta I_{\cup,H_a}(\alpha;T)) \tag{48b}$$

Remark 10. *We show in Lemma A11 of Appendix E that re-scaling the original f-information does not affect the resulting decomposition or transformed operators. Therefore, transforming a Hellinger-information decomposition or a α-information decomposition to a Rényi-information decomposition provides identical results.*

The operational interpretation presented in Section 3.2 is similarly applicable to partial Rényi-information ($\Delta I_{\cup,R_a}$, Equation (48b)), since the function v_a satisfies $v_a(0) = 0$ and $x \leq 0 \Longrightarrow 0 \leq v_a(x)$.

Theorem 5. *The presented definitions for the cumulative loss measure $I_{\cup,R_a}$ provide a non-negative PID on the synergy lattice with an inclusion–exclusion relation under the transformed addition (Definition 29) that satisfies Axioms 1, 2, and 3* for any Rényi-information measure.*

Proof.

- **Axiom 1**: $I_{\cup,R_a}(\alpha;T)$ is invariant to permuting the order of sources, since $I_{\cup,H_a}(\mathbf{S};T)$ satisfies Axiom 1 (see Section 3.2).
- **Axiom 2**: $I_{\cup,R_a}(\alpha;T)$ satisfies monotonicity, since $I_{\cup,H_a}(\mathbf{S};T)$ satisfies Axiom 2 (see Section 3.2) and the transformation function v_a is monotonically increasing for $a \in (0,1) \cup (1,\infty)$.
- **Axiom 3***: Since $I_{\cup,H_a}$ satisfies Axiom 3* (see Section 3.2, Equations (45) and (47)), $I_{\cup,R_a}$ satisfies the self-redundancy axiom by definition, however, at a transformed operator: $I_{\cup,R_a}(\{\mathbf{S}_i\};T) = I_{R_a}(\{\mathbf{V}\};T) \ominus_a I_{R_a}(\{\mathbf{S}_i\};T)$.
- **Non-negativity**: The decomposition of $I_{\cup,R_a}$ is non-negative, since $\Delta I_{\cup,H_a}$ is non-negative (see Section 3.2), the Möbius inverse is computed with transformed operators (Equation (48b)) and the function v_a satisfies $x \leq 0 \Longrightarrow 0 \leq v_a(x)$.

□

Remark 11. *To obtain an equivalent decomposition of Rényi-information on the redundancy lattice, we can correspondingly transform the dual-decomposition from the redundancy lattice of Hellinger-information as shown in Equation (49). The resulting decomposition will satisfy the non-negativity, the axioms of Williams and Beer [1], and an inclusion–exclusion relation under the transformed operators (Definition 29) for the same reasons described above from Theorem 4.*

$$I_{\cap,R_a}(\alpha;T) := v_a(I_{\cap,H_a}(\alpha;T)) \tag{49a}$$

$$\Delta I_{\cap,R_a}(\alpha;T) := v_a(\Delta I_{\cap,H_a}(\alpha;T)) \tag{49b}$$

Remark 12. *The relation between the redundancy and synergy lattice can be used for the definition of a bi-valuation [19] in calculations as discussed in [20]. This is also possible for Rényi-information at transformed operators.*

When taking the limit of Rényi-information for $a \to 1$, we obtain mutual information (I_{KL}). Since mutual information is also an f-information, we expect its operators in the Möbius inverse to be addition. This is indeed the case (Equation (50)), and the measures will be consistent.

$$\begin{aligned} \lim_{a\to 1} x \oplus_a y &= x + y \\ \lim_{a\to 1} x \ominus_a y &= x - y \end{aligned} \tag{50}$$

Finally, the decomposition of Bhattacharyya-information can be obtained by re-scaling the decomposition of Rényi-information at $a = 0.5$, which causes another transform of the addition operator for the inclusion–exclusion relation.

4. Evaluation

A comparison of the proposed decomposition with other methods of the literature can be found in [20] for mutual information. Therefore, this section first compares different f-information measures for typical decomposition examples and discusses the special case of total variation (TV)-information to explain its distinct behavior. Since we can see larger differences between measures in more complex scenarios, we compare the measures by analyzing the information flows in a Markov chain. We provide the implementation used for both dual-decompositions of f-information and the examples used in this work in [30].

4.1. Partial Information Decomposition

4.1.1. Comparison of Different f-Information Measures

We use the examples discussed by Finn and Lizier [13] to compare different f-information decompositions and add a generic example from [20]. All probability distributions used and their abbreviations can be found in Appendix F. We normalize the decomposition results to the f-entropy of the target variable for the visualization in Figure 9.

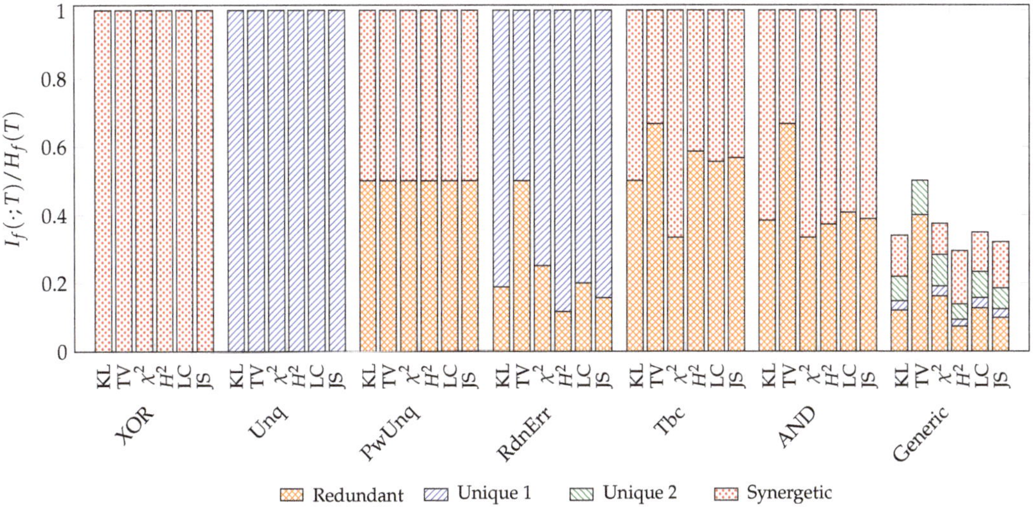

Figure 9. Comparison of different f-information measures normalized to the f-entropy of the target variable. All distributions are shown in Appendix F and correspond to the examples of [13,20]. The example name abbreviations are listed below in Table A1. The measures behave mostly similarly since the decompositions follow an identical structure. However, it can be seen that total variation attributes more information to being redundant than other measures and appears to behave differently in the generic example since it does not attribute any partial information to the first variable or their synergy.

Since all results are based on the same framework, they behave similarly for examples that analyze a specific aspect of the decomposition function (XOR, Unq, PwUnq, RdnErr, Tbc, AND). However, it can be observed that the decomposition of total variation (TV) appears to differ from others: (1) In all examples, total variation attributes more information to being redundant than other measures. (2) In the generic example, total variation is the only measure that does not attribute any information to being unique to variable one or synergetic. We discuss the case of total variation in Section 4.1.2 to explain its distinct behavior.

We visualize the zonogons for the generic example in Figure A2, which shall highlight that the implication of the operational interpretation does not hold in the other direction: the existence of partial information implies an advantage for the expected reward towards some state of the target variable, but an advantage for the expected reward towards some state of the target variable does not imply partial information in the example of total variation.

4.1.2. The Special Case of Total Variation

The behavior of total variation appears different compared to other f-information measures (Figure 9). This is due to total variation measuring the perimeter of a zonogon such that the result corresponds to a linear scaling of the maximal (Euclidean) height h^* that the zonogon reaches above the diagonal, as visualized in Figure 10.

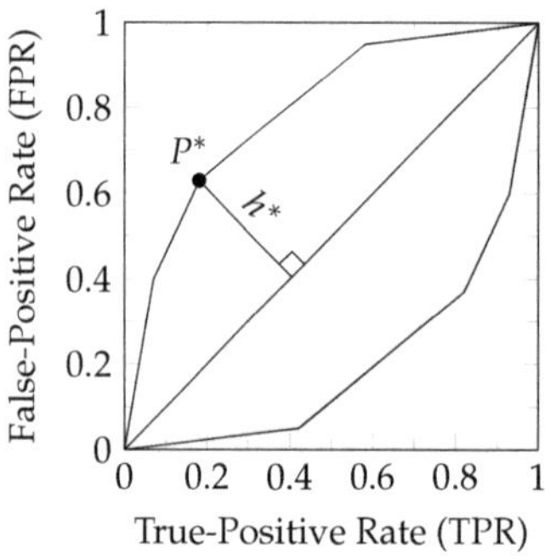

Figure 10. Visualization of the maximal (Euclidean) height h^* at point P^* that a zonogon (blue) reaches above the diagonal.

Remark 13. *From a cost perspective, the height h^* can be interpreted as the performance evaluation of the optimal decision strategy (symmetric point to P^* in the lower zonogon half) for a prediction $\hat{T}$ with minimal expected cost at the cost ratio* $\frac{\text{Cost}(T=t,\hat{T}\neq t)-\text{Cost}(T=t,\hat{T}=t)}{\text{Cost}(T\neq t,\hat{T}=t)-\text{Cost}(T\neq t,\hat{T}\neq t)} = \frac{1-P_T(t)}{P_T(t)}$ *(see Equation (8) of [31]) for each target state individually.*

Lemma 8.

(a) *The pointwise total variation (i_{TV}) is a linear scaling of the maximal (Euclidean) height h^* that the corresponding zonogon reaches above the diagonal, as visualized in Figure 10 (Equation (51a)).*

(b) *For a non-empty set of pointwise channels $\mathbf{A}$, pointwise total variation i_{TV} quantifies the join element to the maximum of its individual channels (Equation (51b)).*

(c) *The loss measure $i_{\cup,TV}$ quantifies the meet for a set of sources on the synergy lattice to their minimum (Equation (51c)).*

$$i_{TV}(p,\kappa) = \frac{1-p}{2}\sum_{v\in\kappa}|v_x - v_y| = (1-p)\frac{h^*}{\sqrt{2}} \tag{51a}$$

$$i_{TV}(p, \bigsqcup_{\kappa\in\mathbf{A}} \kappa) = \max_{\kappa\in\mathbf{A}} i_{TV}(p,\kappa) \tag{51b}$$

$$i_{\cup,TV}(\bigwedge_{\alpha\in\mathbf{A}} \alpha, T, t) = \min_{\alpha\in\mathbf{A}} i_{\cup,TV}(\alpha, T, t) \tag{51c}$$

Proof. The proof of the first two statements (Equations (51a) and (51b)) is provided separately in Appendix G, which imply the third (Equation (51c)) by Definition 26. □

Quantifying the meet element on the synergy lattice to the minimum has the following consequences for total variation: (1) It attributes a minimum amount of synergy, and therefore more information to redundancy than other measures. (2) For each state of the target, at most one variable can provide unique information. In the case of $|\mathcal{T}| = 2$, the pointwise channels are symmetric (see Equation (6)), such that the same variable provides the maximal zonogon height both times. This is the case in the generic example of Figure 9, and the reason why at most one variable can provide unique information in this setting. However, beyond binary targets ($|\mathcal{T}| > 2$), both variables may provide unique information at the same time since different sources can provide the maximal zonogon height for different target states (see the later example in Figure 11).

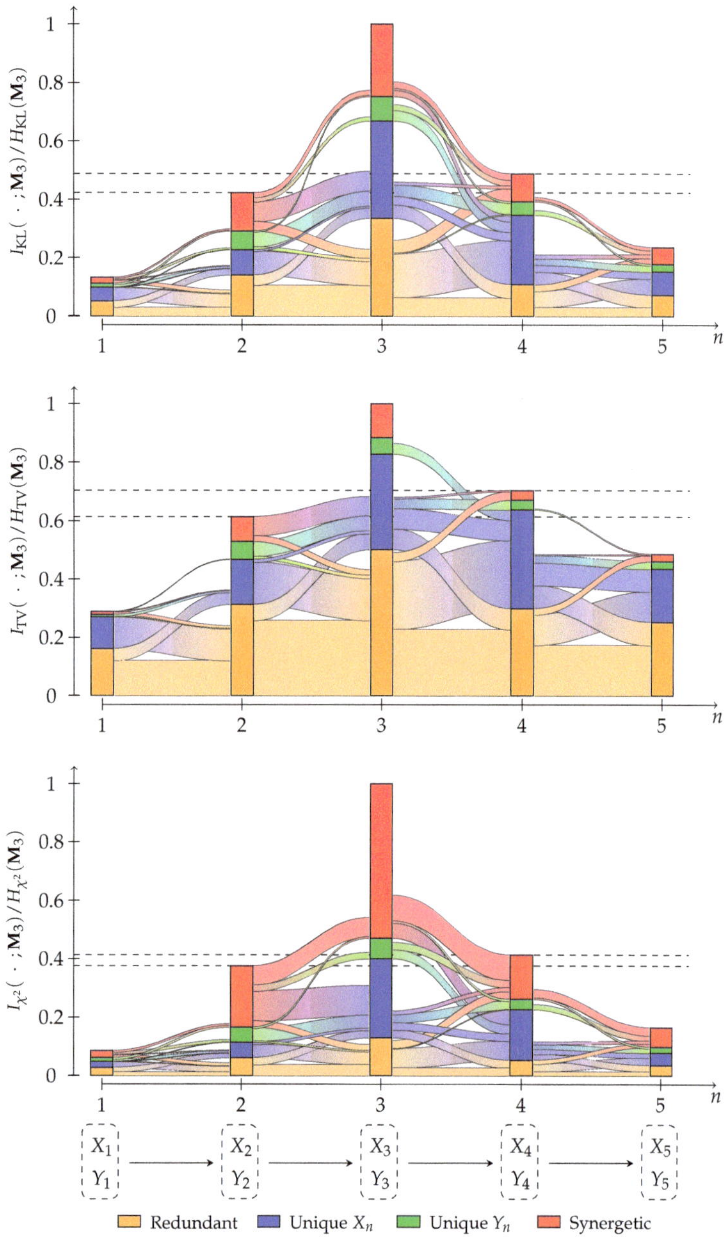

Figure 11. Analysis of the Markov chain information flow (Equation (A47)). Visualized results for the information measures: KL, TV, and χ^2. The remaining results (H^2-, LC-, and JS-information) can be found in Figure A3.

Remark 14. *Using the pointwise minimum on the synergy lattice results in a similar structure to the proposed measure of Williams and Beer [1]. However, TV-information is based on a different pointwise measure i_{TV}, which displays the same behavior (Equation (51b)), unlike pointwise KL-information.*

4.2. Information Flow Analysis

The differences between f-information measures in Section 4.1 appear more visible in complex scenarios. Therefore, this section compares different measures in the information flow analysis of a Markov chain.

Consider a Markov chain $\mathbf{M}_1 \to \mathbf{M}_2 \to \cdots \to \mathbf{M}_5$, where $\mathbf{M}_i = (X_i, Y_i)$ is the joint distribution of two variables. Assume that we are interested in state three, and thus, define $T = \mathbf{M}_3$ as the target variable. Using the approach described in Section 3, we can compute an information decomposition for each state $\mathbf{M}_i$ of the Markov chain with respect to the target. Now, we are additionally interested in how the partial information decomposition from stage $\mathbf{M}_i$ propagates into the next $\mathbf{M}_{i+1}$, as visualized in Figure 11.

Definition 31 (Partial information flow). *The partial information flow of an atom $\alpha \in \mathcal{A}(\mathbf{M}_i)$ into the atom $\beta \in \mathcal{A}(\mathbf{M}_{i+1})$ quantifies the redundancy between the partial contributions of their respective decomposition lattices.*

Notation 8. *We use the notation $I_{\circ,f}$ with $\circ \in \{\cup, \cap\}$ to refer to either the loss measure $I_{\cup,f}$ or redundancy measure $I_{\cap,f}$. The same applies to the functions $J_{\circ\to\circ,f}$ and $J_{\Delta\to\circ,f}$ of Equation (52).*

Let $\alpha \in \mathcal{A}(\mathbf{M}_i)$ and $\beta \in \mathcal{A}(\mathbf{M}_{i+1})$, then we compute information flows equivalently on the redundancy or synergy lattice as shown in Equation (52). When using a redundancy measure $\circ = \cap$, then the strict down-set of $\downarrow_\circ \alpha$ refers to the strict down-set on its redundancy lattice $(\mathcal{A}(\mathbf{M}_i), \preccurlyeq)$, and when using a loss measure $\circ = \cup$, then the strict down-set $\downarrow_\circ \alpha$ refers to the strict down-set on its synergy lattice $(\mathcal{A}(\mathbf{M}_i), \preceq)$. We obtain the intersection of cumulative measures by quantifying their meet, which is on both lattice equivalent to their union of sources ($J_{\circ\to\circ,f}$, Equation (52a)). To obtain how much of the partial contribution of α can be found in the cumulative measure of β ($J_{\Delta\to\circ,f}$), we remove the contributions of its down-set ($\downarrow_\circ \alpha$ on the lattice for $\mathcal{A}(\mathbf{M}_i)$, see Equation (52b)). To finally obtain the flow from the partial contribution of α to the partial contribution of β ($J_{\Delta\to\Delta,f}$), we similarly remove the contributions of the down-set of β ($\downarrow_\circ \beta$ on the lattice for $\mathcal{A}(\mathbf{M}_{i+1})$, see Equation (52c)). The approach can be extended for tracing information flows over multiple steps; however, we will only trace one step in this example.

$$J_{\circ\to\circ,f}(\alpha, \beta, T) := I_{\circ,f}(\alpha \cup \beta; T) \tag{52a}$$

$$J_{\Delta\to\circ,f}(\alpha, \beta, T) := J_{\circ\to\circ,f}(\alpha, \beta, T) - \sum_{\gamma \in \downarrow_\circ \alpha} J_{\Delta\to\circ,f}(\gamma, \beta, T) \tag{52b}$$

$$J_{\Delta\to\Delta,f}(\alpha, \beta, T) := J_{\Delta\to\circ,f}(\alpha, \beta, T) - \sum_{\gamma \in \downarrow_\circ \beta} J_{\Delta\to\Delta,f}(\alpha, \gamma, T) \tag{52c}$$

Remark 15. *The resulting partial information flows are equivalent (dual) between the redundancy and loss measure, except for the bottom element since their functionality differs: The flow from or to the bottom element on the redundancy lattice is always zero. In contrast, the flow from or to the bottom element on the synergy lattice quantifies the information gained or lost in the step.*

Remark 16. *The information flow analysis of Rényi- and Bhattacharyya-information can be obtained as a transformation of the information flow from Hellinger-information. Alternatively, the information flow can be computed directly using Equation (52) under the corresponding definition of addition and subtraction for the information measure used.*

We randomly generate an initial distribution and each row of a transition matrix under the constraint that at least one value shall be above 0.8 to avoid an information decay that is too rapid through the chain. The specific parameters of the example are shown in Appendix H. The event spaces used are $\mathcal{X} = \{0, 1, 2\}$ and $\mathcal{Y} = \{0, 1\}$ such that $|\mathcal{M}_i| = 6$. We construct a Markov chain of five steps with the target $T = \mathbf{M}_3$ and trace each partial information for one step using Equation (52). We visualized the results for KL-, TV-, and

χ^2-information in Figure 11, and the results for H^2-, LC-, and JS-information in Figure A3 of Appendix H.

All results display the expected behavior that the information that $\mathbf{M}_i$ provides about $\mathbf{M}_3$ increases for $1 \leq i \leq 3$ and decreases for $3 \leq i \leq 5$. The information flow results of KL-, H^2-, LC-, and JS-information are conceptually similar. Their main differences appear in the rate at which the information decays and, therefore, how much of the total information we can trace. In contrast, the results of TV- and χ^2-information display different behavior, as shown in Figure 11: TV-information indicates significantly more redundancy, and χ^2-information displays significantly more synergy than the other measures. Additionally, the decomposition of TV-information contains fever information flows. For example, it is the only analysis that does not show any information flow from $\mathbf{M}_2$ into the unique contribution of Y_3 or from $\mathbf{M}_2$ into the synergy of (X_3, Y_3). This demonstrates that the same decomposition method can obtain different behaviors from different f-divergences.

5. Discussion

Using the Blackwell order to construct pointwise lattices and to decompose pointwise information is motivated from the following three aspects:

- All information measures in Section 2.3 are the expected value of the pointwise information (quantification of the Neyman–Pearson region boundary) for an indicator variable of each target state. Therefore, we argue for acknowledging the "pointwise nature" [13] of these information measures and to decompose them accordingly. A similar argument was made previously by Finn and Lizier [13] for the case of mutual information and motivated their proposed pointwise partial information decomposition.
- The Blackwell order does not form a lattice beyond indicator variables since it does not provide a unique meet or join element for $|\mathcal{T}| > 2$ [17]. However, from a pointwise perspective, the informativity (Definition 2) provides a unique representation of union information. This enables separating the definition of redundant, unique, and synergetic information from a specific information measure, which then only serves for its quantification. We interpret these observations as an indication that the Blackwell order should be used to decompose pointwise information based on indicator variables rather than decomposing the expected information based on the full target distribution.
- We can consider where the alternative approach would lead, if we decomposed the expected information from the full target distribution using the Blackwell order: the decomposition would become identical to the method of Bertschinger et al. [9] and Griffith and Koch [10]. For bivariate examples ($|\mathbf{V}| = 2$), this decomposition [9,10] is non-negative and satisfies an additional property (*identity*, proposed by Harder et al. [5]). However, the identity property is inconsistent [32] with the axioms of Williams and Beer [1] and non-negativity for $|\mathbf{V}| > 2$. This causes negative partial information when extending the approach to $|\mathbf{V}| > 2$. The identity property also contradicts the conclusion of Finn and Lizier [13] from studying Kelly Gambling that, "information should be regarded as redundant information, regardless of the independence of the information sources" ([13], p. 26). It also contradicts our interpretation of distinct information through distinct decision regions when predicting an indicator variable for some target state. We do *not* argue that this interpretation should be applicable to the concept of information in general, but acknowledge that this behavior seems present in the information measures studied in this work and construct their decomposition accordingly.

Our critique for the decomposition measure of Williams and Beer [1] focuses on the implication that a less informative variable (Definition 2) about $t \in \mathcal{T}$ provides less pointwise information ($I(S; T = t)$, Equation (15a)): $\kappa(\mathbf{S}_1, T, t) \sqsubseteq \kappa(\mathbf{S}_2, T, t) \implies I(\mathbf{S}_1; T = t) \leq I(\mathbf{S}_2; T = t)$. This implication does not hold in the other direction. Therefore, equal pointwise information does not imply equal informativity and, thus, does not mean being redundant.

We chose to define a notion of pointwise union information based on the join of the Blackwell order since it leads to a meaningful operational interpretation: the convex hull of the pointwise Neyman–Pearson regions is always a subset of their joint distribution. Moreover, it is possible to construct joint distributions for which each individual decision region outside the convex hull becomes inaccessible, even if there may not exist one unique joint distribution at which all synergetic regions are lost simultaneously. This volatility due to the dependence between variables appears suitable for a notion of synergy. Similarly, the resulting unique information appears suitable since it ensures that a variable with unique information must provide access to some additional decision region. Finally, the obtained unique and redundant information is sensible [9] since it only depends on the marginal distributions with the target. The operational interpretation can be strengthened further such that the implication between accessible regions and partial information holds in both directions by revising Lemmas A1 and A2 with a strictly convex generator function.

We perform the decomposition on a pointwise lattice using the Blackwell join since it is possible to represent f-information as the expected value of quantifying the Neyman–Pearson region boundary (zonogon perimeter) for indicator variables (pointwise channels). Since the pointwise measures satisfy a triangle inequality, we mentioned the oversimplified intuition of pointwise f-information as the *length* of the zonogon perimeter. Correspondingly, if we identified an information measure that behaved more like the *area* of the zonogon (which could also maintain their ordering), then we would need to decompose it on a pointwise lattice using the Blackwell meet to achieve non-negativity. We assume that most information measures behave more similar to quantifying the boundary length rather than its area, since the boundary segments can directly be obtained from the conditional probability distribution and do not require an actual construction from the likelihood-ratio test.

In the literature, PIDs have been defined based on different ordering relations [16], the Blackwell order being only one of them. We think that this diversity is desirable since each approach provides a different operational interpretation of redundancy and synergy. For this reason, we wonder if obtaining a non-negative decomposition with the inclusion–exclusion relation for other ordering relations was possible when transferring them to a pointwise perspective or from mutual information to other information measures.

Studying the relations between different information measures for the same decomposition method may provide further insights into their properties, as demonstrated by the example of total variation in Section 4.2. The ability to decompose different information measures is also a necessity to apply the method in a variety of areas, since each information measure can then provide the operational meaning within its respective domains. To ensure consistency between related information measures, we allowed the re-definition of information addition, as demonstrated in the example of Rényi-information in Section 3.6, which also opens new possibilities for satisfying the inclusion–exclusion relation.

There is currently no universally accepted definition of conditional Rényi information. Assuming that $I_{\mathrm{R}_a}(T;\mathbf{S}_i \mid \mathbf{S}_j)$ should capture the information that $\mathbf{S}_i$ provides about T when already knowing the information from $\mathbf{S}_j$, then one could propose that this quantity should correspond to the according partial information contributions (unique/synergetic) and, thus, the definition of Equation (53).

With this in mind, it is also possible to define, model, decompose, and trace *Transfer Entropy* [33], used in the analysis of complex systems, for each presented information measure with the methodology of Section 4.2.

$$I_{\mathrm{R}_a}(T;\mathbf{S}_i \mid \mathbf{S}_j) := I_{\mathrm{R}_a}(T;\mathbf{S}_i,\mathbf{S}_j) \ominus I_{\mathrm{R}_a}(T;\mathbf{S}_j) \tag{53}$$

Finally, studying the corresponding definitions for continuous random variables and identifying suitable information measures for specific applications would be interesting directions for future work.

6. Conclusions

In this work, we demonstrated a non-negative PID in the framework of Williams and Beer [1] for any f-information with practical operational interpretation and the conversion of measures between decomposition lattices. We demonstrated that the decomposition of f-information can be used to obtain a non-negative decomposition of Rényi-information, for which we re-defined the addition to demonstrate that its results satisfy an inclusion–exclusion relation. Finally, we demonstrated how the proposed decomposition method can be used for tracing the flow of information through Markov chains and how the decomposition obtains different properties depending on the chosen information measure.

Author Contributions: Conceptualization, Writing—original draft: T.M.; Analysis of non-negativity: T.M. and E.A.; Writing—review and editing: E.A. and C.R.; Supervision: C.R. All authors have read and agreed to the published version of the manuscript.

Funding: This research was funded by the Swedish Civil Contingencies Agency (grant number MSB 2018-12526) and the Swedish Research Council (grant number VR 2020-04430).

Conflicts of Interest: The authors declare no conflicts of interest. The funders had no role in the design of the study; in the collection, analyses, or interpretation of the data; in the writing of the manuscript; nor in the decision to publish the results.

Appendix A. Quantifying Zonogon Perimeters

Lemma A1. *If the function f is convex, then the function $r_f(p, \vec{v})$ as defined in Equation (28a) is convex in its second argument $\vec{v} \in [0,1]^2$ for a constant $p \in [0,1]$.*

Proof. We use the following definitions for abbreviating the notation. Let $0 \le t \le 1$ and $\vec{v}_i = \left[\begin{smallmatrix} x_i \\ y_i \end{smallmatrix}\right]$:

$$\begin{aligned} a_1 &:= x_1 p + y_1(1-p) \\ a_2 &:= x_2 p + y_2(1-p) \\ b_1 &:= \frac{ta_1}{ta_1 + (1-t)a_2} \\ b_2 &:= \frac{(1-t)a_2}{ta_1 + (1-t)a_2} \end{aligned}$$

The case of $a_i = 0$ is handled by the convention that $0 \cdot f\left(\frac{0}{0}\right) = 0$. Therefore, we can assume that $a_i \neq 0$ and use $0 \le b_1 \le 1$ with $b_2 = 1 - b_1$ to apply the definition of convexity on the function f:

$$\begin{aligned} r_f\left(p, \left[\begin{smallmatrix} tx_1+(1-t)x_2 \\ ty_1+(1-t)y_2 \end{smallmatrix}\right]\right) &= (ta_1 + (1-t)a_2) \cdot f\left(\frac{tx_1 + (1-t)x_2}{ta_1 + (1-t)a_2}\right) \\ &= (ta_1 + (1-t)a_2) \cdot f\left(b_1 \frac{x_1}{a_1} + b_2 \frac{x_2}{a_2}\right) \\ &\le (ta_1 + (1-t)a_2) \cdot \left(b_1 f\left(\frac{x_1}{a_1}\right) + b_2 f\left(\frac{x_2}{a_2}\right)\right) \quad \text{(by convexity of } f\text{)} \\ &= ta_1 \cdot f\left(\frac{x_1}{a_1}\right) + (1-t)a_2 \cdot f\left(\frac{x_2}{a_2}\right) \\ &= t \cdot r_f(p, \left[\begin{smallmatrix} x_1 \\ y_1 \end{smallmatrix}\right]) + (1-t) \cdot r_f(p, \left[\begin{smallmatrix} x_2 \\ y_2 \end{smallmatrix}\right]) \end{aligned}$$

□

Corollary A1. *For $\vec{v}_1, \vec{v}_2, (\vec{v}_1 + \vec{v}_2) \in [0,1]^2$ and a constant $p \in [0,1]$, the function $r_f(p, \vec{v})$ as defined in Equation (28a) satisfies a triangle inequality on its second argument: $r_f(p, \vec{v}_1 + \vec{v}_2) \le r_f(p, \vec{v}_1) + r_f(p, \vec{v}_2)$.*

Proof.

$$\begin{aligned} r_f(p, \ell\vec{v}_1 + (1-\ell)\vec{v}_2) &\leq \ell r_f(p, \vec{v}_1) + (1-\ell) r_f(p, \vec{v}_2) && \text{(be Lemma A1)} \\ r_f(p, 0.5(\vec{v}_1 + \vec{v}_2)) &\leq 0.5\Big(r_f(p, \vec{v}_1) + r_f(p, \vec{v}_2)\Big) && \text{(let } \ell = 0.5) \\ r_f(p, \vec{v}_1 + \vec{v}_2) &\leq r_f(p, \vec{v}_1) + r_f(p, \vec{v}_2) && \text{(by } r_f(p, \ell\vec{v}) = \ell r_f(p, \vec{v})) \end{aligned}$$

□

Lemma A2. *For a constant $p \in [0,1]$, the function i_f maintains the ordering relation from the Blackwell order on binary input channels: $\kappa_1 \sqsubseteq \kappa_2 \Longrightarrow i_f(p, \kappa_1) \leq i_f(p, \kappa_2)$.*

Proof. Let κ_1 be represented by a $2 \times n$ matrix and κ_2 by a $2 \times m$ matrix. By the definition of the Blackwell order ($\kappa_1 \sqsubseteq \kappa_2$, Equation (2)), there exists a stochastic matrix λ such that $\kappa_1 = \kappa_2 \cdot \lambda$. We use the notation $\kappa_2[:, i]$ to refer to the ith column of matrix κ_2 and indicate the element at row $i \in \{1..m\}$ and column $j \in \{1..n\}$ of λ by $\lambda[i, j]$. Since λ is a valid (row) stochastic matrix of dimension $m \times n$, its rows sum to one $\forall i \in \{1..m\}$. $\sum_{j=1}^{n} \lambda[i, j] = 1$.

$$\begin{aligned} i_f(p, \kappa_1) &= \sum_{j=1}^{n} r_f(p, \kappa_1[:, j]) && \text{(by Equation (28b))} \\ &= \sum_{j=1}^{n} r_f(p, \sum_{i=1}^{m} \kappa_2[:, i]\lambda[i, j]) && \text{(by Equation (2))} \\ &\leq \sum_{j=1}^{n} \sum_{i=1}^{m} r_f(p, \kappa_2[:, i]\lambda[i, j]) && \text{(by Corollary A1)} \\ &= \sum_{j=1}^{n} \sum_{i=1}^{m} \lambda[i, j] r_f(p, \kappa_2[:, i]) && \text{(by } r_f(p, \ell\vec{v}) = \ell r_f(p, \vec{v})) \\ &= \sum_{i=1}^{m} r_f(p, \kappa_2[:, i]) && \text{(by } \sum_{j=1}^{n} \lambda[i, j] = 1) \\ &= i_f(p, \kappa_2) && \text{(by Equation (28b))} \end{aligned}$$

□

Lemma A3. *Consider two non-empty sets of binary input channels with equal cardinality ($|\mathbf{A}| = |\mathbf{B}|$) and a constant $p \in [0,1]$. If the Minkowski sum for the zonogons of channels in $\mathbf{A}$ is a subset of the Minkowski sum for the zonogons of channels in $\mathbf{B}$, then the sum of pointwise information for the channels in $\mathbf{A}$ is less than the sum of pointwise information for the channels in $\mathbf{B}$ as shown in Equation (A1).*

$$\sum_{\kappa \in \mathbf{A}} Z(\kappa) \subseteq \sum_{\kappa \in \mathbf{B}} Z(\kappa) \Longrightarrow \sum_{\kappa \in \mathbf{A}} i_f(p, \kappa) \leq \sum_{\kappa \in \mathbf{B}} i_f(p, \kappa) \tag{A1}$$

Proof. Let $n = |\mathbf{A}| = |\mathbf{B}|$. We use the notation $\mathbf{A}[i]$ with $1 \leq i \leq n$ to indicate the channel κ_i within the set $\mathbf{A}$.

$$
\begin{aligned}
\sum_{i=1}^{n} Z(\mathbf{A}[i]) &\subseteq \sum_{i=1}^{n} Z(\mathbf{B}[i]) \\
Z([\mathbf{A}[1] \;\; \ldots \;\; \mathbf{A}[n]]) &\subseteq Z([\mathbf{B}[1] \;\; \ldots \;\; \mathbf{B}[n]]) && \text{(by Equation (4))} \\
Z\left(\frac{1}{n} \cdot [\mathbf{A}[1] \;\; \ldots \;\; \mathbf{A}[n]]\right) &\subseteq Z\left(\frac{1}{n} \cdot [\mathbf{B}[1] \;\; \ldots \;\; \mathbf{B}[n]]\right) && \text{(scale to sum } (1,1)) \\
i_f\left(p, \frac{1}{n} \cdot [\mathbf{A}[1] \;\; \ldots \;\; \mathbf{A}[n]]\right) &\leq i_f\left(p, \frac{1}{n} \cdot [\mathbf{B}[1] \;\; \ldots \;\; \mathbf{B}[n]]\right) && \text{(by Equation (5), Lemma A2)} \\
\sum_{i=1}^{n} i_f\left(p, \frac{1}{n}\mathbf{A}[i]\right) &\leq \sum_{i=1}^{n} i_f\left(p, \frac{1}{n}\mathbf{B}[i]\right) && \text{(by Equation (28b))} \\
\frac{1}{n}\sum_{i=1}^{n} i_f(p, \mathbf{A}[i]) &\leq \frac{1}{n}\sum_{i=1}^{n} i_f(p, \mathbf{B}[i]) && \text{(by } r_f(p, \ell\vec{v}) = \ell r_f(p, \vec{v})) \\
\sum_{\kappa \in \mathbf{A}} i_f(p, \kappa) &\leq \sum_{\kappa \in \mathbf{B}} i_f(p, \kappa)
\end{aligned}
$$

□

Appendix B. Inclusion-Exclusion Inequality of Zonogons

Let $\mathcal{P}(\mathbf{A})$ represent the power set of a non-empty set $\mathbf{A} \neq \emptyset$ and separate the subsets of even ($\mathcal{L}_e$) and odd ($\mathcal{L}_o$) cardinality as shown below. Additionally, let $\mathcal{L}_{\leq 1}$ represent all subsets with cardinality less than or equal to one and $\mathcal{L}_1$ all subsets of cardinality equal to one:

$$
\begin{aligned}
\mathcal{L}_{\leq 1} &:= \{\mathbf{B} \in \mathcal{P}(\mathbf{A}) \;:\; |\mathbf{B}| \leq 1\} \\
\mathcal{L}_1 &:= \{\mathbf{B} \in \mathcal{P}(\mathbf{A}) \;:\; |\mathbf{B}| = 1\} \\
\mathcal{L}_e &:= \{\mathbf{B} \in \mathcal{P}(\mathbf{A}) \;:\; |\mathbf{B}| \text{ even}\} \\
\mathcal{L}_o &:= \{\mathbf{B} \in \mathcal{P}(\mathbf{A}) \;:\; |\mathbf{B}| \text{ odd}\} \\
\mathcal{P}(\mathbf{A}) &= \mathcal{L}_e \cup \mathcal{L}_o \text{ and } \emptyset = \mathcal{L}_e \cap \mathcal{L}_o
\end{aligned} \tag{A2}
$$

The number of subsets with even cardinality is equal to the number of subsets with odd cardinality as shown in Equation (A3).

$$
|\mathcal{L}_e| = \sum_{i=0}^{\left\lfloor \frac{|\mathbf{A}|}{2} \right\rfloor} \binom{|\mathbf{A}|}{2i} = 2^{|\mathbf{A}|-1} = \sum_{i=0}^{\left\lfloor \frac{|\mathbf{A}|}{2} \right\rfloor} \binom{|\mathbf{A}|}{2i+1} = |\mathcal{L}_o| \tag{A3}
$$

Consider a function $g_e : \mathcal{L}_e \to \mathcal{L}_{\leq 1}$, which takes an even subset $\mathbf{E} \in \mathcal{L}_e$ and returns a subset of cardinality $|g_e(\mathbf{E})| = \min(|\mathbf{E}|, 1)$ according to Equation (A4).

$$
\forall \mathbf{E} \in \mathbf{S}_e \;:\; \begin{cases} g_e(\mathbf{E}) = \emptyset & \text{if } \mathbf{E} = \emptyset \\ g_e(\mathbf{E}) = \{e\} \quad \text{s.t. } e \in \mathbf{E} & \text{otherwise} \end{cases} \tag{A4}
$$

Lemma A4. *For any function $g_e \in \mathcal{G}_e$, there exists a function $G : (\mathcal{L}_e, \mathcal{G}_e) \to \mathcal{L}_o$ that satisfies the following two properties:*

(a) For any subset with even cardinality, the function $g_e(\cdot)$ returns a subset of function $G(\cdot)$:

$$
\forall g_e \in \mathcal{G}_e, \mathbf{E} \in \mathcal{L}_e \;:\; g_e(\mathbf{E}) \subseteq G(\mathbf{E}, g_e). \tag{A5}
$$

(b) The function $G(\cdot)$ that satisfies Equation (A5) has an inverse on its first argument $G^{-1} : (\mathcal{L}_o, \mathcal{G}_e) \to \mathcal{L}_e$.

$$
\forall g_e \in \mathcal{G}_e, \mathbf{E} \in \mathcal{L}_e, \exists G^{-1} :\; G^{-1}(G(\mathbf{E}, g_e), g_e) = \mathbf{E}. \tag{A6}
$$

Proof. We construct a function G for an arbitrary g_e and demonstrate that it satisfies both properties (Equations (A5) and A6) by induction on the cardinality of $\mathbf{A}$. We indicate the cardinality of $\mathbf{A}$ with $n = |\mathbf{A}|$ as subscripts $\mathbf{A}_n$, $\mathcal{L}_{e,n}$, $\mathcal{L}_{o,n}$, and G_n:

1. In the base case $\mathbf{A}_1 = \{a\}$, the sets of subsets are $\mathcal{L}_{e,1} = \{\emptyset\}$ and $\mathcal{L}_{o,1} = \{\{a\}\}$. We define the function $G_1(\emptyset, g_e) := \{a\}$ for any g_e to satisfy both required properties:
   (a) The constraints of Equation (A4) ensure that $g_e(\emptyset) = \emptyset$. Since the empty set is the only element in $\mathbf{S}_{e,1}$, the subset relation (requirement of Equation (A5)) is satisfied $g_e(\emptyset) = \emptyset \subseteq \{a\} = G_1(\emptyset, g_e)$.
   (b) The function $G_1 : (\mathcal{L}_{e,1}, \mathcal{G}_e) \to \mathcal{L}_{o,1}$ is a bijection from $\mathcal{L}_{e,1}$ to $\mathcal{L}_{o,1}$ and, therefore, has an inverse on its first argument $G_1^{-1} : (\mathcal{L}_{o,1}, \mathcal{G}_e) \to \mathcal{L}_{e,1}$ (requirement of Equation (A6)).
2. Assume there exists a function G_n that satisfies both required properties (Equations (A5) and (A6)) of sets of cardinality $1 \leq n = |\mathbf{A}_n|$.
3. For the induction step, we show the definition of a function G_{n+1} that satisfies both required properties. For sets $\mathbf{A}_{n+1} = \mathbf{A}_n \cup \{q\}$, the subsets of even and odd cardinality can be expanded as shown in Equation (A7).

$$\begin{aligned} \mathcal{L}_{e,n+1} &= \mathcal{L}_{e,n} \cup \{\mathbf{O} \cup \{q\} : \mathbf{O} \in \mathcal{L}_{o,n}\}, \\ \mathcal{L}_{o,n+1} &= \mathcal{L}_{o,n} \cup \{\mathbf{E} \cup \{q\} : \mathbf{E} \in \mathcal{L}_{e,n}\}. \end{aligned} \tag{A7}$$

We define G_{n+1} for $\mathbf{E} \in \mathcal{L}_{e,n}$ and $\mathbf{O} \in \mathcal{L}_{o,n}$ at any g_e as shown in Equation (A8) using the function G_n and its inverse G_n^{-1} from the induction hypothesis. The function G_{n+1} is defined for any subset in $\mathcal{L}_{e,n+1}$ as can be seen from Equation (A7).

$$\begin{aligned} G_{n+1}(\mathbf{E}, g_e) &:= \begin{cases} \mathbf{E} \cup \{q\} & \text{if } g_e(G_n(\mathbf{E}, g_e) \cup \{q\}) \neq \{q\} \\ G_n(\mathbf{E}, g_e) & \text{if } g_e(G_n(\mathbf{E}, g_e) \cup \{q\}) = \{q\} \end{cases} \\ G_{n+1}(\mathbf{O} \cup \{q\}, g_e) &:= \begin{cases} \mathbf{O} & \text{if } g_e(\mathbf{O} \cup \{q\}) \neq \{q\} \\ G_n^{-1}(\mathbf{O}, g_e) \cup \{q\} & \text{if } g_e(\mathbf{O} \cup \{q\}) = \{q\} \end{cases} \end{aligned} \tag{A8}$$

Figure A1 provides an intuition for the definition of G_{n+1}: the outcome of $g_e(\mathbf{O} \cup \{q\})$ determines if the function G_{n+1} maintains or breaks the mapping of G_n.

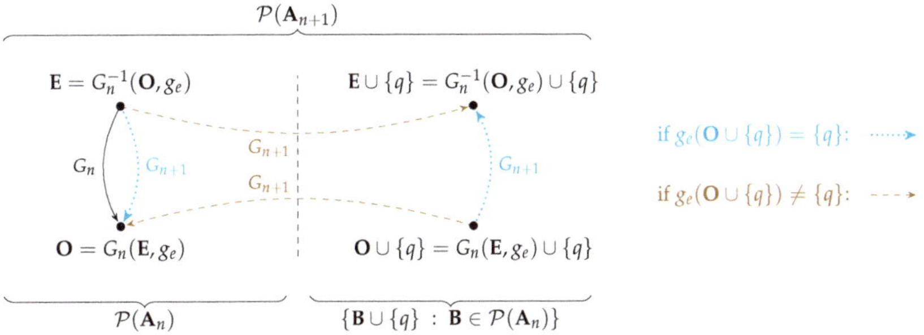

Figure A1. Intuition for the definition of Equation (A8). We can divide the set $\mathcal{P}(\mathbf{A}_{n+1})$ into $\mathcal{P}(\mathbf{A}_n)$ and $\{\mathbf{B} \cup \{q\} : \mathbf{B} \in \mathcal{P}(\mathbf{A}_n)\}$. The definition of function G_{n+1} mirrors G_n if $g_e(\mathbf{O} \cup \{q\}) = \{q\}$ (blue) and otherwise breaks its mapping (orange).

The function F as defined in Equation (A8) satisfies both requirements (Equations (A5) and (A6)) for any g_e:

(a) To demonstrate that the function satisfies the subset relation of Equation (A5), we analyze the four cases for the return value of G_{n+1} as defined in Equation (A8) individually:

- $g_e(\mathbf{E}) \subseteq \mathbf{E} \cup \{q\}$ holds, since the function g_e always returns a subset of its input (Equation (A4)).
- $g_e(\mathbf{E}) \subseteq G_n(\mathbf{E}, g_e)$ holds by the induction hypothesis.
- If $g_e(\mathbf{O} \cup \{q\}) \neq \{q\}$, then $g_e(\mathbf{O} \cup \{q\}) \subseteq \mathbf{O}$: Since the input to function g_e is not the empty set, the function $g_e(\mathbf{O} \cup \{q\})$ returns a singleton subset of its input (Equation (A4)). If the element in the singleton subset is unequal to q, then it is a subset of $\mathbf{O}$.
- If $g_e(\mathbf{O} \cup \{q\}) = \{q\}$, then $g_e(\mathbf{O} \cup \{q\}) \subseteq \{q\} \cup G_n^{-1}(\mathbf{O}, g_e)$ holds trivially.

(b) To demonstrate that the function G_{n+1} has an inverse (Equation (A6)), we show that the function G_{n+1} is a bijection from $\mathcal{L}_{e,n+1}$ to $\mathcal{L}_{o,n+1}$. Since the function G_{n+1} is defined for all elements in $\mathcal{L}_{e,n+1}$ and both sets have the same cardinality ($|\mathcal{L}_{e,n+1}| = |\mathcal{L}_{o,n+1}|$, Equation (A3)), it is sufficient to show that the function G_{n+1} is distinct for all inputs.
The return value of G_{n+1} has four cases, two of which return a set containing q (cases 1 and 4 in Equation (A8)), while the two others do not (cases 2 and 3 in Equation (A8)). Therefore, we have to show that both of these cases cannot coincide for any input:

- Cases 2 and 3 in Equation (A8): If the return value of both cases was equal, then $\mathbf{O} = G_n(\mathbf{E}, g_e)$, and therefore, $g_e(\mathbf{O} \cup \{q\}) = g_e(G_n(\mathbf{E}, g_e) \cup \{q\})$. This leads to a contradiction, since the condition of case 3 ensures $g_e(\mathbf{O} \cup \{q\}) \neq \{q\}$, while the condition of case 2 ensures $g_e(G_n(\mathbf{E}, g_e) \cup \{q\}) = \{q\}$. Hence, the return values of cases 2 and 3 are distinct.
- Cases 1 and 4 in Equation (A8): If the return value of both cases was equal, then $\mathbf{E} = G_n^{-1}(\mathbf{O}, g_e)$, and therefore, $g_e(\mathbf{O} \cup \{q\}) = g_e(G_n(\mathbf{E}, g_e) \cup \{q\})$. This leads to a contradiction, since the condition of case 4 ensures $g_e(\mathbf{O} \cup \{q\}) = \{q\}$, while the condition of case 1 ensures $g_e(G_n(\mathbf{E}, g_e) \cup \{q\}) \neq \{q\}$. Hence, the return values of cases 1 and 4 are distinct.

Since the function G_{n+1} is a bijection, there exists an inverse G_{n+1}^{-1}.

□

Lemma A5. *For a non-empty set of* $2 \times x$ *row stochastic matrices* $\mathbf{A} \neq \emptyset$*:*

$$Z\left(\bigsqcap_{\kappa \in \mathbf{A}} \kappa\right) + \sum_{\substack{\emptyset \neq \mathbf{B} \subseteq \mathbf{A} \\ |\mathbf{B}|\ even}} Z\left(\bigsqcup_{\lambda \in \mathbf{B}} \lambda\right) \subseteq \sum_{\substack{\mathbf{B} \subseteq \mathbf{A} \\ |\mathbf{B}|\ odd}} Z\left(\bigsqcup_{\nu \in \mathbf{B}} \nu\right) \tag{A9}$$

Proof. Consider a function $g_o : \mathcal{L}_o \to \mathcal{L}_1$, where $g_o(\mathbf{O}) \subseteq \mathbf{O}$ such that the function returns a singleton subset for a set of odd cardinality. Equation (A10) can be obtained from the constraints on g_e (Equation (A4)) and Lemma A4.

$$\forall g_e \in \mathcal{G}_e, \mathbf{E} \in \mathcal{L}_e, \exists g_o \in \mathcal{G}_o, G : \begin{cases} g_e(\emptyset) \subseteq g_o(G(\emptyset)) & \text{if } \mathbf{E} = \emptyset \\ g_e(\mathbf{E}) = g_o(G(\mathbf{E})) & \text{otherwise} \end{cases} \tag{A10}$$

Equation (A11a) holds since we can replace $g_e(\emptyset)$ with $g_o(G(\emptyset))$, meaning there exists a $\kappa \in \mathbf{A}$ for creating a (Minkowski) sum over the same set of channel zonogons on both sides of the quality. Equation (A11b) holds since Lemma A4 ensured that the existing function G is a bijection. Equation (A11c) holds since the intersection is a subset of each individual zonogon.

$$\forall g_e \in \mathcal{G}_e, \exists g_o \in \mathcal{G}_o, \kappa \in \mathbf{A}, G: \quad Z(\kappa) + \sum_{\mathbf{E} \in \mathcal{L}_e \setminus \emptyset} Z(g_e(\mathbf{E})) = \sum_{\mathbf{E} \in \mathcal{L}_e} Z(g_o(G(\mathbf{E}))) \tag{A11a}$$

$$\forall g_e \in \mathcal{G}_e, \exists g_o \in \mathcal{G}_o, \kappa \in \mathbf{A}: \quad Z(\kappa) + \sum_{\mathbf{E} \in \mathcal{L}_e \setminus \emptyset} Z(g_e(\mathbf{E})) = \sum_{\mathbf{O} \in \mathcal{L}_o} Z(g_o(\mathbf{O})) \tag{A11b}$$

$$\forall g_e \in \mathcal{G}_e, \exists g_o \in \mathcal{G}_o: \bigcap_{\kappa \in \mathbf{A}} Z(\kappa) + \sum_{\mathbf{E} \in \mathcal{L}_e \setminus \emptyset} Z(g_e(\mathbf{E})) \subseteq \sum_{\mathbf{O} \in \mathcal{L}_o} Z(g_o(\mathbf{O})) \tag{A11c}$$

Equation (A11c) is parameterized by g_e, and the subsets are closed under set union. Therefore, we can combine all choices for g_e and g_o using the set-theoretic union as shown below. For the notation, let $m = 2^{|\mathbf{A}|-1}$, and we indicate subsets of $\mathbf{A}$ with even cardinality as $\mathbf{E}_i \in \mathcal{L}_e$, where $1 \leq i \leq m$. We use the last index for the empty set $\mathbf{E}_m = \emptyset$. The subsets of $\mathbf{A}$ with odd cardinality are correspondingly noted as $\mathbf{O}_i \in \mathcal{L}_o$. For clarity, we note binary input channels from an even subset as $\lambda \in \mathbf{E}$ and binary input channels from an odd subset as $\nu \in \mathbf{O}$.

$$\bigcup_{\substack{\lambda_1 \in \mathbf{E}_1 \\ \lambda_2 \in \mathbf{E}_2 \\ \cdots \\ \lambda_{m-1} \in \mathbf{E}_{m-1}}} \left(\bigcap_{\kappa \in \mathbf{A}} Z(\kappa) + \sum_{i=1}^{m-1} Z(\lambda_i) \right) \subseteq \bigcup_{\substack{\nu_1 \in \mathbf{O}_1 \\ \nu_2 \in \mathbf{O}_2 \\ \cdots \\ \nu_m \in \mathbf{O}_m}} \left(\sum_{j=1}^{m} Z(\nu_j) \right)$$

$$\bigcap_{\kappa \in \mathbf{A}} Z(\kappa) + \sum_{i=1}^{m-1} \bigcup_{\lambda \in \mathbf{E}_i} Z(\lambda) \subseteq \sum_{j=1}^{m} \bigcup_{\nu \in \mathbf{O}_j} Z(\nu) \qquad \left(\text{Minkowski sum distributes over set union}\right)$$

$$\mathrm{Conv}\left(\bigcap_{\kappa \in \mathbf{A}} Z(\kappa) + \sum_{i=1}^{m-1} \bigcup_{\lambda \in \mathbf{E}_i} Z(\lambda) \right) \subseteq \mathrm{Conv}\left(\sum_{j=1}^{m} \bigcup_{\nu \in \mathbf{O}_j} Z(\nu) \right) \qquad \left(\text{if } \mathbf{X} \subseteq \mathbf{Y} \text{ then } \mathrm{Conv}(\mathbf{X}) \subseteq \mathrm{Conv}(\mathbf{Y})\right)$$

$$\bigcap_{\kappa \in \mathbf{A}} Z(\kappa) + \sum_{i=1}^{m-1} \mathrm{Conv}\left(\bigcup_{\lambda \in \mathbf{E}_i} Z(\lambda) \right) \subseteq \sum_{j=1}^{m} \mathrm{Conv}\left(\bigcup_{\nu \in \mathbf{O}_j} Z(\nu) \right) \qquad \left(\text{Convex hull distributes over Minkowski sum}\right)$$

$$Z\left(\bigsqcap_{\kappa \in \mathbf{A}} \kappa \right) + \sum_{i=1}^{m-1} Z\left(\bigsqcup_{\lambda \in \mathbf{E}_i} \lambda \right) \subseteq \sum_{j=1}^{m} Z\left(\bigsqcup_{\nu \in \mathbf{O}_j} \nu \right) \qquad (\text{by Equation (7)})$$

$$Z\left(\bigsqcap_{\kappa \in \mathbf{A}} \kappa \right) + \sum_{\substack{\emptyset \neq \mathbf{E}_i \subseteq \mathbf{A} \\ |\mathbf{E}_i| \text{ even}}} Z\left(\bigsqcup_{\lambda \in \mathbf{E}_i} \lambda \right) \subseteq \sum_{\substack{\mathbf{O}_j \subseteq \mathbf{A} \\ |\mathbf{O}_j| \text{ odd}}} Z\left(\bigsqcup_{\nu \in \mathbf{O}_j} \nu \right) \qquad (\text{replace notation})$$

$$Z\left(\bigsqcap_{\kappa \in \mathbf{A}} \kappa \right) + \sum_{\substack{\emptyset \neq \mathbf{B} \subseteq \mathbf{A} \\ |\mathbf{B}| \text{ even}}} Z\left(\bigsqcup_{\lambda \in \mathbf{B}} \lambda \right) \subseteq \sum_{\substack{\mathbf{B} \subseteq \mathbf{A} \\ |\mathbf{B}| \text{ odd}}} Z\left(\bigsqcup_{\nu \in \mathbf{B}} \nu \right)$$

□

Appendix C. Non-Negativity of Partial f-Information on the Synergy Lattice

The proof of non-negativity can be divided into three parts. First, we show that the loss measure maintains the ordering relation of the synergy lattice and how the quantification of a meet element $i_{\cup,f}(\alpha \wedge \beta, T, t)$ can be computed. Second, we demonstrate how the inclusion–exclusion inequality of zonogons under the Minkowski sum from Appendix B leads to relating pointwise information measures with respect to the Blackwell order. Finally, we combine these two results to demonstrate that an inclusion–exclusion relation using the convex hull of zonogons is greater than their intersection and obtain the non-negativity of the decomposition by transitivity.

Appendix C.1. Properties of the Loss Measure on the Synergy Lattice

Lemma A6. *Any set of sources $\alpha \in \mathcal{P}(\mathcal{P}_1(\mathbf{V}))$ is equivalent ($\cong$) to some atom of the synergy lattice $\gamma \in \mathcal{A}(\mathbf{V})$.*

$$\forall \alpha \in \mathcal{P}(\mathcal{P}_1(\mathbf{V})).\ \exists \gamma \in \mathcal{A}(\mathbf{V}).\ \gamma \cong \alpha$$

The union for two sets of sources is equivalent to the meet of their corresponding atoms on the synergy lattice. Let $\alpha, \beta \in \mathcal{P}(\mathcal{P}_1(\mathbf{V}))$ and $\gamma, \delta \in \mathcal{A}(\mathbf{V})$:

$$\gamma \cong \alpha \text{ and } \delta \cong \beta \Longrightarrow (\gamma \wedge \delta) \cong (\alpha \cup \beta)$$

Proof. The used filter in the definition of an atom ($\mathcal{A}(\mathbf{V}) \subseteq \mathcal{P}(\mathcal{P}_1(\mathbf{V}))$, Equation (8)) only removes sets of cardinality $2 \leq |\alpha|$, and for any removed set of sources, we can construct an equivalent set that contains one less source by removing the subset $\mathbf{S}_a \subset \mathbf{S}_b$ as shown in Equation (A12a). Therefore, all sets of sources $\alpha \in \mathcal{P}(\mathcal{P}_1(\mathbf{V}))$ are equivalent to some atom $\gamma \in \mathcal{A}(\mathbf{V})$ within the lattice (Equation (A12b)).

$$\mathbf{S}_a \subset \mathbf{S}_b \Longrightarrow \alpha \cong (\alpha \setminus \mathbf{S}_a) \qquad \text{where: } \mathbf{S}_a, \mathbf{S}_b \in \alpha \tag{A12a}$$

$$\forall \alpha \in \mathcal{P}(\mathcal{P}_1(\mathbf{V})), \exists \gamma \in \mathcal{A}(\mathbf{V}).\ \alpha \cong \gamma \tag{A12b}$$

The union of two sets of sources $\alpha \in \mathcal{P}(\mathcal{P}_1(\mathbf{V}))$ is inferior to each individual set α and β:

$$(\alpha \cup \beta) \preceq \alpha \qquad \text{(by Equation (10))}$$
$$(\alpha \cup \beta) \preceq \beta \qquad \text{(by Equation (10))}$$

All sets of sources $\varepsilon \in \mathcal{P}(\mathcal{P}_1(\mathbf{V}))$ that are inferior to both α and β ($\varepsilon \preceq \alpha$ and $\varepsilon \preceq \beta$) are also inferior to their union.

$$\varepsilon \preceq \alpha \text{ and } \varepsilon \preceq \beta \Longrightarrow \varepsilon \preceq (\alpha \cup \beta) \qquad \text{(by Equation (10))}$$

Therefore, the union of α and β is equivalent to the meet of their corresponding atoms on the synergy lattice. □

Proof of Lemma 1 from Section 3.2.
For any set of sources $\alpha, \beta \in \mathcal{P}(\mathcal{P}_1(\mathbf{V}))$ and target variable T with state $t \in \mathcal{T}$, the function $\kappa_\sqcup$ (Equation (31)) maintains the ordering from the synergy lattice under the Blackwell order.

$$\alpha \preceq \beta \Longrightarrow \kappa_\sqcup(\beta, T, t) \sqsubseteq \kappa_\sqcup(\alpha, T, t) \tag{A13}$$

Proof. We consider two cases for β:

1. If $\beta = \emptyset$, then the implication holds for any α since the bottom element $\kappa_\sqcup(\emptyset, T, t) = \bot_{\text{BW}}$ is inferior ($\sqsubseteq$) to any other channel.
2. If $\beta \neq \emptyset$, then α is also a non-empty set since $\alpha \preceq \beta \prec \top_{\text{SL}} = \emptyset$.

$$\begin{aligned} & \alpha \preceq \beta \\ \forall \mathbf{S}_b \in \beta, \exists \mathbf{S}_a \in \alpha. \quad & \mathbf{S}_b \subseteq \mathbf{S}_a && \text{(by Equation (10))} \\ \forall \mathbf{S}_b \in \beta, \exists \mathbf{S}_a \in \alpha. \quad & \kappa(\mathbf{S}_b, T, t) \sqsubseteq \kappa(\mathbf{S}_a, T, t) && \text{(by Equation (2))} \\ & \bigsqcup_{\mathbf{S}_b \in \beta} \kappa(\mathbf{S}_b, T, t) \sqsubseteq \bigsqcup_{\mathbf{S}_a \in \alpha} \kappa(\mathbf{S}_a, T, t) \\ & \kappa_\sqcup(\beta, T, t) \sqsubseteq \kappa_\sqcup(\alpha, T, t) \end{aligned}$$

Since the implication holds for both cases, the ordering is maintained. □

Corollary A2. *The defined cumulative loss measures ($i_{\cup,f}$ of Equation (33a) and $I_{\cup,f}$ of Equation (34)) maintain the ordering relation of the synergy lattice for any set of sources $\alpha, \beta \in \mathcal{P}(\mathcal{P}_1(\mathbf{V}))$ and target variable T with state $t \in \mathcal{T}$:*

$$\alpha \preceq \beta \Longrightarrow i_{\cup,f}(\alpha, T, t) \leq i_{\cup,f}(\beta, T, t)$$
$$\alpha \preceq \beta \Longrightarrow I_{\cup,f}(\alpha; T) \leq I_{\cup,f}(\beta; T)$$

Proof. The pointwise monotonicity of the cumulative loss measure ($\alpha \preceq \beta \Longrightarrow i_{\cup,f}(\alpha, T, t) \leq i_{\cup,f}(\beta, T, t)$) is obtained from Lemmas 1 and A2 with Equation (33a). Sine all cumulative pointwise losses $i_{\cup,f}$ are smaller for α than β, so will be their weighted sum ($\alpha \preceq \beta \Longrightarrow I_{\cup,f}(\alpha; T) \leq I_{\cup,f}(\beta; T)$, see Equation (34)). □

Corollary A3. *The cumulative pointwise loss of the meet from two atoms is equivalent to the cumulative pointwise loss of their union for any target variable T with state $t \in \mathcal{T}$:*
$i_{\cup,f}(\alpha \wedge \beta, T, t) = i_{\cup,f}(\alpha \cup \beta, T, t)$.

Proof. The result follows from Lemma A6 and Corollary A2. □

Appendix C.2. The Non-Negativity of the Decomposition

Lemma A7. *Consider a non-empty set of of binary input channel $\mathbf{A} \neq \emptyset$ and $0 \leq p \leq 1$. Quantifying an inclusion–exclusion principle on the pointwise information of their Blackwell join is larger than the pointwise information of their Blackwell meet as shown in Equation (A14).*

$$i_f\left(p, \bigsqcap_{\kappa \in \mathbf{A}} \kappa\right) \leq \sum_{\emptyset \neq \mathbf{B} \subseteq \mathbf{A}} (-1)^{|\mathbf{B}|-1} i_f\left(p, \bigsqcup_{\kappa \in \mathbf{B}} \kappa\right) \tag{A14}$$

Proof.

$$Z\left(\bigsqcap_{\kappa \in \mathbf{A}} \kappa\right) + \sum_{\substack{\emptyset \neq \mathbf{B} \subseteq \mathbf{A} \\ |\mathbf{B}| \text{ even}}} Z\left(\bigsqcup_{\lambda \in \mathbf{B}} \lambda\right) \subseteq \sum_{\substack{\mathbf{B} \subseteq \mathbf{A} \\ |\mathbf{B}| \text{ odd}}} Z\left(\bigsqcup_{\nu \in \mathbf{B}} \nu\right) \quad \text{(by Lemma A5)}$$

$$i_f\left(p, \bigsqcap_{\kappa \in \mathbf{A}} \kappa\right) + \sum_{\substack{\emptyset \neq \mathbf{B} \subseteq \mathbf{A} \\ |\mathbf{B}| \text{ even}}} i_f\left(p, \bigsqcup_{\kappa \in \mathbf{B}} \kappa\right) \leq \sum_{\substack{\emptyset \neq \mathbf{B} \subseteq \mathbf{A} \\ |\mathbf{B}| \text{ odd}}} i_f\left(p, \bigsqcup_{\kappa \in \mathbf{B}} \kappa\right) \quad \text{(by Lemma A3)}$$

$$i_f\left(p, \bigsqcap_{\kappa \in \mathbf{A}} \kappa\right) \leq \sum_{\emptyset \neq \mathbf{B} \subseteq \mathbf{A}} (-1)^{|\mathbf{B}|-1} i_f\left(p, \bigsqcup_{\kappa \in \mathbf{B}} \kappa\right)$$

□

Lemma A8 (Non-negativity on the synergy lattice). *The decomposition of f-information is non-negative on the pointwise and combined synergy lattice for any target variable T with state $t \in \mathcal{T}$:*

$$\forall \alpha \in \mathcal{A}(\mathbf{V}).\, 0 \leq \Delta i_{\cup,f}(\alpha, T, t),$$
$$\forall \alpha \in \mathcal{A}(\mathbf{V}).\, 0 \leq \Delta I_{\cup,f}(\alpha; T).$$

Proof. We show the non-negativity of pointwise partial information ($\Delta i_{\cup,f}(\alpha, T, t)$) in two cases. We write α^{-S} to represent the cover set of α on the synergy lattice and use $p = P_T(t)$ as the abbreviation:

1. Let $\alpha = \bot_{\text{SL}} = \{\mathbf{V}\}$. The bottom element of the synergy lattice is quantified to zero (by Equation (33a), $i_{\cup,f}(\bot_{\text{SL}}, T, t) = 0$), and therefore, also its partial contribution will be zero ($\Delta i_{\cup,f}(\bot_{\text{SL}}, T, t) = 0$), which implies Equation (A15).

$$\alpha = \bot_{\text{SL}} \Longrightarrow 0 \leq \Delta i_{\cup,f}(\alpha, T, t) \tag{A15}$$

2. Let $\alpha \in \mathcal{A}(\mathbf{V}) \setminus \{\bot_{\mathrm{SL}}\}$, then its cover set is non-empty ($\alpha^{-S} \neq \emptyset$). Additionally, we know that no atom in the cover set is the empty set ($\forall \beta \in \alpha^{-S}.\ \beta \neq \emptyset$), since the empty atom is the top element ($\top_{\mathrm{SL}} = \emptyset$).
Since it will be required later, note that the inclusion–exclusion principle of a constant is the constant itself as shown in Equation (A16) since, without the empty set, there exists one more subset of odd cardinality than with even cardinality (see Equation (A3)).

$$i_f(p, \kappa(\mathbf{V}, T, t)) = \sum_{\emptyset \neq \mathbf{B} \subseteq \alpha^{-S}} (-1)^{|\mathbf{B}|-1} i_f(p, \kappa(\mathbf{V}, T, t)) \tag{A16}$$

We can re-write the Möbius inverse as shown in Equation (A17), where Equation (A17b) is obtained from ([23], p. 15)).

$$\begin{aligned}
\Delta i_{\cup,f}(\alpha, T, t) &= i_{\cup,f}(\alpha, T, t) - \sum_{\beta \in \downarrow_S \alpha} \Delta i_{\cup,f}(\beta, T, t) && \text{(by Equation (33b))} \quad \text{(A17a)}\\
&= i_{\cup,f}(\alpha, T, t) - \sum_{\emptyset \neq \mathbf{B} \subseteq \alpha^{-S}} (-1)^{|\mathbf{B}|-1} \cdot i_{\cup,f}\left(\bigwedge_{\beta \in \mathbf{B}} \beta, T, t\right) && \text{(A17b)}\\
&= i_{\cup,f}(\alpha, T, t) - \sum_{\emptyset \neq \mathbf{B} \subseteq \alpha^{-S}} (-1)^{|\mathbf{B}|-1} \cdot i_{\cup,f}\left(\bigcup_{\beta \in \mathbf{B}} \beta, T, t\right) && \text{(by Corollary A3)} \quad \text{(A17c)}\\
&= -\, i_f(p, \kappa_{\sqcup}(\alpha, T, t)) + \sum_{\emptyset \neq \mathbf{B} \subseteq \alpha^{-S}} (-1)^{|\mathbf{B}|-1} \cdot i_f(p, \kappa_{\sqcup}(\bigcup_{\beta \in \mathbf{B}} \beta, T, t)) && \text{(by Equations (33a), (A16))} \quad \text{(A17d)}\\
&= -\, i_f(p, \kappa_{\sqcup}(\alpha, T, t)) + \sum_{\emptyset \neq \mathbf{B} \subseteq \alpha^{-S}} (-1)^{|\mathbf{B}|-1} \cdot i_f(p, \bigsqcup_{\mathbf{S} \in (\bigcup_{\beta \in \mathbf{B}} \beta)} \kappa(\mathbf{S}, T, t)) && \text{(by } \forall \beta \in \alpha^{-S}.\beta \neq \emptyset) \quad \text{(A17e)}\\
&= -\, i_f(p, \kappa_{\sqcup}(\alpha, T, t)) + \sum_{\emptyset \neq \mathbf{B} \subseteq \alpha^{-S}} (-1)^{|\mathbf{B}|-1} \cdot i_f(p, \bigsqcup_{\beta \in \mathbf{B}} \bigsqcup_{\mathbf{S} \in \beta} \kappa(\mathbf{S}, T, t)) && \text{(A17f)}\\
&= -\, i_f(p, \kappa_{\sqcup}(\alpha, T, t)) + \sum_{\emptyset \neq \mathbf{B} \subseteq \{\kappa_{\sqcup}(\beta, T, t)\,:\,\beta \in \alpha^{-S}\}} (-1)^{|\mathbf{B}|-1} \cdot i_f(p, \bigsqcup_{\kappa \in \mathbf{B}} \kappa) && \text{(A17g)}
\end{aligned}$$

Consider the non-empty set of channels $\mathbf{D} = \{\kappa_{\sqcup}(\beta, T, t)\ :\ \beta \in \alpha^{-S}\}$, then we obtain Equation (A18b) from Lemma A7.

$$i_f\left(p, \bigsqcap_{\kappa \in \{\kappa_{\sqcup}(\beta, T, t)\,:\,\beta \in \alpha^{-S}\}} \kappa\right) \leq \sum_{\emptyset \neq \mathbf{B} \subseteq \{\kappa_{\sqcup}(\beta, T, t)\,:\,\beta \in \alpha^{-S}\}} (-1)^{|\mathbf{B}|-1} i_f\left(p, \bigsqcup_{\kappa \in \mathbf{B}} \kappa\right) \tag{A18a}$$

$$i_f\left(p, \bigsqcap_{\beta \in \alpha^{-S}} \kappa_{\sqcup}(\beta, T, t)\right) \leq \sum_{\emptyset \neq \mathbf{B} \subseteq \{\kappa_{\sqcup}(\beta, T, t)\,:\,\beta \in \alpha^{-S}\}} (-1)^{|\mathbf{B}|-1} i_f\left(p, \bigsqcup_{\kappa \in \mathbf{B}} \kappa\right) \tag{A18b}$$

We can construct an upper bound on $i_f(p, \kappa_{\sqcup}(\alpha, T, t))$ based on the cover set α^{-S} as shown in Equation (A19).

$$\begin{aligned}
&\forall \beta \in \alpha^{-S}. && \beta \preceq \alpha && \text{(A19a)}\\
&\forall \beta \in \alpha^{-S}. && \kappa_{\sqcup}(\alpha, T, t) \sqsubseteq \kappa_{\sqcup}(\beta, T, t) && \text{(by Lemma 1)} \quad \text{(A19b)}\\
& && \kappa_{\sqcup}(\alpha, T, t) \sqsubseteq \bigsqcap_{\beta \in \alpha^{-S}} \kappa_{\sqcup}(\beta, T, t) && \text{(A19c)}\\
& && i_f(p, \kappa_{\sqcup}(\alpha, T, t)) \leq i_f\left(p, \bigsqcap_{\beta \in \alpha^{-S}} \kappa_{\sqcup}(\beta, T, t)\right) && \text{(by Lemma A2)} \quad \text{(A19d)}
\end{aligned}$$

By the transitivity of Equations (A18b) and (A19d), we obtain Equation (A20).

$$i_f(p, \kappa_{\sqcup}(\alpha, T, t)) \leq \sum_{\emptyset \neq \mathbf{B} \subseteq \{\kappa_{\sqcup}(\beta, T, t)\,:\,\beta \in \alpha^{-}s\}} (-1)^{|\mathbf{B}|-1} i_f\left(p, \bigsqcup_{\kappa \in \mathbf{B}} \kappa\right) \tag{A20}$$

By Equations (A17) and (A20), we obtain the non-negativity of pointwise partial information as shown in Equation (A21).

$$\alpha \in \mathcal{A}(\mathbf{V}) \setminus \{\perp_{\text{SL}}\}. \qquad 0 \leq \Delta i_{\cup,f}(\alpha, T, t) \tag{A21}$$

From Equations (A15) and (A21), we obtain that pointwise partial information is non-negative for all atoms of the lattice:

$$\forall \alpha \in \mathcal{A}(\mathbf{V}).\, 0 \leq \Delta i_{\cup,f}(\alpha, T) \tag{A22}$$

If all pointwise partial components are non-negative, then their expected value will also be non-negative (see Equation (35)):

$$\forall \alpha \in \mathcal{A}(\mathbf{V}).\, 0 \leq \Delta I_{\cup,f}(\alpha; T) \tag{A23}$$

□

Appendix D. Mappings between Decomposition Lattices and Their Duality

Proof of Lemma 2 from Section 3.4

The function $\Psi(\cdot)$ is a bijection on the redundancy lattice without the bottom element ($\emptyset$) that reverses its order. Let $\alpha, \beta \in \mathcal{A}(\mathbf{V}) \setminus \{\perp_{\text{RL}}\}$:

1. $\Psi(\Psi(\alpha)) \simeq \alpha$;
2. $\alpha \preccurlyeq \beta \iff \Psi(\beta) \preccurlyeq \Psi(\alpha)$.

Proof.

- Property 1: the n-ary Cartesian product (Ψ) provides all combinations of one variable from each source (Definition 28). Let $\gamma = \Psi(\alpha)$, then by Definition 11 ($\simeq$) of equivalence $\Psi(\gamma) \simeq \alpha$, we have to show that both elements are inferior to each other under the redundancy order:
  - $\Psi(\gamma) \preccurlyeq \alpha$: We begin by expanding the definition of the redundancy order as shown in Equation (A24) to highlight that it is sufficient to show that $\alpha \subseteq \Psi(\gamma)$.

    $$\alpha \subseteq \Psi(\gamma) \implies \forall \mathbf{S}_a \in \alpha, \exists \mathbf{S}_b \in \Psi(\gamma), \mathbf{S}_b \subseteq \mathbf{S}_a \implies \Psi(\gamma) \preccurlyeq \alpha \tag{A24}$$

    To show $\alpha \subseteq \Psi(\gamma)$, we have to demonstrate that is is possible to select one variable from each source in γ to reconstruct each source in α:
    * By definition $\gamma = \Psi(\alpha)$, each source in γ contains one variable from each source in α, and all variables from each source in α can be found in some source of γ.
    * By selecting the variable in each source of γ that originated from the same source in α, we can exactly reconstruct each source in α.
    * Therefore, $\alpha \subseteq \Psi(\Psi(\alpha))$, which implies $\Psi(\Psi(\alpha)) \preccurlyeq \alpha$.
  - $\alpha \preccurlyeq \Psi(\gamma)$: We begin by expanding the definition of the redundancy order (Equation (9)) as shown in Equation (A25) to highlight that we have to show that all sources in $\Psi(\gamma)$ are a super-set of some source in α.

    $$\alpha \preccurlyeq \Psi(\gamma) \iff \forall \mathbf{S}_b \in \Psi(\gamma).\, \exists \mathbf{S}_a \in \alpha.\, \mathbf{S}_a \subseteq \mathbf{S}_b \tag{A25}$$

    For a proof by induction, the recursive definition $\Psi'(\alpha)$ as shown in Equation (A26) highlights the relation of interest more clearly. We use the notation $\mathbf{S}[i]$ to indicate the i-th variable in source $\mathbf{S}$. That both functions are equivalent $\Psi'(\alpha) = \Psi(\alpha)$ can directly be seen, since $\Psi'(\alpha)$ recursively combines all possible choices of selecting one variable from each source in α, which is the definition of $\Psi(\alpha)$.

$$\Psi'(\alpha) := \begin{cases} \{\emptyset\} & \text{if } \alpha = \emptyset \\ \bigcup_{i \in 1..|\mathbf{S}|} \{x \cup \{\mathbf{S}[i]\} \; : \; x \in \Psi'(\alpha \setminus \{\mathbf{S}\})\} & \text{otherwise, where } \mathbf{S} \in \alpha \end{cases} \tag{A26}$$

Induction on the cardinality of α:

* *Hypothesis:* It is impossible to choose one variable from each source in $\Psi'(\alpha)$ without selecting all variables of some source $\mathbf{S}_a \in \alpha$:

$$\forall \mathbf{S}_b \in \Psi(\Psi'(\alpha)). \, \exists \mathbf{S}_a \in \alpha. \, \mathbf{S}_a \subseteq \mathbf{S}_b \tag{A27}$$

* Base case $|\alpha| = 1$: The condition is satisfied as shown in Equation (A28), since $\Psi'(\{\mathbf{S}\})$ turns each variable in $\mathbf{S}$ into its own source. The second application $\Psi(\Psi'(\{\mathbf{S}\}))$ recombines them.

$$\begin{aligned} \Psi'(\{\mathbf{S}\}) &= \{\{V\} \; : \; V \in \mathbf{S}\} \\ \Psi(\Psi'(\{\mathbf{S}\})) &= \{\mathbf{S}\} \end{aligned} \tag{A28}$$

* Assume the induction hypothesis holds for $|\alpha| = m$.
* For the induction step, let $\alpha' = \alpha \cup \{\mathbf{S}'\}$: From the recursive definition shown in Equation (A29), we can directly see all relevant options of choosing one element from each resulting source.

$$\Psi'(\alpha') = \bigcup_{i \in 1..|\mathbf{S}'|} \{x \cup \{\mathbf{S}'[i]\} \; : \; x \in \Psi'(\alpha)\} \tag{A29}$$

  · Case 1: From every source in $\Psi'(\alpha')$, we choose the variable $\mathbf{S}'[i]$ that was contributed by the new source $\mathbf{S}'$. The resulting set contains all variables of $\mathbf{S}'$.
  · Case 2: To avoid choosing all variables from $\mathbf{S}'$, we have to select the variables contributed by $x \in \Psi'(\alpha)$ instead for some $\mathbf{S}'[i]$. By the induction hypothesis, choosing one variable from each set in $\Psi'(\alpha)$ leads to choosing all variables of some source $\mathbf{S}_a \in \alpha$.
  · Choosing one variable from each set in $\alpha' = \alpha \cup \{\mathbf{S}'\}$ leads to choosing all variables of $\mathbf{S}'$ or all variables of some source $\mathbf{S}_a \in \alpha$.
  · Thus, the induction hypothesis holds for $|\alpha'| = |\alpha| + 1$.

– As shown above, $\Psi(\Psi(\alpha)) \preccurlyeq \alpha$ and $\alpha \preccurlyeq \Psi(\Psi(\alpha))$, which implies $\alpha \simeq \Psi(\Psi(\alpha))$.

• Property 2: We first expand the definitions:

$$\begin{aligned} \alpha \preccurlyeq \beta &\iff \Psi(\beta) \preccurlyeq \Psi(\alpha) \\ \forall \mathbf{S}_b \in \beta. \, \exists \mathbf{S}_a \in \alpha. \, \mathbf{S}_a \subseteq \mathbf{S}_b &\iff \forall \mathbf{S}_c \in \Psi(\alpha). \, \exists \mathbf{S}_d \in \Psi(\beta). \, \mathbf{S}_d \subseteq \mathbf{S}_c \quad \text{(by Definition 9)} \end{aligned}$$

Then, we view both implications separately:

1. Assume $\forall \mathbf{S}_b \in \beta. \, \exists \mathbf{S}_a \in \alpha. \, \mathbf{S}_a \subseteq \mathbf{S}_b$. Then, there exists a function $w : \mathcal{P}(\mathcal{P}_1(\mathbf{V})) \to \mathcal{P}(\mathcal{P}_1(\mathbf{V}))$ that associates each source in β with a source in α.

$$\forall \mathbf{S}_b \in \beta. \, w(\mathbf{S}_b) \subseteq \mathbf{S}_b \text{ and } w(\mathbf{S}_b) \in \alpha. \tag{A30}$$

All sets $\mathbf{S}_c \in \Psi(\alpha)$ contain one variable of each source in α. Let the function $v_c : \mathcal{P}_1(\mathbf{V}) \to \mathbf{V}$ indicate this selection:

$$\mathbf{S}_c = \{v_c(\mathbf{S}_x) \; : \; \mathbf{S}_x \in \alpha\} \qquad \text{where: } v_c(\mathbf{S}_x) \in \mathbf{S}_x \tag{A31}$$

Define the set $\mathbf{S}_d \in \Psi(\beta)$ using the defined functions above as shown in Equation (A32). The function w is defined for all sources in β, and the selected element is in the original source ($v_c(w(\mathbf{S}_x)) \in \mathbf{S}_x$) by Equation (A30).

$$\mathbf{S}_d = \{v_c(w(\mathbf{S}_x)) \ : \ \mathbf{S}_x \in \beta\} \tag{A32}$$

The constructed set $\mathbf{S}_d \in \Psi(\beta)$ is a subset of $\mathbf{S}_c \in \Psi(\alpha)$, and it can be constructed for each $\mathbf{S}_c \in \Psi(\alpha)$. This proves Equation (A33):

$$\forall \mathbf{S}_b \in \beta.\ \exists \mathbf{S}_a \in \alpha.\ \mathbf{S}_a \subseteq \mathbf{S}_b \Longrightarrow \forall \mathbf{S}_c \in \Psi(\alpha).\ \exists \mathbf{S}_d \in \Psi(\beta).\ \mathbf{S}_d \subseteq \mathbf{S}_c \tag{A33}$$

2. For the other direction, we show Equation (A34) and start with its simplification:

$$\begin{aligned}
\neg(\forall \mathbf{S}_b \in \beta.\ \exists \mathbf{S}_a \in \alpha.\ \mathbf{S}_a \subseteq \mathbf{S}_b) &\Longrightarrow \neg(\forall \mathbf{S}_c \in \Psi(\alpha).\ \exists \mathbf{S}_d \in \Psi(\beta).\ \mathbf{S}_d \subseteq \mathbf{S}_c) \\
\exists \mathbf{S}_b \in \beta.\ \forall \mathbf{S}_a \in \alpha.\ \neg(\mathbf{S}_a \subseteq \mathbf{S}_b) &\Longrightarrow \exists \mathbf{S}_c \in \Psi(\alpha).\ \forall \mathbf{S}_d \in \Psi(\beta).\ \neg(\mathbf{S}_d \subseteq \mathbf{S}_c) \\
\exists \mathbf{S}_b \in \beta.\ \forall \mathbf{S}_a \in \alpha.\ \exists x \in \mathbf{S}_a.\ x \notin \mathbf{S}_b &\Longrightarrow \exists \mathbf{S}_c \in \Psi(\alpha).\ \forall \mathbf{S}_d \in \Psi(\beta).\ \exists x \in \mathbf{S}_d.\ x \notin \mathbf{S}_c
\end{aligned} \tag{A34}$$

The left-hand side states that, for some $\mathbf{S}_b \in \beta$, all sources $\mathbf{S}_a \in \alpha$ contain an element that is not in $\mathbf{S}_b$. Let us fix a particular $\mathbf{S}_b$ and define a function returning this element $v : \mathcal{P}_1(\mathbf{V}) \to \mathbf{V}$:

$$\forall \mathbf{S}_a \in \alpha.\ v(\mathbf{S}_a) \in \mathbf{S}_a \text{ and } v(\mathbf{S}_a) \notin \mathbf{S}_b \tag{A35}$$

Then, we can define the set $\mathbf{S}_c = \{v(\mathbf{S}_a) \ : \ \mathbf{S}_a \in \alpha\}$. The source $\mathbf{S}_c$ selects one variable from each source; thus, $\mathbf{S}_c \in \Psi(\alpha)$, and by definition, $\mathbf{S}_c \cap \mathbf{S}_b = \emptyset$. All sets $\mathbf{S}_d \in \Psi(\beta)$ must select one element from $\mathbf{S}_b$ and, thus, contain one element that is not in $\mathbf{S}_c$. This provides the required implication of Equation (A34).

□

Proof of Lemma 3 from Section 3.4

The function $\Xi(\cdot)$ is a bijection that maintains the ordering of atoms between the redundancy and synergy order. Let $\alpha, \beta \in \mathcal{A}(\mathbf{V})$:

1. $\alpha = \Xi(\Xi(\alpha))$;
2. $\alpha \preccurlyeq \beta \iff \Xi(\alpha) \preceq \Xi(\beta)$.

Proof.

- Property 1 is obtained from Definition 28: the first two cases revert each other, and the third case ($\alpha \neq \emptyset$ and $\alpha \neq \{\mathbf{V}\}$) holds since $\forall \mathbf{S} \in \alpha \ : \ \mathbf{S} = \mathbf{V} \setminus (\mathbf{V} \setminus \mathbf{S})$.
- Property 2:
  - Case 1: If $\alpha = \emptyset = \bot_{\text{RL}}$, then $\Xi(\alpha) = \{\mathbf{V}\} = \bot_{\text{SL}}$. Therefore, $\forall \beta \in \mathcal{A}(\mathbf{V}).\ \bot_{\text{RL}} \preccurlyeq \beta \iff \bot_{\text{SL}} \preceq \beta$.
  - Case 2: If $\alpha = \{\mathbf{V}\} = \top_{\text{RL}}$, then $\Xi(\alpha) = \emptyset = \top_{\text{SL}}$. Therefore, $\forall \alpha \in \mathcal{A}(\mathbf{V}).\ \alpha \preccurlyeq \top_{\text{RL}} \iff \alpha \preceq \top_{\text{SL}}$.
  - Case 3: If $\alpha \neq \emptyset$, then $\beta \neq \emptyset$:

$$\begin{aligned}
\alpha \preccurlyeq \beta &= \forall \mathbf{S}_b \in \beta, \exists \mathbf{S}_a \in \alpha, \mathbf{S}_a \subseteq \mathbf{S}_b && \text{(by Definition 9)} \\
&= \forall \mathbf{S}_b \in \beta, \exists \mathbf{S}_a \in \alpha, (\mathbf{V} \setminus \mathbf{S}_b) \subseteq (\mathbf{V} \setminus \mathbf{S}_a) \\
&= \{\mathbf{V} \setminus \mathbf{S}_a : \mathbf{S}_a \in \alpha\} \preceq \{\mathbf{V} \setminus \mathbf{S}_b : \mathbf{S}_b \in \beta\} && \text{(by Definition 10)} \\
&= \Xi(\alpha) \preceq \Xi(\beta) && \text{(by Definition 28)}
\end{aligned}$$

□

Proof of Lemma 4 from Section 3.4

A redundancy- and synergy-based information decomposition is pointwise dual if, for all $\alpha \in \mathcal{A}(\mathbf{V}) \setminus \{\perp_{\mathrm{RL}}\}$:

$$\begin{aligned} \Delta i_{\cap,f}(\alpha, T, t) &= \Delta i_{\cup,f}(\Xi(\Psi(\alpha)), T, t) \\ \Delta i_{\cap,f}(\perp_{\mathrm{RL}}, T, t) &= 0 = \Delta i_{\cup,f}(\perp_{\mathrm{SL}}, T, t) \end{aligned} \tag{A36}$$

A redundancy- and synergy-based information decomposition is dual if, for all $\alpha \in \mathcal{A}(\mathbf{V}) \setminus \{\perp_{\mathrm{RL}}\}$:

$$\begin{aligned} \Delta I_{\cap,f}(\alpha, T) &= \Delta I_{\cup,f}(\Xi(\Psi(\alpha)), T) \\ \Delta I_{\cap,f}(\perp_{\mathrm{RL}}, T) &= 0 = \Delta I_{\cup,f}(\perp_{\mathrm{SL}}, T) \end{aligned} \tag{A37}$$

Proof.

$$\begin{aligned} \sum_{\beta \in \downarrow_R \alpha} \Delta i_{\cap,f}(\beta, T, t) &= \sum_{\beta \in (\downarrow_R \alpha) \setminus \{\perp_{\mathrm{RL}}\}} \Delta i_{\cap,f}(\beta, T, t) && (\Delta i_{\cap,f}(\perp_{\mathrm{RL}}, T, t) = i_{\cup,f}(\perp_{\mathrm{SL}}, T, t) = 0) \\ &= \sum_{\beta \in \uparrow_S \Xi(\Psi(\alpha))} \Delta i_{\cap,f}(\Psi(\Xi(\beta)), T, t) && \text{(by Corollary 1)} \\ &= \sum_{\beta \in \uparrow_S \Xi(\Psi(\alpha))} \Delta i_{\cup,f}(\Xi(\Psi(\Psi(\Xi(\beta)))), T, t) && \text{(by Equation (38))} \\ &= \sum_{\beta \in \uparrow_S \Xi(\Psi(\alpha))} \Delta i_{\cup,f}(\beta, T, t) \end{aligned}$$

The duality of the pointwise measure $(i_{\cap,f}, i_{\cup,f})$ implies the duality of the combined measure $(I_{\cap,f}, I_{\cup,f})$.

□

Lemma A9. *For $\alpha \in \mathcal{A}(\mathbf{V}) \setminus \{\perp_{RL}\}$ and $\beta \in \mathcal{A}(\mathbf{V})$:*

$$\neg(\exists \mathbf{S}_a \in \alpha.\ \beta \preceq \{\mathbf{S}_a\}) \iff (\Xi(\Psi(\alpha)) \preceq \beta) \tag{A38}$$

Proof.

- Case $\beta = \top_{\mathrm{SL}} = \emptyset$: The condition holds since it implies α to be the minimal element in $\mathcal{A}(\mathbf{V}) \setminus \{\perp_{\mathrm{RL}}\}$.
- Case $\beta \neq \top_{\mathrm{SL}}$: We start by simplifying the expression.

$$\begin{aligned} \neg(\exists \mathbf{S}_a \in \alpha.\ \beta \preceq \{\mathbf{S}_a\}) &\iff (\Xi(\Psi(\alpha)) \preceq \beta) \\ (\forall \mathbf{S}_a \in \alpha.\ \neg(\beta \preceq \{\mathbf{S}_a\})) &\iff (\Xi(\Psi(\alpha)) \preceq \beta) \\ (\forall \mathbf{S}_a \in \alpha.\ \neg(\exists \mathbf{S}_b \in \beta.\ \mathbf{S}_a \subseteq \mathbf{S}_b)) &\iff (\Xi(\Psi(\alpha)) \preceq \beta) && \text{(by Definition 10)} \\ (\forall \mathbf{S}_a \in \alpha.\ \forall \mathbf{S}_b \in \beta.\ \neg(\mathbf{S}_a \subseteq \mathbf{S}_b)) &\iff (\Xi(\Psi(\alpha)) \preceq \beta) \\ (\forall \mathbf{S}_a \in \alpha.\ \forall \mathbf{S}_b \in \beta.\ \neg(\mathbf{S}_a \subseteq \mathbf{S}_b)) &\iff (\Psi(\alpha) \preccurlyeq \Xi(\beta)) && \text{(by Lemma 3)} \\ (\forall \mathbf{S}_a \in \alpha.\ \forall \mathbf{S}_b \in \beta.\ \neg(\mathbf{S}_a \subseteq \mathbf{S}_b)) &\iff (\forall \mathbf{S}_b \in \Xi(\beta).\ \exists \mathbf{S}_c \in \Psi(\alpha).\ \mathbf{S}_c \subseteq \mathbf{S}_b) && \text{(by Definition 9)} \\ (\forall \mathbf{S}_b \in \beta.\ \forall \mathbf{S}_a \in \alpha.\ \neg(\mathbf{S}_a \subseteq \mathbf{S}_b)) &\iff (\forall \mathbf{S}_b \in \beta.\ \exists \mathbf{S}_c \in \Psi(\alpha).\ \mathbf{S}_c \subseteq \mathbf{V} \setminus \mathbf{S}_b) && \text{(by Definition 28)} \\ (\forall \mathbf{S}_b \in \beta.\ \forall \mathbf{S}_a \in \alpha.\ \neg(\mathbf{S}_a \subseteq \mathbf{S}_b)) &\iff (\forall \mathbf{S}_b \in \beta.\ \exists \mathbf{S}_c \in \Psi(\alpha).\ \mathbf{S}_c \cap \mathbf{S}_b = \emptyset) \\ (\forall \mathbf{S}_b \in \beta.\ \forall \mathbf{S}_a \in \alpha.\ \exists x \in \mathbf{S}_a.\ x \notin \mathbf{S}_b) &\iff (\forall \mathbf{S}_b \in \beta.\ \exists \mathbf{S}_c \in \Psi(\alpha).\ \forall x \in \mathbf{S}_c.\ x \notin \mathbf{S}_b) \end{aligned} \tag{A39}$$

  - The left-hand side states that, for all $\mathbf{S}_b \in \beta$, all $\mathbf{S}_a \in \alpha$ must have at least one element that is not in S_b.
  - The right-hand side states that, for all $\mathbf{S}_b \in \beta$, there exists a combination of one variable per source in α such that no element of the resulting collection is in $\mathbf{S}_b$. This is possible if and only if all sources $\mathbf{S}_a \in \alpha$ have at least one element that is not in $\mathbf{S}_b$.

Therefore, both statements imply each other.

□

Lemma A10. *For $\alpha \in \mathcal{A}(\mathbf{V}) \setminus \{\bot_{RL}\}$:*

$$\mathcal{P}_1(\alpha) \ \{\cong\} \left\{ \bigwedge_{\beta \in \mathbf{B}} \beta : \emptyset \neq \mathbf{B} \subseteq \{\{\mathbf{S}\} \ : \ \mathbf{S} \in \alpha\} \right\} \tag{A40}$$

Proof.

$$\begin{aligned}
&= \mathcal{P}_1(\alpha) \\
&= \{\mathbf{B} : \emptyset \neq \mathbf{B} \subseteq \alpha\} \\
&= \left\{ \bigcup_{\beta \in \mathbf{B}} \beta : \emptyset \neq \mathbf{B} \subseteq \{\{\mathbf{S}\} \ : \ \mathbf{S} \in \alpha\} \right\} \\
&\{\cong\} \left\{ \bigwedge_{\beta \in \mathbf{B}} \beta : \emptyset \neq \mathbf{B} \subseteq \{\{\mathbf{S}\} \ : \ \mathbf{S} \in \alpha\} \right\} \quad \text{(by Lemma A6)}
\end{aligned} \tag{A41}$$

□

Proof of Lemma 6 from Section 3.4

The pointwise dual-decomposition for the redundancy lattice of a loss measure on the synergy lattice is defined by:

$$i_{\cap,f}(\alpha, T, t) := \begin{cases} 0 & \text{if } \alpha = \emptyset \\ i_{\cup,f}(\top_{\text{SL}}, T, t) - \sum_{\beta \in \mathcal{P}_1(\alpha)} (-1)^{|\beta|-1} i_{\cup,f}(\beta, T, t) & \text{otherwise} \end{cases} \tag{A42}$$

Proof. The case $\alpha = \emptyset$ is satisfied by definition. Therefore, we proceed assuming $\alpha \neq \emptyset$:

$$\begin{aligned}
i_{\cap,f}(\alpha, T, t) &= \sum_{\gamma \in \downarrow_R \alpha} \Delta i_{\cap,f}(\gamma, T, t) \\
&= \sum_{\gamma \in \uparrow_S \Xi(\Psi(\alpha))} \Delta i_{\cup,f}(\gamma, T, t) && \text{(by Lemma 4)} \\
&= i_{\cup,f}(\top_{\text{SL}}, T, t) - i_{\cup,f}(\top_{\text{SL}}, T, t) + \sum_{\gamma \in \uparrow_S \Xi(\Psi(\alpha))} \Delta i_{\cup,f}(\gamma, T, t) \\
&= i_{\cup,f}(\top_{\text{SL}}, T, t) - \left(\sum_{\gamma \in \mathcal{A}(\mathbf{V})} \Delta i_{\cup,f}(\gamma, T, t) - \sum_{\gamma \in \uparrow_S \Xi(\Psi(\alpha))} \Delta i_{\cup,f}(\gamma, T, t) \right) \\
&= i_{\cup,f}(\top_{\text{SL}}, T, t) - \sum_{\gamma \in \mathcal{A}(\mathbf{V}) \setminus \uparrow_S \Xi(\Psi(\alpha))} \Delta i_{\cup,f}(\gamma, T, t) \\
&= i_{\cup,f}(\top_{\text{SL}}, T, t) - \sum_{\gamma \in \bigcup_{\mathbf{S}_a \in \alpha} \downarrow_S \{\mathbf{S}_a\}} \Delta i_{\cup,f}(\gamma, T, t) && \text{(by Lemma 5)} \\
&= i_{\cup,f}(\top_{\text{SL}}, T, t) - \sum_{\gamma \in \bigcup_{\beta \in \{\{\mathbf{S}_a\} \ : \ \mathbf{S}_a \in \alpha\}} \downarrow_S \beta} \Delta i_{\cup,f}(\gamma, T, t) \\
&= i_{\cup,f}(\top_{\text{SL}}, T, t) - \sum_{\emptyset \neq \mathbf{B} \subseteq \{\{\mathbf{S}_a\} \ : \ \mathbf{S}_a \in \alpha\}} (-1)^{|\beta|-1} i_{\cup,f}(\bigwedge_{\beta \in \mathbf{B}} \beta, T, t) && \text{(by inclusion–exclusion)} \\
&= i_{\cup,f}(\top_{\text{SL}}, T, t) - \sum_{\gamma \in \left\{ \bigwedge_{\beta \in \mathbf{B}} \beta : \ \emptyset \neq \mathbf{B} \subseteq \{\{\mathbf{S}_a\} \ : \ \mathbf{S}_a \in \alpha\} \right\}} (-1)^{|\beta|-1} i_{\cup,f}(\gamma, T, t) \\
&= i_{\cup,f}(\top_{\text{SL}}, T, t) - \sum_{\gamma \in \mathcal{P}_1(\alpha)} (-1)^{|\beta|-1} i_{\cup,f}(\gamma, T, t) && \text{(by Lemma A10)}
\end{aligned} \tag{A43}$$

□

Appendix E. Scaling f-Information Does Not Affect Its Transformation

Lemma A11. *The linear scaling of an f-information does not affect the transformation result and operator: Consider scaling an f-information measure $I_{a_2}(S;T) = k \cdot I_{a_1}(S;T)$ with $k \in (0, \infty)$, then their decomposition transformation to another measure $I_b(S;T)$ will be equivalent.*

Proof. Based on the definitions of Section 3.2, the loss measures scale linearly with the scaling of their f-divergence. Therefore, we obtain two cumulative loss measures, where $I_{\cup,a_1}$ and $I_{\cup,a_2}$ are a linear scaling of each other (Equation (A44a)). They can be transformed into another measure $I_{\cup,b}$, as shown in Equation (A44b).

$$I_{\cup,a_2}(\alpha;T) = k \cdot I_{\cup,a_1}(\alpha;T) \quad \text{(A44a)}$$
$$I_{\cup,b}(\alpha;T) = v_1(I_{\cup,a_1}(\alpha;T)) = v_2(I_{\cup,a_2}(\alpha;T)) \quad \text{(A44b)}$$

Equation (A44b) already demonstrates that their transformation results will be equivalent and that $v_1(z) = v_2(k \cdot z)$ and $k \cdot v_1^{-1}(z) = v_2^{-1}(z)$. Therefore, their operators will also be equivalent as shown below:

$$\begin{aligned} x \oplus_2 y &:= v_2\left(v_2^{-1}(x) \pm v_2^{-1}(y)\right) \\ x \oplus_1 y &:= v_1\left(v_1^{-1}(x) \pm v_1^{-1}(y)\right) \\ &= v_2\left(kv_1^{-1}(x) \pm kv_1^{-1}(y)\right) \\ &= v_2\left(v_2^{-1}(x) \pm v_2^{-1}(y)\right) \\ &= x \oplus_2 y \end{aligned}$$

□

Appendix F. Decomposition Example Distributions

The probability distributions used in Figure 9 can be found in Table A1. For providing an intuition of the decomposition result for $I_{\cup,TV}$ in the generic example, we visualize its corresponding zonogons in Figure A2. It can be seen that the maximal zonogon height is obtained from V_1 (blue), which equals the maximal zonogon height of their joint distribution (V_1, V_2) (red). Therefore, $I_{\cup,TV}$ does not attribute partial information uniquely to V_2 or their synergy by Lemma 8.

Table A1. The distributions used from [13] and the generic example from [20]. The example names are abbreviations for: XOR-gate (XOR), Unique (Unq), Pointwise Unique (PwUnq), Redundant-Error (RdnErr), Two-Bit-copy (Tbc), and the AND-gate (AND) [13].

State			Probability						
V_1	V_2	T	XOR	Unq	PwUnq	RdnErr	Tbc	AND	Generic
0	0	0	1/4	1/4	0	3/8	1/4	1/4	0.0625
0	0	1	-	-	-	-	-	-	0.3000
0	1	0	-	1/4	1/4	1/8	-	1/4	0.1875
0	1	1	1/4	-	-	-	1/4	-	0.1500
0	2	1	-	-	1/4	-	-	-	-
1	0	0	-	-	1/4	-	-	1/4	0.0375
1	0	1	1/4	1/4	-	1/8	-	-	0.0500
1	0	2	-	-	-	-	1/4	-	-
1	1	0	1/4	-	-	-	-	-	0.2125
1	1	1	-	1/4	-	3/8	-	1/4	-
1	1	3	-	-	-	-	1/4	-	-
2	0	1	-	-	1/4	-	-	-	-

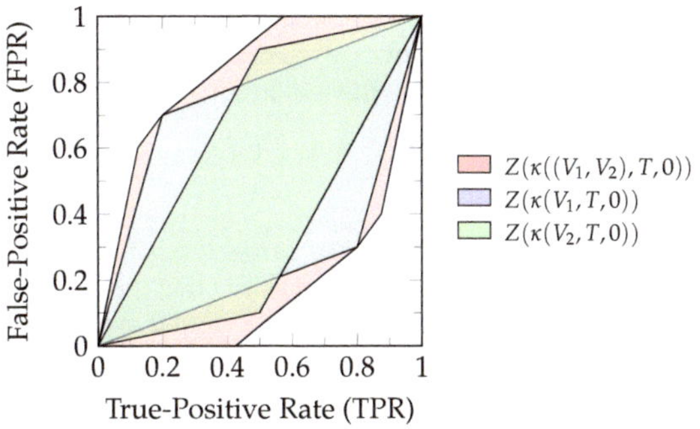

Figure A2. Visualization of the zonogons from the generic example of [20] in state $t = 0$. The target variable T has two states. Therefore, the zonogons of its second state are symmetric (second column of Equation (6)) and have identical heights.

Appendix G. The Relation of Total Variation to the Zonogon Height

Proof of Lemma 8(a) from Section 4.1.2

The pointwise total variation (i_{TV}) is a linear scaling of the maximal (Euclidean) height h^* that the corresponding zonogon $Z(\kappa)$ reaches above the diagonal, as visualized in Figure 10 for any $0 \leq p \leq 1$.

$$i_{\text{TV}}(p,\kappa) = \frac{1-p}{2} \sum_{v \in \kappa} |v_x - v_y| = (1-p)\frac{h^*}{\sqrt{2}}$$

Proof. The point of maximal height P^* that a zonogon $Z(\kappa)$ reaches above the diagonal is visualized in Figure 10 and can be obtained as shown in Equation (A45), where $\Delta\vec{v}$ represents the slope of vector $\vec{v}$.

$$P^* = \sum_{\vec{v} \in \{\vec{v} \in \kappa \,:\, \Delta\vec{v} > 1\}} \vec{v} \tag{A45}$$

The maximal height (Euclidean distance) above the diagonal is calculated as shown in Equation (A46), where $P^* = (P_x^*, P_y^*)$.

$$h^* = \frac{1}{2} \left\| \begin{pmatrix} P_x^* - P_y^* \\ P_y^* - P_x^* \end{pmatrix} \right\|_2 = \sqrt{(P_x^* - P_y^*)^2 + (P_y^* - P_x^*)^2} = \sqrt{2}(P_y^* - P_x^*) \tag{A46}$$

The pointwise total variation i_{TV} can be expressed as the invertible transformation of the maximal euclidean zonogon height above the diagonal as shown below, where $\vec{v} = (\vec{v}_x, \vec{v}_y)$.

$$\begin{aligned}
i_{\text{TV}}(p,\kappa) &= \sum_{\vec{v} \in \kappa} \frac{1}{2} \left| \frac{\vec{v}_x}{p\vec{v}_x + (1-p)\vec{v}_y} - 1 \right| (p\vec{v}_x + (1-p)\vec{v}_y) \\
&= \frac{1-p}{2} \sum_{\vec{v} \in \kappa} |\vec{v}_x - \vec{v}_y| \\
&= \frac{1-p}{2} \left(\sum_{\vec{v} \in \{\vec{v} \in \kappa \,:\, \Delta\vec{v} > 1\}} (\vec{v}_y - \vec{v}_x) + \sum_{\vec{v} \in \{\vec{v} \in \kappa \,:\, \Delta\vec{v} \leq 1\}} (\vec{v}_x - \vec{v}_y) \right) \\
&= \frac{1-p}{2} \Big((P_y^* - P_x^*) + \big((1 - P_x^*) - (1 - P_y^*) \big) \Big) && \text{(by Equation (A45))} \\
&= (1-p)(P_y^* - P_x^*) \\
&= (1-p)\frac{h^*}{\sqrt{2}} && \text{(by Equation (A46))}
\end{aligned}$$

□

Proof of Lemma 8(b) from Section 4.1.2
For a non-empty set of pointwise channel **A** and $0 \leq p \leq 1$, pointwise total variation i_{TV} quantifies the join element to the maximum of its individual channels:

$$i_{\text{TV}}(p, \bigsqcup_{\kappa \in \mathbf{A}} \kappa) = \max_{\kappa \in \mathbf{A}} i_{\text{TV}}(p, \kappa)$$

Proof. The join element $Z(\bigsqcup_{\kappa \in \mathbf{A}} \kappa)$ corresponds to the convex hull of all individual zonogons (see Equation (7)). The maximal height that the convex hull reaches above the diagonal is equal to the maximum of the maximal height that each individual zonogon reaches. Since pointwise total variation is a linear scaling of the (Euclidean) zonogon height above the diagonal (Lemma 8(a) shown above), the join element is valuated to the maximum of its individual channels. □

Appendix H. Information Flow Example Parameters and Visualization

The parameters for the Markov chain used in Section 4.2 are shown in Equation (A47), where $\mathbf{M}_n = (X_n, Y_n)$, $\mathcal{X}_i = \{0, 1, 2\}$, $\mathcal{Y}_i = \{0, 1\}$, $P_{\mathbf{M}_1}$ is the initial distribution, and $P_{\mathbf{M}_{n+1}|\mathbf{M}_n}$ is the transition matrix. The visualized results for the information flow of KL-, TV-, and χ^2-information can be found in Figure 11, and the visualized results of H^2-, LC-, and JS-information in Figure A3.

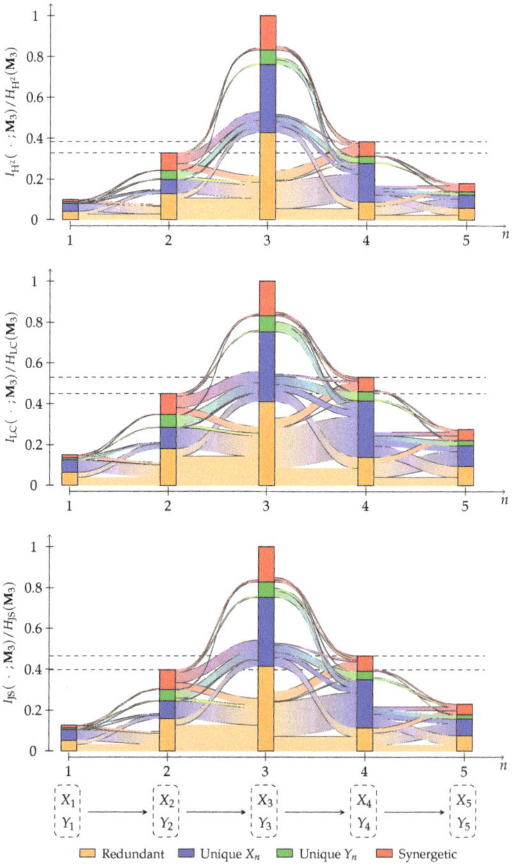

Figure A3. Analysis of the Markov chain information flow (Equation (A47)). Visualized results for the information measures: H^2, LC, and JS. The remaining results (KL, TV, and χ^2) can be found in Figure 11.

$$\text{States } (X_1, Y_1): \quad \begin{matrix} (0,0) & (0,1) & (1,0) & (1,1) & (2,0) & (2,1) \end{matrix} \tag{A47a}$$
$$P_{\mathbf{M}_1} = \begin{bmatrix} 0.01 & 0.81 & 0.00 & 0.02 & 0.09 & 0.07 \end{bmatrix}$$

$$P_{\mathbf{M}_{n+1}|\mathbf{M}_n} = \begin{bmatrix} 0.05 & 0.01 & 0.04 & 0.82 & 0.02 & 0.06 \\ 0.05 & 0.82 & 0.00 & 0.01 & 0.06 & 0.06 \\ 0.04 & 0.01 & 0.82 & 0.05 & 0.04 & 0.04 \\ 0.03 & 0.84 & 0.02 & 0.06 & 0.04 & 0.01 \\ 0.04 & 0.03 & 0.03 & 0.02 & 0.06 & 0.82 \\ 0.07 & 0.04 & 0.01 & 0.03 & 0.81 & 0.04 \end{bmatrix} \tag{A47b}$$

References

1. Williams, P.L.; Beer, R.D. Nonnegative Decomposition of Multivariate Information. *arXiv* **2010**, arXiv:1004.2515.
2. Lizier, J.T.; Bertschinger, N.; Jost, J.; Wibral, M. Information Decomposition of Target Effects from Multi-Source Interactions: Perspectives on Previous, Current and Future Work. *Entropy* **2018**, *20*, 307. [CrossRef] [PubMed]
3. Griffith, V.; Chong, E.K.P.; James, R.G.; Ellison, C.J.; Crutchfield, J.P. Intersection Information Based on Common Randomness. *Entropy* **2014**, *16*, 1985–2000. [CrossRef]
4. Bertschinger, N.; Rauh, J.; Olbrich, E.; Jost, J. Shared Information—New Insights and Problems in Decomposing Information in Complex Systems. In *Proceedings of the European Conference on Complex Systems 2012*; Gilbert, T., Kirkilionis, M., Nicolis, G., Eds.; Springer: Cham, Switzerland, 2013; pp. 251–269.
5. Harder, M.; Salge, C.; Polani, D. Bivariate measure of redundant information. *Phys. Rev. E* **2013**, *87*, 012130. [CrossRef]
6. Finn, C. A New Framework for Decomposing Multivariate Information. Ph.D. Thesis, University of Sydney, Darlington, NSW, Australia, 2019.
7. Polyanskiy, Y.; Wu, Y. *Information Theory: From Coding to Learning*; Book Draft; Cambridge University Press: Cambridge, UK, 2022. Available online: https://people.lids.mit.edu/yp/homepage/data/itbook-2022.pdf (accessed on 13 May 2024).
8. Mironov, I. Rényi Differential Privacy. In Proceedings of the 2017 IEEE 30th Computer Security Foundations Symposium (CSF), Santa Barbara, CA, USA, 21–25 August 2017; pp. 263–275. [CrossRef]
9. Bertschinger, N.; Rauh, J.; Olbrich, E.; Jost, J.; Ay, N. Quantifying Unique Information. *Entropy* **2014**, *16*, 2161–2183. [CrossRef]
10. Griffith, V.; Koch, C., Quantifying Synergistic Mutual Information. In *Guided Self-Organization: Inception*; Springer: Berlin/Heidelberg, Germany, 2014; pp. 159–190. [CrossRef]
11. Goodwell, A.E.; Kumar, P. Temporal information partitioning: Characterizing synergy, uniqueness, and redundancy in interacting environmental variables. *Water Resour. Res.* **2017**, *53*, 5920–5942. [CrossRef]
12. James, R.G.; Emenheiser, J.; Crutchfield, J.P. Unique information via dependency constraints. *J. Phys. A Math. Theor.* **2018**, *52*, 014002. [CrossRef]
13. Finn, C.; Lizier, J.T. Pointwise Partial Information Decomposition Using the Specificity and Ambiguity Lattices. *Entropy* **2018**, *20*, 297. [CrossRef]
14. Ince, R.A.A. Measuring Multivariate Redundant Information with Pointwise Common Change in Surprisal. *Entropy* **2017**, *19*, 318. [CrossRef]
15. Rosas, F.E.; Mediano, P.A.M.; Rassouli, B.; Barrett, A.B. An operational information decomposition via synergistic disclosure. *J. Phys. A Math. Theor.* **2020**, *53*, 485001. [CrossRef]
16. Kolchinsky, A. A Novel Approach to the Partial Information Decomposition. *Entropy* **2022**, *24*, 403. [CrossRef] [PubMed]
17. Bertschinger, N.; Rauh, J. The Blackwell relation defines no lattice. In Proceedings of the 2014 IEEE International Symposium on Information Theory, Honolulu, HI, USA, 29 June–4 July 2014; pp. 2479–2483. [CrossRef]
18. Lizier, J.T.; Flecker, B.; Williams, P.L. Towards a synergy-based approach to measuring information modification. In Proceedings of the 2013 IEEE Symposium on Artificial Life (ALife), Singapore, 16–19 April 2013; pp. 43–51. [CrossRef]
19. Knuth, K.H. Lattices and Their Consistent Quantification. *Ann. Phys.* **2019**, *531*, 1700370. [CrossRef]
20. Mages, T.; Rohner, C. Decomposing and Tracing Mutual Information by Quantifying Reachable Decision Regions. *Entropy* **2023**, *25*, 1014. [CrossRef]
21. Blackwell, D. Equivalent comparisons of experiments. *Ann. Math. Stat.* **1953**, *24*, 265–272. [CrossRef]
22. Neyman, J.; Pearson, E.S. IX. On the problem of the most efficient tests of statistical hypotheses. *Philos. Trans. R. Soc. London. Ser. A Contain. Pap. Math. Phys. Character* **1933**, *231*, 289–337.
23. Chicharro, D.; Panzeri, S. Synergy and Redundancy in Dual Decompositions of Mutual Information Gain and Information Loss. *Entropy* **2017**, *19*, 71. [CrossRef]
24. Csiszár, I. On information-type measure of difference of probability distributions and indirect observations. *Studia Sci. Math. Hungar.* **1967**, *2*, 299–318.

25. Rényi, A. On measures of entropy and information. In Proceedings of the Fourth Berkeley Symposium on Mathematical Statistics and Probability, Volume 1: Contributions to the Theory of Statistics, Berkeley, CA, USA, 20–30 July 1960; University of California Press: Berkeley, NC, USA, 1961; Volume 4, pp. 547–562.
26. Sason, I.; Verdú, S. f-Divergence Inequalities. *IEEE Trans. Inf. Theory* **2016**, *62*, 5973–6006. [CrossRef]
27. Kailath, T. The divergence and Bhattacharyya distance measures in signal selection. *IEEE Trans. Commun. Technol.* **1967**, *15*, 52–60. [CrossRef]
28. Arikan, E. Channel Polarization: A Method for Constructing Capacity-Achieving Codes for Symmetric Binary-Input Memoryless Channels. *IEEE Trans. Inf. Theory* **2009**, *55*, 3051–3073. [CrossRef]
29. Bhattacharyya, A. On a measure of divergence between two statistical populations defined by their probability distribution. *Bull. Calcutta Math. Soc.* **1943**, *35*, 99–110.
30. Mages, T.; Anastasiadi, E.; Rohner, C. Implementation: PID Blackwell Specific Information. 2024. Available online: https://github.com/uu-core/pid-blackwell-specific-information (accessed on 15 March 2024).
31. Cardenas, A.; Baras, J.; Seamon, K. A framework for the evaluation of intrusion detection systems. In Proceedings of the 2006 IEEE Symposium on Security and Privacy (S & P'06), Berkeley, CA, USA, 21–24 May 2006; pp. 15–77. [CrossRef]
32. Rauh, J.; Bertschinger, N.; Olbrich, E.; Jost, J. Reconsidering unique information: Towards a multivariate information decomposition. In Proceedings of the 2014 IEEE International Symposium on Information Theory, Honolulu, HI, USA, 29 June–4 July 2014; pp. 2232–2236. [CrossRef]
33. Bossomaier, T.; Barnett, L.; Harré, M.; Lizier, J.T. *An Introduction to Transfer Entropy*; Springer International Publishing: Cham, Switzerland, 2016. [CrossRef]

entropy

MDPI

Article

Causal Structure Learning with Conditional and Unique Information Groups-Decomposition Inequalities

Daniel Chicharro [1,*] and Julia K. Nguyen [2]

[1] Artificial Intelligence Research Centre, Department of Computer Science, City, University of London, London EC1V 0HB, UK
[2] Department of Neurobiology, Harvard Medical School, Boston, MA 02115, USA
* Correspondence: chicharro31@yahoo.es

Abstract: The causal structure of a system imposes constraints on the joint probability distribution of variables that can be generated by the system. Archetypal constraints consist of conditional independencies between variables. However, particularly in the presence of hidden variables, many causal structures are compatible with the same set of independencies inferred from the marginal distributions of observed variables. Additional constraints allow further testing for the compatibility of data with specific causal structures. An existing family of causally informative inequalities compares the information about a set of target variables contained in a collection of variables, with a sum of the information contained in different groups defined as subsets of that collection. While procedures to identify the form of these groups-decomposition inequalities have been previously derived, we substantially enlarge the applicability of the framework. We derive groups-decomposition inequalities subject to weaker independence conditions, with weaker requirements in the configuration of the groups, and additionally allowing for conditioning sets. Furthermore, we show how constraints with higher inferential power may be derived with collections that include hidden variables, and then converted into testable constraints using data processing inequalities. For this purpose, we apply the standard data processing inequality of conditional mutual information and derive an analogous property for a measure of conditional unique information recently introduced to separate redundant, synergistic, and unique contributions to the information that a set of variables has about a target.

Keywords: causality; directed acyclic graphs; causal discovery; structure learning; causal structures; marginal scenarios; hidden variables; mutual information; unique information; entropic inequalities; data processing inequality

MSC: 62H22; 62D20; 94A15; 94A17

Citation: Chicharro, D.; Nguyen, J.K. Causal Structure Learning with Conditional and Unique Information Groups-Decomposition Inequalities. *Entropy* **2024**, *26*, 440. https://doi.org/10.3390/e26060440

Academic Editor: Richard D. Gill

Received: 13 March 2024
Revised: 12 May 2024
Accepted: 17 May 2024
Published: 23 May 2024

1. Introduction

The inference of the underlying causal structure of a system using observational data is a fundamental question in many scientific domains. The causal structure of a system imposes constraints on the joint probability distribution of variables generated from it [1–4], and these constraints can be exploited to learn the causal structure. Causal learning algorithms based on conditional independencies [1,2,5] allow the construction of a partially oriented graph [6] that represents the equivalence class of all causal structures compatible with the set of conditional independencies present in the distribution of the observable variables (the so-called Markov equivalence class). However, without restrictions on the potential existence and structure of an unknown number of hidden variables that could account for the observed dependencies, Markov equivalence classes may encompass many causal structures compatible with the data.

Conditional independencies impose equality constraints on a joint probability distribution; namely, an independence results in the equality between conditional and unconditional probability distributions, or equivalently, in a null mutual information between independent variables. In addition to the information from independencies between the observed variables, causal information can also be obtained from other functional equality constraints [7], such as dormant independencies that would occur under active interventions [8]. Further causal inference power can be obtained incorporating assumptions on the potential form of the causal mechanisms in order to exploit additional independencies associated with hidden substructures within the generative model [9,10], or independencies related to exogenous noise terms [11–13]. Other approaches have studied the identifiability of specific parametric families of causal models [3,14]. However, these methods only provide additional inference power if the actual causal mechanisms conform to the required parametric form.

Beyond equality constraints, the causal structure may also impose inequality constraints on the distribution of the data [15,16], which reflect non-verifiable independencies involving hidden variables. Figure 1 illustrates this distinction between pairs of causal structures distinguishable based on independence constraints (Figure 1A,B) and causal structures that may be discriminated based on inequality constraints (Figure 1C,D). The structures of Figure 1A,B belong to different Markov equivalence classes because in Figure 1A variables V_1 and V_2 are independent conditioned on S, while in Figure 1B, to obtain an independence it is required to further the condition on V_3. On the other hand, the structures of Figure 1C,D belong to the same equivalence class because no independencies exist between the observable variables $V_i, i = 1, 2, 3$. Nonetheless, if the hidden variables were also observable, these structures would be distinguishable. In Figure 1D, all the dependencies between the observable variables are caused by a single hidden variable U, while in Figure 1C dependencies are created pairwise by different hidden variables. In this case, a testable inequality constraint involving the observable variables reflects the non-verifiable independencies that involve also hidden variables. Intuitively, in Figure 1C, the inequality constraint imposes an upper bound on the overall degree of dependence between the three variables, given that these dependencies arise only in a pairwise manner, while in Figure 1D no such bound exists.

Importantly, unlike equality constraints, inequality constraints provide necessary but not sufficient conditions for the compatibility of data with a certain causal structure. While a certain hypothesized causal structure—like in Figure 1C—may impose the fulfillment of a given inequality intrinsically from its structure, other causal structures—like in Figure 1D—can generate data that, given a particular instantiation of the causal mechanisms, also fulfill the inequality. Accordingly, the causal inference power of inequality constraints lies in the ability to reject hypothesized causal structures that would intrinsically require the fulfillment of an inequality when that inequality is not fulfilled by the data. This means that tighter inequalities have more inferential power, giving the capacity to discard more causal structures.

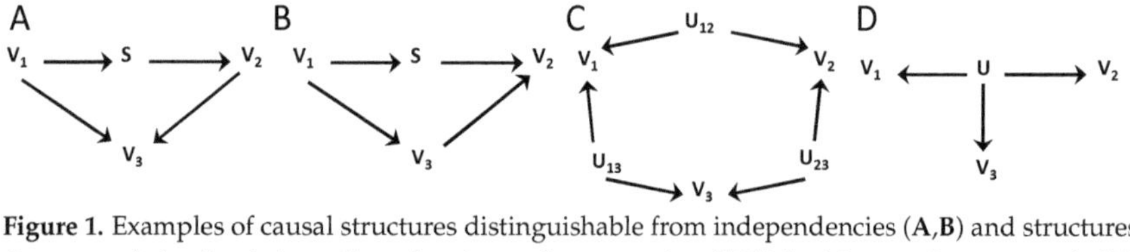

Figure 1. Examples of causal structures distinguishable from independencies (**A**,**B**) and structures that may only be discriminated based on inequality constraints (**C**,**D**). In this case, the structure in (**C**), and not the one in (**D**), intrinsically imposes a constraint due to dependencies between the observable variables $V_i, i = 1, 2, 3$ arising only from pairwise dependencies with hidden common causes.

Two main classes of inequality constraints have been derived. The first class corresponds to inequality constraints in the probability space, which comprise tests of compatibility such as Bell-type inequalities [17,18], instrumental inequalities [19,20], and inequalities that appear on identifiable interventional distributions [21]. The second class corresponds to inequalities involving information-theoretic quantities. The relation between these probabilistic and entropic inequalities has been examined in [22]. One approach to construct entropic inequalities combines the inequalities defining the Shannon entropic cone, i.e., associated with the non-negativity, monotonicity, and submodularity properties of entropy, and additional independence constraints related to the causal structure [23,24]. Additional causally informative inequalities can be derived if considering the so-called Non-Shannon inequalities [25,26]. When the causal structure to be tested involves hidden variables, all non-trivial entropic inequalities in the marginal scenario associated with the set of observable variables can be derived with an algorithmic procedure [23,24] that projects the set of inequalities of all variables into inequalities that only involve the subset of observable variables.

As an alternative approach, information-theoretic inequality constraints can be derived by an explicit analytical formulation [24,27]. In particular, [27] introduced inequalities comparing the information about a target variable contained in a whole collection of variables with a weighted sum of the information contained in groups of variables corresponding to subsets of the collection. Two procedures were introduced to select the composition of these groups. In a first type of inequalities, the composition of the groups is arbitrarily determined, but an inequality only exists under some conditions of independence between the chosen variables, whose fulfillment reflects the underlying causal structure. In a second type, no conditions are required for the existence of an inequality, but the groups must be ancestral sets; that is, must contain all other variables that have a causal effect on any given element of the group. In both cases, [27] showed that the coefficients in the weighted sum of the information contained in groups of variables are determined by the number of intersections between the groups.

In this work, we build upon the results of [27] and generalize their framework of groups-decomposition inequalities in several ways. First, we generalize both types of inequalities to the conditional case, when the inequalities involve conditional mutual information measures instead of unconditional ones. While this extension is trivial for the first type of inequalities, we show that for the second type it requires a definition of augmented ancestral sets. Second, we formulate more flexible conditions of independence for which the first type of inequalities exists. Third, we add flexibility to the construction of the ancestral sets that appear in the second type of inequalities. We show that, given a causal graph and a conditioning set of variables used for the conditional mutual information measures, alternative inequalities exist when determining ancestors in subgraphs that eliminate causal connections from different subsets of the conditioning variables. Furthermore, we determine conditions in which an inequality also holds when removing subsets of ancestors from the whole set of variables, hence relaxing for the second type of inequalities the requirement that the groups correspond to ancestral sets.

Apart from these generalizations, we expand the power of the approach of [27] by considering inequalities whose existence is determined by the partition into groups of a collection of variables that also contains hidden variables. That is, hidden variables can appear not only as hidden common ancestors of the collection but also as part (or even all) of the variables in the collection for which the inequality is defined. To render operational the use of inequalities derived from collections containing hidden variables, we develop procedures that allow mapping those inequalities into testable inequalities that only involve observable variables. While this mapping can be carried out by simply applying the monotonicity of mutual information to remove hidden variables from the groups, this does not work when all variables in the collection are hidden. We show that data processing inequalities [28] can be applied to obtain testable inequalities also in this case, or applied to obtain tighter inequalities than those obtained by simply removing the hidden variables. We illustrate how testable inequalities whose coefficients in the weighted sum depend on intersections among subsets of hidden variables instead of among subsets of observable variables can result into tighter inequalities with higher inferential power.

In order to derive testable groups-decomposition inequalities, we do not only apply the standard data processing inequality of conditional mutual information [28], but we derive an additional data processing inequality for the so-called *unique information* measure introduced in [29]. This measure was introduced in the framework of a decomposition of mutual information into redundant, unique, and synergistic information components [30]. Recently, alternative decompositions have been proposed to decompose the joint mutual information that a set of predictor variables has about a target variable into redundant, synergistic, and unique components [31–35] (among others). These alternative decompositions generally differ in the quantification of each component and differ in whether the measures fulfill certain properties or axioms. However, in our work, we do not apply the unique information measure of [29] as part of a decomposition of the joint mutual information. Instead, we show that it provides an alternative data processing inequality that holds for different causal configurations than the standard data processing inequality of conditional mutual information. In this way, the unique information data processing inequality increases the capability to eliminate hidden variables in order to obtain testable groups-decomposition inequalities. Accordingly, the groups-decomposition inequalities we derive can contain unique information terms apart from the standard mutual information and entropy measures that appear when considering the constraints of the Shannon entropic cone [23,24].

We envisage the application of the causally informative tests here proposed in the following way. Given a data set, a hypothesized causal structure is selected to test its compatibility with the data. First, the set of inequality constraints enforced by that causal structure is determined. Second, their fulfillment is evaluated from the data and the causal structure is discarded if some inequality does not hold. In the first step, the determination of the set of groups-decomposition inequalities enforced by a causal structure requires at different levels the verification of conditional independencies. This is the case, for example, with the conditional independencies that are necessary conditions for the existence of the first type of inequalities introduced by [27]. If all variables involved were observable, this verification could be conducted directly from the data. However, as mentioned above, we here consider groups-decomposition inequalities that may contain hidden variables as part of the collection of variables, which precludes this direct verification. For this reason, we will work under the assumption that statistical independencies can be assessed from the structure of the causal graph, namely with the graphical criterion of separability between nodes in the graph known as *d-separation* [36]. That is, we will rely on the assumption that graphical separability is a sufficient condition for statistical independence and hence characterize the set of groups-decomposition inequalities enforced by a causal structure without using the data. Data would only be used in the second step, in which the actual fulfillment of the inequalities is evaluated.

This paper is organized as follows. In Section 2, we review previous work relevant for our contributions. In Section 3.1, we formulate the data processing inequality for the unique information measure. In Section 3.2, we generalize the first type of inequalities of [27], formulating for the conditional case more general conditions of independence for which a groups-decomposition inequality exists. We also apply data processing inequalities to derive testable groups-decomposition inequalities when collections include hidden variables. In Section 3.3, we generalize the second type of inequalities of [27] as outlined above. In Section 4, we discuss the connection of this work with other approaches to causal structure learning and point to future continuations and potential applications. The Appendix contains proofs of the results (Appendices A and B) and a discussion of the relations between conditional independencies and d-separations required so that the inequalities here derived are applicable to test causal structures (Appendix C).

2. Previous Work on Information-Theoretic Measures and Causal Graphs Relevant for Our Derivations

In this section we review properties of information-theoretic measures and concepts of causal graphs relevant for our work. In Section 2.1, we review basic inequalities of the mutual information and in Section 2.2 the definition and relevant properties of the unique information measure of [29]. We then review in Section 2.3 Directed Acyclic Graphs (DAGs) and their relation to conditional independence through the graphical criterion of *d-separation* [36,37]. Finally, we review the inequalities introduced by [27] to test causal structures from information decompositions involving sums of groups of variables (Section 2.4). We do not aim to more broadly review other types of information-theoretic inequalities [23,24] also used for causal inference. The relation with these other types will be considered in the Discussion.

2.1. Mutual Information Inequalities Associated with Independencies

We present in Lemma 1 two well-known inequalities that will be used in our derivations. This lemma corresponds to Lemma 1 in [27]. For completion, we provide the proof of the lemma.

Lemma 1. *The mutual information fulfills the following inequalities in the presence of the corresponding independencies:*

(i) (Conditional mutual information data processing inequality): Let $\mathbf{A}$, $\mathbf{B}$, $\mathbf{B}'$, *and* $\mathbf{D}$ *be four sets of variables. If* $I(\mathbf{A};\mathbf{B}'|\mathbf{B},\mathbf{D}) = 0$, *then it follows that* $I(\mathbf{A};\mathbf{B}|\mathbf{D}) \geqslant I(\mathbf{A};\mathbf{B}'|\mathbf{D})$.

(ii) (Increase through conditioning on independent sets): Let $\mathbf{A}$, $\mathbf{B}$, $\mathbf{C}$, *and* $\mathbf{Y}$ *be four sets of variables. If* $I(\mathbf{A};\mathbf{C}|\mathbf{B}) = 0$, *then* $I(\mathbf{Y};\mathbf{A}|\mathbf{B}) \leqslant I(\mathbf{Y};\mathbf{A}|\mathbf{B},\mathbf{C})$.

Proof. (i) is proven applying, in two different orders, the chain rule of the mutual information to $I(\mathbf{A};\mathbf{B},\mathbf{B}'|\mathbf{D})$:

$$I(\mathbf{A};\mathbf{B},\mathbf{B}'|\mathbf{D}) = I(\mathbf{A};\mathbf{B}|\mathbf{D}) + I(\mathbf{A};\mathbf{B}'|\mathbf{B},\mathbf{D}) = I(\mathbf{A};\mathbf{B}'|\mathbf{D}) + I(\mathbf{A};\mathbf{B}|\mathbf{B}',\mathbf{D}).$$

Since $I(\mathbf{A};\mathbf{B}'|\mathbf{B},\mathbf{D}) = 0$ and the mutual information is non-negative, this implies the inequality. To prove (ii), the chain rule is applied in different orders to $I(\mathbf{Y},\mathbf{C};\mathbf{A}|\mathbf{B})$:

$$I(\mathbf{Y},\mathbf{C};\mathbf{A}|\mathbf{B}) = I(\mathbf{C};\mathbf{A}|\mathbf{B}) + I(\mathbf{Y};\mathbf{A}|\mathbf{B},\mathbf{C}) = I(\mathbf{Y};\mathbf{A}|\mathbf{B}) + I(\mathbf{C};\mathbf{A}|\mathbf{B},\mathbf{Y}).$$

Since $I(\mathbf{C};\mathbf{A}|\mathbf{B}) = 0$ and the mutual information is non-negative, this implies the inequality. □

2.2. Definition and Properties of the Unique Information

The concept of *unique information* as part of a decomposition of the joint mutual information $I(\mathbf{Y};\mathbf{X})$ that a set of predictor variables $\mathbf{X} = \{\mathbf{X}_1, \ldots, \mathbf{X}_N\}$ has about a target (possibly multivariate) variable $\mathbf{Y}$ was introduced in [30]. In the simplest case of two predictors $\{\mathbf{X}_1, \mathbf{X}_2\}$, this framework decomposes the joint mutual information about $\mathbf{Y}$ into four terms, namely the redundancy of $\mathbf{X}_1$ and $\mathbf{X}_2$, the unique information of $\mathbf{X}_1$ with respect to $\mathbf{X}_2$, the unique information of $\mathbf{X}_2$ with respect to $\mathbf{X}_1$, and the synergy between $\mathbf{X}_1$ and $\mathbf{X}_2$. The predictors share the redundant component, the synergistic one is only obtained by combining the predictors, and unique components are exclusive to each predictor. Several information measures have been proposed to define this decomposition, aiming to comply with a set of desirable properties which were not all fulfilled by the original proposal [29,31–33]. However, in this work we will not study the whole decomposition but specifically apply the bivariate measure of unique information introduced in [29]. In Section 3.1, we derive a data processing inequality for this measure and in Section 3.2 we show how it can help to obtain testable groups-decomposition inequalities for causal structures for which the standard data processing inequality of the mutual information would not allow elimination of the hidden variables. In this Section, we review the definition of the unique information measure of [29], we provide a straightforward generalization to a conditional unique information measure, and state a monotonicity property that will be used to derive the data processing inequality of the unique information. The unique information of $\mathbf{X}_1$ with respect to $\mathbf{X}_2$ about $\mathbf{Y}$ was defined as

$$I(\mathbf{Y};\mathbf{X}_1\backslash\backslash\mathbf{X}_2) \equiv \min_{Q\in\Delta_P} I_Q(\mathbf{Y};\mathbf{X}_1|\mathbf{X}_2), \quad (1)$$

where Δ_P is defined as the set of distributions on $\{\mathbf{Y}, \mathbf{X}_1, \mathbf{X}_2\}$ that preserve the marginals $P(\mathbf{Y}, \mathbf{X}_1)$ and $P(\mathbf{Y}, \mathbf{X}_2)$ of the original distribution $P(\mathbf{Y}, \mathbf{X}_1, \mathbf{X}_2)$. The notation I_Q is used to indicate that the mutual information is calculated on the probability distribution Q. We use $I(\mathbf{Y}; \mathbf{X}_1 \backslash\backslash \mathbf{X}_2)$ to refer to the unique information of $\mathbf{X}_1$ with respect to $\mathbf{X}_2$, compared to $I(\mathbf{Y}; \mathbf{X}_1 | \mathbf{X}_2)$, which is the standard conditional information of $\mathbf{X}_1$ given $\mathbf{X}_2$. We use the notation $\mathbf{X}_1 \backslash\backslash \mathbf{X}_2$ instead of the notation $\mathbf{X}_1 \backslash \mathbf{X}_2$ introduced by [29] to differentiate it from the set notation $\mathbf{X}_1 \backslash \mathbf{X}_2$, which indicates the subset of variables in $\mathbf{X}_1$ that is not contained in $\mathbf{X}_2$, since we will also be using this set notation. This unique information measure is a maximum entropy measure, since all distributions within Δ_P preserve the conditional entropy $H(\mathbf{Y}|\mathbf{X}_2)$, and hence the minimization is equivalent to a maximization of the conditional entropy $H(\mathbf{Y}|\mathbf{X}_1, \mathbf{X}_2)$. The rationale that supports this definition is that the unique information of $\mathbf{X}_1$ with respect to $\mathbf{X}_2$ about $\mathbf{Y}$ has to be determined by the marginal probabilities $P(\mathbf{Y}, \mathbf{X}_1)$ and $P(\mathbf{Y}, \mathbf{X}_2)$, and cannot depend on any additional structure in the joint distribution that contributes to the dependence between $\{\mathbf{X}_1, \mathbf{X}_2\}$ and $\mathbf{Y}$ [29]. This additional contribution is removed by minimizing within Δ_P.

In a straightforward generalization, we define the conditional unique information given another set of variables $\mathbf{Z}$ as

$$I(\mathbf{Y}; \mathbf{X}_1 \backslash\backslash \mathbf{X}_2 | \mathbf{Z}) \equiv \min_{Q \in \Delta_{P'}} I_Q(\mathbf{Y}; \mathbf{X}_1 | \mathbf{X}_2, \mathbf{Z}), \tag{2}$$

where $\Delta_{P'}$ is the set of distributions on $\{\mathbf{Y}, \mathbf{X}_1, \mathbf{X}_2, \mathbf{Z}\}$ that preserve the marginals $P(\mathbf{Y}, \mathbf{X}_1, \mathbf{Z})$ and $P(\mathbf{Y}, \mathbf{X}_2, \mathbf{Z})$ of the original $P(\mathbf{Y}, \mathbf{X}_1, \mathbf{X}_2, \mathbf{Z})$. By construction [29], the conditional unique information is bounded as

$$\min\{I(\mathbf{Y}; \mathbf{X}_1 | \mathbf{Z}), I(\mathbf{Y}; \mathbf{X}_1 | \mathbf{X}_2, \mathbf{Z})\} \geqslant I(\mathbf{Y}; \mathbf{X}_1 \backslash\backslash \mathbf{X}_2 | \mathbf{Z}) \geqslant 0. \tag{3}$$

This is consistent with the intuition of the decomposition that the unique information is a component exclusive of X_1. In Lemma 2, we present a type of monotonicity fulfilled by the conditional unique information. This result is a straightforward extension to the conditional case of the one stated in Lemma 3 of [38]. We include the full proof because it will be useful in the Results section to prove a related data processing inequality for the unique information. To better suit our subsequent use of notation, we consider the two predictors to be $\mathbf{Z}_1$ and $\{\mathbf{X}_1, \mathbf{X}_1'\}$, and the conditioning set to be $\mathbf{Z}_2$.

Lemma 2. *The maximum entropy conditional unique information is monotonic on its second argument, corresponding to the non-conditioning predictor, as follows:*

$$I(\mathbf{Y}; \mathbf{X}_1, \mathbf{X}_1' \backslash\backslash \mathbf{Z}_1 | \mathbf{Z}_2) \geqslant I(\mathbf{Y}; \mathbf{X}_1 \backslash\backslash \mathbf{Z}_1 | \mathbf{Z}_2).$$

Proof. Consider the distribution $P_{1,1'} \equiv P(\mathbf{Y}, \mathbf{X}_1, \mathbf{X}_1', \mathbf{Z}_1, \mathbf{Z}_2)$ and its marginal $P_1 \equiv P(\mathbf{Y}, \mathbf{X}_1, \mathbf{Z}_1, \mathbf{Z}_2)$. Consider any distribution $Q_{1,1'} \in \Delta_{P_{1,1'}}$ and its marginal Q_1 on $(\mathbf{Y}, \mathbf{X}_1, \mathbf{Z}_1, \mathbf{Z}_2)$. Then $Q_1 \in \Delta_{P_1}$. By monotonicity of the mutual information, $I_{Q_{1,1'}}(\mathbf{Y}; \mathbf{X}_1 | \mathbf{Z}_1, \mathbf{Z}_2)$ is lower than or equal to $I_{Q_{1,1'}}(\mathbf{Y}; \mathbf{X}_1, \mathbf{X}_1' | \mathbf{Z}_1, \mathbf{Z}_2)$. Since $I_{Q_{1,1'}}(\mathbf{Y}; \mathbf{X}_1 | \mathbf{Z}_1, \mathbf{Z}_2)$ does not have $\mathbf{X}_1'$ as an argument, it is equal to the information calculated on its marginal $I_{Q_1}(\mathbf{Y}; \mathbf{X}_1 | \mathbf{Z}_1, \mathbf{Z}_2)$. Since this holds for any distribution in $\Delta_{P_{1,1'}}$, it holds in particular for the distribution $Q^*_{1,1'}$ that minimizes $I(\mathbf{Y}; \mathbf{X}_1, \mathbf{X}_1' | \mathbf{Z}_1, \mathbf{Z}_2)$ in $\Delta_{P_{1,1'}}$. Since Q_1^* belongs to Δ_{P_1}, the minimum of $I(\mathbf{Y}; \mathbf{X}_1 | \mathbf{Z}_1, \mathbf{Z}_2)$ in Δ_{P_1} is equal to or smaller than $I_{Q_1^*}(\mathbf{Y}; \mathbf{X}_1 | \mathbf{Z}_1, \mathbf{Z}_2)$ and hence equal to or smaller than $I_{Q^*_{1,1'}}(\mathbf{Y}; \mathbf{X}_1, \mathbf{X}_1' | \mathbf{Z}_1, \mathbf{Z}_2)$. □

2.3. Causal Graphs and Conditional Independencies

We here review basic notions of Directed Acyclic Graphs (DAGs) and the relation between causal structures and dependencies. Consider a set of random variables $\mathbf{V} = \{V_1, \ldots, V_n\}$. A DAG $G = (\mathbf{V}; \mathcal{E})$ consists of nodes $\mathbf{V}$ and edges $\mathcal{E}$ between the nodes. The graph contains $V_i \rightarrow V_j$ for each $(V_i; V_j) \in \mathcal{E}$. We refer to V as both a variable and its corresponding node.

Causal influences can be represented in acyclic graphs given that causal mechanisms are not instantaneous and causal loops can be spanned using separate time-indexed variables. A path in G is a sequence of (at least two) distinct nodes $V_1, \ldots, V_m$, such that there is an edge between V_k and V_{k+1} for all $k = 1, \ldots, m-1$. If all edges are directed as $V_k \rightarrow V_{k+1}$ the path is a causal or directed path. A node V_i is a collider in a path if it has incoming arrows $V_{i-1} \rightarrow V_i \leftarrow V_{i+1}$ and is a noncollider otherwise. A node V_i is called a parent of V_j if there is an arrow $V_i \rightarrow V_j$. The set of parents is denoted $\mathbf{Pa}_{V_j}$. A node V_i is called an ancestor of V_j if there is a directed path from V_i to V_j. Conversely, in this case V_j is a descendant of V_i. For convenience, we define the set of ancestors $an_G(V_i)$ as including V_i itself, and the set of descendants $D_G(V_i)$ as also containing V_i itself.

The link between generative mechanisms and causal graphs relies on the fact that in the graph a variable V_i is a parent of another variable V_j if and only if it is an argument of an underlying functional equation that captures the mechanisms that generate V_j; that is, an argument of $V_j := f_{V_j}(\mathbf{Pa}_{V_j}, \varepsilon_{V_j})$, where ε_{V_j} captures additional sources of stochasticity exogenous to the system. If a DAG constitutes an accurate representation of the causal mechanisms, an isomorphic relation exists between the conditional independencies that hold between variables in the system and a graphical criterion of separability between the nodes, called *d-separation* [36]. Two nodes X and Y are *d-separated* given a set of nodes $\mathbf{S}$ if and only if no $\mathbf{S}$-active paths exist between X and Y. A path is active given the conditioning set $\mathbf{S}$ ($\mathbf{S}$-active) if no noncollider in the path belongs to $\mathbf{S}$ and every collider in the path either is in $\mathbf{S}$ or has a descendant in $\mathbf{S}$. A causal structure G and a generated probability distribution $p(\mathbf{V})$ are *faithful* [1,2] to one another when a conditional independence between X and Y given $\mathbf{S}$—denoted by $X \perp_P Y|\mathbf{S}$—holds if and only if there is no $\mathbf{S}$-active path between them; that is, if X and Y are d-separated given $\mathbf{S}$—denoted by $X \perp_G Y|\mathbf{S}$. Accordingly, faithfulness is assumed in the algorithms of causal inference [1,2] that examine conditional independencies to characterize the Markov equivalence class of causal structures that share a common set of independencies. A well-known example of a system that is unfaithful to its causal structure is the exclusive-OR (X-OR) logic gate, whose output is independent of the two inputs separately but dependent on them jointly.

In contrast to the algorithms that infer Markov equivalence classes, we will show that the applicability of the groups-decomposition inequalities here studied relies on the assumption that d-separability is a sufficient condition for conditional independence. That is, instead of an *if and only if* relation between d-separability and conditional independence, as required in the faithfulness assumption, it is enough to assume that d-separability implies conditional independence. As we further discuss in Appendix C, this is a substantially weaker assumption, since usually faithfulness is violated due to the presence of independencies that are incompatible with the causal structure. This is the case, for example, of the X-OR logic gate, for which faithfulness is violated because the inputs are separately independent of the output despite each having an arrow towards the output in the corresponding causal graph. Conversely, the X-OR gate complies with d-separability being a sufficient condition for independence, since in the graph only the input nodes are d-separated and the corresponding input variables of the X-OR gate are independent. Despite only requiring that d-separability implies independence, to simplify the presentation of our results in the main text we will assume faithfulness and indistinctively use $X \perp Y|\mathbf{S}$ to indicate statistical independence and graphical separability, instead of distinguishing between $X \perp_P Y|\mathbf{S}$ and $X \perp_G Y|\mathbf{S}$. In Appendix C, we will more closely examine how in the proofs of our results the sufficient condition of d-separability for conditional independencies is enough. An important implication of independencies following from d-separability is that, if variables $\{X_1, X_2\}$ are separately independent from Y—namely $Y \perp X_1$ and $Y \perp X_2$—because of the lack of any connection between node Y and both nodes X_1 and X_2, then $\{X_1, X_2\}$ cannot be jointly dependent on Y, namely $Y \not\perp \{X_1, X_2\}$ cannot occur. This is because d-separability between node Y and the set of nodes $\{X_1, X_2\}$ is determined by separately considering the lack of active paths between Y and each node X_1 and X_2. Since the set of paths between Y and $\{X_1, X_2\}$ is the union of the paths between

Y and both X_1 and X_2, considering $\{X_1, X_2\}$ jointly does not add new paths that could create a dependence of Y with $\{X_1, X_2\}$. A dependence can only be created by conditioning on some other variable, which could activate additional paths by activating a collider.

2.4. Inequalities for Sums of Information Terms from Groups of Variables

We now review two results in [27] that are at the foundation of our results. The first corresponds to their Proposition 1. We provide a slightly more general formulation that is useful for subsequent extensions.

Proposition 1. *(Decomposition of information from groups with conditionally independent non-shared components): Consider a collection of groups* $\mathbf{A}_{[n]} \equiv \{\mathbf{A}_1, \ldots, \mathbf{A}_n\}$*, where each group* $\mathbf{A}_i$ *consists of a subset of observable variables* $\mathbf{A}_i \subset \mathcal{O}$*, being* $\mathcal{O}$ *the set of all observable variables. For every* $\mathbf{A}_i \in \mathbf{A}_{[n]}$*, define* d_i *as the maximal value such that* $\mathbf{A}_i$ *has a non-empty intersection where it intersects jointly with* $d_i - 1$ *other distinct groups out of* $\mathbf{A}_{[n]}$*. Consider a conditioning set* $\mathbf{Z}$ *and target variables* $\mathbf{Y}$*. If each group is conditionally independent given* $\mathbf{Z}$ *from the non-shared variables in each other group (i.e.,* $\mathbf{A}_i \perp \mathbf{A}_j \backslash \mathbf{A}_i | \mathbf{Z}, \forall i, j$*), then the conditional information that* $\mathbf{A}_{[n]}$ *has about the target variables* $\mathbf{Y}$ *given* $\mathbf{Z}$ *is bounded from below by*

$$I(\mathbf{Y}; \mathbf{A}_{[n]} | \mathbf{Z}) \geqslant \sum_{i=1}^{n} \frac{1}{d_i} I(\mathbf{Y}; \mathbf{A}_i | \mathbf{Z}).$$

Proof. The proof is presented in Appendix A. It is a generalization to the conditional case of the proof of Proposition 1 in [27] and a slight generalization that allows for dependencies to exist between variables shared by two groups as long as dependencies with non-shared variables do not exist. □

An illustration of Proposition 1 for the unconditional case is presented in Figure 3 of [27], together with further discussion. In Section 3.2 we will provide further illustrations for the extensions of Proposition 1 that we introduce. We will use $\mathbf{d} \equiv \{d_1, \ldots, d_n\}$ to indicate the maximal values for all groups. We will add a subindex $\mathbf{d}_{\mathbf{A}_{[n]}}$ to specify the collection if different collections are compared. A trivial refinement of Proposition 1 would consider $I(\mathbf{Y}; \mathbf{A}_{[n]} \backslash \mathbf{Z} | \mathbf{Z})$ and for each group $I(\mathbf{Y}; \mathbf{A}_i \backslash \mathbf{Z} | \mathbf{Z})$. This may lead to a tighter lower bound by decreasing some values in $\mathbf{d}$ if some intersections between groups occur in $\mathbf{Z}$. We do not present this refinement in order to simplify the presentation.

The second result from [27] that we will be relying on is their Theorem 1. We present a version that is slightly reduced and modified, which is more convenient in order to relate to our own results.

Theorem 1. *(Decomposition of information in ancestral groups.) Let* G *be a DAG model that includes nodes corresponding to the variables in a collection of groups* $\mathbf{A}_{[n]} \equiv \{\mathbf{A}_1, \ldots, \mathbf{A}_n\}$*, which is a subset all observable variables* $\mathcal{O}$*. Let* $an_G(\mathbf{A}_{[n]}) \equiv \{an_G(\mathbf{A}_1), \ldots, an_G(\mathbf{A}_n)\}$ *be the collection of ancestors of the groups, as determined by* G*. For every ancestral set of a group,* $an_G(\mathbf{A}_i)$*, let* $d_i(G)$ *be maximal, such that there is a non-empty joint intersection of* $an_G(\mathbf{A}_i)$ *and other* $d_i(G) - 1$ *distinct ancestral sets out of* $an_G(\mathbf{A}_{[n]})$*. Let* $\mathbf{Y}$ *be a set of target variables. Then the information of* $an_G(\mathbf{A}_{[n]})$ *about* $\mathbf{Y}$ *is bounded as*

$$H(\mathbf{Y}) \geqslant I(\mathbf{Y}; an_G(\mathbf{A}_{[n]})) \geqslant \sum_{i=1}^{n} \frac{1}{d_i(G)} I(\mathbf{Y}; an_G(\mathbf{A}_i)).$$

Proof. The original proof can be found in [27]. □

In contrast to Proposition 1, a generalization to the conditional mutual information is not trivial and will be developed in Section 3.3. We will also propose additional generalizations regarding which graph to use to construct the ancestral sets and conditions to exclude some ancestors from the groups. In their work, [27] conceptualized $\mathbf{Y}$ as corresponding to leaf nodes in the graph, for example providing some noisy measurement of $\mathbf{A}_{[n]}$, with $\mathbf{Y} = \mathbf{A}_{[n]}$ being the case of perfect measurement. While this conceptualization guided their presentation, their results were general, and here we will not assume any concrete causal relation between $\mathbf{Y}$ and $\mathbf{A}_{[n]}$. We have slightly modified the presentation of Theorem 1 from [27] to add the upper bound and to remove some additional subcases with extra assumptions presented in their work. The upper bound is the standard upper bound of mutual information by entropy [28]. In the Results, we will also be interested in cases in which $an_G(\mathbf{A}_{[n]})$ contains hidden variables, so that $I(\mathbf{Y}; an_G(\mathbf{A}_{[n]}))$ cannot be estimated. Given the monotonicity of mutual information, the terms from each ancestral group can be lower bounded by the information in the observable variables within each group and $H(\mathbf{Y})$ is used as a testable upper bound.

There are two main differences between Proposition 1 and Theorem 1. First, Theorem 1 does not impose conditions of independence for the inequality to hold. Second, while the value d_i of each group $\mathbf{A}_i$ is determined in Proposition 1 by the overlap between groups, with no influence of the causal structure relating the variables, on the other hand in Theorem 1 the value $d_i(G)$ depends on the causal structure, since it is determined from the intersections between ancestral sets. Despite these differences, given the relation between causal structure and independencies reviewed in Section 2.3, both types of inequalities can have causal inference power to test the compatibility of certain causal structures with data.

3. Results

In Section 3.1, we introduce a data processing inequality for the conditional unique information measure of [29]. In Section 3.2, we develop new information inequalities involving groups of variables and examine how data processing inequalities can help to derive testable inequalities in the presence of hidden variables. In Section 3.3, we develop new information inequalities involving ancestral sets. The application of these inequalities for causal structure learning is discussed. As justified in the proofs of our results (Appendices A and B) and further discussed in Appendix C, our derivations of groups-decomposition inequalities only rely on the assumption that d-separability implies conditional independence. No further assumptions are used in our work, in particular, our application of the unique information measures of [29] does not require any assumption regarding the precise distribution of the joint mutual information among redundancy, unique, and synergistic components.

3.1. Data Processing Inequality for Conditional Unique Information

Proposition 2. *(Conditional unique information data processing inequality): Let* $\mathbf{A}$, $\mathbf{B}$, $\mathbf{B}'$, $\mathbf{D}$, *and* $\mathbf{E}$ *be five sets of variables. If* $I(\mathbf{A}; \mathbf{B}'|\mathbf{B}, \mathbf{E}) = 0$, *then* $I(\mathbf{A}; \mathbf{B}, \mathbf{B}' \backslash\backslash \mathbf{D}|\mathbf{E}) = I(\mathbf{A}; \mathbf{B} \backslash\backslash \mathbf{D}|\mathbf{E}) \geqslant I(\mathbf{A}; \mathbf{B}' \backslash\backslash \mathbf{D}|\mathbf{E})$.

Proof. Let $P_{BB'} \equiv P(\mathbf{A}, \mathbf{B}, \mathbf{B}', \mathbf{D}, \mathbf{E})$ be the original distribution of the variables and define $\Delta_{P_{BB'}}$ as the set of distributions on $\{\mathbf{A}, \mathbf{B}, \mathbf{B}', \mathbf{D}, \mathbf{E}\}$ that preserve the two marginals $P(\mathbf{A}, \mathbf{B}, \mathbf{B}', \mathbf{E})$ and $P(\mathbf{A}, \mathbf{D}, \mathbf{E})$. Let $P_B \equiv P(\mathbf{A}, \mathbf{B}, \mathbf{D}, \mathbf{E})$ be the marginal of $P_{BB'}$ and Δ_{P_B} be the set of distributions that preserve the marginals $P(\mathbf{A}, \mathbf{B}, \mathbf{E})$ and $P(\mathbf{A}, \mathbf{D}, \mathbf{E})$. By the definition of unique information (Equation (2))

$$\begin{aligned} I(\mathbf{A}; \mathbf{B}, \mathbf{B}' \backslash\backslash \mathbf{D}|\mathbf{E}) &\equiv \min_{Q_{BB'} \in \Delta_{P_{BB'}}} I_{Q_{BB'}}(\mathbf{A}; \mathbf{B}, \mathbf{B}'|\mathbf{D}, \mathbf{E}) \overset{(a)}{=} \\ &\min_{Q_{BB'} \in \Delta_{P_{BB'}}} \left[I_{Q_{BB'}}(\mathbf{A}; \mathbf{B}|\mathbf{D}, \mathbf{E}) + I_{Q_{BB'}}(\mathbf{A}; \mathbf{B}'|\mathbf{B}, \mathbf{D}, \mathbf{E}) \right] \overset{(b)}{=} \\ &\min_{Q_{BB'} \in \Delta_{P_{BB'}}} \left[I_{Q_B}(\mathbf{A}; \mathbf{B}|\mathbf{D}, \mathbf{E}) + I_{Q_{BB'}}(\mathbf{A}; \mathbf{B}'|\mathbf{B}, \mathbf{D}, \mathbf{E}) \right]. \end{aligned} \tag{4}$$

Equality (a) follows from the chain rule of mutual information. Equality (b) holds because $I_{Q_{BB'}}(\mathbf{A};\mathbf{B}|\mathbf{D},\mathbf{E})$ does not depend on $\mathbf{B}'$ and can be calculated with the marginal Q_B, marginalizing $Q_{BB'}$ on $\mathbf{B}'$. Note that $Q_B \in \Delta_{P_B}$. Since $I_{P_{BB'}}(\mathbf{A};\mathbf{B}'|\mathbf{B},\mathbf{E})$ is null, $P(\mathbf{A},\mathbf{B},\mathbf{B}',\mathbf{E})$ factorizes as $P(\mathbf{B}'|\mathbf{B},\mathbf{E})P(\mathbf{A},\mathbf{B},\mathbf{E})$. For any distribution $\tilde{Q}_B \in \Delta_{P_B}$, which preserves $P(\mathbf{A},\mathbf{D},\mathbf{E})$ and $P(\mathbf{A},\mathbf{B},\mathbf{E})$, a distribution can be constructed as $\tilde{Q}_{BB'} \equiv P(\mathbf{B}'|\mathbf{B},\mathbf{E})\tilde{Q}_B$, such that $\tilde{Q}_{BB'} \in \Delta_{P_{BB'}}$, since $\tilde{Q}_{BB'}$ continues to preserve $P(\mathbf{A},\mathbf{D},\mathbf{E})$ and $P(\mathbf{A},\mathbf{B},\mathbf{B}',\mathbf{E})$ is preserved by construction. Also by construction, $I_{\tilde{Q}_{BB'}}(\mathbf{A};\mathbf{B}'|\mathbf{B},\mathbf{D},\mathbf{E}) = 0$ for any $\tilde{Q}_{BB'}$ created from any $\tilde{Q}_B \in \Delta_{P_B}$. In particular, this holds for the distribution $\tilde{Q}^*_{BB'}$ constructed from $\tilde{Q}^*_B$ that minimizes $I_{\tilde{Q}_B}(\mathbf{A};\mathbf{B}|\mathbf{D},\mathbf{E})$, which determines $I(\mathbf{A};\mathbf{B}\backslash\backslash\mathbf{D}|\mathbf{E})$. The distribution $\tilde{Q}^*_{BB'}$ minimizes the first term in the r.h.s of Equation (4) and, given the non-negativity of mutual information, it also minimizes the second term, hence providing the minimum in $\Delta_{P_{BB'}}$. Accordingly, $I(\mathbf{A};\mathbf{B},\mathbf{B}'\backslash\backslash\mathbf{D}|\mathbf{E}) = I(\mathbf{A};\mathbf{B}\backslash\backslash\mathbf{D}|\mathbf{E})$. The monotonicity of unique information on the non-conditioning predictor (Lemma 2) leads to $I(\mathbf{A};\mathbf{B},\mathbf{B}'\backslash\backslash\mathbf{D}|\mathbf{E}) \geqslant I(\mathbf{A};\mathbf{B}'\backslash\backslash\mathbf{D}|\mathbf{E})$. □

A related data processing inequality has already been previously derived for the unconditional unique information in the case of $I(\mathbf{A},\mathbf{D};\mathbf{B}'|\mathbf{B}) = 0$, with $\mathbf{E} = \varnothing$ [39]. Differently, Proposition 2 formulates a data processing inequality for the case $I(\mathbf{A};\mathbf{B}'|\mathbf{B},\mathbf{E}) = 0$. When $\mathbf{E} = \varnothing$, Proposition 2 states a weaker requirement for the existence of an inequality, given the *decomposition axiom* of the mutual information [27]. As we will now see in Section 3.2, Proposition 2 will allow us to apply the unique information data processing inequality in cases in which $I(\mathbf{A};\mathbf{B}'|\mathbf{B},\mathbf{E}) = 0$. In particular, $I(\mathbf{A};\mathbf{B},\mathbf{B}'\backslash\backslash\mathbf{D}|\mathbf{E}) \geqslant I(\mathbf{A};\mathbf{B}'\backslash\backslash\mathbf{D}|\mathbf{E})$ allows us to obtain a lower bound when $\mathbf{B}$ contains hidden variables that we want to eliminate in order to have a testable groups-decomposition inequality. In contrast, the application of the standard data processing inequality of the mutual information $I(\mathbf{A};\mathbf{B},\mathbf{B}'|\mathbf{D},\mathbf{E}) \geqslant I(\mathbf{A};\mathbf{B}'|\mathbf{D},\mathbf{E})$ requires $I(\mathbf{A};\mathbf{B}'|\mathbf{B},\mathbf{D},\mathbf{E}) = 0$, and hence the two types of data processing inequalities may be applicable in different cases to eliminate $\mathbf{B}$. This will be fully appreciated in Propositions 5 and 6. Note that this application of the unique information measure of Equation (2) to eliminate hidden variables is not restrained by the role of the measure in the mutual information decomposition and by considerations about which alternative decompositions optimally quantify the different components [30,35].

3.2. Inequalities Involving Sums of Information Terms from Groups

In this section, we extend Proposition 1 in several ways. Propositions 3–6 present subsequent generalizations, all subsumed by Proposition 6. We present these generalizations progressively to better appreciate the new elements. For these Propositions, examples are displayed in Figures 2 and 3 and explained in text after the enunciation of each Proposition. Which Proposition is illustrated by each example is indicated in the figure caption and in the main text. The objective of these generalizations is twofold: First, to derive new testable inequalities for causal structures not producing a testable inequality from Proposition 1. Second, to find inequalities with higher inferential power, even when some already exist. These objectives are achieved introducing inequalities with less constringent requirements of conditional independence and using data processing inequalities to substitute certain variables from $\mathbf{A}_{[n]}$, so that the conditions of independence are fulfilled or the number of intersections is reduced and lower values in $\mathbf{d}$ are obtained. The first extension relaxes the conditions $\mathbf{A}_i \perp \mathbf{A}_j \backslash \mathbf{A}_i | \mathbf{Z}\ \forall i,j$ required in Proposition 1:

Proposition 3. *(Weaker conditions of independence through group augmentation for a decomposition of information from groups with conditionally independent non-shared components): Consider a collection of groups $\mathbf{A}_{[n]}$, a conditioning set $\mathbf{Z}$, and target variables $\mathbf{Y}$ as in Proposition 1. Consider that for each group $\mathbf{A}_i$ a group $\mathbf{B}_i$ exists, such that $\mathbf{A}_i \subseteq \mathbf{B}_i$ and $\mathbf{B}_i$ can be partitioned in two disjoint subsets $\mathbf{B}_i = \{\mathbf{B}_i^{(1)}, \mathbf{B}_i^{(2)}\}$ such that $\mathbf{B}_i^{(1)}$ fulfills the conditions of independence $\mathbf{B}_i^{(1)} \perp \mathbf{B}_j^{(1)} \backslash \mathbf{B}_i^{(1)} | \mathbf{Z}$ and $\mathbf{B}_i^{(2)}$ the conditions $\mathbf{B}_i^{(2)} \perp \mathbf{B}_j \backslash \mathbf{B}_i^{(2)} | \mathbf{B}_i^{(1)} \mathbf{Z}\ \forall i,j$, and such that $\mathbf{B}_{[n]}^{(1)} \equiv \{\mathbf{B}_1^{(1)}, \ldots, \mathbf{B}_n^{(1)}\}$ and $\mathbf{B}_{[n]}^{(2)} \equiv \{\mathbf{B}_1^{(2)}, \ldots, \mathbf{B}_n^{(2)}\}$ are disjoint. Define the maximal values $d_{\mathbf{B}_i}$ like in Proposition 1 but for* *the augmented groups* $\mathbf{B}_{[n]} \equiv \{\mathbf{B}_1, \ldots, \mathbf{B}_n\}$. *Then, the conditional information that* $\mathbf{B}_{[n]}$ *has about the target variables* $\mathbf{Y}$ *given* $\mathbf{Z}$ *is bounded from below by:*

$$I(\mathbf{Y}; \mathbf{B}_{[n]}|\mathbf{Z}) \geqslant \sum_{i=1}^{n} \frac{1}{d_{\mathbf{B}_i}} I(\mathbf{Y}; \mathbf{B}_i|\mathbf{Z}) \geqslant \sum_{i=1}^{n} \frac{1}{d_{\mathbf{B}_i}} I(\mathbf{Y}; \mathbf{A}_i|\mathbf{Z}).$$

Proof. The proof is provided in Appendix A. □

The contribution of Proposition 3 is to relax the conditional independence requirements $\mathbf{A}_i \perp \mathbf{A}_j \backslash \mathbf{A}_i|\mathbf{Z}$. Analogous conditions remain for $\mathbf{B}_i^{(1)}$, but $\mathbf{B}_i^{(2)}$ needs to fulfill the conditions $\mathbf{B}_i^{(2)} \perp \mathbf{B}_j \backslash \mathbf{B}_i^{(2)}|\mathbf{B}_i^{(1)}\mathbf{Z}\ \forall i, j$. This means that the variables in $\mathbf{B}_i^{(1)}$ are used to separate the variables in $\mathbf{B}_i^{(2)}$ from other groups. If $\mathbf{B}_i^{(2)}$ is empty for all i, Proposition 3 reduces to Proposition 1.

Another difference between Propositions 1 and 3 regards the role of hidden variables. Assume that each $\mathbf{A}_i$ is formed by $\{\mathbf{V}_i, \mathbf{U}_i\}$, where $\mathbf{U}_i$ are hidden variables and $\mathbf{V}_i$ observable variables. In Proposition 1, the requirement that the variables are observable is not fundamental and could be removed. However, to obtain a testable inequality, monotonicity of mutual information would need to be applied to reduce each term $I(\mathbf{Y}; \mathbf{A}_i|\mathbf{Z})$ to its estimable lower bound $I(\mathbf{Y}; \mathbf{V}_i|\mathbf{Z})$ that does not contain the hidden variables $\mathbf{U}_i$. On the other hand, the fulfillment of $\mathbf{A}_i \perp \mathbf{A}_j \backslash \mathbf{A}_i|\mathbf{Z}$ implies $\mathbf{V}_i \perp \mathbf{V}_j \backslash \mathbf{V}_i|\mathbf{Z}$, and reducing $\mathbf{A}_i$ to $\mathbf{V}_i$ can only decrease the number of intersections, and hence $\mathbf{d}_{\mathbf{V}_{[n]}}$ values are equal or smaller than $\mathbf{d}_{\mathbf{A}_{[n]}}$. Therefore, with Proposition 1, there is no advantage in including hidden variables. When testing Proposition 1 for a hypothesis of the underlying causal structure (and related independencies), it is equally or more powerful to use $\mathbf{V}_{[n]}$ than $\mathbf{A}_{[n]}$.

This changes in Proposition 3, since $\mathbf{B}_i^{(1)}$ appears in the conditioning side of the independencies that constrain $\mathbf{B}_i^{(2)}$. If hidden variables within $\mathbf{B}_i^{(1)}$ are necessary to create the independencies for $\mathbf{B}_i^{(2)}$, it is not possible to reduce each group to its subset of observable variables. Note that, for a hypothesized causal structure, whether the independence conditions required by Proposition 3 are fulfilled can be verified without observing the hidden variables by using the d-separation criterion on the causal graph, assuming d-separation implies independence. The actual estimation of mutual information values is only needed when testing an inequality from the data.

If $\mathbf{B}_{[n]}$ includes hidden variables, in general $I(\mathbf{Y}; \mathbf{B}_{[n]}|\mathbf{Z})$ cannot be estimated and $H(\mathbf{Y}|\mathbf{Z})$ is used as an upper bound. For the r.h.s. of the inequality, a lower bound is obtained by monotonicity of the mutual information, removing the hidden variables. In general, a testable inequality has the form

$$H(\mathbf{Y}|\mathbf{Z}) \geqslant \sum_{i=1}^{n} \frac{1}{d_{\mathbf{B}_i}} I(\mathbf{Y}; \mathbf{V}_i|\mathbf{Z}), \tag{5}$$

with $\mathbf{V}_i \subseteq \mathbf{B}_i$ being the observable variables within each group. In the case that $I(\mathbf{Y}; \mathbf{B}_{[n]}|\mathbf{Z}) = I(\mathbf{Y}; \mathbf{V}_{[n]}|\mathbf{Z})$, that is, if the hidden variables do not add information, then a testable tighter upper bound is available using $I(\mathbf{Y}; \mathbf{V}_{[n]}|\mathbf{Z})$. Importantly, the values $\mathbf{d}_{\mathbf{B}_{[n]}}$ are determined using the groups in $\mathbf{B}_{[n]}$. Since $\mathbf{A}_i \subseteq \mathbf{B}_i$, group augmentation comes at the price that $\mathbf{d}_{\mathbf{B}_{[n]}}$ are equal or higher than $\mathbf{d}_{\mathbf{A}_{[n]}}$, but the conditional independence requirements may not be fulfilled without it. Note also that the partition $\mathbf{B}_i = \{\mathbf{B}_i^{(1)}, \mathbf{B}_i^{(2)}\}$ is not known a priori, but determined in the process of finding suitable augmented groups that fulfill the conditions.

We examine some examples before further generalizations. Throughout all figures, we will read independencies from the causal structures using d-separation, assuming faithfulness. In Figure 2A, consider groups $\mathbf{A}_1 = \{V_1, V_2\}$ and $\mathbf{A}_2 = \{V_3, V_4\}$, and $\mathbf{Z} = \varnothing$. Proposition 1 is not applicable due to $V_2 \not\perp V_3$. Augmenting the groups to $\mathbf{B}_1^{(1)} = \mathbf{B}_2^{(1)} = \{U\}$, $\mathbf{B}_1^{(2)} = \{V_1, V_2\}$, and $\mathbf{B}_2^{(2)} = \{V_3, V_4\}$ the conditions of Proposition 3 are fulfilled, as can be verified by d-separation. Coefficients are determined by $\mathbf{d} = \{2,2\}$ due to the intersection of the groups in U. Note that hidden variables are not restricted to be hidden common ancestors, and here U is a mediator between V_2 and V_3. In Figure 2B, consider groups $\mathbf{A}_1 = \{V_1\}$, $\mathbf{A}_2 = \{V_3\}$, $\mathbf{A}_3 = \{V_5\}$, which do not fulfill the conditions of Proposition 1. Augmenting the groups to $\mathbf{B}_1^{(1)} = \{U_2, U_4\}$, $\mathbf{B}_1^{(2)} = \{V_1\}$, $\mathbf{B}_2^{(1)} = \{U_2\}$, $\mathbf{B}_2^{(2)} = \{V_3\}$, $\mathbf{B}_3^{(1)} = \{U_4\}$, and $\mathbf{B}_3^{(2)} = \{V_5\}$ the conditions are fulfilled. Maximal intersection values are $\mathbf{d} = \{2,2,2\}$. In both examples the upper bound is $H(Y)$ since $I(Y; \mathbf{B}_{[n]})$ cannot be estimated due to hidden variables.

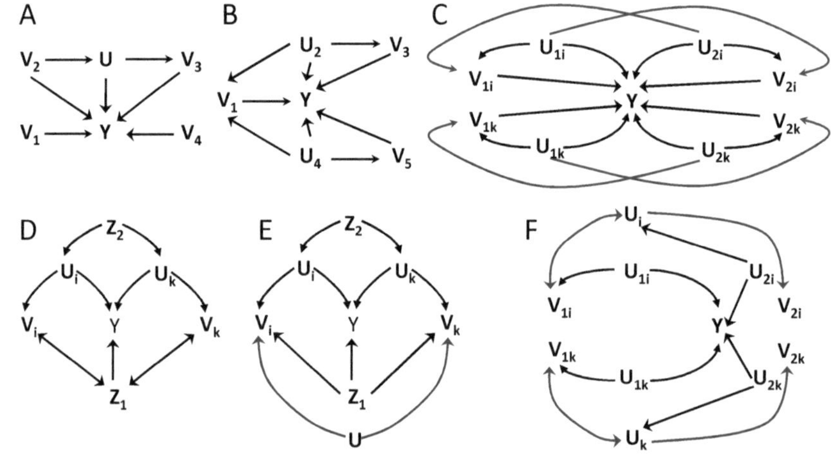

Figure 2. Examples of applications of Proposition 3 (**A–C**) and Proposition 4 (**D–F**) to obtain testable inequalities. The causal graphs allow verifying if the required conditional independence conditions are fulfilled by using d-separation. Variable Y is the target variable, observable variables are denoted by V, hidden variables by U, and conditioning variables by Z. For all examples, the composition of groups is described in the main text. For graphs using subindexes i, k to display two concrete groups, those are representative of the same causal structure for all groups that compose the system. In those graphs, variables with no subindex have the same connectivity with all groups. Bidirectional arrows indicate common hidden parents not included in any group.

We also consider scenarios with more groups. Figure 2C represents $2N$ groups organized in pairs, with subindexes i, k indicating two particular pairs. The $2N$ groups are defined in pairs, with $\mathbf{A}_{1j} = \{V_{1j}\}$ and $\mathbf{A}_{2j} = \{V_{2j}\}$, $j = 1, \ldots, N$. The causal structure is the same across pairs, but the mechanisms generating the variables beyond the causal structure can possibly differ. Proposition 1 is not fulfilled since $V_{1j} \not\perp V_{2j}$. Groups can be augmented to $\mathbf{B}_{j'j}^{(1)} = \{U_{1j}, U_{2j}\}$, $\mathbf{B}_{j'j}^{(2)} = \{V_{j'j}\}$, for $j' = 1, 2$. Proposition 3 then holds with $d = 2$ for all $2N$ groups. The pairs of groups contribute to the sum as $1/2[I(Y; V_{1j}, U_{1j}, U_{2j}) + I(Y; V_{2j}, U_{1j}, U_{2j})]$, which in the testable inequality of the form of Equation (5) reduces to $1/2[I(Y; V_{1j}) + I(Y; V_{2j})]$. The upper bound to the sum of $2N$ terms is $H(Y)$. This inequality provides causal inference power because $V_{1j} \perp V_{2j} | U_{1j}, U_{2j}$ for all j is not directly testable. As previously indicated, the inference power of an inequality emanates from the possibility to discard causal structures that do not fulfill it. Note that for this system an alternative is to define N groups instead of $2N$ groups, each as $\mathbf{A}'_j = \{V_{1j}, V_{2j}\}$. In this case Proposition 1 is already applicable with the coefficients being all 1, since $V_{1i}, V_{2i} \perp V_{1j}, V_{2j}$ for all $i \neq j$. For this inequality, each of the N groups contributes with $I(Y; V_{1j}) + I(Y; V_{2j} | V_{1j})$, and since there are no hidden variables the l.h.s. is $I(Y; \mathbf{A}'_{[n]})$. However, this latter inequality holds for any causal structure that fulfills $V_{1i}, V_{2i} \perp V_{1j}, V_{2j}$ for all $i \neq j$. Given that these independencies do not involve hidden variables, they are directly testable from data, so that the latter inequality does not provide additional inference power, in contrast to the former one.

We now continue with further generalizations. Group augmentation in Proposition 3 cannot decrease the values of the maximal number of intersections. We now describe how the data processing inequalities in Lemma 1(i) and Proposition 2 can be used to substitute variables within the groups, potentially reducing the number of intersections. We start with the data processing inequality for the conditional mutual information.

Proposition 4. *(Decomposition of information from groups modified with the conditional mutual information data processing inequality): Consider a collection of groups $\mathbf{A}_{[n]}$, a conditioning set $\mathbf{Z}$, and target variables $\mathbf{Y}$ as in Proposition 1. Consider that for some group $\mathbf{A}_i$ a group $\mathbf{B}_i$ exists such that $\mathbf{Y} \perp \mathbf{A}_i \backslash \mathbf{B}_i | \mathbf{B}_i \mathbf{Z}$, with $\mathbf{A}_i \backslash \mathbf{B}_i \neq \emptyset$. Define $\mathbf{B}_{[n]}$ as the collection of groups that replaces $\mathbf{A}_i$ by $\mathbf{B}_i$ for those following the previous independence condition. If $\mathbf{B}_{[n]}$ fulfills the conditions of Proposition 3, the inequality derived for $\mathbf{B}_{[n]}$ also provides an upper bound for the sum of the information provided by the groups in $\mathbf{A}_{[n]}$:*

$$H(\mathbf{Y}|\mathbf{Z}) \geqslant I(\mathbf{Y};\mathbf{B}_{[n]}|\mathbf{Z}) \geqslant \sum_{i=1}^{n} \frac{1}{d_{\mathbf{B}_i}} I(\mathbf{Y};\mathbf{B}_i|\mathbf{Z}) \geqslant \sum_{i=1}^{n} \frac{1}{d_{\mathbf{B}_i}} I(\mathbf{Y};\mathbf{A}_i|\mathbf{Z}).$$

Proof. The proof applies Proposition 3 to $\mathbf{B}_{[n]}$ followed by the data processing inequality of Lemma 1(i) to each term within the sum in which $\mathbf{A}_i$ and $\mathbf{B}_i$ are different. Given that $\mathbf{Y} \perp \mathbf{A}_i \backslash \mathbf{B}_i | \mathbf{B}_i \mathbf{Z}$ implies $I(\mathbf{Y};\mathbf{B}_i|\mathbf{Z}) \geqslant I(\mathbf{Y};\mathbf{A}_i|\mathbf{Z})$, their sum is also smaller or equal. □

Proposition 3 envisaged cases in which the conditions of independence of Proposition 1 were not fulfilled for a collection $\mathbf{A}_{[n]}$ and augmentation allowed fulfilling weaker conditions, even if with higher $\mathbf{d}_{\mathbf{B}_{[n]}}$ values compared to $\mathbf{d}_{\mathbf{A}_{[n]}}$. Proposition 4 is useful not only when the conditions of independence are not fulfilled for $\mathbf{A}_{[n]}$, but more generally if some values in $\mathbf{d}_{\mathbf{B}_{[n]}}$ are lower than in $\mathbf{d}_{\mathbf{A}_{[n]}}$, hence providing a tighter inequality. Including hidden variables in $\mathbf{B}_{[n]}$ is beneficiary when replacing observed by hidden variables leads to fewer intersections. The procedures of Proposition 3 and 4 can be combined, that is, starting with $\mathbf{A}_{[n]}$ that contains only observable variables, a new collection can be constructed adding new variables and removing others from $\mathbf{A}_{[n]}$, ending with $\mathbf{B}_{[n]}$ that contains both observable and hidden variables. The collection $\mathbf{B}_{[n]}$ fulfilling the conditions of Proposition 3 may even contain only hidden variables, and a testable inequality is obtained as long as the data processing inequality allows calculating observable lower bounds for all terms in the sum.

Figure 2D–F are examples of Proposition 4. Again we consider cases with N groups with equal causal structure and use indexes i,k to represent two concrete groups. In Figure 2D, with $\mathbf{A}_j = \{V_j\}$, Proposition 3 does not apply for $\mathbf{A}_{[n]}$ conditioning on $\{Z_1, Z_2\}$ because $V_i \not\perp V_j | Z_1, Z_2$, for all i,j. However, given that $Y \perp V_j | U_j, Z_1, Z_2$, each V_j can be replaced to build $\mathbf{B}_j = \{U_j\}$, and since $U_i \perp U_j | Z_1, Z_2$, for all i,j Proposition 3 applies after using Proposition 4 to create $\mathbf{B}_{[n]}$. A testable inequality is derived with upper bound $H(Y|Z_1, Z_2)$ and a sum of terms $I(Y;V_j|Z_1,Z_2)$, each being a lower bound of $I(Y;U_j|Z_1,Z_2)$ given the data processing inequality that follows from $Y \perp V_j | U_j, Z_1, Z_2$. The coefficients are $\mathbf{d}_{\mathbf{B}_{[n]}} = \mathbf{1}$. Therefore, in this case Proposition 4 results in an inequality when no inequality held for $\mathbf{A}_{[n]}$. In Figure 2E, the same procedure relies on $Y \perp V_j | U_j, Z_1, Z_2$ and $U_i \perp U_j | Z_1, Z_2$ to use $\mathbf{B}_j = \{U_j\}$ to create a testable inequality with l.h.s. $H(Y|Z_1,Z_2)$ and the sum of terms $I(Y;V_j|Z_1,Z_2)$ in the r.h.s. with $\mathbf{d}_{\mathbf{B}_{[n]}} = \mathbf{1}$. Note that by U, which has no subindex, we represent in Figure 2E a hidden common driver of all N groups, not only the displayed i,k. In this example Proposition 3 could have been directly applied without using Proposition 4 if augmenting $\mathbf{A}_j = \{V_j\}$ to $\mathbf{B}'_j = \{V_j, U\}$, with $\mathbf{B}_j^{'(1)} = \{U\}$ and $\mathbf{B}_j^{'(2)} = \{V_j\}$, since $V_i \perp V_j | U, Z_1, Z_2$. However, $\mathbf{d}_{\mathbf{B}'_{[n]}} = \mathbf{N}$, since all groups $\mathbf{B}'_j$ intersect in U. Therefore, in this case an inequality already exists without applying Proposition 4, but its use allows replacing $\mathbf{d}_{\mathbf{B}'_{[n]}} = \mathbf{N}$ by $\mathbf{d}_{\mathbf{B}_{[n]}} = \mathbf{1}$, hence creating a tighter inequality with higher causal inference power.

In Figure 2F, again we consider $2N$ groups, consisting of N pairs with the same causal structure across pairs and indices i, k representing two of these pairs. For groups $\mathbf{A}_{j'j} = \{V_{j'j}\}$, with $j' = 1, 2$ and $j = 1, ..., N$, Proposition 3 is directly applicable for $\mathbf{B}^{(1)}_{j'j} = \{U_j\}$ and $\mathbf{B}^{(2)}_{j'j} = \{V_{j'j}\}$, with $\mathbf{d}_{\mathbf{B}_{[n]}} = \mathbf{2}$. The data processing inequalities associated with $Y \perp V_{j'j} | U_{j'j}$ allow applying Proposition 4 to obtain an inequality for the groups $\mathbf{B}'_{j'j} = \mathbf{B}'^{(1)}_{j'j} = \{U_{j'j}\}$, which $\mathbf{d}_{\mathbf{B}'_{[n]}} = \mathbf{1}$.

Proposition 4 relies on the data processing inequality of the conditional mutual information. The data processing inequality of unique information can also be used for the same purpose, and both data processing inequalities can be combined applying them to different groups.

Proposition 5. *(Decomposition of information from groups modified using across different groups the conditional or unique information data processing inequality): Consider a collection of groups* $\mathbf{A}_{[n]}$, *a conditioning set* $\mathbf{Z}$, *and target variables* $\mathbf{Y}$ *as in Proposition 1. Consider a subset of groups such that for* $\mathbf{A}_i$ *a group* $\mathbf{B}_i$ *exists such that, for some* $\mathbf{Z}^{(1)}_i \subseteq \mathbf{Z}$, $\mathbf{Y} \perp \mathbf{A}_i \backslash \mathbf{B}_i | \mathbf{B}_i \mathbf{Z}^{(1)}_i$, *with* $\mathbf{A}_i \backslash \mathbf{B}_i \neq \emptyset$. *Define* $\mathbf{B}_{[n]}$ *as the collection of groups that replaces* $\mathbf{A}_i$ *by* $\mathbf{B}_i$ *for those following the previous independence conditions. Define* $\mathbf{Z}^{(1)}_i \equiv \mathbf{Z}$ *for the unaltered groups and* $\mathbf{Z}^{(2)}_i \equiv \mathbf{Z} \backslash \mathbf{Z}^{(1)}_i$ *for all groups. If* $\mathbf{B}_{[n]}$ *fulfills the conditions of Proposition 3, the inequality derived for* $\mathbf{B}_{[n]}$ *also provides an upper bound for a sum combining conditional and unique information terms for different groups in* $\mathbf{A}_{[n]}$:

$$H(\mathbf{Y}|\mathbf{Z}) \geqslant I(\mathbf{Y}; \mathbf{B}_{[n]}|\mathbf{Z}) \geqslant \sum_{i=1}^{n} \frac{1}{d_{\mathbf{B}_i}} I(\mathbf{Y}; \mathbf{B}_i|\mathbf{Z}) \geqslant$$
$$\sum_{\{i:|\mathbf{Z}^{(2)}_i|=0\}} \frac{1}{d_{\mathbf{B}_i}} I(\mathbf{Y}; \mathbf{A}_i|\mathbf{Z}) + \sum_{\{i:|\mathbf{Z}^{(2)}_i|>0\}} \frac{1}{d_{\mathbf{B}_i}} I(\mathbf{Y}; \mathbf{A}_i \backslash\backslash \mathbf{Z}^{(2)}_i | \mathbf{Z}^{(1)}_i).$$

Proof. The proof applies Proposition 3 to $\mathbf{B}_{[n]}$ and then both types of data processing inequalities depending on which one holds for different groups:

$$\begin{aligned} \sum_{i=1}^{n} \frac{1}{d_{\mathbf{B}_i}} I(\mathbf{Y}; \mathbf{B}_i|\mathbf{Z}) &\overset{(a)}{\geqslant} \sum_{\{i:|\mathbf{Z}^{(2)}_i|=0\}} \frac{1}{d_{\mathbf{B}_i}} I(\mathbf{Y}; \mathbf{B}_i|\mathbf{Z}) + \sum_{\{i:|\mathbf{Z}^{(2)}_i|>0\}} \frac{1}{d_{\mathbf{B}_i}} I(\mathbf{Y}; \mathbf{B}_i \backslash\backslash \mathbf{Z}^{(2)}_i | \mathbf{Z}^{(1)}_i) \overset{(b)}{\geqslant} \\ &\sum_{\{i:|\mathbf{Z}^{(2)}_i|=0\}} \frac{1}{d_{\mathbf{B}_i}} I(\mathbf{Y}; \mathbf{A}_i|\mathbf{Z}) + \sum_{\{i:|\mathbf{Z}^{(2)}_i|>0\}} \frac{1}{d_{\mathbf{B}_i}} I(\mathbf{Y}; \mathbf{A}_i \backslash\backslash \mathbf{Z}^{(2)}_i | \mathbf{Z}^{(1)}_i). \end{aligned} \tag{6}$$

Inequality (a) follows from the unique information always being equal to or smaller than the conditional mutual information (Equation (3)). Inequality (b) applies the conditional mutual information data processing inequality to those groups with $\mathbf{A}_i$ different than $\mathbf{B}_i$ but $|\mathbf{Z}^{(2)}_i| = 0$, and the unique information data processing inequality to those groups with $|\mathbf{Z}^{(2)}_i| > 0$. □

Proposition 5 is useful when the conditions of independence required to apply Proposition 3 do not hold for $\mathbf{A}_{[n]}$. It can also be useful to obtain inequalities with higher causal inferential power if $\mathbf{d}_{\mathbf{B}_{[n]}}$ are smaller than $\mathbf{d}_{\mathbf{A}_{[n]}}$, even if Proposition 3 is directly applicable. By definition, the terms $I(\mathbf{Y}; \mathbf{A}_i \backslash\backslash \mathbf{Z}^{(2)}_i | \mathbf{Z}^{(1)}_i)$ are equal to or smaller than $I(\mathbf{Y}; \mathbf{A}_i|\mathbf{Z})$, which can only decrease the lower bound, but the data processing inequality may hold only for the unique information and not the conditional information term. Note that the partition

$\{\mathbf{Z}_i^{(1)}, \mathbf{Z}_i^{(2)}\}$ can be group-specific and selected such that data processing inequalities can be applied.

Figure 3A shows an example of the application of the data processing inequality of unique information. For $\mathbf{A}_j = \{V_j\}$, Proposition 3 does not apply to $I(Y; \mathbf{A}_{[n]}|Z)$ because $V_i \not\perp V_k|Z$. The data processing inequality of conditional mutual information does not hold with $Y \not\perp V_i|U_i Z$. This data processing inequality could be used adding to U_i the latent common parent in $Y \leftrightarrow Z$, but this variable would be shared by all augmented groups $\mathbf{B}_i$, leading to an intersection of all N groups. Alternatively, the data processing inequality holds for the unique information with $I(Y; U_j \backslash\backslash Z) \geqslant I(Y; V_j \backslash\backslash Z)$, and $U_i \perp U_j|Z$ for all $i \neq j$. Proposition 5 is applied with $\mathbf{Z}_j^{(1)} = \varnothing$, $\mathbf{Z}_j^{(2)} = \{Z\}$, and $\mathbf{B}_j = \mathbf{B}_j^{(1)} = \{U_j\}, \forall j$. This leads to an inequality with $H(Y|Z)$ as upper bound and the sum of terms $I(Y; V_j \backslash\backslash Z)$ at the r.h.s. with coefficients determined by $\mathbf{d}_{\mathbf{B}_{[n]}} = \mathbf{1}$. In Figure 3B, taking $\mathbf{A}_j = \{V_{j1}, V_{j2}\}\ \forall j$ and defining the conditioning set $\mathbf{Z} = \{Z, Z_1, ..., Z_N\}$, we have $V_{i2} \not\perp V_{k2}|\mathbf{Z}$ and $V_{j1}, V_{j2} \not\perp Y|U_j\mathbf{Z}$. On the other hand, $V_{j1}, V_{j2} \perp Y|U_j\mathbf{Z}\backslash Z_j$, so that the data processing can be applied with the unique information and Proposition 5 is applied with $\mathbf{Z}_j^{(1)} = \mathbf{Z}\backslash Z_j$, $\mathbf{Z}_j^{(2)} = \{Z_j\}$ and $\mathbf{B}_j = \mathbf{B}_j^{(1)} = \{U_j\}$. An inequality exists given that $U_i \perp U_k|\mathbf{Z}$, and the testable inequality has an upper bound $H(Y|\mathbf{Z})$ and at the r.h.s. the sum of terms $I(Y; V_{j1}V_{j2} \backslash\backslash Z_j|\mathbf{Z}\backslash Z_j)$, with $\mathbf{d}_{\mathbf{B}_{[n]}} = \mathbf{1}$.

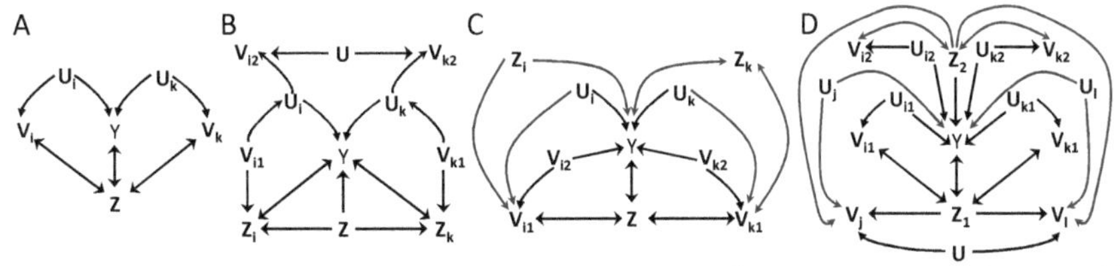

Figure 3. Examples of the application of Proposition 5 (**A–C**) and Proposition 6 (**D**) to obtain testable inequalities. Notation is analogous to Figure 2. The composition of groups is described in the main text.

In Figure 3C, we examine an example in which groups differ in the causal structure of the conditioning variable Z_j: For the groups of the type of group i, Z_i is a common parent of Y and V_{i1}. For the groups of the type of k, Z_k is a collider in a path between Y and V_{k1}. Consider M groups of the former type and $N - M$ of the latter. We examine the existence of an inequality for groups defined as $\mathbf{A}_j = \{V_{j1}, V_{j2}\}\ \forall j$, with $\mathbf{Z} = \{Z, Z_1, \ldots, Z_N\}$. Proposition 3 cannot be applied to $I(Y; \mathbf{A}_{[n]}|\mathbf{Z})$ because $V_{i1} \not\perp V_{j1}|\mathbf{Z}$ for all $i \neq j$. The mutual information data processing inequality is not applicable to substitute V_{j1} because $Y \not\perp V_{j1}|U_jV_{j2}\mathbf{Z}$. However, for the M groups like i, the independence $Y \perp V_{j1}|U_jV_{j2}\mathbf{Z}\backslash Z$ leads to the data processing inequality $I(Y; U_jV_{j2} \backslash\backslash Z|\mathbf{Z}\backslash Z) \geqslant I(Y; V_{j1}V_{j2} \backslash\backslash Z|\mathbf{Z}\backslash Z)$. For these groups, $\mathbf{Z}_j^{(1)} = \mathbf{Z}\backslash Z$ and $\mathbf{Z}_j^{(2)} = \{Z\}$. For the $N - M$ groups like k, the independence $Y \perp V_{j1}|U_jV_{j2}\mathbf{Z}\backslash\{Z, Z_j\}$ leads to $I(Y; U_jV_{j2} \backslash\backslash Z, Z_j|\mathbf{Z}\backslash\{Z, Z_j\}) \geqslant I(Y; V_{j1}V_{j2} \backslash\backslash Z, Z_j|\mathbf{Z}\backslash\{Z, Z_j\})$. For these groups $\mathbf{Z}_j^{(1)} = \mathbf{Z}\backslash\{Z, Z_j\}$ and $\mathbf{Z}_j^{(2)} = \{Z, Z_j\}$. In all cases the modified groups are $\mathbf{B}_j = \mathbf{B}_j^{(1)} = \{U_j, V_{j2}\}$, which fulfill the requirement $U_j, V_{j2} \perp U_i, V_{i2}|\mathbf{Z}$ for all $i \neq j$ needed to apply Proposition 3. The testable inequality that follows from Proposition 5 has upper bound $H(Y|\mathbf{Z})$ and in the sum at the r.h.s. has M terms of the form $I(Y; V_{j1}V_{j2} \backslash\backslash Z|\mathbf{Z}\backslash Z)$ and $N - M$ terms of the form $I(Y; V_{j1}V_{j2} \backslash\backslash Z, Z_j|\mathbf{Z}\backslash\{Z, Z_j\})$. The coefficients are determined by $\mathbf{d}_{\mathbf{B}_{[n]}} = \mathbf{1}$.

Proposition 5 combines both types of data processing inequalities, but only across different groups. Our last extension of Proposition 1 combines both types across and within groups. For each group, we introduce a disjoint partition into m_i subgroups $\mathbf{A}_i = \{\mathbf{A}_i^{(1)}, \ldots, \mathbf{A}_i^{(m_i)}\}$ and define $\mathbf{A}_i^{(0)} \equiv \varnothing$. Subgroups are analogously defined for $\mathbf{Z}_i$, also with $\mathbf{Z}_i^{(0)} \equiv \varnothing$. In general, for any ordered set of vectors we use $\mathbf{V}_i^{[k]} \equiv \{\mathbf{V}_i^{(0)}, \mathbf{V}_i^{(1)}, \ldots, \mathbf{V}_i^{(k)}\}$ to refer to all elements up to k, where in general $\mathbf{V}_i^{(0)}$ can be nonempty.

Proposition 6. *(Decomposition of information from groups modified with the conditional or unique information data processing inequality across and within groups): Consider a collection of groups* $\mathbf{A}_{[n]}$*, a conditioning set* $\mathbf{Z}$*, and a target variable* $\mathbf{Y}$ *as in Proposition 1. Consider that for each group* $\mathbf{A}_i$ *there are disjoint partitions* $\mathbf{A}_i = \{\mathbf{A}_i^{(1)}, \ldots, \mathbf{A}_i^{(m_i)}\}$ *and* $\mathbf{Z} = \{\mathbf{Z}_i^{(1)}, \ldots, \mathbf{Z}_i^{(m_i)}\}$*, and a collection of sets of additional variables* $\mathbf{C}_i = \{\mathbf{C}_i^{(0)}, \mathbf{C}_i^{(1)}, \ldots, \mathbf{C}_i^{(m_i-1)}\}$*, such that* $\mathbf{Y} \perp \mathbf{A}_i^{(k)} | \mathbf{C}_i^{[k]} \mathbf{Z}_i^{[k]} \mathbf{A}_i \backslash \mathbf{A}_i^{[k]}$ *for* $k = 1, \ldots, m_i - 1$*. Define the collection* $\mathbf{B}_{[n]}$ *with the modified groups* $\mathbf{B}_i = \{\mathbf{C}_i, \mathbf{A}_i^{(m_i)}\}$*. If* $\mathbf{B}_{[n]}$ *fulfills the conditions of Proposition 3, the inequality derived for* $\mathbf{B}_{[n]}$ *also provides an upper bound for sums combining conditional and unique information terms for different groups in* $\mathbf{A}_{[n]}$*:*

$$H(\mathbf{Y}|\mathbf{Z}) \geqslant I(\mathbf{Y}; \mathbf{B}_{[n]}|\mathbf{Z}) \geqslant \sum_{i=1}^{n} \frac{1}{d_{\mathbf{B}_i}} I(\mathbf{Y}; \mathbf{B}_i|\mathbf{Z}) \geqslant$$

$$\sum_{i=1}^{n} \frac{1}{d_{\mathbf{B}_i}} I(\mathbf{Y}; \mathbf{C}_i^{[k_i]} \mathbf{A}_i \backslash \mathbf{A}_i^{[k_i]} \backslash\backslash \mathbf{Z} \backslash \mathbf{Z}_i^{[k_i]} | \mathbf{Z}_i^{[k_i]}) \geqslant \sum_{i=1}^{n} \frac{1}{d_{\mathbf{B}_i}} I(\mathbf{Y}; \mathbf{A}_i \backslash\backslash \mathbf{Z} \backslash \mathbf{Z}_i^{(1)} | \mathbf{Z}_i^{(1)}),$$

for $k_i \in \{1, \ldots, m_i - 1\}$*.*

Proof. The proof is provided in Appendix A. □

If $m_i = 1$ for all i, then $\mathbf{A}_i^{(1)} = \mathbf{A}_i$, $\mathbf{Z}_i^{(1)} = \mathbf{Z}$, $\mathbf{B}_i = \{\mathbf{C}_i^{(0)}, \mathbf{A}_i\}$, and Proposition 6 reduces to Proposition 3. If $m_i = 2$ and $\mathbf{Z}_i^{(1)} = \mathbf{Z}$ for all i, we recover Proposition 4, with $\mathbf{B}_i = \{\mathbf{C}_i, \mathbf{A}_i^{(2)}\}$. If $m_i = 2$ for all i and $\mathbf{Z}_i^{(1)} \subset \mathbf{Z}$ for some i, we recover Proposition 5, with $\mathbf{B}_i = \{\mathbf{C}_i, \mathbf{A}_i^{(2)}\}$ and $\mathbf{Z}_i^{(2)} = \mathbf{Z} \backslash \mathbf{Z}_i^{(1)}$. Like for previous propositions, some groups may be unmodified such that $\mathbf{B}_i = \mathbf{A}_i$.

The tightest inequality results from maximizing across $k_i \in \{1, \ldots, m_i - 1\}$ each term in the sum. In the proof of Proposition 6 in Appendix A we show that, when increasing $k_i \in \{1, \ldots, m_i - 1\}$, the terms $I(\mathbf{Y}; \mathbf{C}_i^{[k]} \mathbf{A}_i \backslash \mathbf{A}_i^{[k]} \backslash\backslash \mathbf{Z} \backslash \mathbf{Z}_i^{[k]} | \mathbf{Z}_i^{[k]})$ are monotonically increasing. However, in general $\mathbf{C}_i$ can contain hidden variables, which means that, to obtain a testable inequality, for each $k_i \in \{1, \ldots, m_i - 1\}$ each term needs to be substituted by its lower bound that quantifies the information in the subset of observable variables. For each group, the optimal k_i leading to the tightest inequality will depend on the subset of observable variables $\mathbf{V}_i^{(k_i)} \subseteq \{\mathbf{C}_i^{[k_i]}, \mathbf{A}_i \backslash \mathbf{A}_i^{[k_i]}\}$ and the corresponding values of $I(\mathbf{Y}; \mathbf{V}_i^{(k_i)} \backslash\backslash \mathbf{Z} \backslash \mathbf{Z}_i^{[k_i]} | \mathbf{Z}_i^{[k_i]})$.

Figure 3D shows an example of application of Proposition 6. Like in Figure 3C, there are two types of groups with different causal structure. M groups have the structure of the variables with indexes i, k, and $\mathbf{A}_{j'} = \{V_{j'1}, V_{j'2}\}$. The other $N - M$ groups have the structure of the variables with indexes l, j, and $\mathbf{A}_{j'} = \{V_{j'}\}$. The conditioning set selected is $\mathbf{Z} = \{Z_1, Z_2\}$. Proposition 3 cannot be applied directly because $V_{i1} \not\perp V_{k1}|\mathbf{Z}$ for all $i \neq k$ within the M groups, and $V_j \not\perp V_l|\mathbf{Z}$ for all $j \neq l$ within the $N - M$ groups. Proposition 6 applies as follows. For the $N - M$ groups, $m_{j'} = 2$ with $\mathbf{A}_{j'}^{(1)} = \{V_{j'}\}$, $\mathbf{A}_{j'}^{(2)} = \emptyset$, $\mathbf{Z}_{j'}^{(1)} = \mathbf{Z}$, and $\mathbf{B}_{j'} = \mathbf{C}_{j'}^{(1)} = \{U_{j'}\}$. The independencies $\mathbf{Y} \perp \mathbf{A}_i^{(k)} | \mathbf{C}_i^{[k]} \mathbf{Z}_i^{[k]} \mathbf{A}_i \backslash \mathbf{A}_i^{[k]}$ for $k = 1, \ldots, m_i - 1$ correspond in this case to $Y \perp V_{j'}|\mathbf{Z}U_{j'}$, for $k = 1$. For the other M groups, $m_{j'} = 3$ with $\mathbf{A}_{j'}^{(1)} = \{V_{j'1}\}$, $\mathbf{A}_{j'}^{(2)} = \{V_{j'2}\}$, $\mathbf{A}_{j'}^{(3)} = \emptyset$, $\mathbf{Z}_{j'}^{(1)} = \{Z_2\}$, $\mathbf{Z}_{j'}^{(2)} = \{Z_1\}$, $\mathbf{C}_{j'}^{(1)} = \{U_{j'1}\}$, $\mathbf{C}_{j'}^{(2)} = \{U_{j'2}\}$, and $\mathbf{B}_{j'} = \{U_{j'1}, U_{j'2}\}$. The independencies involved are $Y \perp V_{j'1}|Z_2, U_{j'1}, V_{j'2}$, for $k = 1$, and $Y \perp V_{j'2}|\mathbf{Z}, U_{j'1}, U_{j'2}$, for $k = 2$.

Proposition 6 applies because with $\mathbf{B}_{[n]}$ defined as $\mathbf{B}_{j'} = \{U_{j'}\}$ for the $N - M$ groups and $\mathbf{B}_{j'} = \{U_{j'1}, U_{j'2}\}$ for the M groups, the requirements of independence of Proposition 3 are fulfilled, in particular $\mathbf{B}_i \perp \mathbf{B}_j|\mathbf{Z}$ for all $i \neq j$. The terms $I(Y; \mathbf{B}_{j'}|\mathbf{Z})$ for the $N - M$ groups are $I(Y; U_{j'}|Z_1, Z_2)$ and are substituted by lower bounds $I(Y; V_{j'}|Z_1, Z_2)$ in the testable inequality. For the M groups, we have the subsequent sequence of inequalities: $I(Y; U_{j'1}, U_{j'2}|Z_1, Z_2) \geqslant I(Y; U_{j'1}, V_{j'2}|Z_1, Z_2) \geqslant I(Y; U_{j'1}, V_{j'2} \backslash\backslash Z_1|Z_2) \geqslant I(Y; V_{j'1}, V_{j'2} \backslash\backslash Z_1|Z_2)$. The first inequality follows from the independence for $k = 2$, the second from the unique information being equal or smaller than the conditional information, and the third from the independence for $k = 1$. Considering that a testable inequality can only contain observable variables, for the M groups the terms in the sum can be $I(Y; V_{j'1}, V_{j'2} \backslash\backslash Z_1 | Z_2)$ or $I(Y; V_{j'2} | Z_1, Z_2)$, depending on which one is higher. The coefficients are determined by $\mathbf{d}_{\mathbf{B}_{[n]}} = \mathbf{1}$ and the resulting testable inequality has upper bound $H(Y|Z_1, Z_2)$.

Overall, Propositions 4–6 further extend the cases in which groups-decomposition inequalities of the type of Proposition 1 can be derived. Our Proposition 1 extends Proposition 1 of [27] to allow conditioning sets, Proposition 3 further weakens the conditions of independence required in Proposition 1, and Propositions 4–6 use data processing inequalities to obtain testable inequalities from groups-decompositions derived comprising hidden variables, which can be more powerful than inequalities directly derived without comprising hidden variables. In Figures 2 and 3, we have provided examples of causal structures for which these new groups-decompositions inequalities exist. In all these cases, the use of our groups-decomposition inequalities increases the set of available inequality tests that can be used to reject hypothesized causal structures underlying data.

3.3. Inequalities Involving Sums of Information Terms from Ancestral Sets

We now examine inequalities involving ancestral sets as in Theorem 1 of Steudel and Ay [27], which we reviewed in our Theorem 1 (Section 2.4). We extend this theorem allowing for a conditioning set $\mathbf{Z}$ and adding flexibility on how ancestral sets are constructed, as well as allowing the selection of reduced ancestral sets that exclude some variables. Like for Theorem 1, we will use $an_G(\mathbf{A}_{[n]}) \equiv \{an_G(\mathbf{A}_1), \ldots, an_G(\mathbf{A}_n)\}$ to indicate the collection of all ancestral sets in graph G from the collection of groups $\mathbf{A}_{[n]} \equiv \{\mathbf{A}_1, \ldots, \mathbf{A}_n\}$.

The extension of Theorem 1 to allow for a conditioning set $\mathbf{Z}$ requires an extension of the notion of ancestral set that will be used to determine the coefficients in the inequalities. The intuition for this extension is that conditioning on $\mathbf{Z}$ can introduce new dependencies between groups, in particular when a variable $Z_j \in \mathbf{Z}$ is a common descendant of several ancestral groups, and hence conditioning on it activates paths in which it is a collider. The coefficients need to take into account that common information contributions across ancestral groups can originate from these new dependencies. At the same time, conditioning can also block paths that created dependencies between the ancestral groups. To also account for this, we will not only consider ancestral sets in the original graph G, but in any graph $G' = G_{\underline{\mathbf{Z}'}}$, with $\mathbf{Z}' \subseteq \mathbf{Z}$. The graph $G_{\underline{\mathbf{Z}'}}$ is constructed by removing from G all the outgoing arrows from nodes in $\mathbf{Z}'$. This has an effect equivalent to conditioning on $\mathbf{Z}'$ with regard to eliminating dependencies enabled by paths through $\mathbf{Z}'$ in which the variables in $\mathbf{Z}'$ are noncolliders, since removing those arrows deactivates the paths. To account for these effects of conditioning on $\mathbf{Z}$, for each $Z_j \in \mathbf{Z}$ we define an augmented ancestral set of the groups $\mathbf{A}_i \in \mathbf{A}_{[n]}$ as follows:

$$an_{G'}(\mathbf{A}_i; Z_j) \equiv \begin{cases} an_{G'}(\mathbf{A}_i) & \text{if } an_{G'}(\mathbf{A}_i) \perp an_{G'}(Z_j) \cap an_{G'}(\mathbf{A}_{[n]}) | \mathbf{Z} \\ an_{G'}(\mathbf{A}_i) \cup (an_{G'}(Z_j) \cap an_{G'}(\mathbf{A}_{[n]})) & \text{otherwise.} \end{cases} \tag{7}$$

We then define the set $\mathbf{S}(G'; Z_j) \equiv \{\mathbf{A}_i \in \mathbf{A}_{[n]} : an_{G'}(\mathbf{A}_i) \not\perp an_{G'}(Z_j) \cap an_{G'}(\mathbf{A}_{[n]}) | \mathbf{Z}\}$, that is, the set of groups that have some ancestor not independent from some ancestor of Z_j that is also ancestor of $\mathbf{A}_{[n]}$, given $\mathbf{Z}$.

For each $\mathbf{A}_i$, let $d_i(G'; Z_j)$ be the maximal number such that a non-empty intersection exists between $an_{G'}(\mathbf{A}_i; Z_j)$ and $d_i(G'; Z_j) - 1$ other distinct augmented ancestral sets of $\mathbf{A}_{i_1}, \ldots, \mathbf{A}_{i_{d_i(G';Z_j)-1}}$. Furthermore, we define $d_i(G'; \mathbf{Z})$ as the maximum for all $Z_j \in \mathbf{Z}$:

$$d_i(G'; \mathbf{Z}) \equiv \max_{Z_j \in \mathbf{Z}} d_i(G'; Z_j). \tag{8}$$

We will use $\mathbf{d}(G'; \mathbf{Z})$ to refer to the whole set of maximal values for all groups. If required, we will use $\mathbf{d}_{\mathbf{A}_{[n]}}(G'; \mathbf{Z})$ to specify that the collection is $\mathbf{A}_{[n]}$.

In Figure 4A–D, we consider examples to understand the rationale of how $\mathbf{d}_{\mathbf{A}_{[n]}}(G'; \mathbf{Z})$ is determined in inequalities with a conditioning $\mathbf{Z}$. In Figure 4A, for groups $\mathbf{A}_1 = \{V_1\}$ and $\mathbf{A}_2 = \{V_2\}$, the augmented ancestral sets on graph G are $an_G(\mathbf{A}_1; Z) = \{V_1, Z\}$ and $an_G(\mathbf{A}_2; Z) = \{V_2, Z\}$, which intersect on Z and $d_i(G; \mathbf{Z}) = 2$ for $i = 1, 2$. However, Z is a noncollider in the path creating a dependence between V_1 and V_2, and conditioning on Z renders them independent, so that $d_i(G; \mathbf{Z}) = 2$ overestimates the amount of information the groups may share after conditioning. Alternatively, selecting $G_{\underline{Z}}$ the ancestral sets are $an_{G_{\underline{Z}}}(\mathbf{A}_1; Z) = \{V_1\}$ and $an_{G_{\underline{Z}}}(\mathbf{A}_2; Z) = \{V_2\}$, which do not intersect and $d_i(G_{\underline{Z}}; \mathbf{Z}) = 1$ for $i = 1, 2$ when calculated following Equation (7). A priori, we do not know which graph $G' = G_{\underline{\mathbf{Z}'}}, \mathbf{Z}' \subseteq \mathbf{Z}$, results in a tighter inequality. Here we see that $G_{\underline{Z}}$ leads to an inequality with more causal inference power than G for Figure 4A. In Figure 4B, Z is a collider between V_1 and V_2, so that conditioning on Z creates a dependence between the groups. If the values d_i were determined from the standard ancestral sets, in this case $an_G(\mathbf{A}_i) = an_{G_{\underline{Z}}}(\mathbf{A}_i) = \{V_i\}$, for $i = 1, 2$, which do not intersect, leading to unit coefficients. However, the augmented ancestral sets following Equation (7) are $an_G(\mathbf{A}_i; Z) = an_{G_{\underline{Z}}}(\mathbf{A}_i; Z) = \{V_1, V_2\}$ for $i = 1, 2$, so that $d_i(G; \mathbf{Z}) = d_i(G_{\underline{Z}}; \mathbf{Z}) = 2$. This illustrates that the augmented ancestral sets are necessary to properly determine the coefficients in inequalities with conditioning sets $\mathbf{Z}$, in this case reflecting that $I(Y; V_1|Z)$ and $I(Y; V_2|Z)$ can have redundant information.

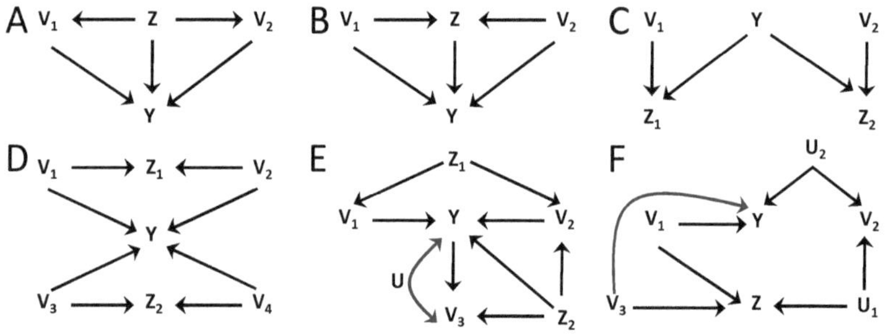

Figure 4. Inequalities involving sums of information terms from ancestral sets. (**A–D**) Examples to illustrate the definition of augmented ancestral sets (Equations (7) and (8)). (**E**,**F**) Examples of the application of Theorem 2 to obtain testable inequalities.

Figure 4C shows a scenario in which conditioning creates dependencies of Y with V_1 and V_2, which were previously independent. The standard ancestral sets $an_{G'}(\mathbf{A}_1) = \{V_1\}$ and $an_{G'}(\mathbf{A}_2) = \{V_2\}$ would not intersect in any $G' = G_{\underline{\mathbf{Z}'}}$, with $\mathbf{Z}' \subseteq \{Z_1, Z_2\}$ and would lead to unit values for d_i. On the other hand, the augmented ancestral sets are $an_{G'}(\mathbf{A}_i; Z_j) = \{V_i\}$ for $i = j$ and $an_{G'}(\mathbf{A}_i; Z_j) = \{V_1, V_2\}$ for $i \neq j$, for all $G' = G_{\underline{\mathbf{Z}'}}$, with $\mathbf{Z}' \subseteq \{Z_1, Z_2\}$. This results in $d_i(G'; \mathbf{Z}) = 2$ in all cases, which appropriately captures that the two groups can have common information about Y when conditioning on $\{Z_1, Z_2\}$. The example of Figure 4D illustrates why each value $d_i(G'; Z_j)$ is determined separately (Equation (7)) first, and only after is the maximum calculated (Equation (8)). Four groups are defined as $\mathbf{A}_i = V_i$ for $i = 1, \ldots, 4$. If $d_i(G'; \mathbf{Z})$ were to be determined directly from Equation (7) but using $\mathbf{Z} = \{Z_1, Z_2\}$, instead of using separately Z_1 and Z_2, then for all the ancestral sets the augmented ancestral set would include all variables, since $an_{G'}(\mathbf{Z}) \cap an_{G'}(\mathbf{A}_{[n]})$ is equal to $an_{G'}(\mathbf{A}_{[n]})$. This would lead to $d_i = 4, \forall i$. However, that determination would overestimate how many groups become dependent when conditioning on $\mathbf{Z}$, since Z_1 creates a dependence between V_1 and V_2 and Z_2 between V_3 and V_4, but no dependencies across these pairs are created. The determination of $\mathbf{d}(G'; \mathbf{Z}) = \mathbf{2}$ from Equations (7) and (8) properly leads to a tighter inequality than the one obtained if considering jointly both conditioning variables.

Equipped with this extended definition of $\mathbf{d}_{\mathbf{A}_{[n]}}(G';\mathbf{Z})$, we now present our generalization of Theorem 1:

Theorem 2. *Let G be a DAG model containing nodes corresponding to a set of (possibly hidden) variables $\mathcal{X}$. Let $\mathbf{Y} \in \mathcal{X}$ be a set of observable target variables, and $\mathbf{Z} = \{Z_1, \ldots, Z_m\}$ a conditioning set of observable variables, with $\mathbf{Z} \subset \mathcal{X}$. Let $\mathbf{A}_{[n]} = \{\mathbf{A}_1, \ldots, \mathbf{A}_n\}$ be a collection of (possibly overlapping) groups of (possibly hidden) variables $\mathbf{A}_i \subset \mathcal{X}$. Consider a DAG G' selected as $G' = G_{\underline{\mathbf{Z}'}}$ with $\mathbf{Z}' \subseteq \mathbf{Z}$, constructed by removing from graph G all the outgoing arrows from nodes in $\mathbf{Z}'$. Following Equation (7), define an augmented ancestral set in G' for each group $\mathbf{A}_i \in \mathbf{A}_{[n]}$ for each variable in the conditioning set, $Z_j \in \mathbf{Z}$. Following Equation (8), determine $d_i(G';\mathbf{Z})$ for each group, given the intersections of the augmented ancestral sets $an_{G'}(\mathbf{A}_i; Z_j)$. Select a variable $W_0 \in an_{G'}(\mathbf{A}_{[n]})$ and a group of variables $\mathbf{W} \subseteq D_{G'}(W_0) \cap an_{G'}(\mathbf{A}_{[n]})$, possibly $\mathbf{W} = \varnothing$. Define the reduced ancestral sets $\tilde{an}_{G'}(\mathbf{A}_i) \equiv an_{G'}(\mathbf{A}_i) \backslash \mathbf{W}$ for each $\mathbf{A}_i \in \mathbf{A}_{[n]}$, and the reduced collection $\tilde{an}_{G'}(\mathbf{A}_{[n]}) \equiv an_{G'}(\mathbf{A}_{[n]}) \backslash \mathbf{W}$. The information about $\mathbf{Y}$ in this reduced collection when conditioning on $\mathbf{Z}$ is bounded from below by*

$$I(\mathbf{Y}; \tilde{an}_{G'}(\mathbf{A}_{[n]})|\mathbf{Z}) \geqslant \sum_{i=1}^{n} \frac{1}{d_i(G';\mathbf{Z})} I(\mathbf{Y}; \tilde{an}_{G'}(\mathbf{A}_i)|\mathbf{Z}). \tag{9}$$

Proof. The proof is provided in Appendix B. □

Theorem 2 provides several extensions of Theorem 1. First, it allows for a conditioning set $\mathbf{Z}$. Second, given a hypothesis of the generative causal graph G underlying the data, Theorem 2 can be applied to any $G' = G_{\underline{\mathbf{Z}'}}$ with $\mathbf{Z}' \subseteq \mathbf{Z}$, and hence offers a set of inequalities potentially adding causal inference power. As we have discussed in relation to Figure 4A–D, the selection of G' that leads to the tightest inequality in some cases will be determined by the causal structure, but in general it also depends on the exact probability distribution of the variables. Third, Theorem 2 allows excluding some variables $\mathbf{W}$ from the ancestral sets, although imposing constraints in the causal structure of $\mathbf{W}$. The role of these constraints is clear in the proof at Appendix B. The case of Theorem 1 corresponds to $\mathbf{Z} = \varnothing$, $\mathbf{W} = \varnothing$, and $G' = G$.

Excluding some variables $\mathbf{W}$ can be advantageous. For example, if $\mathbf{Y}$ is univariate and it overlaps with some ancestral sets, as it is the case when some groups include descendants of Y, then the upper bound $I(Y; an_{G'}(\mathbf{A}_{[n]})|\mathbf{Z})$ is equal to $H(Y|\mathbf{Z})$ and also $I(Y; an_{G'}(\mathbf{A}_i)|\mathbf{Z})$ is equal to $H(Y|\mathbf{Z})$ for all ancestral sets that include Y. Excluding $\mathbf{W} = Y$ provides a tighter upper bound $I(Y; an_{G'}(\mathbf{A}_{[n]}) \backslash Y|\mathbf{Z})$ and may provide more causal inferential power. Another scenario in which a reduced collection can be useful is when excluding $\mathbf{W}$ removes all hidden variables from $an_{G'}(\mathbf{A}_{[n]})$, such that $\tilde{an}_{G'}(\mathbf{A}_{[n]})$ is observable, giving $I(\mathbf{Y}; \tilde{an}_{G'}(\mathbf{A}_{[n]})|\mathbf{Z})$ as a testable upper bound instead of $H(\mathbf{Y}|\mathbf{Z})$. When comparing inequalities with different sets $\mathbf{W}$, in some cases the form of the causal structure and the specification of which variables are hidden or observable will a priori determine an order of causal inference power among the inequalities. However, like for the comparison across $G' = G_{\underline{\mathbf{Z}'}}$ with $\mathbf{Z}' \subseteq \mathbf{Z}$, in general the power of the different inequalities depends on the details of the generated probability distributions. Formulating general criteria to rank inequalities with different $\mathbf{Z}$, G', and $\mathbf{W}$ in terms of their inferential power is beyond the scope of this work.

Note that we have formulated Theorem 2 explicitly allowing for hidden variables. Also, in Theorem 1 (as a subcase of Theorem 2) the restriction of $\mathbf{A}_{[n]}$ being observable variables can be removed. In any case, the inclusion of hidden variables can only increase the causal inference power if combined with data processing inequalities to obtain a testable inequality. Propositions 4–6 indicate how to possibly tighten an inequality derived from Proposition 1 by substituting $\mathbf{A}_{[n]}$ by a new collection $\mathbf{B}_{[n]}$ that, including hidden variables, leads to $\mathbf{d}_{\mathbf{B}_{[n]}}$ smaller than $\mathbf{d}_{\mathbf{A}_{[n]}}$. The same application of data processing inequalities of the unique and conditional mutual information can be used for Theorem 2 to determine a $\mathbf{B}_{[n]}$ with $\mathbf{d}_{\mathbf{B}_{[n]}}(G';\mathbf{Z})$ smaller than $\mathbf{d}_{\mathbf{A}_{[n]}}(G';\mathbf{Z})$. The use of data processing inequalities is necessary because they allow substituting some of the observable variables by hidden variables, instead of only adding hidden variables. When only adding variables, the number of intersections between ancestral groups can only increase, hence not decreasing $\mathbf{d}(G'; \mathbf{Z})$. On top of this, a testable inequality replaces information terms of ancestral groups by their lower bounds given by observable subsets of variables. This means that, adding hidden variables, the testable inequality will contain the same information terms of the observable variables, but possibly smaller coefficients, hence resulting in a looser inequality. This is not the case any more when hidden variables are not added but instead substitute some of observable variables, thanks to data processing inequalities. This substitution may decrease the number of intersections between ancestral groups, and the coefficients in the sum may be higher. We will not describe this procedure in detail, since the use of data processing inequalities is analogous to their use in Propositions 4–6.

We now illustrate the application of Theorem 2. In Figure 4E, with $\mathbf{Z} = \{Z_1, Z_2\}$, the conditions of independence required by Proposition 6 do not hold for any set of groups, either $\mathbf{A}_i = \{V_i\}$, $i = 1,2,3$, or, with $i \neq j \neq k$, $\mathbf{A}_1 = \{V_i, V_j\}$, $\mathbf{A}_2 = \{V_i, V_k\}$ or $\mathbf{A}_1 = \{V_i, V_j\}$, $\mathbf{A}_2 = \{V_k\}$. No data processing inequalities can be applied to replace some variables to fulfill the conditions. On the other hand, Theorem 2 can always be applied, since it does not require the fulfillment of some conditions of independence. For example, for $\mathbf{A}_i = \{V_i\}$, $i = 1,2,3$ and for $G' = G_{\underline{Z_1 Z_2}}$, we have $an_{G'}(V_1) = \{V_1\}$, $an_{G'}(V_2) = \{V_2\}$, $an_{G'}(V_3) = \{V_1, V_2, V_3, U, Y\}$, and following Equation (7) $an_{G'}(V_1; Z_j) = \{V_1\}$, $an_{G'}(V_2; Z_j) = \{V_2\}$, and $an_{G'}(V_3; Z_j) = \{V_1, V_2, V_3, U, Y\}$, for $j = 1,2$. This leads to $\mathbf{d}(G'; \mathbf{Z}) = \{2,2,3\}$. For illustration purpose, we focus on $\mathbf{W}$ equal to $\{Y, U\}$ or any of its subsets. In all cases $\tilde{an}_{G'}(V_i) = an_{G'}(V_i)$, for $i = 1,2$, contributing terms $1/2I(Y; V_1|Z_1, Z_2)$ and $1/2I(Y; V_2|Z_1, Z_2)$. For $\mathbf{W} = \{Y, U\}$ or $\mathbf{W} = \{Y\}$, the contribution of the observable lower bound of the third group is $1/3I(Y; V_1, V_2, V_3|Z_1, Z_2)$. For $\mathbf{W} = \{U\}$ or $\mathbf{W} = \emptyset$, the third group contributes $1/3H(Y|Z_1, Z_2)$. For $\mathbf{W} = \{Y, U\}$, $\tilde{an}_{G'}(\mathbf{A}_{[n]}) = \{V_1, V_2, V_3\}$, which is observable and the upper bound is $I(Y; V_1, V_2, V_3|Z_1, Z_2)$. For any other subset of $\{Y, U\}$ the upper bound in the testable inequality is $H(Y|Z_1, Z_2)$. Because the terms in the sum for groups 1 and 2 are equal for all the $\mathbf{W}$ compared, in this case it can be checked that selecting $\mathbf{W} = \{Y, U\}$ leads to the tightest inequality. This example illustrates the utility of being able to construct inequalities for reduced ancestral sets.

While in the previous example only Theorem 2 and not Proposition 6 was applicable, more generally, a causal structure will involve the fulfillment of a set of inequalities, some obtained using Proposition 6 and some using Theorem 2. Which inequalities have higher inferential power will depend on the causal structure and the exact probability distribution of the data, and neither Theorem 2 nor Proposition 6 are more powerful a priori. In Figure 4F, Proposition 6 cannot be applied using $\mathbf{A}_i = \{V_i\}$, $i = 1,2,3$ and conditioning on Z, because $V_i \not\perp V_j|Z, \forall i,j$ and no data processing inequalities help to substitute these variables. On the other hand, Theorem 2 can be applied with $\mathbf{A}_i = \{V_i\}$, leading to $an_{G'}(V_1) = \{V_1\}$, $an_{G'}(V_3) = \{V_3\}$, and $an_{G'}(V_2) = \{V_2, U_1, U_2\}$, for all $G' = G_{\underline{Z'}}$. The augmented ancestral sets are $an_{G'}(V_1; Z) = \{V_1, V_3, U_1\} = an_{G'}(V_3; Z)$, and $an_{G'}(V_2; Z) = \{V_1, V_2, V_3, U_1, U_2\}$, also for all G', resulting in $\mathbf{d}(G'; Z) = \mathbf{3}$. Focusing on the case of $\mathbf{W} = \{Y, U_2\}$, or any subset of it, in all cases the associated testable inequality has $H(Y|Z)$ as upper bound and in the r.h.s. the sum of terms $1/3I(Y; V_i|Z)$, $i = 1,2,3$. Alternatively, defining $\mathbf{A}_1 = \{V_1, V_3, U_1\}$ and $\mathbf{A}_2 = \{V_2, U_1\}$, Proposition 3 is applicable with the two groups intersecting in U_1 and $V_1, V_3 \perp V_2|Z, U_1$. The associated testable inequality has the same upper bound $H(Y|Z)$ and in the r.h.s. the sum of terms $1/2I(Y; V_1, V_3|Z)$ and $1/2I(Y; V_2|Z)$. In this case, which inequality has more causal inferential power will depend on the exact distribution of the data.

Overall, Theorem 2 extends Theorem 1 of [27], allowing conditioning sets and providing more flexible conditions to form the groups. In the examples of Figure 4, we have illustrated how Theorem 2 substantially increases the number of groups-decomposition inequalities that can be tested to reject hypothesized causal structures to be compatible with a certain data set.

4. Discussion

We have presented several generalizations of the type of groups-decomposition inequalities introduced by [27], which compare the information about target variables contained in a collection of variables with a weighted sum of the information contained in subsets of the collection. These generalizations include an extension to allow for conditioning sets and methods to identify existing inequalities that involve collections and subsets selected with less restrictive criteria. This comprises less restrictive conditions of independence, the use of ancestral sets from subgraphs of the causal structure of interest, and the removal of some variables from the ancestral sets. We have also shown how to exploit inequalities identified for collections containing hidden variables—which are not directly testable—by converting them into testable inequalities using data processing inequalities.

Our use of data processing inequalities to derive testable groups-decomposition inequalities when collections contain hidden variables is not entirely new. We found inspiration for this approach in the proof of Theorem 1 in [24]. This theorem derives a causally informative inequality from a particular type of causal structure, namely common ancestor graphs in which all dependencies between observable variables are caused by hidden common ancestors. The inequality presented in the theorem corresponds to the setting of a univariate target variable and groups composed by different single observable variables. In their simplest case, each hidden ancestor only has two children, which are observable variables. Their proof uses the mutual information data processing inequality to convert a sum of information terms involving the observable variables into a sum of terms involving the hidden ancestors. The final inequality can equally be proven applying our Proposition 4 by deriving an inequality for the collection of hidden variables and then converting it into a testable inequality using data processing inequalities. The same final inequality can also be derived as an application of our Theorem 2 followed by the use of the data processing inequality.

We have expanded the applicability of data processing inequalities by showing that this type of inequality also holds for conditional unique information measures [29]. For a given causal structure, a testable causally informative inequality may be obtained substituting hidden variables by observable variables thanks to the data processing inequality of the unique information, in cases in which the data processing inequality of mutual information is not applicable. As shown in Proposition 6, the unique information data processing inequalities are particularly powerful for deriving groups-decomposition inequalities with a conditioning set, since they can iteratively be applied to replace different subsets of hidden variables by observable variables choosing which variables are kept as conditioning variables and which ones are taken as reference variables for different unique information measures. This use of unique information indicates how other types of information-theoretic measures could be similarly incorporated to derive causally informative inequalities. Recent developments in the decomposition of mutual information into redundant, synergistic, and unique contributions [30] provide candidate measures whose utility for this purpose needs to be further explored [31–35,40,41] (among others). Furthermore, while this type of decomposition has been extensively debated recently [35,42,43], aspects of its characterization are still unsolved and an understanding of how the terms are related to the causal structure can provide new insights.

One particular domain in which our generalizations can be useful is to study causal interactions among dynamical processes [23,44], for which causal interactions are characterized from time series both in the temporal [45] and spectral domain [46–48]. When studying high-dimensional multivariate dynamical processes, such as brain dynamics (e.g., [49–51]) or econometric data [52,53], an important question is to determine whether correlations between time series are related to causal influences or to hidden common influences. For highly interconnected systems with many hidden variables, the number of independencies may be small, hence providing limited information about the causal structure. In this case, inequality constraints can help to substantially narrow down the set of causal structures compatible with the data. Accordingly, our generalization to formulate conditional inequalities may play an important role in combination with measures to quantify partial dependencies between time series [54,55]. We expect this approach to be easily adaptable to non-stationary time-series, as it is often the case in the presence of unit roots and co-integrated time series [56–58]. This can be carried out by selecting collections and groups consistent with the temporal partitioning in non-stationary information-theoretic measures of causality in time-series [59,60]. Another area to extend the applicability of our proposal is to study non-classical quantum systems [16,61–63]. In this case, an extended d-separation criterion [64] and adapted faithfulness considerations [65] have been proposed to take into account the particularities of quantum systems. Further exploration will be required to determine if and how our derivations that rely on d-separation leading to statistical independence (Appendix C) are also applicable when considering generalized causal structures for quantum systems.

Besides the extension to particular domains, an important question yet to be addressed regards the relation between the causal inferential power of different inequalities. Our proposal considerably enlarges the number of groups-decomposition inequalities of the type of [27] available to test the compatibility of a causal structure with a given data set. We have seen in our analysis some examples of how, under certain conditions, the causal structure imposes an ordering to the power of alternative inequalities. Future work should aim to derive broader criteria to rank the inferential power of inequalities, for example in terms of the relation between the conditioning sets or the constituency of the groups that appear in each inequality. Formulating criteria to rank the inferential power of different inequalities would help to simplify the set of inequalities that needs to be tested when the compatibility of a certain causal structure with the data is to be examined.

Apart from a characterization of how groups-decomposition inequalities are related among themselves, future work should also examine the relation and embedding of this type of inequalities with those derived with other approaches. In our understanding, the algorithmic projection procedure of [23,24] could equally retrieve some of the inequalities here described, but without the advantage of having a constructive procedure to derive the form of an inequality directly reading a causal graph, and instead requiring costly computations that may limit the derivation of inequalities for large systems. The incorporation of constraints for other types of information-theoretic measures, such as constraints involving unique information measures, would require an extension of the algorithmic approach. Among other approaches, the so-called *Inflation technique* [66] stands out as capable of providing asymptotically sufficient tests of causal compatibility [67]. The inflation method creates a new causal structure with multiple copies of the original structure and symmetry constraints on the ancestral properties of the different copies, in such a way that testable constraints on the inflated graph can be mapped back to the compatibility of the original causal structure. However, despite the ongoing advances in its theoretical developments and implementation [68], to our knowledge it is not straightforward to identify the order of inflation and the specific inflation structure adequate to discriminate between certain causal structures. The availability of inequalities easily derived by reading the original causal structure can also be helpful in combination with the inflation method, in order to discard as many candidate causal structures as possible before the design of additional inflated graphs. The connection with other approaches [69–74] also deserves further investigation, ultimately to determine minimal sets of inequality constraints with equivalent inferential power.

Beyond the derivation of existing testable causally informative inequalities, a crucial issue for their application is the implementation of the corresponding tests. This implementation depends on the estimation of information-theoretic measures from data. A ubiquitous challenge for the application of mutual information measures is that they are positively biased and their estimation is data-demanding [75,76]. These biases scale with the dimensionality of the variables, and hence can hinder the applicability of information-theoretic inequalities for large collections of variables, or for variables with high cardinality. However, recent advances in the estimation of mutual information for high-dimensional data can help to attenuate these biases [77]. Furthermore, the implementation of the tests can take advantage of the existence of both upper-bound and lower-bound estimators of mutual information [78], using opposite bounds at the two sides of the inequalities. These technical aspects of the implementation of the tests are important to apply all types of information-theoretic inequalities [23–27,71]. Despite these common challenges, our extension of groups-decomposition inequalities does not come at the price of having to test inequalities that intrinsically are more difficult to estimate. Our contribution can substantially increase the number of inequalities available to be tested, and we have provided examples in Figures 2–4 of new inequalities in which—in particular thanks to the use of data processing inequalities—the dimensionality of the collections is not increased. Future work is required to determine how to efficiently combine all available tests. In the goal to determine minimal sets of inequality tests that are maximally informative, the statistical power of the tests will need to be considered together with their discrimination power among causal structures.

Author Contributions: All authors contributed to the design of the research. The research was carried out by D.C. The manuscript was written by D.C. with the contribution of J.K.N. All authors have read and agreed to the published version of the manuscript.

Funding: This research received no external funding.

Conflicts of Interest: The authors declare no conflicts of interest.

Appendix A. Proofs of Propositions 1, 3, and 6

Proof of Proposition 1. Given a collection $\mathbf{A}_{[n]} = \{\mathbf{A}_1, \ldots, \mathbf{A}_n\}$, define $\mathbf{X}_{[r]}$ as the set of r variables that are part of at least a group in $\mathbf{A}_{[n]}$. We have that

$$\begin{aligned}
&I(\mathbf{Y}; \mathbf{A}_{[n]}|\mathbf{Z}) \overset{(a)}{=} I(\mathbf{Y}; \mathbf{X}_{[r]}|\mathbf{Z}) \overset{(b)}{=} \sum_{k=1}^{r} I(\mathbf{Y}; X_k|\mathbf{X}_{[k-1]}, \mathbf{Z}) \overset{(c)}{\geqslant} \\
&\sum_{k=1}^{r} I(\mathbf{Y}; X_k|\mathbf{X}_{[k-1]}, \mathbf{Z}) \left(\sum_{\mathbf{A}_i : X_k \in \mathbf{A}_i} \frac{1}{d_i} \right) \overset{(d)}{=} \sum_{i=1}^{n} \frac{1}{d_i} \sum_{X_k \in \mathbf{A}_i} I(\mathbf{Y}; X_k|\mathbf{X}_{[k-1]}, \mathbf{Z}) \overset{(e)}{\geqslant} \\
&\sum_{i=1}^{n} \frac{1}{d_i} \sum_{X_k \in \mathbf{A}_i} I(\mathbf{Y}; X_k|(\mathbf{X}_{[k-1]} \cap \mathbf{A}_i), \mathbf{Z}) \overset{(f)}{=} \sum_{i=1}^{n} \frac{1}{d_i} I(\mathbf{Y}; \mathbf{A}_i|\mathbf{Z})
\end{aligned} \tag{A1}$$

Equality (a) follows from $\mathbf{X}_{[r]}$ containing the same variables as $\mathbf{A}_{[n]}$. Equality (b) follows from the iterative application of the chain rule for mutual information, where $X_{[0]} \equiv \varnothing$ and $\mathbf{X}_{[k-1]} = \{X_0, \ldots, X_{k-1}\}$. Inequality (c) follows from the definition of d_i as maximal, such that the number of groups that contain X_k is equal or smaller than d_i for all $\mathbf{A}_i$ containing X_k, and hence $\sum_{\mathbf{A}_i : X_k \in \mathbf{A}_i} 1/d_i \leqslant 1$. Equality (d) groups together into the inner sum variables within the same group. Inequality (e) follows from Lemma 1(ii). In more detail, $\mathbf{A}_i \perp \mathbf{A}_j \backslash \mathbf{A}_i | \mathbf{Z}\ \forall i,j$, combined with the weak union property of independencies [27], ensures that for each $X_k \in \mathbf{A}_i$, $X_k \perp (\mathbf{X}_{[k-1]} \cap \mathbf{A}_j) \backslash \mathbf{A}_i | (\mathbf{X}_{[k-1]} \cap \mathbf{A}_i), \mathbf{Z}, \forall j \neq i$. Assuming faithfulness, this implies $X_k \perp \mathbf{X}_{[k-1]} \backslash \mathbf{A}_i | (\mathbf{X}_{[k-1]} \cap \mathbf{A}_i), \mathbf{Z}$. Lemma 1 (ii) applies with $A = X_k$, $\mathbf{B} = \{(\mathbf{X}_{[k-1]} \cap \mathbf{A}_i), \mathbf{Z}\}$, and $\mathbf{C} = \mathbf{X}_{[k-1]} \backslash \mathbf{A}_i$. Equality (f) follows applying the chain rule within each group $\mathbf{A}_i$. □

Proposition 1 of [27] is included in the case $\mathbf{Z} = \varnothing$. The faithfulness assumption allows relaxing their assumption $X_k \perp X_{[r]} \backslash X_k \forall k$ to $\mathbf{A}_i \perp \mathbf{A}_j \backslash \mathbf{A}_i | \mathbf{Z}\ \forall i,j$. A tighter bound can be obtained in some cases if some variables are trimmed. In particular, for a variable X', $\mathbf{A}_j$ can be trimmed to $\mathbf{A}_j \backslash X'$ for all groups such that $I(\mathbf{Y}; \mathbf{A}_j|\mathbf{Z}) = I(\mathbf{Y}; \mathbf{A}_j \backslash X'|\mathbf{Z})$ and possibly lower d_j values can be obtained after trimming. We do not explicitly include this trimming process in the definition of d_j to simplify the formulation.

Proof of Proposition 3. Consider a collection of groups $\mathbf{B}_{[n]} = \{\mathbf{B}_1, \ldots, \mathbf{B}_n\}$, each with a partition in disjoint subsets $\mathbf{B}_i = \{\mathbf{B}_i^{(1)}, \mathbf{B}_i^{(2)}\}$ that fulfill the conditions $\mathbf{B}_i^{(1)} \perp \mathbf{B}_j^{(1)} \backslash \mathbf{B}_i^{(1)} | \mathbf{Z}$ and $\mathbf{B}_i^{(2)} \perp \mathbf{B}_j \backslash \mathbf{B}_i^{(2)} | \mathbf{B}_i^{(1)} \mathbf{Z}$ $\forall i, j$, and such that $\mathbf{B}_{[n]}^{(1)} = \{\mathbf{B}_1^{(1)}, \ldots, \mathbf{B}_n^{(1)}\}$ and $\mathbf{B}_{[n]}^{(2)} = \{\mathbf{B}_1^{(2)}, \ldots, \mathbf{B}_n^{(2)}\}$ are disjoint. Define $\mathbf{X}_{[r_k]}^{(k)}$ as the set of r_k variables part of at least a group in $\mathbf{B}_{[n]}^{(k)}$, for $k = 1, 2$. We have that

$$
\begin{aligned}
& I(\mathbf{Y}; \mathbf{B}_{[n]} | \mathbf{Z}) \overset{(a)}{=} I(\mathbf{Y}; \mathbf{X}_{[r_1]}^{(1)}, \mathbf{X}_{[r_2]}^{(2)} | \mathbf{Z}) \overset{(b)}{=} \\
& \sum_{X_k \in \mathbf{X}_{[r_1]}^{(1)}} I(\mathbf{Y}; X_k | \mathbf{X}_{[k-1]}^{(1)}, \mathbf{Z}) + \sum_{X_k \in \mathbf{X}_{[r_2]}^{(2)}} I(\mathbf{Y}; X_k | \mathbf{X}_{[k-1]}^{(2)}, \mathbf{X}_{[r_1]}^{(1)}, \mathbf{Z}) \overset{(c)}{\geqslant} \\
& \sum_{i=1}^{n} \frac{1}{d_i} I(\mathbf{Y}; \mathbf{B}_i^{(1)} | \mathbf{Z}) + \sum_{i=1}^{n} \frac{1}{d_i} \sum_{X_k \in \mathbf{B}_i^{(2)}} I(\mathbf{Y}; X_k | \mathbf{X}_{[k-1]}^{(2)}, \mathbf{X}_{[r_1]}^{(1)}, \mathbf{Z}) \overset{(d)}{\geqslant} \\
& \sum_{i=1}^{n} \frac{1}{d_i} I(\mathbf{Y}; \mathbf{B}_i^{(1)} | \mathbf{Z}) + \sum_{i=1}^{n} \frac{1}{d_i} \sum_{X_k \in \mathbf{B}_i^{(2)}} I(\mathbf{Y}; X_k | (\mathbf{X}_{[k-1]}^{(2)} \cap \mathbf{B}_i^{(2)}), \mathbf{B}_i^{(1)}, \mathbf{Z}) \overset{(e)}{=} \\
& \sum_{i=1}^{n} \frac{1}{d_i} I(\mathbf{Y}; \mathbf{B}_i^{(1)} | \mathbf{Z}) + \sum_{i=1}^{n} \frac{1}{d_i} I(\mathbf{Y}; \mathbf{B}_i^{(2)} | \mathbf{B}_i^{(1)} \mathbf{Z}) \overset{(f)}{=} \sum_{i=1}^{n} \frac{1}{d_i} I(\mathbf{Y}; \mathbf{B}_i | \mathbf{Z}).
\end{aligned} \tag{A2}
$$

Equality (a) holds because $\{\mathbf{X}_{[r_1]}^{(1)}, \mathbf{X}_{[r_2]}^{(2)}\}$ contains the same variables as $\mathbf{B}_{[n]}$. Equality (b) is an iterative application of the chain rule. Inequality (c) is as follows: For the sum in $\mathbf{X}_{[r_1]}^{(1)}$, steps (c) to (f) of Equation (A1) are all combined, substituting sets $\mathbf{A}_i$ by $\mathbf{B}_i^{(1)}$ and given that these variables fulfill conditions of independence equivalent to Proposition 1. For the sum in $\mathbf{X}_{[r_2]}^{(2)}$, only steps (c) and (d) of Equation (A1) are applied, substituting sets $\mathbf{A}_i$ by $\mathbf{B}_i^{(2)}$. Inequality (d) holds applying Lemma 1 (ii). In more detail, $\mathbf{B}_i^{(2)} \perp \mathbf{B}_j \backslash \mathbf{B}_i^{(2)} | \mathbf{B}_i^{(1)} \mathbf{Z}$ $\forall i, j$ combined with the weak union property of independencies [27] mean that for each $X_k \in \mathbf{B}_i^{(2)}$, $X_k \perp \{\mathbf{B}_j^{(1)}, (X_{[k-1]}^{(2)} \cap \mathbf{B}_j^{(2)}) \backslash \mathbf{B}_i^{(2)}\} | (X_{[k-1]}^{(2)} \cap \mathbf{B}_i^{(2)}), \mathbf{B}_i^{(1)}, \mathbf{Z}$ $\forall j \neq i$. Assuming faithfulness, this implies $X_k \perp \{(\mathbf{X}_{[r_1]}^{(1)} \backslash \mathbf{B}_i^{(1)}), (X_{[k-1]}^{(2)} \backslash \mathbf{B}_i^{(2)})\} | (X_{[k-1]}^{(2)} \cap \mathbf{B}_i^{(2)}), \mathbf{B}_i^{(1)}, \mathbf{Z}$. Accordingly, Lemma 1 (ii) applies with $A = X_k$, $\mathbf{B} = \{(X_{[k-1]}^{(2)} \cap \mathbf{B}_i^{(2)}), \mathbf{B}_i^{(1)}, \mathbf{Z}\}$, and $\mathbf{C} = \{(\mathbf{X}_{[r_1]}^{(1)} \backslash \mathbf{B}_i^{(1)}), (X_{[k-1]}^{(2)} \backslash \mathbf{B}_i^{(2)})\}$. Equalities (e) and (f) follow from the chain rule of mutual information. □

Before continuing with the proof of Proposition 6, we formulate in Lemma A1 a property of the unique information that will be used in the proof.

Lemma A1. *(Conditioning on reference variables increases conditional unique information): The conditional unique information $I(\mathbf{Y}; \mathbf{X} \backslash\backslash \mathbf{Z}_1 \mathbf{Z}_2 | \mathbf{Z}_3)$ is smaller than or equal to $I(\mathbf{Y}; \mathbf{X} \backslash\backslash \mathbf{Z}_1 | \mathbf{Z}_2 \mathbf{Z}_3)$, where $\mathbf{Z}_2$ moves from the set of reference predictors of the unique information to the conditioning set.*

Proof of Lemma A1. The unique information $I(\mathbf{Y}; \mathbf{X} \backslash\backslash \mathbf{Z}_1 \mathbf{Z}_2 | \mathbf{Z}_3)$ is by definition (Equation (2)) the minimum information $I(\mathbf{Y}; \mathbf{X} | \mathbf{Z}_1 \mathbf{Z}_2 \mathbf{Z}_3)$ among the distributions that preserve $P(\mathbf{Y}, \mathbf{X}, \mathbf{Z}_3)$ and $P(\mathbf{Y}, \mathbf{Z}_1, \mathbf{Z}_2, \mathbf{Z}_3)$, and $I(\mathbf{Y}; \mathbf{X} \backslash\backslash \mathbf{Z}_1 | \mathbf{Z}_2 \mathbf{Z}_3)$ is the minimum information $I(\mathbf{Y}; \mathbf{X} | \mathbf{Z}_1 \mathbf{Z}_2 \mathbf{Z}_3)$ among the distributions that preserve $P(\mathbf{Y}, \mathbf{X}, \mathbf{Z}_2, \mathbf{Z}_3)$ and $P(\mathbf{Y}, \mathbf{Z}_1, \mathbf{Z}_2, \mathbf{Z}_3)$. Since the latter constraints subsume the former ones, the minimum can only be equal or higher. □

Proof of Proposition 6. For iterations $k = 1, ..., m_i - 1$, consider the following:

$$I(\mathbf{Y}; \mathbf{C}_i^{[k-1]} \mathbf{A}_i \backslash \mathbf{A}_i^{[k-1]} \backslash\backslash \mathbf{Z} \backslash \mathbf{Z}_i^{[k-1]} | \mathbf{Z}_i^{[k-1]}) \overset{(a)}{\leqslant} I(\mathbf{Y}; \mathbf{C}_i^{[k]} \mathbf{A}_i \backslash \mathbf{A}_i^{[k-1]} \backslash\backslash \mathbf{Z} \backslash \mathbf{Z}_i^{[k-1]} | \mathbf{Z}_i^{[k-1]}) \overset{(b)}{\leqslant}$$
$$I(\mathbf{Y}; \mathbf{C}_i^{[k]} \mathbf{A}_i \backslash \mathbf{A}_i^{[k-1]} \backslash\backslash \mathbf{Z} \backslash \mathbf{Z}_i^{[k]} | \mathbf{Z}_i^{[k]}) \overset{(c)}{=} I(\mathbf{Y}; \mathbf{C}_i^{[k]} \mathbf{A}_i \backslash \mathbf{A}_i^{[k]} \backslash\backslash \mathbf{Z} \backslash \mathbf{Z}_i^{[k]} | \mathbf{Z}_i^{[k]}). \tag{A3}$$

Inequality (a) holds from monotonicity, information cannot decrease if adding $\mathbf{C}_i^{(k)}$ to $\mathbf{C}_i^{[k-1]}$. Inequality (b) holds from Lemma A1, moving $\mathbf{Z}_i^{(k)}$ from the set of reference predictors of the unique information to the conditioning set. Equality (c) follows from $\mathbf{A}_i \backslash \mathbf{A}_i^{[k-1]} = \{\mathbf{A}_i^{(k)}, \mathbf{A}_i \backslash \mathbf{A}_i^{[k]}\}$ and the assumption in Proposition 6 that $\mathbf{Y} \perp \mathbf{A}_i^{(k)} | \mathbf{C}_i^{[k]} \mathbf{Z}_i^{[k]} \mathbf{A}_i \backslash \mathbf{A}_i^{[k]}$ holds. Accordingly, the unique information is preserved removing $\mathbf{A}_i^{(k)}$ (Proposition 2). This leads to the inequality $I(\mathbf{Y}; \mathbf{C}_i^{[k-1]} \mathbf{A}_i \backslash \mathbf{A}_i^{[k-1]} \backslash\backslash \mathbf{Z} \backslash \mathbf{Z}_i^{[k-1]} | \mathbf{Z}_i^{[k-1]}) \leqslant I(\mathbf{Y}; \mathbf{C}_i^{[k]} \mathbf{A}_i \backslash \mathbf{A}_i^{[k]} \backslash\backslash \mathbf{Z} \backslash \mathbf{Z}_i^{[k]} | \mathbf{Z}_i^{[k]})$. Equation (A3) iterated for $k = 1, \ldots, m_i - 1$ leads to $I(\mathbf{Y}; \mathbf{B}_i \backslash\backslash \mathbf{Z}_i^{(m_i)} | \mathbf{Z}_i^{[m_i-1]})$, with $\mathbf{B}_i = \{\mathbf{C}_i^{[m_i-1]}, \mathbf{A}_i^{(m_i)}\}$. Finally, this unique information by construction is smaller than $I(\mathbf{Y}; \mathbf{B}_i | \mathbf{Z})$. The terms $I(\mathbf{Y}; \mathbf{A}_i \backslash\backslash \mathbf{Z} \backslash \mathbf{Z}_i^{(1)} | \mathbf{Z}_i^{(1)})$ are obtained removing $\mathbf{C}_i^{[1]}$ from $I(\mathbf{Y}; \mathbf{C}_i^{[k]} \mathbf{A}_i \backslash \mathbf{A}_i^{[k-1]} \backslash\backslash \mathbf{Z} \mathbf{Z}_i^{[k]} | \mathbf{Z}_i^{[k]})$ by monotonicity, from step $k = 1$. □

Appendix B. Proof of Theorem 2

Proof of Theorem 2. The proof proceeds by induction like the proof of Theorem 1 in [27]. To render the notation less heavy, we simplify $an_{G'}(\mathbf{A}_i)$ to $an(\mathbf{A}_i)$ and $d_i(G'; \mathbf{Z})$ to d_i, with both G' and $\mathbf{Z}$ fixed. Define $\mathbf{V}_Z = \{\mathbf{V}_Z^{(1)}, \ldots, \mathbf{V}_Z^{(m)}\}$, with $\mathbf{V}_Z^{(j)} \equiv (an(Z_j) \cap an(\mathbf{A}_{[n]})) \backslash \mathbf{W}$. Without loss of generality, for $j = 1, \ldots, m$ we sequentially apply the chain rule to separate the information that each subset $\mathbf{V}_Z^{(j)}$ provides about $\mathbf{Y}$ after the chain rule has already been applied to $\mathbf{V}_Z^{[j-1]} \equiv \{\mathbf{V}_Z^{(1)}, ..., \mathbf{V}_Z^{(j-1)}\}$. At the j-th iteration, we obtain

$$I(\mathbf{Y}; \tilde{an}(\mathbf{A}_{[n]}) | \mathbf{Z}, \mathbf{V}_Z^{[j-1]}) = I(\mathbf{Y}; \mathbf{V}_Z^{(j)} | \mathbf{Z}, \mathbf{V}_Z^{[j-1]}) + I(\mathbf{Y}; \tilde{an}(\mathbf{A}_{[n]}) | \mathbf{Z}, \mathbf{V}_Z^{[j]}). \tag{A4}$$

The iterative induction step proceeds as follows. Assume that the inequality of Theorem 2 holds for

$$I(\mathbf{Y}; \tilde{an}(\mathbf{A}_{[n]}) | \mathbf{Z}, \mathbf{V}_Z^{[j]}) \geqslant \sum_{i=1}^{n} \frac{1}{d_i} I(\mathbf{Y}; \tilde{an}(\mathbf{A}_i) | \mathbf{Z}, \mathbf{V}_Z^{[j]}). \tag{A5}$$

We show that then the inequality also holds for $I(\mathbf{Y}; \tilde{an}(\mathbf{A}_{[n]}) | \mathbf{Z}, \mathbf{V}_Z^{[j-1]})$. First, if $\mathbf{V}_Z^{(j)} \subseteq \{\mathbf{Z}, \mathbf{V}_Z^{[j-1]}\}$ then $\{\mathbf{Z}, \mathbf{V}_Z^{[j-1]}\} = \{\mathbf{Z}, \mathbf{V}_Z^{[j]}\}$ and Equation (A5) already provides the desired inequality. We continue with $\mathbf{V}_Z^{(j)} \nsubseteq \{\mathbf{Z}, \mathbf{V}_Z^{[j-1]}\}$. Split the sum in Equation (A5) into two sums, one containing groups in the set $\mathbf{S}(G'; Z_j)$ (see its definition below Equation (7)), and the other groups not in $\mathbf{S}(G'; Z_j)$. For the sake of simplifying notation, we use $\mathbf{S}_{Z_j}$ for $\mathbf{S}(G'; Z_j)$, given that G' is fixed. We first consider the sum of groups in $\mathbf{S}_{Z_j}$:

$$\begin{aligned}
&\sum_{\mathbf{A}_i \in \mathbf{S}_{Z_j}} \frac{1}{d_i} I(\mathbf{Y}; \tilde{an}(\mathbf{A}_i) | \mathbf{Z}, \mathbf{V}_Z^{[j]}) \overset{(a)}{=} \\
&\sum_{\mathbf{A}_i \in \mathbf{S}_{Z_j}} \frac{1}{d_i} \left[I(\mathbf{Y}; \tilde{an}(\mathbf{A}_i), \mathbf{V}_Z^{(j)} | \mathbf{Z}, \mathbf{V}_Z^{[j-1]}) - I(\mathbf{Y}; \mathbf{V}_Z^{(j)} | \mathbf{Z}, \mathbf{V}_Z^{[j-1]}) \right] \overset{(b)}{\geqslant} \\
&\left[\sum_{\mathbf{A}_i \in \mathbf{S}_{Z_j}} \frac{1}{d_i} I(\mathbf{Y}; \tilde{an}(\mathbf{A}_i), \mathbf{V}_Z^{(j)} | \mathbf{Z}, \mathbf{V}_Z^{[j-1]}) \right] - I(\mathbf{Y}; \mathbf{V}_Z^{(j)}) | \mathbf{Z}, \mathbf{V}_Z^{[j-1]}) \overset{(c)}{\geqslant} \\
&\left[\sum_{\mathbf{A}_i \in \mathbf{S}_{Z_j}} \frac{1}{d_i} I(\mathbf{Y}; \tilde{an}(\mathbf{A}_i) | \mathbf{Z}, \mathbf{V}_Z^{[j-1]}) \right] - I(\mathbf{Y}; \mathbf{V}_Z^{(j)}) | \mathbf{Z}, \mathbf{V}_Z^{[j-1]}).
\end{aligned} \tag{A6}$$

Equality (a) follows from the chain rule. Inequality (b) follows from the definition of $d_i(G';\mathbf{Z})$ (in short d_i) in Equation (8). By construction $d_i(G';\mathbf{Z})$ is equal to or higher than all $d_i(G';Z_j)$ and $d_i(G';Z_j)$ is the maximal number of groups intersecting together with $an(\mathbf{A}_i;Z_j)$ (Equation (7)). For any group i within $\mathbf{S}(G';Z_j)$, $an(\mathbf{A}_i;Z_j)$ includes $an(Z_j) \cap an(\mathbf{A}_{[n]})$ and hence $d_i(G';Z_j) \geqslant |\mathbf{S}(G';Z_j)|$, so that $\sum_{\mathbf{A}_i \in \mathbf{S}_{Z_j}} 1/d_i \leqslant 1$. Inequality (c) follows from the monotonicity property of the mutual information. For the other sum

$$\sum_{\mathbf{A}_i \notin \mathbf{S}_{Z_j}} \frac{1}{d_i} I(\mathbf{Y};\tilde{an}(\mathbf{A}_i)|\mathbf{Z},\mathbf{V}_Z^{[j]}) \overset{(a)}{\geqslant} \sum_{\mathbf{A}_i \notin \mathbf{S}_{Z_j}} \frac{1}{d_i} I(\mathbf{Y};\tilde{an}(\mathbf{A}_i)\backslash \mathbf{V}_Z^{(j)}|\mathbf{Z},\mathbf{V}_Z^{[j-1]}) \overset{(b)}{=} \sum_{\mathbf{A}_i \notin \mathbf{S}_{Z_j}} \frac{1}{d_i} I(\mathbf{Y};\tilde{an}(\mathbf{A}_i)|\mathbf{Z},\mathbf{V}_Z^{[j-1]}). \tag{A7}$$

Inequality (a) follows from applying Lemma 1 (ii), with $\mathbf{A} = \tilde{an}(\mathbf{A}_i)\backslash\{\mathbf{Z},\mathbf{V}_Z^{[j]}\}$, $\mathbf{B} = \{\mathbf{Z},\mathbf{V}_Z^{[j-1]}\}$, and $\mathbf{C} = \mathbf{V}_Z^{(j)}\backslash\{\mathbf{Z},\mathbf{V}_Z^{[j-1]}\}$. Independence $\mathbf{A} \perp \mathbf{C}|\mathbf{B}$ holds because $\mathbf{A}_i \notin \mathbf{S}(G';Z_j)$ means $an(\mathbf{A}_i) \perp an(Z_j) \cap an(\mathbf{A}_{[n]})|\mathbf{Z}$ (Equation (7)), which implies $\tilde{an}(\mathbf{A}_i) \perp \mathbf{V}_Z^{(j)}|\mathbf{Z}$, given that $\mathbf{V}_Z^{(j)} \equiv (an(Z_j) \cap an(\mathbf{A}_{[n]}))\backslash\mathbf{W}$. Assuming faithfulness, since all the variables in $\mathbf{V}_Z^{[j-1]}$ are ancestors of $\mathbf{Z}$, conditioning on $\{\mathbf{Z},\mathbf{V}_Z^{[j-1]}\}$ does not create any new dependence (activating colliders) that did not exist conditioning on $\mathbf{Z}$. Equality (b) holds because given Equation (7) an overlap between $\tilde{an}(\mathbf{A}_i)\backslash\mathbf{Z}$ and $\mathbf{V}_Z^{(j)}\backslash\mathbf{Z}$ is in contradiction with $\mathbf{A}_i \notin \mathbf{S}(G';Z_j)$. Combining Equations (A6) and (A7) in the r.h.s of Equation (A5), we obtain that

$$I(\mathbf{Y};\tilde{an}(\mathbf{A}_{[n]})|\mathbf{Z},\mathbf{V}_Z^{[j]}) \geqslant \left[\sum_{i=1}^{n} \frac{1}{d_i} I(\mathbf{Y};\tilde{an}(\mathbf{A}_i)|\mathbf{Z},\mathbf{V}_Z^{[j-1]})\right] - I(\mathbf{Y};\mathbf{V}_Z^{(j)}|\mathbf{Z},\mathbf{V}_Z^{[j-1]}). \tag{A8}$$

We then insert this inequality in Equation (A4) to obtain the final desired inequality:

$$I(\mathbf{Y};\tilde{an}(\mathbf{A}_{[n]})|\mathbf{Z},\mathbf{V}_Z^{[j-1]}) \geqslant \sum_{i=1}^{n} \frac{1}{d_i} I(\mathbf{Y};\tilde{an}(\mathbf{A}_i)|\mathbf{Z},\mathbf{V}_Z^{[j-1]}). \tag{A9}$$

After subtracting $\mathbf{V}_Z = \{\mathbf{V}_Z^{(1)},\ldots,\mathbf{V}_Z^{(m)}\}$, the validity of the inequality of Theorem 2 depends on the validity of

$$I(\mathbf{Y};\tilde{an}(\mathbf{A}_{[n]})|\mathbf{Z},an(\mathbf{Z}) \cap \tilde{an}(\mathbf{A}_{[n]})) \geqslant \sum_{i=1}^{n} \frac{1}{d_i} I(\mathbf{Y};\tilde{an}(\mathbf{A}_i)|\mathbf{Z},an(\mathbf{Z}) \cap \tilde{an}(\mathbf{A}_{[n]})). \tag{A10}$$

At each iterations, if $\tilde{an}(\mathbf{A}_{[n]})\backslash\{\mathbf{Z},\mathbf{V}_Z^{[j]}\}$ is empty, the corresponding assumption in Equation (A5) is trivially fulfilled and the proof ends. Otherwise, the proof by induction continues further subtracting variables from $\tilde{an}(\mathbf{A}_{[n]})\backslash an(\mathbf{Z})$. We define the set of groups whose ancestral set in G' overlaps with $\mathbf{W}$:

$$\mathbf{S}_{\mathbf{W}} \equiv \{\mathbf{A}_i \in \mathbf{A}_{[n]} : an_{G'}(\mathbf{A}_i) \cap \mathbf{W} \neq \varnothing\}. \tag{A11}$$

We select subsets of variables to be subtracted using the same criterion used in the proof of Theorem 1 of [27], but restricting the groups used as reference in each iteration to be in the complementary set $\overline{\mathbf{S}}_{\mathbf{W}}$, i.e., with $an(\mathbf{A}_i) = \tilde{an}(\mathbf{A}_i)$. In more detail, consider without loss of generality that in the first iteration the j-th group $\mathbf{A}_j$ is taken as reference. Define $\mathbf{V}^{(0)} \equiv \mathbf{V}_Z$, where $\mathbf{V}_Z = \{\mathbf{V}_Z^{(1)},\ldots,\mathbf{V}_Z^{(m)}\}$ has already been subtracted from $\tilde{an}(\mathbf{A}_{[n]})$. With $\mathbf{A}_j$ as reference, find the joint intersection of $\tilde{an}(\mathbf{A}_j)\backslash\mathbf{V}^{(0)}$ with a maximal number of other groups $\tilde{an}(\mathbf{A}_{j'})\backslash\mathbf{V}^{(0)}$, $j' \neq j$. Define $\mathbf{S}_j^{(1)}$ as the set of groups in this intersection. The superindex indicates that this set is associated with the first iteration of this part of the induction procedure, while the subindex indicates that the j-th group is the reference. The subindex will be omitted when the group used as reference is not relevant. Define $\mathbf{V}_j^{(1)} \equiv \bigcap_{\mathbf{A}_i \in \mathbf{S}_j^{(1)}} \tilde{an}(\mathbf{A}_i) \backslash \mathbf{V}^{(0)}$ as the set of variables contained in this intersection. This subset is subtracted in the first iteration. Analogously, consider that in the k-th iteration $\mathbf{V}^{[k-1]} \equiv \{\mathbf{V}^{(0)}, ..., \mathbf{V}^{(k-1)}\}$ has already been subtracted and the j-th group is taken as reference. Then $\mathbf{S}_j^{(k)}$ is determined by the joint intersection of $\tilde{an}(\mathbf{A}_j) \backslash \mathbf{V}^{[k-1]}$ with a maximal number of other groups $\tilde{an}(\mathbf{A}_{j'}) \backslash \mathbf{V}^{[k-1]}$, $j' \neq j$. The subset of variables subtracted in the k-th iteration is $\mathbf{V}_j^{(k)} \equiv \bigcap_{\mathbf{A}_i \in \mathbf{S}_j^{(k)}} \tilde{an}(\mathbf{A}_i) \backslash \mathbf{V}^{[k-1]}$. By construction $\mathbf{V}_j^{(k)} \subseteq \tilde{an}_{G'}(\mathbf{A}_{[n]}) \backslash \mathbf{V}^{[k-1]}$. Furthermore, $|\mathbf{S}_j^{(k)}| \leqslant d_j(G'; \mathbf{Z})$, since $d_j(G'; \mathbf{Z})$ is maximal among $d_j(G'; Z_i)$ for $i = 1, \ldots, m$ (Equation (8)) for all intersections of the augmented ancestral sets defined in Equation (7), while $\mathbf{S}_j^{(k)}$ is determined by only intersections with no support in $\mathbf{V}^{[k-1]}$ and only among the reduced ancestral sets. So far, we have described the selection of subsets to be subtracted. We now look at the iterative induction step when removing a subset $\mathbf{V}_j^{(k)}$ after the previous $k-1$ iterations have already been performed. Consider

$$
\begin{aligned}
&I(\mathbf{Y}; \tilde{an}(\mathbf{A}_{[n]})|\mathbf{Z}, \mathbf{V}^{[k-1]}) \overset{(a)}{=} I(\mathbf{Y}; \tilde{an}(\mathbf{A}_{[n]})\mathbf{V}_j^{(k)}|\mathbf{Z}, \mathbf{V}^{[k-1]}) \\
&\overset{(b)}{=} I(\mathbf{Y}; \mathbf{V}_j^{(k)}|\mathbf{Z}, \mathbf{V}^{[k-1]}) + I(\mathbf{Y}; \tilde{an}(\mathbf{A}_{[n]})|\mathbf{Z}, \mathbf{V}^{[k]}).
\end{aligned}
\tag{A12}
$$

Equality (a) follows from $\mathbf{V}_j^{(k)} \subseteq \tilde{an}(\mathbf{A}_{[n]}) \backslash \mathbf{V}^{[k-1]}$. Equality (b) is an application of the chain rule. We now show that under the assumption that

$$
I(\mathbf{Y}; \tilde{an}(\mathbf{A}_{[n]})|\mathbf{Z}, \mathbf{V}^{[k]}) \geqslant \sum_{i=1}^{n} \frac{1}{d_i} I(\mathbf{Y}; \tilde{an}(\mathbf{A}_i)|\mathbf{Z}, \mathbf{V}^{[k]}),
\tag{A13}
$$

the analogous inequality holds for $I(\mathbf{Y}; \tilde{an}(\mathbf{A}_{[n]})|\mathbf{Z}, \mathbf{V}^{[k-1]})$. We again break down the sum of the groups into two sums, one containing groups in $\mathbf{S}_j^{(k)}$ and the other the rest. We first consider the sum of groups in $\mathbf{S}_j^{(k)}$:

$$
\begin{aligned}
&\sum_{\mathbf{A}_i \in \mathbf{S}_j^{(k)}} \frac{1}{d_i} I(\mathbf{Y}; \tilde{an}(\mathbf{A}_i)|\mathbf{Z}, \mathbf{V}^{[k]}) \overset{(a)}{=} \\
&\sum_{\mathbf{A}_i \in \mathbf{S}_j^{(k)}} \frac{1}{d_i} \left[I(\mathbf{Y}; \tilde{an}(\mathbf{A}_i)\mathbf{V}_j^{(k)}|\mathbf{Z}, \mathbf{V}^{[k-1]}) - I(\mathbf{Y}; \mathbf{V}_j^{(k)}|\mathbf{Z}, \mathbf{V}^{[k-1]}) \right] \overset{(b)}{\geqslant} \\
&\left[\sum_{\mathbf{A}_i \in \mathbf{S}_j^{(k)}} \frac{1}{d_i} I(\mathbf{Y}; \tilde{an}(\mathbf{A}_i)\mathbf{V}_j^{(k)}|\mathbf{Z}, \mathbf{V}^{[k-1]}) \right] - I(\mathbf{Y}; \mathbf{V}_j^{(k)}|\mathbf{Z}, \mathbf{V}^{[k-1]}) \overset{(c)}{\geqslant} \\
&\left[\sum_{\mathbf{A}_i \in \mathbf{S}_j^{(k)}} \frac{1}{d_i} I(\mathbf{Y}; \tilde{an}(\mathbf{A}_i)|\mathbf{Z}, \mathbf{V}^{[k-1]}) \right] - I(\mathbf{Y}; \mathbf{V}_j^{(k)}|\mathbf{Z}, \mathbf{V}^{[k-1]}).
\end{aligned}
\tag{A14}
$$

Equality (a) follows from the chain rule. Inequality (b) holds because $|\mathbf{S}_j^{(k)}| \leqslant d_i(G'; \mathbf{Z})$ for all $\mathbf{A}_i \in \mathbf{S}_j^{(k)}$. This is because the intersection that determines $\mathbf{S}_j^{(k)}$ contains variables from $\mathbf{A}_j$ and from all other groups $\mathbf{A}_i \in \mathbf{S}_j^{(k)}$, and hence for all these groups it also determines $d_i(G'; \mathbf{Z})$ unless an intersection with more groups exists for $\mathbf{A}_i$. Given $|\mathbf{S}_j^{(k)}| \leqslant d_i(G'; \mathbf{Z})$ for all $\mathbf{A}_i \in \mathbf{S}_j^{(k)}$, it follows that $\sum_{\mathbf{A}_i \in \mathbf{S}_j^{(k)}} 1/d_i(G'; \mathbf{Z}) \leqslant \sum_{\mathbf{A}_i \in \mathbf{S}_j^{(k)}} 1/|\mathbf{S}_j^{(k)}| = 1$. Inequality (c)

follows from monotonicity of mutual information. We now consider the sum involving groups that do not belong to $\mathbf{S}_j^{(k)}$:

$$\sum_{\mathbf{A}_i \notin \mathbf{S}_j^{(k)}} \frac{1}{d_i} I(\mathbf{Y}; \tilde{an}(\mathbf{A}_i)|\mathbf{Z}, \mathbf{V}^{[k]}) \geqslant \sum_{\mathbf{A}_i \notin \mathbf{S}_j^{(k)}} \frac{1}{d_i} I(\mathbf{Y}; \tilde{an}(\mathbf{A}_i)|\mathbf{Z}, \mathbf{V}^{[k-1]}). \tag{A15}$$

The inequality holds applying Lemma 1(ii) with $\mathbf{A} = \tilde{an}(\mathbf{A}_i)\backslash\{\mathbf{Z}, \mathbf{V}^{[k]}\}$, $\mathbf{B} = \{\mathbf{Z}, \mathbf{V}^{[k-1]}\}$, and $\mathbf{C} = \mathbf{V}_j^{(k)}\backslash\{\mathbf{Z}, \mathbf{V}^{[k-1]}\}$. By construction, $\mathbf{V}_j^{(k)} \cap \{\mathbf{Z}, \mathbf{V}^{[k-1]}\} = \varnothing$ and hence $\mathbf{C} = \mathbf{V}_j^{(k)}$. Furthermore, $\tilde{an}(\mathbf{A}_i)\backslash\{\mathbf{Z}, \mathbf{V}^{[k-1]}\}$ is equal to $\tilde{an}(\mathbf{A}_i)\backslash\{\mathbf{Z}, \mathbf{V}^{[k]}\}$ given that $\mathbf{A}_i \notin \mathbf{S}_j^{(k)}$. An intersection of $\tilde{an}(\mathbf{A}_i)\backslash\{\mathbf{Z}, \mathbf{V}^{[k-1]}\}$ and $\mathbf{V}_j^{(k)}$ is contradictory with the definition of $\mathbf{V}_j^{(k)}$, since $|\mathbf{S}_j^{(k)}|$ is determined to be maximal, but would increase to $|\mathbf{S}_j^{(k)}| + 1$ if defined by that intersection, and that would lead to $\mathbf{A}_i \in \mathbf{S}_j^{(k)}$ instead. Lemma 1(ii) applies given the independence $\mathbf{A} \perp \mathbf{C}|\mathbf{B}$. We now prove that this independence holds. We proceed discarding the presence of all types of paths in G that would create a dependence $\mathbf{A} \not\perp \mathbf{C}|\mathbf{B}$. Under the faithfulness assumption, we examine the four different types of paths in G that could create a dependence. First, there is a variable $X_r \in \mathbf{C}$ and a variable $X_l \in \mathbf{A}$ with an active directed path in G from X_r to X_l, not blocked by $\mathbf{B}$. If this path is active in G conditioning on $\mathbf{B} = \{\mathbf{Z}, \mathbf{V}^{[k-1]}\}$, it also exists in any $G' = G_{\underline{\mathbf{Z}'}}$, with $\mathbf{Z}' \subseteq \mathbf{Z}$, since the removal of outgoing arrows has the same effect as conditioning for the paths in which the conditioning variables are noncolliders (i.e., do not have two incoming arrows). This active directed path means that X_r would be an ancestor of X_l in G'. Therefore, given $X_l \in \mathbf{A}$ and $X_r \in \mathbf{C}$, X_r itself would be part of $\tilde{an}_{G'}(\mathbf{A}_i)\backslash\mathbf{V}^{[k-1]}$. However, as argued above, an intersection of $\tilde{an}_{G'}(\mathbf{A}_i)\backslash\mathbf{V}^{[k-1]}$ and $\mathbf{V}_j^{(k)}$ is contradictory with $\mathbf{A}_i \notin \mathbf{S}_j^{(k)}$. Second, there is a variable $X_r \in \mathbf{C}$ and a variable $X_l \in \mathbf{A}$ with an active directed path in G from X_l to X_r, not blocked by $\mathbf{B}$. Again, this path being active in G when conditioning on $\mathbf{B} = \{\mathbf{Z}, \mathbf{V}^{[k-1]}\}$, means that it also exists in any $G' = G_{\underline{\mathbf{Z}'}}$, with $\mathbf{Z}' \subseteq \mathbf{Z}$. Therefore, X_l would be an ancestor of X_r in G'. This is again a contradiction with the definition of $\mathbf{V}_j^{(k)}$ because it could be redefined to include $|\mathbf{S}_j^{(k)}| + 1$ groups, since X_l would be an ancestor of all groups intersecting in $\mathbf{V}_j^{(k)}$. Third, there is a variable $X_r \in \mathbf{C}$, a variable $X_l \in \mathbf{A}$, and another variable X_h that is not part of $\mathbf{A}$ nor $\mathbf{C}$ with an active directed path in G from X_h to X_r and an active directed path from X_h to X_l, both not blocked by $\mathbf{B}$. This would also imply that these directed paths exist in $G' = G_{\underline{\mathbf{Z}'}}$, with $\mathbf{Z}' \subseteq \mathbf{Z}$, and hence X_h is an ancestor of $\mathbf{A}$ and $\mathbf{C}$ in G'. Since X_h is an ancestor of $\mathbf{A} = \tilde{an}(\mathbf{A}_i)\backslash\{\mathbf{Z}, \mathbf{V}^{[k-1]}\}$ but by construction $X_h \notin \mathbf{A}$, this means that X_h has to be part of $\{\mathbf{Z}, \mathbf{V}^{[k-1]}\}$ or of $\mathbf{W}$, since any ancestor of $an(\mathbf{A}_i)$ is part of $an(\mathbf{A}_i)$. If $X_h \in \{\mathbf{Z}, \mathbf{V}^{[k-1]}\}$, conditioning on $\mathbf{B} = \{\mathbf{Z}, \mathbf{V}^{[k-1]}\}$ would prevent from having active directed paths from X_h to X_r and from X_h to X_l, leading to a contradiction. We now consider the case $X_h \in \mathbf{W}$. Since X_h is an ancestor of $\mathbf{C} = V_j^{(k)}$, by construction of $V_j^{(k)}$, X_h is an ancestor of $\tilde{an}(\mathbf{A}_j)\backslash\{\mathbf{Z}, \mathbf{V}^{[k-1]}\}$. This means that $an(\mathbf{A}_j)$ includes $X_h \in \mathbf{W}$ which, given Equation (A11), is in contradiction with the criterion for selection of reference groups such that $\mathbf{A}_j \in \overline{\mathbf{S}}_{\mathbf{W}}$. In these three types of cases, an active path would exist despite conditioning on $\mathbf{B}$. In the last type, a path would be activated by conditioning on $\mathbf{B}$. At least one variable $X_h \in \mathbf{B} = \{\mathbf{Z}, \mathbf{V}^{[k-1]}\}$ has to be a collider or a descendant of a collider along the path that conditioning activates. Consider first that a single collider X_h is involved. For the collider to activate the path, it must exist an active directed subpath to X_h from a variable X_r that is part of $\mathbf{C}$ or part of its ancestor set in G'. Since this directed subpath is active in G when conditioning on $\mathbf{B}$, it is also active in G'. This means that X_r would be an ancestor of X_h in G'. If X_h is part of $\mathbf{Z}$ or part of $\mathbf{V}^{(0)} \equiv (an_{G'}(\mathbf{Z}) \cap an_{G'}(\mathbf{A}_{[n]}))\backslash\mathbf{W}$, then X_r being an ancestor of X_h means that it is part of $an_{G'}(\mathbf{Z}) \cap an_{G'}(\mathbf{A}_{[n]})$. Accordingly, by definition of $\mathbf{V}^{(0)}$, X_r would be part of $\mathbf{V}^{(0)}$ or of $\mathbf{W}$. The former option leads to a contradiction because

$\mathbf{V}^{(0)}$ has already been removed from $\tilde{an}(\mathbf{A}_{[n]})$ and is part of the conditioning variables, so that the subpath from X_r to X_h could not be part of the path activated by conditioning on the collider. The latter option, X_r being part of $\mathbf{W}$, is in contradiction with it being an ancestor of $\mathbf{C} = \mathbf{V}_j^{(k)}$, since this means being an ancestor of the group $\mathbf{A}_j$ taken as reference to build $\mathbf{V}_j^{(k)}$, which by construction is chosen from $\bar{S}_{\mathbf{W}}$. We continue considering that X_h is part of $\mathbf{V}^{(k')} \in \mathbf{V}^{[k-1]}$, for $0 < k' \leqslant k-1$. In this case, X_r being an ancestor of X_h would mean that either X_r is in $\mathbf{W}$ or it would have been possible to define $\mathbf{V}^{(k')}$ to include X_r. In the former case, this leads to a contradiction because for $0 < k' \leqslant k-1$ all $\mathbf{V}^{(k')}$ have been constructed taking as reference a group belonging to $\bar{S}_{\mathbf{W}}$. In the latter case, this leads to a contradiction because $\mathbf{V}^{(k')}$ is constructed to include all variables in the intersection with the maximum number of groups. The same reasoning holds if the activated path contains more than one collider from $\mathbf{B}$, by selecting the collider X_h closest to a variable in $\mathbf{C}$ along the path. Since for all four types of paths that could lead to $\mathbf{A} \not\perp \mathbf{C}|\mathbf{B}$ we reach a contradiction, $\mathbf{A} \perp \mathbf{C}|\mathbf{B}$ holds and Lemma 1(ii) can be applied to obtain the inequality in Equation (A15). Combining Equations (A14) and (A15) with the r.h.s. of Equation (A13), we obtain that

$$I(\mathbf{Y};\tilde{an}(\mathbf{A}_{[n]})|\mathbf{Z},\mathbf{V}^{[k]}) \geqslant \left[\sum_{i=1}^{n}\frac{1}{d_i}I(\mathbf{Y};\tilde{an}(\mathbf{A}_i)|\mathbf{Z},\mathbf{V}^{[k-1]})\right] - I(\mathbf{Y};\mathbf{V}_j^{(k)}|\mathbf{Z},\mathbf{V}^{[k-1]}). \tag{A16}$$

We then insert this inequality in Equation (A12) to obtain the desired inequality:

$$I(\mathbf{Y};\tilde{an}(\mathbf{A}_{[n]})|\mathbf{Z},\mathbf{V}^{[k-1]}) \geqslant \sum_{i=1}^{n}\frac{1}{d_i}I(\mathbf{Y};\tilde{an}(\mathbf{A}_i)|\mathbf{Z},\mathbf{V}^{[k-1]}). \tag{A17}$$

After the completion of these iterations, all variables in $(an(\mathbf{Z}) \cap an(\mathbf{A}_{[n]}))\backslash\mathbf{W}$ and in groups from $\bar{\mathbf{S}}_{\mathbf{W}}$ have been subtracted from $\tilde{an}(\mathbf{A}_{[n]})$. The proof ends if after some iteration $\tilde{an}(\mathbf{A}_{[n]})\backslash\mathbf{V}^{[k]}$ is empty. In particular, the proof ends if $\mathbf{W}$ is empty and hence all groups are already subtracted. Otherwise, assume that m' iterations have been carried out when finishing this step. The proof by induction continues with a single additional step for the remaining groups $\mathbf{S}_{\mathbf{W}}$. Select a single variable X_0 out of $\tilde{an}(\mathbf{A}_{[n]})\backslash\mathbf{V}^{[m']}$ that is only contained in groups in $\mathbf{S}_{\mathbf{W}}$ and apply the chain rule

$$\begin{aligned} I(\mathbf{Y};\tilde{an}(\mathbf{A}_{[n]})|\mathbf{Z},\mathbf{V}^{[m']}) &= I(\mathbf{Y};\tilde{an}(\mathbf{A}_{[n]})\backslash X_0|\mathbf{Z},\mathbf{V}^{[m']}) + I(\mathbf{Y};X_0|\mathbf{Z},\tilde{an}(\mathbf{A}_{[n]})\backslash X_0) = \\ & I(\mathbf{Y};\tilde{an}(\mathbf{A}_{[n]})\backslash X_0|\mathbf{Z},\mathbf{V}^{[m']}) + I(\mathbf{Y};\tilde{an}(\mathbf{A}_{[n]})|\mathbf{Z},\tilde{an}(\mathbf{A}_{[n]})\backslash X_0). \end{aligned} \tag{A18}$$

The iterative induction step should prove that if the inequality of the theorem holds for $I(\mathbf{Y};\tilde{an}(\mathbf{A}_{[n]})|\mathbf{Z},\tilde{an}(\mathbf{A}_{[n]})\backslash X_0)$ it is also true for $I(\mathbf{Y};\tilde{an}(\mathbf{A}_{[n]})|\mathbf{Z},\mathbf{V}^{[m']})$. We will prove this below. Before we show that the inequality

$$I(\mathbf{Y};\tilde{an}(\mathbf{A}_{[n]})|\mathbf{Z},\tilde{an}(\mathbf{A}_{[n]})\backslash X_0) \geqslant \sum_{i=1}^{n}\frac{1}{d_i}I(\mathbf{Y};\tilde{an}(\mathbf{A}_i)|\mathbf{Z},\tilde{an}(\mathbf{A}_{[n]})\backslash X_0) \tag{A19}$$

always holds, and hence it provides the base case for the induction proof. The base case is true because

$$\begin{aligned} \sum_{i=1}^{n}\frac{1}{d_i}I(\mathbf{Y};\tilde{an}(\mathbf{A}_i)|\mathbf{Z},\tilde{an}(\mathbf{A}_{[n]})\backslash X_0) &\overset{(a)}{=} \sum_{i:X_0\in\tilde{an}(\mathbf{A}_i)}\frac{1}{d_i}I(\mathbf{Y};X_0|\mathbf{Z},\tilde{an}(\mathbf{A}_{[n]})\backslash X_0) \\ &\overset{(b)}{=} I(\mathbf{Y};X_0|\mathbf{Z},\tilde{an}(\mathbf{A}_{[n]})\backslash X_0)\left[\sum_{i:X_0\in\tilde{an}(\mathbf{A}_i)}\frac{1}{d_i}\right] \overset{(c)}{\leqslant} I(\mathbf{Y};X_0|\mathbf{Z},\tilde{an}(\mathbf{A}_{[n]})\backslash X_0). \end{aligned} \tag{A20}$$

Equality (a) holds because $I(\mathbf{Y}; \tilde{an}(\mathbf{A}_i)|\mathbf{Z}, \tilde{an}(\mathbf{A}_{[n]})\backslash X_0)$ is zero for the terms that do not contain X_0. Equality (b) holds because the information term is the same across the sum and can be factorized. Inequality (c) is justified as follows. Let N_0 be the number of groups that contain X_0, and hence that intersect in X_0. For these groups, $d_i(G'; \mathbf{Z})$ is higher than or equal to N_0. This means that $\sum_{i: X_0 \in \tilde{an}(\mathbf{A}_i)} 1/d_i(G'; \mathbf{Z}) \leqslant 1$. We now complete the proof of the last iterative induction step:

$$\begin{aligned}
&\sum_{i=1}^{n} \frac{1}{d_i} I(\mathbf{Y}; \tilde{an}(\mathbf{A}_i)|\mathbf{Z}, \tilde{an}(\mathbf{A}_{[n]})\backslash X_0) \overset{(a)}{=} \sum_{\mathbf{A}_i \in \mathbf{S_W}} \frac{1}{d_i} I(\mathbf{Y}; \tilde{an}(\mathbf{A}_i)|\mathbf{Z}, \tilde{an}(\mathbf{A}_{[n]})\backslash X_0) \overset{(b)}{=} \\
&\sum_{\mathbf{A}_i \in \mathbf{S_W}} \frac{1}{d_i} \left[I(\mathbf{Y}; \tilde{an}(\mathbf{A}_i), \tilde{an}(\mathbf{A}_{[n]})\backslash X_0 | \mathbf{Z}, \mathbf{V}^{[m']}) - I(\mathbf{Y}; \tilde{an}(\mathbf{A}_{[n]})\backslash X_0 | \mathbf{Z}, \mathbf{V}^{[m']}) \right] \overset{(c)}{\geqslant} \\
&\left[\sum_{\mathbf{A}_i \in \mathbf{S_W}} \frac{1}{d_i} I(\mathbf{Y}; \tilde{an}(\mathbf{A}_i), \tilde{an}(\mathbf{A}_{[n]})\backslash X_0 | \mathbf{Z}, \mathbf{V}^{[m']}) \right] - I(\mathbf{Y}; \tilde{an}(\mathbf{A}_{[n]})\backslash X_0 | \mathbf{Z}, \mathbf{V}^{[m']}) \overset{(d)}{\geqslant} \\
&\left[\sum_{\mathbf{A}_i \in \mathbf{S_W}} \frac{1}{d_i} I(\mathbf{Y}; \tilde{an}(\mathbf{A}_i) | \mathbf{Z}, \mathbf{V}^{[m']}) \right] - I(\mathbf{Y}; \tilde{an}(\mathbf{A}_{[n]})\backslash X_0 | \mathbf{Z}, \mathbf{V}^{[m']}) \overset{(e)}{=} \\
&\left[\sum_{i=1}^{n} \frac{1}{d_i} I(\mathbf{Y}; \tilde{an}(\mathbf{A}_i) | \mathbf{Z}, \mathbf{V}^{[m']}) \right] - I(\mathbf{Y}; \tilde{an}(\mathbf{A}_{[n]})\backslash X_0 | \mathbf{Z}, \mathbf{V}^{[m']}).
\end{aligned} \tag{A21}$$

Equality (a) holds because X_0 is selected to be contained only in groups in $\mathbf{S_W}$. Equality (b) follows from the chain rule and from $\mathbf{V}^{[m']} \subseteq \tilde{an}(\mathbf{A}_{[n]})\backslash X_0$. Inequality (c) holds because, for all $\mathbf{A}_i \in \mathbf{S_W}$, $d_i(G'; \mathbf{Z})$ is higher than or equal to $|\mathbf{S_W}|$, since their ancestral sets intersect at W_0, which is an ancestor of all variables in $\mathbf{W}$. This means that $\sum_{\mathbf{A}_i \in \mathbf{S_W}} 1/d_i(G'; \mathbf{Z}) \leqslant 1$. Inequality (d) follows from the monotonicity of mutual information, and equality (e) holds because $\tilde{an}(\mathbf{A}_i) \subseteq \{\mathbf{Z}, \mathbf{V}^{[m']}\}$ for all $\mathbf{A}_i \notin \mathbf{S_W}$. We use the last expression in Equation (A21) at the r.h.s of Equation (A19), and combine it with Equation (A18) to obtain

$$I(\mathbf{Y}; \tilde{an}(\mathbf{A}_{[n]})|\mathbf{Z}, \mathbf{V}^{[m']}) \geqslant \sum_{i=1}^{n} \frac{1}{d_i} I(\mathbf{Y}; \tilde{an}(\mathbf{A}_i)|\mathbf{Z}, \mathbf{V}^{[m']}). \tag{A22}$$

This completes the iterative induction step of the proof. Since the validity of the base case has also been proven, this completes the proof. □

Appendix C. On Required Assumptions Relating Independencies and d-Separation

In this Section, we discuss more closely the requirements on the relation between graphical d-separation and statistical independencies needed for the applicability of the derived inequality constraints. As indicated in Section 2.3, so far we have invoked the faithfulness assumption [1,2] in order to simplify the presentation, that is, we have not distinguished between $X \perp_P Y|\mathbf{S}$ and $X \perp_G Y|\mathbf{S}$. We will now make this distinction and reconsider all cases of the proofs of Appendices A and B where faithfulness has been invoked, showing that in fact it is only required to assume that d-separation is a sufficient condition for statistical independence.

We start with the role that the assumption of d-separation implying independence has in the proof of Propositions 1 and 3. As discussed in Section 1, we envisage the implementation of the tests such that conditional independence requirements of Proposition 1 or 3 are verified in terms of graphical separability for the hypothesized causal structure. In particular, a test from Proposition 1 is to be applied when verifying that for the selected collection and groups it holds that $\mathbf{A}_i \perp_G \mathbf{A}_j\backslash\mathbf{A}_i|\mathbf{Z}\ \forall i,j$. It is then assumed that this implies $\mathbf{A}_i \perp_P \mathbf{A}_j\backslash\mathbf{A}_i|\mathbf{Z}\ \forall i,j$. In the proof of Proposition 1, in step (e) of Equation (A1), Lemma 1(ii) has been applied invoking faithfulness to guarantee that for $X_k \in \mathbf{A}_i$, independencies $X_k \perp_P (\mathbf{X}_{[k-1]} \cap \mathbf{A}_j)\backslash\mathbf{A}_i|(\mathbf{X}_{[k-1]} \cap \mathbf{A}_i), \mathbf{Z}, \forall j \neq i$ imply the independence $X_k \perp_P \mathbf{X}_{[k-1]}\backslash\mathbf{A}_i|(\mathbf{X}_{[k-1]} \cap \mathbf{A}_i), \mathbf{Z}$. However, while this implication needs to be assumed at the level of independencies, at the level of graphical separability,

$X_k \perp_G (\mathbf{X}_{[k-1]} \cap \mathbf{A}_j)\backslash\mathbf{A}_i|(\mathbf{X}_{[k-1]} \cap \mathbf{A}_i), \mathbf{Z}, \forall j \neq i$ straightforwardly implies the joint separability $X_k \perp_G \mathbf{X}_{[k-1]}\backslash\mathbf{A}_i|(\mathbf{X}_{[k-1]} \cap \mathbf{A}_i), \mathbf{Z}$. This is because the separability of $\mathbf{X}_{[k-1]}\backslash\mathbf{A}_i$ follows from the lack of active paths for each of the nodes it contains, and hence is equivalent to the separability of $(\mathbf{X}_{[k-1]} \cap \mathbf{A}_j)\backslash\mathbf{A}_i$ for all j, which jointly comprise the same nodes. The assumption that d-separation implies independence guarantees the independence $X_k \perp_P \mathbf{X}_{[k-1]}\backslash\mathbf{A}_i|(\mathbf{X}_{[k-1]} \cap \mathbf{A}_i), \mathbf{Z}$ from $X_k \perp_G \mathbf{X}_{[k-1]}\backslash\mathbf{A}_i|(\mathbf{X}_{[k-1]} \cap \mathbf{A}_i), \mathbf{Z}$, without the need to more broadly require faithfulness. The proof of Proposition 3 relies on an analogous way on the assumption that d-separation implies independence, using it to guarantee the conditional independencies involving the subsets in $\mathbf{B}^{(1)}_{[n]}$ and $\mathbf{B}^{(2)}_{[n]}$. In step (d) of Equation (A2), the fact that separability for a joint set of nodes is straightforwardly guaranteed by the separability of each of its nodes is again applied and then mapped to the existence of an independence using this assumption. The fact that conditions $\mathbf{B}^{(1)}_i \perp_G \mathbf{B}^{(1)}_j\backslash\mathbf{B}^{(1)}_i|\mathbf{Z}$ and $\mathbf{B}^{(2)}_i \perp_G \mathbf{B}_j\backslash\mathbf{B}^{(2)}_i|\mathbf{B}^{(1)}_i\mathbf{Z}\ \forall i, j$ can be verified using d-separation instead of estimating independencies from data is crucial in the case that the groups include hidden variables, which precludes the direct evaluation of these independencies.

The next result whose derivation relies on the assumption that d-separation implies independence is Theorem 2. In step (a) of Equation (A7), faithfulness was invoked to guarantee that conditioning on some ancestors of $\mathbf{Z}$ cannot create new dependencies that were not already created by conditioning on $\mathbf{Z}$ itself. In more detail, it was assumed that if the independence $\tilde{an}(\mathbf{A}_i) \perp_P \mathbf{V}^{(j)}_Z|\mathbf{Z}$ holds then also $\tilde{an}(\mathbf{A}_i) \perp_P \mathbf{V}^{(j)}_Z|\{\mathbf{Z}, \mathbf{V}^{[j-1]}_Z\}$ holds, where $\mathbf{V}^{[j-1]}_Z$ are by construction ancestors of $\mathbf{Z}$. Again, at the level of graphical separability this implication is straightforward and does not require any assumption. This is because by definition of d-separation a path is activated both when conditioning on a collider or on any descendant of the collider, and $\mathbf{V}^{[j-1]}_Z$ being ancestors of $\mathbf{Z}$ means that $\mathbf{Z}$ contains a descendant for each node in $\mathbf{V}^{[j-1]}_Z$. Accordingly, no assumption is needed to ensure $\tilde{an}(\mathbf{A}_i) \perp_G \mathbf{V}^{(j)}_Z|\{\mathbf{Z}, \mathbf{V}^{[j-1]}_Z\}$ from $\tilde{an}(\mathbf{A}_i) \perp_G \mathbf{V}^{(j)}_Z|\mathbf{Z}$. The assumption that d-separation implies independence is then used to ensure $\tilde{an}(\mathbf{A}_i) \perp_P \mathbf{V}^{(j)}_Z|\{\mathbf{Z}, \mathbf{V}^{[j-1]}_Z\}$ from $\tilde{an}(\mathbf{A}_i) \perp_G \mathbf{V}^{(j)}_Z|\{\mathbf{Z}, \mathbf{V}^{[j-1]}_Z\}$. Faithfulness is also invoked in the proof of Theorem 2 to justify the application of Lemma 1(ii) in Equation (A15). In this case, the existence of an independence $\mathbf{A} \perp_P \mathbf{C}|\mathbf{B}$ is directly justified in terms of the nonexistence of active paths in the graph, hence guaranteeing $\mathbf{A} \perp_G \mathbf{C}|\mathbf{B}$ and subsequently using the assumption that d-separation implies independence to derive $\mathbf{A} \perp_P \mathbf{C}|\mathbf{B}$.

The considerations above show that the assumption that d-separation implies statistical independence is enough to derive the existence of groups-decomposition inequalities under the conditions of Propositions 1 and 3, and of Theorem 2. Furthermore, if unfaithful independencies are present in the data that do not follow from the causal structure, this may decrease the power to reject causal structures testing the inequalities, but will not lead to incorrect rejections. This differs from the impact of unfaithful independencies on the inference of the Markov equivalence class from data [1,2]. In that case, unfaithful independencies can lead to an incorrect reconstruction of the skeleton of the graph or result in contradictory rules for edge orientation. The assumption that d-separation implies statistical independence is substantially weaker than the reverse assumption also included in the faithfulness assumption, namely that statistical independence implies d-separation. The X-OR logic gate is an example that the latter assumption can be violated. Conversely, if the causal graph is meant to reflect the underlying structure of actual physical mechanisms involved in generating the variables, all statistical dependencies need to originate from some paths of influence between the variables. Accordingly, a d-separation that does not lead to an independence can be taken as an indicator that some structure is missing in the causal graph, namely associated with the paths that create the observed dependence. In this regard, it is appropriate to reject a causal structure if it does not fulfill an inequality constraint because graphical separability is not reflected in the corresponding independencies found in the data.

References

1. Spirtes, P.; Glymour, C.N.; Scheines, R. *Causation, Prediction, and Search*, 2nd ed.; MIT Press: Cambridge, MA, USA, 2000.
2. Pearl, J. *Causality: Models, Reasoning, Inference*, 2nd ed.; Cambridge University Press: New York, NY, USA, 2009.
3. Peters, J.; Janzing, D.; Schölkopf, B. *Elements of Causal Inference: Foundations and Learning Algorithms*; MIT Press: Cambridge, MA, USA, 2017.
4. Malinsky, D.; Danks, D. Causal discovery algorithms: A practical guide. *Philos. Compass* **2018**, *13*, e12470. [CrossRef]
5. Verma, T. *Graphical Aspects of Causal Models*; Technical Report R-191; Computer Science Department, UCLA: Los Angeles, CA, USA, 1993.
6. Zhang, J. On the completeness of orientation rules for causal discovery in the presence of latent confounders and selection bias. *Artif. Intell.* **2008**, *172*, 1873–1896. [CrossRef]
7. Tian, J.; Pearl, J. On the testable implications of causal models with hidden variables. In Proceedings of the Eighteenth Conference on Uncertainty in Artificial Intelligence, San Francisco, CA, USA, 1–4 August 2002.
8. Verma, T.; Pearl, J. Equivalence and synthesis of causal models. In Proceedings of the Sixth Conference on Uncertainty in Artifial Intelligence, Cambridge, MA, USA, 27–29 July 1990; pp. 220–227.
9. Chicharro, D.; Besserve, M.; Panzeri, S. Causal learning with sufficient statistics: An information bottleneck approach. *arXiv* **2020**, arXiv:2010.05375.
10. Parbhoo, S.; Wieser, M.; Wieczorek, A.; Roth, V. Information bottleneck for estimating treatment effects with systematically missing covariates. *Entropy* **2020**, *22*, 389. [CrossRef]
11. Hoyer, P.O.; Janzing, D.; Mooij, J.M.; Peters, J.; Schölkopf, B. Nonlinear causal discovery with additive noise models. In Proceedings of the 21st Conference on Advances in Neural Information Processing Systems (NIPS 2008), Vancouver, BC, Canada, 8–11 December 2008; pp. 689–696.
12. Zhang, K.; Hyvärinen, A. On the identifiability of the post-nonlinear causal model. In Proceedings of the 25th Annual Conference on Uncertainty in Artificial Intelligence (UAI), Montreal, QC, Canada, 18–21 June 2009; pp. 647–655.
13. Chicharro, D.; Panzeri, S.; Shpitser, I. Conditionally-additive-noise models for structure learning. *arXiv* **2019**, arXiv:1905.08360
14. Shimizu, S.; Inazumi, T.; Sogawa, Y.; Hyvärinen, A.; Kawahara, Y.; Washio, T.; Hoyer, P.O.; Bollen, K. DirectLiNGAM: A direct method for learning a linear non-Gaussian structural equation model. *J. Mach. Learn. Res.* **2011**, *12*, 1225–1248.
15. Evans, R.J. Graphs for margins of Bayesian networks. *Scand. J. Stat.* **2015**, *43*, 625. [CrossRef]
16. Weilenmann, M.; Colbeck, R. Analysing causal structures with entropy. *Proc. Roy. Soc. A* **2017**, *473*, 20170483. [CrossRef]
17. Bell, J.S. On the Einstein-Podolsky-Rosen paradox. *Physics* **1964**, *1*, 195–200. [CrossRef]
18. Clauser, J.F.; Horne, M.A.; Shimony, A.; Holt, R.A. Proposed experiment to test local hidden-variable theories. *Phys. Rev. Lett.* **1969**, *23*, 880. [CrossRef]
19. Pearl, J. On the testability of causal models with latent and instrumental variables. In Proceedings of the Eleventh Conference on Uncertainty in Artificial Intelligence, Montreal, QC, Canada, 18–20 August 1995; pp. 435–443.
20. Bonet, B. Instrumentality tests revisited. In Proceedings of the 17th Conference on Uncertainty in Artificial Intelligence (UAI), San Francisco, CA, USA, 2–5 August 2001; pp. 48–55.
21. Kang, C.; Tian, J. Inequality constraints in causal models with hidden variables. In Proceedings of the 22nd Conference on Uncertainty in Artificial Intelligence, Cambridge, MA, USA, 13–16 July 2006; pp. 233–240.
22. Chaves, R.; Luft, L.; Gross, D. Causal structures from entropic information: Geometry and novel scenarios. *New J. Phys.* **2014**, *16*, 043001. [CrossRef]
23. Fritz, T.; Chaves, R. Entropic inequalities and marginal problems. *IEEE Trans. Inf. Theory* **2013**, *59*, 803–817. [CrossRef]
24. Chaves, R.; Luft, L.; Maciel, T.O.; Gross, D.; Janzing, D.; Schölkopf, B. Inferring latent structures via information inequalities. In Proceedings of the 30th Conference on Uncertainty in Artificial Intelligence, Quebec City, QC, Canada, 23–27 July 2014; pp. 112–121.
25. Dougherty, R.; Freiling, C.; Zeger, K. Six new non-Shannon information inequalities. In Proceedings of the IEEE International Symposium on Information Theory, Seattle, WA, USA, 9–14 July 2006; pp. 233–236.
26. Weilenmann, M.; Colbeck, R. Non-Shannon inequalities in the entropy vector approach to causal structures. *Quantum* **2018**, *2*, 57. [CrossRef]
27. Steudel, B.; Ay, N. Information-theoretic inference of common ancestors. *Entropy* **2015**, *17*, 2304–2327. [CrossRef]
28. Cover, T.M.; Thomas, J.A. *Elements of Information Theory*, 2nd ed.; John Wiley and Sons: Hoboken, NJ, USA, 2006.
29. Bertschinger, N.; Rauh, J.; Olbrich, E.; Jost, J.; Ay, N. Quantifying unique information. *Entropy* **2014**, *16*, 2161–2183. [CrossRef]
30. Williams, P.L.; Beer, R.D. Nonnegative decomposition of multivariate information. *arXiv* **2010**, arXiv:1004.2515.
31. Harder, M.; Salge, C.; Polani, D. Bivariate measure of redundant information. *Phys. Rev. E* **2013**, *87*, 012130. [CrossRef] [PubMed]
32. Ince, R.A.A. Measuring multivariate redundant information with pointwise common change in surprisal. *Entropy* **2017**, *19*, 318. [CrossRef]
33. James, R.G.; Emenheiser, J.; Crutchfield, J.P. Unique Information via dependency constraints. *J. Phys. A Math. Theor.* **2019**, *52*, 014002. [CrossRef]
34. Ay, N.; Polani, D.; Virgo, N. Information decomposition based on cooperative game theory. *Kybernetika* **2020**, *56*, 979–1014. [CrossRef]
35. Kolchinsky, A. A novel approach to the partial information decomposition. *Entropy* **2022**, *24*, 403. [CrossRef]

36. Pearl, J. Fusion, propagation, and structuring in belief networks. *Artif. Intell.* **1986**, *29*, 241–288. [CrossRef]
37. Geiger, D.; Verma, T.; Pearl, J. d-Separation: From theorems to algorithms. In Proceedings of the Fifth Annual Conference on Uncertainty in Artificial Intelligence, Amsterdam, The Netherlands, 18–20 August 1989; pp. 118–125.
38. Rauh, J.; Bertschinger, N.; Olbrich, E.; Jost, J. Reconsidering unique information: Towards a multivariate information decomposition. In Proceedings of the IEEE International Symposium on Information Theory (ISIT 2014), Honolulu, HI, USA, 29 June–4 July 2014; pp. 2232–2236.
39. Banerjee, P.K.; Olbrich, E.; Jost, J.; Rauh, J. Unique Informations and Deficiencies. *arXiv* **2019**, arXiv:1807.05103v3.
40. Chicharro, D.; Panzeri, S. Synergy and redundancy in dual decompositions of mutual information gain and information loss. *Entropy* **2017**, *19*, 71. [CrossRef]
41. Chicharro, D. Quantifying multivariate redundancy with maximum entropy decompositions of mutual information. *arXiv* **2017**, arXiv:1708.03845.
42. Pica, G.; Piasini, E.; Chicharro, D.; Panzeri, S. Invariant components of synergy, redundancy, and unique information among three variables. *Entropy* **2017**, *19*, 451. [CrossRef]
43. Chicharro, D.; Pica, G.; Panzeri, S. The identity of information: How deterministic dependencies constrain information synergy and redundancy. *Entropy* **2018**, *20*, 169. [CrossRef]
44. Chicharro, D.; Ledberg, A. Framework to study dynamic dependencies in networks of interacting processes. *Phys. Rev. E* **2012**, *86*, 041901. [CrossRef]
45. Lütkepohl, H. *New Introduction to Multiple Time Series Analysis*; Springer: Berlin/Heidelberg, Germany, 2006.
46. Geweke, J.F. Measurement of linear dependence and feedback between multiple time series. *J. Am. Stat. Assoc.* **1982**, *77*, 304–313. [CrossRef]
47. Chicharro, D. On the spectral formulation of Granger causality. *Biol. Cybern.* **2011**, *105*, 331–347. [CrossRef]
48. Chicharro, D. Parametric and non-parametric criteria for causal inference from time-series. In *Directed Information Measures in Neuroscience*; Wibral, M., Vicente, R. Lizier, J.T., Eds.; Springer: Berlin/Heidelberg, Germany, 2014; pp. 195–223.
49. Brovelli, A.; Ding, M.; Ledberg, A.; Chen, Y.; Nakamura, R.; Bressler, S.L. Beta oscillations in a large-scale sensorimotor cortical network: Directional influences revealed by Granger causality. *Proc. Natl. Acad. Sci. USA* **2004**, *101*, 9849–9854. [CrossRef] [PubMed]
50. Brovelli, A.; Chicharro, D.; Badier, J.M.; Wang, H.; Jirsa, V. Characterization of cortical networks and corticocortical functional connectivity mediating arbitrary visuomotor mapping. *J. Neurosci.* **2015**, *35*, 12643–12658. [CrossRef] [PubMed]
51. Celotto, M.; Bím, J.; Tlaie, A.; De Feo, V.; Toso, A.; Lemke, S.M.; Chicharro, D.; Nili, H.; Bieler, M.; Hanganu-Opatz, I.L.; et al. An information-theoretic quantification of the content of communication between brain regions. In Proceedings of the Thirty-Seventh Conference on Neural Information Processing Systems, New Orleans, LA, USA, 10–16 December 2023.
52. Granger, C.W.J. Investigating causal relations by econometric models and cross-spectral methods. *Econometrica* **1969**, *37*, 424–438. [CrossRef]
53. Hiemstra, C.; Jones, J.D. Testing for linear and nonlinear Granger causality in the stock price-volume relation. *J. Financ.* **1994**, *49*, 1639–1664.
54. Hlaváčková-Schindler, K.; Paluš, M.; Vejmelka, M.; Bhattacharya, J. Causality detection based on information-theoretic approaches in time-series analysis. *Phys. Rep.* **2007**, *441*, 1–46. [CrossRef]
55. Geweke, J.F. Measures of conditional linear dependence and feedback between time series. *J. Am. Stat. Assoc.* **1984**, *79*, 907–915. [CrossRef]
56. Caporale, M.C.; Hassapis, C.; Pittis, N. Unit roots and long-run causality: Investigating the relationship between output, money and interest rates. *Econ. Model.* **1998**, *15*, 91–112. [CrossRef]
57. Caporale, M.C.; Pittis, N. Efficient estimation of cointegrating vectors and testing for causality in vector auto-regressions. *J. Econ. Surv.* **1999**, *13*, 3–35.
58. Hacker, R.S.; Hatemi, J.A. Tests for causality between integrated variables using asymptotic and bootstrap distributions: Theory and application. *Appl. Econ.* **2006**, *38*, 1489–1500. [CrossRef]
59. Massey, J.L. Causality, feedback and directed information. In Proceedings of the 1990 IEEE International Symposium Information Theory and Its Applications, Honolulu, HI, USA, 10–15 June 1990; Volume 27, pp. 303–305.
60. Amblard, P.O.; Michel, O. On directed information theory and Granger causality graphs. *J. Comput. Neurosci.* **2011**, *30*, 7–16. [CrossRef]
61. Chaves, R.; Majenz, C.; Gross, D. Information-theoretic implications of quantum causal structures. *Nat. Commun.* **2015**, *6*, 5766. [CrossRef]
62. Wolfe, E.; Schmid, D.; Sainz, A.B.; Kunjwal, R.; Spekkens, R.W. Quantifying Bell: The resource theory of nonclassicality of common-cause boxes. *Quantum* **2020**, *4*, 280. [CrossRef]
63. Tavakoli, A.; Pozas-Kerstjens, A.; Luo, M.; Renou, M.O. Bell nonlocality in networks. *Rep. Prog. Phys.* **2022**, *85*, 056001. [CrossRef] [PubMed]
64. Henson, J.; Lal, R.; Pusey, M.F. Theory-independent limits on correlations from generalized Bayesian networks. *New J. Phys.* **2014**, *16*, 113043. [CrossRef]
65. Wood, C.J.; Spekkens, R.W. The lesson of causal discovery algorithms for quantum correlations: Causal explanations of Bell-inequality violations require fine-tuning. *New J. Phys.* **2015**, *17*, 033002. [CrossRef]

66. Wolfe, E.; Spekkens, R.W.; Fritz, T. The Inflation Technique for causal inference with latent variables. *J. Caus. Inf.* **2019**, *7*, 20170020. [CrossRef]
67. Navascués, M.; Wolfe, E. The Inflation Technique completely solves the causal compatibility problem. *J. Causal Infer.* **2020**, *8*, 70–91. [CrossRef]
68. Boghiu, E.C.; Wolfe, E.; Pozas-Kerstjens, A. Inflation: A Python library for classical and quantum causal compatibility. *Quantum* **2023**, *7*, 996. [CrossRef]
69. Evans, R.J. Graphical methods for inequality constraints in marginalized DAGs. In Proceedings of the IEEE International Workshop on Machine Learning for Signal Processing (MLSP), Santander, Spain, 23–26 September 2012; pp. 1–6.
70. Fraser, T.C. A combinatorial solution to causal compatibility. *J. Causal Inference* **2020**, *8*, 22. [CrossRef]
71. Finkelstein, N.; Zjawin, B.; Wolfe, E.; Shpitser, I.; Spekkens, R.W. Entropic inequality constraints from e-separation relations in directed acyclic graphs with hidden variables. In Proceedings of the Thirty-Seventh Conference on Uncertainty in Artificial Intelligence, Online, 27–29 July 2021; pp. 1045–1055.
72. Evans, R.J. Latent-free equivalent mDAGs. *Algebr. Stat.* **2023**, *14*, 3–16. [CrossRef]
73. Khanna, S.; Ansanelli, M.M.; Pusey, M.F.; Wolfe, E. Classifying causal structures: Ascertaining when classical correlations are constrained by inequalities. *Phys. Rev. Res.* **2024**, *6*, 023038. [CrossRef]
74. Rodari, G.; Poderini, D.; Polino, E.; Suprano, A.; Sciarrino, F.; Chaves, R. Characterizing hybrid causal structures with the exclusivity graph approach. *arXiv* **2023**, arXiv:2401.00063.
75. Treves, A.; Panzeri, S. The upward bias in measures of information derived from limited data samples. *Neural Comput.* **1995**, *7*, 399–407. [CrossRef]
76. Paninski, L. Estimation of entropy and mutual information. *Neural Comput.* **2003**, *17*, 1191–1253. [CrossRef]
77. Belghazi, M.I.; Baratin, A.; Rajeshwar, S.; Ozair, S.; Bengio, Y.; Courville, A.; Hjelm, R.D. Mutual Information Neural Estimation. In Proceedings of the Thirty-Fifth International Conference on Machine Learning, Stockholm, Sweden, 10–15 July 2018; pp. 531–540.
78. Poole, B.; Ozair, S.; van den Oord, A.; Alemi, A.A.; Tucker, G. On Variational Bounds of Mutual Information. In Proceedings of the Thirty-Sixth International Conference on Machine Learning, Long Beach, CA, USA, 10–15 June 2019; pp. 5171–5180.

entropy

MDPI

Article

Partial Information Decomposition: Redundancy as Information Bottleneck

Artemy Kolchinsky [1,2]

[1] ICREA-Complex Systems Lab, Universitat Pompeu Fabra, 08003 Barcelona, Spain; artemyk@gmail.com
[2] Universal Biology Institute, The University of Tokyo, Tokyo 113-0033, Japan

Abstract: The partial information decomposition (PID) aims to quantify the amount of redundant information that a set of sources provides about a target. Here, we show that this goal can be formulated as a type of information bottleneck (IB) problem, termed the "redundancy bottleneck" (RB). The RB formalizes a tradeoff between prediction and compression: it extracts information from the sources that best predict the target, without revealing which source provided the information. It can be understood as a generalization of "Blackwell redundancy", which we previously proposed as a principled measure of PID redundancy. The "RB curve" quantifies the prediction–compression tradeoff at multiple scales. This curve can also be quantified for individual sources, allowing subsets of redundant sources to be identified without combinatorial optimization. We provide an efficient iterative algorithm for computing the RB curve.

Keywords: partial information decomposition; information bottleneck; rate distortion; redundancy

Citation: Kolchinsky, A. Partial Information Decomposition: Redundancy as Information Bottleneck. *Entropy* **2024**, *26*, 546. https://doi.org/10.3390/e26070546

Academic Editor: Daniel Chicharro

Received: 13 May 2024
Revised: 20 June 2024
Accepted: 21 June 2024
Published: 26 June 2024

1. Introduction

Many research fields that study complex systems are faced with multivariate probabilistic models and high-dimensional datasets. Prototypical examples include brain imaging data in neuroscience, gene expression data in biology, and neural networks in machine learning. In response, various information-theoretic frameworks have been developed in order to study multivariate systems in a universal manner. Here, we focus on two such frameworks, *partial information decomposition* and the *information bottleneck.*

The *partial information decomposition* (PID) considers how information about a target random variable Y is distributed among a set of source random variables $X_1, \dots, X_n$ [1–4]. For example, in neuroscience, the sources $X_1, \dots, X_n$ might represent the activity of n different brain regions and Y might represent a stimulus, and one may wish to understand how information about the stimulus is encoded in different brain regions. A central idea of the PID is that the information provided by the sources can exhibit *redundancy*, when the same information about Y is present in each source, and *synergy*, when information about Y is found only in the collective outcome of all sources. Moreover, it has been shown that standard information-theoretic quantities, such as entropy and mutual information, are not sufficient to quantify redundancy and synergy [1,5]. However, finding the right measures of redundancy and synergy has proven difficult. In recent work [4], we showed that such measures can be naturally defined by formalizing the analogy between set theory and information theory that lies at the heart of the PID [5]. We then proposed a measure of redundant information (*Blackwell redundancy*) that is motivated by algebraic, axiomatic, and operational considerations. We argued that Blackwell redundancy overcomes many limitations of previous proposals [4].

The *information bottleneck* (IB) [6,7] is a method for extracting compressed information from one random variable X that optimally predicts another target random variable Y. For instance, in the neuroscience example with stimulus Y and brain activity X, the IB method could be used to quantify how well the stimulus can be predicted using only one bit of information about brain activity. The overall tradeoff between the prediction of Y and compression of X is captured by the so-called *IB curve*. The IB method has been employed in various domains, including neuroscience [8], biology [9], and cognitive science [10]. In recent times, it has become particularly popular in machine learning applications [7,11–14].

In this paper, we demonstrate a formal connection between PID and IB. We focus in particular on the relationship between the IB and PID redundancy, leaving the connection to other PID measures (such as synergy) for future work. To begin, we show that Blackwell redundancy can be formulated as an information-theoretic constrained optimization problem. This optimization problem extracts information from the sources that best predict the target, under the constraint that the solution does not reveal which source provided the information. We then define a generalized measure of Blackwell redundancy by relaxing the constraint. Specifically, we ask how much predictive information can be extracted from the sources without revealing more than a certain number of bits about the identity of the source. Our generalization leads to an IB-type tradeoff between the prediction of the target (generalized redundancy) and compression (leakage of information about the identity of the source). We refer to the resulting optimization problem as the *redundancy bottleneck* (RB) and to the manifold of optimal solutions at different points on the prediction/compression tradeoff as the *RB curve*. We also show that the RB prediction and compression terms can be decomposed into contributions from individual sources, giving rise to an individual RB curve for each source.

Besides the intrinsic theoretical interest of unifying PID and the IB, our approach brings about several practical advantages. In particular, the RB curve offers a fine-grained analysis on PID redundancy, showing how redundant information emerges at various scales and across different sources. This fine-grained analysis can be used to uncover sets of redundant sources without performing intractable combinatorial optimization. Our approach also has numerical advantages. The original formulation of Blackwell redundancy was based on a difficult optimization problem that becomes infeasible for larger systems. By reformulating Blackwell redundancy as an IB-type problem, we are able to solve it efficiently using an iterative algorithm, even for larger systems (code available at https://github.com/artemyk/pid-as-ib, accessed on 12 May 2024). Finally, the RB has some attractive formal properties. For instance, unlike the original Blackwell redundancy, the RB curve is continuous in the underlying probability distributions.

This paper is organized as follows. In the next section, we provide the background on the IB, PID, and Blackwell redundancy. In Section 3, we introduce the RB, illustrate it with several examples, and discuss its formal properties. In Section 4, we introduce an iterative algorithm to solve the RB optimization problem. We discuss the implications and possible future directions in Section 5. All proofs are found in the Appendix A.

2. Background

We begin by providing relevant background on the information bottleneck, partial information decomposition, and Blackwell redundancy.

2.1. *Information Bottleneck (IB)*

The information bottleneck (IB) method provides a way to extract information that is present in one random variable X that is relevant for predicting another target random variable Y [6,15,16]. To do so, the IB posits a "bottleneck variable" Q that obeys the Markov condition $Q - X - Y$. This Markov condition guarantees that Q does not contain any information about Y that is not found in X. The quality of any particular choice of bottleneck variable Q is quantified via two mutual information terms: $I(X;Q)$, which decreases when Q provides a more compressed representation of X, and $I(Y;Q)$, which increases when Q allows a better prediction of Y. The IB method selects Q to maximize prediction given a constraint on compression [15–17]:

$$I_{\mathrm{IB}}(R) = \max_{Q:Q-X-Y} I(Y;Q) \quad \text{where} \quad I(X;Q) \leq R. \tag{1}$$

The values of $I_{\text{IB}}(R)$ for different R specify the *IB curve*, which encodes the overall tradeoff between prediction and compression.

In practice, the IB curve is usually explored by considering the Lagrangian relaxation of the constrained optimization problem (1):

$$F_{\text{IB}}(\beta) := \max_{Q} I(Y;Q) - \frac{1}{\beta} I(X;Q) \tag{2}$$

Here, $\beta \geq 0$ is a parameter that controls the tradeoff between compression cost (favored for $\beta \to 0$) and prediction benefit (favored for $\beta \to \infty$). The advantage of the Lagrangian formulation is that it avoids the non-linear constraint in Equation (1). If the IB curve is strictly concave, then the two Equations (1) and (2) are equivalent, meaning that there is a one-to-one map between the solutions of both problems [18]. When the IB curve is not strictly concave, a modified objective such as the "squared Lagrangian" or "exponential Lagrangian" should be used instead; see Refs. [18–20] for more details.

Since the original proposal, many reformulations, generalizations, and variants of the IB have been developed [7]. Notable examples include the "conditional entropy bottleneck" (CEB) [13,21], the "multi-view IB" [22], the "distributed IB" [23], as well as a large family of objectives called the "multivariate IB" [24]. All of these approaches consider some tradeoff between two information-theoretic terms: one that quantifies the prediction of target information that should be maximized and one that quantifies the compression of unwanted information that should be minimized. We refer to an optimization that involves a tradeoff between information-theoretic prediction and compression terms as an *IB-type problem*.

2.2. Partial Information Decomposition

The PID considers how information about a target random variable Y is distributed across a set of source random variables $X_1, \ldots, X_n$. One of the main goals of the PID is to quantify redundancy, the amount of shared information that is found in each of the individual sources. The notion of redundancy in PID was inspired by an analogy between sets and information that has re-appeared in various forms throughout the history of information theory [25–31]. Specifically, if the amount of information provided by each source is conceptualized as the size of a set, then the redundancy is conceptualized as the size of the intersection of those sets [1,4,5]. Until recently, however, this analogy was treated mostly as an informal source of intuition, rather than a formal methodology.

In a recent paper [4], we demonstrated that the terms of PID can be defined by formalizing this analogy to set theory. Recall that, in set theory, the intersection of sets $A_1, \ldots, A_n$ is defined as the largest set B that is contained in each set A_s for $s \in \{1 \ldots n\}$. Thus, the size of the intersection of finite sets $A_1, \ldots, A_n$ is

$$\left| \bigcap_{s=1}^{n} A_s \right| = \max_{B} |B| \quad \text{where} \quad B \subseteq A_s \quad \forall s \in \{1 \ldots n\}.$$

We showed that PID redundancy can be defined in a similar way: the redundancy between sources $X_1, \ldots, X_n$ is the maximum mutual information in any random variable Q that is less informative about the target Y than each individual source [4]:

$$I_{\cap}^{\sqsubseteq} := \max_{Q} I(Q;Y) \quad \text{where} \quad Q \sqsubseteq X_s \quad \forall s \in \{1 \ldots n\}. \tag{3}$$

The notation $Q \sqsubseteq X_s$ indicates that Q is "less informative" about the target than X_s, given some pre-specified ordering relation $\sqsubseteq$. The choice of the ordering relation completely determines the resulting redundancy measure $I_{\cap}^{\sqsubseteq}$. We discuss possible choices in the following subsection.

We used a similar approach to define "union information", which in turn leads to a principled measure of synergy [4]. Note that union information and redundancy are related algebraically but not numerically; in particular, unlike in set theory, the principle of inclusion–exclusion does not always hold.

As mentioned above, here, we focus entirely on redundancy and leave the exploration of connections between IB and union information/synergy for future work.

2.3. Blackwell Redundancy

Our definition of PID redundancy (3) depends on the definition of the "less informative" relation $\sqsubseteq$. Although there are many relations that can be considered [25,32–35], arguably the most natural choice is the *Blackwell order*.

The Blackwell order is a preorder relation over "channels", that is conditional distributions with full support. A channel $\kappa_{B|Y}$ is said to be less informative than $\kappa_{C|Y}$ in the sense of the Blackwell order if there exists some other channel $\kappa_{B|C}$ such that

$$\kappa_{B|Y} = \kappa_{B|C} \circ \kappa_{C|Y}. \tag{4}$$

Throughout, we use the notation $\circ$ to indicate the composition of channels, as defined via matrix multiplication. For instance, $\kappa_{B|Y} = \kappa_{B|C} \circ \kappa_{C|Y}$ is equivalent to the statement $\kappa_{B|Y}(b|y) = \sum_c \kappa_{B|C}(b|c)\kappa_{C|Y}(c|y)$ for all b and y. Equation (4) implies that $\kappa_{B|Y}$ is less informative than $\kappa_{C|Y}$ if $\kappa_{B|Y}$ can be produced by downstream stochastic processing of the output of channel $\kappa_{C|Y}$. We use the notation

$$\kappa_{B|Y} \preceq \kappa_{C|Y}, \tag{5}$$

to indicate that $\kappa_{B|Y}$ is less Blackwell-informative than $\kappa_{C|Y}$. The Blackwell order can also be defined over random variables rather than channels. Given a target random variable Y with full support, random variable B is said to be less Blackwell-informative than random variable C, written as

$$B \preceq_Y C, \tag{6}$$

when their corresponding conditional distributions obey the Blackwell relation, $p_{B|Y} \preceq p_{C|Y}$ [36]. It is not hard to verify that any random variable B that is independent of Y is lowest under the Blackwell order, obeying $B \preceq_Y C$ for all C.

The Blackwell order plays a fundamental role in statistics, and it has an important operational characterization in decision theory [36–38]. Specifically, $p_{B|Y} \preceq p_{C|Y}$ if and only if access to channel $p_{C|Y}$ is better for every decision problem than access to channel $p_{B|Y}$. See Refs. [4,39] for details of this operational characterization and Refs. [4,36,39–42] for more discussion of the relation between the Blackwell order and the PID.

Combining the Blackwell order (6) with Equation (3) gives rise to *Blackwell redundancy* [4]. Blackwell redundancy, indicated here as $I_\cap$, is the maximal mutual information in any random variable that is less Blackwell-informative than each of the sources:

$$I_\cap := \max_Q I(Q;Y) \quad \text{where} \quad Q \preceq_Y X_s \ \forall s. \tag{7}$$

The optimization is always well defined because the feasible set is not empty, given that any random variable Q that is independent of Y satisfies the constraints. (Note also that, for continuous-valued or countably infinite sources, max may need to be replaced by a sup; see also Appendix A.)

$I_\cap$ has many attractive features as a measure of PID redundancy, and it overcomes several problems with previous approaches [4]. For instance, it can be defined for any number of sources, it uniquely satisfies a natural set of PID axioms, and it has fundamental statistical and operational interpretations. Statistically, it is the maximum information transmitted across any channel that can be produced by downstream processing of any one of the sources. Operationally, it is the maximum information that any random variable can have about Y without being able to perform better on any decision problem than any one of the sources.

As we showed [4], the optimization problem (7) can be formulated as the maximization of a convex function subject to a set of linear constraints. For a finite-dimensional system, the feasible set is a finite-dimensional polytope, and the maximum will lie on one of its extreme points; therefore, the optimization can be solved exactly by enumerating the vertices of the feasible set and choosing the best one [4]. However, this approach is limited to small systems, because the number of vertices of the feasible set can grow exponentially.

Finally, it may be argued that Blackwell redundancy is actually a measure of redundancy in the channels $p_{X_1|Y}, \dots, p_{X_n|Y}$, rather than in the random variables $X_1, \dots, X_n$. This is because the joint distribution over $(Y, X_1, \dots, X_n)$ is never explicitly invoked in the definition of $I_\cap$; in fact, any joint distribution is permitted as long as it is compatible with the correct marginals. (The same property holds for several other redundancy measures ([4], Table 1), and Ref. [39] even suggested this property as a requirement for any valid measure of PID redundancy.) In some cases, the joint distribution may not even exist, for instance when different sources represent mutually exclusive conditions. To use a neuroscience example, imagine that $p_{X_1|Y}$ and $p_{X_2|Y}$ represent the activity of some brain region X in response to stimulus Y, measured either in younger ($p_{X_1|Y}$) or older ($p_{X_2|Y}$) subjects. Even though there is no joint distribution over (Y, X_1, X_2) in this case, redundancy is still meaningful as the information about the stimulus that can be extracted from the brain activity of either age group. In the rest of this paper, we generally work within the channel-based interpretation of Blackwell redundancy.

3. Redundancy Bottleneck

In this section, we introduce the redundancy bottleneck (RB) and illustrate it with examples. Generally, we assume that we are provided with the marginal distribution p_Y of the target random variable Y, as well as n source channels $p_{X_1|Y}, \dots, p_{X_n|Y}$. Without loss of generality, we assume that p_Y has full support. We use calligraphic letters (like $\mathcal{Y}$ and $\mathcal{X}_s$) to indicate the set of outcomes of random variables (like Y and X_s). For simplicity, we use notation appropriate for discrete-valued variables, such as in Equation (4), though most of our results also apply to continuous-valued variables.

3.1. Reformulation of Blackwell Redundancy

We first reformulate Blackwell redundancy (7) in terms of a different optimization problem. Our reformulation will make use of the random variable Y, along with two additional random variables, S and Z. The outcomes of S are the indexes of the different sources, $\mathcal{S} = \{1, \dots, n\}$. The set of outcomes of Z is the union of the outcomes of the individual sources, $\mathcal{Z} = \bigcup_{s=1}^{n} \mathcal{X}_s$. For example, if there are two sources with outcomes $\mathcal{X}_1 = \{0,1\}$ and $\mathcal{X}_2 = \{0,1,2\}$, then $\mathcal{S} = \{1,2\}$ and $\mathcal{Z} = \{0,1\} \cup \{0,1,2\} = \{0,1,2\}$. The joint probability distribution over (Y, S, Z) is defined as

$$p_{YSZ}(y,s,z) = \begin{cases} p_Y(y)\nu_S(s)p_{X_s|Y}(z|y) & \text{if } z \in \mathcal{X}_s \\ 0 & \text{otherwise} \end{cases} \tag{8}$$

In other words, y is drawn from the marginal p_Y, the source s is then drawn independently from the distribution ν_S, and finally z is drawn from the channel $p_{X_s|Y}(z|y)$ corresponding to source s. In this way, the channels corresponding to the n sources ($p_{X_1|Y}, \dots, p_{X_n|Y}$) are combined into a single conditional distribution $p_{Z|SY}$.

We treat the distribution ν_S as an arbitrary fixed parameter, and except where otherwise noted, we make no assumptions about this distribution except that it has full support. As we will see, different choices of ν_S cause the different sources to be weighed differently in the computation of the RB. We return to the question of how to determine this distribution below.

Note that, under the distribution defined in Equation (8), Y and S are independent, so

$$I(Y;S) = 0. \tag{9}$$

Actually, many of our results can be generalized to the case where there are correlations between S and Y. We leave exploration of this generalization for future work.

In addition to Y, Z, and S, we introduce another random variable Q. This random variable obeys the Markov condition $Q-(Z,S)-Y$, which ensures that Q does not contain any information about Y that is not contained in the joint outcome of Z and S. The full joint distribution over (Y,S,Z,Q) is

$$p_{YSZQ}(y,s,z,q) = p_{YSZ}(y,s,z)p_{Q|SZ}(q|s,z). \tag{10}$$

We sometimes refer to Q as the "bottleneck" random variable.

The set of joint outcomes of (S,Z) with non-zero probability is the disjoint union of the outcomes of the individual sources. For instance, in the example above with $\mathcal{X}_1 = \{0,1\}$ and $\mathcal{X}_2 = \{0,1,2\}$, the set of joint outcomes of (S,Z) with non-zero probability is $\{(1,0),(1,1),(2,0),(2,1),(2,2)\}$. Because Q depends jointly on S and Z, our results do not depend on the precise labeling of the source outcomes, e.g., they are the same if $\mathcal{X}_2 = \{0,1,2\}$ is relabeled as $\mathcal{X}_2 = \{2,3,4\}$.

Our first result shows that Blackwell redundancy can be equivalently expressed as a constrained optimization problem. Here, the optimization is over bottleneck random variables Q, i.e., over conditional distributions $p_{Q|SZ}$ in Equation (10).

Theorem 1. *Blackwell redundancy (7) can be expressed as*

$$I_\cap = \max_{Q:Q-(Z,S)-Y} I(Q;Y|S) \quad \textit{where} \quad I(Q;S|Y) = 0. \tag{11}$$

Importantly, Theorem 1 does not depend on the choice of the distribution ν_S, as long as it has full support.

In Theorem 1, the Blackwell order constraint in Equation (7) has been replaced by an information-theoretic constraint $I(Q;S|Y) = 0$, which states that Q does not provide any information about the identity of source S, additional to that already provided by the target Y. The objective $I(Q;Y)$ has been replaced by the conditional mutual information $I(Q;Y|S)$. Actually, the objective can be equivalently written in either form, since $I(Q;Y|S) = I(Q;Y)$ given our assumptions (see the proof of Theorem 1 in the Appendix A). However, the conditional mutual information form will be useful for further generalization and decomposition, as discussed in the next sections.

3.2. Redundancy Bottleneck

To relate Blackwell redundancy to the IB, we relax the constraint in Theorem 1 by allowing the leakage of R bits of conditional information about the source S. This defines the *redundancy bottleneck* (RB) at compression rate R:

$$I_{\mathrm{RB}}(R) := \max_{Q:Q-(Z,S)-Y} I(Q;Y|S) \quad \text{where} \quad I(Q;S|Y) \le R. \tag{12}$$

We note that, for $R > 0$, the value of $I_{\mathrm{RB}}(R)$ does depend on the choice of the source distribution ν_S.

Equation (12) is an IB-type problem that involves a tradeoff between prediction $I(Q;Y|S)$ and compression $I(Q;S|Y)$. The prediction term $I(Q;Y|S)$ quantifies the generalized Blackwell redundancy encoded in the bottleneck variable Q. The compression term $I(Q;S|Y)$ quantifies the amount of conditional information that the bottleneck variable leaks about the identity of the source. The set of optimal values of $(I(Q;S|Y), I(Q;Y|S))$ defines the *redundancy bottleneck curve* (RB curve) that encodes the overall tradeoff between prediction and compression.

We prove a few useful facts about the RB, starting from monotonicity and concavity.

Theorem 2. *$I_{\mathrm{RB}}(R)$ is non-decreasing and concave as a function of R.*

Since $I_{\text{RB}}(R)$ is non-decreasing in R, the lowest RB value is achieved in the $R = 0$ regime, when it equals the Blackwell redundancy (Theorem 1):

$$I_{\text{RB}}(R) \geq I_{\text{RB}}(0) = I_{\cap}. \tag{13}$$

The largest value is achieved as $R \to \infty$, when the compression constraint vanishes. It can be shown that $I(Q;Y|S) \leq I(Z;Y|S) = I(Y;Z,S)$ using the Markov condition $Q-(Z,S)-Y$ and the data-processing inequality (see the next subsection). This upper bound is achieved by the bottleneck variable $Q = Z$. Combining implies

$$I_{\text{RB}}(R) \leq I(Z;Y|S) = \sum_{s} \nu_S(s) I(X_s;Y), \tag{14}$$

where we used the form of the distribution p_{YSZ} in Equation (8) to arrive at the last expression. The range of necessary compression rates can be restricted as $0 \leq R \leq I(Z;S|Y)$.

Next, we show that, for finite-dimensional sources, it suffices to consider finite-dimensional Q. Thus, for finite-dimensional sources, the RB problem (12) involves the maximization of a continuous objective over a compact domain, so the maximum is always achieved by some Q. (Conversely, in the more general case of infinite-dimensional sources, it may be necessary to replace max with sup in Equation (12); see Appendix A.)

Theorem 3. *For the optimization problem (12), it suffices to consider Q of cardinality* $|\mathcal{Q}| \leq \sum_s |\mathcal{X}_s| + 1$.

Interestingly, the cardinality bound for the RB is the same as for the IB if we take $X = (Z,S)$ in Equation (1) [16,20]. It is larger than the cardinality required for Blackwell redundancy (7), where $|\mathcal{Q}| \leq (\sum_s |\mathcal{X}_s|) - n + 1$ suffices [4].

The Lagrangian relaxation of the constrained RB problem (12) is given by

$$F_{\text{RB}}(\beta) = \max_{Q:Q-(Z,S)-Y} I(Q;Y|S) - \frac{1}{\beta} I(Q;S|Y). \tag{15}$$

The parameter β controls the tradeoff between prediction and compression. The $\beta \to 0$ limit corresponds to the $R = 0$ regime, in which case, Blackwell redundancy is recovered, while the $\beta \to \infty$ limit corresponds to the $R = \infty$ regime, when the compression constraint is removed. The RB Lagrangian (15) is often simpler to optimize than the constrained optimization (12). Moreover, when the RB curve $I_{\text{RB}}(R)$ is strictly concave, there is a one-to-one relationship between the solutions to the two optimization problems (12) and (15). However, when the RB curve is not strictly concave, there is no one-to-one relationship and the usual Lagrangian formulation is insufficient. This can be addressed by optimizing a modified objective that combines prediction and compression in a nonlinear fashion, such as the "exponential Lagrangian" [19]:

$$F_{\text{RB}}^{\text{exp}}(\beta) = \max_{Q:Q-(Z,S)-Y} I(Q;Y|S) - \frac{1}{\beta} e^{I(Q;S|Y)}. \tag{16}$$

(See an analogous analysis for IB in Refs. [18,19].)

3.3. Contributions from Different Sources

Both the RB prediction and compression terms can be decomposed into contributions from different sources, leading to an individual RB curve for each source. As we show in the examples below, this decomposition can be used to identify groups of redundant sources without having to perform intractable combinatorial optimization.

Let Q be an optimal bottleneck variable at rate R, so that $I_{\mathrm{RB}}(R) = I(Q;Y|S)$ and $I(Q;S|Y) \le R$. Then, the RB prediction term can be expressed as the weighted average of the prediction contributions from individual sources:

$$I_{\mathrm{RB}}(R) = I(Q;Y|S) = \sum_s \nu_S(s) I(Q;Y|S=s). \tag{17}$$

Here, we introduce the specific conditional mutual information:

$$I(Q;Y|S=s) := D(p_{Q|Y,S=s} \| p_{Q|S=s}), \tag{18}$$

where $D(\cdot\|\cdot)$ is the Kullback–Leibler (KL) divergence. To build intuitions about this decomposition, we may use the Markov condition $Q - (Z,S) - Y$ to express the conditional distributions in Equation (18) as compositions of channels:

$$p_{Q|Y,S=s} = p_{Q|Z,S=s} \circ p_{Z|Y,S=s}$$
$$p_{Q|S=s} = p_{Q|Z,S=s} \circ p_{Z|S=s}$$

Using the data-processing inequality for the KL divergence and Equation (8), we can then write

$$I(Q;Y|S=s) \le D(p_{Z|Y,S=s} \| p_{Z|S=s}) = D(p_{X_s|Y} \| p_{X_s}).$$

The last term is simply the mutual information $I(Y;X_s)$ between the target and source s. Thus, the prediction contribution from source s is bounded between 0 and the mutual information provided by that source:

$$0 \le I(Q;Y|S=s) \le I(Y;X_s). \tag{19}$$

The difference between the mutual information and the actual prediction contribution:

$$I(Y;X_s) - I(Q;Y|S=s) \ge 0,$$

quantifies the unique information in source s. The upper bound in Equation (19) is achieved in the $R \to \infty$ limit by $Q = Z$, leading to Equation (14). Conversely, for $R = 0$, $p_{Q|Y,S=s} = p_{Q|Y}$ (from $I(Q;S|Y) = 0$) and $p_{Q|S=s} = p_Q$ (from Equation (9)), so

$$I(Q;Y|S=s) = I(Q;Y) = I_{\mathrm{RB}}(0) = I_\cap.$$

Thus, when $R = 0$, the prediction contribution from each source is the same, and it is equal to the Blackwell redundancy.

The RB compression cost can also be decomposed into contributions from individual sources:

$$I(Q;S|Y) = \sum_s \nu_S(s) I(Q;S=s|Y). \tag{20}$$

Here, we introduce the specific conditional mutual information:

$$I(Q;S=s|Y) := D(p_{Q|Y,S=s} \| p_{Q|Y}). \tag{21}$$

The source compression terms can be related to so-called *deficiency*, a quantitative generalization of the Blackwell order. Although various versions of deficiency can be defined [43–45], here we consider the "weighted deficiency" induced by the KL divergence. For any two channels $p_{B|Y}$ and $p_{C|Y}$, it is defined as

$$\delta_D(p_{C|Y}, p_{B|Y}) := \min_{\kappa_{B|C}} D(\kappa_{B|C} \circ p_{C|Y} \| p_{B|Y}). \tag{22}$$

This measure quantifies the degree to which two channels violate the Blackwell order, vanishing when $\kappa_{B|Y} \preceq \kappa_{C|Y}$. To relate the source compression terms (20) to deficiency, observe that $p_{Q|Y,S=s} = p_{Q|Z,S=s} \circ p_{Z|Y,S=s}$ and that $p_{Z|Y,S=s} = p_{X_s|Y}$. Given Equation (21), we then have

$$I(Q; S = s|Y) \geq \delta_D(p_{X_s|Y}, p_{Q|Y}). \tag{23}$$

Thus, each source compression term is lower bounded by the deficiency between the source channel $p_{X_s|Y}$ and the bottleneck channel $p_{Q|Y}$. Furthermore, the compression constraint in the RB optimization problem (12) sets an upper bound on the deficiency of $p_{Q|Y}$ averaged across all sources.

Interestingly, several recent papers have studied the relationship between deficiency and PID redundancy in the restricted case of two sources [38,41,45–47]. To our knowledge, we provide the first link between deficiency and redundancy for the general case of multiple sources. Note also that previous work considered a slightly different definition of deficiency where the arguments of the KL divergence are reversed. Our definition of deficiency is arguably more natural, since it is more natural to minimize the KL divergence over a convex set with respect to the first argument [48].

Finally, observe that, in both decompositions (17) and (20), the source contributions are weighted by the distribution $\nu_S(s)$. Thus, the distribution ν_S determines how different sources play into the tradeoff between prediction and compression. In many cases, ν_S can be chosen as the uniform distribution. However, other choices of ν_S may be more natural in other situations. For example, in a neuroscience context where different sources correspond to different brain regions, $\nu_S(s)$ could represent the proportion of metabolic cost or neural volume assigned to region s. Alternatively, when different sources represent mutually exclusive conditions, as in the age group example mentioned at the end of Section 2, $\nu_S(s)$ might represent the frequency of condition s found in the data. Finally, it may be possible to set ν_S in an "adversarial" manner so as to maximize the resulting value of $I_{RB}(R)$ in Equation (12). We leave the exploration of this adversarial approach for future work.

3.4. Examples

We illustrate our approach using a few examples. For simplicity, in all examples, we use a uniform distribution over the sources, $\nu_S(s) = 1/n$. The numerical results are calculated using the iterative algorithm described in the next section.

Example 1. *We begin by considering a very simple system, called the "UNIQUE gate" in the PID literature. Here, the target Y is binary and uniformly-distributed, $p_Y(y) = 1/2$ for $y \in \{0,1\}$. There are two binary-valued sources, X_1 and X_2, where the first source is a copy of the target, $p_{X_1|Y}(x_1|y) = \delta_{x_1,y}$, while the second source is an independent and uniformly-distributed bit, $p_{X_2|Y}(x_1|y) = 1/2$. Thus, source X_1 provides 1 bit of information about the target, while X_2 provides none. The Blackwell redundancy is $I_\cap = 0$ [4], because it is impossible to extract any information from the sources without revealing that this information came from X_1.*

We performed RB analysis by optimizing the RB Lagrangian $F_{RB}(\beta)$ (15) at different β. Figure 1a,b show the prediction $I(Q;Y|S)$ and compression $I(Q;S|Y)$ values for the optimal bottleneck variables Q. At small β, the prediction converges to the Blackwell redundancy, $I(Q;Y|S) = I_\cap = 0$, and there is complete loss of information about source identity, $I(Q;S|Y) = 0$. At larger β, the prediction approaches the maximum $I(Q;Y|S) = 0.5 \times I(X_1;Y) = 0.5$ bit, and compression approaches $I(Q;S|Y) = I(Z;S|Y)$ ≈ 0.311 bit. Figure 1c shows the RB curve, illustrating the overall tradeoff between prediction and compression.

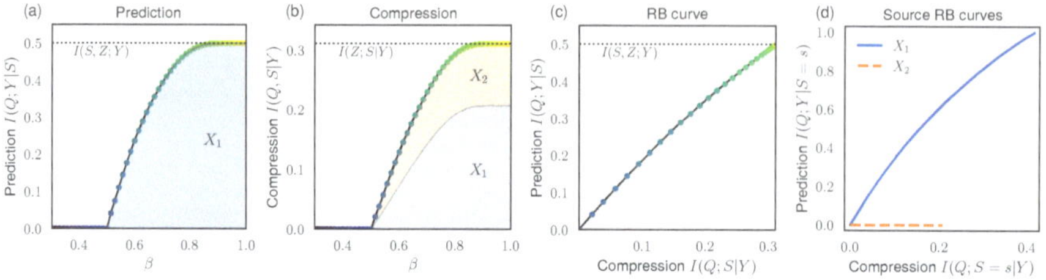

Figure 1. RB analysis for the UNIQUE gate (Example 1). (**a**) Prediction values found by optimizing the RB Lagrangian (15) at different β. Colored regions indicate contributions from different sources, $\nu_S(s)I(Q;Y|S=s)$ from Equation (17). For this system, only source X_1 contributes to the prediction. (**b**) Compression costs found by optimizing the RB Lagrangian at different β. Colored regions indicate contributions from different sources, $\nu_S(s)I(Q;S=s|Y)$ from Equation (20). (**c**) The RB curve shows the tradeoff between optimal compression and the prediction values; the marker colors correspond to the β values as in (**a**,**b**). All bottleneck variables Q must fall within the accessible grey region. (**d**) RB curves for individual sources.

In the shaded regions of Figure 1a,b, we show the additive contributions to the prediction and compression terms from the individual sources, $\nu_S(s)I(Q;Y|S=s)$ from Equation (17) and $\nu_S(s)I(Q;S=s|Y)$ from Equation (20), respectively. We also show the resulting RB curves for individual sources in Figure 1d. As expected, only source X_1 contributes to the prediction at any level of compression.

To summarize, if some information about the identity of the source can be leaked (non-zero compression cost), then improved prediction of the target is possible. At the maximum needed compression cost of 0.311, it is possible to extract 1 bit of predictive information from X_1 and 0 bits from X_2, leading to an average of 0.5 bits of prediction.

Example 2. *We now consider the "AND gate", another well-known system from the PID literature. There are two independent and uniformly distributed binary sources, X_1 and X_2. The target Y is also binary-valued and determined via $Y = X_1$ AND X_2. Then, $p_Y(0) = 3/4$ and $p_Y(1) = 1/4$, and both sources have the same channel:*

$$p_{X_s|Y}(x|y) = \begin{cases} 2/3 & \textit{if } y=0, x=0 \\ 1/3 & \textit{if } y=0, x=1 \\ 0 & \textit{if } y=1, x=0 \\ 1 & \textit{if } y=1, x=1 \end{cases}$$

Because the two source channels are the same, the Blackwell redundancy obeys $I_\cap = I(Y;X_1) = I(Y;X_2) = 0.311$ bits [4]. From Equations (13) and (14), we see that $I_{RB}(R) = I_\cap$ across all compression rates. In this system, all information provided by the sources is redundant, so there is no strict tradeoff between prediction and compression. The RB curve (not shown) consists of a single point, $(I(Q;Y|S), I(Q;S|Y)) = (0.311, 0)$.

Example 3. *We now consider a more sophisticated example with four sources. The target is binary-valued and uniformly distributed, $p_Y(y) = 1/2$ for $y \in \{0,1\}$. There are four binary-valued sources, where the conditional distribution of each source $s \in \{1,2,3,4\}$ is a binary symmetric channel with error probability ϵ_s:*

$$p_{X_s|Y}(x|y) = \begin{cases} 1-\epsilon_s & \textit{if } y = x \\ \epsilon_s & \textit{if } y \neq x \end{cases} \tag{24}$$

We take $\epsilon_1 = \epsilon_2 = 0.1$, $\epsilon_3 = 0.2$, and $\epsilon_4 = 0.5$. Thus, sources X_1 and X_2 provide most information about the target; X_3 provides less information; X_4 is completely independent of the target.

We performed our RB analysis and plot the RB prediction values in Figure 2a and the compression values in Figure 2b, as found by optimizing the RB Lagrangian at different β. At small β, the prediction converges to the Blackwell redundancy, $I(Q;Y|S) = I_\cap = 0$, and there is complete loss of information about source identity, $I(Q;S|Y) = 0$. At large β, the prediction is equal to the maximum $I(Z;Y|S) \approx 0.335$ bit, and compression is equal to $I(Q;S|Y) \approx 0.104$ bit. Figure 2c shows the RB curve.

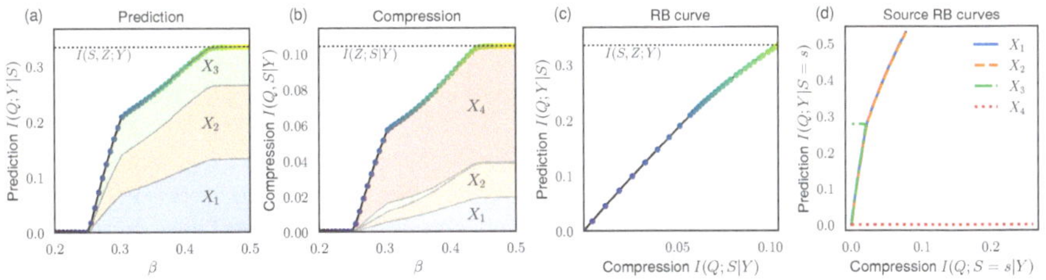

Figure 2. RB analysis for the system with 4 binary symmetric channels (Example 3). (**a**,**b**) Prediction and compression values found by optimizing the RB Lagrangian (15) at different β. Contributions from individual sources are shown as shaded regions. (**c**) The RB curve shows the tradeoff between optimal compression and prediction values; marker colors correspond to the β values as in (**a**,**b**). (**d**) RB curves for individual sources.

In Figure 2a,b, we show the additive contributions to the prediction and compression terms from the individual sources, $\nu_S(s)I(Q;Y|S=s)$ and $\nu_S(s)I(Q;S=s|Y)$, respectively, as shaded regions. We also show the resulting RB curves for individual sources in Figure 2d.

As expected, source X_4 does not contribute to the prediction at any level of compression, in accord with the fact that $I(Q;Y|S=s) \leq I(X_4;Y) = 0$. Sources X_1 and X_2 provide the same amount of prediction and compression at all points, up to the maximum $I(X_1;Y) = I(X_2;Y) \approx 0.531$. Source X_3 provides the same amount of prediction and compression as sources X_1 and X_2, until it hits its maximum prediction $I(X_3;Y) \approx 0.278$. As shown in Figure 2d, at this point, X_3 splits off from sources X_1 and X_2 and its compression contribution decreases to 0; this is compensated by increasing the compression cost of sources X_1 and X_2. The same behavior can also be seen in Figure 2a,b, where we see that the solutions undergo phase transitions as different optimal strategies are uncovered at increasing β. Importantly, by considering the prediction/compression contributions from the the individual sources, we can identify that sources X_1 and X_2 provide the most redundant information.

Let us comment on the somewhat surprising fact that, at larger β, the compression cost of X_3 decreases—even while its prediction contribution remains constant and the prediction contribution from X_1 and X_2 increases. At first glance, this appears counter-intuitive if one assumes that, in order to increase prediction from X_1 and X_2, the bottleneck channel $p_{Q|Y}$ should approach $p_{X_1|Y} = p_{X_2|Y}$, thereby increasing the deficiency $\delta_D(p_{X_3|Y}, p_{Q|Y})$ and the compression cost of X_3 via the bound (23). In fact, this is not the case, because the prediction is quantified via the conditional mutual information $I(Q;Y|S)$, not the mutual information $I(Q;Y)$. Thus, it is possible that the prediction contributions from X_1 and X_2 are large, even when the bottleneck channel $p_{Q|Y}$ does not closely resemble $p_{X_1|Y} = p_{X_2|Y}$.

More generally, this example shows that it is possible for the prediction contribution from a given source to stay the same, or even increase, while its compression cost decreases. In other words, as can be seen from Figure 2d, it is possible for the RB curves of the individual sources to be non-concave and non-monotonic. It is only the overall RB curve, Figure 2c, representing the optimal prediction–compression tradeoff on average, that must be concave and monotonic.

Example 4. *In our final example, the target consists of three binary spins with a uniform distribution, so* $Y = (Y_1, Y_2, Y_3)$ *and* $p_Y(y) = 1/8$ *for all* y*. There are three sources, each of which contains two binary spins. Sources* X_1 *and* X_2 *are both equal to the first two spins of the target* Y, $X_1 = X_2 = (Y_1, Y_2)$*. Source* X_3 *is equal to the first and last spin of the target,* $X_3 = (Y_1, Y_3)$*.*

Each source provides $I(Y; X_s) = 2$ bits of mutual information about the target. The Blackwell redundancy $I_\cap$ is 1 bit, reflecting the fact that there is a single binary spin that is included in all sources (Y_1).

We performed our RB analysis and plot the RB prediction values in Figure 3a and the compression values in Figure 3b, as found by optimizing the RB Lagrangian at different β. At small β, the prediction converges to the Blackwell redundancy, $I(Q; Y|S) = I_\cap = 1$, and $I(Q; S|Y) = 0$. At large β, the prediction is equal to the maximum $I(Z; Y|S) = 2$ bit, and compression is equal to $I(Z; S|Y) \approx 0.459$. Figure 3c shows the RB curve. As in the previous example, the RB curve undergoes phase transitions as different optimal strategies are uncovered at different β.

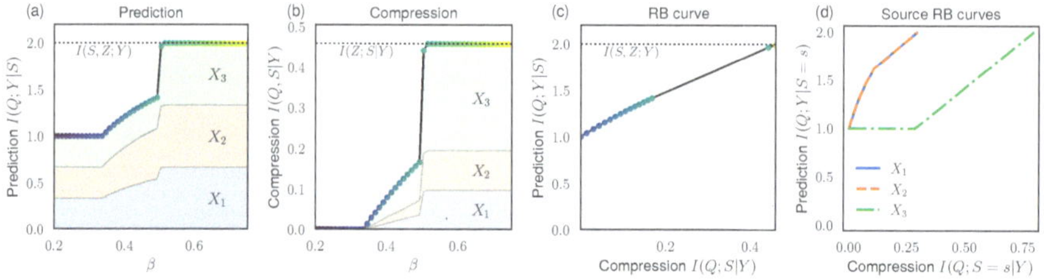

Figure 3. RB analysis for the system with a 3-spin target (Example 4). (**a**,**b**) Prediction and compression values found by optimizing the RB Lagrangian (15) at different β. Contributions from individual sources are shown as shaded regions. (**c**) The RB curve shows the tradeoff between optimal compression and prediction values; marker colors correspond to the β values as in (**a**,**b**). (**d**) RB curves for individual sources.

In Figure 3a,b, we show the additive contributions to the prediction and compression terms from the individual sources, $\nu_S(s) I(Q; Y|S = s)$ and $\nu_S(s) I(Q; S = s|Y)$, as shaded regions. We also show the resulting RB curves for individual sources in Figure 3d.

Observe that sources X_1 and X_2 provide more redundant information at a given level of compression. For instance, as shown in Figure 3d, at source compression $I(Q; S = s|Y) \approx .25$, X_1 and X_2 provide 2 bits of prediction, while X_3 provides only a single bit. This again shows how the RB source decomposition can be used for identifying sources with high levels of redundancy.

3.5. Continuity

It is known that the Blackwell redundancy $I_\cap$ can be discontinuous as a function of the probability distribution of the target and source channels [4]. In Ref. [4], we explain the origin of this discontinuity in geometric terms and provide sufficient conditions for Blackwell redundancy to be continuous. Nonetheless, the discontinuity of $I_\cap$ is sometimes seen as an undesired property.

On the other hand, as we show in this section, the value of RB is continuous in the probability distribution for all $R > 0$.

Theorem 4. *For finite-dimensional systems and* $R > 0$, $I_{RB}(R)$ *is a continuous function of the probability values* $p_{X_s|Y}(x|y)$, $p_Y(y)$, *and* $\nu_S(s)$.

Thus, by relaxing the compression constraint in Theorem 1, we "smooth out" the behavior of Blackwell redundancy and arrive at a continuous measure. We illustrate this using a simple example.

Example 5. *We consider the COPY gate, a standard example in the PID literature. Here, there are two binary-valued sources jointly distributed according to*

$$p_{X_1X_2}(x_1,x_2) = \begin{cases} 1/2-\epsilon/4 & \textit{if } x_1 = x_2 \\ \epsilon/4 & \textit{if } x_1 \neq x_2 \end{cases}$$

The parameter ϵ controls the correlation between the two sources, with perfect correlation at $\epsilon = 0$ and complete independence at $\epsilon = 1$. The target Y is a copy of the joint outcome of the two sources, $Y = (X_1, X_2)$.

It is known that Blackwell redundancy $I_\cap$ is discontinuous for this system, jumping from $I_\cap = 1$ at $\epsilon = 0$ to $I_\cap = 0$ for $\epsilon > 0$ [4]. On the other hand, the RB function $I_{\text{RB}}(R)$ is continuous for $R > 0$. Figure 4 compares the behavior of Blackwell redundancy and RB as a function of ϵ, at $R = 0.01$ bits. In particular, it can be seen that $I_{\text{RB}}(R) = 1$ at $\epsilon = 0$ and then decays continuously as ϵ increases.

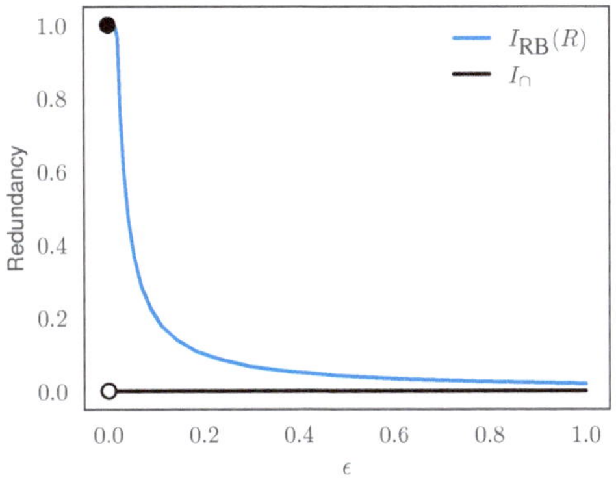

Figure 4. The RB function $I_{\text{RB}}(R)$ is continuous in the underlying probability distribution for $R > 0$, while Blackwell redundancy can be discontinuous. Here illustrated on the COPY gate, $Y = (X_1, X_2)$, as a function of correlation strength ϵ between X_1 and X_2 (perfect correlation at $\epsilon = 0$, independence at $\epsilon = 1$). Blackwell redundancy jumps from $I_\cap = 1$ at $\epsilon = 0$ to $I_\cap = 0$ at $\epsilon > 0$, while $I_{\text{RB}}(R)$ (at $R = 0.01$) decays continuously.

4. Iterative Algorithm

We provide an iterative algorithm to solve the RB optimization problem. This algorithm is conceptually similar to the Blahut–Arimoto algorithm, originally employed for rate distortion problems and later adapted to solve the original IB problem [6]. A Python implementation of our algorithm is available at https://github.com/artemyk/pid-as-ib; there, we also provide updated code to exactly compute Blackwell redundancy (applicable to small systems).

To begin, we consider the RB Lagrangian optimization problem, Equation (15). We rewrite this optimization problem using the KL divergence:

$$F_{\text{RB}}(\beta) = \max_{r_{Q|SZ}} D(r_{Y|QS} \| p_{Y|S}) - \frac{1}{\beta} D(r_{Q|SY} \| r_{Q|Y}). \tag{25}$$

Here, notation like $r_{Q|Y}$, $r_{Y|QS}$, etc., refers to distributions that include Q and therefore depend on the optimization variable $r_{Q|SZ}$, while notation like $p_{Y|S}$ refers to distributions that do not depend on Q and are not varied under the optimization. Every choice of conditional distribution $r_{Q|SZ}$ induces a joint distribution $r_{YSZQ} = p_{YSZ} r_{Q|SZ}$ via Equation (10).

We can rewrite the first KL term in Equation (25) as

$$D(r_{Y|QS}\|p_{Y|S}) = D(r_{Y|QS}\|p_{Y|S}) - \min_{\omega_{YSZQ}} D(r_{Y|QS}\|\omega_{Y|QS})$$
$$= \max_{\omega_{YSZQ}} \mathbb{E}_{p_{YSZ}r_{Q|SZ}}\left[\ln\frac{\omega(y|q,s)}{p(y|s)}\right].$$

where $\mathbb{E}$ indicates the expectation, and we introduced the variational distribution ω_{YSZQ}. The maximum is achieved by $\omega_{YSZQ} = r_{YSZQ}$, which gives $\omega_{Y|QS} = r_{Y|QS}$. We rewrite the second KL term in Equation (25) as

$$D(r_{Q|SY}\|r_{Q|Y}) = D(r_{Q|SY}r_{Z|SYQ}\|r_{Q|Y}r_{Z|SYQ})$$
$$= \min_{\omega_{YSZQ}} D(r_{Q|SY}r_{Z|SYQ}\|\omega_{Q|Y}\omega_{Z|SYQ}).$$

Here, we introduce the variational distribution ω_{YSZQ}, where the minimum is achieved by $\omega_{YSZQ} = r_{YSZQ}$. The term $r_{Q|SY}r_{Z|SYQ}$ can be rewritten as

$$r(q|s,y)r(z|s,y,q) = \frac{r(z,s,y,q)}{p(s,y)} = \frac{r(q|s,z)p(z,s,y)}{p(s,y)} = r(q|s,z)p(z|s,y)$$

where we used the Markov condition $Q - (S,Z) - Y$. In this way, we separate the contribution from the conditional distribution $r_{Q|SZ}$ being optimized.

Combining the above allows us to rewrite Equation (25) as

$$F_{\mathrm{RB}}(\beta) = \max_{r_{Q|ZS},\omega_{YSZQ}} \mathbb{E}_{p_{YSZ}r_{Q|SZ}}\left[\ln\frac{\omega(y|q,s)}{p(y|s)}\right] - \frac{1}{\beta}D(r_{Q|SZ}p_{Z|SY}\|\omega_{Q|Y}\omega_{Z|SYQ}). \tag{26}$$

We now optimize this objective in an iterative and alternating manner with respect to $r_{Q|SZ}$ and ω_{YSZQ}. Formally, let $\mathcal{L}(r_{Q|SZ},\omega_{YSZQ})$ refer to the objective in Equation (26). Then, starting from some initial guess $r^{(0)}_{Q|SZ}$, we generate a sequence of solutions

$$\omega^{(t+1)}_{YSZQ} = \arg\max_{\omega_{YSZQ}} \mathcal{L}(r^{(t)}_{Q|SZ},\omega_{YSZQ}) \tag{27}$$
$$r^{(t+1)}_{Q|SZ} = \arg\max_{r_{Q|SZ}} \mathcal{L}(r_{Q|SZ},\omega^{(t+1)}_{YSZQ}) \tag{28}$$

Each optimization problem can be solved in closed form. As already mentioned, the optimizer in Equation (27) is

$$\omega^{(t+1)}_{YSZQ} = r^{(t)}_{YSZQ} = r^{(t)}_{Q|SZ}p_{SZY}.$$

The optimization (28) can be solved by taking derivatives, giving

$$r^{(t+1)}(q|s,z) \propto e^{\sum_y p(y|s,z)\left[\beta\ln\omega^{(t)}(y|q,s) - \ln\frac{p(z|s,y)}{\omega^{(t)}(q|y)\omega^{(t)}(z|s,y,q)}\right]},$$

where the proportionality constant in $\propto$ is fixed by normalization $\sum_q r^{(t+1)}(q|s,z) = 1$.

Each iteration increases the value of objective $\mathcal{L}$. Since the objective is upper bounded by $I(Z;Y|S)$, the algorithm is guaranteed to converge. However, as in the case of the original IB problem, the objective is not jointly convex in both arguments, so the algorithm may converge to a local maximum or a saddle point, rather than a global maximum. This can be partially alleviated by running the algorithm several times starting from different initial guesses $r^{(0)}_{Q|SZ}$.

When the RB is not strictly concave, it is more appropriate to optimize the exponential RB Lagrangian (16) or another objective that combines the prediction and compression terms in a nonlinear manner [18,19]. The algorithm described above can be used with such objectives after a slight modification. For instance, for the exponential RB Lagrangian, we modify (26) as

$$F_{\mathrm{RB}}^{\exp}(\beta) = \max_{r_{Q|SZ},\omega_{YSZQ}} \mathbb{E}_{p_{YSZ}r_{Q|SZ}}\left[\ln \frac{\omega(y|q,s)}{p(y|s)}\right] - \frac{1}{\beta} e^{D(r_{Q|ZS}p_{Z|SY}\|\omega_{Q|Y}\omega_{Z|SYQ})}. \tag{29}$$

A similar analysis as above leads to the following iterative optimization scheme:

$$\begin{aligned} \omega_{YSZQ}^{(t+1)} &= r_{Q|SZ}^{(t)} p_{SZY} \\ r^{(t+1)}(q|s,z) &\propto e^{\sum_y p(y|s,z)\left[\beta^{(t)} \ln \omega^{(t)}(y|q,s) - \ln \frac{p(z|s,y)}{\omega^{(t)}(q|y)\omega^{(t)}(z|s,y,q)}\right]}, \end{aligned}$$

where $\beta^{(t)} = \beta e^{-I_{r^{(t)}}(Q;S|Y)}$ is an effective inverse temperature. (Observe that, unlike the squared Lagrangian [18], the exponential Lagrangian leads to an effective inverse temperature $\beta^{(t)}$ that is always finite and converges to β as $I_{r^{(t)}}(Q;S|Y) \to 0$.)

When computing an entire RB curve, as in Figure 1a–c, we found good results by annealing, that is by re-using the optimal $r_{Q|SZ}$ found for one β as the initial guess at higher β. For quantifying the value of the RB function $I_{\mathrm{RB}}(R)$ at a fixed R, as in Figure 4, we approximated $I_{\mathrm{RB}}(R)$ via a linear interpolation of the RB prediction and compression values recovered from the RB Lagrangian at varying β.

5. Discussion

In this paper, we propose a generalization of Blackwell redundancy, termed the redundancy bottleneck (RB), formulated as an information-bottleneck-type tradeoff between prediction and compression. We studied some implications of this formulation and proposed an efficient numerical algorithm to solve the RB optimization problem.

We briefly mention some directions for future work.

The first direction concerns our iterative algorithm. The algorithm is only applicable to systems where it is possible to enumerate the outcomes of the joint distribution p_{QYSZ}. This is impractical for discrete-valued variables with very many outcomes, as well as continuous-valued variables as commonly found in statistical and machine learning settings. In future work, it would be useful to develop RB algorithms suitable for such datasets, possibly by exploiting the kinds of variational techniques that have recently gained traction in machine learning applications of IB [11–13].

The second direction would explore connections between the RB and other information-theoretic objectives for representation learning. To our knowledge, the RB problem is novel to the literature. However, it has some similarities to existing objectives, including among others the conditional entropy bottleneck [13], multi-view IB [22], and the privacy funnel and its variants [49]. Showing formal connections between these objectives would be of theoretical and practical interest, and could lead to new interpretations of the concept of PID redundancy.

Another direction would explore the relationship between RB and information-theoretic measures of causality [50,51]. In particular, if the different sources represent some mutually exclusive conditions—such as the age group example provided at the end of Section 2—then redundancy could serve as a measure of causal information flow that is invariant to the conditioning variable.

Finally, one of the central ideas of this paper is to treat the identity of the source as a random variable in its own right, which allows us to consider what information different bottleneck variables reveal about the source. In this way, we convert the search for topological or combinatorial structure in multivariate systems into an interpretable and differential information-theoretic objective. This technique may be useful in other problems that consider how information is distributed among variables in complex systems, including other PID measures such as synergy [4], information-theoretic measures of modularity [52,53], and measures of higher-order dependency [54,55].

Funding: This project has received funding from the European Union's Horizon 2020 research and innovation programme under the Marie Skłodowska-Curie Grant Agreement No. 101068029.

Institutional Review Board Statement: Not applicable.

Informed Consent Statement: Not applicable.

Data Availability Statement: No research data was used in this study.

Acknowledgments: I thank Nihat Ay, Daniel Polani, Fernando Rosas, and especially, André Gomes for useful feedback. I also thank the organizers of the "Decomposing Multivariate Information in Complex Systems" (DeMICS 23) workshop at the Max Planck Institute for the Physics of Complex Systems (Dresden, Germany), which inspired this work.

Conflicts of Interest: The author declares no conflicts of interest.

Appendix A

We provide proofs of the theorems in the main text. Throughout, we use D for the Kullback–Leibler (KL) divergence, H for the Shannon entropy, and I for the mutual information.

Appendix A.1. Proof of Theorem 1

We begin by proving a slightly generalized version of Theorem 1, that is we show the equivalence between the two optimization problems:

$$I_\cap = \sup_Q I(Q;Y) \quad \text{where} \quad Q \preceq_Y X_s \ \forall s \tag{A1}$$

$$I_\cap = \sup_{Q:Q-(Z,S)-Y} I(Q;Y|S) \quad \text{where} \quad I(Q;S|Y) = 0. \tag{A2}$$

The slight generalization comes from replacing max by sup, so that the result also holds for systems with infinite-dimensional sources, where the supremum is not guaranteed to be achieved. For finite-dimensional systems, the supremum is always achieved, and we reduce to the simpler case of Equations (7) and (11).

Proof. Let V_1 indicate the supremum in Equation (A1) and V_2 the supremum in Equation (A2), given some $\nu_S(s)$ with full support. We prove that $V_1 = V_2$.

We will use that, for any distribution that has the form of Equation (10) and obeys $I(Q;S|Y) = 0$, the following holds:

$$\begin{aligned} I(Q;Y|S) &= H(Q|S) - H(Q|S,Y) \\ &= H(Q) - H(Q|Y) = I(Q;Y) \end{aligned} \tag{A3}$$

Here, we used the Markov condition $Q - Y - S$, as well as $I(Q;S) = H(Q) - H(Q|S) = 0$, as follows from Equation (9) and the data-processing inequality.

Let Q be a feasible random variable that comes within $\epsilon \geq 0$ of the objective in (A1), $I(Q;Y) \geq V_1 - \epsilon$. Define the joint distribution:

$$p_{QYSZ}(q,y,s,z) = \kappa_{Q|X_s}(q|z)p_Y(y)\nu_S(s)p_{X_s|Y}(z|y)$$

whenever $z \in \mathcal{X}_s$, otherwise $p_{QYSZ}(q,y,s,z) = 0$. Here, we used the channels $\kappa_{Q|X_s}$ associated with the Blackwell relation $Q \preceq_Y X_s$, so that $p_{Q|Y} = \kappa_{Q|X_s} \circ p_{X_s|Y}$. Under the distribution p_{QYSZ}, the Markov conditions $Q - (S,Z) - Y$ and $Q - Y - S$ hold, the latter since

$$p_{QS|Y}(q,s|y) = p_{Q|Y}(q|y)\nu_S(s). \tag{A4}$$

Therefore, this distribution has the form of Equations (8) and (10) and satisfies the constraints in Equation (A2). Using Equation (A3), we then have

$$V_1 - \epsilon \leq I(Q;Y) = I(Q;Y|S) \leq V_2.$$

Conversely, let p_{YSZQ} be a feasible joint distribution for the optimization of Equation (A2) that comes within $\epsilon \geq 0$ of the supremum, $I(Q;Y|S) \geq V_2 - \epsilon$. Using the form of this joint distribution from Equation (10), we can write

$$\begin{aligned}
p_{Q|Y}(q|y) &\stackrel{(a)}{=} p_{Q|YS}(q|y,s) \\
&= \sum_z p_{Q|YSZ}(q|y,s,z) p_{Z|YS}(z|y,s) \\
&\stackrel{(b)}{=} \sum_z p_{Q|SZ}(q|z,s) p_{Z|YS}(z|y,s) \\
&\stackrel{(c)}{=} \sum_z p_{Q|SZ}(q|z,s) p_{X_s|Y}(z|y)
\end{aligned}$$

In (a), we used $I(Q;S|Y) = 0$; in (b), we used $Q - (S,Z) - Y$; in (c), we used that $p_{Z|YS=s} = p_{X_s|Y}$. This implies that $p_{Q|Y} \preceq p_{X_s|Y}$ for all s. Therefore, $p_{Q|Y}$ satisfies the constraints in Equation (A1), so $I(Q;Y) \leq V_1$. Combining with Equation (A3) implies

$$V_2 - \epsilon \leq I(Q;Y|S) = I(Q;Y) \leq V_1.$$

Taking the limit $\epsilon \to 0$ gives the desired result. □

Appendix A.2. Proof of Theorem 2

We now prove a slightly generalized version of Theorem 2. We show that the solution to the following optimization problem is non-decreasing and concave in R:

$$I_{\mathrm{RB}}(R) := \sup_{Q:Q-(Z,S)-Y} I(Q;Y|S) \quad \text{where} \quad I(Q;S|Y) \leq R. \tag{A5}$$

The slight generalization comes from replacing max in Equation (12) by sup, so that the result also holds for systems with infinite-dimensional sources where the supremum is not guaranteed to be achieved.

Proof. $I_{\mathrm{RB}}(R)$ is non-decreasing in R because larger R give weaker constraints (larger feasible set) in the maximization problem (A5).

To show concavity, consider any two points on the RB curve as defined by Equation (A5): $(R, I_{\mathrm{RB}}(R))$ and $(R', I_{\mathrm{RB}}(R'))$. For any $\epsilon > 0$, there exist Q and Q' such that

$$\begin{aligned}
I(Q;S|Y) &\leq R & \qquad I(Q;Y|S) &\geq I_{\mathrm{RB}}(R) - \epsilon \\
I(Q';S|Y) &\leq R' & \qquad I(Q';Y|S) &\geq I_{\mathrm{RB}}(R') - \epsilon
\end{aligned}$$

Without loss of generality, suppose that both variables have the same set of outcomes $\mathcal{Q}$. Then, we define a new random variable Q_λ with outcomes $\mathcal{Q}_\lambda = \{1,2\} \times \mathcal{Q}$, as well as a family of conditional distributions parameterized by $\lambda \in [0,1]$:

$$\begin{aligned}
p_{Q_\lambda|ZS}(1,q|z,s) &= \lambda p_{Q|ZS}(q|z,s) \\
p_{Q_\lambda|ZS}(2,q|z,s) &= (1-\lambda) p_{Q'|ZS}(q|z,s)
\end{aligned}$$

In this way, we define Q_λ via a disjoint convex mixture of Q and Q' onto non-overlapping subspaces, with λ being the mixing parameter. With a bit of algebra, it can be verified that, for every λ,

$$H(Q_\lambda|Y) = \lambda H(Q|Y) + (1-\lambda) H(Q'|Y),$$

and similarly for $H(Q_\lambda|Y,S)$ and $H(Q_\lambda|S)$. Therefore,

$$\begin{aligned} I(Q_\lambda;S|Y) &= \lambda I(Q;S|Y) + (1-\lambda)I(Q';S|Y) \\ &\leq \lambda R + (1-\lambda)R' \\ I(Q_\lambda;Y|S) &= \lambda I(Q;Y|S) + (1-\lambda)I(Q';Y|S) \\ &\geq \lambda I_{\mathrm{RB}}(R) + (1-\lambda)I_{\mathrm{RB}}(R') - \epsilon \end{aligned}$$

Since I_{RB} is defined via a maximization, we have

$$I_{\mathrm{RB}}(\lambda R + (1-\lambda)R') \geq I(Q_\lambda;Y|S) \geq \lambda I_{\mathrm{RB}}(R) + (1-\lambda)I_{\mathrm{RB}}(R') - \epsilon.$$

Taking the limit $\epsilon \to 0$ proves the concavity. □

Appendix A.3. Proof of Theorem 3

Proof. We show that, for any Q that achieves $I(Q;S|Y) \leq R$, there is another Q' with cardinality $|\mathcal{Q}'| \leq \sum_s |\mathcal{X}_s| + 1$ that satisfies $I(Q';S|Y) \leq R$ and $I(Q';Y|S) \geq I(Q;Y|S)$.

Consider any joint distribution p_{QSZY} from Equation (10) that achieves $I(Q;S|Y) \leq R$, and let $\mathcal{Q}$ be the corresponding set of outcomes of Q. Fix the corresponding conditional distribution $p_{SZ|Q}$, and note that it also determines the conditional distributions:

$$p_{YSZ|Q}(y,s,z|q) = p_{Y|SZ}(y|s,z)p_{SZ|Q}(s,z|q) \tag{A6}$$

$$= \frac{\nu_S(s)p_{X_s|Y}(z|y)p_Y(y)}{p_{SZ}(s,z)} p_{SZ|Q}(s,z|q) \tag{A7}$$

$$p_{Y|SQ}(y|s,q) = \frac{\sum_z p_{YSZ|Q}(y,s,z|q)}{\sum_{z,y'} p_{YSZ|Q}(y',s,z|q)} \tag{A8}$$

$$p_{S|YQ}(s|y,q) = \frac{\sum_z p_{YSZ|Q}(y,s,z|q)}{\sum_{z,s'} p_{YSZ|Q}(y,s',z|q)} \tag{A9}$$

Next, consider the following linear program:

$$V = \max_{\omega_{Q'} \in \Delta} \sum_q \omega_{Q'}(q) D(P_{Y|SQ=q} \| P_{Y|S}) \tag{A10}$$

$$\text{where} \sum_q \omega_{Q'}(q) p_{SZ|Q}(s,z|q) = p_{SZ}(s,z)\ \forall s,z \tag{A11}$$

$$\sum_q \omega_{Q'}(q) H(S|Y,Q=q) = H(S|Y,Q) \tag{A12}$$

where Δ is the $|\mathcal{Q}|$-dimensional unit simplex, and we use the notation $H(S|Y,Q=q) = -\sum_{y,s} p_{YS|Q}(y,s|q) \ln p_{S|YQ}(s|y,q)$. The first set of constraints (A11) guarantees that $\omega_{Q'} p_{YSZ|Q}$ belongs to the family (10) and, in particular, that the marginal over (S,Z,Y) is $\nu_S(s)p_{X_s|Y}(z|y)p_Y(y)$ (see Equation (A7)). There are $\sum_s |\mathcal{X}_s|$ possible outcomes of (s,z), but $\sum_{s,z} p_{SZ}(s,z) = 1$ by the conservation of probability. Therefore, Equation (A11) effectively imposes $\sum_s |\mathcal{X}_s| - 1$ constraints. The last constraint (A12) guarantees that $H(S|Y,Q') = H(S|Y,Q)$; hence,

$$\begin{aligned} I(Q';S|Y) &= H(S|Y) - H(S|Y,Q') \\ &= H(S|Y) - H(S|Y,Q) = I(Q;S|Y) \leq R. \end{aligned}$$

Equation (A10) involves a maximization of a linear function over the simplex, subject to $\sum_s |\mathcal{X}_s|$ hyperplane constraints. The feasible set is compact, and the maximum is achieved at one of the extreme points of the feasible set. By Dubin's theorem [56], any extreme point of this feasible set can be expressed as a convex combination of at most $\sum_s |\mathcal{X}_s| + 1$ extreme points of Δ. Thus, the maximum is achieved by a marginal distribution $\omega_{Q'}$ with support on at most $\sum_s |\mathcal{X}_s| + 1$ outcomes. This distribution satisfies:

$$\sum_q \omega_{Q'}(q) D(P_{Y|SQ=q} \| P_{Y|S}) \geq \sum_q p_Q(q) D(P_{Y|SQ=q} \| P_{Y|S})$$

since the actual marginal distribution p_Q is an element of the feasible set. Finally, note that

$$\sum_q \omega_{Q'}(q) D(P_{Y|SQ=q} \| P_{Y|S}) = I(Q'; Y|S)$$
$$\sum_q p_Q(q) D(P_{Y|SQ=q} \| P_{Y|S}) = I(Q; Y|S);$$

therefore, $I(Q'; Y|S) \geq I(Q; Y|S)$. □

Appendix A.4. Proof of Theorem 4

Proof. For a finite-dimensional system, we may restrict the optimization problem in Theorem 1 to Q with cardinality $|\mathcal{Q}| \leq \sum_s |\mathcal{X}_s| + 1$ (Theorem 3). In this case, the feasible set can be restricted to a compact set, and the objective is continuous; therefore, the maximum will be achieved.

Now, consider a tuple of random variables (S, Z, Y, Q) that obey the Markov conditions $S - Y - Z$ and $Q - (S, Z) - Y$. Suppose that Q achieves the maximum in Theorem 1 for a given $R > 0$:

$$I(Q; Y|S) = I_{\text{RB}}(R), \qquad I(Q; S|Y) \leq R. \tag{A13}$$

Consider also a sequence of random variables (S_k, Z_k, Y_k, Q_k) for $k = 1, 2, 3 \ldots$ where each tuple has the same outcomes as (S, Z, Y, Q) and obeys the Markov conditions $S_k - Y_k - Z_k$ and $Q_k - (S_k, Z_k) - Y_k$. Let $I^k_{\text{RB}}(R)$ indicate the redundancy bottleneck defined in Theorem 1 for random variables Z_k, Y_k, S_k, and suppose that Q_k achieves the optimum for problem k:

$$I(Q_k; Y_k|S_k) = I^k_{\text{RB}}(R) \qquad I(Q_k; S_k|Y_k) \leq R. \tag{A14}$$

To prove continuity, we assume that the joint distribution of (S_k, Z_k, Y_k) approaches the joint distribution of (S, Z, Y),

$$\lim_k \| p_{S_k Z_k Y_k} - p_{SXY} \|_1 = 0.$$

We first show that

$$I_{\text{RB}}(R) \geq \lim_k I^k_{\text{RB}}(R). \tag{A15}$$

First, observe that given our assumption that p_{SZ} has full support, we can always take k sufficiently large so that each $p_{S_k Z_k}$ has full support. Next, we define the random variable Q'_k that obeys the Markov condition $Q'_k - (S, Z) - Y$, with conditional distribution:

$$p_{Q'_k|SZ}(q|s, z) := p_{Q_k|S_k Z_k}(q|s, z).$$

This conditional distribution is always well-defined, given that $p_{S_k Z_k}$ has the same support as p_{SZ}. By assumption, $p_{S_k Z_k Y_k} \to p_{SZY}$; therefore,

$$p_{Q'_k SZY} - p_{Q_k S_k Z_k Y_k} \to 0. \tag{A16}$$

Conditional mutual information is (uniformly) continuous due to the (uniform) continuity of entropy (Theorem 17.3.3, [57]). Therefore,

$$0 = \lim_k [I(Q_k; S_k|Y_k) - I(Q'_k; S|Y)] \leq R - \lim_k I(Q'_k; S|Y), \tag{A17}$$

where we used Equation (A14). We also define another random variable Q^α_k, which also obeys the Markov condition $Q^\alpha_k - (S,Z) - Y$, whose conditional distribution is defined in terms of the convex mixture:

$$\begin{aligned} p_{Q^\alpha_k|SZ}(q|s,z) &:= \alpha_k p_{Q'|SX}(q|s,z) + (1-\alpha_k) p_U(q), \\ \alpha_k &:= \min\left\{1, \frac{R}{I(Q'_k; S|Y)}\right\} \in [0,1] \end{aligned} \tag{A18}$$

Here, $p_U(q) = 1/|\mathcal{Q}|$ is a uniform distribution over an auxiliary independent random variable U with outcomes $\mathcal{Q}$. From the convexity of conditional mutual information [58],

$$I(Q^\alpha_k; S|Y) \leq \alpha_k I(Q'_k; S|Y) + (1-\alpha_k) I(U; S|Y) \leq R.$$

In the last inequality, we used $I(U;S|Y) = 0$ and plugged in the definition of α_k. Observe that the random variable Q^α_k falls in the feasible set of the maximization problem that defines I_{RB}, so

$$I_{\mathrm{RB}}(R) \geq I(Q^\alpha_k; Y|S). \tag{A19}$$

Combining Equations (A17) and (A18), and $R > 0$ implies that $\alpha_k \to 1$, so

$$p_{Q^\alpha_k SZY} - p_{Q'_k SZY} \to 0.$$

Combining with Equations (A14), (A16) and (A19), along with continuity of conditional mutual information, gives

$$I_{\mathrm{RB}}(R) \geq \lim_k I(Q^\alpha_k; Y|S) = \lim_k I(Q'_k; Y|S) = \lim_k I(Q_k; Y_k|S_k) = \lim_k I^k_{\mathrm{RB}}(R).$$

We now proceed in a similar way to prove

$$I_{\mathrm{RB}}(R) \leq \lim_k I^k_{\mathrm{RB}}(R). \tag{A20}$$

We define the random variable Q'' that obeys the Markov condition $Q'' - (S_k, Z_k) - Y_k$, with conditional distribution

$$p_{Q''_k|S_k Z_k}(q|s,z) = p_{Q|SX}(q|s,z).$$

Since $p_{S_k Z_k Y_k} \to p_{SZY}$ by assumption,

$$p_{Q''_k S_k Z_k Y_k} - p_{QSZY} \to 0. \tag{A21}$$

We then have

$$0 = \lim_k [I(Q; S|Y) - I(Q''_k; S_k|Y_k)] \leq R - \lim_k I(Q''_k; S_k|Y_k). \tag{A22}$$

where we used Equation (A13). We also define the random variable $Q^{\alpha\prime}$ that obeys the Markov condition $Q^{\alpha\prime} - (S_k, Z_k) - Y_k$, with conditional distribution

$$\begin{aligned} p_{Q^{\alpha\prime}_k|S_k Z_k}(q|s,z) &= \alpha'_k p_{Q''|S_k Z_k}(q|s,z) + (1-\alpha'_k) p_U(q), \\ \alpha'_k &:= \min\left\{1, \frac{R}{I(Q''_k; S_k|Y_k)}\right\} \in [0,1] \end{aligned} \tag{A23}$$

Using the convexity of conditional mutual information, $I(U; S_k; Y_k) = 0$, and the definition of α'_k, we have

$$I(Q_k^{\alpha'}; S_k|Y_k) \le \alpha'_k I(Q''_k; S_k|Y_k) + (1-\alpha'_k) I(U; S_k|Y_k) \le R.$$

Therefore, the random variable $Q_k^{\alpha'}$ falls in the feasible set of the maximization problem that defines I_{RB}^k, so

$$I_{\mathrm{RB}}^k(R) \ge I(Q_k^{\alpha'}; Y_k|S_k). \tag{A24}$$

Combining Equations (A22) and (A23), and $R > 0$ implies $\alpha'_k \to 1$; therefore,

$$p_{Q_k^{\alpha'} S_k Z_k Y_k} - p_{Q''_k S_k Z_k Y_k} \to 0.$$

Combining this with Equations (A13), (A21) and (A24), along with the continuity of conditional mutual information, gives

$$\lim_k I_{\mathrm{RB}}^k(R) \ge \lim_k I(Q_k^{\alpha'}; Y_k|S_k) = \lim_k I(Q''_k; Y_k|S_k) = I(Q; Y|S) = I_{\mathrm{RB}}(R).$$

□

References

1. Williams, P.L.; Beer, R.D. Nonnegative decomposition of multivariate information. *arXiv* **2010**, arXiv:1004.2515.
2. Wibral, M.; Priesemann, V.; Kay, J.W.; Lizier, J.T.; Phillips, W.A. Partial information decomposition as a unified approach to the specification of neural goal functions. *Brain Cogn.* **2017**, *112*, 25–38. [CrossRef] [PubMed]
3. Lizier, J.; Bertschinger, N.; Jost, J.; Wibral, M. Information decomposition of target effects from multi-source interactions: Perspectives on previous, current and future work. *Entropy* **2018**, *20*, 307. [CrossRef] [PubMed]
4. Kolchinsky, A. A Novel Approach to the Partial Information Decomposition. *Entropy* **2022**, *24*, 403. [CrossRef]
5. Williams, P.L. Information Dynamics: Its Theory and Application to Embodied Cognitive Systems. Ph.D. Thesis, Indiana University, Bloomington, IN, USA, 2011.
6. Tishby, N.; Pereira, F.; Bialek, W. The information bottleneck method. In Proceedings of the 37th Allerton Conference on Communication, Monticello, IL, USA, 22–24 September 1999.
7. Hu, S.; Lou, Z.; Yan, X.; Ye, Y. A Survey on Information Bottleneck. *IEEE Trans. Pattern Anal. Mach. Intell.* **2024**, 1–20. [CrossRef] [PubMed]
8. Palmer, S.E.; Marre, O.; Berry, M.J.; Bialek, W. Predictive information in a sensory population. *Proc. Natl. Acad. Sci. USA* **2015**, *112*, 6908–6913. [CrossRef]
9. Wang, Y.; Ribeiro, J.M.L.; Tiwary, P. Past–future information bottleneck for sampling molecular reaction coordinate simultaneously with thermodynamics and kinetics. *Nat. Commun.* **2019**, *10*, 3573. [CrossRef] [PubMed]
10. Zaslavsky, N.; Kemp, C.; Regier, T.; Tishby, N. Efficient compression in color naming and its evolution. *Proc. Natl. Acad. Sci. USA* **2018**, *115*, 7937–7942. [CrossRef] [PubMed]
11. Alemi, A.A.; Fischer, I.; Dillon, J.V.; Murphy, K. Deep variational information bottleneck. In Proceedings of the International Conference on Learning Representations (ICLR), Toulon, France, 24–26 April 2017. Available online: https://openreview.net/forum?id=HyxQzBceg (accessed on 12 May 2024).
12. Kolchinsky, A.; Tracey, B.D.; Wolpert, D.H. Nonlinear information bottleneck. *Entropy* **2019**, *21*, 1181. [CrossRef]
13. Fischer, I. The conditional entropy bottleneck. *Entropy* **2020**, *22*, 999. [CrossRef]
14. Goldfeld, Z.; Polyanskiy, Y. The information bottleneck problem and its applications in machine learning. *IEEE J. Sel. Areas Inf. Theory* **2020**, *1*, 19–38. [CrossRef]
15. Ahlswede, R.; Körner, J. Source Coding with Side Information and a Converse for Degraded Broadcast Channels. *IEEE Trans. Inf. Theory* **1975**, *21*, 629–637. [CrossRef]
16. Witsenhausen, H.; Wyner, A. A conditional entropy bound for a pair of discrete random variables. *IEEE Trans. Inf. Theory* **1975**, *21*, 493–501. [CrossRef]
17. Gilad-Bachrach, R.; Navot, A.; Tishby, N. An Information Theoretic Tradeoff between Complexity and Accuracy. In *Learning Theory and Kernel Machines*; Goos, G., Hartmanis, J., van Leeuwen, J., Schölkopf, B., Warmuth, M.K., Eds.; Springer: Berlin/Heidelberg, Germany, 2003; Volume 2777, pp. 595–609. [CrossRef]
18. Kolchinsky, A.; Tracey, B.D.; Van Kuyk, S. Caveats for information bottleneck in deterministic scenarios. In Proceedings of the International Conference on Learning Representations (ICLR), New Orleans, LA, USA, 6–9 May 2019. Available online: https://openreview.net/forum?id=rke4HiAcY7 (accessed on 12 May 2024).
19. Rodríguez Gálvez, B.; Thobaben, R.; Skoglund, M. The convex information bottleneck lagrangian. *Entropy* **2020**, *22*, 98. [CrossRef] [PubMed]

20. Benger, E.; Asoodeh, S.; Chen, J. The cardinality bound on the information bottleneck representations is tight. In Proceedings of the 2023 IEEE International Symposium on Information Theory (ISIT), Taipei, Taiwan, 25–30 June 2023; pp. 1478–1483.
21. Geiger, B.C.; Fischer, I.S. A comparison of variational bounds for the information bottleneck functional. *Entropy* **2020**, *22*, 1229. [CrossRef] [PubMed]
22. Federici, M.; Dutta, A.; Forré, P.; Kushman, N.; Akata, Z. Learning robust representations via multi-view information bottleneck. *arXiv* **2020**, arXiv:2002.07017.
23. Murphy, K.A.; Bassett, D.S. Machine-Learning Optimized Measurements of Chaotic Dynamical Systems via the Information Bottleneck. *Phys. Rev. Lett.* **2024**, *132*, 197201. [CrossRef] [PubMed]
24. Slonim, N.; Friedman, N.; Tishby, N. Multivariate Information Bottleneck. *Neural Comput.* **2006**, *18*, 1739–1789. [CrossRef]
25. Shannon, C. The lattice theory of information. *Trans. IRE Prof. Group Inf. Theory* **1953**, *1*, 105–107. [CrossRef]
26. McGill, W. Multivariate information transmission. *Trans. IRE Prof. Group Inf. Theory* **1954**, *4*, 93–111. [CrossRef]
27. Reza, F.M. *An Introduction to Information Theory*; Dover Publications: Mineola, NY, USA, 1961.
28. Ting, H.K. On the amount of information. *Theory Probab. Its Appl.* **1962**, *7*, 439–447. [CrossRef]
29. Han, T. Linear dependence structure of the entropy space. *Inf. Control* **1975**, *29*, 337–368. [CrossRef]
30. Yeung, R.W. A new outlook on Shannon's information measures. *IEEE Trans. Inf. Theory* **1991**, *37*, 466–474. [CrossRef]
31. Bell, A.J. The co-information lattice. In Proceedings of the Fifth International Workshop on Independent Component Analysis and Blind Signal Separation: ICA, Nara, Japan, 1–4 April 2003; Volume 2003.
32. Gomes, A.F.; Figueiredo, M.A. Orders between Channels and Implications for Partial Information Decomposition. *Entropy* **2023**, *25*, 975. [CrossRef] [PubMed]
33. Griffith, V.; Koch, C. Quantifying synergistic mutual information. In *Guided Self-Organization: Inception*; Springer: Berlin/Heidelberg, Germany, 2014; pp. 159–190.
34. Griffith, V.; Chong, E.K.; James, R.G.; Ellison, C.J.; Crutchfield, J.P. Intersection information based on common randomness. *Entropy* **2014**, *16*, 1985–2000. [CrossRef]
35. Griffith, V.; Ho, T. Quantifying redundant information in predicting a target random variable. *Entropy* **2015**, *17*, 4644–4653. [CrossRef]
36. Bertschinger, N.; Rauh, J. The Blackwell relation defines no lattice. In Proceedings of the 2014 IEEE International Symposium on Information Theory, Honolulu, HI, USA, 29 June–4 July 2014; pp. 2479–2483.
37. Blackwell, D. Equivalent comparisons of experiments. *Ann. Math. Stat.* **1953**, *24*, 265–272. [CrossRef]
38. Rauh, J.; Banerjee, P.K.; Olbrich, E.; Jost, J.; Bertschinger, N.; Wolpert, D. Coarse-Graining and the Blackwell Order. *Entropy* **2017**, *19*, 527. [CrossRef]
39. Bertschinger, N.; Rauh, J.; Olbrich, E.; Jost, J.; Ay, N. Quantifying unique information. *Entropy* **2014**, *16*, 2161–2183. [CrossRef]
40. Rauh, J.; Banerjee, P.K.; Olbrich, E.; Jost, J.; Bertschinger, N. On extractable shared information. *Entropy* **2017**, *19*, 328. [CrossRef]
41. Venkatesh, P.; Schamberg, G. Partial information decomposition via deficiency for multivariate gaussians. In Proceedings of the 2022 IEEE International Symposium on Information Theory (ISIT), Espoo, Finland, 26 June–1 July 2022; pp. 2892–2897.
42. Mages, T.; Anastasiadi, E.; Rohner, C. Non-Negative Decomposition of Multivariate Information: From Minimum to Blackwell Specific Information. *Entropy* **2024**, *26*, 424. [CrossRef]
43. Le Cam, L. Sufficiency and approximate sufficiency. *Ann. Math. Stat.* **1964**, *35*, 1419–1455. [CrossRef]
44. Raginsky, M. Shannon meets Blackwell and Le Cam: Channels, codes, and statistical experiments. In Proceedings of the 2011 IEEE International Symposium on Information Theory, St. Petersburg, Russia, 31 July–5 August 2011; pp. 1220–1224.
45. Banerjee, P.K.; Olbrich, E.; Jost, J.; Rauh, J. Unique informations and deficiencies. In Proceedings of the 2018 56th Annual Allerton Conference on Communication, Control, and Computing (Allerton), Monticello, IL, USA, 2–5 October 2018; pp. 32–38.
46. Banerjee, P.K.; Montufar, G. The Variational Deficiency Bottleneck. In Proceedings of the 2020 International Joint Conference on Neural Networks (IJCNN), Glasgow, UK, 19–24 July 2020; pp. 1–8. [CrossRef]
47. Venkatesh, P.; Gurushankar, K.; Schamberg, G. Capturing and Interpreting Unique Information. In Proceedings of the 2023 IEEE International Symposium on Information Theory (ISIT), Taipei, Taiwan, 25–30 June 2023; pp. 2631–2636. [CrossRef]
48. Csiszár, I.; Matus, F. Information projections revisited. *IEEE Trans. Inf. Theory* **2003**, *49*, 1474–1490. [CrossRef]
49. Makhdoumi, A.; Salamatian, S.; Fawaz, N.; Médard, M. From the information bottleneck to the privacy funnel. In Proceedings of the 2014 IEEE Information Theory Workshop (ITW 2014), Hobart, Australia, 2–5 November 2014; pp. 501–505.
50. Janzing, D.; Balduzzi, D.; Grosse-Wentrup, M.; Schölkopf, B. Quantifying causal influences. *Ann. Stat.* **2013**, *41*, 2324–2358. [CrossRef]
51. Ay, N. Confounding ghost channels and causality: A new approach to causal information flows. *Vietnam. J. Math.* **2021**, *49*, 547–576. [CrossRef]
52. Kolchinsky, A.; Rocha, L.M. Prediction and modularity in dynamical systems. In Proceedings of the European Conference on Artificial Life (ECAL), Paris, France, 8–12 August 2011. Available online: https://direct.mit.edu/isal/proceedings/ecal2011/23/65/111139 (accessed on 12 May 2024).
53. Hidaka, S.; Oizumi, M. Fast and exact search for the partition with minimal information loss. *PLoS ONE* **2018**, *13*, e0201126. [CrossRef] [PubMed]
54. Rosas, F.; Ntranos, V.; Ellison, C.J.; Pollin, S.; Verhelst, M. Understanding interdependency through complex information sharing. *Entropy* **2016**, *18*, 38. [CrossRef]

55. Rosas, F.E.; Mediano, P.A.; Gastpar, M.; Jensen, H.J. Quantifying high-order interdependencies via multivariate extensions of the mutual information. *Phys. Rev. E* **2019**, *100*, 032305. [CrossRef]
56. Dubins, L.E. On extreme points of convex sets. *J. Math. Anal. Appl.* **1962**, *5*, 237–244. [CrossRef]
57. Cover, T.M.; Thomas, J.A. *Elements of Information Theory*; John Wiley & Sons: Hoboken, NJ, USA, 2006.
58. Timo, R.; Grant, A.; Kramer, G. Lossy broadcasting with complementary side information. *IEEE Trans. Inf. Theory* **2012**, *59*, 104–131. [CrossRef]

entropy

MDPI

Article

Synergy Makes Direct Perception Inefficient

Miguel de Llanza Varona [1,*,†] and Manolo Martínez [2,†]

1 School of Engineering and Informatics, University of Sussex, Brighton BN1 9RH, UK
2 Philosophy Department, Universitat de Barcelona, 08001 Barcelona, Spain; manolomartinez@ub.edu
* Correspondence: m.de-llanza-varona@sussex.ac.uk
† These authors contributed equally to this work.

Abstract: A typical claim in anti-representationalist approaches to cognition such as ecological psychology or radical embodied cognitive science is that ecological information is sufficient for guiding behavior. According to this view, affordances are immediately perceptually available to the agent (in the so-called "ambient energy array"), so sensory data does not require much further inner processing. As a consequence, mental representations are explanatorily idle: perception is immediate and direct. Here we offer one way to formalize this direct-perception claim and identify some important limits to it. We argue that the claim should be read as saying that successful behavior just implies picking out affordance-related information from the ambient energy array. By relying on the Partial Information Decomposition framework, and more concretely on its development of the notion of synergy, we show that in multimodal perception, where various energy arrays carry affordance-related information, the "just pick out affordance-related information" approach is very inefficient, as it is bound to miss all synergistic components. Efficient multimodal information combination requires transmitting sensory-specific (and not affordance-specific) information to wherever it is that the various information streams are combined. The upshot is that some amount of computation is necessary for efficient affordance reconstruction.

Keywords: synergy; affordances; direct perception; ecological information

Citation: de Llanza Varona, M.; Martínez, M. Synergy Makes Direct Perception Inefficient. *Entropy* **2024**, *26*, 708. https://doi.org/10.3390/e26080708

Academic Editor: Daniel Chicharro

Received: 7 May 2024
Revised: 31 July 2024
Accepted: 15 August 2024
Published: 21 August 2024

1. Introduction

Cognition is often taken to be (among other things, but centrally) involved in the generation of "adaptive behavior" ([1], ([2] p. 359)]), which is sensitive to "the structure of the environment and the goals of the [cognitive agent]" ([3], p. 3). One natural way to think of cognition, then, is as the transformation and combination of information relevant to the production of behavior (some of it incoming from the environment, some of it encoding agent goals, etc.) into an actual moment-by-moment behavioral plan.

The most popular approach to the investigation of this process is what [4] calls *mainstream representationalism* [5–7]: the view that this transmission and combination of information depends on computations over representations. What exactly representations are is a matter of much debate; for our current purposes, we can simply think of them as signals that carry information about, among other things, the agent's current environment, or their current goals, to downstream areas where these streams of information are combined and transformed in ways increasingly relevant to the production of behavior.

While representationalism is both popular and scientifically successful [8], it is not the only game in town. Alternatives to representationalist cognitive science include *radical embodied* [9,10] cognitive science. This approach is part of a package of views in cognitive science that is steadily gaining in influence: so-called *4E* approaches to cognition [11] downplay the importance of internal computation, and highlight the fact that, sometimes at least, behavior-relevant information can be simply picked up from the environment with very little "post-processing". This shift of focus has allowed embodied cognitive scientists, for example, to redescribe interceptive actions, such as a baseball outfielder catching a ball [10,12]: instead of the outfielder's brain solving the physics problem of predicting the position and time at which the ball will impact the ground from some estimated initial conditions, the outfielder can simply "align themselves with the path of the ball and run so as to make the ball appear to move with constant velocity" ([10], p. 5). This is less computationally intensive, and potentially more ecologically plausible, than the kind of physics-based calculations that classical cognitive science would traditionally gravitate towards.

Embodied cognitive science, therefore, stresses the role that agent–environment dynamics play in cognition. We talk of "stressing the role" rather than "substituting representations with" advisedly: we don't think that representationalism and these alternative approaches are in conflict—perhaps *contra* their proponents, and the overall tenor of the debate surrounding them. Rather we believe, with [13], that they should be thought of as complementary, largely compatible tools in the cognitive-scientific toolbox.

Under this light, one important task for theorists of cognitive science consists in charting the range of applicability of these different approaches: that they are all useful certainly need not mean that they all be everywhere and universally useful. It might very well be, for example, that representation-based analyses happen not to be illuminating in the description and explanation of some particular cognitive process (e.g., perhaps sudden "Aha!" moments of mathematical insight, as described in [14]), and it might equally well be that there are limits to the explanatory usefulness of non-representational strategies.

In this paper, in particular, we discuss, from this vantage point, one of the main themes in radical embodied cognitive science and ecological psychology [15,16]: the claims that, first, the contents of perception are determined by a set of regularities present in the environment, called "affordances" [17]; and, second, that information about affordances can be *directly perceived* by the agent, without the need for any inner processing or computation [15,18,19]. Here we will show that there are some limits to this putatively direct, non-computational, non-representational information pickup.

2. The Direct Perception of Affordances

In keeping with the notion, discussed above, that cognition is intimately linked to the generation of adaptive behavior, radical embodied cognitive scientists and ecological psychologists think of perception as being essentially for action: agents explore their environment so that, through action, they can modify it. Specifically, agents actively engage with their environment through the perception of affordances: possibilities for action *afforded by* the environment, such as climbability (that affords climbing), drinkability (that affords drinking), etc.

How do we perceive affordances? There is a "set of structures and regularities in the environment that allow an animal to engage with [them]" ([19], p. 5232). These structures and regularities are what ecological psychologists call *ecological information*. Ecological information inheres on an *ambient energy array*: highly structured patterns of, e.g., ambient light, or of sound waves, that carry information about present affordances [17]. What we may call, in turn, the *direct perception hypothesis* [20] is the claim that perceivers can directly pick up this ecological information in the environment without the need to compute over it, manipulate it or enrich it in any way [18]—without doing what ([9], p. 18) calls "mental gymnastics". A few complications are important here:

First, affordances are agent-relative (or, interchangeably for our purposes, co-constituted by the agent and the environment). When we say that the ambient energy array carries information about affordances, we should be read as saying that it does so when we keep a certain agent fixed, or that it does so as parameterized by a concrete agent.

Second, there is some debate in the literature about whether the presence or absence of affordances should be nomologically necessitated by the ambient energy array [21]. That is to say, whether the probability of the presence of a certain affordance given a certain configuration of the ambient energy array should always be 0 or 1—what [18] call *specification*—or just made highly (im)probable by it [9]. In the model we develop in the sequel, we follow Chemero in endorsing this latter probabilistic characterization, which we take to be ecologically more plausible, as it does not require that the ambient energy array be always and everywhere unambiguous. In any event, nomological necessitation is a special case of probabilistic correlation.

Finally, it is common for ecological psychologists to claim that "[t]he idea of ecological information developed by J. J. Gibson has no aspects in common with the idea of information as it is understood by cognitivism" ([17], p. 49), echoing ([15], p. 232). If "information as understood by cognitivism" means information as described in Shannon's theory of information (see below), this is an exaggeration. If the ambient energy array makes the presence of an affordance more (un)likely, or even necessitates its presence (absence), then, trivially, the mutual information between a random variable, the values of which are possible configurations of the ambient energy array, and another random variable, the values of which are the presence or absence of a certain target affordance, is necessarily nonzero. See Section 4 for the characterization of mutual information.

3. Multi-Modal Perception and Synergistic Affordances

There are simple scenarios in which ecological information about some affordance is present in the structured energy of *only one* ambient energy array, pertaining to only one sensory modality. (What counts as a sensory modality is itself a vexed question in this debate. We can assume an ecological-psychology understanding thereof, perhaps along the lines developed in [22].)

For example, a walkable surface can be perceived as such by relying only on the set of regularities in ambient light that can be taken in visually. For the purposes of this paper, we can grant that, in these simple cases, perception of affordances results from the direct pickup of ecological information. This can be seen as a stipulation: when there is only one source of affordance-related information, perception counts as direct. We note, in passing, that this is conceding a lot to the defender of direct perception: deep learning [23] teaches us that extracting ecologically relevant features (e.g., the presence of food, or of stairs) from a single source (e.g., an array of pixels) is a computationally complex process, far from direct under any reasonable definition of "direct". See [24].

In any case, ecological information about affordances is often the result of complex interactions between several ambient energy arrays, targeted by several different sensory modalities, in a multi-dimensional space, that do not meet this definition of "direct". One way to develop this idea is Stoffregen and Bardy's notion of a *global array* [18]. The main idea is that, in the general case, the value of an affordance can be recovered only from ecological information present in all ambient energy arrays considered jointly, but possibly not in subsets thereof. By only considering each of them separately it is not necessarily (and perhaps not typically) possible to pinpoint affordance values to the best available accuracy. We will call these *multimodal affordances*.

Ref. [18] claims that the perception of multimodal affordances in the global array is *also* direct. We do not feel that direct perception has been characterized in a clear enough manner to reach a verdict on this issue. What we propose to do in what follows is to develop a formalization of some of the key notions in the debate, in terms of the so-called *partial information decomposition* framework, so that the trade-offs of taking some act of perception as direct are more sharply in view.

4. Information Theory and Lossy Communication

4.1. Basic Concepts

As we have seen, the perception of multimodal affordances relies upon the pickup of information present in patterns in the global array. We now introduce tools to quantify to which extent each of the ambient energy arrays that jointly constitute the global array carries affordance-related information, and to which (possibly different) extent the global array does too. We will rely on information theory for this.

Information theory [25] is a mathematical framework that characterizes optimal transmission of information through a typically noisy channel. In this framework, information is a quantity that measures the degree of uncertainty in a random variable. In this work, we treat single ambient energy arrays as random variables that are combined into another random variable—the global array. Thus, multimodal affordance perception is constrained by how these random variables interact with each other. The way information theory formalizes the dependency between two random variables X and Z is *mutual information*, $I(X;Z)$:

$$I(X;Z) = \mathbb{E}_{x,z}[\log \frac{p(x,z)}{p(x)p(z)}] \quad (1)$$

$$= H(X) - H(X|Z) \quad (2)$$

where the entropy of a random variable X, or $H(X)$, is defined as

$$H(X) = -\mathbb{E}_{p(x)}[\log p(x)] \quad (3)$$

One way to think of the mutual information between X and Z is as the reduction in uncertainty (i.e., entropy) of X once the value of Z is known. Mutual information is symmetric, so it can also be formulated in the other direction; that is, as the reduction in uncertainty about Z when X is known.

As can be seen, Equation (1) only considers two random variables, which makes it inadequate for our current purposes, where at least three random variables are involved: two (or more) single ambient energy arrays, and the resulting global array.

4.2. PID and Synergistic Information

In such higher-dimensional systems, where the information flows from at least two random variables to a third one, we can make use of multivariate mutual information, which, for three random variables, is defined as

$$I(X,Z;Y) = I(Y;X) - I(Y;Z|X) \quad (4)$$

One problem with Equation (4) is that it neglects the possibility of information interaction between the set of random variables. It may be, for example, that both X and Z carry the same pieces of information about Y (say, that for some particular ecological situation, what ambient light says about the current landscape of affordances, and what sound waves say about it, is pretty much the same). It may also be that each of X and Z carries a unique piece of information about Y; or that each carries no information about Y on their own, but *when put together* they do. Any arbitrary combination of these three possibilities might be the case as well.

Unfortunately, this inquiry goes beyond the scope of classic information theory. The framework of *partial information decomposition* (also PID henceforth, [26]) has been recently formulated as an effort to formalize precisely the ways in which information flows in such multivariate systems. In particular, PID defines three possible interactions between the random variables of a system, informally introduced above, corresponding to three different kinds of information (groups of) variables can carry: redundant, unique, and synergistic. Unique information measures the amount of information that is only present in one random variable, but not the others. Redundant information measures the amount of information available in more than one random variable. Finally, synergistic information measures the amount of information carried by a group of random variables as a whole, but not contained in their individual contributions. Our analyses in this paper rely chiefly on the synergistic components in the PID.

The PID approach is still relatively new, and its formal underpinnings still in flux. Several definitions of synergistic information (and the attendant unique and redundant information notions) have been offered in recent years, all of them with advantages and shortcomings. Among these, we will rely on the mathematical definition of synergistic information provided by [27,28]. Given a set of n random variables $\mathbf{X} = \{X_1, X_2, \ldots, X_n\}$, where $n \geq 2$, and a random variable Y, they define the synergistic information in $\mathbf{X}$ about Y as follows:

$$I_{syn}(\{X_1, \ldots, X_n\}; Y) = I(X_{1\ldots n}; Y) - I_{union}(\{X_1, \ldots, X_n\}; Y) \quad (5)$$

where union information is computed as follows:

$$I_{union}(\{X_1, \ldots, X_n\}; Y) \equiv \min_{\substack{Pr^*(X_1, \ldots, X_n, Y) \\ \text{subject to: } Pr^*(X_i, Y) = Pr(X_i, Y)\ \forall i}} I^*(X_{1\ldots n}; Y) \quad (6)$$

We can use the Lagrangian method (as we do in a maximum entropy problem) to approximate the optimal distribution in the minimization of the right-hand side [27–29]. This definition captures the intuitive idea of synergistic information: the information, $I(X_{1\ldots n}; Y)$, that the system as a whole (or joint random variable) $X_{1\ldots n}$ carries about a target variable Y is greater than the information, I_{union}, that the aggregation of all individual variables, $\{X_1, \ldots, X_n\}$, does: the difference, in Equation (5), is the synergistic component. One important reason to rely on this definition of synergy is that it has well-defined bounds. In particular, it is an upper bound on the WholeMinusSum (WMS) synergy [30], which underestimates the synergy in a system, and a lower bound on the S_{max} measure [26], which overestimates it. In addition, Equation (5) exhibits some desirable properties, such as nonnegativity, which early attempts at quantifying interaction information, such as the *interaction information* [31], do not have. (Another recently proposed measure of interactions and dependencies is the so-called *O-information* [32,33]. We will restrict ourselves here to measures in the PID tradition. We would like to thank an anonymous reviewer for pointing us to this alternative body of work).

A common example of a synergistic system is the XOR logic gate, defined by the truth table in Table 1. We can use this simple example to illustrate how synergistic information is not stored in either of the random variables, X_1 and X_2, alone but in their combination. First, let us evaluate the information that each input random variable X_i carries about the target variable Y. Assuming all inputs are uniformly distributed, the mutual information between each input and output is

$$I(X_i; Y) = H(X_i) - H(X_i|Y) \quad (7)$$
$$= H(X_i) - H(X_i) = 0 \quad (8)$$

Looking closely at Table 1, we see that knowing the value of X_i (where $i \in \{1,2\}$) does not reduce the initial 1 bit uncertainty of Y. For example, knowing that $X_1 = 0$ does not change the initial probabilities $p(Y = 0)$ and $p(Y = 1)$, which entails $H(X_1|Y) = H(X_1)$. *Mutatis mutandis* for X_2. Thus, adding the mutual information of the individual components of the XOR gate leads to zero information about the output variable: $I(X_1; Y) + I(X_2; Y) = 0$.

Table 1. Truth table of an XOR gate.

X_1	X_2	Y
0	0	0
0	1	1
1	0	1
1	1	0

We now evaluate the mutual information between the target variable Y when both inputs are considered as a whole $\{X_1, X_2\}$:

$$I(\{X_1, X_2\}; Y) = 1 \tag{9}$$

In this case, the uncertainty about the Y is completely resolved once both X_1 and X_2 are known. Since the information about Y is not in any random variable in isolation, but only in their union, information can only flow when the system is considered as a whole, rather than the sum of its parts. This is precisely the intuition behind synergistic information.

4.3. Communication

In our model, affordance-related information (e.g., about the presence of food) is conveyed by two energy arrays (e.g., ambient light and sound waves) that causally affect distinct sensory modalities (visual and auditory, in the example). We model the multimodal perception of affordances according to Shannon's mathematical theory of communication [25]. Roughly speaking, a communication pipeline consists of (a) a source that generates messages; (b) an encoder that sends an encoded signal of the messages through a typically noisy channel; and (c) a decoder that generates faithful estimates of the source messages based on the incoming encoded signals.

(As an aside, we note that Shannon's communication theory does not require the source messages and the decoder's estimates to lie in the same dimensional space. For example, we could design a communication pipeline where the source messages are sensory observations at the retinal level and the output of the decoder is an action that depends on visual input. In this scenario, the dimensionality of the source messages is going to be significantly higher than the space of possible actions: $\mathbb{R}_{messages} \gg \mathbb{R}_{actions}$).

For our specific case of study, we treat each encoder as a sensory modality that receives inputs from a single ambient energy array; the signals can be thought of as neural patterns of activation, perhaps; and the decoder as some cognitive sub-system downstream that generates the affordance percept.

In this multimodal-affordance perception setup, we slightly extend the main Shannonian model by introducing *two* distinct sources (one per energy array) along with their corresponding encoders (one per sensory modality). Each source message is transmitted to its corresponding encoder, which produces a signal. Finally, a single decoder takes incoming pairs of signals from the encoders to generate an affordance estimate (see Figure 1). We can examine the information interaction between the encoded signals and the affordance by using the tools described in Section 4.2.

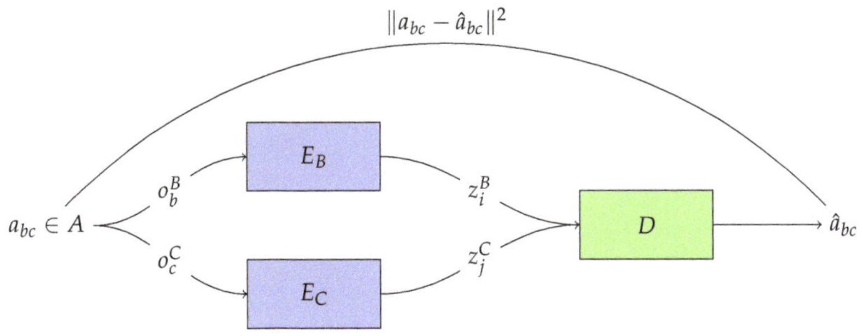

Figure 1. Communication model used to formalize the perception of multimodal affordances. An affordance, a_{bc}, is co-instantiated by the energy array states o_b^B and o_c^C. Then, encoders E_B and E_C encode each sensory observation as z_i^B and z_j^C, respectively. Given those signals, the decoder D generates an estimate, $\hat{a}_{bc}$, of the affordance value a_{bc}.

4.4. Lossy Compression

Shannon's lossless source coding theorem [25] states that any source can be compressed up to its entropy with negligible error. For example, given a discrete random variable X that can take four possible states with the following probability distribution $p(X) = \{0.5, 0.2, 0.2, 0.1\}$, applying Equation (3), we observe that the maximum achievable error-free compression is 1.76 bits. When that is the case, all the information at the source can be perfectly recovered at the end of the communication pipeline by the decoder.

However, cognition operates under limited cognitive resources (due to the cost of metabolic processes, and other biological constraints, [34–37]), which makes lossless compression, and therefore, lossless communication, rarely achievable. To model such limitations, we impose a capacity constraint: the two modality-specific encoders cannot simply relay all of the information present in their target energy array to the downstream decoder. Formally, this means that the maximum transmission rate R (i.e., number of transmitted bits per symbol) achievable by the channel is lower than the entropy of the energy array O: $R < H(O)$.

What this means is that the encoder cannot uniquely encode the source messages (i.e., different source messages are mapped onto the same signal). This creates some uncertainty at the decoder, thus making perfect reconstruction of the affordance matrix unfeasible in general. When lossless communication is not viable, a sub-field of information theory called *rate-distortion theory* [38] defines optimal lossy compression. The core idea underlying this theory is that fidelity in communication is governed by the trade-off between transmitted information and the expected distortion level of the source estimates. Formally, this trade-off is captured by the rate-distortion function, which defines the minimum mutual information $I(X;Z)$ (i.e., maximum level of compression) between two random variables X and Z (source input and its compressed representation, respectively) given some tolerable expected distortion $\mathcal{L}$ of the source estimates $\hat{X}$ generated from Z. To avoid confusion in our notation, we will use D to refer to the decoder (Section 5), and $\mathcal{L}$ to refer to the expectation over any arbitrary loss function or distortion measure (e.g., MSE or Hamming distance). The rate-distortion function is ([39], chapter 10):

$$R(\mathcal{L}) = \min_{q(z|x):\mathcal{L}_{q(x,z)} \leq \mathcal{L}} I(X;Z) \tag{10}$$

where q is the optimal encoding distribution over Z that satisfies the expected distortion constraint and the rate R is an upper bound on the mutual information

$$R \geq I(X;Z) \tag{11}$$

which follows from the data processing inequality. The measure of distortion $\mathcal{L}$ is arbitrary and will depend on the actual task to which the lossily compressed information will be put.

The goal in lossy compression is to minimize the rate R without exceeding a given expected distortion $\mathcal{L}$. For our case study of multimodal affordances, each encoder can only send a maximum of L *different* signals such that $R_L < H(O)$. This is, of course, precisely what happens in brains, where the information present, e.g., at the retina, cannot be losslessly reconstructed from the activity of any downstream neural population. Under such constraint, a perfect estimate $\hat{A}$ of the multimodal affordance A becomes unachievable; that is, $\mathcal{L}(A, \hat{A}) > 0$. It is now clear why our multimodal perception scenario can be seen as a rate-distortion problem. Even though we are not explicitly computing the rate-distortion function in our experiments, we approximate it algorithmically by minimizing the expected distortion of the affordance estimates given a fixed transmission rate at the encoders (see Section 5.3).

Importantly, while the rate-distortion function is an optimal way to quantify the amount of compression given some distortion constraint, it does not provide any insight into the specific algorithmic implementation to achieve such optimal compression. For this reason, we not only quantify the amount of information transmitted but also examine how these resources are utilized, by calculating the *spatial entropy* of signals (see Section 4.5).

4.5. Spatial Entropy

In our model, signals are distributed both probabilistically and spatially. Due to the constraints mentioned above, each encoder has fewer available signals than there are possible energy array states, which forces them to subsume sets of states under single sensory estimates. The spatial distribution of the signals provides insight into which states of the energy array are being represented as which states. To measure this, we use spatial entropy, as characterized in [40], to account for this spatial information:

$$H_{CI}(X) = -\sum_{i=1}^{n} d_i p(x_i) \log p(x_i) \tag{12}$$

Here d_i is the average Euclidean distance between signal x_i and all other signals. By doing this, we can weight the entropy definition in Equation (3) using the average distance between each sensory signal in the encoding space. Intuitively, for a given distribution over signals, the more spatially spread they are (i.e., the higher d is), the higher the spatial entropy. Higher spread among signals suggests that the encoder is giving a fuller picture of the energy array. Conversely, the more densely packed signals in the encoding space are, the fewer spatially distinct aspects of the energy array are being captured.

5. Methods

5.1. Model Description

This is how we model global arrays: we express an "affordance landscape" as a 2-dimensional, $m \times n$ matrix A, where each dimension corresponds to one ambient energy array (we will also call these dimensions *basic properties* in what follows). We can think of these dimensions as the model equivalents to, respectively, ambient light and ambient sound, for example. The first dimension (energy array) has m possible states; the second one, n possible states.

Sensory observations, $O^B \in \mathbb{R}^m$ and $O^C \in \mathbb{R}^n$, record the possible values each energy array can take, such that $O^B = [o_1^B, o_2^B, \ldots, o_m^B]$ and $O^C = [o_1^C, o_2^C, \ldots, o_n^C]$. We define an affordance matrix $A \in \mathbb{R}^{m \times n}$ as follows:

$$A = \begin{bmatrix} a_{11} & a_{12} & \cdots & a_{1n} \\ a_{21} & a_{22} & \cdots & a_{2n} \\ \vdots & \vdots & \ddots & \vdots \\ a_{m1} & a_{m2} & \cdots & a_{mn} \end{bmatrix} \tag{13}$$

where each entry a_{bc} gives the value of the target affordance when the two ambient energy arrays are observed to be in state o_b^B, and o_c^C, respectively.

Modality-specific encoders $E_B : o_b^B \mapsto z_i^B$ and $E_C : o_c^C \mapsto z_j^C$ receive these observations, o_b^B and o_c^C, respectively, and map them to encoded signals, z_i^B and z_j^C, respectively, that are sent downstream to a decoder $D : (z_i^B, z_j^C) \mapsto \hat{a}_{bc}$, that generates an estimate $\hat{a}_{bc}$ of the current affordance value a_{bc}. A, O, Z, and $\hat{A}$ are random variables, while E and D are functions. The communication pipeline for a 1-dimensional affordance specified by O^B is assumed to form the following Markov chain

$$A \xmapsto{f} O^B \xmapsto{E_B} Z^B \xmapsto{D} \hat{A} \tag{14}$$

where each component is only conditionally dependent on the previous one. The end goal of the system is to transmit just as much mutual information $I(A; \hat{A})$ as needed to generate faithful enough estimates $\hat{a}$ of the target affordance value a.

Encoders are not *directly* causally sensible to the affordance, but only through the basic properties that co-specify the affordance. Whatever we take "direct perception" to imply, it has to be compatible with this fact. Still, the property of interest for the agent is the affordance value: it is with this property that it has to engage in order to generate adaptive behavior. That is to say, the agent's goal (as ecological psychologists and embodied cognitive scientists rightly point out) is not to reconstruct sensory stimuli (i.e., basic properties), but to minimize their uncertainty about the current value of the affordance.

Once each encoder sends the signals downstream, the decoder's job is to generate a faithful estimate of the property of interest. We assume that the codebook is shared by the encoder and decoder, so the decoder knows the inverse mapping from encoded signals back to sensory observations and therefore can reconstruct the optimal expected affordance value given that information. To evaluate the "goodness" of those estimates, we use the Mean Squared Error (MSE) between A and $\hat{A}$ as a distortion measure $\mathcal{L}$ of the generated estimates:

$$\mathcal{L}_{MSE}(A, \hat{A}) = \frac{1}{|O|} \sum_{bc \in O} (a_{bc} - \hat{a}_{bc})^2 \quad \text{where} \quad O = [(o_b^B, o_c^C) \mid b \in O^B, c \in O^C] \tag{15}$$

which computes the squared distance between each estimate and the actual affordance value. We define each decoder's estimate $\hat{a}_{bc}$ as the expected affordance value corresponding to the observations encoded under the same signal:

$$D(z_i^B, z_j^C) = \hat{a}_{bc} = \frac{1}{|O|} \sum_{bc \in O} a_{bc} \quad \text{where} \quad O = [(o_b^B, o_c^C) \mid b \in E_B^{-1}(z_i^B), c \in E_C^{-1}(z_j^C)] \tag{16}$$

where z_i^B and z_j^C are the ith and jth signals encoding observations o_b^B and o_c^C, respectively, via the mappings $E_B(o_b^B)$ and $E_C(o_c^C)$. The above expression estimates each affordance value by taking the expectation over all affordance values that correspond to each pair of observations encoded in each modality. We use O to refer to the set of pairs of the Cartesian product between the observations obtained through the inverse mapping of the encoders. As a crucial part of this work is to understand whether the perception of multimodal affordances entails any intermediate processing of the energy arrays, we also measure whether the whole system is keeping track of sensory observations. In particular, we compute the sensory estimates that the decoder can generate via the encoder's inverse mapping:

$$\hat{o}_b^B = \frac{1}{|O|} \sum_{o \in O} o \quad \text{where} \quad O = [o_b^B \mid b \in E_B^{-1}(z_i^B)] \tag{17}$$

where, similarly as before, $z_i^B \in Z^B$ is the ith signal that encodes the sensory observation o_b^B. This expression computes each sensory estimate by averaging over all observations O^B that are mapped onto the same signal z_i^B.

5.2. Encoding Strategies

We investigate two different encoding strategies. First, we evaluate the *direct encoding* strategy, which tries to maximize information about the property of interest (i.e., the affordance value). In this strategy, each encoder generates a mapping such that the content of the signals directly maximizes affordance information. Since each encoder is only sensitive to one dimension of the affordance matrix, the best they can do is to transmit as much information about the expected affordance value of the dimension they are causally sensitive to. Formally, the expected affordance value corresponding to dimension B (and, *mutatis mutandis*, C) can be defined as

$$A^B = \mathbb{E}_c[a_{bc}] \quad \forall b \in O^B \tag{18}$$

Given this, the *direct encoding* strategy can be formalized as follows:

$$\arg\max_{Z^B} I(A^B; \hat{A}^B) \tag{19}$$

In particular, each one-dimensional affordance estimate can be obtained by

$$\hat{A}_b^B = D\Big(E_B(o_b^B)\Big) = \frac{1}{|O|}\sum_{o\in O} \mathbb{E}_c[a_{oc}] \quad \text{where} \quad O = [o_b^B \mid b \in E_B^{-1}(z_i^B)] \tag{20}$$

We intend for this strategy to be a formalization of the direct perception claim that affordance-related information can be simply picked up from the energy array. Our two direct encoders do just that: simply pick up as much affordance-related information from their proprietary arrays as they can. For our toy example, we directly compute $I(A^B; \hat{A}^B)$. However, we observe that in a more complex scenario, the spatial distribution of the signals is key to determining the *usefulness* of the encoding strategy (see Section 4.5), which we address below. Thus, to provide a simple measure for Equation (19), we approximate this quantity through $\mathcal{L}_{MSE}(A^B, \hat{A}^B)$ as follows:

$$\begin{aligned} I(A^B; \hat{A}^B) &= H(A^B) - H(A^B|\hat{A}^B) && (21)\\ &= H(A^B) + \mathbb{E}_p[p(a^B|\hat{a}^B)] && (22)\\ &\geq H(A^B) + \mathbb{E}_p[q(a^B|\hat{a}^B)] && (23)\\ &\approx -\mathcal{L}_{MSE}(A^B, \hat{A}^B) && (24) \end{aligned}$$

where we choose a Gaussian distribution q as an approximation to the true distribution p. As $H(A^B)$ is a constant (i.e., the affordance matrix does not change), maximizing mutual information amounts to minimizing the mean-squared error.

In contrast to direct encoding, we examine an *indirect encoding* strategy that merely aims at supplying the decoder with the signals that will allow *the decoder* to come up with the best possible reconstruction of affordance value. In this strategy, encoders do not make any assumptions as to whether this requires them to squeeze as much affordance-related information as possible or not. The main question to analyze is how much *sensory* information signals carry when encoders follow this strategy. In particular, we want to understand to what extent information in the signals depends on

$$\arg\max_{Z^B} I(O^B; \hat{O}^B) \tag{25}$$

which would imply that indirect encoders end up prioritizing the transmission of information about sensory data. If that is the case, then the perception of affordance-related information would be mediated by the integration of the sensory signals of each modality, and therefore, indirect. Similarly to $\hat{A}^B$, each sensory estimate in $\hat{O}^B$ can be computed using Equation (17). We approximate Equation (25) using the mean-squared error, as performed before, and the spatial entropy. The justification for using the mean-squared error is equivalent to the one provided before. Regarding the spatial entropy, we use it to examine how the spatial distribution of signals contributes to minimizing $\mathcal{L}_{MSE}(O^B, \hat{O}^B)$. As mutual information is symmetric, we follow the other direction to obtain the entropy of the sensory estimates:

$$\begin{aligned} I(O^B; \hat{O}^B) &= H(\hat{O}^B) - \underbrace{H(\hat{O}^B|O^B)}_{=0} && (26)\\ &= H(\hat{O}^B) && (27) \end{aligned}$$

where the last term in the right-hand side of Equation (26) arises from using a deterministic encoder. Then, we simply replace $H(\hat{O}^B)$ by its spatial entropy counterpart $H_{CI}(\hat{O}^B)$

defined in Section 4.5. Using spatial entropy can provide a deeper understanding of how the spatial distribution of signals contributes to achieving (near) optimal encoding strategies, beyond just considering the probability distribution of signals.

For the sake of simplicity, throughout the whole model description and further experiments, we assume that (i) all random variables are discrete; (ii) both O^B and O^C are uniformly distributed; and, (iii) the distribution of the other random variables (O, $\hat{O}$, Z, A, $\hat{A}$) is given by the frequency of its values.

5.3. Encoder Optimization

In our experiments, we run a simple optimization algorithm to approximate optimal encoder strategies. Suppose we have two encoders, each of which has a repertoire of n possible signals. The pseudocode for this optimization is given in Algorithm 1. As for the "relevant MSE" in line 14 of Algorithm 1: in the direct perception scenario we use MSE_DIRECT: each encoder is individually optimized to minimize their MSE; while in the indirect case, we use MSE_INDIRECT: we find the pair of encoders that *jointly* minimize it.

Algorithm 1 Encoder Optimization

1: $b \leftarrow$ dimension of O^B energy array
2: $c \leftarrow$ dimension of O^C energy array
3: $m \leftarrow$ number of signals available for the E^B encoder
4: $n \leftarrow$ number of signals available for the E^C encoder
5: $A \leftarrow b \times c$ matrix ▷ affordance landscape
6: $A_b \leftarrow$ a vector with the means of A rows ▷ affordance landscape as seen by the E^B encoder
7: $A_c \leftarrow$ a vector with the means of A columns ▷ affordance landscape as seen by the E^C encoder
8: RUNS $\leftarrow$ how many different random starting points
9: LENGTHOFRUN $\leftarrow$ how many optimization steps
10: **for** RUNS times **do**
11: $ENC_1 \leftarrow$ random vector of integers from 1 to m, of size b
12: $ENC_2 \leftarrow$ random vector of integers from 1 to n, of size c ▷ Random initialization of the two encoders
13: **for** LENGTHOFRUN times **do**
14: Compute the relevant MSEs (see explanation in main text).
15: For each encoder: randomly modify the signal to which one particular (also random) observation is mapped. If the resulting MSE is lower than the one calculated above, keep the new encoder; otherwise, discard it.
16: **end for**
17: **end for**
18: Keep the encoders with the lowest MSE

19: **function** MSE_DIRECT(encoder)
20: decoder $\leftarrow$ all zeros vector with size <number of signals available at the encoder>
21: $\hat{A} \leftarrow$ all zeros vector with size <length of encoder (i.e., number of observations)>
22: MSE s$\leftarrow$ all zeros vector with size <length of encoder (i.e., number of observations)>
23: **for** $i \leftarrow 1$ to number of signals available at the encoder **do**
24: decoder$[i] \leftarrow$ the mean of all observations (from 1 to length of encoder) that the encoder maps onto signal i
25: **end for**
26: **for** $i \leftarrow 1$ to length of encoder **do**
27: $\hat{A}[i] \leftarrow$ decoder[encoder$[i]$] ▷ what the decoder produces given the signal
28: $MSEs[i] \leftarrow (A[i] - \hat{A}[i])^2$
29: **end for**
30: Return the mean of $MSEs$
31: **end function**

32: **function** MSE_INDIRECT(encoder1, encoder2)
33: $\hat{A} \leftarrow$ all zeros matrix with dimensions equal to affordance map A
34: decoder $\leftarrow$ all zeros matrix with dimensions $< m \times n >$ ▷ the decoded value given a pair of signals
35: $MSEs \leftarrow$ an all zeros matrix with dimensions equal to affordance map A
36: **for** $i \leftarrow 1$ to m **do**
37: **for** $j \leftarrow 1$ to n **do**
38: decoder$[i, j] \leftarrow$ the mean of all observations that the encoders maps onto signals i and j respectively
39: **end for**
40: **end for**
41: **for** $i \leftarrow 1$ to b **do**
42: **for** $j \leftarrow 1$ to c **do**

Algorithm 1 *Cont.*

```
            Â[i] ← decoder[encoder1[i],encoder2[j]]        ▷ what the decoder produces given the signals
            MSEs[i] ← (A[i] − Â[i])^2
        end for
    end for
    Return the mean of MSEs
end function
```

While there is no guarantee that this algorithm will find the optimal encoders, first, in our tests it consistently lands on encoders that are optimal or close to optimal; and, second, it is the same procedure for all tests so results for different strategies are (barring some unexpected bias) fully comparable.

It is not always easy to reconstruct an algorithm from this kind of pseudocode. The fully explicit code is available on the following Github repository: https://github.com/MigueldeLlanza/SynergisticPerception (accessed on 3 May 2024).

5.4. Information-Theoretic Measures

We rely on the BROJA measure from the *dit* python package [41] to compute the synergistic measure defined in Equation (5). Similarly, we adapt the code from the *Spatentropy* R package [42] to measure the spatial entropy measure defined by Equation (12).

5.5. Data

We first evaluate the direct-perception claim with a toy example using a synthetic 4×4 affordance matrix that exhibits synergistic properties. This simple scenario is useful to examine in detail how information is processed in each encoding strategy. Then, we further investigate the direct perception claim using realistic images from the CIFAR-100 dataset [43]. We chose the "people" superclass of CIFAR-100 as the data source due to its simplicity compared to other classes. When solving Equation (5), each unique RGB pixel value in the range $[0, 255]$ is treated as a different value of the random variable A. For this reason, calculating the synergy becomes computationally intractable. To overcome these computational demands we transform each image to grayscale and reduce the number of unique pixel values to 5 using K-means clustering. Here we assume the following tradeoff: calculating the synergy becomes tractable at the expense of reducing the image quality. The goal in this second scenario is to explore information processing in a context with plausible sensory inputs (visual in this case). To make an artificial multimodal setup, we consider each dimension of an image as a different energy array that causally affects each encoder independently. That is to say, we interpret each image as a 2-dimensional affordance matrix, where each pixel value (i.e., affordance value) is assumed to be co-defined by the instantiation of each energy array. For example, the top-right pixel value of an $m \times n$ image is co-defined by the first value of the first energy array (i.e., row 0) and the last value of the second energy array (i.e., column n).

6. Results

6.1. Toy Example

In this section, we first analyze a toy model of a cognitively bounded agent whose goal is to perceive a multimodal affordance. In this setup, the maximum achievable rate is less than the entropy of the receptor fields, so the encoders cannot account for all the variability in the input, which makes it a rate-distortion problem. In addition, each encoder is only sensitive to one dimension of the affordance matrix, corresponding to the one basic property it is causally sensitive to. Following the previous description, for a $A \in \mathbb{R}^{m \times n}$, and a set of observations O^B, the dimensionality of the encoded signals will be $Z^B \in \mathbb{R}^m$:

$$Z^B = [E_B(o_1^B), E_B(o_2^B), \ldots, E_B(o_m^B)] \tag{28}$$

where the set of signals for a specific energy array (O^B in this case) is a vector of encoded observations. If we think of the energy array O^B as color, then an instantiation of that random variable o_1^B could be read as *color red* (i.e., $B =$ *color* and $1 =$ *red*). As the constrained encoder cannot send a different signal per color, some colors will be subsumed under the same signal following a *many-to-one* mapping. In this scenario, the decoder has to deal with some uncertainty about what sensory observations caused the received encoded signals, so we assume that the decoding process relies on the expected affordance value corresponding to all the observations mapped onto the same signal.

Finally on to our toy example. Assume the following 4×4 affordance matrix A

O^B \ O^C	1	2	3	4
1	0	0	1	1
2	0	0	2	1
3	1	2	0	0
4	1	1	0	0

(29)

that depends on two energy arrays $O^B = [1,2,3,4]$ and $O^C = [1,2,3,4]$ that we can think of as, e.g., color and loudness. Assuming a channel capacity of 1 bit, each encoder can only send two signals (0 and 1). As mentioned before, each encoder is sensitive to the expected affordance value per dimension: $A_b^B = \mathbb{E}_c[a_{bc}]$ and $A_c^C = \mathbb{E}_b[a_{bc}]$, respectively. For example, the expected affordance values corresponding to dimension B are:

$$A_1^B = \mathbb{E}_c[a_{1c}] = \frac{1}{4}[0+0+1+1] = 0.5 \tag{30}$$

$$A_2^B = \frac{1}{4}[0+0+2+1] = 0.75 \tag{31}$$

$$A_3^B = \frac{1}{4}[1+2+0+0] = 0.75 \tag{32}$$

$$A_4^B = \frac{1}{4}[1+1+0+0] = 0.5 \tag{33}$$

Each encoder alone could potentially discriminate two different expected affordance values, 0.5 and 0.75. Similarly, each encoder is only able to discriminate between two different energy array states (i.e., two different colors or two different sound levels), as it can transmit 1 bit of information.

6.1.1. Direct Encoding

Under this strategy, each encoder sends signals that maximize affordance information. In this example, E_B and E_C generate the following mappings:

$$E_B(o_b^B) = \left\{ \begin{array}{ll} 0, & \text{if } o_b^B \in \{1,4\} \\ 1, & \text{if } o_b^B \in \{2,3\} \end{array} \right\} \tag{34}$$

$$E_C(o_c^C) = \left\{ \begin{array}{ll} 0, & \text{if } o_c^C \in \{1,4\} \\ 1, & \text{if } o_c^C \in \{2,3\} \end{array} \right\} \tag{35}$$

For example, if the affordance value a_{13} is the case, then o_1^B (e.g., red color) and o_3^C (e.g., loud sound), and the encoded signals will be $Z^B = 0$ and $Z^C = 1$. Here, each encoder is trying to maximize affordance information given the receptive field it is sensitive to. For instance, subsuming energy array states 2 and 3 under the same signal can be understood as attributing high affordance value to those states, and low affordance value to the pair of values 1 and 4. This is an intuitive strategy to follow, as each encoder is trying to provide as much relevant information as possible on its own.

As shown before, given a pair of signals, the best the decoder can do is to apply Equation (16) to compute the expectation of the affordance value corresponding to the sensory observations mapped onto those signals. In the current example, the decoded expected affordance $\hat{a}_{13}$ is:

$$D(Z^B = 0, Z^C = 1) = \frac{1}{4}[a_{12} + a_{13} + a_{42} + a_{43}] \tag{36}$$

$$= \frac{1}{4}[0 + 1 + 1 + 0] = \frac{2}{4} = 0.5 \tag{37}$$

Following the same procedure for all affordance values and corresponding sensory observations, we end up with the following estimate $\hat{A}$ of the affordance matrix:

O^B \ O^C	1	2	3	4
1	0.5	0.5	0.5	0.5
2	0.5	1	1	0.5
3	0.5	1	1	0.5
4	0.5	0.5	0.5	0.5

(38)

whose expected distortion can be evaluated by computing Equation (15):

$$\mathcal{L}_{MSE}(A, \hat{A}) = 0.44 \tag{39}$$

Here, the strategy of the encoders is to maximize affordance information as each signal maximizes the expected affordance value along its basic property dimension. In particular, the expected affordance value is higher when the basic property value is either 2 or 3, and lower when it is 1 or 4. Computing Equation (17) for all possible O^B, we have the following expected decoder's receptive field estimate:

O^B	1	2	3	4
Z^B	0	1	1	0
$\hat{O}^B$	2.5	2.5	2.5	2.5

(40)

so when $O^B \in \{2,3\}$, it entails a high affordance value and the opposite when $O^B \in \{1,4\}$. The same holds for O^C (as the affordance matrix in this toy example is symmetric, all the results shown for the energy array B hold for C). Interestingly, maximizing affordance information is at odds with conveying information about the basic property. All sensory information is destroyed by this encoding strategy since the decoder collapses all possible sensory states into the same estimate 2.5; that is, no matter what signals are sent downstream, the best the decoder can do is to map them onto the same value, thus destroying all the information in the receptive fields. This type of encoder is the one we call *direct*, as it does not at all keep track of the sensory stimuli it is sensitive to:

$$I(O^B; \hat{O}^B) = H(O^B) - H(O^B|\hat{O}^B) \tag{41}$$

$$= H(O^B) - H(O^B) = 0 \tag{42}$$

but, instead, tries to capture as much information as possible about the property of interest A:

A^B	0.5	0.75	0.75	0.5
$\hat{A}^B$	0.5	0.75	0.75	0.5

(43)

leading to $I(A^B; \hat{A}^B) = 1$. (Note that $p(O^B, \hat{O}^B) = p(O^B)$ because the encoder is deterministic: $p(O^B, \hat{O}^B) = p(\hat{O}^B|O^B)p(O^B) = p(O^B)$).

6.1.2. Indirect Encoding

Can we do better with the same resources? The answer is yes. We now examine whether Equation (25) is needed to capture the synergistic interactions in the system. In this example, a synergistic strategy is achieved by the following mappings:

$$E_B(o_b^B) = \begin{Bmatrix} 0, & \text{if } o_b^B \in \{1,2\} \\ 1, & \text{if } o_b^B \in \{3,4\} \end{Bmatrix} \tag{44}$$

$$E_C(o_c^C) = \begin{Bmatrix} 0, & \text{if } o_c^C \in \{1,2\} \\ 1, & \text{if } o_c^C \in \{3,4\} \end{Bmatrix} \tag{45}$$

Following the same steps as in the direct encoding, the expected affordance estimate is (see Figure 2, which shows the raw affordance matrix along with the corresponding direct and synergistic estimates)

O^B \ O^C	1	2	3	4
1	0	0	1.25	1.25
2	0	0	1.25	1.25
3	1.25	1.25	0	0
4	1.25	1.25	0	0

(46)

which leads to a better-expected distortion compared to the direct strategy:

$$\mathcal{L}_{MSE}(A, \hat{A}) = 0.09 \tag{47}$$

How much receptive field information is transmitted in this scenario? Again, using Equation (17) the decoder's estimate of the receptive field inputs given the received encoded signals is:

O^B	1	2	3	4
Z^B	0	0	1	1
$\hat{O}^B$	1.5	1.5	3.5	3.5

(48)

As can be seen, *all* the information about the sensory states that can be captured with a 1-bit encoder is preserved

$$I(O^B; \hat{O}^B) = H(O^B) - H(O^B | \hat{O}^B) \tag{49}$$

$$= 2 - 1 = 1 \tag{50}$$

as there is 1 bit of information transmitted through the whole communication pipeline. In particular, the decoder's receptive field estimate is 1.5 when $O^B \in \{1,2\}$, and 3.5 otherwise. In this scenario, the encoded signals can be interpreted as carrying information about the receptive fields rather than directly about the affordance value. Importantly, this strategy leads to an efficient use of the available resources, as the system transmits at its maximum capacity, which is a 1 bit rate (i.e., sending either a 0 or 1, which is then translated by the decoder as 1.5 or 3.5). Symmetrically, no affordance information is stored in any of the encoders alone:

A^B	0.5	0.75	0.75	0.5
$\hat{A}^B$	0.625	0.625	0.625	0.625

(51)

as $I(A^B; \hat{A}^B) = 0$. This is why indirect encoding works better: as the information of the affordance value is carried synergistically by the two energy arrays, it pays off to relay an estimate of those very arrays so that the downstream decoder can then reconstruct these synergistic components. If each encoder tries to maximize affordance-related information directly, "going it alone", the synergistic components will not be transmitted, and the decoder will not be able to exploit them. Table 2 summarizes the results shown for each strategy in the toy example.

Table 2. Results of the two encoding strategies for affordance reconstruction, synergistic information, sensory state information, and uni-dimensional affordance information.

Strategy	$\mathcal{L}_{MSE}(A,\hat{A})$	$I_{syn}(\{Z^B,Z^C\};A)$	$I(O^B;\hat{O}^B)$	$I(O^C;\hat{O}^C)$	$I(A^B;\hat{A}^B)$	$I(A^C;\hat{A}^C)$
Direct	0.44	0.25	0	0	1	1
Indirect	0.09	1	1	1	0	0

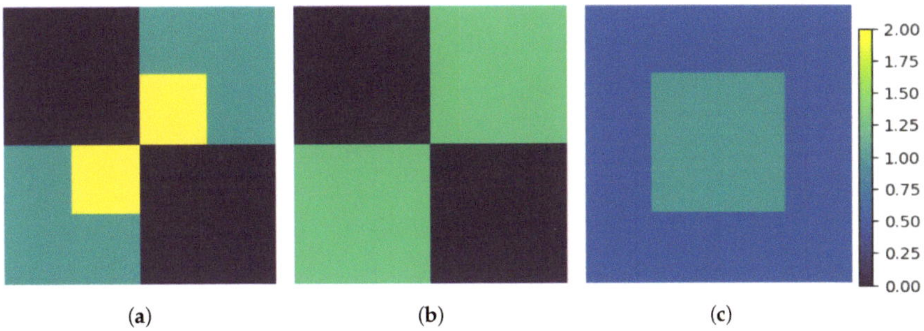

Figure 2. Affordance estimates of the toy model. (**a**) Affordance matrix. (**b**) Indirect estimate. (**c**) Direct estimate.

(Note that one could swap entries a_{42} and a_{23} of Equation (29) to create an affordance matrix with synergistic information, where both strategies would result in the same affordance estimate).

This toy model is, of course, constructed precisely to show clearly what we want it to show. In the next section we make the same point, but now relying on statistically natural stimuli.acces

6.2. CIFAR-100

After showing the behavior of each encoding strategy in a toy model, we now show the results using CIFAR-100 data as affordance landscapes. To evaluate the direct perception of synergistic affordances, we examine how sensory information is related to affordance information under each encoding–decoding strategy (i.e., direct and indirect). In Figure 3, we show the results for the case in which the maximum capacity is constrained to 3 bits per encoder. (We stick to 3 bits due to the computational costs of solving Equation 5). That is, each encoder can only encode 8 dimensions (using 2^3 signals) out of the 32 possible they are causally sensitive to (CIFAR-100 images have a 32×32 dimension). In particular, each energy array is defined as $O^B = [0, 1, \ldots, 31]$ (sensible to the image rows; i.e., horizontal information) and $O^C = [0, 1, \ldots, 31]$ (sensible to the image columns, i.e., vertical information).

We show the following results grouped by strategy for each encoder dimension: (i) Figure 3a shows the correlation between sensory estimates ("MSE sensory estimates") and sensory spatial entropy; (ii) Figure 3b shows the correlation between sensory estimates and synergistic information; (iii) Figure 3c shows the correlation between sensory estimates and estimates of each dimension of the affordance; (iv) Figure 3d illustrates how affordance estimates ("MSE Affordance Estimate") are correlated with sensory estimates; and (v) Figure 3e shows the correlation between affordance estimates and synergistic information.

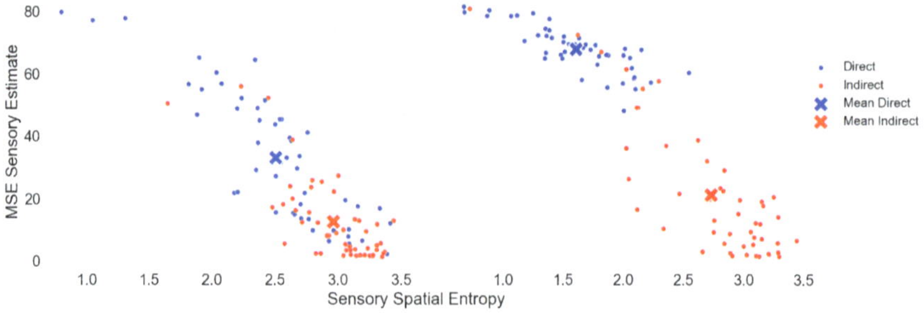
MSE Sensory Estimate
Sensory Spatial Entropy
Direct
Indirect
Mean Direct
Mean Indirect

(**a**)

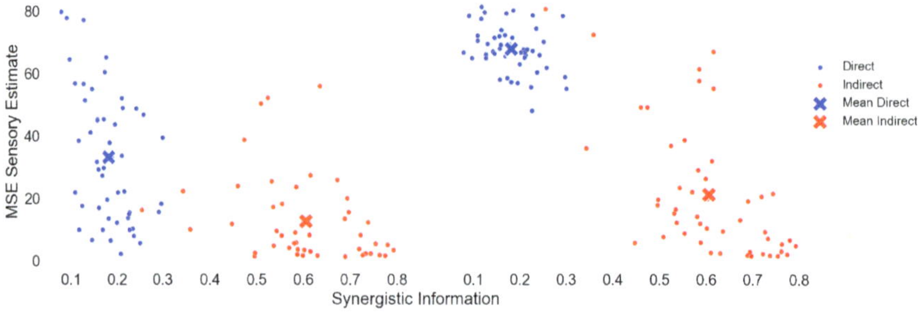
MSE Sensory Estimate
Synergistic Information
Direct
Indirect
Mean Direct
Mean Indirect

(**b**)

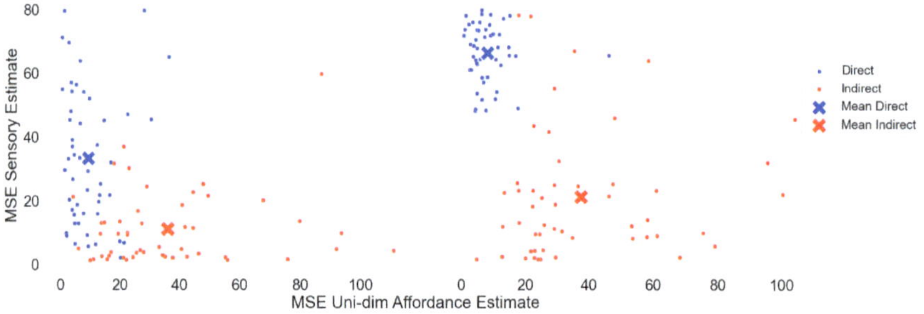
MSE Sensory Estimate
MSE Uni-dim Affordance Estimate
Direct
Indirect
Mean Direct
Mean Indirect

(**c**)

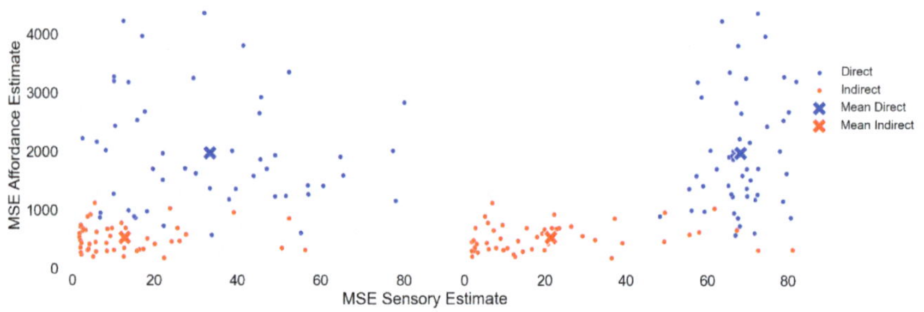
MSE Affordance Estimate
MSE Sensory Estimate
Direct
Indirect
Mean Direct
Mean Indirect

(**d**)

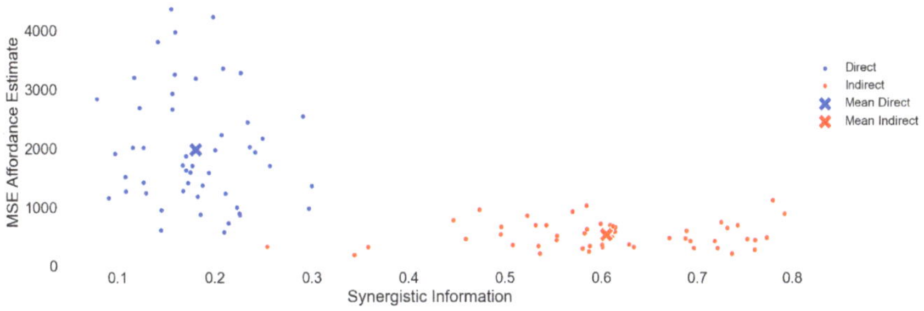

(**e**)

Figure 3. Results for different metrics for both the direct and the indirect encoding strategies when the capacity constraint is set to 8 signals per encoder; that is, each encoder can, at most, encode 8 out of 32 dimensions of the input. In (**a–d**), the left plot corresponds to the results obtained for encoder B, while the right plots correspond to the results for encoder C. In each plot, we show the results per data point (i.e., CIFAR-100 images) and the mean corresponds to the point of the means of each dimension. (**a**) Sensory accuracy as a function of spatial entropy. (**b**) Sensory accuracy as a function of synergistic information. (**c**) Sensory accuracy as a function of uni-dimensional affordance accuracy. (**d**) Affordance accuracy as a function of sensory accuracy. (**e**) Affordance accuracy as a function of synergistic information.

The main source of evidence supporting the claim that the direct perception of multi-modal synergistic affordances is suboptimal can be found in Figure 3e. There it is shown how minimizing affordance distortion is achieved by maximizing the synergistic information (i.e., $I_{syn}(\{Z^B, Z^C\}; A)$) present in the affordance matrix, thus supporting the claim that *synergy makes direct perception inefficient*. In the same line, Figure 3d shows how indirect encoders (red dots) manage to significantly minimize the expected distortion of the affordance value by minimizing the expected distortion of the sensory observations. This suggests that, at least in some contexts, *a near-optimal encoding strategy has to keep track of sensory observations to improve the estimates of the property of interest.*

What kind of information does each encoding strategy aim to maximize? Figure 3c shows a trade-off between sensory and affordance information: maximizing one quantity (Equation (21)) is at the expense of minimizing the other (Equation (17)), in line with Section 5.2. Encoders following the direct strategy seem to individually maximize affordance information to the detriment of discarding sensory information, while the ones following the indirect strategy behave oppositely.

Figure 3a shows how encoders that minimize the sensory distortion maximize their spatial entropy to account for as much variability about the sensory observations as possible. Thus, examining the spatial distribution of signals is necessary to account for the encoding behavior. All this is consistent with the efficient coding claim that neurons are tuned to the statistical properties of their sensory input by maximizing their information capacity (i.e., entropy) [44,45], which in this case is captured by their spatial entropy. As can be seen, in Figure 4, indirect encoders create a more spread encoding of the signals compared to the direct strategy. Note that the strategy found by the algorithm can sometimes have some degree of redundancy. This happens when information conveyed by more than one signal is collapsed onto the same dimension of the sensory observation. In the direct strategy shown in Figure 4, $I(O; \hat{O}) < 3$, since less than 8 dimensions of the sensory dimensions are being captured. Therefore, spatial entropy sheds some light on how the encoders have to map the inputs onto signals to convey the relevant information downstream.

Next, we explore whether the relation between sensory and affordance distortion is related to the synergistic nature of the affordance matrix. In Figure 3b, we see how the synergistic information is tightly related to sensory distortion. In particular, indirect encoders capture sensory information by increasing the synergistic information they carry about the affordance matrix, compared to the direct ones.

Note that in Figure 3a–d, the difference between each strategy is greater between encoders C (figures on the right). This is mainly due to the structure of the data. Encoders C are sensible to the vertical dimension of CIFAR-100 data, which is more likely to contain most of its pixel variability in fewer dimensions. For instance, an image of a standing person has its main vertical variance along the pixel columns where the person is standing. However, the horizontal dimension of that same image contains variability in a wider range of pixel rows. A direct strategy will use most of its information capacity to capture high-density regions of affordance-related information, at the expense of missing sensory-related information, which leads to an encoding that is highly penalized in synergistic contexts.

In addition, we also computed the p-values to evaluate the statistical significance of the results shown in each of the subplots in Figure 3. For example, we computed the p-value to evaluate the statistical significance of the synergistic strategy over the direct one regarding the "MSE Sensory Estimate" results. For all measures, the results of the indirect encoding–decoding pair were statistically significant compared to the direct behavior ($p \ll 0.05$).

These results suggest that the perception of synergistic multimodal affordances heavily relies on keeping track of sensory information, which is needed to capture as much synergistic information as possible. Direct strategies cannot capture synergistic interactions because most of the sensory information is destroyed by the encoders, leading to inefficiency. Thus, optimal multimodal perception of synergistic affordances cannot be direct; it requires a modicum of computation to properly combine different streams of information.

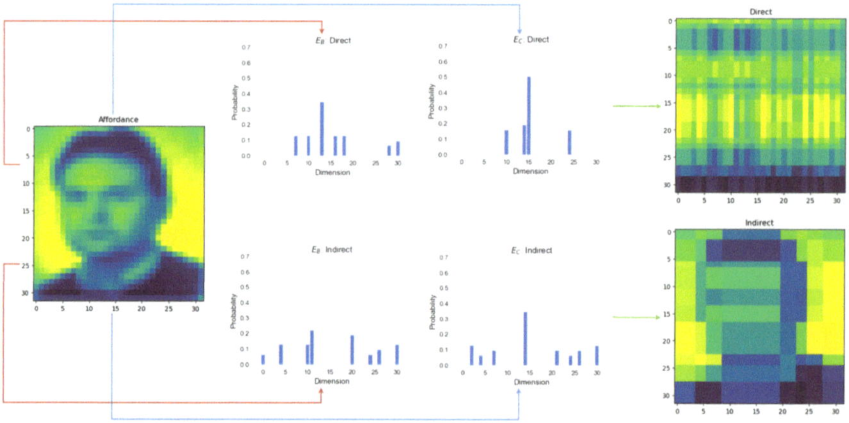

Figure 4. Encoded signals of a CIFAR-100 image used as an affordance landscape (left) and the resulting estimates (right) per each encoding–decoding strategy: direct (top) and indirect (bottom). As can be seen, the indirect encoded signals are more spread out across their possible states (32 dimensions) and have higher entropy (i.e., closer to a uniform distribution) than the direct encoding. Thus, indirect encodings exhibit a higher spatial entropy.

7. Discussion

7.1. Direct Perception and Synergistic Information in Nature

In this work, we have shown how direct perception of synergistic multimodal affordances results in an inefficient pickup of affordance-related information. One could retort that, even if somewhat inefficient, direct perception might still, as a matter of fact, be the prevalent perceptual mechanism underlying adaptive behavior and that, therefore, perception is not mediated by any computational process. While we agree that direct perception might be all there is in certain contexts, there is wide evidence of synergistic multimodal affordances in nature and cognition. For example, [46] provides some evidence that woodboring insects synergistically integrate multimodal cues during host selection. They suggest that these insects synergistically combine both visual and olfactory cues when making host-selection decisions. Another example of multimodal perception can be found in [47]. In their research, they study how rats categorize the orientation of grids (horizontal or vertical) when they rely on either visual, tactile, or visual-tactile information. They show that visual-tactile information is synergistically combined, which results in better performance when categorizing the orientation of the grids. According to our model and results presented above, to properly perceive these synergistic multimodal cues, some degree of inner processing or computation is needed: at least to that extent, perception is indirect.

7.2. Direct Perception and the Global Array

What about the possibility, rehearsed above, of directly perceiving the global array in its entirety? We have shown how the global array contains synergistic information that depends on energy arrays that have to be combined through some computations. Could there be a mechanism that allows the direct perception of the global array, without relying on energy-array specific information? At least in some important cases, neurophysiology prevents this—sensory surfaces are quite simply not in physical contact. This is all we are assuming in our model. For one prominent example, the organ of Corti connects to the cortex via the auditory nerve; and the retina connects to the cortex via the optical nerve. Any informational combination of these two sensory inputs has to happen *after* information is relayed through those two, plausibly not fully lossless, nerves. Of course, there is ample evidence that brains integrate information from different sensory modalities in order to guide behavior [48–51]; and, as an anonymous reviewer has reminded us, this combination can happen as soon as V1 (e.g., [52]). This suggests that cognitive systems generate a single percept by combining incoming signals from each modality in some downstream region [53]. This combination of, first, lossy transmission of sensory information and, then, downstream combination of this information, is what we aim at capturing with our model.

7.3. Real Multimodal Data to Study Information Interaction

In this study, we have not used real multimodal data, but interpreted CIFAR-100 images "multimodally", by considering vertical and horizontal informations independently. For subsequent work, we expect to run similar models on naturalistic, *bona-fide* multimodal data.

Author Contributions: Conceptualization, M.M. and M.d.L.V.; methodology, M.M. and M.d.L.V.; software, M.d.L.V. and M.M.; validation, M.d.L.V.; formal analysis, M.d.L.V. and M.M.; data curation, M.d.L.V.; writing—original draft preparation, M.d.L.V. and M.M.; writing—review and editing, M.M. and M.d.L.V.; visualization, M.d.L.V.; supervision, M.M.; funding acquisition, M.M. All authors have read and agreed to the published version of the manuscript.

Funding: Financial support was provided by the Spanish Ministry of Science and Innovation, through grants [PID2021-127046NA-I00] and [CEX2021-001169-M MCIN/AEI/10.13039/501100011033], and by the Generalitat de Catalunya, through grant [2021-SGR-00276]. M.d.L.V. gratefully acknowledges the financial support provided by VERSES AI.

Data Availability Statement: All of the code necessary to reproduce the figures and analyses in this paper can be found at https://github.com/MigueldeLlanza/SynergisticPerception (accessed on 3 May 2024).

Acknowledgments: We would like to thank Miguel Ángel Sebastián and audiences in Barcelona, Athens, and Geneva for their comments on earlier drafts.

Conflicts of Interest: The authors declare no conflicts of interest.

References

1. Akagi, M. Cognition as the Sensitive Management of an Agent's Behavior. *Philos. Psychol.* **2022**, *35*, 718–741. [CrossRef]
2. Barack, D.L.; Krakauer, J.W. Two Views on the Cognitive Brain. *Nat. Rev. Neurosci.* **2021**, *22*, 359–371. [CrossRef]
3. Anderson, J.R. *The Adaptive Character of Thought*; Lawrence Erlbaum Associates, Publishers: Hillsdale, NJ, USA, 1990.

4. Favela, L.H.; Machery, E. Investigating the Concept of Representation in the Neural and Psychological Sciences. *Front. Psychol.* **2023**, *14*, 1165622.
5. Fodor, J.A. *The Language of Thought*, 1st ed.; Harvard University Press: Cambridge, MA, USA, 1980.
6. Millikan, R.G. *Language, Thought and Other Biological Categories;* The MIT Press: Cambridge, MA, USA, 1984.
7. Shea, N. *Representation in Cognitive Science;* Oxford University Press: Oxford, UK, 2018.
8. Quilty-Dunn, J.; Porot, N.; Mandelbaum, E. The Best Game in Town: The Reemergence of the Language-of-Thought Hypothesis across the Cognitive Sciences. *Behav. Brain Sci.* **2023**, *46*, e261. [CrossRef]
9. Chemero, A. *Radical Embodied Cognitive Science;* MIT Press: Cambridge, MA, USA, 2011.
10. Wilson, A.D.; Golonka, S. Embodied Cognition Is Not What You Think It Is. *Front. Psychol.* **2013**, *4*, 58. [CrossRef]
11. Newen, A.; Bruin, L.D.; Gallagher, S. (Eds.) *The Oxford Handbook of 4E Cognition;* Oxford Library of Psychology, Oxford University Press: Oxford, UK, 2018.
12. Fajen, B.R.; Riley, M.A.; Turvey, M.T. Information, Affordances, and the Control of Action in Sport. *Int. J. Sport Psychol.* **2008**, *40*, 79–107.
13. Beer, R.D.; Williams, P.L. Information Processing and Dynamics in Minimally Cognitive Agents. *Cogn. Sci.* **2015**, *39*, 1–38. [CrossRef]
14. Stephen, D.G.; Boncoddo, R.A.; Magnuson, J.S.; Dixon, J.A. The Dynamics of Insight: Mathematical Discovery as a Phase Transition. *Mem. Cogn.* **2009**, *37*, 1132–1149. [CrossRef]
15. Gibson, J.J. *The Ecological Approach to Visual Perception: Classic Edition;* Psychology Press: London, UK, 2014.
16. Turvey, M.T.; Shaw, R.E.; Reed, E.S.; Mace, W.M. Ecological Laws of Perceiving and Acting: In Reply to Fodor and Pylyshyn (1981). *Cognition* **1981**, *9*, 237–304. [PubMed]
17. Heras-Escribano, M. *The Philosophy of Affordances;* Springer International Publishing: Berlin, Germany, 2019. [CrossRef]
18. Stoffregen, T.A.; Bardy, B.G. On Specification and the Senses. *Behav. Brain Sci.* **2001**, *24*, 195–213. [CrossRef]
19. Bruineberg, J.; Chemero, A.; Rietveld, E. General ecological information supports engagement with affordances for 'higher'cognition. *Synthese* **2019**, *196*, 5231–5251. [PubMed]
20. Mace, W.M. JJ Gibson's Ecological Theory of Information Pickup: Cognition from the Ground Up. In *Approaches to Cognition: Contrasts and Controversies;* Knapp, T.J., Robertson, L.C., Eds.; Lawrence Erlbaum Associates, Publishers: Hillsdale, NJ, USA, 1986; pp. 137–157.
21. Shaw, R.; Turvey, M.T.; Mace, W.M. Ecological Psychology: The Consequence of a Commitment to Realism. In *Cognition and the Symbolic Processes;* Weimer, W., Palermo, D., Eds.; Lawrence Erlbaum Associates, Inc.: Hillsdale, NJ, USA, 1982; Volume 2, pp. 159–226.
22. Gibson, J. The Senses Considered as Perceptual Systems. In *The Senses Considered as Perceptual Systems;* Houghton Mifflin: Boston, MA, USA, 1966.
23. Goodfellow, I.; Bengio, Y.; Courville, A. *Deep Learning;* MIT Press: Cambridge, MA, USA, 2016.
24. Ehrlich, D.A.; Schneider, A.C.; Priesemann, V.; Wibral, M.; Makkeh, A. A Measure of the Complexity of Neural Representations Based on Partial Information Decomposition. *arXiv* **2023**, arXiv:2209.10438.
25. Shannon, C.E. A Mathematical Theory of Communication. *Bell Syst. Tech. J.* **1948**, *27*, 379–423.
26. Williams, P.L.; Beer, R.D. Nonnegative decomposition of multivariate information. *arXiv* **2010**, arXiv:1004.2515.
27. Griffith, V.; Koch, C. Quantifying Synergistic Mutual Information. In *Guided Self-Organization: Inception;* Prokopenko, M., Ed.; Emergence, Complexity and Computation; Springer: Berlin/Heidelberg, Germany, 2014; pp. 159–190. [CrossRef]
28. Bertschinger, N.; Rauh, J.; Olbrich, E.; Jost, J.; Ay, N. Quantifying Unique Information. *Entropy* **2014**, *16*, 2161–2183. [CrossRef]
29. Jaynes, E.T. On the rationale of maximum-entropy methods. *Proc. IEEE* **1982**, *70*, 939–952.
30. Chechik, G.; Globerson, A.; Anderson, M.; Young, E.; Nelken, I.; Tishby, N. Group redundancy measures reveal redundancy reduction in the auditory pathway. In *Advances in Neural Information Processing Systems;* NIPS: Cambridge, MA, USA, 2001; Volume 14.
31. McGill, W. Multivariate Information Transmission. *Trans. IRE Prof. Group Inf. Theory* **1954**, *4*, 93–111. [CrossRef]
32. Rosas, F.E. Quantifying High-Order Interdependencies via Multivariate Extensions of the Mutual Information. *Phys. Rev. E* **2019**, *100*, 032305. [CrossRef] [PubMed]
33. Varley, T.F.; Pope, M.; Faskowitz, J.; Sporns, O. Multivariate Information Theory Uncovers Synergistic Subsystems of the Human Cerebral Cortex. *Commun. Biol.* **2023**, *6*, 1–12. [CrossRef]
34. Sims, C.R. Rate–Distortion Theory and Human Perception. *Cognition* **2016**, *152*, 181–198.
35. Genewein, T.; Leibfried, F.; Grau-Moya, J.; Braun, D.A. Bounded rationality, abstraction, and hierarchical decision-making: An information-theoretic optimality principle. *Front. Robot. AI* **2015**, *2*, 27.
36. Lieder, F.; Griffiths, T.L. Resource-rational analysis: Understanding human cognition as the optimal use of limited computational resources. *Behav. Brain Sci.* **2020**, *43*, e1.
37. Zhou, D.; Lynn, C.W.; Cui, Z.; Ciric, R.; Baum, G.L.; Moore, T.M.; Roalf, D.R.; Detre, J.A.; Gur, R.C.; Gur, R.E.; et al. Efficient coding in the economics of human brain connectomics. *Netw. Neurosci.* **2022**, *6*, 234–274.
38. Shannon, C.E. Coding theorems for a discrete source with a fidelity criterion. *IRE Nat. Conv. Rec.* **1959**, *4*, 1.
39. Cover, T.M.; Thomas, J.A. *Elements of Information Theory;* Wiley: New York, NY, USA, 2006.

40. Claramunt, C. A spatial form of diversity. In Proceedings of the Spatial Information Theory: International Conference, COSIT 2005, Ellicottville, NY, USA, 14–18 September 2005; Proceedings 7; Springer: Berlin, Germany, 2005; pp. 218–231.
41. James, R.G.; Ellison, C.J.; Crutchfield, J.P. dit: A Python package for discrete information theory. *J. Open Source Softw.* **2018**, *3*, 738. [CrossRef]
42. Altieri, L.; Cocchi, D.; Roli, G. Spatentropy: Spatial entropy measures in r. *arXiv* **2018**, arXiv:1804.05521.
43. Krizhevsky, A.; Hinton, G. *Learning Multiple Layers of Features from Tiny Images*; University of Toronto: Toronto, ON, Canada, 2009.
44. Laughlin, S. A Simple Coding Procedure Enhances a Neuron's Information Capacity. *Zeitschrift für Naturforschung C* **1981**, *36*, 910–912. [CrossRef]
45. Barlow, H.B. *Possible Principles Underlying the Transformation of Sensory Messages*; MIT Press: Cambridge, MA, USA, 1961; Volume 1, pp. 217–234.
46. Campbell, S.A.; Borden, J.H. Additive and synergistic integration of multimodal cues of both hosts and non-hosts during host selection by woodboring insects. *Oikos* **2009**, *118*, 553–563.
47. Nikbakht, N.; Tafreshiha, A.; Zoccolan, D.; Diamond, M.E. Supralinear and supramodal integration of visual and tactile signals in rats: Psychophysics and neuronal mechanisms. *Neuron* **2018**, *97*, 626–639. [PubMed]
48. Noppeney, U. Perceptual inference, learning, and attention in a multisensory world. *Annu. Rev. Neurosci.* **2021**, *44*, 449–473.
49. Chen, Y.; Spence, C. Assessing the role of the 'unity assumption' on multisensory integration: A review. *Front. Psychol.* **2017**, *8*, 445.
50. Choi, I.; Lee, J.Y.; Lee, S.H. Bottom-up and top-down modulation of multisensory integration. *Curr. Opin. Neurobiol.* **2018**, *52*, 115–122. [PubMed]
51. Stein, B.E.; Stanford, T.R. Multisensory integration: Current issues from the perspective of the single neuron. *Nat. Rev. Neurosci.* **2008**, *9*, 255–266. [PubMed]
52. Watkins, S.; Shams, L.; Tanaka, S.; Haynes, J.D.; Rees, G. Sound Alters Activity in Human V1 in Association with Illusory Visual Perception. *NeuroImage* **2006**, *31*, 1247–1256. [CrossRef]
53. Ernst, M.O.; Bülthoff, H.H. Merging the senses into a robust percept. *Trends Cogn. Sci.* **2004**, *8*, 162–169.

Article

Synergy as the Failure of Distributivity

Ivan Sevostianov * and Ofer Feinerman

Department of Physics of Complex Systems, Weizmann Institute of Science, Rehovot 7610001, Israel; ofer.feinerman@weizmann.ac.il
* Correspondence: ivan.sevostianov@weizmann.ac.il

Abstract: The concept of emergence, or synergy in its simplest form, is widely used but lacks a rigorous definition. Our work connects information and set theory to uncover the mathematical nature of synergy as the failure of distributivity. For the trivial case of discrete random variables, we explore whether and how it is possible to get more information out of lesser parts. The approach is inspired by the role of set theory as the fundamental description of part–whole relations. If taken unaltered, synergistic behavior is forbidden by the set-theoretic axioms. However, random variables are not a perfect analogy of sets: we formalize the distinction, highlighting a single broken axiom—union/intersection distributivity. Nevertheless, it remains possible to describe information using Venn-type diagrams. The proposed multivariate theory resolves the persistent self-contradiction of partial information decomposition and reinstates it as a primary route toward a rigorous definition of emergence. Our results suggest that non-distributive variants of set theory may be used to describe emergent physical systems.

Keywords: emergence; information diagrams; decomposition

Citation: Sevostianov, I.; Feinerman, O. Synergy as the Failure of Distributivity. *Entropy* **2024**, *26*, 916. https://doi.org/10.3390/e26110916

Academic Editor: Daniel Chicharro

Received: 15 September 2024
Revised: 16 October 2024
Accepted: 26 October 2024
Published: 28 October 2024

Copyright: © 2024 by the authors. Licensee MDPI, Basel, Switzerland. This article is an open access article distributed under the terms and conditions of the Creative Commons Attribution (CC BY) license (https://creativecommons.org/licenses/by/4.0/).

1. Introduction

Reductionism is a standard scientific approach in which a system is studied by breaking it into smaller parts. However, some of the most interesting phenomena in physics and biology appear to resist such disentanglement. In these cases, complexity emerges from intricate interactions between many predominantly simple components [1]. Such *synergic* systems are typically described as "a whole that is greater than the sum of its parts". To pour quantitative meaning into this equation-like definition, it is natural to borrow tools from the mathematical theory that describes part–whole relationships, namely set theory. Unfortunately, for finite sets, a simple Venn diagram suffices to demonstrate that the size of the whole ($A \cup B$) can never exceed the sum of the sizes of its parts (A and B):

$$|A \cup B| = |A| + |B| - |A \cap B| \leq |A| + |B| \qquad (1)$$

In fact, the trivial interaction, $A \cap B$, between the two parts of the system decreases the size of the whole rather than increasing it.

To allow for more intricate interactions, one can turn to the realm of random variables. It is well known that measuring the outcome of two random variables can provide more information than the sum of what is obtained when measuring each separately. Moreover, the textbook description of the interactions between random variables often involves set-theoretical-like Venn diagrams [2]. These two facts lead to the intriguing possibility that random variables may lend themselves to a mathematical description of non-trivial whole–part relationships.

Take two discrete variables W and Z: the information W contains about Z is determined by the mutual information function $I(W;Z)$ [3]. Cases for which W can be presented as a joint random variable $W = (X,Y)$ allow us to compare the whole against its parts:

$$I((X,Y);Z) \mathrel{\substack{\leq \\ = \\ \geq}} I(X;Z) + I(Y;Z) \qquad (2)$$

In other words, looking at both system parts together can convey either more or less information than their added values. Therefore, and in contrast to Equation (1), this formalism can be used to describe synergy.

In their seminal paper [4], Williams and Beer proposed the framework of *partial information decomposition* as a way of assessing the underlying structure of a two discrete random variable system and quantifying the amount of synergy between its parts. They suggested that, much like a set of elements, each variable can be decomposed into separate information "subsets". These *information atoms* are assumed to have non-negative size and represent the information that is shared between two variables (R), uniquely present in only one of them (U_X, U_Y):

$$\begin{aligned} &I(X;Z) = R + U_X, \\ &I(Y;Z) = R + U_Y, \\ &I((X,Y);Z) = R + U_X + U_Y + S, \\ &R, U_X, U_Y, S \geq 0 \end{aligned} \tag{3}$$

See Figure 1 for clarification. An additional synergy term (S) was artificially introduced to provide a simple mechanism that allows the whole to be greater than the sum of its parts:

$$I((X,Y);Z) - I(X;Z) - I(Y;Z) = S - R > 0 \text{ iff } S > R \tag{4}$$

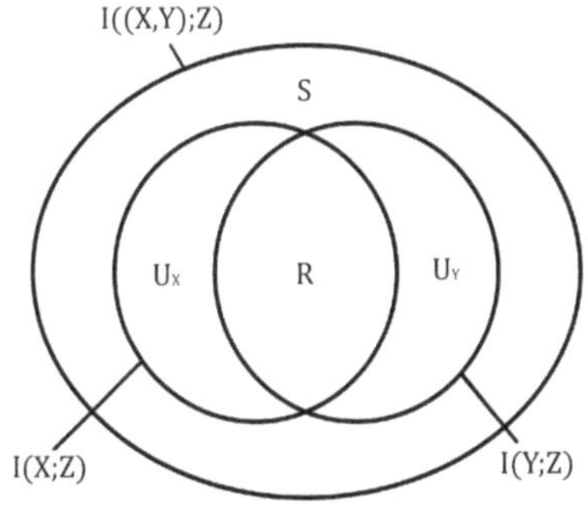

Figure 1. This diagram illustrates how information in two variables X, Y about a third variable Z can be decomposed into different information atoms. The amount of such information in X, Y and joint variable (X, Y) is measured using the mutual information $I(X;Z), I(Y;Z)$, and $I((X,Y);Z)$ correspondingly. Redundant information R is information that is shared between X and Y such that knowing one of them suffices in deducing this information about Z. Unique information U_X is found only in X, U_Y—only in Y. The synergistic information S that X and Y hold about Z is only contained in the joint variable, but not individual sources on their own.

A series of papers [5–7] focused on calculating these atoms' sizes by fixing the single remaining degree of freedom in Equation (3). No consensus has yet been reached regarding a single physical solution. Meanwhile, the field of applications is getting wider [8,9]. Recent works extend the theory to continuous variables [10,11], introduce causality [12,13], and consider quantum information [14].

Unfortunately, partial information decomposition has a significant drawback that puts the whole approach into question: no extension beyond two variables is possible without a fundamental self-contradiction [15]. Some authors attempted to resolve this by abandoning the basic properties required of information atoms, including their non-negativity [16,17].

In what follows, we reconsider the foundations of partial information decomposition and pinpoint the source of its long-standing self-contradictions. To do this, we follow H. K. Ting [18] to establish a rigorous relation between information and set theories and highlight a fundamental distinction between them: random variables, unlike sets, do not adhere to the union/intersection distributivity axiom [19]. This leads us to study a distributivity-free variant of set theory as a possible self-consistent theory of information atoms. Within this framework, we demonstrate that the presence of synergistic properties is a direct consequence of the broken axiom. In the case of $N = 3$ random variables, we show that the amount of synergistic information precisely coincides with the extent to which distributivity is breached. The acquired understanding allows us to resolve the contradictions and suggest a coherent multivariate theory, which may provide the foundations for quantifying emergence in large systems.

2. Set-Theoretic Approach to Information

In this section, we formalize the distinction between finite sets and discrete random variables. Clearly, it is linked to the synergistic behavior of the latter. We will first focus on a special illustrative example: the XOR gate. This system contains neither redundant nor unique information, which will emphasize the peculiar properties of synergy. A more general discussion, including arbitrary random variables, will be presented in the next section.

2.1. Basic Random Variable Operations

Some set-theoretic operations have straightforward extensions to random variables [18,20,21]. The first of these relies on the similarity between Equations (1) and (2) and identifies taking the joint variable with the union operator ($\cup$). One can now go on to define random variable inclusion as:

$$X \subseteq Y \Leftrightarrow \exists Z : X \cup Z = Y \tag{5}$$

which is, actually, equivalent to X being a deterministic function of Y.

The inclusion–exclusion formula ([22], Chapter 3.1) applied to two random variables reveals mutual information as the size of the intersection between two random variables:

$$H(X \cup Y) = H(X) + H(Y) - I(X;Y), \tag{6}$$

where Shannon entropy H is regarded as a measure on the random variable space. Indeed, it complies with many properties required of a mathematical measure ([23], Chapter 1.4): non-negativity, monotonicity, and subadditivity. Furthermore, entropy is zero only for deterministic variables, which play the role of an empty set (Appendix A, Lemma A1):

$$\begin{aligned} &H(X) \geq 0, \\ &X \subseteq Y \Rightarrow H(X) \leq H(Y), \\ &H\left(\bigcup_{i=1}^{N} X_i\right) \leq \sum_{i=1}^{N} H(X_i), \\ &H(X) = 0 \Leftrightarrow X = \varnothing \end{aligned} \tag{7}$$

A rigorous definition of intersection ($\cap$) needs to comply with the inclusion order (5) $X \cap Y \subseteq X, X \cap Y \subseteq Y$, in addition to the size constraint. Unfortunately, a random variable satisfying both conditions does not always exist [24]. Nonetheless, a physically sensible intersection may be inferred in several cases:

$$\begin{aligned} &H(X \cup Y) = H(X) + H(Y) \Leftrightarrow X \cap Y = \varnothing, \\ &X \subseteq Y \Leftrightarrow H(X) = I(X;Y) \Leftrightarrow X \cap Y = X \end{aligned} \tag{8}$$

These simple parallels between information theory and set theory are enough to study information decomposition in a random variable XOR gate.

2.2. The Simplest Synergic System: XOR Gate

Consider three pairwise independent fair coins O_1, O_2, O_3 with an additionally imposed higher order interaction–parity rule $O_3 = O_1 \oplus O_2$. It fixes the value of the third variable to be 0 whenever the values of O_1 and O_2 coincide, and 1 otherwise.

Probability	O_1	O_2	O_3
1/4	0	0	0
0	0	0	1
0	0	1	0
1/4	0	1	1
0	1	0	0
1/4	1	0	1
1/4	1	1	0
0	1	1	1

One can easily calculate the amount of information O_1, O_2 and (O_1, O_2) convey about O_3. The comparison of these contributions shows that the system is indeed synergic:

$$\begin{aligned}
&I(O_1; O_3) = 0\,\text{bit},\\
&I(O_2; O_3) = 0\,\text{bit},\\
&I((O_1, O_2); O_3) = 1\,\text{bit},\\
&I((O_1, O_2); O_3) > I(O_1; O_3) + I(O_2; O_3)
\end{aligned} \tag{9}$$

Moreover, by substituting the above result into the decomposition Equation (3), we find that the system contains only a single non-zero information atom $S = 1$ bit. This allows us to study synergy separately from any other contributions on this example.

2.3. Subdistributivity

When taking a closer look at the XOR gate, our set-theoretic intuition for random variables breaks down even further. The pairwise independence dictates $O_2 \cap O_3 = O_1 \cap O_3 = \varnothing$, while the parity rule makes O_3 a deterministic function of the joint variable (O_1, O_2):

$$O_3 \subseteq (O_1 \cup O_2) \Rightarrow (O_1 \cup O_2) \cap O_3 = O_3 \tag{10}$$

A simple conclusion from these facts is that the XOR-gate variables do not comply with the set-theoretic axiom of distributivity:

$$(O_1 \cup O_2) \cap O_3 = O_3 \neq \varnothing = (O_1 \cap O_3) \cup (O_2 \cap O_3) \tag{11}$$

Nevertheless, it can be shown that a weaker relation of *subdistributivity* holds for any three random variables (Appendix A, Lemma A2):

$$(X \cup Y) \cap Z \supset (X \cap Z) \cup (Y \cap Z) \tag{12}$$

Even though it is evident that random variables are quite different from sets, we argue that some of the logic behind partial information decomposition may be recovered by extending set-theoretic notions, such as the inclusion–exclusion principle and Venn diagrams, to non-distributive systems.

2.4. Inclusion–Exclusion Formulas

The inclusion–exclusion formula for the XOR gate can be obtained by repeatedly applying the two-variable Equation (6) and using that $I(X; Y) = H(X \cap Y)$ when the intersection exists:

$$\begin{aligned} &H(O_1 \cup O_2 \cup O_3) = \\ &= H(O_1 \cup O_2) + H(O_3) - H((O_1 \cup O_2) \cap O_3) = \\ &= H(O_1) + H(O_2) + H(O_3) - H((O_1 \cup O_2) \cap O_3) \end{aligned} \tag{13}$$

It disagrees with the analogous set-theoretic formula (for non-intersecting sets) only in the last term, which is non-zero precisely due to the subdistributivity. Note that while the rest of the terms are symmetric with respect to the permutation of indices, expression $(O_1 \cup O_2) \cap O_3$ is not as it explicitly depends on the order of derivation. This essentially leads to three different inclusion–exclusion formulas. Nonetheless, the size of the distributivity-breaking term remains invariant:

$$H((O_1 \cup O_2) \cap O_3) = H((O_1 \cup O_3) \cap O_2) = H((O_2 \cup O_3) \cap O_1) \tag{14}$$

2.5. Construction of Venn-Type Diagram for XOR Gate

The non-uniqueness of inclusion–exclusion formulas complicates the construction of Venn diagrams. A way of tackling this as well as some further intuition can be traced via our XOR gate example.

In set theory, Venn diagrams act as graphical representations of the inclusion–exclusion principle ([22], Chapter 3.1). The inclusion–exclusion formula computes the size of union as a sum of all possible intersections between the participating sets. For correct bookkeeping, this is achieved with alternating signs that account for the *covering number*—the number of times each intersection is counted as a part of some set. In classical set theory, the covering number of an intersection is trivially the number of sets which are being intersected. However, (13) includes the distributivity-breaking term, which is absent from this classical theory and whose covering number is not evident. It appears with a negative sign which signifies an even-times covered region. In this three variable system, the only even alternative is a 2-covered region. From another perspective, in each of the three possible formulas O_k is covered once by itself and one more time by the union $O_i \cup O_j$ (though not by O_i or O_j individually). As for the size of this region, independent of k, it measures at 1 bit of information. Denoting this area as Π_s, we have:

$$\Pi_s[2] = H((O_i \cup O_j) \cap O_k) = H(O_k) = 1 \text{ bit}, \tag{15}$$

where the covering number is indicated in the brackets $[]$. To find the rest of our diagram's regions, we borrow two properties of set-theoretic diagrams.

First of all, in a system of N arbitrary random variables $X_1, \dots X_N$, the total entropy of the system is equal to the sum of all diagram regions $\Pi_i[c_i]$:

$$H(X_1, \dots X_N) = \sum_i \Pi_i[c_i] \tag{16}$$

Second, the sum of individual variables' entropies is equal to the sum of region sizes times their corresponding covering numbers c_i:

$$H(X_1) + H(X_2) + \dots + H(X_N) = \sum_i c_i \Pi_i[c_i] \tag{17}$$

These properties may be viewed as the *information conservation law*: adding new sources should either introduce new information or increase the covering of existing regions.

Let us assume that in addition to Π_s the diagram of the XOR gate contains several more regions $\Pi_{j \neq s}$. To calculate their sizes and coverings we apply (16) and (17):

$$\sum_{j \neq s} (c_j - 1)\Pi_j[c_j] = 0 \text{ bit} \tag{18}$$

We use the fact that information is non-negative and discard meaningless empty regions. The above equation then allows for a single 1-bit region, which is covered once:

$$\Pi_g[1] = 1 \text{ bit} \tag{19}$$

To respect the physical meaning behind the diagram regions as pieces of information, we demand the structure of the diagram to be well-defined. In other words, despite the existence of three different versions of inclusion–exclusion formula (13), they are all assumed to describe the *same* system. Indeed, our result remains invariant with respect to index permutations in terms of region sizes and covering numbers.

In regard to the shape of the Venn diagram, this assumption dictates along with (15) that region Π_s corresponds to all variables at the same time:

$$\Pi_s = H(O_1) = H(O_2) = H(O_3) \tag{20}$$

One can think of Π_s as a 2-covered triple intersection between O_1, O_2, and O_3. This is a drastic divergence from classical set theory, where an intersection between n sets is covered exactly n times. As we shall see, without distributivity, n variables can have multiple intersection regions with different covering numbers $1 \leq c \leq n$.

Moving on to the second region in this system: Π_g appears as a leftover when taking the difference between the whole system and Π_s and by set-theoretic intuition, it does not intersect with O_k for any k. As such, it is not a part of any single variable.

Finally, we combine all findings into a system of equations, which generates the Venn-type diagram of the information distribution inside the XOR gate (Figure 2):

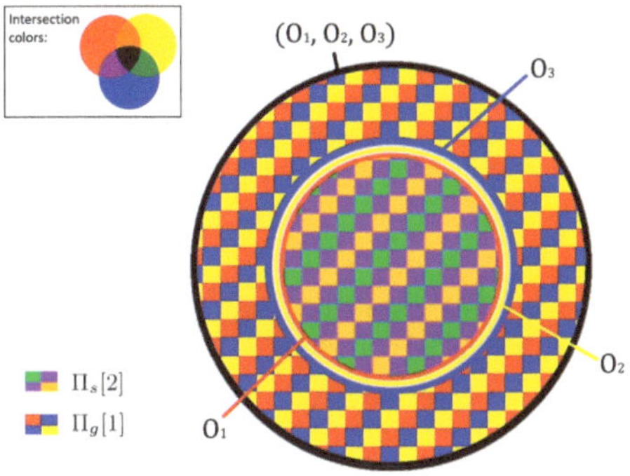

Figure 2. A Venn-type diagram for the XOR gate. Each variable is represented by a primary color circle (red, yellow, blue) while the outer circle outlines the whole system. Of the total 2 bits of the XOR gate, one is covered two times and is represented by the inner disk. Since it is covered twice, this area is colored by pairwise color-blends (orange, purple, and green). Since it is covered by three variables, it includes patches of all three possible blends. A critical difference between this diagram and a set-theoretic one is that even though the three variables have no pairwise intersections, the inner disk representing the mutual content of all three variables is non-empty. The remaining 1 bit is covered once and resides only inside the joint variable. Since this area is covered once, it is colored by primary colors. Patches of all three colors are used since this area does not belong to any single variable.

$$\begin{aligned}
&H(O_1) = \Pi_s,\\
&H(O_2) = \Pi_s,\\
&H(O_3) = \Pi_s,\\
&H(O_1 \cup O_2) = \Pi_s + \Pi_g,\\
&H(O_2 \cup O_3) = \Pi_s + \Pi_g,\\
&H(O_1 \cup O_3) = \Pi_s + \Pi_g,\\
&H(O_1 \cup O_2 \cup O_3) = \Pi_s + \Pi_g
\end{aligned} \tag{21}$$

In usual Venn diagrams, intersections represent correlations between different parts. Similarly, in the XOR gate the higher-order parity interaction added on top of the non-correlated variables is responsible for the appearance of a 2-covered triple intersection.

2.6. Synergy as an Information Atom

We can compare our set-theory-inspired results against the expectations of the partial information decomposition. Namely, Equations (3) state that the information O_1 and O_2 carry about O_3 can be described by the atoms $R = U_1 = U_2 = 0$ bit, $S = 1$ bit. The left side of each line in (3) may be rewritten by definition as an intersection of random variables:

$$\begin{aligned} I(X;Z) &= H(X \cap Z), \\ I(Y;Z) &= H(Y \cap Z), \\ I((X,Y);Z) &= H((X \cup Y) \cap Z) \end{aligned} \tag{22}$$

For the XOR gate, the former two are empty, while the last line links the original definition of synergistic information to the non-set-theoretic term of the inclusion–exclusion Formula (13) and the peculiar region of the corresponding diagram:

$$S = I((O_1, O_2); O_3) = H((O_1 \cup O_2) \cap O_3) = \Pi_s \tag{23}$$

Curiously, synergistic behavior of mutual information does not contradict the sub-additivity of entropy. The synergistic information piece S is not new to the system and is always contained in the variables' full entropy.

The nature of *ghost atom* $G = \Pi_g$ is deeply connected to this outcome, even though it does not explicitly participate in the decomposition. Consider the individual contributions by each of the sources O_1, O_2:

$$I(O_{i=1,2}; O_3) = H(O_i) + H(O_3) - H(O_i \cup O_3) \tag{24}$$

Using (21), we can rewrite this in terms of information atoms:

$$I(O_i; O_3) = \Pi_s + \Pi_s - (\Pi_s + \Pi_g) = S - G = 0 \tag{25}$$

The equality between the synergistic and ghost atoms ensures that the former is exactly canceled from the individual contribution by each source. Synergistic information is, of course, still present in the "whole" (23). This circumstance is responsible for creating the illusion of synergy appearing out of nowhere when sources are combined.

3. General Trivariate Decomposition

The XOR gate example studied above is a degenerate example with a sole synergistic information atom. We will now expand our description into a system with non-synergistic components with the aim to characterize any three variables using information atoms.

3.1. Extended Random Variable Space

The lack of a proper description for information intersections severely limits our ability to decompose the information content of more general random variable systems. Our solution for this issue is inspired by an elegant duality between set theory and information quantities found by H. K. Ting in [18] and further elaborated in [21]. It simply extends the space of random variables to include all elements produced by operations $\cup, \cap, \setminus$ (2), (8) and (28). Entropy is extended as a (non-negative) measure $\hat{H}$ such that:

$$\begin{aligned} &\hat{H}(X) = 0 \Leftrightarrow X = \varnothing, \\ &X \cap Y = \varnothing \Leftrightarrow \hat{H}(X \cup Y) = \hat{H}(X) + \hat{H}(Y) \end{aligned} \tag{26}$$

To approach the problem of characterizing information atoms in the trivariate case, we derive the corresponding inclusion–exclusion formula. As stated previously, the bivariate version (6) holds without alterations (Appendix A, Lemma A3). Now, in contrast, we get a distributivity-breaking difference term, which, to make matters even worse, depends on the order of derivation (Appendix A, Theorem A1). One possible variant of this formula is portrayed in Figure 3:

$$\begin{aligned}
&\hat{H}(X_1 \cup X_2 \cup X_3) = \\
&= \hat{H}(X_1) + \hat{H}(X_2) + \hat{H}(X_3) - \\
&- \hat{H}(X_1 \cap X_2) - \hat{H}(X_1 \cap X_3) - \hat{H}(X_2 \cap X_3) + \\
&+ \hat{H}(X_1 \cap X_2 \cap X_3) - \Delta\hat{H},
\end{aligned} \tag{27}$$

where $\Delta\hat{H} = \hat{H}(((X_{\sigma(1)} \cup X_{\sigma(2)}) \cap X_{\sigma(3)}) \backslash ((X_{\sigma(1)} \cap X_{\sigma(3)}) \cup (X_{\sigma(2)} \cap X_{\sigma(3)})))$ for any permutation of indices σ. The difference is defined as:

$$D = X \backslash Y \Leftrightarrow D \cap Y = \emptyset, D \cup (X \cap Y) = X \tag{28}$$

In general, due to subdistributivity the difference may not be unique (Appendix A, (A20)). Its size, on the other hand, is fixed as $\hat{H}(X \backslash Y) = \hat{H}(X) - \hat{H}(X \cap Y)$.

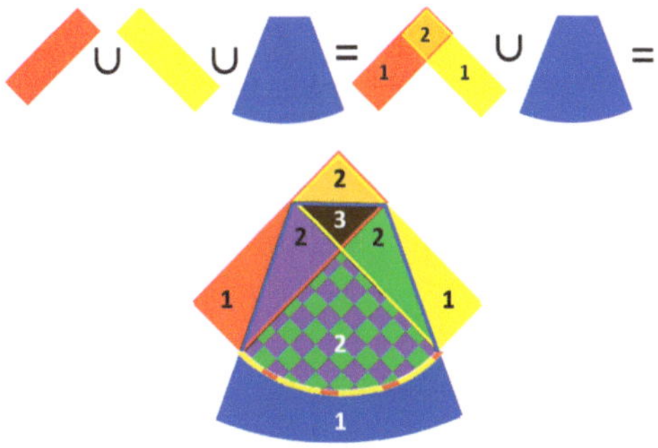

Figure 3. A single realization of the inclusion–exclusion principle for three variables. The new region, corresponding to the distributivity-breaking difference is represented via a checkered pattern. Covering numbers are written for each sector and highlighted by the colors. This is not a full Venn-type diagram that defines the information atoms, and hence, its structure is clearly not invariant with respect to variable permutations.

3.2. Set-Theoretic Solution

Before going to arbitrary variables, consider a system where distributivity axiom holds. Under such condition the setup becomes effectively equivalent to set theory. A trivariate system can, therefore, be illustrated by the same Venn diagram as that of three sets:

$$\begin{aligned}
&H(X_1) = \Pi_{\{1\}} + \Pi_{\{1\}\{2\}} + \Pi_{\{1\}\{3\}} + \Pi_{\{1\}\{2\}\{3\}}, \\
&H(X_2) = \Pi_{\{2\}} + \Pi_{\{1\}\{2\}} + \Pi_{\{2\}\{3\}} + \Pi_{\{1\}\{2\}\{3\}}, \\
&H(X_3) = \Pi_{\{3\}} + \Pi_{\{1\}\{3\}} + \Pi_{\{2\}\{3\}} + \Pi_{\{1\}\{2\}\{3\}}, \\
&H(X_1, X_2) = \Pi_{\{1\}} + \Pi_{\{2\}} + \Pi_{\{1\}\{2\}} + \Pi_{\{1\}\{3\}} + \Pi_{\{2\}\{3\}} + \Pi_{\{1\}\{2\}\{3\}}, \\
&H(X_1, X_3) = \Pi_{\{1\}} + \Pi_{\{3\}} + \Pi_{\{1\}\{2\}} + \Pi_{\{1\}\{3\}} + \Pi_{\{2\}\{3\}} + \Pi_{\{1\}\{2\}\{3\}}, \\
&H(X_2, X_3) = \Pi_{\{2\}} + \Pi_{\{3\}} + \Pi_{\{1\}\{2\}} + \Pi_{\{1\}\{3\}} + \Pi_{\{2\}\{3\}} + \Pi_{\{1\}\{2\}\{3\}}, \\
&H(X_1, X_2, X_3) = \\
&= \Pi_{\{1\}} + \Pi_{\{2\}} + \Pi_{\{3\}} + \Pi_{\{1\}\{2\}} + \Pi_{\{1\}\{3\}} + \Pi_{\{2\}\{3\}} + \Pi_{\{1\}\{2\}\{3\}}
\end{aligned} \tag{29}$$

By calculating the sizes of atoms, we derive (Appendix B, (A29)) the criterion for their non-negativity: the whole must be less or equal to the sum of the parts:

$$I(X_1, X_2; X_3) - I(X_1; X_3) - I(X_2; X_3) \leq 0 \tag{30}$$

3.3. Main Result: Arbitrary Trivariate System

At this point, we have studied two opposite cases: a completely synergic system (XOR gate) and one without any synergy (set-theoretic solution). To describe three arbitrary variables, any general decomposition must be able to replicate both of them. It turns out that a combination of the already known atoms (Figure 4) suffices in providing a non-negative decomposition (presented in detail in Appendix B (A47); for the proof see Lemma A6):

$$\begin{aligned} H(X_i) &= \Pi_s + \sum_{\text{set-theor. atoms}} \Pi, \\ H(X_i, X_{j\neq i}) &= \Pi_s + \Pi_g + \sum_{\text{s.t. atoms}} \Pi, \\ H(X_1, X_2, X_3) &= \Pi_s + \Pi_g + \sum_{\text{s.t. atoms}} \Pi, \\ \Pi_s &= \Pi_g \end{aligned} \tag{31}$$

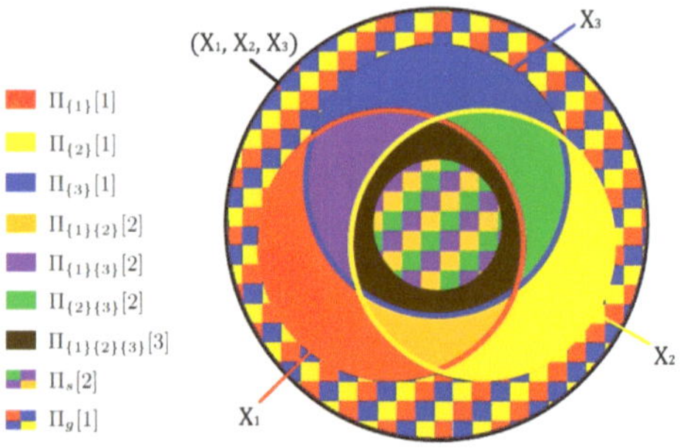

Figure 4. A graphical illustration for the general solution of the trivariate problem. Compared to the Venn diagram for three sets, two new regions here are the 2-covered part of triple intersection Π_s (synergistic atom) and a ghost atom Π_g, which is not a part of any single initial variable. Similarly to Figure 3, colors indicate the coverings: three primary colors (red, yellow, blue, or their checkered combination) correspond to 1-covered atoms, the overlay of any two colors (orange, purple, green or their checkered combination) is 2-covered, and the overlay of all three colors (brown) is 3-covered.

This is the minimal solution to the problem as it contains the smallest set of necessary atoms. The whole and parts are now related by the difference of two terms:

$$I((X_1, X_2); X_3) - I(X_1; X_3) - I(X_2; X_3) = \Pi_s - \Pi_{\{1\}\{2\}\{3\}} \lesseqgtr 0 \tag{32}$$

We can gain major insight by substituting the left side using the inclusion–exclusion formulas (6) and (27):

$$\Delta\hat{H} - \hat{H}(X_1 \cap X_2 \cap X_3) = \Pi_s - \Pi_{\{1\}\{2\}\{3\}} \tag{33}$$

Remember that the only 3-covered area in the system is $X_1 \cap X_2 \cap X_3$. Therefore, the size of Π_s is determined by the distributivity-breaking difference:

$$\begin{aligned} \Pi_{\{1\}\{2\}\{3\}} &= \hat{H}(X_1 \cap X_2 \cap X_3), \\ \Pi_s &= \Delta\hat{H} \end{aligned} \tag{34}$$

To find the physical meaning behind the recovered solution, we once again compare it to the partial information decomposition of the same system. Only four of the diagram regions (Figure 4) appear in the corresponding equations:

$$I(X_1; X_3) = \Pi_{\{1\}\{2\}\{3\}} + \Pi_{\{1\}\{3\}},$$

$$I(X_2; X_3) = \Pi_{\{1\}\{2\}\{3\}} + \Pi_{\{2\}\{3\}},$$
$$I((X_1, X_2); X_3) = \Pi_{\{1\}\{2\}\{3\}} + \Pi_s + \Pi_{\{1\}\{3\}} + \Pi_{\{2\}\{3\}} \tag{35}$$

The result fully captures the structure behind Williams and Beer's definitions [4]:

$$\Pi_{\{1\}\{2\}\{3\}} \equiv \text{Redundancy},$$
$$\Pi_{\{1\}\{3\}} \equiv \text{Unique information in } X_1,$$
$$\Pi_{\{2\}\{3\}} \equiv \text{Unique information in } X_2,$$
$$\Pi_s \equiv \text{Synergy} \tag{36}$$

We have, thus, shown how information synergy naturally follows from set-theoretic arguments. The synergistic contribution is contained in the entropy of the parts and is precisely equal to the distributivity-breaking difference $\Delta\hat{H}$. The interaction responsible for the synergistic contribution is depicted on the Venn diagram as an intersection with unconventional covering number Π_s. Finally, the illusion of a whole being greater than the sum of its parts comes from the fact that the mutual information terms on the left-hand size of Equation (3) do not account for all regions of the Venn-diagram (Figure 4).

4. Towards a Multivariate Information Decomposition

In this section, we lay the foundation for a consistent theory of multivariate decomposition and resolve the contradictions between partial information decomposition axioms [15].

4.1. Information Atoms Based on Part–Whole Relations

To rigorously define the information atoms, we may think of them as basic pieces of information, which make up all more complex quantities. Previously, we have used the inclusion–exclusion principle to break down the entropy of the whole system into smaller parts step by step. Even without writing the formula for N variables, one can find the general form of the terms participating in this process:

$$\Xi[C] = \bigcap\left(\bigcup X_i\right) \tag{37}$$

The covering number C is defined trivially as the number of intersecting union-brackets in (37) and determines the sign of the associated term by the inclusion–exclusion principle. Similarly to the Möbius inversion used in set theory [25], the decomposition of non-distributive space will rely on the inclusion order lattice $(L^{\Xi}, \subseteq)$ of terms Ξ. A general description of the decomposition through part–whole relations was proposed in [26] in the form of the *parthood table*. It is a matrix with entries 0 or 1, which define whether a given atom Π is a part of a particular larger information piece, i.e., the inclusion–exclusion term (37):

$$\hat{H}(\Xi_i[C_i]) = \sum_j f_{ij}\Pi_j[c_j],$$
$$f_{ij} = 0, 1 \tag{38}$$

The parthood table depends on the initial variables through the *monotonicity* axiom, or compliance with the inclusion lattice $(L^{\Xi}, \subseteq)$:

$$\Xi_i \subseteq \Xi_j \Rightarrow \forall k\, f_{ik} \leq f_{jk} \tag{39}$$

It relates the table's entries within themselves by a simple rule: if one Ξ term is included in the other, all the atoms from the decomposition of former should be present in the decomposition of the latter.

The summands Π are non-negative functions and represent the sizes of atoms. The covering number c_j of each atom is defined by the coverings of inclusion–exclusion terms C_i:

$$c_j = \max_{i:f_{ij}=1} C_i \tag{40}$$

This rule remains unchanged from the classical set theory.

The information conservation law (17) is the final condition that preserves the physical meaning of the covering numbers—the number of times the same information appears in the system.

The existence of a general solution for N variables is not guaranteed. Besides, linear system (38) is undetermined for $N > 2$. For a specific set of degenerate cases it is, however, still possible to calculate the sizes of all atoms. We will next list several such examples while specifying how information is distributed among their different parts.

Set-Theoretic Solution for N Variables

In a distributive system, the solution is a particular case of Möbius inversion [25] (Appendix B, (A30)). Mutual information as a function of random variables becomes sub-additive (Appendix B, Lemma A5) proving that the lack of distributivity is a necessary condition for emergence.

XOR Gate

The solution found for the XOR gate is unique in the parthood table formalism (Appendix B, Theorem A2). This reinforces our proposal of synergistic and ghost atoms as physical entities.

N-Parity

Generalizing the XOR gate to an arbitrary number of variables yields the N-parity setup. It allows a solution of the similar form (Appendix B, (A42)–(A46)):

$$\begin{aligned} &\Pi_s[2] = 1 \text{ bit}, \\ &\Pi_{g_{n=\overline{1,N-2}}}[1] = 1 \text{ bit}, \\ &\forall n, \sigma \; H(X_{\sigma(1)}, X_{\sigma(2)}, \ldots X_{\sigma(n)}) = \Pi_s + \sum_{i=2}^{n-1} \Pi_{g_i} \end{aligned} \tag{41}$$

4.2. *Resolving the Partial Information Decomposition Self-Contradiction*

The existence of any multivariate decomposition was previously believed to be disproved [15] by employing a simple example that could not be solved without discarding one of the partial information decomposition axioms. The information inside three XOR variables, O_1, O_2, O_3, about their joint variable $O_4 = (O_1, O_2, O_3)$ was claimed to be grouped into three 1-bit synergistic atoms that, using our notation, corresponding to $O_1 \cap (O_2 \cup O_3) \cap O_4$, $O_2 \cap (O_1 \cup O_3) \cap O_4$, and $O_3 \cap (O_1 \cup O_2) \cap O_4$. These were summed up to give three bits of information—more than the total of two bits present in the entire system. The authors of [15] concluded that the non-negativity of information was not respected.

To resolve this discrepancy, first notice that partial information decomposition atoms are a subset of of the full set of atoms $\{\Pi\}$. In the system with N sources of information $X_1, \ldots X_N$ and target X_{N+1} they lie inside the intersection $I(X_1, \ldots, X_N; X_{N+1}) = \hat{H}((X_1 \cup \cdots \cup X_N) \cap X_{N+1})$ and are defined by the submatrix of the full parthood table $f_{ij} : \Xi_i \subseteq (X_1 \cup X_2 \cup \ldots X_N) \cap X_{N+1}$. In particular, when the output is equal to the joint variable of all inputs, the entropy of inputs coincides with mutual information, and hence, all atoms appear in the partial information decomposition (Appendix C, Lemma A7). The set of atoms $\{\Pi\}$ itself is then identical to that of the system $X_1, \ldots X_N$ alone with the exception of all covering numbers being increased by one to comply with the additional cover of X_{N+1} (Appendix C, Theorem A3). This is exactly the type of system that was used in [15]. Using the solution of the XOR gate, we find:

$$\begin{aligned}
&\Pi_s[3] = 1\text{ bit},\\
&\Pi_g[2] = 1\text{ bit},\\
&I(O_1;O_4) = \Pi_s,\\
&I(O_2;O_4) = \Pi_s,\\
&I(O_3;O_4) = \Pi_s,\\
&I((O_1,O_2);O_4) = \Pi_s + \Pi_g,\\
&I((O_1,O_3);O_4) = \Pi_s + \Pi_g,\\
&I((O_2,O_3);O_4) = \Pi_s + \Pi_g,\\
&I((O_1,O_2,O_3);O_4) = \Pi_s + \Pi_g
\end{aligned} \tag{42}$$

In place of three, there is only one symmetric atom $\Pi_s[3]$. The confusion in [15] occurred since different forms of the inclusion–exclusion principle were considered separately and it was assumed that each version would create its own synergistic atom.

5. Discussion

Previous attempts for studying synergistic information using set-theoretic intuition have led to self-contradictions. In this work, we point out that the non-distributivity of random variables corresponds to a well-defined variant of set-theory. We employ our results to construct a Venn-like diagram for an arbitrary three-variable system and demonstrate how synergism to be a direct consequence of distributivity breaking.

Our results do not fully solve the problem at hand. First, precise calculation of atom sizes was left unanswered and might require a more explicit description of information intersections. Another caveat is that although we constructed the equations that describe a self-consistent multivariate information decomposition, the existence of a solution for N arbitrary random variables is yet to be proven.

Nevertheless, this work lays the basis for a self-consistent multivariate theory. Our analysis reestablishes the concept of information decompositions as a foundation for further enquiry in quantifying emergence. In this context, information theory serves as a mere illustration: the mechanism we describe offers an explanation of the nature of synergy which uses solely set-theoretic concepts and can be applied to any emergent physical system.

From the physical standpoint, synergistic properties of information are a consequence of entropy reordering inside the system of inputs and outputs. However, this is only possible because the mathematical entities under consideration (discrete random variables) possess the property of subdistributivity, whose origin and interpretation in terms of the underlying physical system is yet to be found. One could also take a different function to represent the size of random variables. This might lead to additional positive (synergic) or negative (redundant) contributions and requires further investigation. Examples of measures other than entropy that still obey set-theoretic logic are discussed in [21].

Author Contributions: I.S. and O.F. developed the theory and wrote the paper. All authors have read and agreed to the published version of the manuscript.

Funding: This work has received funding from the European Research Council (ERC) under the European Union's Horizon 2020 research and innovation program (grant agreement No. 770964), the Israeli Science Foundation grant 1727/20, and the Minerva Foundation. O.F. is the incumbent of the Henry J Leir Professorial chair.

Institutional Review Board Statement: Not applicable.

Data Availability Statement: Data is contained within the article.

Acknowledgments: We wish to thank Rotem Shalev, Amir Shpilka, and Gregory Falkovich for their insightful comments.

Conflicts of Interest: The authors declare no conflicts of interest. The funders had no role in the design of the study; in the collection, analyses, or interpretation of data; in the writing of the manuscript; or in the decision to publish the results.

Abbreviations

The following abbreviations are used in this manuscript:

PID	Partial Information Decomposition
XOR	Exclusive OR
RV	Random variable

Appendix A. Properties of the Extended Random Variable (RV) Space

Lemma A1. *In the set-inspired algebra (Section 2.1), all deterministic variables are equal between each other and obey the property of the empty set ([27], Chapter 5): for any random variable X:*

$$\varnothing \subseteq X \tag{A1}$$

Proof. Let V be a deterministic variable. It is therefore also a deterministic function of any random variable X, which by (5) implies $V \subseteq X$.

Now, for any two deterministic variables V_1, V_2, we have $V_1 \subseteq V_2$ and $V_2 \subseteq V_1$; hence, in set-theoretic view:

$$V_1 = V_2 \tag{A2}$$

□

Corollary A1. *Other properties of the empty set are equivalent to (A1): for any random variable X and deterministic variable $\varnothing$:*

$$\begin{aligned} X \cup \varnothing &= X, \\ X \cap \varnothing &= \varnothing \end{aligned} \tag{A3}$$

While the postulate of distributivity is independent of the other axioms in set theory, a weaker condition of subdistributivity of union over intersection ought to hold in random variable space even without it:

Lemma A2. *For any three random variables X, Y, Z:*

$$(X \cap Z) \cup (Y \cap Z) \subseteq (X \cup Y) \cap Z \tag{A4}$$

Proof. We start by showing that if variables X_1, X_2 are both included in X_3, then also $(X_1 \cup X_2) \subseteq X_3$. Indeed, by the definition of inclusion (5), whenever X_1 and X_2 are deterministic functions of X_3, the joint variable (X_1, X_2) is also such.

Now notice that for arbitrary variables X, Y, Z we have:

$$\begin{aligned} &(X \cap Z) \cap ((X \cup Y) \cap Z) = (X \cup Y) \cap (Z \cap (X \cap Z)) = \\ &= (X \cup Y) \cap (X \cap Z) = (X \cap Z), \end{aligned} \tag{A5}$$

therefore, by (8), $(X \cap Z) \subseteq (X \cup Y) \cap Z$. Likewise, $(Y \cap Z) \subseteq (X \cup Y) \cap Z$.

Combining the above results, we get the statement of the lemma:

$$(X \cap Z) \cup (Y \cap Z) \subseteq (X \cup Y) \cap Z \tag{A6}$$

□

Corollary A2. *The subdistributivity (or, more correctly, superdistributivity) of intersection over union also holds:*

$$(X \cap Y) \cup Z \subseteq (X \cup Z) \cap (Y \cup Z) \tag{A7}$$

In the extended RV space, the inclusion–exclusion principle for two variables, as expected, remains unaffected by the lack of distributivity

Lemma A3. *The size of the union of two extended RV space members is related to their own sizes and the size of their intersection as:*

$$\hat{H}(X \cup Y) = \hat{H}(X) + \hat{H}(Y) - \hat{H}(X \cap Y) \tag{A8}$$

Proof. We will rewrite the left side $H(X \cup Y)$ as a union of two disjoint pieces:

$$X \cup (Y \backslash X) = X \cup (X \cap Y) \cup (Y \backslash X) = X \cup Y \tag{A9}$$

At the same time, by definition $X \cap (Y \backslash X) = \varnothing$. We may use the additivity of the measure (26) to write the size of union as a sum of sizes of its disjoint parts:

$$\hat{H}(X \cup Y) = \hat{H}(X) + \hat{H}(Y \backslash X) \tag{A10}$$

Repeating the same steps in order to decompose the second summand into two more terms concludes the proof:

$$\begin{aligned} &(Y \backslash X) \cap (X \cap Y) = ((Y \backslash X) \cap X) \cap Y = \varnothing, \\ &(Y \backslash X) \cup (X \cap Y) = Y, \\ &\hat{H}(Y) = \hat{H}(Y \backslash X) + \hat{H}(X \cap Y) \end{aligned} \tag{A11}$$

□

The inclusion–exclusion principle for three variables, along with all the terms from the set-theoretic version, contains a peculiar extra term related to the failure of distributivity

Theorem A1. *The size of triple union is related to the sizes of individual terms, their intersections, and the distributivity-breaking difference $\Delta\hat{H}$:*

$$\begin{aligned} &\hat{H}(X_1 \cup X_2 \cup X_3) = \\ &= \hat{H}(X_1) + \hat{H}(X_2) + \hat{H}(X_3) - \\ &- \hat{H}(X_1 \cap X_2) - \hat{H}(X_1 \cap X_3) - \hat{H}(X_2 \cap X_3) + \\ &+ \hat{H}(X_1 \cap X_2 \cap X_3) - \Delta\hat{H}, \end{aligned} \tag{A12}$$

where the last term is found as:

$$\Delta\hat{H} = \hat{H}(((X_{\sigma(1)} \cup X_{\sigma(2)}) \cap X_{\sigma(3)}) \backslash ((X_{\sigma(1)} \cap X_{\sigma(3)}) \cup (X_{\sigma(2)} \cap X_{\sigma(3)}))) \tag{A13}$$

and stays invariant with respect to permutations of indices σ.

Proof. We begin by choosing two of three variables (or extended RV space members) on the left side and grouping them in order to use the result of the previous lemma (A8):

$$\hat{H}((X_1 \cup X_2) \cup X_3) = \hat{H}(X_1 \cup X_2) + \hat{H}(X_3) - \hat{H}((X_1 \cup X_2) \cap X_3) \tag{A14}$$

The first term is easily decomposed further using Lemma A3. In order to proceed with the third term, we define the distributivity-breaking difference as $\Delta X_{123} = \big((X_1 \cup X_2) \cap X_3\big) \backslash \big((X_1 \cap X_3) \cup (X_2 \cap X_3)\big)$ and apply the second axiom of the measure:

$$\begin{aligned} &\hat{H}((X_1 \cup X_2) \cap X_3) = \\ &= \hat{H}(((X_1 \cap X_3) \cup (X_2 \cap X_3)) \cup \Delta X_{123}) = \\ &= \hat{H}((X_1 \cap X_3) \cup (X_2 \cap X_3)) + \hat{H}(\Delta X_{123}) \end{aligned} \tag{A15}$$

Applying (A8) once again:

$$\begin{aligned} &\hat{H}((X_1 \cap X_3) \cup (X_2 \cap X_3)) = \\ &= \hat{H}(X_1 \cap X_3) + \hat{H}(X_2 \cap X_3) - \hat{H}(X_1 \cap X_2 \cap X_3) \end{aligned} \tag{A16}$$

and combining everything into the final form:

$$\begin{aligned} &\hat{H}(X_1 \cup X_2 \cup X_3) = \\ &= \hat{H}(X_1) + \hat{H}(X_2) + \hat{H}(X_3) - \\ &- \hat{H}(X_1 \cap X_2) - \hat{H}(X_1 \cap X_3) - \hat{H}(X_2 \cap X_3) + \\ &+ \hat{H}(X_1 \cap X_2 \cap X_3) - \hat{H}(\Delta X_{123}) \end{aligned} \tag{A17}$$

The only term that depends on the order of putting brackets in (A14) is $\hat{H}(\Delta X_{123})$. Due to the associativity and commutativity of both union and intersection, we conclude that it is the only part of the equation that is not symmetric with respect to the permutations of indices:

$$\Delta X_{123} \neq \Delta X_{132} \neq \Delta X_{231}, \tag{A18}$$

Its size is, therefore, bound to be the same in all three cases. Defining a single function equal to this value concludes the proof:

$$\Delta \hat{H} = \hat{H}(\Delta X_{123}) \tag{A19}$$

□

The operation of taking the difference $\backslash$ in extended RV space may have more than one outcome. It can be shown already on the XOR gate example. Taking the variable that represents the whole system $W = O_1 \cup O_2 \cup O_3$, we have two candidates O_2, O_3 for the result of the difference $W \backslash O_1$. Substituting them into the definition (28), we find out that both are valid, despite being explicitly unequal:

$$\begin{aligned} &O_{i=2,3} \cap O_1 = \varnothing, \\ &O_i \cup (W \cap O_1) = O_i \cup O_1 = W \end{aligned} \tag{A20}$$

Appendix B. Information Atoms

A convenient notation of antichains was proposed in the partial information decomposition [4,15] to describe pieces of information. Let us denote each joint variable by the collection of variables' indices:

$$(X_{i_1}, X_{i_2}, \ldots, X_{i_m}) \to \{i_1 i_2 \ldots i_m\} = \mathbf{A} \tag{A21}$$

There is a trivial partial order $\mathbf{A} \preceq \mathbf{B} \Leftrightarrow \forall i \in \mathbf{A}\ i \in \mathbf{B}$ and we can use it to represent the intersections. A set of strong antichains $\alpha \in \mathcal{A}(N)$ is taken on the above poset:

$$\alpha = \mathbf{A}_1 \mathbf{A}_2 \ldots \mathbf{A}_n = \{i_{11} \ldots i_{1m_1}\}\{i_{21} \ldots i_{2m_2}\} \ldots \{i_{n1} \ldots i_{nm_n}\}, \tag{A22}$$

where all indices are chosen from $\overline{1,N}$ and never coincide $i_{ab} \neq i_{cd}$. The partial order $\preceq$ can be extended to antichains:

$$\alpha \preceq \beta \Leftrightarrow \forall \mathbf{B} \in \beta\ \exists \mathbf{A} \in \alpha : \mathbf{A} \preceq \mathbf{B} \tag{A23}$$

Now, a general inclusion–exclusion term (37) in an N-variable system can be denoted by an antichain $\alpha \in \mathcal{A}(N)$:

$$\Xi_\alpha[C = n] = \bigcap_{j=1}^{n} \left(\bigcup_{k=1}^{m_j} X_{i_{jk}} \right) \tag{A24}$$

The covering C is always equal to the cardinality of the corresponding antichain (the number of brackets $\{\}$):

$$C = n = |\alpha| \tag{A25}$$

The inclusion order on Ξ-terms follows from the antichain order $\preceq$. The latter is independent of the chosen random variables and holds for every system:

$$\alpha \preceq \beta \Rightarrow \Xi_\alpha \subseteq \Xi_\beta \tag{A26}$$

The new notation allows us to replace the first index of the parthood table f_{ij} with an antichain and simplify the formulation of the multivariate theory's axioms:

$$\begin{aligned}
&\hat{H}(\Xi_\alpha) = \sum_i f_{\alpha i} \Pi_i[c_i],\\
&\Xi_\alpha \subseteq \Xi_\beta \Rightarrow \forall i\ f_{\alpha i} \leq f_{\beta i},\\
&c_i = \max_{\alpha : f_{\alpha i} = 1} |\alpha|\\
&\sum_{k=1}^{N} H(X_k) = \sum_i c_i \Pi_i[c_i]
\end{aligned} \tag{A27}$$

Lemma A4. *Two inclusion–exclusion terms that are equal as members of extended RV space have identical parthood matrix rows:*

$$\Xi_\alpha = \Xi_\beta \Rightarrow \forall i : \Pi_i > 0\ f_{\alpha i} = f_{\beta i} \tag{A28}$$

Set-Theoretic Solution

This is a complete replica of set theory, fully compliant with the distributivity axiom. For $N = 3$ variables, condition (30) is necessary and sufficient for non-negativity of all atoms:

$$\begin{aligned}
&\Pi_{\{1\}\{2\}\{3\}} = I(X_1; X_3) + I(X_2; X_3) - I(X_1, X_2; X_3) \geq 0,\\
&\Pi_{\{i\}\{j\}} = I(X_i; X_j | X_k) \geq 0,\\
&\Pi_{\{i\}} = -H(X_j, X_k) + H(X_1, X_2, X_3) \geq 0
\end{aligned} \tag{A29}$$

For an arbitrary number of variables N, there is no variability in the inclusion–exclusion formulas and the atoms are recovered via the Möbius inversion with respect to the antichain order $\preceq$. Let us also denote the atoms by a special subset of antichains ι with a single index in each bracket:

$$\begin{aligned}
&\hat{H}(\Xi_\alpha) = \sum_{\iota \preceq \alpha} \Pi_\iota[n], \qquad \iota = \{i_1\}\{i_2\}\ldots\{i_n\},\\
&\Pi_\iota = \sum_{m=n}^{N} (-1)^{m-n} \sum_{i_{n+1},\ldots i_m} I_m(X_{i_1}; \ldots X_{i_m}),
\end{aligned} \tag{A30}$$

where I_m is the mth order interaction information function defined as a sign-changing sum of entropies $\sum_{k=1}^{m}(-1)^{k-1}\sum_{j_1,\ldots j_k} H(X_{j_1}, X_{j_2}, \ldots, X_{j_k})$.

Set-theoretic systems never exhibit synergistic properties. The following result can be understood in the sense that the lack of distributivity is a necessary condition for the existence of synergy in any N-variable system

Lemma A5. *In a set-theoretic system, mutual information is always subadditive:*

$$I((X_1, \ldots X_N); X_{N+1}) \leq \sum_{i=1}^{N} I(X_i; X_{N+1}) \tag{A31}$$

Proof. Let us substitute the atoms (A30) into the inequality:

$$\sum_{\iota \preceq \{12\ldots N\}\{N+1\}} \Pi_\iota \leq \sum_{k=1}^{N} \sum_{\iota' \preceq \{k\}\{N+1\}} \Pi_{\iota'} \tag{A32}$$

For any atom on the left side, we have by (A23):

$$\iota \preceq \{12\ldots N\}\{N+1\} \Rightarrow \exists \{i_a\}, \{i_b\} \in \iota : \begin{cases} \{i_a\} \preceq \{12\ldots N\} \\ \{i_b\} \preceq \{N+1\} \end{cases} \tag{A33}$$

Since ι is composed of single indices, we have:

$$\begin{aligned} i_a &= \overline{1, N}, \\ i_b &= N+1 \end{aligned} \tag{A34}$$

Then, this term can also be found on the right side of (A32):

$$\exists \iota' \preceq \{i_a\}\{N+1\} : \iota = \iota' \tag{A35}$$

The non-negativity of all atoms concludes the proof. □

XOR Gate

The XOR gate contains a completely different set of atoms. With three pairwise independent initial variables, the set of inclusion–exclusion terms simplifies to:

$$\begin{aligned} \Xi_{\{123\}}[1] &= O_1 \cup O_2 \cup O_3 & \hat{H}(\Xi_{\{123\}}) &= 2, \\ \Xi_{\{ij\}}[1] &= O_i \cup O_j & \hat{H}(\Xi_{\{ij\}}) &= 2, \\ \Xi_{\{i\}}[1] &= O_i & \hat{H}(\Xi_{\{i\}}) &= 1, \\ \Xi_{\{ij\}\{k\}}[2] &= (O_i \cup O_j) \cap O_k & \hat{H}(\Xi_{\{ij\}\{k\}}) &= 1 \end{aligned}$$

In the extended RV space $\Xi_{\{ij\}\{k\}} = \Xi_{\{k\}}, \Xi_{\{ij\}} = \Xi_{\{123\}}$ and by Lemma A4, we only need to find decompositions of $\Xi_{\{i\}}$ and $\Xi_{\{123\}}$. Due to the symmetry of the problem, decomposition of $\Xi_{\{i\}}$ may contain three types of atoms: three distinct atoms Π_i, each being a part of only the respective Ξ_i; three distinct atoms $\Pi_{i,j}$, each being a part of both specified terms; or one symmetrically shared Π_s, as we have guessed in (15)

$$\hat{H}(\Xi_{\{ij\}\{k\}}[2]) = \hat{H}(\Xi_{\{k\}}[1]) = \Pi_k[2] + \Pi_{i,k}[2] + \Pi_{j,k}[2] + \Pi_s[2] \tag{A36}$$

The coverings are calculated by definition (A27). For $\Xi_{\{123\}}$, one more atom Π_g may be added:

$$\begin{aligned} &\hat{H}(\Xi_{\{ij\}}[1]) = \hat{H}(\Xi_{\{123\}}[1]) = \\ &= \Pi_1[2] + \Pi_2[2] + \Pi_3[2] + \Pi_{1,2}[2] + \Pi_{2,3}[2] + \Pi_{1,3}[2] + \Pi_s[2] + \Pi_g[1] \end{aligned} \tag{A37}$$

The following parthood table contains columns for all atoms discussed above.

f	Π_s	Π_g	Π_1	Π_2	Π_3	$\Pi_{1,2}$	$\Pi_{1,3}$	$\Pi_{2,3}$
{1}{2}{3}	0	0	0	0	0	0	0	0
{1}{2}	0	0	0	0	0	0	0	0
{1}{3}	0	0	0	0	0	0	0	0
{2}{3}	0	0	0	0	0	0	0	0
{12}{3}	1	0	0	0	1	0	1	1
{13}{2}	1	0	0	1	0	1	0	1
{23}{1}	1	0	1	0	0	1	1	0
{1}	1	0	1	0	0	1	1	0
{2}	1	0	0	1	0	1	0	1
{3}	1	0	0	0	1	0	1	1
{12}	1	1	1	1	1	1	1	1
{13}	1	1	1	1	1	1	1	1
{23}	1	1	1	1	1	1	1	1
{123}	1	1	1	1	1	1	1	1

In a symmetric solution, the atom sizes are invariant with respect to index permutations, and hence, let:

$$\begin{aligned}
&\Pi_s = x, \\
&\Pi_{i,k} = y, \\
&\Pi_i = 1 - 2y - x, \\
&\Pi_g = 2 - x - 3y - 3(1 - 2y - x) = 2x + 3y - 1
\end{aligned} \tag{A38}$$

Substituting this into the information conservation law:

$$\begin{aligned}
&\sum_i H(X_i) = 3 = 2x + 2 * 3y + 2 * 3 * (1 - 2y - x) + 2x + 3y - 1 = 5 - 2x - 3y, \\
&2x + 3y = 2
\end{aligned} \tag{A39}$$

However, we know that all atoms have non-negative sizes, which means that most atoms disappear from the solution (have zero sizes):

$$\begin{aligned}
&\Pi_i = 1 - 2y - x = -0.5y \geq 0, \\
&y = 0, \\
&x = 1
\end{aligned} \tag{A40}$$

Theorem A2. *The XOR gate has a unique symmetric decomposition:*

$$\begin{aligned}
&\Pi_s[2] = 1\ bit, \\
&\Pi_g[1] = 1\ bit
\end{aligned} \tag{A41}$$

f	Π_s	Π_g
$\{1\}\{2\}\{3\}$	0	0
$\{1\}\{2\}$	0	0
$\{1\}\{3\}$	0	0
$\{2\}\{3\}$	0	0
$\{12\}\{3\}$	1	0
$\{13\}\{2\}$	1	0
$\{23\}\{1\}$	1	0
$\{1\}$	1	0
$\{2\}$	1	0
$\{3\}$	1	0
$\{12\}$	1	1
$\{13\}$	1	1
$\{23\}$	1	1
$\{123\}$	1	1

N-Parity

A generalization of the XOR gate is the N-parity setup, also a symmetric system, for which one of the variables is fully determined by the combination of all the others:

$$X_{\overline{1,N}} = \begin{cases} 0, & 50\% \\ 1, & 50\% \end{cases}, \qquad \forall i = \overline{1,N}\ X_i \equiv \sum_{j \neq i} X_j \mod 2 \tag{A42}$$

The set of inclusion–exclusion terms is quite simple: 1-covered terms coinciding with the entropies, whose size is equal to the number of participating variables (for N variables it remains at $N+1$ bits since the last variable is deterministic of the rest):

$$\begin{aligned} \Xi_{\{i_1 i_2 \dots i_n\}}[1] &= \bigcup_{k=\overline{1,n}} X_{i_k}, \\ \hat{H}(\Xi_{\{i_1 i_2 \dots i_n\}}) &= \min(n, N-1) \end{aligned} \tag{A43}$$

and 1-bit 2-covered intersections between two unions:

$$\begin{aligned} \Xi_{\{i_1 i_2 \dots i_n\}\{i_{n+1} \dots i_N\}}[2] &= \left(\bigcup_{k=\overline{1,n}} X_{i_k} \right) \cap \left(\bigcup_{l=\overline{n+1,N}} X_{i_l} \right), \\ \hat{H}(\Xi_{\{i_1 i_2 \dots i_n\}\{i_{n+1} \dots i_N\}}) &= 1 \end{aligned} \tag{A44}$$

The rest of Ξ-terms are empty. A solution can be easily guessed: a single symmetric 2-covered atom $\Pi_s[2] = 1$ and a set of $N-2$ ghost atoms $\Pi_{g_k}[1] = 1, k = \overline{1, N-2}$, such that:

$$\begin{aligned} \hat{H}(\Xi_{\{i_1 i_2 \dots i_n\}\{i_{n+1} \dots i_N\}}) &= \Pi_s, \\ \hat{H}(\Xi_{\{i_1 i_2 \dots i_n\}}) &= \Pi_s + \sum_{k=1}^{n-2} \Pi_{g_k} \end{aligned} \tag{A45}$$

We immediately see that the information conservation law is satisfied:

$$\sum_i H(X_i) = N = 2\Pi_s + \sum_{k=1}^{N-2} \Pi_{g_k} \tag{A46}$$

Arbitrary Trivariate System

A Venn-type diagram for any three variables can be constructed using the following universal system of equations and parthood table (Table A1).

$$H(X_1) = \Pi_{\{1\}\{2\}\{3\}}[3] + \Pi_s[2] + \Pi_{\{1\}\{2\}}[2] + \Pi_{\{1\}\{3\}}[2] + \Pi_{\{1\}}[1],$$

$$\begin{aligned}
&H(X_2) = \Pi_{\{1\}\{2\}\{3\}}[3] + \Pi_s[2] + \Pi_{\{1\}\{2\}}[2] + \Pi_{\{2\}\{3\}}[2] + \Pi_{\{2\}}[1], \\
&H(X_3) = \Pi_{\{1\}\{2\}\{3\}}[3] + \Pi_s[2] + \Pi_{\{1\}\{3\}}[2] + \Pi_{\{2\}\{3\}}[2] + \Pi_{\{3\}}[1], \\
&H(X_1, X_2) = \Pi_{\{1\}\{2\}\{3\}}[3] + \Pi_s[2] + \Pi_{\{1\}\{2\}}[2] + \Pi_{\{1\}\{3\}}[2] + \Pi_{\{2\}\{3\}}[2] + \\
&+\Pi_{\{1\}}[1] + \Pi_{\{2\}}[1] + \Pi_g[1], \\
&H(X_1, X_3) = \Pi_{\{1\}\{2\}\{3\}}[3] + \Pi_s[2] + \Pi_{\{1\}\{2\}}[2] + \Pi_{\{1\}\{3\}}[2] + \Pi_{\{2\}\{3\}}[2] + \\
&+\Pi_{\{1\}}[1] + \Pi_{\{3\}}[1] + \Pi_g[1], \\
&H(X_2, X_3) = \Pi_{\{1\}\{2\}\{3\}}[3] + \Pi_s[2] + \Pi_{\{1\}\{2\}}[2] + \Pi_{\{1\}\{3\}}[2] + \Pi_{\{2\}\{3\}}[2] + \\
&+\Pi_{\{2\}}[1] + \Pi_{\{3\}}[1] + \Pi_g[1], \\
&H(X_1, X_2, X_3) = \Pi_{\{1\}\{2\}\{3\}}[3] + \Pi_s[2] + \Pi_{\{1\}\{2\}}[2] + \Pi_{\{1\}\{3\}}[2] + \Pi_{\{2\}\{3\}}[2] + \\
&+\Pi_{\{1\}}[1] + \Pi_{\{2\}}[1] + \Pi_{\{3\}}[1] + \Pi_g[1], \\
&\Pi_s[2] = \Pi_g[1]
\end{aligned} \tag{A47}$$

Table A1. Parthood table for a universal trivariate decomposition.

f	$\Pi_{\{1\}\{2\}\{3\}}$	Π_s	$\Pi_{\{1\}\{2\}}$	$\Pi_{\{1\}\{3\}}$	$\Pi_{\{2\}\{3\}}$	$\Pi_{\{1\}}$	$\Pi_{\{2\}}$	$\Pi_{\{3\}}$	Π_g
{1}{2}{3}	1	0	0	0	0	0	0	0	0
{1}{2}	1	0	1	0	0	0	0	0	0
{1}{3}	1	0	0	1	0	0	0	0	0
{2}{3}	1	0	0	0	1	0	0	0	0
{12}{3}	1	1	0	1	1	0	0	0	0
{13}{2}	1	1	1	0	1	0	0	0	0
{23}{1}	1	1	1	1	0	0	0	0	0
{1}	1	1	1	1	0	1	0	0	0
{2}	1	1	1	0	1	0	1	0	0
{3}	1	1	0	1	1	0	0	1	0
{12}	1	1	1	1	1	1	1	0	1
{13}	1	1	1	1	1	1	0	1	1
{23}	1	1	1	1	1	0	1	1	1
{123}	1	1	1	1	1	1	1	1	1

Lemma A6. *Any system of three random variables can be decomposed into a set of non-negative atoms (A47).*

Proof. One can find the sizes of atoms $\Pi_{\{i\}}$ from the last four equations in the system:

$$\begin{aligned}
\Pi_{\{1\}} &= H(X_1, X_2, X_3) - H(X_2, X_3) \geq 0, \\
\Pi_{\{2\}} &= H(X_1, X_2, X_3) - H(X_1, X_3) \geq 0, \\
\Pi_{\{3\}} &= H(X_1, X_2, X_3) - H(X_1, X_2) \geq 0
\end{aligned} \tag{A48}$$

For the rest of the set-theoretic atoms, we have:

$$\begin{aligned}
I(X_1; X_2) &= \Pi_{\{1\}\{2\}\{3\}} + \Pi_{\{1\}\{2\}}, \\
I(X_1; X_3) &= \Pi_{\{1\}\{2\}\{3\}} + \Pi_{\{1\}\{3\}}, \\
I(X_2; X_3) &= \Pi_{\{1\}\{2\}\{3\}} + \Pi_{\{2\}\{3\}}
\end{aligned} \tag{A49}$$

To satisfy the non-negativity requirement, we need:

$$\begin{aligned}
\Pi_{\{1\}\{2\}} &= I(X_1; X_2) - \Pi_{\{1\}\{2\}\{3\}} \geq 0, \\
\Pi_{\{1\}\{3\}} &= I(X_1; X_3) - \Pi_{\{1\}\{2\}\{3\}} \geq 0, \\
\Pi_{\{2\}\{3\}} &= I(X_2; X_3) - \Pi_{\{1\}\{2\}\{3\}} \geq 0,
\end{aligned} \tag{A50}$$

which is equivalent to:

$$0 \leq \Pi_{\{1\}\{2\}\{3\}} \leq \min(I(X_1;X_2), I(X_1;X_3), I(X_2;X_3)) \tag{A51}$$

The last independent equation can be written using a third-order information interaction function:

$$I_3(X_1;X_2;X_3) = \Pi_{\{1\}\{2\}\{3\}} - \Pi_s, \tag{A52}$$

therefore:

$$\Pi_s = \Pi_g = \Pi_{\{1\}\{2\}\{3\}} - I_3(X_1;X_2;X_3) \geq 0 \tag{A53}$$

The obtained set of conditions is indeed self-consistent, as:

$$\min(I(X_1;X_2), I(X_1;X_3), I(X_2;X_3)) \geq I_3(X_1;X_2;X_3) \tag{A54}$$

□

Appendix C. Partial Information Decomposition (PID)

The partial information decomposition atoms are only a subset of all atoms Π. Yet, for some systems, it may be equal to the full set. Indeed, when the output is exactly the joint variable of all inputs, it essentially "covers" the whole diagram of the system of inputs. The entropies of inputs completely turn into mutual information about the output.

Lemma A7. *The partial information decomposition with inputs $X_1, \ldots X_N$ and their joint variable chosen as an output $X_{N+1} = (X_1, \ldots, X_N)$ contains all information atoms Π of the system $X_1, \ldots X_{N+1}$.*

Proof. The PID atoms are by definition the ones contained in the intersection of the form:

$$(X_1 \cup X_2 \cup \cdots \cup X_N) \cap X_{N+1} \tag{A55}$$

By conditions of the lemma, in extended random variable space, we have:

$$\begin{aligned} &(X_1 \cup X_2 \cup \cdots \cup X_N) \cap X_{N+1} = (X_1 \cup X_2 \cup \cdots \cup X_N) = \\ &= (X_1 \cup X_2 \cup \cdots \cup X_N) \cup X_{N+1} \end{aligned} \tag{A56}$$

Applying Lemma A4 concludes the proof. □

A stronger statement can be made that the whole structure of the resulting $N+1$ variable decomposition is equivalent to the lesser decomposition of just the inputs $X_1, \ldots X_N$ with a single extra covering added to each atom to account for the output X_{N+1}, covering the whole system one more time.

Theorem A3. *A decomposition for the $N+1$ variable system $X_1, \ldots X_{N+1}$ with:*

$$X_{N+1} = X_1 \cup X_2 \cup \cdots \cup X_N \tag{A57}$$

defined by a set of atoms $\{\Pi_i[c_i]\}_{i \in I}$ and parthood table f can be obtained from the decomposition $\{\tilde{\Pi}_j[\tilde{c}_j]\}_{j \in J}, \tilde{f}$ of the N variable system $X_1, \ldots X_N$ as:

$$\forall \alpha \in \mathcal{A}(N+1), i \in I \begin{cases} f_{\alpha i} = \tilde{f}_{F(\alpha)j(i)} \\ \Pi_i = \tilde{\Pi}_{j(i)} \\ c_i = \tilde{c}_{j(i)} + 1 \end{cases} \tag{A58}$$

where $j(i)$ is a bijection of indices and (surjective) function $F : \mathcal{A}(N+1) \to \mathcal{A}(N)$ removes a bracket from an antichain if this bracket contains index $N+1$.

Proof. Examining the inclusion–exclusion terms, we find that:

$$\forall \alpha \in \mathcal{A}(N+1)\ \Xi_\alpha = \Xi_{F(\alpha)} \tag{A59}$$

By Lemma A4, this guarantees the equivalence of the corresponding parthood table rows:

$$\forall i \in I, \alpha \in \mathcal{A}(N+1)\ f_{\alpha i} = f_{F(\alpha)i} \tag{A60}$$

Now, we need to determine the parthood table rows only for $\alpha \in \text{Im}(F) = \mathcal{A}(N)$. Knowing the solution $\{\tilde{\Pi}\}_{j\in J}$ for the N-variable system, we substitute the same atoms into the larger $N+1$ variable system and define a bijection of indices $j(i)$:

$$\begin{gathered}\hat{H}(\Xi_\alpha) = \hat{H}(\Xi_{F(\alpha)}) = \sum_{j\in J} \tilde{f}_{F(\alpha)j}\tilde{\Pi}_j = \sum_{i\in I} f_{\alpha i}\Pi_i, \\ \forall i \in I, \alpha \in \mathcal{A}(N+1)\ \Pi_i = \tilde{\Pi}_{j(i)}, f_{\alpha i} = \tilde{f}_{F(\alpha)j(i)}\end{gathered} \tag{A61}$$

Finally, to ensure the validity of the new solution, we check its compliance with axioms (A27):

1. Monotonicity:

$$\Xi_\alpha \subseteq \Xi_\beta \Rightarrow \Xi_{F(\alpha)} \subseteq \Xi_{F(\beta)} \Rightarrow \forall i \in I\ f_{\alpha i} = \tilde{f}_{F(\alpha)j(i)} \le \tilde{f}_{F(\beta)j(i)} = f_{\beta i} \tag{A62}$$

2. Covering numbers:

$$\begin{cases} N+1 \in \alpha \Rightarrow |\alpha| = |F(\alpha)| + 1 \\ N+1 \notin \alpha \Rightarrow |\alpha| = |F(\alpha)| \end{cases} \tag{A63}$$

$$c_i = \max_{\alpha\in\mathcal{A}(N+1):f_{\alpha i}=1} |\alpha| = \max_{\beta\in\mathcal{A}(N):\tilde{f}_{\beta j(i)}=1} |\beta| + 1 = \tilde{c}_{j(i)} + 1 \tag{A64}$$

3. Information conservation law:

$$\begin{gathered} H(X_{N+1}) = H(X_1, \dots X_N) = \sum_{j\in J} \tilde{\Pi}_j, \\ \sum_{k=1}^{N} H(X_k) = \sum_{j\in J} \tilde{c}_j \tilde{\Pi}_j, \\ \sum_{k=1}^{N+1} H(X_k) = \sum_{j\in J} \tilde{c}_i \tilde{\Pi}_i + H(X_{N+1}) = \sum_{j\in J} (\tilde{c}_j + 1)\tilde{\Pi}_j = \sum_{i\in I} c_i \Pi_i \end{gathered} \tag{A65}$$

□

References

1. Artime, O.; De Domenico, M. From the origin of life to pandemics: Emergent phenomena in complex systems. *Philos. Trans. R. Soc. A Math. Phys. Eng. Sci.* **2022**, *380*, 20200410. [CrossRef] [PubMed]
2. Cover, T.M.; Thomas, J.A. *Elements of Information Theory*; Wiley Series in Telecommunications and Signal Processing; Wiley-Interscience: Hoboken, NJ, USA, 2006.
3. Shannon, C. A Mathematical Theory of Communication. *Bell Labs Tech. J.* **1948**, *27*, 379–423. [CrossRef]
4. Williams, P.; Beer, R. Nonnegative Decomposition of Multivariate Information. *arXiv* **2010**, arXiv:1004.2515.
5. Harder, M.; Salge, C.; Polani, D. Bivariate measure of redundant information. *Phys. Rev. E Stat. Nonlinear Soft Matter Phys.* **2013**, *87*, 012130. [CrossRef] [PubMed]
6. Bertschinger, N.; Rauh, J.; Olbrich, E.; Ay, N. Quantifying Unique Information. *Entropy* **2013**, *16*, 2161. [CrossRef]
7. Kolchinsky, A. A Novel Approach to the Partial Information Decomposition. *Entropy* **2022**, *24*, 403. [CrossRef] [PubMed]

8. Mediano, P.; Rosas, F.; Luppi, A.; Jensen, H.; Seth, A.; Barrett, A.; Carhart-Harris, R.; Bor, D. Greater than the parts: A review of the information decomposition approach to causal emergence. *Philos. Trans. R. Soc. A Math. Phys. Eng. Sci.* **2022**, *380*, 20210246. [CrossRef] [PubMed]
9. Lizier, J.; Bertschinger, N.; Wibral, M. Information Decomposition of Target Effects from Multi-Source Interactions: Perspectives on Previous, Current and Future Work. *Entropy* **2018**, *20*, 307. [CrossRef] [PubMed]
10. Ehrlich, D.A.; Schick-Poland, K.; Makkeh, A.; Lanfermann, F.; Wollstadt, P.; Wibral, M. Partial information decomposition for continuous variables based on shared exclusions: Analytical formulation and estimation. *Phys. Rev. E* **2024**, *110*, 014115. [CrossRef] [PubMed]
11. Schick-Poland, K.; Makkeh, A.; Gutknecht, A.; Wollstadt, P.; Sturm, A.; Wibral, M. A partial information decomposition for discrete and continuous variables. *arXiv* **2021**, arXiv:2106.12393.
12. Rosas, F.; Mediano, P.; Jensen, H.; Seth, A.; Barrett, A.; Carhart-Harris, R.; Bor, D. Reconciling emergences: An information-theoretic approach to identify causal emergence in multivariate data. *PLoS Comput. Biol.* **2020**, *16*, e1008289. [CrossRef] [PubMed]
13. Balduzzi, D.; Tononi, G. Integrated Information in Discrete Dynamical Systems: Motivation and Theoretical Framework. *PLoS Comput. Biol.* **2008**, *4*, e1000091. [CrossRef] [PubMed]
14. van Enk, S.J. Quantum partial information decomposition. *Phys. Rev. A* **2023**, *108*, 062415. [CrossRef]
15. Rauh, J.; Bertschinger, N.; Olbrich, E. Reconsidering unique information: Towards a multivariate information decomposition. *IEEE Int. Symp. Inf. Theory—Proc.* **2014**, *2014*, 2232–2236. [CrossRef]
16. Finn, C.; Lizier, J. Pointwise Partial Information Decomposition Using the Specificity and Ambiguity Lattices. *Entropy* **2018**, *20*, 297. [CrossRef] [PubMed]
17. Ince, R.A.A. The Partial Entropy Decomposition: Decomposing multivariate entropy and mutual information via pointwise common surprisal. *arXiv* **2017**, arXiv:1702.01591.
18. Ting, H.K. On the Amount of Information. *Theory Probab. Its Appl.* **1962**, *7*, 439–447. [CrossRef]
19. Tao, T. Special Cases of Shannon Entropy. Blogpost. 2017. Available online: https://terrytao.wordpress.com/2017/03/01/special-cases-of-shannon-entropy/ (accessed on 1 September 2024).
20. Yeung, R. A new outlook on Shannon's information measures. *IEEE Trans. Inf. Theory* **1991**, *37*, 466–474. [CrossRef]
21. Lang, L.; Baudot, P.; Quax, R.; Forr'e, P. Information Decomposition Diagrams Applied beyond Shannon Entropy: A Generalization of Hu's Theorem. *arXiv* **2022**, arXiv:2202.09393.
22. Mazur, D.R. *AMS/MAA Textbooks*; American Mathematical Society: Providence, RI, USA, 2010. [CrossRef]
23. Tao, T. *An Introduction to Measure Theory*; American Mathematical Society: Providence, RI, USA, 2011; Volume 126.
24. Wolf, S.; Wullschleger, J. Zero-error information and applications in cryptography. In Proceedings of the Information Theory Workshop, San Antonio, TX, USA, 24–29 October 2004; pp. 1–6.
25. Stanley, R. *Enumerative Combinatorics: Volume 1*; Cambridge Studies in Advanced Mathematics; Cambridge University Press: Cambridge, UK, 1997.
26. Gutknecht, A.; Wibral, M.; Makkeh, A. Bits and pieces: Understanding information decomposition from part-whole relationships and formal logic. *Proc. R. Soc. A Math. Phys. Eng. Sci.* **2021**, *477*, 20210110. [CrossRef] [PubMed]
27. Stoll, R. *Set Theory and Logic*; Dover Books on Advanced Mathematics; Dover Publications: Mineola, NY, USA, 1979.

entropy

MDPI

Article

Unique Information Through the Lens of Channel Ordering: An Introduction and Review

Pradeep Kr. Banerjee

Institute for Data Science Foundations, Blohmstraße 15, 21079 Hamburg, Germany; pradeep.banerjee@tuhh.de

Abstract: The problem of constructing information measures with a well-defined interpretation is of fundamental significance in information theory. A good definition of an information measure entails certain desirable properties while also providing answers to operational problems. In this work, we investigate the properties of the unique information, an information measure that quantifies a deviation from the Blackwell order. Beyond providing an accessible introduction to the topic from a channel ordering perspective, we present a novel resource-theoretic characterization of unique information in a cryptographic task related to secret key agreement. Our operational view of unique information entails rich physical intuition that leads to new insights into secret key agreement in the context of non-negative decompositions of the mutual information into redundant and synergistic contributions. Through this lens, we illuminate new directions for research in partial information decompositions and information-theoretic cryptography.

Keywords: comparison of channels; unique information; Blackwell order; information-theoretic cryptography; secret key rate; secrecy monotones; synergy; redundancy; Le Cam deficiency; resource theories

1. Introduction

Shannon's pioneering work [1] characterized the capacity of a physical channel by way of maximum mutual information. Since then, information theory has had a special relation to communication engineering, even though ideas and tools from information theory have been successfully applied in many other research fields, such as cryptography, statistics, machine learning, complex systems, and biology, to name a few.

Despite significant progress in information theory, many fundamental questions remain regarding the nature of information. One of the primary challenges is that information is not a conserved quantity, making it difficult to track and describe its distribution across composite systems. A composite system consists of multiple interacting subsystems, each of which may hold *unique* (or exclusive) information, or share *redundant* (or shared) information. Additionally, there are cases where some information is not directly accessible to any individual subsystem but can only be determined by considering the entire system. For example, a checksum for a set of digits can only be computed when all the digits are known. Such *synergistic* effects are especially relevant in cryptography, where the objective is for the encrypted message to reveal no information about the original message without the corresponding key.

How should the amount of unique, shared, and synergistic information be measured? This question can be approached from two different points of view, namely, the *axiomatic* and the *operational* [2]. In an *axiomatic* approach, one posits certain desirable properties that a measure of information should satisfy. This point of view goes back to Shannon [1],

Academic Editor: Daniel Chicharro

Received: 11 October 2024
Revised: 18 December 2024
Accepted: 26 December 2024
Published: 1 January 2025

Citation: Banerjee, P.K. Unique Information Through the Lens of Channel Ordering: An Introduction and Review. *Entropy* **2025**, *27*, 29. https://doi.org/10.3390/e27010029

who showed that his definition of entropy is the only one that satisfies certain intuitively appealing properties. Shannon notes that such an axiomatic characterization is *"in no way necessary for the theory"* but *"lends a certain plausibility"* to the definitions and that the *"real justification of these definitions, however, will reside in their implications"* [1]. Thus, in Shannon's view, the ultimate criterion for accepting some quantity as a measure of information is whether it provides answers to interesting problems. This is an *operational* or *pragmatic* view of information. For example, Shannon's coding theorems endow the entropy and mutual information with concrete meaning in operational tasks related to data compression and transmission. Rényi [2,3] and Csiszár [4,5] comment that for problems that lay outside the scope of these theorems, both the axiomatic and the operational points of view deserve attention and can, in fact, be used to "control" or inform the other when constructing new measures of information. Understanding the properties of these measures helps clarify the fundamental limits of operational problems. Dually, analyzing such problems motivates the quest for new information measures.

This review investigates the properties of the unique information (UI), an information measure introduced by Bertschinger et al. [6], which quantifies deviations from the Blackwell order. We adopt Shannon's pragmatic stance, focusing on an operational view of unique information from a channel ordering perspective. This builds on the original definition of UI in [6], which is motivated by the idea that unique information should be "useful". Bertschinger et al. formalized this idea in terms of decision problems: Whenever Bob has unique information about something Alice knows (which is not accessible to Eve), there is a decision problem in which Bob has an advantage over Eve. By leveraging tools from resource theories [7–11], we provide a concrete formalization of this conceptual framework.

Resource theories provide an abstract operational framework for studying what physical transformations between a given set of objects are possible under restrictions that follow from the nature of the system under investigation. Within this framework, resources are measured by *monotones*, quantities that do not increase under allowed operations. We present a novel resource-theoretic characterization of UI in a fundamental cryptographic task related to secret key agreement, showing that UI functions similarly to classical *secret key rates* [12–15], and is in fact a monotone that quantifies the "resourcefulness" or secrecy content of a source distribution. This operational characterization not only extends the applicability of UI in cryptographic settings but also opens up new avenues for its study within resource theory.

Our resource-theoretic approach represents a significant departure from existing frameworks on bivariate partial information decompositions, offering a fresh perspective on how UI can be leveraged in the broader context of information-theoretic cryptography. While most existing approaches have focused on the shared information within these decompositions using an axiomatic framework, we shift the focus to an operational view of UI, grounded in the context of channel preorders. Shannon emphasized that the value of an information measure should be judged by its implications in practical tasks, rather than its adherence to abstract properties alone. Following this viewpoint, we argue that UI's significance emerges most clearly when applied in concrete settings like decision-making or cryptographic problems, where operational utility takes precedence over purely axiomatic considerations.

This work serves as both a review and a formalization of existing research on UI and related measures based on channel orderings, with a particular focus on interpreting these insights through the lens of resource theories. The focus of this review is primarily on measures akin to UI, particularly those rooted in channel orderings, and does not extend to other types of information measures that fall outside this framework. We draw extensively from previously published works [16–21] and integrate key insights from unpublished portions of the author's PhD thesis [22], which are not available in the public domain. By synthesizing these contributions, this review not only provides a comprehensive overview of prior research on UI and channel preorders, but also introduces novel resource-theoretic perspectives, offering a fresh and compelling advancement in the study of bivariate partial information decompositions and information-theoretic cryptography.

Outline. The paper is organized as follows: Section 2 provides a brief review of prior work on non-negative bivariate information decompositions and presents a formal description of the problem, with a focus on the properties of the function UI as introduced by Bertschinger et al. [6]. Section 3 offers a self-contained exposition on channel orderings in information theory. In Section 4, we review Le Cam deficiencies and their generalizations [23–25], which exhibit properties analogous to the UI. These deficiencies quantify the cost of approximating one channel by another through randomization, capturing deviations from output- and input-degraded channel orderings. This provides insight into the distinctions between the bivariate decompositions of Bertschinger et al. [6] and Harder et al. [26]. In Section 5, we review the operational significance of UI in a cryptographic task related to secret key agreement [16,17]. Finally, Section 6 presents a novel resource-theoretic characterization of the main results from Section 5, demonstrating that the UI serves as a resource "monotone" quantifying the secrecy content of a given distribution under a specific class of allowed operations.

2. Bivariate Partial Information Decompositions

Notation and conventions. We shall use notation that is commonly used in information theory [27,28]. We assume that random variables S, Y, Z, etc., are finite, as are all other random variables in this work. The set of all probability measures on a finite set $\mathcal{S}$ is denoted by $\mathbb{P}_{\mathcal{S}}$. A *channel* μ from $\mathcal{S}$ to $\mathcal{Z}$ is a family $\mu = \{\mu_s\}_{s\in\mathcal{S}}$ of probability distributions on $\mathcal{Z}$, one for each possible input $s \in \mathcal{S}$. We write $\mathsf{M}(\mathcal{S};\mathcal{Z})$ to denote the space of all channels from $\mathcal{S}$ to $\mathcal{Z}$. Given two channels, $\mu \in \mathsf{M}(\mathcal{S};\mathcal{Z})$ and $\rho \in \mathsf{M}(\mathcal{Z};\mathcal{Y})$, the composition $\rho\circ\mu \in \mathsf{M}(\mathcal{S};\mathcal{Y})$ of μ with ρ is defined as follows: $\rho\circ\mu_s(y) = \sum_{z\in\mathcal{Z}} \rho_z(y)\mu_s(z)$ for all $s \in \mathcal{S}$, $z \in \mathcal{Z}$. A *binary symmetric channel* with parameter p, denoted as $\mathsf{BSC}(p)$, is a channel from $\mathcal{S} = \{0,1\}$ to $\mathcal{Y} = \{0,1\}$ that flips each bit independently with some error probability $p \in [0, \frac{1}{2}]$. A *binary erasure channel* on $\mathcal{S} = \{0,1\}$ with erasure probability $\epsilon \in [0,1]$, denoted as $\mathsf{BEC}(\epsilon)$, is a channel from $\mathcal{S}$ to $\mathcal{Y} = \mathcal{S}\cup\{\mathsf{e}\}$ such that $Y = S$ with probability $1-\epsilon$ and $Y = \mathsf{e}$ with probability ϵ. Given two distributions P and Q, the Kullback–Leibler (KL) divergence from P to Q is denoted as $D(P\|Q)$. $H(S)$ denotes the Shannon entropy of random variable S. $h(\cdot)$ is the binary entropy function, $h(p) = -p\log p - (1-p)\log(1-p)$ for $p \in (0,1)$ and $h(0) = h(1) = 0$.

The mutual information of two random variables S and Y is defined as

$$I(S;Y) = H(S) + H(Y) - H(SY). \tag{1}$$

I measures the total amount of correlation between S and Y and possesses the following key properties [28,29]:

$$I(S;Y) = I(Y;S) \quad \textit{(symmetry)}, \tag{2a}$$

$$I(S;Y) \geq 0;\ I(S;Y) = 0 \iff S \textit{ is independent of } Y \quad \textit{(non-negativity)}, \tag{2b}$$

$$I(S;YZ) \geq I(S;Y) \quad \textit{(strong subadditivity)}. \tag{2c}$$

Strong subadditivity is equivalent to the non-negativity of the conditional mutual information:

$$I(S;Z|Y) \geq 0;\ I(S;Z|Y) = 0 \iff S - Y - Z,$$

where $S - Y - Z$ denotes that S, Y, and Z form a Markov chain in that order. Strong subadditivity also implies the following key property of the mutual information, namely, its monotonicity with respect to data processing

$$S - Z - Y \implies I(S;Z) \geq I(S;Y), \text{ with equality if and only if } S - Y - Z \quad (\textit{data processing inequality}).$$

Another integral property of the mutual information is the following equality, which is called the chain rule:

$$I(S;YZ) = I(S;Y) + I(S;Z|Y) \qquad (\textit{chain rule}). \tag{3}$$

In general, conditioning on an additional random variable can either increase or decrease the mutual information. We consider three canonical distributions to illustrate this point. Each of these distributions capture a fundamentally different kind of interaction between three jointly distributed random variables.

Example 1. *The* RDN, XOR, *and the* COPY *distributions.*

RDN: *If S, Y, and Z are uniformly distributed binary random variables with $S = Y = Z$, then conditioning on Z decreases the mutual information between S and Y. This is an instance of a purely* redundant *interaction where Y and Z convey the same information about S.*

XOR: *If S and Y are independent binary random variables, and $Z = S \oplus Y$ (where $\oplus$ denotes the binary* XOR *operation), then conditioning on Z increases the mutual information between S and Y. This is an instance of a purely* synergistic *interaction where neither Y nor Z individually conveys any information about S, but jointly, they fully determine S.*

COPY: *If Y and Z are independent uniformly distributed binary random variables, and $S = (Y, Z)$ then $I(S;Y) = I(S;Y|Z) = H(Y) = 1$ bit, and $I(S;Z) = I(S;Z|Y) = H(Z) = 1$ bit. This is an instance of an interaction that is neither redundant nor synergistic, but purely* unique, *for now, Y and Z each uniquely conveys 1 bit of information about S.*

In general, all three forms of interaction—unique, redundant, and synergistic—can coexist simultaneously. Our goal is to disentangle the individual contributions to the mutual information between S and (Y, Z) arising from these interactions. Specifically, we distinguish S as the *target* variable of interest, with Y and Z serving as *predictor* variables.

Let $\widetilde{UI}$, $\widetilde{SI}$, and $\widetilde{CI}$ be non-negative functions that depend continuously on the joint distribution of (S, Y, Z). The mutual information between S and Y can be decomposed into two components: information Y has about S that is *unknown* to Z (referred to as the *unique* or *exclusive* information of Y with respect to Z), and information Y has about S that is *known* to Z (referred to as the *shared* or *redundant* information). This decomposition is given by the following:

$$I(S;Y) = \underbrace{\widetilde{UI}(S;Y\backslash Z)}_{\text{unique } Y \text{ with respect to } Z} + \underbrace{\widetilde{SI}(S;Y,Z)}_{\text{shared (redundant)}} . \tag{4}$$

Conditioning on Z eliminates the shared information but introduces *complementary* (or *synergistic*) information arising from the interaction between Y and Z. This is expressed as follows:

$$I(S;Y|Z) = \underbrace{\widetilde{UI}(S;Y\backslash Z)}_{\text{unique } Y \text{ with respect to } Z} + \underbrace{\widetilde{CI}(S;Y,Z)}_{\text{complementary (synergistic)}} . \tag{5}$$

The unique information can be interpreted either as the conditional mutual information without synergy or as the mutual information without redundancy. Applying the chain rule for mutual information, the total mutual information between S and (Y, Z) can be decomposed into four distinct terms, as illustrated in Figure 1:

$$I(S;YZ) = \widetilde{UI}(S;Y\backslash Z) + \widetilde{SI}(S;Y,Z) + \widetilde{UI}(S;Z\backslash Y) + \widetilde{CI}(S;Y,Z). \quad (6)$$

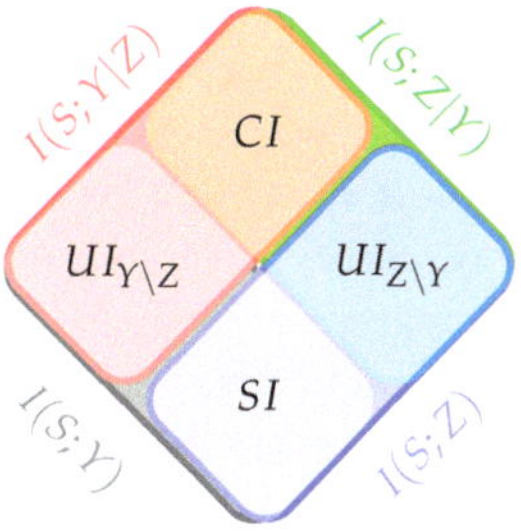

Figure 1. An illustration of the information decomposition in Equations (4)–(6).

Equations (4)–(6) leave only a single degree of freedom; i.e., it suffices to specify either a measure for $\widetilde{SI}$, for $\widetilde{CI}$, or for $\widetilde{UI}$. Any definition of the measure $\widetilde{UI}$ fixes two of the terms in (6), which, in turn, also determines the other terms by (4) and (5). This gives rise to the following *consistency condition*:

$$I(S;Y) + \widetilde{UI}(S;Z\backslash Y) = I(S;Z) + \widetilde{UI}(S;Y\backslash Z). \quad (7)$$

The *coinformation* [30] is defined as the difference between the shared and synergistic information. It serves as a symmetric measure of correlation among three random variables:

$$CoI(S;Y;Z) = \widetilde{SI}(S;Y,Z) - \widetilde{CI}(S;Y,Z) = I(S;Y) - I(S;Y|Z). \quad (8)$$

Coinformation is called *interaction information* (with a change of sign) in [31] and *multiple mutual information* in [32]. The XOR distribution in Example 1 shows that CoI can be negative. Coinformations and entropies are related by a Möbius inversion [30]. Equation (8) can equivalently be written as a linear combinations of entropies:

$$CoI(S;Y;Z) = H(S) + H(Y) + H(Z) - H(SY) - H(SZ) - H(YZ) + H(SYZ). \quad (9)$$

Yeung [33] discusses properties of the CoI as a signed measure using analogies between sets and random variables. Te Sun [34] studies the more general question of what linear combinations of entropies are always non-negative.

Yet, another way to express the CoI is in terms of mutual informations:

$$CoI(S;Y;Z) = I(S;Y) + I(S;Z) - I(S;YZ). \quad (10)$$

Equation (10) shows that CoI can be interpreted as a measure of the "extensivity" of mutual information, i.e., how the mutual information increases as we combine Y and Z [35]: If $CoI = 0$, then the mutual information is exactly extensive in the sense that $I(S;YZ)$ is the sum of the mutual informations $I(S;Y)$ and $I(S;Z)$. If $CoI > 0$, then the mutual information is subextensive and the shared component dominates the synergistic component. Conversely, if $CoI < 0$, then the mutual information is superextensive and the synergistic component dominates the shared component.

Coinformation is a widely utilized measure in neuroscience and related fields, with positive values interpreted as redundancy and negative values as synergy [36–45]. However, it cannot detect interactions where redundancy and synergy are perfectly balanced [46].

The *correlational importance*, a non-negative measure for evaluating the role of correlations in neural coding [47–49] (see also [50]), aligns conceptually with complementary information. Notably, it can sometimes exceed the total mutual information, as demonstrated in specific examples [51].

Non-negative decompositions of the form (4)–(6) that seek to disentangle the synergistic and redundant contributions to the total information that a pair of predictors convey about the target S were first considered by Williams and Beer [46]. Some notable follow-up works include [6,26,52–59]. For the general case of k finite predictor variables, Williams and Beer proposed the *partial information lattice* framework to decompose the mutual information between the target and predictors into a sum of non-negative terms corresponding to the different ways in which combinations of the predictor variables convey shared, unique, or complementary information about S. The lattice is a consequence of certain natural properties of the shared information, sometimes called the *Williams–Beer axioms*. The underlying idea is that any information about S can be classified according to "who knows what", i.e., which information about S is shared by which subsets of the predictors [59]. Specializing to the bivariate case ($k = 2$), the Williams–Beer axioms only put crude bounds on the values of the functions $\widetilde{SI}$, $\widetilde{UI}$, and $\widetilde{CI}$ in (4)–(6). Additional axioms have been proposed in [26,60]. See Appendix A for a brief review of these axioms. Unfortunately, some of these axioms contradict each other, and the question for the right axiomatic characterization of shared information is still open.

Bertschinger et al. [6] proposed a pragmatic approach to decompositions of the form (4)–(6) based on the idea that if Y has unique information about S with respect to Z, then there must be a situation or task where such unique information is useful. This idea is formalized in terms of decision problems. We recall the definitions in [6].

Definition 1 ([6]). *For some finite state spaces $\mathcal{Y}$, $\mathcal{Z}$, and $\mathcal{S}$, let $\mathbb{P}_{\mathcal{S}\times\mathcal{Y}\times\mathcal{Z}}$ be the set of all joint distributions of (S, Y, Z). Given $P \in \mathbb{P}_{\mathcal{S}\times\mathcal{Y}\times\mathcal{Z}}$, let*

$$\Delta_P := \{Q \in \mathbb{P}_{\mathcal{S}\times\mathcal{Y}\times\mathcal{Z}} \colon Q_{SY}(s,y) = P_{SY}(s,y) \text{ and } Q_{SZ}(s,z) = P_{SZ}(s,z)\} \tag{11}$$

denote the set of all joint distributions of (S, Y, Z) that have the same marginals on (S, Y) and (S, Z) as P. The unique information that Y conveys about S with respect to Z is defined as

$$UI(S; Y\backslash Z) = \min_{Q\in\Delta_P} I_Q(S; Y|Z), \tag{12a}$$

where the subscript Q in I_Q denotes the joint distribution on which the function is computed. Specifying (12a) *fixes the other three functions in* (6)*, which are then*

$$UI(S; Z\backslash Y) = \min_{Q\in\Delta_P} I_Q(S; Z|Y), \tag{12b}$$

$$SI(S; Y, Z) = \max_{Q\in\Delta_P} CoI_Q(S; Y; Z), \tag{12c}$$

$$CI(S; Y, Z) = I(S; Y|Z) - UI(S; Y\backslash Z). \tag{12d}$$

The functions UI, SI, and CI are non-negative and satisfy (4)–(6) (and hence (7)). Furthermore, the function SI satisfies the bivariate Williams–Beer axioms [6] (see Appendix A):

$$
\begin{aligned}
&SI(S;Y,Z) = SI(S;Z,Y) && \textit{(symmetry)}, \\
&SI(S;Y) = I(S;Y) && \textit{(self-redundancy)}, \\
&SI(S;Y,Z) \leq SI(S;Y) \text{ with equality if } Z \text{ is a function of } Y && \textit{(bivariate monotonicity)}.
\end{aligned} \tag{13}
$$

The definition of the function UI is rooted in a notion of channel domination due to Blackwell [61]. Intuitively, one channel dominates another if the latter can be "simulated" by the former by some stochastic degradation. UI satisfies the following key property which we call the *Blackwell property* (see Definition 10):

Lemma 1 (Vanishing UI [6], Lemma 6)**.** *For a given joint distribution P_{SYZ}, $UI(S;Y\backslash Z)$ vanishes if and only if there exists a random variable Y' such that $S - Z - Y'$ is a Markov chain and $P_{SY'} = P_{SY}$.*

Blackwell's theorem [61,62] establishes that $UI(S;Y\backslash Z) = 0$ is equivalent to the assertion that, for any decision problem involving the prediction of S, having access to Z provides the same predictive capability as having access to Y (see Theorem 1).

Given $(S,Y,Z) \sim P$, let

$$
Q^0(s,y,z) = \begin{cases} \dfrac{P(s,y)P(s,z)}{P(s)}, & \text{if } P(s) > 0, \\ 0, & \text{else.} \end{cases} \tag{14}
$$

Observe that $Q^0 \in \Delta_P$. Moreover, Q^0 defines a Markov chain $Y - S - Z$. The following lemma gives conditions under which the function SI vanishes:

Lemma 2 (Vanishing SI [6], Lemma 9)**.** *SI vanishes if and only if $I_{Q^0}(Y;Z) = 0$.*

Lemma 3 characterizes the quantities UI, SI, and CI among alternative definitions of information decompositions.

Lemma 3 ([6], Lemma 3)**.** *Let $\widetilde{UI}(S;Y\backslash Z)$, $\widetilde{UI}(S;Z\backslash Y)$, $\widetilde{SI}(S;Y,Z)$, and $\widetilde{CI}(S;Y,Z)$ be non-negative functions on $\mathbb{P}_{\mathcal{S}\times\mathcal{Y}\times\mathcal{Z}}$ satisfying equations (4)–(6), and assume that the following holds:*

$(*)$ *$\widetilde{UI}$ depends only on the marginal distributions of the pairs (S,Y) and (S,Z).*

Then, $\widetilde{UI} \leq UI$, $\widetilde{SI} \geq SI$, and $\widetilde{CI} \geq CI$ with equality if and only if there exists $Q \in \Delta_P$ such that $\widetilde{CI}_Q(S;Y,Z) = 0$.

By Lemma 3, (12a–12d) is the *only* information decomposition that satisfies $(*)$ and the following property:

$(**)$ For each $P \in \Delta$, there is $Q \in \Delta_P$ with $CI_Q(S;Y,Z) = 0$.

Assumption $(*)$ in Lemma 3 is motivated by the Blackwell property, which also depends only on the marginal distributions of the pairs (S,Y) and (S,Z).

Given $(S,Y,Z) \sim P$, let

$$
Q^* \in \operatorname*{arg\,min}_{Q\in\Delta_P} I_Q(S;Y|Z). \tag{15}
$$

By definition, $I_{Q^*}(S;Y|Z) = UI(S;Y\backslash Z)$. The distribution Q^* is called a *minimum synergy distribution* as

$$
CI_P(S;Y,Z) = 0 \text{ if and only if } P \in \operatorname*{arg\,min}_{Q\in\Delta_P} I_Q(S;Y|Z). \tag{16}
$$

Although theoretically promising, the operational significance of the UI is not immediately evident, except in cases where it vanishes, reflecting the Blackwell property. One of our main aims is to address this gap by examining UI's operational relevance in practical model systems through the following key observations:

- The Blackwell relation induces a partial order on channels with the same input alphabet. Most channels are incomparable, meaning one cannot always simulate another by degradation. In such cases, UI quantifies the degree of deviation from simulating one channel by another.
- Weaker notions of channel comparison, such as the "less noisy" property [63], have operational significance through vanishing C_S, where C_S is the secrecy capacity of the wiretap channel [64,65]. Similar to how C_S measures deviation from the less noisy order, a nonvanishing UI quantifies a deviation from the Blackwell order and bounds operational quantities in secret key agreement tasks. In particular, UI acts as a *secrecy monotone*, never increasing under local operations in one-way secret key agreement protocols, making it an upper bound on the *one-way secret key rate* $S_{\rightarrow}$ [66]. This endows the UI with operational significance.
- Finally, the best-known upper bounds on the *two-way secret key rate* $S_{\leftrightarrow}$ involve a secret key decomposition [67]. We show that UI satisfies a similar property, ensuring UI is never greater than the best-known computable upper bound on $S_{\leftrightarrow}$. We conjecture that UI serves as a lower bound on $S_{\leftrightarrow}$ and identify a class of distributions where they coincide.

3. Comparison of Channels

Given two channels that convey information about the same random variable, a natural question is "which channel is better?". Depending on the task at hand, some orderings are more natural or mathematically more appealing than others. For example, ordering channels according to their capacity is often too coarse to be useful in practice. In a seminal paper [61], David Blackwell introduced an ordering of channels in terms of risks of statistical decision rules. Blackwell showed that such an ordering can be equivalently characterized in terms of a purely probabilistic relation between the channels. Blackwell formulated his result in terms of a decision problem, where a decision maker or agent reacts to the outcome of a statistical experiment. In information-theoretic parlance, a statistical experiment is just a noisy channel [4,25]. Shannon [68] independently introduced a criterion for ordering communication channels from a random coding perspective, which is weaker than Blackwell's criterion.

We provide a self-contained introduction to channel orderings in information theory. Such orderings are a well-studied subject in network information theory [69]. For instance, the capacity region of broadcast channels (without feedback) depends only on the component channels and is known for a number of special cases when one of the components is "better" than the other in some well-defined sense (see, e.g., [70,71]).

The Blackwell order. The Blackwell order evaluates channels with a common input alphabet by comparing the minimal expected loss a rational agent incurs when making decisions based on their outputs. This concept is formalized through decision problems under uncertainty (see [24] for an in-depth discussion).

Consider a *decision problem* $(\pi_S, \mathcal{A}, \ell)$, where $\mathcal{A}$ is the set of possible actions, $\ell(s,a)$ represents the bounded loss incurred when the agent chooses action $a \in \mathcal{A}$ in state $s \in \mathcal{S}$, and π_S is the prior distribution over the state space $\mathcal{S}$.

The agent observes a random variable Z via a channel $\mu : \mathcal{S} \to \mathcal{Z}$ before choosing an action. A rational agent selects a strategy $\rho \in \mathsf{M}(\mathcal{Z};\mathcal{A})$ to minimize the *expected loss* (or *risk*), defined as follows:

$$R(\pi_S, \mu, \rho, \ell) := \sum_{s\in\mathcal{S}} \pi_S(s) \sum_{a\in\mathcal{A}} \rho \circ \mu_s(a)\ell(s, a). \quad (17)$$

The *optimal risk* for channel μ is as follows:

$$R(\pi_S, \mu, \ell) := \min_{\sigma\in\mathcal{A}_\mu} \sum_{s\in\mathcal{S}} \pi_S(s) \sum_{a\in\mathcal{A}} \sigma_s(a)\ell(s, a). \quad (18)$$

where $\mathcal{A}_\mu = \{\rho \circ \mu : \rho \in \mathsf{M}(\mathcal{Z}; \mathcal{A})\}$. Optimal strategies can always be chosen deterministically, so it suffices to consider deterministic strategies.

Now, suppose the agent has access to another random variable Y via a second channel $\kappa \in \mathsf{M}(\mathcal{S}; \mathcal{Y})$ with the same input alphabet $\mathcal{S}$. The agent will *always* prefer Z to Y if, for any decision problem, the optimal risk using Z is no greater than that using Y. This leads to the following definition.

Definition 2. *Given $\mu \in \mathsf{M}(\mathcal{S}; \mathcal{Z})$, $\kappa \in \mathsf{M}(\mathcal{S}; \mathcal{Y})$, and a probability distribution π_S on $\mathcal{S}$ such that $P_{SZ}(s, z) = \pi_S(s)\mu_s(z)$ and $P_{SY}(s, y) = \pi_S(s)\kappa_s(y)$, we say that Z is* always more informative *about S than Y and write $Z \sqsupseteq_S Y$ if $R(\pi_S, \kappa, \ell) \geq R(\pi_S, \mu, \ell)$ for any decision problem (with π_S fixed as above).*

The variables can also be ranked probabilistically: Z is *always* preferred over Y if, given access to Z, a single use of Y can be simulated by sampling $y' \in \mathcal{Y}$ after each observation $z \in \mathcal{Z}$. This implies that Y provides no additional utility beyond what Z already offers.

Definition 3. *Write $Z \sqsupseteq'_S Y$ if there exists a random variable Y' such that the pairs (S, Y) and (S, Y') are statistically indistinguishable, and $S - Z - Y'$ is a Markov chain.*

Intuitively, Z knows everything that Y knows about S in both these situations. Blackwell showed the equivalence of these two relations [61]. The following is a statement of Blackwell's theorem for random variables [62]:

Theorem 1 (Blackwell's theorem for random variables). $Z \sqsupseteq_S Y \iff Z \sqsupseteq'_S Y$.

The original statement of Blackwell's theorem [61] allows us to directly compare the channels κ and μ and the input distribution on $\mathcal{S}$ can be arbitrary.

Definition 4. *We say that μ is* always more informative *than κ and write $\mu \sqsupseteq_{\mathcal{S}} \kappa$ if $R(\pi_S, \kappa, \ell) \geq R(\pi_S, \mu, \ell)$ for any $(\pi_S, \mathcal{A}, \ell)$.*

Definition 5. *We say that κ is* output-degraded *(or* post-garbled*)* from *μ and write $\mu \sqsupseteq_{\mathcal{S}}^{odeg} \kappa$ if $\kappa = \lambda \circ \mu$ for some $\lambda \in \mathsf{M}(\mathcal{Z}; \mathcal{Y})$.*

The relation $\sqsupseteq_{\mathcal{S}}^{\mathrm{odeg}}$ is also called the *degradation order* (see, e.g., [72]).

Theorem 2 (Blackwell's Theorem (1953) [61]). $\mu \sqsupseteq_{\mathcal{S}} \kappa \iff \mu \sqsupseteq_{\mathcal{S}}^{odeg} \kappa$.

See [73] for a simple proof of Blackwell's theorem.

If π_S has full support, then $\mu \sqsupseteq_{\mathcal{S}} \kappa \iff Z \sqsupseteq_S Y$ (Theorem 4 in [62]) and it suffices to look only at different loss functions. In the sequel, we assume that π_S has full support, and we call $\sqsupseteq_{\mathcal{S}}$ and $\sqsupseteq_S$ the *Blackwell orders*.

Strictly speaking, the Blackwell order is only a preorder rather than a partial order as there exist channels $\kappa \neq \mu$ that satisfy $\kappa \sqsupseteq_{\mathcal{S}} \mu \sqsupseteq_{\mathcal{S}} \kappa$ (when κ arises from μ by permuting the output alphabet). However, for our purposes, such channels can be treated as equivalent.

We write $\mu \sqsupset_{\mathcal{S}} \kappa$ if $\mu \sqsupseteq_{\mathcal{S}} \kappa$ and $\kappa \not\sqsupseteq_{\mathcal{S}} \mu$. By Blackwell's theorem, this indicates that μ performs at least as well as κ in any decision problem and that there exist decision problems in which μ outperforms κ.

A related order is the *zonotope order*, which is weaker than the Blackwell order [62,74]. For the special case of binary-valued channel inputs, i.e., $|\mathcal{S}| = 2$, the Blackwell order defines a lattice and is identical to the zonotope order [62,74] and its generalization, the k-decision order [61].

The Shannon order. Shannon proposed a criterion for simulating one channel from another based on a random coding argument [68]. Shannon's criterion allows for randomization at *both* the input and the output of the simulating channel as well as for shared randomness between its input and output.

Definition 6 ([68]). *Given two channels $\kappa \in \mathsf{M}(\mathcal{S}';\mathcal{Y})$ and $\mu \in \mathsf{M}(\mathcal{S};\mathcal{Z})$, we say that μ* includes *κ and write $\mu \sqsupseteq^{inc} \kappa$ if for some $k \in \mathbb{N}$, there exists a probability distribution $g \in \mathbb{P}_{[k]}$ and k pairs of pre- and post-channels $(\alpha_i, \beta_i) \in \mathsf{M}(\mathcal{S}';\mathcal{S}) \times \mathsf{M}(\mathcal{Z};\mathcal{Y})$, $1 \le i \le k$, such that $\kappa = \sum_{i=1}^{k} g(i)(\beta_i \circ \mu \circ \alpha_i)$.*

Shannon showed that if $\mu \sqsupseteq^{inc} \kappa$, then the existence of a good coding scheme for κ implies the existence of a good coding scheme for μ, where "goodness" is measured in the sense of low probability of error. Let Σ be the set of all convex combinations of products of the channels in $\mathsf{M}(\mathcal{S}';\mathcal{S})$ with those in $\mathsf{M}(\mathcal{Z};\mathcal{Y})$, i.e.,

$$\Sigma = \operatorname{conv}\left(\alpha \otimes \beta \in \mathsf{M}(\mathcal{S}' \times \mathcal{Z};\mathcal{S} \times \mathcal{Y}) : \alpha \in \mathsf{M}(\mathcal{S}';\mathcal{S}),\ \beta \in \mathsf{M}(\mathcal{Z};\mathcal{Y})\right), \tag{19}$$

where conv(C) denotes the convex hull of C, and $(\alpha \otimes \beta)_{s',z}(s,y) = \alpha_{s'}(s)\beta_z(y)$ for each $s \in \mathcal{S}$, $s' \in \mathcal{S}'$, $z \in \mathcal{Z}$, and $y \in \mathcal{Y}$. By Carathéodory's theorem [75], any channel $\chi \in \Sigma$ can be represented as a convex combination of at most $|\mathcal{S}' \times \mathcal{Z} \times \mathcal{S} \times \mathcal{Y}| + 1$ product channels. Given $\mu \in \mathsf{M}(\mathcal{S};\mathcal{Z})$ and $\chi \in \Sigma$, define the *skew-composition* $\chi \circ_s \mu \in \mathsf{M}(\mathcal{S}';\mathcal{Y})$ of μ with χ as follows: $\chi \circ_s \mu(y|s') = \sum_{s \in \mathcal{S}, z \in \mathcal{Z}} \chi_{s',z}(s,y)\mu_s(z)$ for all $s' \in \mathcal{S}'$, $y \in \mathcal{Y}$. We then have the following equivalent characterization of the Shannon order:

Proposition 1 ([76]). *$\mu \sqsupseteq^{inc} \kappa$ if and only if there exists $\chi \in \Sigma$ such that $\kappa = \chi \circ_s \mu$.*

Nasser [76] gave a characterization of the Shannon order that is similar to Blackwell's theorem.

In Definition 6, the input and output alphabets of both κ and μ may be different. If the channels share a common input alphabet, i.e., $\mathcal{S}' = \mathcal{S}$, then $\mu \sqsupseteq^{\mathsf{odeg}}_{\mathcal{S}} \kappa \implies \mu \sqsupseteq^{inc} \kappa$. The converse implication is not true in general and the Shannon order is weaker than the Blackwell order [25].

The input-degraded order. Given two channels that share a common output alphabet, Nasser [77] introduced the following ordering:

Definition 7 ([77]). *Let $\bar{\kappa} \in \mathsf{M}(\mathcal{Y};\mathcal{S})$ and $\bar{\mu} \in \mathsf{M}(\mathcal{Z};\mathcal{S})$ be two channels with a common output alphabet. We say that $\bar{\kappa}$* is input-degraded from *$\bar{\mu}$ and write $\bar{\mu} \sqsupseteq^{ideg}_{\mathcal{S}} \bar{\kappa}$ if $\bar{\kappa} = \bar{\mu} \circ \bar{\lambda}$ for some $\bar{\lambda} \in \mathsf{M}(\mathcal{Y};\mathcal{Z})$.*

Proposition 2 ([77]).

$$\bar{\mu} \sqsupseteq^{ideg}_{\mathcal{S}} \bar{\kappa} \iff \operatorname{conv}(\{\bar{\kappa}_y\}_{y \in \mathcal{Y}}) \subset \operatorname{conv}(\{\bar{\mu}_z\}_{z \in \mathcal{Z}})$$

where conv(C) *denotes the convex hull of* C*.*

Nasser [77] gave a characterization of the input-degraded order that is similar to Blackwell's theorem.

The more capable and less noisy orders. Given two channels $\kappa \in \mathsf{M}(\mathcal{S};\mathcal{Y})$ and $\mu \in \mathsf{M}(\mathcal{S};\mathcal{Z})$ with a common input alphabet, Körner and Marton introduced the following two orderings [63]:

Definition 8. *μ is said to be* more capable *than κ, denoted $\mu \sqsupseteq^{mc} \kappa$, if $I(S;Z) \geq I(S;Y)$ for every probability distribution $P_S \in \mathbb{P}_{\mathcal{S}}$.*

Definition 9. *μ is said to be* less noisy *than κ, denoted $\mu \sqsupseteq^{ln} \kappa$, if $I(U;Z) \geq I(U;Y)$ for every P_{US} such that $U - S - YZ$ is a Markov chain.*

An equivalent characterization of the less noisy relation is the following [78]: $\mu \sqsupseteq^{\mathsf{ln}} \kappa$ if and only if $I(S;Z) - I(S;Y)$ is a concave function of the input probability distribution P_S.

We note the following relationship between the Blackwell, less noisy and the more capable preorders:

Proposition 3 ([63]).

$$\mu \sqsupseteq_{\mathcal{S}}^{odeg} \kappa \implies \mu \sqsupseteq^{ln} \kappa \implies \mu \sqsupseteq^{mc} \kappa. \tag{20}$$

As the following examples show, the converse of neither implication is true in general [63].

Example 2 (Broadcast channel consisting of a BSC and a BEC [69,79])**.** *A memoryless broadcast channel model $(\mathcal{S}, \xi_s(y,z), \mathcal{Y} \times \mathcal{Z})$ consists of three sets $\mathcal{S}$, $\mathcal{Y}$, and $\mathcal{Z}$, and a channel $\xi \in \mathsf{M}(\mathcal{S};\mathcal{Y} \times \mathcal{Z})$. Let $\kappa_s(y) := \sum_{z\in\mathcal{Z}} \xi_s(y,z)$ and $\mu_s(z) := \sum_{y\in\mathcal{Y}} \xi_s(y,z)$ be the two components of ξ.*

Consider a broadcast channel with $\kappa = \mathsf{BSC}(p)$ with crossover probability $p \in (0, 1/2)$, and $\mu = \mathsf{BEC}(\epsilon)$ with erasure probability $\epsilon \in (0,1)$. Then, the following hold:

1. *For $0 < \epsilon \leq 2p$, Y is output-degraded from Z.*
2. *For $2p < \epsilon \leq 4p(1-p)$, Z is less noisy than Y, but Y is not output-degraded from Z.*
3. *For $4p(1-p) < \epsilon \leq h(p)$, Z is more capable than Y, but not less noisy.*
4. *For $h(p) < \epsilon < 1$, ξ does not belong to any of the three classes.*

Example 3 (Doubly symmetric binary erasure (DSBE) source [12,80])**.** *A DSBE source with parameters (p,ϵ) is defined as follows: $P_{SYZ}(s,y,z) = P_{SY}(s,y)p_{Z|SY}(z|s,y)$ where $P_{SY}(0,0) = P_{SY}(1,1) = p/2$, $P_{SY}(0,1) = P_{SY}(1,0) = (1-p)/2$, and $P_{Z|SY}(z|s,y)$ is an erasure channel, i.e., $Z = SY$ with probability $1-\epsilon$ and $Z = \mathsf{e}$ with probability ϵ. Without loss of generality, we may assume $p > \frac{1}{2}$. Then, the following hold:*

1. *For $0 < \epsilon \leq 2(1-p)$, Y is output-degraded from Z.*
2. *For $2(1-p) < \epsilon \leq 4p(1-p)$, Z is less noisy than Y, but Y is not output-degraded from Z.*
3. *For $4p(1-p) < \epsilon \leq h(p)$, Z is more capable than Y, but not less noisy.*
4. *For $h(p) < \epsilon < 1$, a $\mathsf{DSBE}(p,\epsilon)$ source does not belong to any of the three classes.*

4. Unique Information and Channel Deficiencies

How can we determine whether Y possesses unique information about S that is not available to Z? Consider the channels κ and μ with a *common input* alphabet $\mathcal{S}$, as illustrated in Figure 2a. If μ can be reduced to κ by appending a post-channel λ at its *output*, then μ can be said to *include* κ. Similarly, for the channels $\bar{\kappa}$ and $\bar{\mu}$ with a *common output* alphabet $\mathcal{S}$, as shown in Figure 2b, $\bar{\mu}$ can be considered to include $\bar{\kappa}$ if it reduces to $\bar{\kappa}$ by adding a pre-channel $\bar{\lambda}$ at its *input*.

In both cases, one would expect Y to provide no unique information about S relative to Z. A nonzero unique information would then serve as a measure of the extent to which one channel deviates from being an inclusion or randomization of the other.

Figure 2. (**a**) Simulation of the channel κ through a randomization at the output of μ, where κ and μ share a *common input* alphabet $\mathcal{S}$. (**b**) Simulation of the channel $\bar{\kappa}$ through a randomization at the input of $\bar{\mu}$, where $\bar{\kappa}$ and $\bar{\mu}$ share a *common output* alphabet $\mathcal{S}$.

The function UI in Definition 1 is based on the idea of approximating one channel by randomizing its *output* (see Figure 2a). In contrast, Harder et al. [26] defined a measure of shared information through a difference in two KL divergence terms, where one term involves randomization at the *input* (see Figure 2b). In both cases, the resulting decompositions of the total mutual information are non-negative.

Banerjee et al. [16] introduce two quantities that generalize Le Cam's notion of *weighted deficiency* [23–25] between channels. Weighted deficiencies quantify the cost of approximating one channel from another via randomizations and are closely related to the function UI. Depending on whether the randomization occurs at the output or input, two different forms of weighted deficiency arise: the *weighted output KL deficiency* and the *weighted input KL deficiency*. Both of these induce non-negative bivariate decompositions [16]. Interestingly, the decomposition corresponding to the weighted input deficiency coincides with the one introduced by Harder et al. [26] (see Proposition 8).

4.1. Generalized Le Cam Deficiencies

The Blackwell order provides a natural criterion to determine if a variable Y has unique information about S with respect to Z or not; see Definitions 2 and 3.

Definition 10 (Blackwell property). *Y has no unique information about S with respect to $Z :\Longleftrightarrow Z \sqsupseteq'_S Y$.*

The function UI satisfies the Blackwell property (see Lemma 1). When $UI(S;Y\backslash Z)$ vanishes, we say that Z is *Blackwell-sufficient* for Y with respect to S.

Theorem 1 states that if the relation $Z \sqsupseteq_S Y$ (resp. $Y \sqsupseteq_S Z$) does not hold, then there exist a loss function and a set of actions that render Y (resp. Z) more useful. This statement motivates the following definition [6]:

Definition 11. *Y has unique information about S with respect to Z if there exists a set of actions $\mathcal{A}$ and a loss function $\ell(s,a) \in \mathbb{R}^{\mathcal{S}\times\mathcal{A}}$ such that $R(\pi_S,\kappa,\ell) < R(\pi_S,\mu,\ell)$.*

The relation $\sqsupseteq_{\mathcal{S}}^{\mathsf{odeg}}$ is a preorder on the family of all channels with the same input alphabet $\mathcal{S}$ (see Definition 5). In general, we cannot always simulate one channel by a randomization of the other. To be able to compare any two channels, Lucien Le Cam introduced the notion of channel *deficiencies* [23,24]:

Definition 12. *Given $\mu \in \mathsf{M}(\mathcal{S};\mathcal{Z})$ and $\kappa \in \mathsf{M}(\mathcal{S};\mathcal{Y})$, the* Le Cam deficiency of μ with respect to κ *is*

$$\delta(\mu,\kappa) := \inf_{\lambda\in\mathsf{M}(\mathcal{Z};\mathcal{Y})} \sup_{s\in\mathcal{S}} \|\lambda\circ\mu_s - \kappa_s\|_{\mathsf{TV}}. \tag{21}$$

where $\|\cdot\|_{\mathsf{TV}}$ *denotes the total variation distance.*

Note that $\delta(\mu,\kappa) = 0$ if and only if $\mu \sqsupseteq_{\mathcal{S}}^{\mathsf{odeg}} \kappa$.

Definition 13. *Given* $\mu \in \mathsf{M}(\mathcal{S};\mathcal{Z})$, $\kappa \in \mathsf{M}(\mathcal{S};\mathcal{Y})$ *and a probability distribution* π_S *on* $\mathcal{S}$*, the* weighted Le Cam deficiency of μ with respect to κ *is*

$$\delta^{\pi}(\mu,\kappa) := \inf_{\lambda \in \mathsf{M}(\mathcal{Z};\mathcal{Y})} \mathbb{E}_{s\sim\pi_S} \|\lambda \circ \mu_s - \kappa_s\|_{\mathsf{TV}}. \tag{22}$$

The *Le Cam randomization criterion* [23] establishes that deficiencies quantify the maximal gap in optimal risks between decision problems when using the channel μ instead of κ.

Theorem 3 ([23])**.** *Fix* $\mu \in \mathsf{M}(\mathcal{S};\mathcal{Z})$, $\kappa \in \mathsf{M}(\mathcal{S};\mathcal{Y})$*, and a probability distribution* π_S *on* $\mathcal{S}$*, and write* $\|\ell\|_\infty = \max_{s,a} \ell(s,a)$*. For every* $\epsilon > 0$, $\delta^{\pi}(\mu,\kappa) \le \epsilon$ *if and only if* $R(\pi_S,\mu,\ell) - R(\pi_S,\kappa,\ell) \le \epsilon\|\ell\|_\infty$ *for any set of actions* $\mathcal{A}$ *and any bounded loss function* ℓ*.*

Raginsky [25] introduced a broad class of deficiency-like quantities based on a "generalized" divergence between probability distributions that maintains a monotonicity property with respect to data processing. Specializing this to the KL divergence, we have the following definition:

Definition 14. *The* output KL deficiency of μ with respect to κ *is*

$$\delta_o(\mu,\kappa) := \inf_{\lambda \in \mathsf{M}(\mathcal{Z};\mathcal{Y})} \sup_{s\in\mathcal{S}} D(\kappa_s \| \lambda \circ \mu_s), \tag{23}$$

where the subscript o in δ_o *emphasizes the fact that the randomization is at the* output *of the channel* μ*.*

In a spirit similar to [25] and Section 6.2 in [24], one can define a weighted output KL deficiency [16]:

Definition 15. *The* weighted output KL deficiency of μ with respect to κ *is*

$$\delta_o^{\pi}(\mu,\kappa) := \min_{\lambda \in \mathsf{M}(\mathcal{Z};\mathcal{Y})} D(\kappa \| \lambda \circ \mu | \pi_S). \tag{24}$$

The weighted output KL deficiency quantifies the cost of approximating one observed variable from the other (and vice versa) through Markov kernels. Notably, $\delta_o^{\pi}(\mu,\kappa) = 0$ if and only if $Z \sqsupseteq_S' Y$, capturing the intuition that a small value of $\delta_o^{\pi}(\mu,\kappa)$ implies that Z is *approximately Blackwell-sufficient* for Y with respect to S. Using Pinsker's inequality, we obtain the following:

$$\delta^{\pi}(\mu,\kappa) \le \sqrt{\tfrac{\ln(2)}{2}\delta_o^{\pi}(\mu,\kappa)}. \tag{25}$$

Bounding the weighted output KL deficiency is sufficient to guarantee that the differences in optimal risks remain bounded for any decision problem of interest [16]:

Proposition 4. *Fix* $\mu \in \mathsf{M}(\mathcal{S};\mathcal{Z})$, $\kappa \in \mathsf{M}(\mathcal{S};\mathcal{Y})$*, and a prior probability distribution* π_S *on* $\mathcal{S}$*, and write* $\|\ell\|_\infty = \max_{s,a} \ell(s,a)$*. For every* $\epsilon > 0$*, if* $\delta_o^{\pi}(\mu,\kappa) \le \epsilon$*, then* $R(\pi_S,\mu,\ell) - R(\pi_S,\kappa,\ell) \le \sqrt{\epsilon\frac{\ln(2)}{2}}\|\ell\|_\infty$ *for any set of actions* $\mathcal{A}$ *and any bounded loss function* ℓ*.*

Recall the data processing inequality for the mutual information:

$$Z - Y - W \implies I(Z;W) \leq \min\{I(Z;Y), I(Y;W)\}. \tag{26}$$

Lemma 4 shows that the weighted output KL deficiency satisfies a similar inequality:

Lemma 4. *Let $\mu \in \mathsf{M}(\mathcal{S};\mathcal{Z})$, $\kappa \in \mathsf{M}(\mathcal{S};\mathcal{Y})$, and $\nu \in \mathsf{M}(\mathcal{S};\mathcal{W})$ be three channels with a common input alphabet and let π_S be a given distribution on $\mathcal{S}$. Then,*

$$Z \sqsupseteq_S Y \sqsupseteq_S W \implies \delta_o^{\pi}(\mu,\nu) \leq \min\{\delta_o^{\pi}(\mu,\kappa), \delta_o^{\pi}(\kappa,\nu)\}.$$

See Appendix B for a proof. One can also define a weighted deficiency for the input-degraded order in Definition 7 [16].

Definition 16. *The* weighted input KL deficiency of $\bar{\mu}$ with respect to $\bar{\kappa}$ *is*

$$\delta_i^{\pi}(\bar{\mu},\bar{\kappa}) := \min_{\bar{\lambda} \in \mathsf{M}(\mathcal{Y};\mathcal{Z})} D(\bar{\kappa} \| \bar{\mu} \circ \bar{\lambda} | \pi_Y), \tag{27}$$

where the subscript i in δ_i emphasizes the fact that the randomization is at the input *of the channel $\bar{\mu}$.*

The weighted input KL deficiency satisfies the following monotonicity property:

Lemma 5. *Let $\bar{\mu} \in \mathsf{M}(\mathcal{Z};\mathcal{S})$, $\bar{\kappa} \in \mathsf{M}(\mathcal{Y};\mathcal{S})$, and $\bar{\nu} \in \mathsf{M}(\mathcal{W},\mathcal{S})$ be three channels with a common output alphabet, and let π_W be a given distribution on $\mathcal{W}$. Then,*

$$\bar{\mu} \sqsupseteq_S^{ideg} \bar{\kappa} \implies \delta_i^{\pi}(\bar{\mu},\bar{\nu}) \leq \delta_i^{\pi}(\bar{\kappa},\bar{\nu}).$$

The proof is similar to the first part of the proof of Lemma 4 and is omitted.

4.2. Non-Negative Mutual Information Decompositions

Given an information measure that captures some aspect of unique information but does not satisfy the consistency condition (7), we can construct the corresponding bivariate information decomposition as follows:

Lemma 6 ([81], Proposition 9). *Let $\delta : \mathbb{P}_{\mathcal{S}\times\mathcal{Y}\times\mathcal{Z}} \to \mathbb{R}$ be a non-negative function that satisfies*

$$\delta(S;Y \setminus Z) \leq \min\{I(S;Y), I(S;Y|Z)\}.$$

Then, a bivariate information decomposition is given by

$$\begin{aligned}
UI_\delta(S;Y \setminus Z) &= \max\{\delta(S;Y \setminus Z), \delta(S;Z \setminus Y) + I(S;Y) - I(S;Z)\}, \\
UI_\delta(S;Z \setminus Y) &= \max\{\delta(S;Z \setminus Y), \delta(S;Y \setminus Z) + I(S;Z) - I(S;Y)\}, \\
SI_\delta(S;Z,Y) &= \min\{I(S;Y) - \delta(S;Y \setminus Z), I(S;Z) - \delta(S;Z \setminus Y)\}, \\
CI_\delta(S;Z,Y) &= \min\{I(S;Y|Z) - \delta(S;Y \setminus Z), I(S;Z|Y) - \delta(S;Z \setminus Y)\}.
\end{aligned}$$

We refer to the construction in Lemma 6 as the *UI construction*. The unique information UI_δ generated by this construction is the smallest UI function among all bivariate information decompositions with $UI \geq \delta$.

This construction can be used to derive new non-negative bivariate decompositions.

4.2.1. Decomposition Based on the Weighted Output KL Deficiency

Proposition 5 ([16]). *Let $(S, Y, Z) \sim P$, and let π_S be the marginal distribution of S. Let $\kappa \in \mathsf{M}(\mathcal{S}; \mathcal{Y})$ resp. $\mu \in \mathsf{M}(\mathcal{S}; \mathcal{Z})$ be two channels describing the conditional distribution of Y resp. Z, given S. Define*

$$\delta(S; Y \setminus Z) = \delta_o^{\pi}(\mu, \kappa), \tag{28}$$

where δ_o is the weighted output KL deficiency (24). Then, the functions UI_δ, SI_δ, and CI_δ in Lemma 6 define a non-negative bivariate decomposition.

Lemma 7 ([16]). *Define*

$$UI_o(S; Y \backslash Z) = \max\{\delta_o^{\pi}(\mu, \kappa), \delta_o^{\pi}(\kappa, \mu) + I(S; Y) - I(S; Z)\}. \tag{29}$$

Then, $UI_o(S; Y \backslash Z)$ vanishes if and only if Y has no unique information about S with respect to Z (according to Definition 10).

From Lemma 3, we have the following relationship between the different quantities:

Lemma 8.

$$\delta_o^{\pi}(\mu, \kappa) \leq UI_o(S; Y \backslash Z) \leq UI(S; Y \backslash Z),$$

The next proposition follows from Lemmas 1 and 7, and Definition 15.

Proposition 6.

$$\delta_o^{\pi}(\mu, \kappa) = 0 \iff UI_o(S; Y \backslash Z) = 0 \iff UI(S; Y \backslash Z) = 0.$$

4.2.2. Decomposition Based on the Weighted Input KL Deficiency

Proposition 7 ([16]). *Let $(S, Y, Z) \sim P$, and let π_Y resp. π_Z be the induced marginal distributions of Y resp. Z, both assumed to have full support. Let $\bar{\kappa} \in \mathsf{M}(\mathcal{Y}; \mathcal{S})$ and $\bar{\mu} \in \mathsf{M}(\mathcal{Z}; \mathcal{S})$ be two channels such that $\bar{\kappa} = P_{S|Y}$ and $\bar{\mu} = P_{S|Z}$. Define*

$$\delta(S; Y \setminus Z) = \delta_i^{\pi}(\bar{\mu}, \bar{\kappa}), \tag{30}$$

where δ_i is the weighted input KL deficiency (27). Then, the functions UI_δ, SI_δ, and CI_δ in Lemma 6 define a non-negative bivariate decomposition.

Harder et al. [26] introduced a measure of *shared information* based on reverse information (rI) projections [82] onto a convex set of probability measures.

Definition 17. *For $C \subset \mathbb{P}_{\mathcal{S}}$, let* conv$(C)$ *denote the convex hull of C. Let*

$$Q_{y \searrow Z}(S) \in \underset{Q \in \mathrm{conv}(\{\bar{\mu}_z\}_{z \in \mathcal{Z}}) \subset \mathbb{P}_{\mathcal{S}}}{\arg\min} D(\bar{\kappa}_y \| Q)$$

be the rI-projection of $\bar{\kappa}_y$ onto the convex hull of the points $\{\bar{\mu}_z\}_{z \in \mathcal{Z}} \in \mathbb{P}_{\mathcal{S}}$. Define the projected information of Y onto Z with respect to S *as*

$$I_S(Y \searrow Z) := \mathbb{E}_{(s,y) \sim \bar{\kappa} \times \pi_Y} \log \frac{Q_{y \searrow Z}(s)}{\bar{\kappa} \circ \pi_Y(s)}, \tag{31}$$

and the shared information as

$$SI_{red}(S;Y,Z) := \min\{I_S(Y \searrow Z), I_S(Z \searrow Y)\}. \tag{32}$$

Proposition 8 states that implicit in the above construction is the weighted input KL deficiency $\delta_i^{\pi}(\bar{\mu},\bar{\kappa})$.

Proposition 8 ([16]). $I_S(Y \searrow Z) = I(S;Y) - \delta_i^{\pi}(\bar{\mu},\bar{\kappa})$.

An immediate consequence of Proposition 8 is that the decomposition proposed by Harder et al. [26] and that in Proposition 7 are equivalent.

Remark 1 (SI_{red} is not continuous). *$I_S(Y \searrow Z)$ and $I_S(Z \searrow Y)$ are defined in terms of conditional probability $\bar{\kappa}_y = P_{S|Y=y}$ and $\bar{\mu}_z = P_{S|Z=z}$, which are only defined for those y,z with $\pi_Y(y) > 0$ and $\pi_Z(z) > 0$. Therefore, $I_S(Y \searrow Z)$ and $I_S(Z \searrow Y)$ are discontinuous when probabilities tend to zero. For a concrete example, see Example 3 in* [18].

Remark 2 (Vanishing sets of UI and deficiencies). *The Blackwell order compares two channels with a* common input *alphabet. This order has found applications in network information theory* [69,79]. *In wiretap channel models* [64,65] *(see Section 5.2), one considers a memoryless broadcast channel $\xi : \mathcal{S} \to \mathcal{Y} \times \mathcal{Z}$ where Alice selects the inputs to ξ, while Bob and Eve observe, resp., the Y-outputs and the Z-outputs. Bob's component channel is defined as $\kappa_s(y) = \sum_{z\in\mathcal{Z}} \xi_s(y,z)$ and Eve's as $\mu_s(z) = \sum_{y\in\mathcal{Y}} \xi_s(y,z)$. The secrecy capacity of the wiretap channel, C_S, quantifies a deviation from the less noisy order and depends on ξ only through the component channels κ and μ (see Proposition 9). Likewise, when the distribution of the input to ξ is fixed, the UI and weighted output deficiency δ_o^{π} quantify a deviation from the Blackwell order and depend on ξ only through κ and μ. Proposition 6 shows that the sets on which UI and δ_o^{π} vanish are the same.*

On the other hand, the weighted input deficiency δ_i^{π} quantifies a deviation from the input-degraded order, which compares two channels with a common output *alphabet. This ordering appears more natural in some settings, e.g., when learning a classifier (see, e.g.,* [81]*). We can again define a channel model $\bar{\xi} : \mathcal{Y} \times \mathcal{Z} \to \mathcal{S}$. The associated component channels $\bar{\kappa}(s|y)$ and $\bar{\mu}(s|z)$ are, however, not uniquely determined by $\bar{\xi}$ (also see Remark 1). In Theorem 22 of* [6]*, it was claimed that the vanishing sets of δ_i^{π} and UI coincide. However, Banerjee et al. [83] showed that this assertion is incorrect (see Example 28b in [83]).*

Remark 3 (Decompositions based on known bounds on the secret key rates). *In Section 5, we show that the function UI shares conceptual similarities with secret key rates* [12,84]. *The UI construction can be used to obtain bivariate information decompositions from the one-way ($S_{\to}$,* (42)*) and two-way secret key rates ($S_{\leftrightarrow}$), as well as from related information functions defined as bounds on these rates. These functions include the secrecy capacity of the wiretap channel C_S* (36)*, the* intrinsic information $I_{\downarrow}$ (47)*, the* reduced intrinsic information $I_{\downarrow\downarrow}$ (50)*, and the* minimum intrinsic information B_1 (52)*. Each of these bounds can be expressed as optimization problems over Markov kernels of bounded size. For the complete chain of inequalities, see* (57)*. Like UI, both $S_{\to}$ and C_S depend solely on the marginal distributions of the pairs (S,Y) and (S,Z). However, unlike UI, none of these functions satisfy the consistency condition* (7)*. Nevertheless, since these bounds are upper-bounded by* $\min\{I(S;Y), I(S;Y|Z)\}$*, we can utilize the UI construction outlined in Lemma 6 to derive new non-negative decompositions. An analysis of the properties of these decompositions is reserved for future study.*

5. Unique Information and Secrecy Monotones

The contents of this section have a distinct cryptographic flavor. Our main goal is to establish the operational significance of the UI in Definition 1. In order to keep the exposition reasonably self-contained, we collect all relevant definitions and models in Section 5.2. Theorem 8, the triangle inequality for the UI (Property P.7), and Theorem 9 are the main results in this section. Theorem 8 was first derived in [16], while the contents of Sections 5.4 and 5.5 expands on the work in [16,17].

5.1. Motivation and Synopsis

Consider the *source model* for secret key agreement between Alice and Bob, who are distant from each other and must communicate over a noiseless but insecure (public) channel in the presence of an adversary, Eve [12,85]. Alice, Bob, and Eve observe i.i.d. copies of random variables S, Y, and Z, respectively, where $(S,Y,Z) \sim P$. Alice and Bob aim to agree on a secret key by exchanging messages over the public channel according to a predefined protocol. Eve is aware of the protocol and can intercept and read all the messages exchanged. The maximum rate at which Alice and Bob can compute a key such that Eve's total information (from both Z and the entire communication) about the key is negligibly small is referred to as the *two-way secret key rate*, $S_{\leftrightarrow}$. If Alice is allowed to send only one message and Bob sends none, the corresponding key rate is called the *one-way secret key rate*, $S_{\rightarrow}$.

The secret key rates are conceptually similar to the function UI. While $UI(S;Y\backslash Z)$ is interpreted as the *information about S known to Y, but not to Z*, $S_{\leftrightarrow}(S;Y|Z)$ can be interpreted as the *information common to S and Y, which is unique with respect to Z*.

For example, consider the RDN distribution from Example 1, where Alice, Bob, and Eve each share one uniformly random bit. In this case, since Eve knows the exact values of S and Y, Alice and Bob cannot share a secret. This is reflected in the values of $UI(S;Y\backslash Z)$ and $UI(Y;S\backslash Z)$, both of which are zero.

As another example, consider the XOR distribution in Example 1, where the values of any two variables in (S,Y,Z) determine the third. Clearly, if Alice can only observe S and Bob can only observe Y, they cannot generate a secret key. This is also apparent from the values of $UI(S;Y\backslash Z)$ and $UI(Y;S\backslash Z)$, both of which are zero. However, if Alice is also able to observe Z, she can compute Y, which can then be used as a key that is perfectly secret from Eve, since Eve's variable Z is independent of the key Y.

Intuitively, when Alice and Bob share some common information that is unique with respect to Eve, they can *exploit* this information to generate a secret key. A distribution combining elements of the XOR and RDN models exemplifies the potential advantage of such a setup:

Example 4 (The XORRDN distribution [12,84]). *Consider the following distribution:* $P_{SYZ}(0,0,0) = P_{SYZ}(0,1,1) = P_{SYZ}(1,0,1) = P_{SYZ}(1,1,0) = \frac{1}{8}$, *and* $P_{SYZ}(2,2,2) = P_{SYZ}(3,3,3) = \frac{1}{4}$. *The table below shows the distribution (with Z's value in parentheses):*

	S			
Y (Z)	0	1	2	3
0	1/8 (0)	1/8 (1)	.	.
1	1/8 (1)	1/8 (0)	.	.
2	.	.	1/4 (2)	.
3	.	.	.	1/4 (3)

If Eve observes 2 or 3, she can determine the exact values of S and Y. When she observes 0 or 1, she can infer that Alice and Bob's values lie within $\{0,1\}$*, but within this range, their observations are independent. Consequently, no secret key agreement is possible in this case. This is reflected in the values of* $UI(S;Y\backslash Z)$ *and* $UI(Y;S\backslash Z)$*, both of which are zero.*

Consider now the modified distribution: $P_{SYZ}(0,0,0) = P_{SYZ}(0,1,1) = P_{SYZ}(1,0,1) = P_{SYZ}(1,1,0) = \frac{1}{8}$*, and* $P_{SYZ}(2,2,0) = P_{SYZ}(3,3,1) = \frac{1}{4}$*, where Eve's variable Z can only assume binary values.*

	S			
Y (Z)	0	1	2	3
0	1/8 (0)	1/8 (1)	.	.
1	1/8 (1)	1/8 (0)	.	.
2	.	.	1/4 (0)	.
3	.	.	.	1/4 (1)

Now Bob (resp. Alice) has 1 bit of unique information about Alice's (resp. Bob's) values with respect to Eve (namely, the ability to distinguish whether Alice sees values in the XOR *or the* RDN *quadrant) which can be used to agree on 1 bit of secret.*

A computable characterization of the one-way secret key rate is known [66] (see Theorem 6). In contrast, determining the two-way key rate for a given distribution, or even the condition when it is positive, seems difficult, and its value is known only for a handful of distributions [66,67,86,87]. For protocols with unbounded communication, computing the two-way key rate for a general distribution is a fundamental and open area of inquiry in information-theoretic cryptography.

A standard technique for deriving upper bounds on the two-way key rate is to consider functions of joint distributions called *secrecy monotones* or simply *monotones*, which satisfy the following property: In any secret key agreement protocol, a monotone can *never increase* if Alice and Bob are only allowed to perform a well-defined class of physical operations called local operations (LOs) and public communication (PC) [14,67,88]. Theorem 8 shows that the UI is an upper bound on the one-way secret key rate. This is a consequence of the fact that the function UI is a monotone when the class of allowed operations is local operations and one-way public communication.

The state-of-the-art upper bounds on the two-way key rate are based on the following key property (see Theorem 4 in [67]): For any tuple (S,Y,Z,Z'),

$$S_{\leftrightarrow}(S;Y\|Z) \leq S_{\leftrightarrow}(S;Y\|Z') + S_{\rightarrow}(SY;Z'\|Z). \tag{33}$$

In [67,89], a heuristic interpretation of this decomposition is provided: Let $s = S_{\leftrightarrow}(S;Y\|Z)$. Consider a fourth party, Charlie, who receives i.i.d. copies of Z' but does not have access to the public channel. If we decompose s into two parts: s_1, which Charlie does not know, and $s_2 = s - s_1$, which Charlie knows about the shared secret key between S and Y with respect to Z, then s_1 is at most $S_{\leftrightarrow}(S;Y\|Z')$, while s_2 is at most $S_{\rightarrow}(SY;Z'\|Z)$.

Gohari et al. [80] gave an alternative interpretation of (33): For any $(S,Y,Z,Z') \sim P$, if the induced channel $P_{Z|SY}$ dominates $P_{Z'|SY}$ in the *less noisy* sense (see Definition 9), then the second term $S_{\rightarrow}(SY;Z'\|Z)$ vanishes. Thus, $S_{\rightarrow}(SY;Z'\|Z)$ represents the "penalty" for deviating from the less noisy condition when substituting $P_{Z|SY}$ with $P_{Z'|SY}$.

The function UI satisfies a triangle inequality, which implies the following property that resembles (33): For any (S,Y,Z,Z'),

$$UI(S;Y\backslash Z) \leq UI(S;Y\backslash Z') + UI(SY;Z'\backslash Z). \tag{34}$$

From (34), we conclude that the UI is never greater than the best-known computable upper bound on $S_{\leftrightarrow}$. We also give an example where the UI is not lower than the best-known lower bound on the two-way rate. We conjecture that the UI lower-bounds the two-way key rate and discuss implications of the conjecture.

5.2. Information-Theoretic Secrecy Models

We begin by reviewing some fundamental models in information-theoretic cryptography. Some excellent references include [13–15] and Section 17.3 in [27].

Suppose that Alice wishes to transmit a message to Bob over a *noiseless* channel such that an adversary, Eve, who has access to the channel, obtains no information about the message. The channel is assumed to be *authenticated* in the sense that Eve has only read access to the channel and cannot modify or insert messages without being detected. Authentication can be guaranteed, for instance, if Alice and Bob initially share a short secret key [90]. The assumption that the channel is noiseless entails no loss of practicality if we assume that powerful error correction schemes exist, so that the message can be recovered with an arbitrarily small probability of error. This assumption is convenient because it allows us to focus solely on secrecy without having to worry about communication efficiency. We will call such a noiseless and authenticated channel the *public channel*. The terminology is, of course, suggestive of the fact that the channel is insecure. While it is often impractical to assume that a secure channel (e.g., a trusted courier) is always available whenever such a need arises, without loss of generality, we will assume that insecure public channels (e.g., telephone lines) are always available.

The Shannon model. Shannon introduced a simple model of a cryptosystem [91] as follows. Let random variables $M \in \mathcal{M}$ and $C \in \mathcal{C}$ model, resp., the message and the codeword or ciphertext. Alice and Bob share a common secret key modeled by a random variable $K \in \mathcal{K}$. We assume that K is independent of M. Let $e : \mathcal{M} \times \mathcal{K} \to \mathcal{C}$ and $d : \mathcal{C} \times \mathcal{K} \to \mathcal{M}$ denote, resp., Alice's encoding and Bob's decoding function. The pair (e, d) is called a *coding scheme*. We assume that Eve has no knowledge of the key but knows the coding scheme and that Bob can decode messages without error, i.e., $M = d(C, K)$ if $C = e(M, K)$. Alice encodes M into a ciphertext C using the secret key before sending it over the public channel. Since the channel is public, Eve receives an identical copy of C as Bob. A coding scheme is said to achieve *perfect secrecy* if Eve's equivocation about the message given the ciphertext as measured by the conditional entropy $H(M|C)$ equals her a priori uncertainty about the message, i.e., $H(M|C) = H(M)$, or, equivalently $I(M;C) = 0$. Shannon gave a necessary condition for communication in perfect secrecy.

Theorem 4 ([91]). *If a coding scheme achieves perfect secrecy, then $H(K) \geq H(M)$.*

To see this, note that by assumption, $H(M) = H(M|C)$. Since Bob can decode messages without error, we have $H(M|CK) = 0$. The claim follows from $H(M) = H(M|C) = H(M|C) - H(M|CK) = I(K;M|C) \leq H(K|C) \leq H(K)$.

From an algorithmic perspective, perfect secrecy can be realized using a public channel and a secret key by means of a simple coding scheme called the *one-time pad* (OTP) [92]:

Example 5 (OTP). *The message M is a l-bit string and the key K is a uniformly distributed l-bit string which is independent of the message. Alice computes $C = M \oplus K$ and Bob computes $C \oplus K$, where $\oplus$ denotes a bit-wise* XOR *operation. Alice's encoding guarantees that $H(C) = l$. Also, $H(C|M) = H(K|M) = H(K) = l$, since there is a one-to-one mapping between C and K given M, and K is independent of M. We thus have $I(M;C) = H(C) - H(C|M) = 0$, which shows that the OTP achieves perfect secrecy.*

The OTP guarantees that Eve can do no better than randomly guess M and that there exists *no* algorithm that could extract any information about M from C. The OTP is *unconditionally secure* in the sense that this is true even when Eve has unlimited computing power. The OTP is also provably secure in the sense that very precise statements can be made about the information that is leaked to Eve under some well-defined notion of statistical independence (or near-independence) of the message from Eve's observations.

Contrast this with *computationally secure* cryptosystems which are based on computational complexity theory [93,94]. The security of these systems is based on the following assumptions: (a) Eve's computational resources, specified by some model of computation, are bounded and, (b) certain one-way functions exist that are computationally "hard" to invert (see Chapter 2 in [95]). The existence of such one-way functions is an open conjecture [96]. Candidates for one-way functions are the discrete-logarithm and the integer factorization problem which form, resp., the basis of the Diffie–Hellman key exchange [93] and the RSA public-key cryptosystem [94]. Efficient randomized algorithms are known for the discrete-logarithm and the integer factorization problem on quantum computers [97]. Hence, public-key cryptosystems are not only provably insecure in theory, but also potentially in practice.

The OTP implements unconditional secrecy with low complexity. However, its applicability is limited in practice since Alice and Bob must share a secret key in advance. Furthermore, the key must at least be as long as the message and can be used only once. Theorem 4, however, shows that the OTP is optimal with respect to key length. Hence, any unconditionally secure cryptosystem is necessarily as impractical as the OTP.

On the other hand, the assumption that the Eve has precisely the *same* information as Bob (except for the secret key) is unrealistic in general. This is, for instance, the case in computational security schemes, which assume that Eve's channel is noiseless, but her computational resources are bounded. Physical communication channels are noisy, and in real systems, Eve has some minimal uncertainty about the signal received by Bob. The following example shows that if Eve's observation is in some sense "noisier" than Bob's, then information-theoretically secure communication is possible even when Alice and Bob do *not* share a secret key in advance.

Example 6 (The binary erasure wiretap channel [13,64]). *Consider the following simplistic scenario: Alice wishes to send one bit of information to Bob over a binary public channel. Eve's channel is not as perfect as Bob's: she observes a corrupted version of the bit at the output of a* $\mathsf{BEC}(\epsilon)$. *Hence, Eve knows the bit with probability* $1-\epsilon$, *and her equivocation equals* ϵ.

Let us assume that Alice has access to a source of private randomness which is independent of the message and the channel. To augment Eve's equivocation, Alice chooses a message M uniformly at random from the set $\{0,1\}$ *and employs the following coding scheme: She takes the set of all n-bit sequences* $\{0,1\}^n$ *and splits them into two* bins, b_0 *and* b_1, *which comprise all n-bit sequences with odd, resp., even parity. To send a message* $m \in \{0,1\}$, *Alice transmits a codeword* S^n *chosen uniformly at random in* b_m. *The rate of the code is* $\frac{1}{n}$ *bits per transmitted channel symbol.*

Clearly, Bob can recover the correct message by determining the parity of the received codeword. Eve, however, observes a sequence $Z^n \in \{0,1,\mathsf{e}\}^n$ *that has* $n\epsilon$ *erasures on average. Define a binary random variable E such that* $E=0$ *if* Z^n *contains no erasures and* $E=1$ *otherwise. If* $E=0$, *Eve can decode the message correctly. However, if* $E=1$, *the parity of the erased bits is equally likely to be odd or even. We can lower bound Eve's equivocation as follows:*

$$\begin{aligned} H(M|Z^n) \geq H(M|Z^n,E) &\overset{(a)}{=} H(M|Z^n,E=1)(1-(1-\epsilon)^n) \\ &= H(M)(1-(1-\epsilon)^n) = 1-(1-\epsilon)^n, \end{aligned}$$

where equality (a) follows from the fact that $Pr[E = 1] = 1 - (1 - \epsilon)^n$ *and* $H(M|Z^n, E = 0) = 0$. *Hence,* $I(M; Z^n) \le (1 - \epsilon)^n$, *which vanishes exponentially fast in* n. *By repeating this process, Alice and Bob can agree on a secret key of arbitrary length.*

The coding scheme in Example 6 is secure in an asymptotic sense since it requires that the *total* amount of information leaked to Eve vanishes as n goes to infinity, i.e., $\lim_{n\to\infty} I(M; Z^n) = 0$. This is less stringent than requiring an exact statistical independence of M and Z^n and is often mathematically more tractable [13]. We call this the *strong secrecy* condition. Alternatively, one can require that the *rate* at which information is leaked to Eve vanishes as n goes to infinity, i.e., $\lim_{n\to\infty} \frac{1}{n} I(M; Z^n) = 0$. We call this the *weak secrecy* condition. This requirement is weaker than the strong secrecy condition since it is satisfied as long as $I(M; Z^n)$ grows at most sublinearly in n.

The wiretap channel model. Example 6 shows that one can use a noisy channel as a "cryptographic resource". We now consider a more general case first considered by Wyner [64] and subsequently generalized by Csiszár and Körner [65], where the main channel from Alice to Bob is no longer noiseless. Given a broadcast channel $\xi \in \mathsf{M}(\mathcal{S}; \mathcal{Y} \times \mathcal{Z})$, let $\kappa_s(y) := \sum_{z\in\mathcal{Z}} \xi_s(y, z)$ and $\mu_s(z) := \sum_{y\in\mathcal{Y}} \xi_s(y, z)$ be the two components of ξ. Alice chooses the input to ξ, and we refer to κ as the "main channel" and μ as "Eve's channel".

Alice uses a stochastic encoder to map the message M into an input S^n to the channels κ and μ. Bob and Eve observe, resp., the corresponding outputs Y^n and Z^n. Bob wishes to decode the message with a small probability of error such that Eve's information about the message is arbitrarily small. The largest achievable rate at which Alice can send a message to Bob is called the *secrecy capacity* $C_S(S; Y|Z)$. We give a formal definition.

Definition 18 ([65]). *The secrecy capacity of the wiretap channel is the largest rate R such that for every* $\epsilon > 0$, $\delta > 0$, *and sufficiently large n, there exist random variables* M, S^n, Y^n, *and* Z^n *satisfying* $M - S^n - Y^n Z^n$, *where* Y^n *and* Z^n *are connected with* S^n *via the channels* κ *and* μ, *resp., and M is distributed on a set* $\mathcal{M}$ *with* $\frac{1}{n}\log|\mathcal{M}| > R - \delta$ *and with a suitable (deterministic) decoder* $d : \mathcal{Y}^n \to \mathcal{M}$,

$$Pr[d(Y^n) \neq M] < \epsilon \qquad \textit{(reliability)}, \tag{35a}$$

$$H(M|Z^n) > \log|\mathcal{M}| - \epsilon \qquad \textit{(strong secrecy)}. \tag{35b}$$

Equation (35a) ensures that the Bob's probability of error is arbitrarily small while (35b) ensures that Eve has negligible information about the message.

The secrecy capacity of the wiretap channel admits the following characterization.

Theorem 5 ([65], Corollary 2). *The secrecy capacity* $C_S(S; Y|Z)$ *of the wiretap channel is*

$$C_S(S; Y|Z) = \max[I(U; Y) - I(U; Z)] \tag{36}$$

for random variables (U, S, Y, Z) *such that* $U - S - YZ$ *is a Markov chain and* $P_{Y|S} = \kappa$, $P_{Z|S} = \mu$. *The auxiliary variable U may be assumed to have a range of size at most* $|\mathcal{S}|$.

C_S depends on ξ only through its marginals κ and μ [65]. When the distribution of the input to ξ is fixed, C_S depends only on the marginal distributions of the pairs (S, Y) and (S, Z). Hence, we can analyze if secure communication is possible or not by restricting our attention to Δ_P (see Definition 1). Proposition 9 shows that one can interpret the quantity C_S as quantifying a deviation from the less noisy order.

Proposition 9 ([65], Corollary 3).

$$\mu \sqsupseteq^{ln} \kappa \iff C_S(S;Y|Z) = 0. \tag{37}$$

The setting originally considered by Wyner [64] is a special case of the wiretap channel model where Eve's channel is *physically degraded* from the main channel in the sense that $\xi = \kappa \times \lambda$ for some $\lambda \in \mathsf{M}(\mathcal{Y};\mathcal{Z})$. We call this the *degraded wiretap channel* model. The binary erasure wiretap channel in Example 6 is an instance of this model where κ is a noiseless channel and $\mu = \mathsf{BEC}(\epsilon)$. The coding scheme in this example is apparently not that useful since the transmission rate goes to zero as n goes to infinity, albeit more slowly than does $I(M;Z^n)$. Nevertheless, the example suggests that when Alice is allowed to use a *stochastic* encoder, she can map a given message to a bin of codewords, and then select one of them at random to "confuse" Eve and achieve some secrecy guarantee. This intuition is brought to bear by Wyner, who showed that it is possible to transmit at a rate bounded away from zero and still achieve some secrecy guarantee by using a random binning scheme.

The secrecy capacity of the degraded wiretap channel is

$$C_S^w(S;Y|Z) = \max_{P_S}[I(S;Y) - I(S;Z)] = \max_{P_S} I(S;Y|Z), \tag{38}$$

where the second equality follows from the fact $S - Y - Z$ is a Markov chain by assumption. Note that $C_S(S;Y|Z) \geq C_S^w(S;Y|Z)$ since $U = S$ is a valid choice in (36). Also note that if Eve obtains the same information as Bob; i.e., if $Z = Y$, then $C_S^w = C_S = 0$. This is consistent with our analysis of Shannon's model and the general idea that it is *impossible* to realize unconditional security "from scratch", i.e., if only public channels are available.

For jointly distributed random variables $(S,Y,Z) \sim P$, $I(S;Y|Z)$ is a concave function of P_S for fixed $P_{YZ|S}$ (see Lemma 3.3 in [13]). Thus, the optimization problem in (38) is a convex program. We can also relate C_S^w to the main channel capacity $C_\kappa := \max_{P_S} I(S;Y)$ and to Eve's channel capacity $C_\mu := \max_{P_S} I(S;Z)$ as follows:

$$C_S^w(S;Y|Z) = \max_{P_S}[I(S;Y) - I(S;Z)] \geq \max_{P_S} I(S;Y) - \max_{P_S} I(S;Z) = C_\kappa - C_\mu.$$

The secrecy capacity of the degraded wiretap channel is hence at least as large as the difference between the main channel capacity and Eve's channel capacity. Note that if μ is physically degraded from κ, then $\kappa \sqsupseteq_S^{\mathsf{odeg}} \mu$, but not conversely. However, since C_S and C_S^w depend on ξ only through its marginals κ and μ, there is no real difference between output-degraded channels and physically degraded channels from the point of view of secure communication.

For the models discussed so far, a necessary condition for Alice and Bob to be able to communicate in secrecy is that they have an explicit *physical advantage* over Eve. In Shannon's model, for instance, Alice and Bob need to share a secret key in advance, while in Wyner's model, the main channel must be less noisier than Eve's. An obvious weakness of these models is that in a practical application, it may not often be possible to guarantee such an advantage. A key question is whether Alice and Bob can exchange messages in secrecy when they do *not* have a physical advantage to start with. Consider the following example:

Example 7 (Binary broadcast channel with independent BSCs, Lemma 1 in [85]). *Let* $\xi = \kappa \times \mu$ *where* $\kappa = \mathsf{BSC}(\epsilon)$ *and* $\mu = \mathsf{BSC}(\delta)$ *and* $\epsilon \leq \frac{1}{2}, \delta \leq \frac{1}{2}$. *The secrecy capacity of* ξ *is*

$$C_S(S;Y|Z) = \begin{cases} h(\delta) - h(\epsilon), & \text{if } \delta > \epsilon \\ 0, & \text{otherwise} \end{cases} \tag{39}$$

C_S vanishes whenever Bob's channel is noisier than Eve's in the sense that $\delta \leq \epsilon$. Here, $h(\cdot)$ is the binary entropy function.

Consider now a variation in the scenario in Example 7, where Bob can also send messages to Alice over an insecure public channel. We are interested in whether secrecy guarantees are possible in the range $0 < \delta \leq \epsilon < \frac{1}{2}$ for this augmented scenario. The following example, due to Maurer [85], shows an ingenious trick to achieve this.

Example 8 (Public feedback from Bob to Alice increases secrecy capacity [85]). *Alice inputs a random bit S to the "real" channel ξ where $S \sim \text{Bernoulli}\left(\frac{1}{2}\right)$. Let $E \sim \text{Bernoulli}(\epsilon)$ and $D \sim \text{Bernoulli}(\delta)$ be, resp., the independent error bits of the main channel and Eve's channel. Bob observes $Y = S \oplus E$ and Eve observes $Z = S \oplus D$. We assume that the main channel is noisier than Eve's in the sense that $\delta \leq \epsilon$.*

To send a message bit C, Bob computes $W = C \oplus Y = C \oplus S \oplus E$ and sends it over the public channel. Since Alice knows S, she computes $W \oplus S = C \oplus E$. Eve, on the other hand, only knows Z, and she computes $W \oplus Z = C \oplus E \oplus D$. In effect, this procedure simulates a "conceptual" broadcast channel from Bob to Alice and Eve, where the conceptual main channel (to Alice) is equivalent to the real main channel and Eve's conceptual channel is a composition of the real main channel and Eve's real channel. This corresponds exactly to Wyner's degraded wiretap channel scenario, where Eve's conceptual channel is physically degraded from the main channel, thus allowing for some positive secrecy rate. Maurer showed that a suitably modified notion of secrecy capacity (called the secrecy capacity with public discussion*) for this augmented scenario is equal to $h(\epsilon + \delta - 2\epsilon\delta) - h(\epsilon)$, which is strictly positive unless $\epsilon = \frac{1}{2}$, $\delta = 0$ or $\delta = 1$, (see Proposition 1 in* [85]*).*

Example 8 highlights the important fact that noiseless feedback can increase the secrecy capacity. This is true even when the feedback is known to Eve and she has a physical advantage over Bob. Crucially, the latter finding suggests that the necessity of the condition that Bob has a physical advantage over Eve to achieve a positive secrecy capacity in Example 7 stems from a restriction imposed by rate-limited one-way communication. These observations motivate the study of more general models of secret key agreement using two-way or interactive public communication.

The source model for secret key agreement using public discussion. Maurer introduced the *source model* for secret key agreement [12,85]. In this model, Alice, Bob, and Eve observe n i.i.d. copies of random variables S, Y, and Z, respectively, where (S, Y, Z) follows a joint distribution known to all parties, referred to as the *source*. Alice and Bob aim to agree on a common secret key by communicating interactively over a public channel that is observable by Eve.

The *two-way* public communication protocol proceeds in rounds, with Alice and Bob alternately exchanging messages. Alice sends messages in the odd-numbered rounds, and Bob sends messages in the even-numbered rounds. Each message is a function of the sender's observation and all previously exchanged messages. At the conclusion of the protocol, Alice (resp. Bob) computes a key K (resp. K') as a function of S^n (resp. Y^n) and C, the set of all exchanged messages.

Definition 19 ([85]). *The* two-way secret key rate *for the source model, denoted as $S_{\leftrightarrow}(S;Y|Z)$, is the maximum rate R such that for every $\epsilon > 0$ and sufficiently large n, there exists a two-way* *public communication protocol that outputs keys K and K′ (ranging over some common set $\mathcal{K}$) satisfying*

$$Pr[K = K'] \geq 1 - \epsilon \qquad \text{(reliability)}, \tag{40a}$$
$$\tfrac{1}{n} I(K; C, Z^n) \leq \epsilon \qquad \text{(weak secrecy)}, \tag{40b}$$
$$\tfrac{1}{n} H(K) > \tfrac{1}{n} \log |\mathcal{K}| - \epsilon \qquad \text{(uniformity)}, \tag{40c}$$

and achieving $\frac{1}{n}H(K) \geq R - \epsilon$, where C is the amount of public communication consumed in the protocol.

Equations (40a) and (40c) ensure, resp., that the keys are equal to each other with high probability and that they are almost uniformly distributed. Equation (40b) ensures that the *rate* at which Eve learns information about the keys is negligibly small. A still stronger definition requires that Eve's *total* information about the key is negligibly small, i.e.,

$$I(K; C, Z^n) \leq \epsilon; \qquad \text{(strong secrecy)}. \tag{41}$$

Both these definitions give the same secret key rate [98]. Moreover, this rate is achievable without using private randomness at either Alice's or Bob's end. This is unlike the wiretap channel model, where coding schemes for the strong secrecy and the weak secrecy condition are very different [13] and randomness in the encoding process plays a crucial role in enabling secure communication.

Note that Definition 19 of the two-way rate says nothing about the amount of public communication (i.e., the number of rounds) required to agree on a secret key, which can be arbitrarily large. However, models imposing some restriction on the possible communication are also of interest. We say that the protocol is *one-way* if Alice is allowed to send only one message and Bob none. The corresponding key rate is called the *one-way secret key rate* $S_{\rightarrow}(S;Y|Z)$. The one-way key rate is a lower bound on the two-way key rate. $S_{\rightarrow}$ admits the following characterization.

Theorem 6 ([66], Theorem 1)**.** *The* one-way secret key rate $S_{\rightarrow}(S;Y|Z)$ *for the source model is the solution of the following optimization problem:*

$$S_{\rightarrow}(S;Y|Z) = \max_{P_{UV|SYZ}: V - U - S - YZ} I(U;Y|V) - I(U;Z|V). \tag{42}$$

In this optimization problem, it suffices to restrict the range of the random variables U and V to sizes $|\mathcal{S}|^2$ and $|\mathcal{S}|$, respectively.

The bounds on the cardinalities imply that the optimization domain is a set of stochastic matrices of finite size, which makes it possible to turn this theorem into an algorithm to compute $S_{\rightarrow}$.

The following trivial bounds on the two-way rate are known [85]:

Proposition 10.

$$\max\{I(S;Y) - I(S;Z), I(Y;S) - I(Y;Z)\} \leq S_{\leftrightarrow}(S;Y|Z) \leq \min\{I(S;Y), I(S;Y|Z)\}.$$

For some sources, the lower bound in Proposition 10 can be negative (see [99] for an operational interpretation of the lower bound when such is the case). If neither $I(S;Y) > I(S;Z)$ nor $I(Y;S) > I(Y;Z)$ holds, then Alice and Bob can exploit the authenticity of the public channel to "distill" observations for which Alice and Bob have an advantage over Eve.

Maurer [85] and Maurer and Wolf [100] considered a scenario where a satellite broadcasts random bits at a low signal power and earthlings Alice, Bob, and Eve receive these bits over independent binary channels. Secret key agreement is *always* possible in this scenario unless Eve's channel is noiseless or either Alice or Bob receives no information at all about these bits. The following example describes an advantage distillation strategy called the "repeat-code protocol" for this scenario.

Example 9 (The "satellite" source with independent BSCs [85,100]). *Let* $R \sim \text{Bernoulli}\left(\frac{1}{2}\right)$. *We pass R through three independent binary symmetric channels with parameters* α, β, *and* ϵ, *resp., to obtain S, Y, and Z. We assume that* $0 \leq \alpha, \beta < \frac{1}{2}$, *and* $0 < \epsilon < \min\{\alpha, \beta\}$. *Thus, Eve has an initial advantage over Alice and Bob in the sense that* $I(S;Z) > I(S;Y)$ *and* $I(Y;Z) > I(Y;S)$.

Given n realizations of the source, Alice and Bob exploit the authenticity of the public channel to reverse Eve's advantage as follows: Alice generates a bit $C \sim \text{Bernoulli}\left(\frac{1}{2}\right)$ *and sends* $S^n \oplus C^n$ *over the public channel, where* $\oplus$ *denotes a bit-wise* XOR *operation and* C^n *is a vector consisting of n repetitions of the bit C. Bob computes* $(S^n \oplus C^n) \oplus Y^n$ *and publicly "accepts" if and only if his output is equal to either* $(0,0,\ldots,0)$ *or* $(1,1,\ldots,1)$, *when Alice retains C; or else, Alice discards C. In other words, Alice and Bob make use of a code comprising two n-bit codewords* $(0,0,\ldots,0)$ *and* $(1,1,\ldots,1)$ *and retain a bit only if their observations are either highly correlated or highly anti-correlated. Eve computes* $(S^n \oplus C^n) \oplus Z^n$ *and her optimal guess for C is 0 if at least half of the bits in her string is 0, and 1 otherwise. As n goes to infinity, Bob's average error probability when guessing the bit C sent by Alice decreases asymptotically faster than Eve's and that the secret key rate is strictly positive in this scenario. This protocol can be used over multiple rounds to further reduce Eve's information.*

The design of practical secret key agreement protocols turns out to be a simpler problem than the construction of wiretap channel codes [13]. A wiretap code needs to *simultaneously* guarantee reliable communication of a message to Bob (35a) and secrecy against Eve (35b). On the other hand, keys are random strings that are not meant to convey any information by themselves and do not need to be known in advance. Alice and Bob can freely shuffle, combine, or discard their observations. This allows for the design of *sequential* key distillation strategies that handle the reliability constraint (40a) and secrecy constraint (40b) *independently*. Since one can always post-process weakly secret keys, strong secrecy comes "for free," i.e., a rate achievable under the weak secrecy condition (40b) is also achievable under the strong secrecy condition (41) (see Theorem 1 in [98]).

A typical key agreement protocol operates in sequential phases [13]: First, Alice, Bob, and Eve observe n realizations of a source. Second, if neither Alice nor Bob has an initial advantage over Eve, they use an *advantage distillation* strategy to reverse Eve's advantage. Third, Alice and Bob exchange messages over the public channel and apply error correction techniques to process their observations and agree on a common bit string. This phase is called *information reconciliation*. Since the error correction information is public, the common bits are only partially secret from Eve. Fourth, Alice and Bob use a suitable hash function to distill a (shorter) highly secret string about which Eve has virtually no information. This phase is called *privacy amplification by public discussion* [101]. Finally, they use the key as an OTP for secure encryption.

The channel model for secret key agreement using public discussion. A *channel model* for secret key agreement generalizes the source model [66,85]. The model involves a channel $\xi \in \mathsf{M}(\mathcal{S};\mathcal{Y} \times \mathcal{Z})$. Alice selects the inputs to ξ, while Bob and Eve observe, resp., the corresponding Y-outputs and the Z-outputs of ξ. Alice and Bob also have access to a public channel. The definitions of the two-way and one-way secret key rates are similar to those for the source model (see Section 17.3 in [27]). Given a channel model, Alice can emulate the associated source model by choosing i.i.d. copies of a random variable S as inputs to ξ. The corresponding channel outputs are i.i.d. copies of Y and Z. Hence, any key rate achieved by a source model with generic variables (S, Y, Z) subject to $P_{YZ|S} = \xi$ is also achieved by the associated channel model [66].

The wiretap channel model may be regarded as a channel model where no public communication is allowed. Clearly, the secret key rate for the channel model defined by ξ is at least as large as the secrecy capacity C_S of the associated wiretap channel defined by the components κ and μ of ξ (see Theorem 5). Ahlswede and Csiszár [66] showed that the one-way secret key rate for the channel model is equal to the secrecy capacity of the associated wiretap channel model. Thus, the one-way rate depends on ξ only through κ and μ. Note, however, that the same is not true for the two-way rate [27].

The secret key rate for the channel model is sometimes called the secrecy capacity with public discussion [85] (e.g., see Example 8). This denomination is slightly misleading because the former characterizes a secret key rate, not a secure communication rate [13].

In the sequel, we shall concern ourselves primarily with the source model.

5.3. *Known Bounds on the Two-Way Secret Key Rate*

5.3.1. Lower Bounds

The best-known lower bound on $S_{\leftrightarrow}$ uses two-way public communication [67,80]. Given random variables $U_1, U_2, \cdots, U_k$ satisfying the Markov chain conditions

$$U_i - SU_{1:i-1} - YZ, \text{ for odd } i \tag{43}$$

$$U_i - YU_{1:i-1} - SZ, \text{ for even } i \tag{44}$$

and for any integer ζ such that $1 \leq \zeta \leq k$, we have $S_{\leftrightarrow}(S;Y|Z) \geq L(S;Y|Z)$ where

$$L(S;Y|Z) = \sum_{\substack{i\geq\zeta \\ \text{odd } i}} I(U_i;Y|U_{1:i-1}) - I(U_i;Z|U_{1:i-1}) + \sum_{\substack{i\geq\zeta \\ \text{even } i}} I(U_i;S|U_{1:i-1}) - I(U_i;Z|U_{1:i-1}), \tag{45}$$

and the cardinality bounds on $U_1, U_2, \ldots, U_k$ satisfy

$$|\mathcal{U}_i| \leq \begin{cases} |\mathcal{S}| \prod_{l=1}^{i-1} |\mathcal{U}_l| & \text{for } i \text{ odd,} \\ |\mathcal{Y}| \prod_{l=1}^{i-1} |\mathcal{U}_l| & \text{for } i \text{ even.} \end{cases} \tag{46}$$

The bound (45) is difficult to evaluate but is quite intuitive: depending on whether i is odd or even, the individual terms can be understood from the form of the one-way secret key rate in Theorem 6 when either Alice or Bob sends a public message.

5.3.2. Upper Bounds

As noted in Proposition 10, a trivial upper bound on $S_{\leftrightarrow}(S;Y|Z)$ is $\min\{I(S;Y), I(S;Y|Z)\}$ [85].

The two-way rate equals the conditional mutual information when Eve helps Alice and Bob by announcing her variable, i.e., $S_{\leftrightarrow}(SZ;YZ|Z) = I(S;Y|Z)$. This ascribes an operational meaning to $I(S;Y|Z)$ as the key rate obtained when Alice and Bob have an explicit advantage over Eve.

If Eve sends Z through a channel $P_{Z'|Z}$, then the key rate cannot decrease. Thus, we have $S_{\leftrightarrow}(S;Y|Z) \leq S_{\leftrightarrow}(S;Y|Z') \leq I(S;Y|Z')$ for any $P_{Z'|Z}$ [12]. This observation motivates an improved bound by way of the *intrinsic information*, $I_{\downarrow}$:

$$S_{\leftrightarrow}(S;Y|Z) \leq I(S;Y{\downarrow}Z) := \min_{P_{Z'|Z}:\, SY-Z-Z'} I(S;Y|Z'). \tag{47}$$

where Z' may be assumed to have a range of size at most $|\mathcal{Z}|$ [102]. Unlike the UI, which depends only on the marginal distributions of the pairs (S,Y) and (S,Z), $I_{\downarrow}$ depends on the full joint distribution, and also does not satisfy the consistency condition (7). Proposition 11 shows that $I_{\downarrow}$ is never lower than the UI.

Proposition 11. $UI(S;Y\backslash Z) \leq I(S;Y{\downarrow}Z)$.

See Appendix B for a proof.

Renner and Wolf [84] noted that the intrinsic information exhibits a property called "locking"; i.e., it can drop by an arbitrarily large amount on giving away a bit of information to Eve. In contrast, the two-way rate satisfies

$$S_{\leftrightarrow}(S;Y|ZU) \geq S_{\leftrightarrow}(S;Y|Z) - H(U) \tag{48}$$

for jointly distributed random variables (S,Y,Z,U) (see Theorem 3 in [84]), and the conditional mutual information satisfies an analogous property:

$$I(S;Y|ZU) \geq I(S;Y|Z) - H(U). \tag{49}$$

Renner and Wolf [84] proposed an improved upper bound called the *reduced intrinsic information* $I_{\downarrow\downarrow}$, which does not exhibit locking:

$$\begin{aligned} I(S;Y{\downarrow\downarrow}Z) &:= \inf_{P_{U|SYZ}} I(S;Y{\downarrow}ZU) + H(U) \\ &\geq \inf_{P_{U|SYZ}} S_{\leftrightarrow}(S;Y|ZU) + H(U) = S_{\leftrightarrow}(S;Y|Z). \end{aligned} \tag{50}$$

Choosing U to be a constant, one immediately obtains $I(S;Y{\downarrow\downarrow}Z) \leq I(S;Y{\downarrow}Z)$. $I(S;Y{\downarrow\downarrow}Z)$ does not lock since

$$\begin{aligned} I(S;Y{\downarrow\downarrow}Z) = \inf_{P_{V|SYZ}} I(S;Y{\downarrow}ZV) + H(V) &\leq \inf_{P_{U'|SY(Z,U)}} I(S;Y{\downarrow}ZUU') + H(UU') \\ &\leq I(S;Y{\downarrow\downarrow}ZU) + H(U), \end{aligned}$$

where the inequality in the second step follows from restricting the infimum to random variables $V = UU'$.

The tightest known upper bound on the two-way rate is [67]

$$B_2(S;Y|Z) := \inf_{P_{Z'|SYZ}} I(S;Y|Z') + S_{\rightarrow}(SY;Z'|Z). \tag{51}$$

Unfortunately, B_2 cannot be computed explicitly, as no bound on the size of Z' is known.

A slightly weaker but computable upper bound is given by the *minimum intrinsic information* [67].

$$B_1(S;Y|Z) := \min_{P_{Z'|SYZ}} I(S;Y|Z') + I(SY;Z'|Z), \tag{52}$$

where $|\mathcal{Z}'| \leq |\mathcal{S}||\mathcal{Y}||\mathcal{Z}|$.

Summarizing, we have the following chain of bounds on the two-way rate.

$$\begin{aligned} C_S(S;Y|Z) \leq S_{\rightarrow}(S;Y|Z) \leq L(S;Y|Z) \leq S_{\leftrightarrow}(S;Y|Z) \\ \leq B_2(S;Y|Z) \leq B_1(S;Y|Z) \\ \leq I(S;Y{\downarrow\downarrow}Z) \leq I(S;Y{\downarrow}Z) \leq I(S;Y|Z). \end{aligned} \tag{53}$$

5.4. Properties of the UI

In this section, we show that the function UI shares some fundamental properties of the secret key rate.

We first recall the trivial bounds on the UI [6]:

$$I(S;Y) - I(S;Z) \leq UI(S;Y\backslash Z) \leq \min\{I(S;Y), I(S;Y|Z)\}. \tag{54}$$

These bounds match the trivial bounds on the two-way secret key rate in Proposition 10 (note that $S_{\leftrightarrow}(S;Y|Z)$ is symmetric under permutations of S and Y, while $UI(S;Y\backslash Z)$ is not). In the adversarial setting in Example 4, if either Eve has less information about S than Bob or, by symmetry, less information about Y than Alice, then Alice and Bob can exploit this difference to extract a secret key.

Property P.1 states that the UI does not exhibit locking.

P.1 (*UI does not lock*). For jointly distributed random variables (S,Y,Z,U),

$$UI(S;Y\backslash ZU) \geq UI(S;Y\backslash Z) - H(U). \tag{55}$$

This property is useful as it ensures that the unique information that Y has about S with respect to an adversary Z cannot "unlock", i.e., drop by an arbitrarily large amount on giving away some information to Z.

Property P.1 and Proposition 11 together imply that $UI(S;Y\backslash Z) \leq I(S;Y{\downarrow\downarrow}Z)$, a fact that will be generalized later in Theorem 9.

Property P.2 states that UI can never increase under local operations of Alice and Bob. The counterpart of this property for the secret key rate is Lemma 4 in [12]. On a related note, in Section 6.3, we discuss a construction that enforces monotonicity under local operations for an arbitrary information measure.

P.2 (*Monotonicity under local operations (LOs) of Alice and Bob*). For all (S,S',Y,Z) such that YZ–S–S' is a Markov chain, $UI(S;Y\backslash Z) \geq UI(S';Y\backslash Z)$. Likewise, for all (S,Y,Y',Z) such that SZ–Y–Y' is a Markov chain, $UI(S;Y\backslash Z) \geq UI(S;Y'\backslash Z)$.

Suppose Alice publicly announces the value of a random variable. Then, Property P.3 states that UI can never increase.

P.3 (*Monotonicity under public communication (PC) by Alice*). For all (S,Y,Z) and functions f over the support of S, $UI((S,f(S));(Y,f(S))\backslash(Z,f(S))) \leq UI(S;Y\backslash Z)$.

The basic unit of secrecy is the "secret bit" Φ. This is any distribution defined on the sets $\{0,1\} \times \{0,1\} \times \mathcal{Z}$ such that

$$\Phi(s,y,z) := \tfrac{1}{2}\delta_{s,y} \times Q_Z(z), \tag{56}$$

where Q_Z is an arbitrary distribution.

For the secret bit, UI satisfies an intuitive normalization property:

P.4 (*Normalization*). $UI_\Phi(S;Y\backslash Z) = UI_\Phi(Y;S\backslash Z) = 1$.

Given many independent copies of $(S,Y,Z) \sim P$, the goal of a secret key agreement protocol is to distill as many copies of Φ as possible. The following two properties, additivity and asymptotic continuity, are important since we are concerned with the asymptotic rate of secret key distillation.

P.5 (*Additivity on tensor products*). Let random variables (S, S', Y, Y', Z, Z') be such that (S, Y, Z) is independent of (S', Y', Z'). Then, $UI(SS'; YY' \backslash ZZ') = UI(S; Y \backslash Z) + UI(S'; Y' \backslash Z')$.

Property P.5 is shown in Lemma 19 of [6].

Asymptotic continuity is a stronger form of continuity that takes into account convergence in relation to the dimension of the underlying state space [11,18,103–105]. Specifically, a function f is said to be asymptotically continuous if

$$|f(P) - f(P')| \leq C\epsilon \log |\mathcal{S}| + \zeta(\epsilon)$$

for all joint distributions $P, P' \in \mathbb{P}_{\mathcal{S}}$, where C is a constant, $\epsilon = \frac{1}{2}\|P - P'\|_1$, and $\zeta : [0, 1] \to \mathbb{R}_+$ is a continuous function that converges to zero as $\epsilon \to 0$ [11].

As an example, entropy is asymptotically continuous (see, e.g., Lemma 2.7 in [27]): for any $P, P' \in \mathbb{P}_{\mathcal{S}}$, if $\frac{1}{2}\|P - P'\|_1 \leq \epsilon$, then

$$|H_P(S) - H_{P'}(S)| \leq \epsilon \log |\mathcal{S}| + h(\epsilon),$$

where $h(\cdot)$ is the binary entropy function. Likewise, the conditional mutual information satisfies asymptotic continuity in the following sense [84,106]: for any $P, P' \in \mathbb{P}_{\mathcal{S}\times\mathcal{Y}\times\mathcal{Z}}$, if $\frac{1}{2}\|P - P'\|_1 \leq \epsilon$, then

$$|I_P(S; Y|Z) - I_{P'}(S; Y|Z)| \leq \epsilon \log \min\{|\mathcal{S}|, |\mathcal{Y}|\} + 2h(\epsilon).$$

Note that the right-hand side of the above inequality does not depend explicitly on the cardinality of Z.

The function UI is as asymptotically continuous:

P.6 (*Asymptotic continuity*). For any $P, P' \in \mathbb{P}_{\mathcal{S}\times\mathcal{Y}\times\mathcal{Z}}$ and $\epsilon \in [0, 1]$, if $\|P - P'\|_1 = \epsilon$, then $UI_{P'}(S; Y \backslash Z) - UI_P(S; Y \backslash Z) \leq \zeta(\epsilon) + \frac{5}{2}\epsilon \log \min\{|\mathcal{S}|, |\mathcal{Y}|\}$ for some bounded, continuous function $\zeta : [0, 1] \to \mathbb{R}_+$ such that $\zeta(0) = 0$.

The function UI satisfies a triangle inequality:

P.7 (*Triangle inequality*). For any (S, Y, Z, Z'),

$$UI(S; Y \backslash Z) \leq UI(S; Y \backslash Z') + UI(S; Z' \backslash Z).$$

An intuitive understanding of Property (P.7) can be gained by iterating the fundamental idea of information decomposition as follows: In the presence of a fourth variable Z', we aim to decompose $u := UI(S; Y \backslash Z)$ into two components—a part u_1, which is also known to Z', and the remainder $u_2 = u - u_1$, which Z' does not know. Clearly, u_1 should be upper-bounded by $UI(S; Z' \backslash Z)$, as Z' alone knows what Z' and Y share. Moreover, $u_2 \leq UI(S; Y \backslash Z')$, since what neither Z nor Z' knows is less than what Z' does not know. Together, these observations provide a heuristic argument for why the triangle inequality should hold.

Property P.7 relies on the following monotonicity property: UI can only increase under local operations by Eve.

P.8 (*Monotonicity under local operations of Eve*). For all (S, Y, Z, Z') such that $SY–Z–Z'$ is a Markov chain, $UI(S; Y \backslash Z) \leq UI(S; Y \backslash Z')$.

Using Property P.7 and Property P.2, we conclude:

Corollary 1. *For any* (S, Y, Z, Z'), $UI(S; Y \backslash Z) \leq UI(S; Y \backslash Z') + UI(SY; Z' \backslash Z)$.

We can interpret Corollary 1 like inequality (33): Given $(S, Y, Z, Z') \sim P$, if the induced channel $P_{Z|SY}$ dominates the channel $P_{Z'|SY}$ in the Blackwell sense, then the second term $UI(SY; Z' \backslash Z)$ vanishes (see Lemma 1). One can interpret $UI(SY; Z' \backslash Z)$ as quantifying a deviation from the Blackwell order when we replace $P_{Z|SY}$ with $P_{Z'|SY}$.

5.5. *UI*-Based Bounds on Secret Key Rates

General properties of upper bounds on secret key rates have been studied within the framework of secrecy or protocol monotones—non-negative real-valued functionals of joint distributions that remain non-increasing throughout the execution of a protocol (see, e.g., [14,67,88,89,107]). For example, the *intrinsic information* in (47) is a protocol monotone [84]. We defer a more general discussion on protocol monotones in the context of *resource theories* to Section 6.

The following theorem gives sufficient conditions for a function to be an upper bound for the secret key rate.

Theorem 7 (Theorem 3.1 in [107], Lemma 2.10 in [88])**.** *Let M be a non-negative real-valued function of the joint distribution of the triple (S, Y, Z) that satisfies Properties P.2–P.6. Then, M is an upper bound for the one-way secret key rate.*

If, in addition, M does not increase under public communication by Bob (Property P.3, with $f(S)$ replaced by $g(Y)$ for some function g over the support of Y), then M is an upper bound for the two-way secret key rate.

Like the UI, $S_{\rightarrow}$ depends only on the marginal distributions of the pairs (S, Y) and (S, Z) [66]. Since UI satisfies Properties P.2–P.6, the following result is immediate from Theorem 7:

Theorem 8. *$UI(S; Y \backslash Z)$ is an upper bound for the one-way secret key rate $S_{\rightarrow}(S; Y \| Z)$.*

Corollary 1 implies the following result.

Proposition 12. *$UI(S; Y \backslash Z) \leq B_1(S; Y|Z)$.*

From Theorem 8 and Proposition 12, we have the following chain of inequalities relating the bounds on the two-way rate.

Theorem 9.

$$\begin{aligned} C_S(S; Y|Z) \leq S_{\rightarrow}(S; Y \| Z) &\leq UI(S; Y \backslash Z) \leq B_1(S; Y|Z) \\ &\leq I(S; Y \downarrow\downarrow Z) \leq I(S; Y \downarrow Z) \leq I(S; Y|Z). \end{aligned} \tag{57}$$

Remark 4. *Given $(S, Y, Z) \sim P$, let*

$$Q^* \in \underset{Q \in \Delta_{P(S,Y,Z)}}{\arg\min} \; I_Q(S; Y|Z). \tag{58}$$

By definition, $I_{Q^*}(S; Y|Z) = UI(S; Y \backslash Z)$. Recall that the distribution Q^* is a minimum synergy *distribution (see Equation (16)). An immediate consequence of Theorem 9 is as follows: choosing $P = Q^*$, all known upper bounds on the two-way rate collapse to the UI and the conditional mutual information, respectively.*

The following example [80,108] shows that there exists a distribution for which $UI(S;Y\backslash Z)$ is *not* lower than $L(S;Y|Z)$, the best-known lower bound on the two-way rate (see (45)).

Example 10 (Doubly symmetric binary erasure (DSBE) source)**.** *Consider the DSBE source with parameters (p,ϵ) in Example 3.*

If $\epsilon = 0$, we have $Z = SY$ and $S_{\leftrightarrow}(S;Y\|Z) = 0$, while if $\epsilon = 1$, we have $Z = \mathtt{e}$ and $S_{\leftrightarrow}(S;Y\|Z) = I(S;Y)$.

For this source, the two-way rate vanishes if and only if (see Theorem 14 in [12])

$$\epsilon \leq \frac{1-p}{p}. \tag{59}$$

On the other hand, both the one-way secret key rate $S_{\rightarrow}(S;Y\|Z)$ and the best-known lower bound $L(S;Y|Z)$ vanish if and only if (see Theorem 7 in [80])

$$\epsilon \leq 4p(1-p), \tag{60}$$

while both $UI(S;Y\backslash Z)$ and $UI(Y;S\backslash Z)$ vanish if and only if

$$\epsilon \leq 2(1-p). \tag{61}$$

For $p > \frac{1}{2}$, we have $\frac{1-p}{p} < 2(1-p) < 4p(1-p)$. Figure 3 illustrates these bounds for a DSBE$(0.6,\epsilon)$ source.

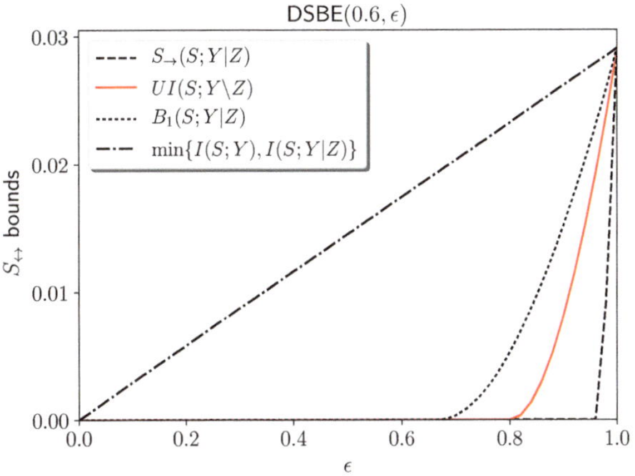

Figure 3. Bounds on the two-way secret key rate for a DSBE$(0.6,\epsilon)$ source.

On the other hand, the following example shows that UI is *not* an upper bound on $S_{\leftrightarrow}$ (see also Example 12).

Example 11 (Satellite source with independent BECs [86])**.** *Let $R \sim \text{Bernoulli}\left(\frac{1}{2}\right)$. We pass R through three independent erasure channels with parameter ϵ to obtain S, Y, and Z. Thus, $P_{SYZR}(s,y,z,r) = P_R(r)P_{S|R}(s|r)P_{Y|R}(y|r)P_{Z|R}(z|r)$. Observe that $P_{SY}(a,b) = P_{SZ}(a,b) = P_{YZ}(a,b)$ for all $a,b \in \{0,1,e\}$. Therefore, all the UIs vanish. Gohari and Anantharam [86] showed that a secret key agreement protocol exists such that $S_{\leftrightarrow}(S;Y\|Z) = I(S;Y|Z) = \epsilon(1-\epsilon)^2$ is an achievable rate. $\epsilon(1-\epsilon)^2$ is strictly positive for $\epsilon \in (0,1)$.*

We make the following conjecture:

Conjecture 1. *$UI(S;Y\backslash Z) \leq S_{\leftrightarrow}(S;Y\|Z)$.*

Remark 5 (Sandwich bound on $S_{\leftrightarrow}(S;Y|Z)$)**.** *If Conjecture 1 is true, then*

$$UI(S;Y\backslash Z) = I_{Q^*}(S;Y|Z) \leq S_{\leftrightarrow}(S;Y|Z) \leq I_P(S;Y|Z). \quad (62)$$

Equation (62) implies that the set of all Q^* as in (58) is a set of distributions for which the UI equals the two-way rate.

A related work [87] gives necessary conditions for when the two-way rate equals the conditional mutual information.

Definition 20. *Define the following functions on $\mathbb{P}_{\mathcal{S}\times\mathcal{Y}\times\mathcal{Z}}$.*

$$B_{sUI}(S;Y|Z) := \inf_{P_{Z'|SYZ}} UI(S;Y\backslash Z') + UI(SY;Z'\backslash Z).$$

$$B_{gUI}(S;Y|Z) := \inf_{P_{Z'|SYZ}} I(S;Y|Z') + UI(SY;Z'\backslash Z).$$

As the following proposition shows, $B_{gUI}(S;Y|Z)$ is a new upper bound on the two-way rate which is juxtaposed between the two best-known bounds B_2 and B_1.

Proposition 13.

$$B_{sUI}(S;Y|Z) = UI(S;Y\backslash Z) \leq B_{gUI}(S;Y|Z) \quad (63)$$

$$B_2(S;Y|Z) \leq B_{gUI}(S;Y|Z) \leq B_1(S;Y|Z) \quad (64)$$

It remains to be seen if there exist scenarios where the B_{gUI} bound is strictly better than the B_1 bound. This remains a scope for future study.

5.6. The Blackwell Property and Secret Key Agreement Against Active Adversaries

In the source model for secret key agreement, we assume that the public channel is authenticated; i.e., Eve is only a passive adversary. In practice, this is guaranteed by authentication schemes that require Alice and Bob to share a short secret key in advance [90]. However, if this assumption is no longer valid and Eve gains both read and write access to the public channel, Maurer and Wolf [109] established an all-or-nothing result: either the same secret key rate as in the authenticated channel case can be achieved, or no key can be established at all. Maurer introduced the following property of a joint distribution to characterize the impossibility of secret key agreement in the presence of an active adversary:

Definition 21. *Given $(S,Y,Z) \sim P$, we say that Y* is simulatable by Z with respect to S *and write $\mathrm{sim}_S(Z \to Y)$ if there exists a random variable Y' such that the pairs (S,Y) and (S,Y') are statistically indistinguishable, and $S - Z - Y'$ is a Markov chain.*

It is immediately apparent that $\mathrm{sim}_S(Z \to Y)$ and $Z \sqsupseteq'_S Y$ in Definition 3 are equivalent. We now restate Maurer's impossibility result in terms of the function UI. We write $S^*_{\leftrightarrow}$ to denote the secret key rate in the active adversary scenario.

Theorem 10 ([109], Theorem 11)**.** *Let (S,Y,Z) be a triple of random variables such that $S_{\leftrightarrow}(S;Y|Z) > 0$. If either $UI(S;Y\backslash Z) = 0$ or $UI(Y;S\backslash Z) = 0$, then $S^*_{\leftrightarrow}(S;Y|Z) = 0$, else $S^*_{\leftrightarrow}(S;Y|Z) = S_{\leftrightarrow}(S;Y|Z)$.*

Remark 6. *Theorem 10 gives another operational interpretation of the vanishing UI; namely, if either S or Y possesses no unique information about each other with respect to Z, then Alice and Bob have no advantage in a secret key agreement task against an active Eve.*

Example 12 shows a distribution for which $S_{\leftrightarrow}(S;Y|Z) > 0$ but $S^*_{\leftrightarrow}(S;Y|Z) = 0$.

Example 12 ([110], Example 4). *Consider the distribution* $P_{SYZ}(0,0,0) = P_{SYZ}(0,0,1) = P_{SYZ}(0,1,0) = P_{SYZ}(1,0,0) = P_{SYZ}(1,1,1) = \frac{1}{5}$. *This distribution has* $I(S;Y\downarrow Z) = 0.02$. *Gisin and Wolf [110] showed that a secret key agreement protocol exists such that* $S_{\leftrightarrow}(S;Y|Z) > 0$. *However, since the pairwise marginal distributions of* (S,Y), (S,Z), *and* (Y,Z) *are all identical, all the unique informations vanish. Thus,* $S^*_{\leftrightarrow}(S;Y|Z) = 0$.

For the passive key agreement scenario, Example 9 shows that two-round protocols can be strictly better than one-round protocols. In general, there exists no upper bound on the number of rounds required to agree on a secret key [111]. Orlitsky and Wigderson [112], however, gave a necessary and sufficient condition for the existence of a secret key: $S_{\leftrightarrow} > 0$, if and only if $S_{\leftrightarrow}$ is positive with only *two rounds* of communication. Property P.3 shows that the UI can never increase in a one-round secret key agreement protocol where Alice sends a public message to Bob. An analysis of the behavior of the UI in two-round protocols, where, in addition, Bob feeds a message back to Alice, is reserved for future study.

6. Resource Theories of Secrecy

In this concluding section, we sketch the resource-theoretic underpinnings behind Theorem 8. Resource theories study a set of objects endowed with a preorder. Classical and quantum information theories can be viewed as examples of resource theories [113]. A resource-theoretic formulation of thermodynamics is implicit in Lieb and Yngvason's axiomatic derivation of the second law of thermodynamics [114]. We refer the reader to [7–11] for detailed exposition on resource theories. We next study the problem of interconvertibility between a given pair of source and target distributions from a resource-theoretic perspective. This is similar in spirit to the work in [52] that briefly studied interconversions between the different partial information terms in (6) under local operations.

6.1. Theories of Resource Convertibility

Resource theories provide an abstract operational framework for studying what physical transformations between objects are possible under a certain class of constraints. The set of all possible operations on these objects can be divided into those that can be implemented in a cheap or simple way (called "free operations"), and those that entail a costly implementation. Given access to the set of free operations. the theory seeks to study the structure that is induced on the objects. We say that objects A and B are ordered as $A \to B$, if A can be converted to B by free operations. An object is *free* if it can be generated from scratch using only free operations; all other objects are *resources*. The resource content of an object cannot increase under free operations.

For example, in the source model for secret key agreement (Section 5.2), the objects of interest are the set of all source distributions. The set of free operations is local operations and public communication (LOPC) by Alice and Bob. The free objects are the set of all distributions under which Alice and Bob's observations are mutually independent; all other objects are *resources*. The basic resource unit is the secret bit Φ (see (56)). Resources are valuable in the sense that when combined with free operations, they can generate other resources or simulate non-free operations. For example, one can simulate a one-time pad (OTP) using LOPC and a secret bit (see Example 5).

Any non-negative, real-valued function M that respects the preorder in the sense that if $A \to B$, then $M(A) \geq M(B)$ is called a *monotone*. M can be interpreted as an assignment of a value to each object in a way that is consistent with the preorder. If $M(A) < M(B)$, then a conversion of A to B is not possible. This property is useful in practice for checking the infeasibility of a conversion.

When an *exact* conversion of A to B is not possible, we can instead ask for an *approximate* conversion at a many-copy level: convert n independent realizations of A to B' which is close to m independent realizations of the desired target B, i.e., $A^{\otimes n} \to B' \simeq B^{\otimes m}$ under the free operations. The *rate* or *yield* of this conversion is $\gamma := \frac{m}{n}$. The existence of a monotone that satisfies certain additivity and continuity properties allows us to obtain an upper bound on the rate of such conversions (Theorem 7).

The UI is a monotone that quantifies the resourcefulness or secrecy content of a source distribution when the set of free operations is local operations by Alice and Bob and one-way public communication by Alice. In particular, UI is non-increasing under this set of free operations. A consequence of this property is that the UI is an upper bound on the one-way secret key rate $S_{\rightarrow}$ (Theorem 8).

We now study two other "symmetric" monotones, the total correlation (TC) (see (65)) and the dual total correlation (DTC) (see (66)), which can be viewed as multipartite generalizations of the mutual information.

6.2. Total Correlation and Dual Total Correlation

Given $(S, Y, Z) \sim P$, the *total correlation (TC)* [115] is defined as follows:

$$\begin{aligned} TC(S;Y;Z) &= D(P_{SYZ} \| P_S \times P_Y \times P_Z) \\ &= H(S) + H(Y) + H(Z) - H(SYZ) \\ &= I(S;Y) + I(Y;Z) + I(Z;S) - CoI(S;Y;Z). \end{aligned} \tag{65}$$

TC measures the total amount of correlations between S, Y, and Z. TC is symmetric in its arguments, non-negative, and vanishes if and only if $P_{SYZ} = P_S \times P_Y \times P_Z$. Total correlation is called multi-information in [116,117] and stochastic interaction in [117].

Te Sun [34] defined a related quantity called the *dual total correlation (DTC)* based on the lattice-theoretic duality of Shannon information measures [32]:

$$\begin{aligned} DTC(S;Y;Z) &= H(SYZ) - H(S|YZ) + H(Y|SZ) - H(Z|SY) \\ &= I(S;Y|Z) + I(Y;Z|S) + I(Z;S|Y) + CoI(S;Y;Z). \end{aligned} \tag{66}$$

Like the TC, DTC is symmetric in its arguments, non-negative, and vanishes if and only if $P_{SYZ} = P_S \times P_Y \times P_Z$ [34]. From (65) and (66), we have the following relation between TC and DTC:

$$TC(S;Y;Z) + DTC(S;Y;Z) = I(S;YZ) + I(Y;SZ) + I(Z;SY). \tag{67}$$

TC and DTC capture different aspects of the correlations between S, Y, and Z. To see this, consider the RDN and XOR distributions in Example 1: The correlations in the RDN distribution can be attributed purely to pairwise interactions since S, Y, and Z are identical random variables. On the other hand, correlations in the XOR distribution arise purely due to triplewise interactions, since S, Y, and Z are pairwise independent. For the RDN, we have $TC = 2\log 2 > \log 2 = DTC$, and for the XOR, we have $DTC = 2\log 2 > \log 2 = TC$. For distributions where S, Y, and Z have binary supports, TC is maximized by the RDN distribution, while DTC is maximized by the XOR distribution [117].

Te Sun [34] studied higher-dimensional analogs of these quantities and argued that TC is effective in measuring "local" lower-order correlations, whereas DTC is effective in measuring overall higher-order correlations (see, e.g., Example 6.2 in [34]). For many practical distributions of interest, most of the TC resides in the lower-order correlations [118]. Austin [119] studied the different nature of the structures induced by small values of TC and DTC on a metric space of probability measures: if a joint distribution P has a small

TC, then P is close to a product measure, where closeness is in the sense of the Wasserstein distance; on the other hand, if P has a small DTC, then it is close to a mixture of product measures.

Interconvertibility between probability distributions under LOPC. Of immediate interest to us are the monotonicity properties of TC and DTC in relation to the problem of converting a given probability distribution to another. Concretely, we consider the following setup: Three collaborating parties, Alice, Bob, and Charlie observe i.i.d. copies of random variables S, Y, and Z, resp., distributed according to some known source distribution P. The goal is to convert P into a target distribution P' when the set of free operations is LOPC by Alice, Bob, and Charlie.

Cerf et al. [120] showed that TC and DTC are monotones under LOPC. In particular, in the tripartite case, $TC(S;Y;Z)$, $DTC(S;Y;Z)$, $I(S;YZ)$, $I(Y;SZ)$, and $I(Z;SY)$ are five monotones. From (67), it is shown that these monotones are not all linearly independent. However, none of these monotones can be expressed as a linear combination of the others with only positive coefficients. Hence, for a given source–target pair, these five monotones set independent constraints on the possible interconversions under LOPC.

Table 1 lists the values of the monotones for some distributions in Example 1. We see, for instance, that the conversion XOR $\rightarrow$ RDN is not feasible since TC increases from 1 to 2 while going from XOR to RDN. Likewise, RDN $\rightarrow$ XOR is not feasible since DTC increases from 1 to 2 while going from RDN to XOR.

Table 1. Values of the five tripartite monotones for the secret bit Φ, and the RDN and XOR distributions [120].

	$I(S;YZ)$	$I(Y;SZ)$	$I(Z;YS)$	$DTC(S;Y;Z)$	$TC(S;Y;Z)$
Φ	1	1	0	1	1
RDN	1	1	1	**1**	**2**
XOR	1	1	1	**2**	**1**

On the other hand, the following conversions are feasible and can be achieved using simple protocols [120]:

- XOR $\rightarrow \Phi$: Charlie publicly announces the value of his bit.
- RDN $\rightarrow \Phi$: Charlie forgets his bit (e.g., sends Z through a channel that completely randomizes it).
- XOR$^{\otimes 2} \rightarrow$ RDN: Alice, Bob, and Charlie observe, resp., the bits (s,s'), (y,y'), and (z,z'), where $z = s \oplus y$ and $z' = s' \oplus y'$. Alice publicly announces s and Bob y'. Since Charlie knows (z,z'), she computes $z \oplus s = y$ and $z' \oplus y' = s'$ and publicly announces $w = y \oplus s'$. Finally, since Alice knows s', she computes $s' \oplus w = y$. Thus, Alice, Bob, and Charlie end up sharing the bit y.
- RDN$^{\otimes 2} \rightarrow$ XOR: Alice, Bob, and Charlie observe, resp., the bits (s,s'), (y,y'), and (z,z'). Alice and Bob forget, resp., s and y', while Charlie computes $z \oplus z'$ and forgets the values z and z'.

Cerf et al. [120] considered the more general question of a reversible interconversion between an arbitrary P_{SYZ} and the distributions Φ_{SY}, Φ_{YZ}, Φ_{ZS}, RDN, and XOR, where we write Φ_{SY} for the secret bit shared between S and Y, and likewise for Φ_{YZ} and Φ_{ZS}. More concretely, does there exist yields $\gamma_1, \dots, \gamma_5$ such that the following reversible conversion is feasible under LOPC?

$$P_{SYZ} \rightleftharpoons \Phi_{SY}^{\otimes \gamma_1} \otimes \Phi_{YZ}^{\otimes \gamma_2} \otimes \Phi_{ZS}^{\otimes \gamma_3} \otimes \mathrm{XOR}^{\otimes \gamma_4} \otimes \mathrm{RDN}^{\otimes \gamma_5}. \tag{68}$$

Cerf et al. [120] showed that the five monotones in Table 1 do not forbid, in principle, the following reversible conversions under LOPC:

- If $CoI = 0$, then $P_{SYZ} \rightleftharpoons \Phi_{SY}^{\otimes \gamma_1} \otimes \Phi_{YZ}^{\otimes \gamma_2} \otimes \Phi_{ZS}^{\otimes \gamma_3}$.
- If $CoI > 0$, then $P_{SYZ} \rightleftharpoons \Phi_{SY}^{\otimes \gamma_1} \otimes \Phi_{YZ}^{\otimes \gamma_2} \otimes \Phi_{ZS}^{\otimes \gamma_3} \otimes \text{RDN}^{\otimes \gamma_5}$.
- If $CoI < 0$, then $P_{SYZ} \rightleftharpoons \Phi_{SY}^{\otimes \gamma_1} \otimes \Phi_{YZ}^{\otimes \gamma_2} \otimes \Phi_{ZS}^{\otimes \gamma_3} \otimes \text{XOR}^{\otimes \gamma_4}$,

where $CoI = SI - CI$ is the coinformation (see (8)). It is, however, plausible that additional monotones exist that might render some of these conversions infeasible (see, e.g., [84,121]). One natural candidate for such a monotone is an "extractable" version of the function SI in Definition 1, which we describe next.

6.3. Extractable Shared Information and Monotonicity Under Local Operations

Rauh et al. [52] and Bertschinger et al. [60] argue that shared information should never increase under local operations (e.g., coarse graining) of the target and/or the predictors. Specifically, for local operations of the predictors, the function SI in Definition 1 satisfies the following property called *right monotonicity* (see A.7 in Appendix A):

$$SI(S;Y,Z) \geq SI(S;f_1(Y),f_2(Z)) \tag{69}$$

for all functions f_1 and f_2. However, for local operations on the target, SI does not exhibit a corresponding property, referred to as *left monotonicity* (see A.8 in Appendix A). Rauh et al. [19] proposed a construction that enforces left monotonicity. Define

$$\overline{SI}(S;Y,Z) = \sup_{f:\mathcal{S}\to\mathcal{S}'} SI(f(S);Y,Z), \tag{70}$$

where the supremum runs over all functions $f\colon \mathcal{S} \to \mathcal{S}'$ from the domain of S to an arbitrary finite set $\mathcal{S}'$. By construction, $\overline{SI}$ satisfies left monotonicity, and $\overline{SI}$ is the smallest function bounded from below by SI that satisfies left monotonicity. One can interpret $\overline{SI}$ as a measure of "extractable" shared information [19]. The intuition is that $\overline{SI}$ is the maximal possible amount of SI one can extract from (Y,Z) by transforming S locally. Furthermore, one can generalize the construction to define a probabilistic version of extractability by replacing f by a stochastic matrix. This leads to the definition

$$\overline{\overline{SI}}(S;Y,Z) := \sup_{P_{S'|S}\colon YZ-S-S'} SI(S';Y,Z). \tag{71}$$

By definition, $\overline{\overline{SI}}$ is monotone under local operations. A study of the monotonicity properties of $\overline{\overline{SI}}$ with respect to public communication is reserved for future study.

Remark 7. *More generally, one can apply the "extractable" construction to arbitrary information measures. Furthermore, by iterating the construction, one can construct an information measure that is monotonic in all arguments* [19]. *An example of this construction is the intrinsic information* $I_\downarrow$ *in* (47). *The use of* min *instead of* max *in Definition* (47) *reflects that* $I_\downarrow$ *can only increase under local operations by Eve, a monotonicity property it shares with the function* UI *(see Property P.8 and Proposition 11). Work in a similar vein include* [103], *where a construction called "arrowing" is used for building probabilistically extractable versions of a given function (see also* [122]*). Galla and Gühne* [123] *discuss probabilistic extractability for a measure of correlation called the "connected correlation"* [124–128], *which are based on projections onto exponential families* [129].

6.4. Left Monotonic Information Decompositions

Is it possible to construct an information decomposition where all measures satisfy left monotonicity? The seemingly simple strategy of starting with an arbitrary decomposition and replacing each partial information measure with its extractable counterpart fails, as this would increase all partial measures (unless already extractable), leading to an overall increase in their sum. For instance, if $\widetilde{SI}$ is replaced by a larger function, then $\widetilde{UI}$ must be reduced due to constraint (4).

As argued in [52], it is intuitive that $\widetilde{UI}$ be left monotonic. In particular, the function UI in Definition 1 satisfies left monotonicity (see Property P.2 in Section 5.4). Likewise, it is also desirable that $\widetilde{SI}$ be left monotonic [52,60]. The intuition for synergy is much less clear. The extractable construction cannot be directly generalized to ensure left monotonicity for both unique and shared information. However, such a decomposition may still exist, with left monotonicity affecting the measure of shared information. Suppose that $\widetilde{SI}$, $\widetilde{UI}$, and $\widetilde{CI}$ define a bivariate information decomposition satisfying (4)–(6), and suppose that $\widetilde{SI}$ and $\widetilde{UI}$ satisfy left monotonicity. Then,

$$\widetilde{SI}(f(Y,Z);Y,Z) \leq I(Y;Z) \tag{72}$$

for any function f [19]. Inequality (72) is related to the identity axiom (see A.6 in Appendix A). Indeed, it is easy to derive (72) from the identity axiom and from the assumption that $\widetilde{SI}$ is left monotonic. None of the non-negative information decompositions proposed so far satisfies (72). Griffith et al. [130] proposed a function $I_\curlywedge$ as a measure of shared information that satisfies left monotonicity. However, this function does not induce a non-negative information decomposition (see A.4 in Appendix A).

The next proposition shows that left monotonicity of the shared information is not consistent with the Blackwell property of the unique information:

Proposition 14 ([19,20])**.** *There is no bivariate information decomposition satisfying* (4)–(6) *in which $\widetilde{UI}$ satisfies the Blackwell property and $\widetilde{SI}$ satisfies left monotonicity.*

A resource-theoretic characterization of the complementary information appears challenging. The problem resides with the fact that it is difficult to postulate how the complementary information should behave if, say, one or more parties perform some local operations on their subsystems. Two studies in this direction deserve notice: Rauh et al.'s Section IV.C in [52] show that the measure CI in Definition 1 can either increase or decrease under local operations of the targets and/or the sources. Another work is a decomposition of the total correlation (TC) due to Amari [124]. The total correlation among three variables can be decomposed into a sum of two non-negative terms that quantify, resp., the amount of correlations arising from purely pairwise and purely triplewise interactions [124] (Equation 78). The latter term can be interpreted as the synergistic component of the total correlation. However, examples are known where this component violates monotonicity under local operations [123]. Finally, an axiomatic approach to information flow in computational systems is motivated in [131], where it is shown that the CI in Definition 1 provides an intuitive and insightful measure of information flow volume. This warrants further investigation.

Funding: A part of this research was funded by the European Research Council (ERC) under the EU's Horizon 2020 research and innovation program (grant agreement no 757983).

Data Availability Statement: The original contributions presented in the study are included in the article, further inquiries can be directed to the author.

Acknowledgments: The author gratefully acknowledges Johannes Rauh, Eckehard Olbrich, Jürgen Jost, Guido Montúfar, Nils Bertschinger, Tobias Fritz, and David Wolpert for their valuable insights and helpful discussions throughout the development of this work.

Conflicts of Interest: The author declares no conflicts of interest.

Appendix A. The Axiomatic Approach to Shared Information

An axiomatic approach to the concept of shared information was pioneered by Williams and Beer [46]. Recall that the shared information can be interpreted as mutual information without the unique information; see (4).

For the general case of k finite predictor variables $Y_1, \ldots, Y_k$, Williams and Beer [46] proposed the *partial information lattice* framework to decompose the total mutual information $I(S; Y_1, \ldots, Y_k)$ into a sum of terms (called *partial information terms*) corresponding to the different ways in which combinations of the variables $Y_1, \ldots, Y_k$ convey shared, unique, or complementary information about the target S. When $k = 2$, writing $Y_1 \equiv Y$ and $Y_2 \equiv Z$, the decomposition has the form given by (4)–(6).

The partial information lattice is a consequence of certain natural properties of the shared information (sometimes called the *Williams–Beer axioms*). The underlying idea is that any information about S can be classified according to "who knows what", i.e., which information about S is shared by which subsets of $\{Y_1, \ldots, Y_k\}$. This idea resonates with *secret-sharing schemes*, a fundamental tool used in many cryptographic protocols [132]. A secret-sharing scheme involves a secret (S), a finite set $\mathcal{K} = \{1, \ldots, k\}$ of parties, and a family $\mathcal{A}$ of (nonempty) subsets of $\mathcal{K}$ called the *access structure* that is closed to taking supersets. The goal is to distribute the secret (S) among k parties such that only elements of $\mathcal{A}$ can reconstruct the secret, while all other subsets of $\mathcal{K}$ obtain no information about the secret. There is a one-to-one correspondence between the partial information terms of Williams and Beer's decomposition scheme and the set of access structures of secret-sharing schemes with k parties [59].

Let $\widetilde{SI}(S; Y_1, \ldots, Y_k)$ denote the information about S that is shared among the random variables $Y_1, \ldots, Y_k$. It is natural to demand that $\widetilde{SI}$ satisfies the following properties [46]:

A.1 (*Symmetry*). $\widetilde{SI}(S; Y_1, \ldots, Y_k)$ is symmetric under permutations of $Y_1, \ldots, Y_k$.

A.2 (*Self-redundancy*). $\widetilde{SI}(S; Y_1) = I(S; Y_1)$.

A.3 (*Monotonicity*). $\widetilde{SI}(S; Y_1, \ldots, Y_{k-1}, Y_k) \leq \widetilde{SI}(S; Y_1, \ldots, Y_{k-1})$, with equality if $Y_i = f(Y_k)$ for some $i < k$ and some function f.

We refer to properties A.1–A.3 as the *Williams–Beer axioms*. Any function satisfying these axioms is non-negative [46]. The axioms, however, do not uniquely characterize the function $\widetilde{SI}$. When $\widetilde{SI}$ is defined, we can associate with each element of the partial information lattice a "local" quantity (the partial information term) that is uniquely determined from $\widetilde{SI}$ by a Möbius inversion. The total mutual information $I(S; Y_1, \ldots, Y_k)$ is then a sum of these local terms [46]. In general, however, the local terms can be negative. For a non-negative decomposition, we require the following additional property:

A.4 (*Local positivity*). All the partial information terms in the induced decomposition are non-negative.

Williams and Beer defined a function

$$
\begin{aligned}
I_{\min}(S; Y_1, \ldots, Y_k) &= \sum_s P_S(s) \min_i \Big\{ \sum_{y_i} P_{Y_i|S}(y_i|s) \log \frac{P_{S|Y_i}(s|y_i)}{P_S(s)} \Big\} \\
&= \sum_s \min_i \Big\{ \sum_{y_i} P_{SY_i}(s, y_i) \log \frac{P_{SY_i}(s, y_i)}{P_S(s) P_{Y_i}(y_i)} \Big\}, \qquad \text{(A1)}
\end{aligned}
$$

and showed that $I_{\min}$ satisfies A.1–A.3 and that the decomposition induced by I_{min} satisfies A.4. While the measure $I_{\min}$ has subsequently been criticized for "not measuring the right thing" [26,53,60], there has been no successful attempt to find better measures, except for the bivariate case ($k = 2$) [6,26]. One problem seems to be the lack of a clear consensus on the values of the shared information for some paradigmatic examples. For example, it seems natural that the shared information is zero for the COPY distribution in Example 1 since Y and Z are independent [6,26,60]. However, $I_{\min}$ assigns 1 bit of shared information in this case. The second problem relates to the difficulty of coming up with a minimal number of "natural" and "essential" properties for the shared information.

Bertschinger et al. [60] proposed the following additional axiom:

A.5 (*Left chain rule*). $\widetilde{SI}(SS';Y_1,\dots,Y_k) = \widetilde{SI}(S;Y_1,\dots,Y_k) + \widetilde{SI}(S';Y_1,\dots,Y_k|S)$, where $\widetilde{SI}(S';Y_1,\dots,Y_k|S) = \sum_{s\in\mathcal{S}} P_S(s)\widetilde{SI}(S';Y_1,\dots,Y_k|s)$.

A.5 is a natural generalization of the chain rule of mutual information (3).

Specializing to the bivariate case, A.4 and A.5 together imply the following property [60], which was first proposed in [26]:

A.6 (*Identity*). $\widetilde{SI}((Y,Z);Y,Z) = I(Y;Z)$.

The identity property states that if S is an identical copy of the predictor variables, i.e., if $S = (Y,Z)$, then the shared information should equal the mutual information between Y and Z. Rauh et al. [52], however, showed that A.6 is incompatible with A.4 for $k \geq 3$. This implies that A.4 and A.5 are not compatible for $k \geq 3$.

Rauh et al. [52] argue that shared information should never increase if the target and/or the predictors perform some *local* operation (e.g., coarse graining) on their subsystems. For local operations of the predictors, the Williams–Beer axioms imply the following property:

A.7 *(Right monotonicity).* $\widetilde{SI}(S;Y_1,\dots,Y_k) \geq \widetilde{SI}(S;f_1(Y_1),\dots,f_k(Y_k))$ *for all functions* $f_1,\dots,f_k$.

On the other hand, the left chain rule A.5 implies the following property [60]:

A.8 (*Left monotonicity*). $\widetilde{SI}(S;Y_1,\dots,Y_k) \geq \widetilde{SI}(f(S);Y_1,\dots,Y_k)$ for all functions f.

Appendix B. Deferred Proofs

Proof of Lemma 4. Since $Z \sqsupseteq_S Y$, there exists some $\lambda' \in \mathsf{M}(\mathcal{Z};\mathcal{Y})$ such that $\kappa = \lambda' \circ \mu$. Hence,

$$\begin{aligned}
\delta_o^\pi(\kappa,\nu) &= \min_{\lambda\in\mathsf{M}(\mathcal{Y};\mathcal{W})} D(\nu\|\lambda\circ\kappa|\pi_S) \\
&= \min_{\lambda\in\mathsf{M}(\mathcal{Y};\mathcal{W})} D(\nu\|\lambda\circ\lambda'\circ\mu|\pi_S) \\
&\geq \min_{\lambda\in\mathsf{M}(\mathcal{Z};\mathcal{W})} D(\nu\|\lambda\circ\mu|\pi_S) = \delta_o^\pi(\mu,\nu).
\end{aligned}$$

Since $Y \sqsupseteq_S W$, there exists some $\lambda' \in \mathsf{M}(\mathcal{Y};\mathcal{W})$ such that $\nu = \lambda' \circ \kappa$. Hence,

$$\begin{aligned}
\delta_o^\pi(\mu,\nu) &= \min_{\lambda\in\mathsf{M}(\mathcal{Z};\mathcal{W})} D(\nu\|\lambda\circ\mu|\pi_S) \\
&= \min_{\lambda\in\mathsf{M}(\mathcal{Z};\mathcal{W})} D(\lambda'\circ\kappa\|\lambda\circ\mu|\pi_S) \\
&\leq \min_{\lambda\in\mathsf{M}(\mathcal{Z};\mathcal{Y})} D(\lambda'\circ\kappa\|\lambda'\circ\lambda\circ\mu|\pi_S) \\
&\leq \min_{\lambda\in\mathsf{M}(\mathcal{Z};\mathcal{Y})} D(\kappa\|\lambda\circ\mu|\pi_S) = \delta_o^\pi(\mu,\kappa),
\end{aligned}$$

where the inequality in the last step follows from the data processing inequality for the KL divergence (Theorem 2.2 in [28]). □

Proof of Proposition 11. We shall use the following variational characterization of the UI, which follows from Property P.8:

$$UI(S;Y\backslash Z) = \min_{P_{Z'|Z}:SY-Z-Z'} UI(S;Y\backslash Z'). \tag{A2}$$

Let $(S,Y,Z) \sim P$ and let $(S,Y,Z') \sim P'$ such that $P' = P \cdot P_{Z'|Z} \equiv \sum_{z \in \mathcal{Z}} P_{SYZ} P_{Z'|Z}$. Let $Q \in \Delta_P$ and $Q' = Q \cdot P_{Z'|Z} \in \Delta_{P'}$. We then have

$$\begin{aligned}
UI(S;Y\backslash Z) &= \min_{P_{Z'|Z}:SY-Z-Z'} UI(S;Y\backslash Z') \\
&= \min_{P_{Z'|Z}:SY-Z-Z'} \min_{Q' \in \Delta_{P'}} I_{Q'}(S;Y|Z') \\
&\leq \min_{P_{Z'|Z}:SY-Z-Z'} \min_{Q \in \Delta_P} I_{Q \cdot P_{Z'|Z}}(S;Y|Z') \\
&= \min_{Q \in \Delta_P} \min_{P_{Z'|Z}:SY-Z-Z'} I_{Q \cdot P_{Z'|Z}}(S;Y|Z') \\
&= \min_{Q \in \Delta_P} I_Q(S;Y\downarrow Z) \leq I_P(S;Y\downarrow Z),
\end{aligned}$$

where the first step is just (A2), and the inequality in the third step follows since for any $Q \in \Delta_P$, Q' lies in $\Delta_{P'}$. □

References

1. Shannon, C.E. A mathematical theory of communication. *Bell Syst. Tech. J.* **1948**, *27*, 379–423. [CrossRef]
2. Rényi, A. On the foundations of information theory. *Rev. L'Institut Int. Stat.* **1965**, *33*, 1–14. [CrossRef]
3. Rényi, A. On measures of entropy and information. In *Proceedings of the Fourth Berkeley Symposium on Mathematical Statistics and Probability, Volume 1: Contributions to the Theory of Statistics*; University of California Press: Berkeley, CA, USA, 1961; pp. 547–561.
4. Csiszár, I. A class of measures of informativity of observation channels. *Period. Math. Hung.* **1972**, *2*, 191–213. [CrossRef]
5. Csiszár, I. Axiomatic characterizations of information measures. *Entropy* **2008**, *10*, 261–273. [CrossRef]
6. Bertschinger, N.; Rauh, J.; Olbrich, E.; Jost, J.; Ay, N. Quantifying Unique Information. *Entropy* **2014**, *16*, 2161–2183. [CrossRef]
7. Coecke, B.; Fritz, T.; Spekkens, R.W. A mathematical theory of resources. *Inf. Comput.* **2016**, *250*, 59–86. [CrossRef]
8. Fritz, T. Resource convertibility and ordered commutative monoids. *Math. Struct. Comput. Sci.* **2017**, *27*, 850–938. [CrossRef]
9. Del Rio, L.; Kraemer, L.; Renner, R. Resource theories of knowledge. *arXiv* **2015**, arXiv:1511.08818.
10. Goold, J.; Huber, M.; Riera, A.; del Rio, L.; Skrzypczyk, P. The role of quantum information in thermodynamics—A topical review. *J. Phys. Math. Theor.* **2016**, *49*, 143001. [CrossRef]
11. Chitambar, E.; Gour, G. Quantum resource theories. *Rev. Mod. Phys.* **2019**, *91*, 025001. [CrossRef]
12. Maurer, U.M.; Wolf, S. Unconditionally Secure Key Agreement and the Intrinsic Conditional Information. *IEEE Trans. Inf. Theory* **1999**, *45*, 499–514. [CrossRef]
13. Bloch, M.; Barros, J. *Physical-Layer Security: From Information Theory to Security Engineering*; Cambridge University Press: Cambridge, UK, 2011.
14. Narayan, P.; Tyagi, H. Multiterminal secrecy by public discussion. *Found. Trends Commun. Inf. Theory* **2016**, *13*, 129–275. [CrossRef]
15. Tyagi, H.; Watanabe, S. *Information-Theoretic Cryptography*; Cambridge University Press: Cambridge, UK, 2023.
16. Banerjee, P.K.; Olbrich, E.; Jost, J.; Rauh, J. Unique informations and deficiencies. In Proceedings of the 56th Annual Allerton Conference on Communication, Control and Computing, Monticello, IL, USA, 2–5 October 2018; pp. 32–38.
17. Rauh, J.; Banerjee, P.K.; Olbrich, E.; Jost, J. Unique information and secret key decompositions. In Proceedings of the IEEE International Symposium on Information Theory (ISIT), Paris, France, 7–12 July 2019; pp. 3042–3046.
18. Rauh, J.; Banerjee, P.K.; Olbrich, E.; Montúfar, G.; Jost, J. Continuity and additivity properties of information decompositions. *Int. J. Approx. Reason.* **2023**, *161*, 108979. [CrossRef]
19. Rauh, J.; Banerjee, P.K.; Olbrich, E.; Jost, J.; Bertschinger, N. On extractable shared information. *Entropy* **2017**, *19*, 328. [CrossRef]
20. Rauh, J.; Banerjee, P.K.; Olbrich, E.; Jost, J.; Bertschinger, N.; Wolpert, D. Coarse-graining and the Blackwell order. *Entropy* **2017**, *19*, 527. [CrossRef]
21. Banerjee, P.K.; Rauh, J.; Montúfar, G. Computing the unique information. In Proceedings of the IEEE International Symposium on Information Theory (ISIT), Vail, CO, USA, 17–22 June 2018; pp. 141–145.
22. Banerjee, P.K. Unique Information and the Blackwell Order. Ph.D. Thesis, Max Planck Institute for Mathematics in the Sciences, Leipzig, Germany, 2020.
23. Le Cam, L. Sufficiency and approximate sufficiency. *Ann. Math. Stat.* **1964**, *35*, 1419–1455. [CrossRef]
24. Torgersen, E. *Comparison of Statistical Experiments*; Cambridge University Press: Cambridge, UK, 1991; Volume 36.

25. Raginsky, M. Shannon meets Blackwell and Le Cam: Channels, codes, and statistical experiments. In Proceedings of the IEEE International Symposium on Information Theory (ISIT), St. Petersburg, Russia, 31 July–5 August 2011; pp. 1220–1224.
26. Harder, M.; Salge, C.; Polani, D. A Bivariate measure of redundant information. *Phys. Rev. E* **2013**, *87*, 012130. [CrossRef]
27. Csiszár, I.; Körner, J. *Information Theory: Coding Theorems for Discrete Memoryless Systems*; Cambridge University Press: Cambridge, UK, 2011.
28. Polyanskiy, Y.; Wu, Y. Lecture Notes on Information Theory. Lecture Notes for ECE563 (UIUC) and 6.441 (MIT), 2012–2017. Available online: https://ocw.mit.edu/courses/6-441-information-theory-spring-2016/pages/lecture-notes/ (accessed on 12 November 2024).
29. Wehrl, A. General properties of entropy. *Rev. Mod. Phys.* **1978**, *50*, 221. [CrossRef]
30. Bell, A.J. The Co-Information Lattice. In Proceedings of the Fourth International Symposium on Independent Component Analysis and Blind Signal Separation (ICA 03), Charleston, SC, USA, 5–8 March 2003.
31. McGill, W. Multivariate information transmission. *IRE Trans. Inf. Theory* **1954**, *4*, 93–111.
32. Han, T.S. Linear dependence structure of the entropy space. *Inf. Control.* **1975**, *29*, 337–368. [CrossRef]
33. Yeung, R.W. A new outlook on Shannon's information measures. *IEEE Trans. Inf. Theory* **1991**, *37*, 466–474. [CrossRef]
34. Han, T.S. Nonnegative entropy measures of multivariate symmetric correlations. *Inf. Control.* **1978**, *36*, 133–156. [CrossRef]
35. Hayden, P.; Headrick, M.; Maloney, A. Holographic mutual information is monogamous. *Phys. Rev. D* **2013**, *87*, 046003. [CrossRef]
36. Brenner, N.; Strong, S.P.; Koberle, R.; Bialek, W.; Steveninck, R.R.d.R.v. Synergy in a neural code. *Neural Comput.* **2000**, *12*, 1531–1552. [CrossRef] [PubMed]
37. Averbeck, B.B.; Latham, P.E.; Pouget, A. Neural correlations, population coding and computation. *Nat. Rev. Neurosci.* **2006**, *7*, 358. [CrossRef] [PubMed]
38. Gat, I.; Tishby, N. Synergy and redundancy among brain cells of behaving monkeys. *Adv. Neural Inf. Process. Syst.* **1999**, *11*, 111–117.
39. Reich, D.S.; Mechler, F.; Victor, J.D. Independent and redundant information in nearby cortical neurons. *Science* **2001**, *294*, 2566–2568. [CrossRef]
40. Schneidman, E.; Puchalla, J.L.; Segev, R.; Harris, R.A.; Bialek, W.; Berry, M.J. Synergy from silence in a combinatorial neural code. *J. Neurosci.* **2011**, *31*, 15732–15741. [CrossRef] [PubMed]
41. Chechik, G.; Anderson, M.J.; Bar-Yosef, O.; Young, E.D.; Tishby, N.; Nelken, I. Reduction of information redundancy in the ascending auditory pathway. *Neuron* **2006**, *51*, 359–368. [CrossRef] [PubMed]
42. Anastassiou, D. Computational analysis of the synergy among multiple interacting genes. *Mol. Syst. Biol.* **2007**, *3*, 83. [CrossRef]
43. Kontoyiannis, I.; Lucena, B. Mutual information, synergy and some curious phenomena for simple channels. In Proceedings of the IEEE International Symposium on Information Theory (ISIT), Adelaide, SA, Australia, 4–9 September 2005; pp. 1651–1655.
44. Steudel, B.; Ay, N. Information-theoretic inference of common ancestors. *Entropy* **2015**, *17*, 2304–2327. [CrossRef]
45. Jakulin, A.; Bratko, I. Quantifying and Visualizing Attribute Interactions: An Approach Based on Entropy. *arXiv* **2003**, arXiv:cs/0308002.
46. Williams, P.; Beer, R. Nonnegative Decomposition of Multivariate Information. *arXiv* **2010**, arXiv:1004.2515v1.
47. Latham, P.E.; Nirenberg, S. Synergy, Redundancy, and Independence in Population Codes, Revisited. *J. Neurosci.* **2005**, *25*, 5195–5206. [CrossRef] [PubMed]
48. Pola, G.; Thiele, A.; Hoffmann, K.P.; Panzeri, S. An exact method to quantify the information transmitted by different mechanisms of correlational coding. *Network Comput. Neural Syst.* **2003**, *14*, 35–60. [CrossRef] [PubMed]
49. Oizumi, M.; Ishii, T.; Ishibashi, K.; Hosoya, T.; Okada, M. Mismatched decoding in the brain. *J. Neurosci.* **2010**, *30*, 4815–4826. [CrossRef] [PubMed]
50. Steeg, G.V.; Brekelmans, R.; Harutyunyan, H.; Galstyan, A. Disentangled representations via synergy minimization. In Proceedings of the 55th Annual Allerton Conference on Communication, Control and Computing, Monticello, IL, USA, 3–6 October 2017; pp. 180–187.
51. Schneidman, E.; Bialek, W.; Berry, M.J. Synergy, redundancy, and independence in population codes. *J. Neurosci.* **2003**, *23*, 11539–11553. [CrossRef]
52. Rauh, J.; Bertschinger, N.; Olbrich, E.; Jost, J. Reconsidering unique information: Towards a multivariate information decomposition. In Proceedings of the IEEE International Symposium on Information Theory (ISIT), Honolulu, HI, USA, 29 June–4 July 2014; pp. 2232–2236.
53. Griffith, V.; Koch, C. Quantifying Synergistic Mutual Information. In *Guided Self-Organization: Inception*; Emergence, Complexity and Computation; Springer: Berlin/Heidelberg, Germany, 2014; Volume 9, pp. 159–190.
54. Barrett, A.B. Exploration of synergistic and redundant information sharing in static and dynamical Gaussian systems. *Phys. Rev. E* **2015**, *91*, 052802. [CrossRef]
55. Olbrich, E.; Bertschinger, N.; Rauh, J. Information decomposition and synergy. *Entropy* **2015**, *17*, 3501–3517. [CrossRef]

56. Chicharro, D.; Panzeri, S. Synergy and redundancy in dual decompositions of mutual information gain and information loss. *Entropy* **2017**, *19*, 71. [CrossRef]
57. Chicharro, D. Quantifying multivariate redundancy with maximum entropy decompositions of mutual information. *arXiv* **2017**, arXiv:1708.03845.
58. Pica, G.; Piasini, E.; Safaai, H.; Runyan, C.; Harvey, C.; Diamond, M.; Kayser, C.; Fellin, T.; Panzeri, S. Quantifying how much sensory information in a neural code is relevant for behavior. *Adv. Neural Inf. Process. Syst.* **2017**, *30*, 3689–3699.
59. Rauh, J. Secret sharing and shared information. *Entropy* **2017**, *19*, 601. [CrossRef]
60. Bertschinger, N.; Rauh, J.; Olbrich, E.; Jost, J. Shared Information—New Insights and Problems in Decomposing Information in Complex Systems. In *Proceedings ECCS 2012*; Springer: Berlin/Heidelberg, Germany, 2013; pp. 251–269.
61. Blackwell, D. Equivalent Comparisons of Experiments. *Ann. Math. Stat.* **1953**, *24*, 265–272. [CrossRef]
62. Bertschinger, N.; Rauh, J. The Blackwell relation defines no lattice. In Proceedings of the IEEE International Symposium on Information Theory (ISIT), Honolulu, HI, USA, 29 June–4 July 2014; pp. 2479–2483.
63. Körner, J.; Marton, K. Comparison of two noisy channels. In *Topics in Information Theory*; Colloquia Mathematica Societatis Janos Bolyai: Keszthely, Hungary, 1975; Volume 16, pp. 411–423.
64. Wyner, A.D. The wire-tap channel. *Bell Syst. Tech. J.* **1975**, *54*, 1355–1387. [CrossRef]
65. Csiszár, I.; Körner, J. Broadcast channels with confidential messages. *IEEE Trans. Inf. Theory* **1978**, *24*, 339–348. [CrossRef]
66. Ahlswede, R.; Csiszár, I. Common randomness in information theory and cryptography–Part I: Secret sharing. *IEEE Trans. Inf. Theory* **1993**, *39*, 1121–1132. [CrossRef]
67. Gohari, A.A.; Anantharam, V. Information-theoretic key agreement of multiple terminals–Part I. *IEEE Trans. Inf. Theory* **2010**, *56*, 3973–3996. [CrossRef]
68. Shannon, C.E. A note on a partial ordering for communication channels. *Inf. Control.* **1958**, *1*, 390–397. [CrossRef]
69. El Gamal, A.; Kim, Y.H. *Network Information Theory*; Cambridge University Press: Cambridge, UK, 2011.
70. El Gamal, A. The capacity of a class of broadcast channels. *IEEE Trans. Inf. Theory* **1979**, *25*, 166–169. [CrossRef]
71. Geng, Y.; Nair, C.; Shitz, S.S.; Wang, Z.V. On broadcast channels with binary inputs and symmetric outputs. *IEEE Trans. Inf. Theory* **2013**, *59*, 6980–6989. [CrossRef]
72. Cohen, J.; Kemperman, J.; Zbăganu, G. *Comparisons of Stochastic Matrices with Applications in Information Theory, Statistics, Economics, and Population Sciences*; Birkhäuser: Basel, Switzerland, 1998.
73. de Oliveira, H. Blackwell's informativeness theorem using diagrams. *Games Econ. Behav.* **2018**, *109*, 126–131. [CrossRef]
74. Dahl, G. Matrix majorization. *Linear Algebra Its Appl.* **1999**, *288*, 53–73. [CrossRef]
75. Rockafellar, R.T. *Convex Analysis*; Princeton University Press: Princeton, NJ, USA, 2015.
76. Nasser, R. Characterizations of Two Channel Orderings: Input-Degradedness and the Shannon Ordering. *IEEE Trans. Inf. Theory* **2018**, *64*, 6759–6770. [CrossRef]
77. Nasser, R. On the input-degradedness and input-equivalence between channels. In Proceedings of the IEEE International Symposium on Information Theory (ISIT), Aachen, Germany, 25–30 June 2017; pp. 2453–2457.
78. Van Dijk, M. On a special class of broadcast channels with confidential messages. *IEEE Trans. Inf. Theory* **1997**, *43*, 712–714. [CrossRef]
79. Nair, C. Capacity Regions of Two New Classes of Two-Receiver Broadcast Channels. *IEEE Trans. Inf. Theory* **2010**, *56*, 4207–4214. [CrossRef]
80. Gohari, A.; Günlü, O.; Kramer, G. Coding for positive rate in the source model key agreement problem. *IEEE Trans. Inf. Theory* **2020**, *66*, 6303–6323. [CrossRef]
81. Banerjee, P.K.; Montúfar, G. The variational deficiency bottleneck. In Proceedings of the International Joint Conference on Neural Networks (IJCNN), Glasgow, UK, 19–24 July 2020; pp. 1–8.
82. Csiszár, I.; Matúš, F. Information projections revisited. *IEEE Trans. Inf. Theory* **2003**, *49*, 1474–1490. [CrossRef]
83. Banerjee, P.K.; Olbrich, E.; Jost, J.; Rauh, J. Unique Informations and Deficiencies. *arXiv* **2018**, arXiv:1807.05103.
84. Renner, R.; Wolf, S. New Bounds in Secret-Key Agreement: The Gap between Formation and Secrecy Extraction. In Proceedings of the Advances in Cryptology—EUROCRYPT 2003, Warsaw, Poland, 4–8 May 2003; pp. 562–577.
85. Maurer, U.M. Secret key agreement by public discussion from common information. *IEEE Trans. Inf. Theory* **1993**, *39*, 733–742. [CrossRef]
86. Gohari, A.A.; Anantharam, V. Comments On "Information-Theoretic Key Agreement of Multiple Terminals–Part I". *IEEE Trans. Inf. Theory* **2017**, *63*, 5440–5442. [CrossRef]
87. Chitambar, E.; Fortescue, B.; Hsieh, M.H. Distributions attaining secret key at a rate of the conditional mutual information. In *Proceedings of the Annual Cryptology Conference*; Springer: Berlin/Heidelberg, Germany, 2015; pp. 443–462.
88. Maurer, U.M.; Renner, R.; Wolf, S. Unbreakable keys from random noise. In *Security with Noisy Data*; Springer: Berlin/Heidelberg, Germany, 2007; pp. 21–44.

89. Keykhosravi, K.; Mahzoon, M.; Gohari, A.A.; Aref, M.R. From source model to quantum key distillation: An improved upper bound. In Proceedings of the IEEE IWCIT, Tehran, Iran, 7–8 May 2014; pp. 1–6.
90. Wegman, M.N.; Carter, J.L. New hash functions and their use in authentication and set equality. *J. Comput. Syst. Sci.* **1981**, *22*, 265–279. [CrossRef]
91. Shannon, C.E. Communication theory of secrecy systems. *Bell Syst. Tech. J.* **1949**, *28*, 656–715. [CrossRef]
92. Vernam, G.S. Cipher printing telegraph systems for secret wire and radio telegraphic communications. *Trans. Am. Inst. Electr. Eng.* **1926**, *45*, 295–301. [CrossRef]
93. Diffie, W.; Hellman, M. New directions in cryptography. *IEEE Trans. Inf. Theory* **1976**, *22*, 644–654. [CrossRef]
94. Rivest, R.L.; Shamir, A.; Adleman, L. A method for obtaining digital signatures and public-key cryptosystems. *Commun. ACM* **1978**, *21*, 120–126. [CrossRef]
95. Goldreich, O. *Foundations of Cryptography: Basic Tools*; Cambridge University Press: Cambridge, UK, 2001.
96. Impagliazzo, R. A personal view of average-case complexity. In Proceedings of the Structure in Complexity Theory, Tenth Annual IEEE Conference, Minneapolis, MN, USA, 19–22 June 1995; pp. 134–147.
97. Shor, P.W. Polynomial-time algorithms for prime factorization and discrete logarithms on a quantum computer. *SIAM Rev.* **1999**, *41*, 303–332. [CrossRef]
98. Maurer, U.M.; Wolf, S. From Weak to Strong Information-Theoretic Key Agreement. In Proceedings of the IEEE International Symposium on Information Theory (ISIT), Sorrento, Italy, 25–30 June 2000; p. 18.
99. Oppenheim, J.; Spekkens, R.W.; Winter, A. A classical analogue of negative information. *arXiv* **2005**, arXiv:quant-ph/0511247.
100. Maurer, U.M.; Wolf, S. Towards characterizing when information-theoretic secret key agreement is possible. In *Proceedings of the International Conference on the Theory and Application of Cryptology and Information Security*; Springer: Berlin/Heidelberg, Germany, 1996; pp. 196–209.
101. Bennett, C.H.; Brassard, G.; Crépeau, C.; Maurer, U.M. Generalized privacy amplification. *IEEE Trans. Inf. Theory* **1995**, *41*, 1915–1923. [CrossRef]
102. Christandl, M.; Renner, R.; Wolf, S. A property of the intrinsic mutual information. In Proceedings of the IEEE International Symposium on Information Theory (ISIT), Yokohama, Japan, 29 June–4 July 2003; p. 258.
103. Synak-Radtke, B.; Horodecki, M. On asymptotic continuity of functions of quantum states. *J. Phys. A Math. Gen.* **2006**, *39*, L423. [CrossRef]
104. Fannes, M. A continuity property of the entropy density for spin lattice systems. *Commun. Math. Phys.* **1973**, *31*, 291–294. [CrossRef]
105. Winter, A. Tight uniform continuity bounds for quantum entropies: Conditional entropy, relative entropy distance and energy constraints. *Commun. Math. Phys.* **2016**, *347*, 291–313. [CrossRef]
106. Christandl, M.; Winter, A. Squashed entanglement—An additive entanglement measure. *J. Math. Phys.* **2004**, *45*, 829–840. [CrossRef]
107. Christandl, M.; Ekert, A.; Horodecki, M.; Horodecki, P.; Oppenheim, J.; Renner, R. Unifying classical and quantum key distillation. In *Proceedings of the Theory of Cryptography Conference*; Springer: Berlin/Heidelberg, Germany, 2007; pp. 456–478.
108. Maurer, U.M.; Wolf, S. Secret-key agreement over unauthenticated public channels–Part II: The simulatability condition. *IEEE Trans. Inf. Theory* **2003**, *49*, 832–838. [CrossRef]
109. Maurer, U.M.; Wolf, S. Secret-key agreement over unauthenticated public channels–Part I: Definitions and a completeness result. *IEEE Trans. Inf. Theory* **2003**, *49*, 822–831. [CrossRef]
110. Gisin, N.; Wolf, S. Linking classical and quantum key agreement: Is there bound information? In *Proceedings of the Annual International Cryptology Conference*; Springer: Berlin/Heidelberg, Germany, 2000; pp. 482–500.
111. Chitambar, E.; Hsieh, M.H. Round complexity in the local transformations of quantum and classical states. *Nat. Commun.* **2017**, *8*, 2086. [CrossRef]
112. Orlitsky, A.; Wigderson, A. Secrecy enhancement via public discussion. In Proceedings of the IEEE International Symposium on Information Theory (ISIT), San Antonio, TX, USA, 17–22 January 1993; p. 155.
113. Devetak, I.; Harrow, A.W.; Winter, A.J. A resource framework for quantum Shannon theory. *IEEE Trans. Inf. Theory* **2008**, *54*, 4587–4618. [CrossRef]
114. Lieb, E.H.; Yngvason, J. A guide to entropy and the second law of thermodynarnics. *Not. Am. Math. Soc.* **1998**, *45*, 571–581.
115. Watanabe, S. Information theoretical analysis of multivariate correlation. *IBM J. Res. Dev.* **1960**, *4*, 66–82. [CrossRef]
116. Studený, M.; Vejnarová, J. The multiinformation function as a tool for measuring stochastic dependence. In *Learning in Graphical Models*; Springer: Berlin/Heidelberg, Germany, 1998; pp. 261–297.
117. Wennekers, T.; Ay, N. Spatial and temporal stochastic interaction in neuronal assemblies. *Theory Biosci.* **2003**, *122*, 5–18. [CrossRef]
118. Schneidman, E.; Berry, M.J.; Segev, R.; Bialek, W. Weak pairwise correlations imply strongly correlated network states in a neural population. *Nature* **2006**, *440*, 1007. [CrossRef]
119. Austin, T. Measures of correlation and mixtures of product measures. *arXiv* **2018**, arXiv:1809.10272.

120. Cerf, N.J.; Massar, S.; Schneider, S. Multipartite classical and quantum secrecy monotones. *Phys. Rev. A* **2002**, *66*, 042309. [CrossRef]
121. Prabhakaran, V.M.; Prabhakaran, M.M. Assisted common information with an application to secure two-party sampling. *IEEE Trans. Inf. Theory* **2014**, *60*, 3413–3434. [CrossRef]
122. Horodecki, K.; Horodecki, M.; Horodecki, P.; Oppenheim, J. Locking entanglement with a single qubit. *Phys. Rev. Lett.* **2005**, *94*, 200501. [CrossRef] [PubMed]
123. Galla, T.; Gühne, O. Complexity measures, emergence, and multiparticle correlations. *Phys. Rev. E* **2012**, *85*, 046209. [CrossRef]
124. Amari, S.I. Information geometry on hierarchy of probability distributions. *IEEE Trans. Inf. Theory* **2001**, *47*, 1701–1711. [CrossRef]
125. Schneidman, E.; Still, S.; Berry, M.J., II; Bialek, W. Network information and connected correlations. *Phys. Rev. Lett.* **2003**, *91*, 238701. [CrossRef]
126. Kahle, T.; Olbrich, E.; Jost, J.; Ay, N. Complexity measures from interaction structures. *Phys. Rev. E* **2009**, *79*, 026201. [CrossRef]
127. Linden, N.; Popescu, S.; Wootters, W.K. Almost every pure state of three qubits is completely determined by its two-particle reduced density matrices. *Phys. Rev. Lett.* **2002**, *89*, 207901. [CrossRef]
128. Zhou, D.L. Irreducible multiparty correlations can be created by local operations. *Phys. Rev. A* **2009**, *80*, 022113. [CrossRef]
129. Ay, N.; Jost, J.; Vân Lê, H.; Schwachhöfer, L. *Information Geometry*; Springer: Berlin/Heidelberg, Germany, 2017; Volume 8.
130. Griffith, V.; Chong, E.K.P.; James, R.G.; Ellison, C.J.; Crutchfield, J.P. Intersection Information Based on Common Randomness. *Entropy* **2014**, *16*, 1985–2000. [CrossRef]
131. Venkatesh, P.; Dutta, S.; Grover, P. How should we define information flow in neural circuits? In Proceedings of the IEEE International Symposium on Information Theory (ISIT), Paris, France, 7–12 July 2019; pp. 176–180.
132. Beimel, A. Secret-sharing schemes: A survey. In *Proceedings of the International Conference on Coding and Cryptology*; Springer: Berlin/Heidelberg, Germany, 2011; pp. 11–46.

MDPI AG
Grosspeteranlage 5
4052 Basel
Switzerland
Tel.: +41 61 683 77 34

Entropy Editorial Office
E-mail: entropy@mdpi.com
www.mdpi.com/journal/entropy

www.ingramcontent.com/pod-product-compliance
Lightning Source LLC
LaVergne TN
LVHW072322090526
838202LV00019B/2333